Adventurously eclectic, authoritative and thought-provoking, this new handbook, organised in geographic and thematic chapters, is freshly up to date. It will be valued by specialist business historians wanting to catch up on missed recent work in related areas and social scientists aiming to deepen their research by adding a business historical dimension.

Leslie Hannah, Visiting Professor, London School of Economics

The contributions to this collection provide concise and insightful overviews of the development, current state and future research directions of key aspects of the field of business history. Taken together, they capture the methodological, thematic and geographic diversity of a vibrant scholarly discipline with roots in and links to the broader fields of history, economics, management studies and sociology.

Ray Stokes, Professor of Business History, University of Glasgow; Director, Centre for Business History in Scotland; and Executive Editor, *Business History*

The Routledge Companion to Business History

The Routledge Companion to Business History is a definitive work of reference, and authoritative, international source on business history. Compiled by leading scholars in the field, it offers both researchers and students an introduction and overview of current scholarship in this expanding discipline.

Drawing on a wealth of international contributions, this volume expands the field and explores how business history interacts theoretically and methodologically with other fields. It charts the origins and development of business history and its global reach from Latin America and Africa, to North America and Europe. With this multi-perspective approach, it illustrates the unique contribution of business history and its relationship with a range of other disciplines, from finance and banking to gender issues in corporations.

The Routledge Companion to Business History is a vital source of reference for students and researchers in the fields of business history, corporate governance and business ethics.

John F. Wilson is Pro Vice Chancellor (Business & Law) at Northumbria University, Newcastle, UK.

Steven Toms is Professor and Chair in Accounting at the University of Leeds, UK.

Abe de Jong is Professor of Corporate Finance and Corporate Governance at Erasmus University Rotterdam, the Netherlands.

Emily Buchnea is a Research Assistant at the Newcastle University Business School, UK.

Routledge Companions in Business, Management and Accounting

Routledge Companions in Business, Management and Accounting are prestige reference works providing an overview of a whole subject area or sub-discipline. These books survey the state of the discipline including emerging and cutting-edge areas. Providing a comprehensive, up-to-date, definitive work of reference, Routledge Companions can be cited as an authoritative source on the subject.

A key aspect of these Routledge Companions is their international scope and relevance. Edited by an array of highly regarded scholars, these volumes also benefit from teams of contributors which reflect an international range of perspectives.

Individually, Routledge Companions in Business, Management and Accounting provide an impactful one-stop-shop resource for each theme covered. Collectively, they represent a comprehensive learning and research resource for researchers, postgraduate students and practitioners.

Published titles in this series include:

The Routledge Companion to Philanthropy
Edited by Tobias Jung, Susan Phillips and Jenny Harrow

The Routledge Companion to Marketing History
Edited by D. G. Brian Jones and Mark Tadajewski

The Routledge Companion to Reinventing Management Education
Edited by Chris Steyaert, Timon Beyes and Martin Parker

The Routledge Companion to the Professions and Professionalism
Edited by Mike Dent, Ivy Bourgeault, Jean-Louis Denis and Ellen Kuhlmann

The Routledge Companion to Contemporary Brand Management
Edited by Francesca Dall'Olmo Riley, Jaywant Singh and Charles Blankson

The Routledge Companion to Banking Regulation and Reform
Edited by Ismail Ertürk and Daniela Gabor

The Routledge Companion to the Makers of Modern Entrepreneurship
Edited by David B. Audretsch and Erik E. Lehmann

The Routledge Companion to Business History
Edited by John F. Wilson, Steven Toms, Abe de Jong and Emily Buchnea

The Routledge Companion to Business History

Edited by John F. Wilson, Steven Toms,
Abe de Jong and Emily Buchnea

Routledge
Taylor & Francis Group

LONDON AND NEW YORK

First published 2017
by Routledge
2 Park Square, Milton Park, Abingdon, Oxon OX14 4RN

and by Routledge
605 Third Avenue, New York, NY 10017

First issued in paperback 2021

Routledge is an imprint of the Taylor & Francis Group, an informa business

British Library Cataloguing-in-Publication Data
A catalogue record for this book is available from the British Library

Library of Congress Cataloging-in-Publication Data
A catalog record for this book has been requested

Typeset in Bembo
by codeMantra

ISBN 13: 978−1−03−224230−9 (pbk)
ISBN 13: 978−0−415−85556−3 (hbk)

DOI: 10.4324/9780203736036

Contents

Contents

Figures

Tables

Contributors

Gareth Austin, University of Cambridge, UK.

Emily Buchnea, Newcastle University, UK.

Catherine Casson, University of Manchester, UK.

Mark Casson, University of Reading, UK.

Andrea Colli, Bocconi University, Italy.

Chris Colvin, Queen's University Belfast, UK.

Abe de Jong, Erasmus University Rotterdam, the Netherlands.

Helen Doe, University of Exeter, UK.

Pierre Gervais, Université Sorbonne Nouvelle - Paris 3, France.

David Higgins, Newcastle University, UK.

Matthias Kipping, York University, Canada.

Martin Kragh, Uppsala University, Sweden.

Takafumi Kurosawa, Kyoto University, Japan.

Mitchell J. Larson, University of Central Lancashire, UK.

Cheryl McWatters, University of Ottawa, Canada.

Bernard Mees, RMIT University, Australia.

David Merrett, The University of Melbourne, Australia.

Rory Miller, University of Liverpool, UK.

Bob Millward, University of Manchester, UK.

John Quail, University of York, UK.

Keetie Sluyterman, Utrecht University, the Netherlands.

Andrew Smith, University of Liverpool, UK.

Kevin Tennent, University of York, UK.

Anna Tilba, Newcastle University, UK.

Contributors

Steve Toms, University of Leeds, UK.

Hugo van Driel, Erasmus University Rotterdam, the Netherlands.

Simon Ville, University of Wollongong, Australia.

Dan Wadhwani, University of the Pacific, USA.

Tony Webster, Northumbria University, Newcastle, UK.

Gerarda Westerhuis, Utrecht University, the Netherlands.

John Wilson, Northumbria University, Newcastle, UK.

Mark Wilson, University of North Carolina at Charlotte, USA.

Part I
The discipline of business history

1

Introduction

John F. Wilson, Steven Toms, Abe de Jong and Emily Buchnea

Rationale

In putting together this *Companion*, the editors were motivated by the desire to expand current thinking on the discipline of business history and to produce a comprehensive and current work of reference which can be cited as an authoritative, international source on the subject. While we recognize the impossible nature of covering every single topic or region that has been researched by business historians, we wanted to showcase the rich variety of work that is being done, contrasting methodological approaches, international settings, multiple periods of history, ancient and modern and cross-cutting themes. This multi-perspective approach illustrates the unique appeal of business history and underlines its contribution to a number of adjacent disciplines. In achieving this set of aims, we were also keen to demonstrate how business history now interacts with other fields, theoretically and methodologically, in a much more dynamic way. While extensive work needs to be done in these respects, by bringing together a highly talented group of business historians we are progressing the discipline's research agenda, enhancing knowledge and understanding and offering researchers and students an introduction to, and overview of, current scholarship in a discipline that has moved out of the shadow of economic history into a fully fledged genre with its own identity.

Indeed, business history has made enormous strides in the last twenty-five years, with vibrant professional associations operating across several Continents, all of which converged on Bergen for the inaugural World Business History Conference in August 2016. Similarly, the journals closely linked to business history continue to flourish, increasing both the number of issues published each year and their readership, especially in other disciplines. One of the most significant benefits arising from this process of evolution has been a significant switch in emphasis away from the study of single firms into a much richer study of business systems and the context in which they evolved over much longer time periods. Journal editors have played an instrumental role in fashioning these changes, while the increasing move of business historians into business schools has prompted a reevaluation of methodologies and perspectives in order to link much more closely to the social sciences.

Consonant with previous efforts to define the discipline of business history (Wilson, 1996; Jones and Zeitlin, 2008), the editors have based their work on the premise that business history is concerned with understanding how business organizations evolve, in their institutional, national and international contexts through managerial process, by engaging with a variety of source material. The intersection between business history and the broad field of business studies has also opened up fresh areas for research, including the study of international business and globalization, business networks and clusters, corporate governance and entrepreneurial behavior. This most recent phase has also expanded the range of methodologies that business historians can employ, complementing the traditional use of archival research by incorporating new sources of quantitative and qualitative data, including oral history, visual records and statistical and financial data.

The broad intention behind this *Companion* is to provide a framework for the study of all these dimensions of business history, accommodating the best traditions with new perspectives that have been driven by a rapidly increasing flow of contributions from the wider social sciences and business schools. As a consequence, the scope of the book goes beyond the traditional and reflects increased international scope and a wider range of methodologies. This will provide an introduction to, and overview of, current scholarship in the expanding discipline of business history, using a structure that builds the research agenda and at the same time offering thematic perspectives on major business issues and problems. The expectation is that the approach will benefit a wide range of scholars, most obviously business historians, but more importantly scholars whose background may be in the social sciences, other branches of history or who are indeed entirely new to the discipline. For the general reader, it will provide an introduction to the historical dimensions of a range of issues that permeate the concerns and policy agendas of today's entrepreneurs, managers and regulators.

In this context, while we do not intend to provide an extensive business history bibliography, it is worthwhile highlighting some of the key stages in the discipline's development. This theme is elaborated further in Chapter 3 by Kipping, Kurosawa and Wadhwani, but it is worth noting that of central importance to the way in which the discipline has matured relates to the way in which business historians have progressively moved away from the large American corporation-oriented work of Alfred Chandler, a scholar who dominated the discipline up to the 1990s. Chandler's work has now largely been overridden by a range of alternative approaches that have generated much more effective ways of understanding business evolution in a range of international contexts. Chandler's last major publication was in 1990 (*Scale and Scope*), following which business historians in several countries not only challenged his paradigm, but also offered alternative approaches to a model of business evolution that owed much to a preoccupation with big business operating in a distinctly American fashion. Wilson (1996) produced the first textbook on British business history in the mid-1990s, while Jones (1996) published a history of international business in the same year. These works stimulated widespread debate about the nature of business history, and especially the extent to which it could be regarded as a social science, given the increasing tendency of especially scholars of organization studies to delve into the field.

One of the key features of this new dimension to business history research was a desire to offer a fresh interpretation of business evolution. This was at the centre of work by Toms and Wilson (2003), who while using the Chandlerian focus on scale and scope economies, outlined through the use of a two-by-two matrix the need to incorporate a wider range of influences that included accountability and governance perspectives, the development of efficient capital markets and the impact of globalization. At the same time, scholars such as Clark and Rowlinson (2004) and Usdiken and Kiesr (2004) were focusing social scientists' attention on what is now referred to as a culturalist 'historic turn' in organization studies, providing a platform for work that is continuing to generate deep insights into both a business history methodology and the way in which business organisations have evolved. It was also apparent that by the beginning of the twenty-first century a significant majority of business historians were located in business schools, rather than history departments, revealing a further motive to link more closely with social science research methodologies. More recently, Scranton and Fridenson (2013) filled many of the gaps in Chandler's paradigm by offering an innovative theme-based approach to reimagining business history, including a critique of traditional practices. Similarly, Amatori and Colli (2013) have also challenged previous perspectives. A highly novel approach was mooted by Bucheli and Wadhwani (2014), who adopted a structure based on the theories and methods of management research, prompting the emergence of a fresh interest in temporality as a means of opening up new opportunities that management scholars such as Suddaby, Kipping and Rowlinson (all of whom feature in Bucheli and Wadhwani, 2014) have seized effectively. This is exciting research that will no doubt continue to provoke strong feelings amongst historians and social scientists alike, indicating how business history has the potential to stimulate debate and attract the brightest minds. Indeed, there is an increasing expectation that business historians need to develop much greater fluency in bridging the gap between historical and social science research, as well as incorporating more theoretical approaches in developing insights into longitudinal studies (Maclean et al., 2015).

While an integration of all of these approaches is difficult to achieve comprehensively, it is nonetheless necessary if the present state of the art of business history is to be truly represented. The present work consequently complements these contributions by offering fresh themes, international overviews and methodologies, thus providing a crucial bridging mechanism with other social sciences and contributing to the broad aim of linking business history with complementary disciplines, broadening the audience for our work and reinvigorating established approaches.

Structure and contents

The proposed structure will achieve these objectives through the exploration of the following key themes:

- The discipline of business history (agendas, historiography, debates, interdisciplinary approaches and methodology)
- Business ownership (looking at various organisations, including private, public, family and not-for-profit)
- International varieties of capitalism (regional and national perspectives)
- Institutions (from pre-industrial to de-industrial and global)
- Management and ethics (culture, ethics, organisation, etc.)

The rapid expansion of the discipline referred to earlier suggests the value of a structure based on key themes, in that it is necessary to showcase the rich variety of business history. This multi-perspective approach thereby illustrates the unique appeal of business history and underlines its contribution to a number of adjacent disciplines. Key themes running through the sections and chapters will be: new approaches and emerging issues, sources, methodologies and the emergence of new subject areas within business history; areas which have become pertinent to the current business landscape (for example, corporate governance policy, CSR and sustainability); applying new methodologies (networks); revisiting well-worn topics with fresh perspectives (pre-modern business history, gender and globalization); and identifying areas for further research. Clearly, a chronology would have been more ambitious, if not impossible, in view of the international scope, interactions of business and economic institutions, sector specialisms and the *dramatis personae* of individuals involved. Instead, the themes provide a selection of direct entry points and bridges between business history and other fields of enquiry.

As has been noted recently (Rowlinson et al., 2009), business and management scholars moving into business history lack methodological guidance, not least from historians. Part I of the *Companion* addresses that gap, whilst also providing an overview of principle debates and controversies in business history. In Chapter 2, Toms and Wilson provide specific guidance on the methods and potential pitfalls of archival research and the use of historical evidence of all types to inform wider debates. This theme is taken further in Chapter 3 by Kipping, Kurosawa and Wadhwani, who note that business history has evolved as a discipline in its own right and has bolstered its relationships with cognate disciplines. It goes on to provide deep insights into the role of business history as nested in the evolution of other disciplines, extending the coverage outside the USA and Western Europe to demonstrate a broad international and cross-disciplinary nature of business history. In Chapter 4, de Jong et al. review the most influential recent papers in business history, providing an introduction and insight into key business history publications whilst gauging their impact through a citation analysis. Taken together the chapters in this section provide an overview and introduction to the main debates and methodologies in business history.

Part II is organised around different models of business ownership, drawing on the extensive business history and adjacent literature that has explored the reasons why businesses fall under different types of ownership at different stages of national and international economic and institutional development. In Chapter 5, Colli defines personal capitalism and presents a model in which this form of capitalism can be a stage in development, where technology, culture and institutions induce a diffusion of firm types, leading to multiple varieties of personal capitalism. Chapter 6 by Quail introduces managerial capitalism, where the business owners are mere financiers and companies are managed by professional executives. The historical overview shows that over time a variety of forms of managerial capitalism have prevailed. Chapter 7 by Colvin is different in nature, as he describes how the history of banking has been studied over the twentieth century. Simultaneously, this chapter discusses the main contributions to banking history. Smith and Tennant in Chapter 8 present the historical development of financial capitalism, and in particular the contributions by business historians to the debate about financialization. Finally, Webster completes the overview in Chapter 9, discussing the so-called third sector, namely, co-operatives, mutuals, charities and social enterprises. The five chapters demonstrate the rich contributions of business history to ongoing debates about business ownership and control.

As business history can be used to explain the evolution of such arrangements within a variety of international contexts, Part III offers an important contribution to the debate about which models of capitalism work and why nations succeed or fail economically, linking closely with the 'varieties of capitalism' debate. This encapsulates a series of such contrasts by taking a broadly continental perspective (with the exception of Asia, which proved impossible to cover as a single entity), including hitherto neglected regions. Austin in Chapter 10 demonstrates this graphically, emphasizing how in Sub-Saharan Africa such is the dominance of subsistence production and exchange that firms are significantly less dominant than in industrialised economies, a problem compounded, for the purposes of historical investigation, by the paucity of archive material. Ville and Merrett in Chapter 11 are more concerned with how Australia fits into the 'varieties of capitalism' debate, revealing that while managerial capitalism emerged in Australia, the lack of a strong managerial class limited this development, while collaboration across firms persisted throughout the twentieth century. Kragh in Chapter 12 offers deep insights into the dominance of large-scale enterprise ('gigantism') in Soviet and Chinese business, while at the same time demonstrating that in spite of strong central government control an informal form of collaboration (respectively, *blat* and *guanxi*) were extensively used by the business communities. While state ownership was also a common feature of Latin American business development up to the 1980s, in Chapter 13 Miller highlights how the increasingly dominant private business groups have evolved into major players on the global scene, fueled by privatization and foreign direct investment. In his discussion of North American capitalism (including Canada and Mexico), Wilson in Chapter 15 highlights the constantly changing nature of business, and especially the recent demise of large-scale manufacturing concerns, the dominance of finance and the links with government regulation. Finally, in tracing the extensive differences between Western European economies, Sluyterman and Westerhuis in Chapter 16 reflect on the 'varieties of capitalism' debate and its focus on institutional issues, linking these to the various stages of industrialization through which many have passed.

In the penultimate part of the Companion, we turn to the role of institutions within business history by providing coverage of business structures of the pre-modern era, informal networks which govern business behaviour, the growing prominence of corporate governance procedures and the influence of globalisation. In the opening chapter of this section, Casson and Casson offer an in-depth overview of themes more commonly found in modern business history and by doing so, illuminate the potential for further research into such themes in the pre-1750 period. Using a host of interesting examples, the authors shed light on many aspects of the business institutions, enterprise and practices of the pre-modern and early modern period. Buchnea in Chapter 18 also incorporates aspects of pre-modern business, examining how networks have determined business growth and practices in a number of contexts. Focusing on informal network arrangements, this chapter highlights the importance of relationships in influencing business from the early modern to the present period. Continuing the thread of influential relationships, in Chapter 19 Millward presents an impressive overview of business and government relations in Europe, Japan and the US from the nineteenth century. Through this detailed exploration, Millward addresses fundamental questions about the needs and wants of businesses and how respective governments have responded to these. Building on this discussion of intervention in business, in Chapter 20 Tilba explores an emergent strand of business history research: the development of corporate governance in the UK as it pertains to corporate ownership. In this section, structures which influence firm behaviour persist as a central theme and the final chapter on globalisation takes a particularly novel approach to this. In this chapter, Gervais and McWatters examine not only how businesses have been shaped by an increasing 'globalised' world, but also how business historians have continued to focus on this conception of 'globalisation' and the resultant divergence of ideas regarding the periodisation and contemporary perception of globalisation, which continues to constrain histories of global business.

The final part is inspired by recent events in the ever-changing landscape of British business. These chapters focus on two separate but related issues: the role of individuals in business and the importance of accountability in business. In examining these topics, the authors highlight useful frameworks and areas for further research within the history of management, corporate social responsibility (CSR), and contexts of managerial behaviour. In Chapter 22, Larson examines the progression of management professionalization through a thorough chronological analysis of the contributions made by scholars writing in the twentieth century. Importantly, Larson addresses many of the critics of management education and the profession itself and explores how the divergence in opinions with regards to the role of manager has impacted upon the field of business history and business studies in general. The following chapter by Doe continues this theme of 'roles' by examining the ways in which women have been perceived in business and what their actual contributions have been. Here, Doe challenges old definitions, suggesting that women have been passed over frequently in histories of business because of a persistent focus on 'Big Business'. The final two chapters in the section shed light on areas in which management and ethics intersect. Through an inventive approach, Toms' chapter on financial fraud and scandals examines how business history can inform issues of malfeasance in the financial sector. After a useful longitudinal overview, Toms presents a helpful conceptual framework using historical incidences of financial fraud to determine the interaction between opportunity and impediment. In a contrasting examination, Mees takes a meaningful look at the foundations of business ethics and changing perceptions of what is 'ethical' which have given rise to several areas which require further exploration by business historians, namely the new prominence of CSR and issues of sustainability.

Conclusion

To repeat a point made in the first paragraph, it would have been impossible to cover every country, region and topic that has been researched by business historians. Nevertheless, the editors believe that we have brought together a collection that will stand the test of time by presenting deep insights into a discipline that continues to evolve, and especially by both extending its coverage and building much stronger links with the social sciences. While little has been said about the way in which business historians continue to work closely with adjacent areas such as management history, accounting history and labour history, it remains true to claim that this provides further fertile ground in which the discipline can flourish. Indeed, as this *Companion* demonstrates business history continues to go from strength to strength, offering much to a wide range of scholars and students seeking to understand the dynamics of business evolution and its relationship with an ever-changing environment.

References

Amatori, F., & Colli, A. (2013). *Business history: Complexities and comparisons*. Abingdon: Routledge.

Bucheli, M. & Wadhwani, R. D. (2014). *Organizations in time: History, theory, methods*. Oxford: Oxford University Press.

Chandler, A. D. (1990). *Scale and scope: The dynamics of industrial capitalism*. Cambridge: Harvard Business School.

Clark, P., & Rowlinson, M. (2004). The treatment of history in organisation studies: towards an 'historic turn'? *Business History*, *46*(3), 331–352.

Jones, G. (1996). *Evolution of International Business*. Abingdon: Routledge.

Jones, G. & Zeitlin, J. (2008). *The Oxford handbook of business history*. Oxford: Oxford University Press.

Maclean, M., Harvey, C., & Clegg, S. (2015). Conceptualizing historical organization studies. *Academy of Management Review*, *41*(4), (Oct 2016), 609–632.

Rowlinson, M., Stager J. R. & Booth, C. (2009). Critical Management and Organizational History. In M. Alvesson, H. Willmott & T. Bridgman (Eds.), *Handbook of Critical Management Studies* (pp. 286–303). Oxford: Oxford University Press.

Scranton, P. & Fridenson, P. (2013). *Reimagining business history*. Baltimore, MD: JHU Press.

Toms, S. & Wilson, J. (2003). Scale, scope and accountability: Towards a new paradigm of British business history. *Business History*, *45*(4), 1–23.

Üsdiken, B., & Kieser, A. (2004). Introduction: History in organisation studies. *Business History*, *46*(3), 321–330.

Wilson, J. F. (1996). *British Business History, 1720–1995*. Manchester: Manchester University Press.

2

Business history
Agendas, historiography and debates

Steven Toms and John Wilson

Introduction

Business history has developed rapidly in recent decades to incorporate a wide range of methodologies in a variety of international contexts. The discipline began as a branch of economic history in the USA in the 1920s and in Britain in the 1950s (Supple, 1977; Wilson, 1995). Its emergence in Britain followed the publication of a series of influential company histories and the establishment of the journal *Business History* in 1958 at the University of Liverpool. The most influential of these early company histories was Charles Wilson's *History of Unilever*, the first volume of which was published in 1954. Other examples included Coleman's work on Courtaulds and artificial fibres, Alford on Wills and the tobacco industry and Barker on Pilkington's and glass manufacture (for an overview, see Hannah, 1983; Wilson, 1995; Wilson and Toms, 2008). These early studies were conducted primarily by economic historians interested in the role of leading firms in the development of the wider industry, and therefore went beyond mere corporate histories. European and Japanese business historians were not slow to follow these models, engaging extensively in both corporate and broader industrial studies, providing a much richer range of material on which to start developing typologies of business evolution in different contexts (Farnie et al., 2000; Rowlinson, Toms and Wilson, 2007).

Business history has more recently become more embedded in business schools and the wider social sciences, thereby expanding its research agenda to incorporate questions of interest to a wide range of academics, policy makers and practitioners. More recently, it has accommodated, firstly, the 'historical turn in organizational studies' (Clark and Rowlinson, 2004), potentially opening up the discipline to a new range of philosophical and methodological approaches, and secondly, 'new business history' which utilises a range of methodologies with the objective of obtaining generalisable results (de Jong et al., 2015). These alternative perspectives provide the opportunity for the debates (for example, Taylor et al., 2010; Toms and Wilson, 2010) that indicate the health and continuing development of any *sui generis* discipline. They have also made available a variety of methodologies that can be applied to the understanding of history. Alternatively, the historical method can be used to inform the investigation of present-day research agendas, involving the approaches less familiar perhaps to mainstream scholars of business and social scientists.

Notwithstanding the progress of business history as a discipline, these developments create a potential minefield of methodologies. They have also created some discussion about the role of the methodology that has for many years provided the main tool for business historians, namely, archival research. This chapter discusses archival research and then considers some of the criticisms of this approach and assesses the potential complementary solutions of alternative approaches. Another important methodological focus for business historians has traditionally been the case study. Again, this has been the focus of some criticism, prompting suggestions in favour of complementarity with alternative approaches. It is consequently necessary in this chapter to provide a review of archival case-oriented methodologies and the potential viability of alternatives.

To make sense of such a varied agenda, and to exemplify alternative methodologies, the chapter also considers one of the most significant debates in both economic and business history, namely, entrepreneurship and the growth of the firm. By adopting this single issue as the cornerstone of this chapter, we can also consider a set of major research questions that have occupied business historians over several decades, and to the extent that they are unresolved, continue to do so. Originating with a discussion about the determinants of the long-run decline of the British economy, it is vital to emphasise that the subject of entrepreneurship and the growth of the firm has attracted enormous interest from economic and business historians for well over fifty years, providing a consistently provocative range of interpretations and methodological approaches. One should also add that this debate not only illustrates the relevance of business history to understanding the big issues that dominate the policy agenda today and our collective understanding of the past, but also provides a useful illustration of the methodological issues that confront the business historian.

To incorporate these complementary perspectives, the chapter begins with a discussion of the conventional archival method and the specific advantages it provides to business historians and to business history relative to other disciplines. It then goes on to critique archival approaches and examine the merits of alternative methodologies, including oral history, textual analysis and the application of scientific methods. A further section revisits the debates on entrepreneurial failure and British industrial decline as an example of the business history method as a contribution to debates in wider disciplines.

Archival and case study research

Archival research refers to research conducted using existing data, usually curated in a location and independent of the researcher. In practice, this means that archival data has been collected and stored for some purpose other than the specific objective of any particular researcher. The motives of and procedures of the curator are therefore important points for the business historian's attention and critical scrutiny. Archival data, certainly for business historians, often exists in unmodified form. For example, the accounting records of a business are preserved in the form that they were originally created. As a consequence, the researcher may need to collate the records so that further analysis can be undertaken. In some cases, some collation may have already occurred, for example where data has been submitted by participating firms to an industry organization or government agency, or has been subject to analysis for the purposes of inclusion in journals, newspapers and reports. These collations may exist in published or unpublished forms.

Because the archive has been created in non-random fashion for some other purpose, care is required to align the research question or hypothesis with the content of the archive. If the archive is inappropriate to the search for an answer to specific research questions, alternative approaches are preferable. Verification of historical records, frequently referred to as triangulation, is an important skill and must demonstrate good command of corroborating evidence. Things can go wrong, as the experience of authenticating the fraudulent 'Hitler diaries' demonstrated. A critical and indeed sceptical mindset should accompany the business historian into the archives, to ascertain their provenance, and demonstrate a critical understanding of why the record was created, by whom and why it has survived. This will be especially important when the historian attempts to add oral evidence to what is available in written form, through interviews and/or questionnaire exercises of extant individuals with knowledge of the firm/industry. As we will note later, oral evidence must carry with it an academic health warning, given the propensity of some individuals to relate a narrative that does not necessarily tally with the written record, creating major problems for the historian when attempting to produce an objective conclusion.

Many archives exist because old books, correspondence, memoranda, minutes of meetings, statistical reports and so on, have been retained for posterity by organizations wishing to maintain their corporate memory. However, the mere existence of an archive does not justify investigation for its own sake, even if the objective is simply to create a 'coffee table monograph' about the company in question. Even here, some judgement of context is required. Genuine research questions, however, must build on context so that they are developed and guided by a literature review conducted prior to the selection of archival records. Hazards still remain, of course, in terms of the content of the archive, which once investigated can diverge significantly from what is implied in index records and hand-lists.

Discussion of how the archive, once identified, is actually investigated is rare, both in historical and social science research methods texts (Gunn and Faire, 2012, p. 5). A likely reason is that such processes are guided by practical considerations (King, 2012, p. 19), often including the time and resource issues associated with access, ranging from the cost of professional transcription and translation services to the use of appropriate contacts to access private sources. Where such issues are significant, considerations of methodological purity may be set aside, such that research questions are modified according to what can actually be ascertained. Where accession costs are significant, and the content eclectic, historians may be tempted to let the archive speak, quickly developing questions on the basis of chance discoveries relevant either to other important agendas or to a range of agendas not directly focused on specific research questions at all. The issues raised by such pure empiricism, including the possibility that new knowledge can be created independently of existing theoretical frameworks, are returned to below.

Independence of creation can be an important advantage where relevant variables cannot be generated through experimental methods or where there would otherwise be ethical barriers to the subject of investigation. In business history, this might mean variables associated with different models of corporate governance, for example one-shareholder-one-vote cannot be investigated without legislation to create such models. On the other hand, if an archive documents the experience of using such models in the past, then archival research would be a useful method (for example, Toms, 2001, 2012). Similarly, an important potential contribution is where the interrogation of this archive provides the opportunity to answer a research question that cannot be answered using other often more recent data sources, or where such sources do not necessarily enhance the debate. For example, to investigate the effects of the length of the working week on worker efficiency a recent study (Penceval, 2014) used data from the Health of Munition Workers Committee (HMWC) set up in 1915. The context in which new, unskilled workers were recruited against the backdrop of a lifting of peacetime restrictions on the working week meant the episode had useful experimental features on which to draw generalisations. The archival data on output and working hours had been collected with the same purpose as the research questions interested in present-day manifestations of this relationship, allowing variables to be measured that were subject to statistical analysis. Notwithstanding the earlier removal of restrictions, the HMWC recommended the re-imposition of maximum working hours on the grounds of maximising total output, supporting the generalizable conclusion that it is efficient for businesses to self-impose restrictions on working time in the absence of legislation.

Case studies have dominated business history research. The reasons for this are easy to understand. Cases provide the opportunity to research micro relationships within and between firms that may otherwise elude the economic historian's typical dataset. These advantages at the same time create limitations, particularly when applying a scientific method to produce robust generalisations. For de Jong et al. (2015) the solution is to develop methodologies that build knowledge incrementally through the accumulation of case-related knowledge, thereby allowing the development of theoretical perspectives and widening its appeal in the social sciences (Toms and Wilson, 2011). The call for a 'new business history' is important, not least because of the increasing critique of business histories that rely on case studies underpinned only by archival research.

Critique of archival research and new research methods in business history

Notwithstanding the ability of historical research to answer important research questions and to adapt social science methodologies to do so, a recent critique of traditional business history has developed based on its apparent neglect of methodology. According to this view, not only do business historians frequently treat their archival method as implicit, or indeed fail to articulate it entirely, but also historical methodology, including archival research, is increasingly absent from methodological textbooks. An important reason is that business historians have been reluctant to debate methodological issues amongst themselves (Bell and Taylor, 2013, pp. 128–129).

Acknowledging this vacuum, a number of methodologies have emerged based on the potential of a more rigorous approach to business history. These include actor network theory, for example, using the sociology of translation to explain business leaders' adoption of the ideas of the Human Relations School. Using this approach, Callon's four moments of problematization provide an analytical framework for the investigation of published and archival evidence (Bruce and Nyland, 2011; Callon, 1986). Oral history offers the possibility of a 'history from below', which although increasingly adopted by business historians (Wilson et al. 2013) has already been significantly developed in other fields (Walton, 2010), creating additional sources that can complement, or indeed question, the content of corporate archives (Robertson, 2009). The value of this approach then is its ability not just to generate additional evidence, but in doing so develop new perspectives and deeper understanding.

Having noted the potential benefits of oral evidence, it is equally vital to assess its drawbacks and highlight why business historians must be extremely cautious when applying this material to either narrative-building or detailed analysis. The most obvious initial point is that memories fade, necessitating a careful triangulation of oral evidence against other primary and secondary sources. More worrying, however, is the purposeful misdirection of the interviewer, resulting in a skewed interpretation of events that severely clouds any objective judgement. This is often regarded as a major flaw in commissioned histories, in that the executives who employ a historian to write such a monograph can be accused of influencing the outcome, usually in their favour. Alternatively, in providing only selective access to material, and especially limiting access to the most recent archive which could well be regarded as commercially-sensitive, historians are limited in the degree to which they can follow the analysis of key decisions.

An excellent example of this form of manipulation is the way in which the 150th anniversary history of The Co-operative Group was written (Wilson et al. 2013). While the historians were provided with access to a copious archive, the most recent material was not made available, resulting in an excessive reliance on oral and secondary evidence to provide insights into events and trends. The publication of this monograph also coincided with major financial problems within The Group, with the collapse of The Co-operative Bank and a whole series of attendant issues. Although The Group's senior executives were well aware of the impending problems, they chose not to reveal them to the historians, resulting in a concluding chapter that lacks credibility when compared to The Group's real position. It is also worth adding that many other business historians have experienced similar problems when attempting to write about more recent developments, highlighting a general problem with commissioned business history, and indeed any work that is dependent upon sources that are not entirely reliable.

A discussion of such fundamental issues reveals the need for business historians to be much more versatile in both methodological and analytical senses. One alternative is to employ discourse analysis, as a means of pursuing a more detailed analysis of what can either be found in documents or provided in oral evidence. Discourse analysis examines a literature on the basis of theoretically or pre-determined criteria, identifying specific aspects for the purposes of further scrutiny. For example, analysing the history of strategic management, Thomas et al. (2013) use four categories: historiographic methodology; vocabulary and metaphor; modality; and intertextuality. They conduct a qualitative analysis of a sample of strategic management texts that allow the discipline's history to be traced, highlighting a series of limitations that are also characteristic of the recent wave of criticism of traditional business history itself, including an unquestioning and often teleological view of progress and an associated lack of engagement with critical perspectives and reflexivity.

Such methods have the potential to add to business history by either generating additional evidence or reanalysing existing evidence. Being critical or reflexive should not be an end in itself, nor should research effort be concerned merely with establishing the relevance of a particular method for its own sake. Moreover, when applied to historical analysis, specific philosophical perspectives, which also imply a research methodology, can enrich debates by bringing fresh perspectives to business history research.

On the other hand, these accounts can also be one-sided interpretations, partly because their embedded methodology precludes and even promotes a reluctance to critique the underlying epistemological assumptions, whether Foucauldian, Marxist or rationalist/institutionalist. For these reasons it is important to be aware of critical analysis of philosophical positions when considering such research. Using Foucault as an example, business historians would do well to take account of studies that analyse the weaknesses of totalising methodological approaches. Rowlinson and Carter (2002) provide such a critical analysis of the methodologies employed by Foucauldian researchers, including ambivalence, error and neglect of historiography, as an obstacle to the successful investigation of history in organisation studies. Another obstacle is narrow focus and mono-causality. Hoskin and Macve (1988) use a Foucauldian genealogical perspective to reinterpret the genesis of management in the industrial revolution by changing the traditional focus of Pollard's (1965) pioneering study to the arms manufacturers of ante-bellum USA. Here, military administrators transferred the discourse of West Point examinations to the objectives of manufacturing efficiency and accountability. Analysis of such discourse offers a tightly focused understanding of the genesis of management, but necessarily excludes issues of political patronage, governance and financial (mis)appropriation that should probably send researchers elsewhere in their quest to identify the first modern management (Toms and Fleischman, 2015). Recognition of alternatives, whether mainstream or radical, managerialist or anti-managerialist, can provide schemes for analysing the literature and testing competing theories (Rowlinson, Toms and Wilson, 2007).

Indeed, such eclecticism has long characterised what might still be described as mainstream business history. One reason for this is that the overwhelming focus of these studies advocating new methodologies has, unsurprisingly, been on the relevance of the methodology itself, rather than testable research questions. In some cases, researchers have investigated archives with a new methodology in mind, but without considering how the theoretical concepts implied by the methodology might help constitute research questions (Rowlinson and Hassard, 2013, p. 113). Conversely, the HMWC example above illustrates how research questions that are related only exogenously to the methodology, or more strictly the method, stand a priori to the choice of specific investigative tools. Maintaining such an approach whilst being open-minded about the methodology, offers a useful way forward for business history, whilst maintaining its engagement with related disciplines. Studies that simply interrogate an archive on the 'Everest' justification, on the other hand, stand guilty of the empiricism that is the normal focus of the recent methodological critique, while at the same time becoming hostage to the problems outlined earlier with regard to oral and more recent evidence.

Another criticism of 'mainstream' business history that has gathered pace in recent years has concerned its apparent narrow scope, based on its attention to core industries and large firms. For researchers new to business history, this presents itself as a plethora of possible new perspectives. These include alternative business organisations such as co-operatives, not-for-profit, charity and voluntary organisations and public corporations, including their governance and finance. Labour history and social history are other adjacent neglected fields that are entirely suitable for analysis, particularly where concepts like 'Disneyfication', 'McDonaldization' (Walton, 2010, pp. 4–5; Ritzer, 2006) and indeed globalization are strongly influenced by the contemporary business agenda. Scranton and Fridenson (2013) echo these and other suggestions, highlighting promising themes ranging from fraud to trust and co-operation, as well as empires to emerging nations and subaltern studies. Moreover, abandoning the traditional practices of business history and adopting new thematic domains might be the best way to study such themes. These changing foci of investigation are determined in part by the decline of once dominant business organisations (U.S. Steel, General Motors, DuPont, Sears) in the US that informed the dominant Chandlerian narrative up to the 1990s (Scranton and Fridenson, 2013, pp. 5–6). Notwithstanding these clear trends, there are nonetheless justifications for reaffirming the Chandlerian model. Important reasons are the strong relationship between big business and national economic performance, the incremental, if discontinuous role of technology and the recent economic resurgence of the US at the expense of Japan and Europe (Amatori and Colli, 2011, pp. 7–8). These differences reflect in part the increasing divergence of business history internationally, and against this backdrop it is perhaps unsurprising that only some business historians find virtue in the once dominant Chandlerian and US models.

Reconsidering these agendas returns us to the major on-going debates in business history. No doubt they can be addressed or at least nuanced by using new methodologies or the alternative perspectives discussed above. The next section considers a major debate, chosen for its importance to business history and the wider policy agenda, as well as its ability to illustrate the methodological issues highlighted in the discussion thus far.

Entrepreneurship and the growth of the firm

As the previous section has shown, business history has the potential to accommodate methodologies and extend its own toolkit. Indeed, new approaches have done much to enhance the potential of the discipline in recent years. At the same time, the scope of the discipline has expanded, and in recent years has ranged from the trading methods of the ancient Greeks (Peacock, 2013) to analyses of the role of venture capital up to and including the 2008 financial crisis (Toms et al., 2015).

Business history and economic performance

The theory of the firm, and the role of the entrepreneur within the firm, has long been and remains a central topic of business history enquiry (Amatori and Colli, 2011, p. 3). As business history emerged as a discipline in its own right, it aimed to explain what could not be explained by economics, namely, the qualitative dimensions of firm growth. For this reason, an important initial focus was the role of the entrepreneur, or the residual, an unexplained factor in the economist's model of production efficiency. At the same time, it directed attention to the rise and fall of industrial economies and international differences in competitiveness, which were and remain key issues for economic historians. With a focus on the reasons for the relative decline of the British economy from the late nineteenth century onwards, the entrepreneurial failure hypothesis offered a potentially plausible interpretation.

The entrepreneurial failure hypothesis dominated these discussions for a long period, leading to a series of case studies of core industries, including coal, textiles and steel, supported in turn by archival research into the performance of a plethora of individual enterprises (Aldcroft, 1964; McCloskey and Sandberg, 1972). Many of these were collated in Chandler's (1990) *Scale and Scope*, which attributed the success of the American model to investment in technology and marketing capability supported by integrated organisational structures, with British firms allegedly failing to make similar investments.

The Lancashire cotton textile industry, which had been the leading take-off sector in the industrial revolution, but which was slow to invest in subsequent technical developments, became an important focus of debate on this subject. Mass and Lazonick (1990), for example, argued that cotton textile entrepreneurs in Britain failed to develop larger integrated plants on the American model; also a conclusion reached by Chandler (1990) in his synthesis of a number of comparative case studies. Since then, research using new archival sources has offered alternative interpretations. A major omission from a debate about poor economic performance was an absence of studies using firm-level financial data. Analysis of such data and collations from a number of sources, including corporate archives, government repositories of accounting records and contemporary press sources, suggested that firms were making good profits in the two decades before 1914 (Toms, 1998). Their individual investment decisions therefore made more sense than the Chandlerian critique suggested, not just in core industries like cotton textiles but also in the wider economy. Moreover, financial speculation and events that followed the First World War are more relevant in these accounts than the traditional account of entrepreneurial failure (Arnold and McCartney, 2010; Higgins, Toms and Filatotchev, 2015). Methodological concerns that influence this conclusion included counter-factual analysis using only information that entrepreneurs had at the time, incorporating relevant path dependencies and issues associated with the subjectivity of accounting information, assessed not in terms of its accuracy per se, but whether or not the figures were believed to be accurate by economic decision-makers (Higgins and Toms, 1997; Higgins and Toms, 2003; Toms and Beck, 2007).

The entrepreneurial failure debates reveal not only the hazards of mixing economics with history, but also reveal how business-level analysis can resolve conflicts arising from their different methodological traditions. History provides what the economist lacks, namely, a theory of change. Being concerned not with 'origins, but transitions' (Butterfield, 1931), history explores the paths that to the classical economist are simply movements from one state of equilibrium to another. Thus, Mass and Lazonick (1990) criticised Sandberg (1974) for applying 'static' neo-classical equilibrium models to the cotton industry, suggesting instead that history and economics should develop a dynamic theory of institutional change. One might also add that simple acceptance of the dominance of economics places potential limitations on conclusions, since where the economist, or social scientist, might count heads and create categories, the historian cannot escape the requirement, in addition to focus on particular individuals (Elton and Sunderland, 1967, p. 28). Keynes (1971, p. 151), as an economist, was careful to recognise the need for a wider context for his own discipline when he postulated that economics is a method rather than a doctrine. Indeed, thorough analysis of the documentary sources without any reliance on formal economic models and a conscious neutrality vis a vis contradictory ideological interpretation remains a viable alternative standpoint (for example, Farnie, 1979). However, both history and economics share the common problem of incompleteness (Hawke, 1980), the former in terms of evidence, the latter in terms of the restrictive assumptions necessary for the analysis of isolated economic relationships.

The obvious and uncontroversial solution is to combine the best aspects of both disciplines; using economic models and data to add to the evidence where appropriate, while using historical context to qualify the conclusions drawn from economic analysis. For example, to argue that contemporary entrepreneurs would have made decisions according to the realisable rate of return on investment calculated according to the assumptions of marginal economics is a possible model for analysing the decision-making process. For the historian, noting that decision-makers in a market economy behave according to certain rational principles, perhaps governed by the simplifying static assumptions of equilibrium, can be a useful means of understanding the past. It is not the same thing as endorsing ideologically-charged precepts of apparently rational behaviour, such as self-interest. Rather, it is the acceptance of their use as a tool of historical investigation. A neo-classical economist using neo-classical economic models to investigate historical problems is one thing; a historian examining the same problem with the same model, because that model was used by historical actors, and aware of the limitations and context of that model, is quite another.

Conclusions

Identifying and researching an archive offers an important distinguishing feature of research into business problems using an historical dimension. At the same time, business historians need to be fully aware of the dangers associated with both relying on what a company has bothered to retain and the extent to which other evidence is required in order to triangulate what is in the written record. Furthermore, if one of these alternative sources is oral evidence, then even greater care needs to be taken in the way that this is applied to an objective analysis of the firm's performance. Above all, though, and especially if business historians want to contribute to broader debates, for example entrepreneurial performance, it is essential to engage with a variety of methodologies, whether from economics or other social sciences, in order to make the material relevant. As we have noted above, business historians (de Jong et al., 2015) are also venturing into the methodological field, offering creative techniques that can be effectively applied to the analysis of historical evidence, whether written or oral. This reflects the enormous progress that business history as a discipline has made over the course of the last seventy years, and especially in Western Europe, where more creative approaches to methodology are developing rapidly.

References

Aldcroft, D. H. (1964). The Entrepreneur and the British Economy, 1870–1914. *The Economic History Review*, 17(1), 113–134.

Amatori, F. & Colli, A. (2011). *Business History: Complexities and Comparisons*. Abingdon: Routledge.

Arnold, T. & McCartney, S. (2010). Can macro-economic sources be used to define UK business performance, 1855–1914? *Business History*, 52 (4), 564–589.

Bell, E. & Taylor, S. (2013). Writing history into management research. *Management & Organizational History*, 8(2), 127–136.

Bruce, K. & Nyland, C. (2011). Elton Mayo and the Deification of Human Relations. *Organization Studies*, 32(3), 383–405.

Butterfield, H. (1931). *The Whig Interpretation of History*. London: Bell.

Callon, M. (1986). Some elements of a sociology of translation: domestication of the scallops and the fishermen of St. Brieuc Bay, in J. Law (ed.), *Power, Action and Belief: A New Sociology of Knowledge? Sociological Review*, Monograph № 32, 196–233. London: Routledge.

Chandler, A. (1990). *Scale and Scope: The Dynamics of Industrial Capitalis*m. Cambridge: Belknap Press.

Clark, P. & Rowlinson, M. (2004). The treatment of history in organization studies: towards an 'historic turn'? *Business History*, 46, 331–352.

de Jong, A., Higgins, D. M. & van Driel, H. (2015). Towards a new business history? *Business History*, 57(1), 5–29.

Elton, G. R. & Sunderland, H. (1967). *The Practice of History* (p. 169). Sydney: Sydney University Press.

Farnie, D. A. (1979). *English Cotton Industry and the World Market, 1815–1896*. Oxford: Clarendon.

Farnie, D. A., Nakaoka, T., Jeremy, D., Wilson J.F. & Abe, T. (2000). *Region and strategy in Britain and Japan: business in Lancashire and Kansai, 1890–1990* Abingdon: Routledge.

Gunn, S. & Faire, L. (eds.). (2012). *Research Methods for History*. Edinburgh: Edinburgh University Press.

Hannah, L. (1983). New issues in British business history. *Business History Review*, 57(2), 165–174.

Hawke, G. R. (1980). *Economics for Historians*. Cambridge: Cambridge University Press.

Higgins, D. & Toms, S. (1997). Firm structure and financial performance: the Lancashire textile industry, c. 1884-c. 1960. *Accounting, Business & Financial History*, 7(2), 195–232.

Higgins, D. & Toms, S. (2003). Financial distress, corporate borrowing, and industrial decline: the Lancashire cotton spinning industry, 1918–38. *Accounting, Business & Financial History*, 13(2), 207–232.

Higgins, D., Toms, S., & Filatotchev, I. (2015). Ownership, financial strategy and performance: the Lancashire cotton textile industry, 1918–1938. *Business History*, 57(1), 97–121.

Hoskin, K. W. & Macve, R. H. (1988). The genesis of accountability: the West Point connections. *Accounting, Organizations and Society*, 13(1), 37–73.

Keynes, J. M. (1971). *The Collected Works of John Maynard Keynes*. Vol. 12. London: Macmillan.

King, M. (2012). 'Working with/in the archives' in Gunn, S., & Faire, L. (eds.). (2012). *Research methods for history*. Edinburgh: Edinburgh University Press.

Maclean, M., Harvey, C., & Clegg, S. (2015). Conceptualizing historical organization studies. *Academy of Management Review*, 41(4), (Oct 2016), 609–632.

Mass, W. & Lazonick, W. (1990). The british cotton industry and international competitive advantage: the state of the debates, *Business History*, XXXII(4), 9–65.

McCloskey, D. N. & Sandberg, L. G. (1972). From damnation to redemption: judgments on the late Victorian entrepreneur. *Explorations in Economic History*, 9, 89–108.

Peacock, M. S. (2013). Accounting for money: the legal presuppositions of money and accounting in ancient Greece. *Business History*, 55(2), 280–301.

Penceval, J. (2014). The Productivity of Working Hours, Stanford University Discussion Paper No. 8129.

Pollard, S. (1965). *The Genesis of Modern Management: a Study of the Industrial Tevolution in Great Britain* (p. 209). Cambridge: Harvard University Press.

Ritzer, G. (2006). *McDonaldization: The Reader*. Thousand Oaks: Pine Forge Press.

Robertson, E. (2009). *Chocolate, Women and Empire: a Social and Cultural History*. Manchester: Manchester University Press.

Rowlinson, M. & Carter, C. (2002). Foucault and history in organization studies. *Organization, 9*(4), 527–547.

Rowlinson, M. & Hassard, J. S. (2013). Historical neo-institutionalism or neo-institutionalist history? Historical research in management and organization studies. *Management & Organizational History, 8*(2), 111–126.

Rowlinson, M., Toms, S. & Wilson, J. F. (2007). Competing perspectives on the "managerial revolution": from "managerialist" to "anti-managerialist". *Business History, 49*(4), 464–482.

Sandberg, L. G. (1974). *Lancashire in Decline: a Study in Entrepreneurship, Technology, and International Trade*. Columbus: Ohio State University Press.

Scranton, P. & Fridenson, P. (2013). *Reimagining Business History*. Baltimore: Johns Hopkins.

Supple, B. (1977). Introduction: approaches to business history, in Supple, B. (ed.) *Essays in British Business History*. Oxford: Clarendon, 1–8.

Taylor, S., Bell, E. & Cooke, B. (2009). Business history and the historiographical operation. *Management & Organizational History, 4*(2), 151–166.

Thomas, P., Wilson, J. & Leeds, O. (2013). Constructing "the history of strategic management": a critical analysis of the academic discourse. *Business History, 55*(7), 1119–1142.

Toms, S. (1998). Windows of opportunity in the textile industry: the business strategies of Lancashire entrepreneurs, 1880–1914. *Business History, 40*(1), 1–25.

Toms, S. (2001). Information content of earnings in an unregulated market: the co-operative cotton mills of Lancashire, 1880–1900. *Accounting and Business Research, 31*(3), 175–190.

Toms, S. (2012). Producer co-operatives and economic efficiency: evidence from the nineteenth-century cotton textile industry. *Business History, 54*(6), 855–882.

Toms, S. & Beck, M. (2007). The limitations of economic counterfactuals: The case of the Lancashire textile industry. *Management & Organizational History, 2*(4), 315–330.

Toms, S. & Fleischman, R. K. (2015). Accounting fundamentals and accounting change: Boulton & Watt and the Springfield Armory. *Accounting, Organizations and Society*. 41, 1–20.

Toms, S. & Wilson, J. (2010). In defence of business history: a reply to Taylor, Bell and Cooke. *Management & Organizational History, 5*(1), 109–120.

Toms, S. & Wilson, J. (2011). Business history: sustaining excellence. *Business History, 54*(1), 1–5.

Toms, S., Wilson, N. & Wright, M. (2015). The evolution of private equity: corporate restructuring in the UK, c. 1945–2010. *Business History, 57*(5), 736–768.

Walton, J. K. (2010). New directions in business history: themes, approaches and opportunities. *Business History, 52*(1), 1–16.

Whittle, A. & Wilson, J.F. (2014). Ethnomethodology and the production of history: studying "history-in-action". *Business History, 56*(1), 2015, 1–15.

Wilson, J. F. (1995). *British Business History, 1720–1994*. Manchester: Manchester University Press.

Wilson, J. F. & Toms, S. (2008). Fifty years of business history. *Business History, 50*(2), 125–126.

Wilson, J. F., Webster, A. & Vorberg-Rugh, R. (2013). The co-operative movement in Britain: from crisis to "Renaissance", 1950–2010. *Enterprise and Society, 14*(2), 271–302.

Wilson, J. F., Webster, A., & Vorberg-Rugh, R. (2013). *Building Co-operation: A Business History of the Co-operative Group, 1863–2013*. Oxford: Oxford University Press.

3

A revisionist historiography of business history

A richer past for a richer future

Matthias Kipping, Takafumi Kurosawa and R. Daniel Wadhwani[1]

Introduction

Business historians have recently devoted considerable attention to the future of their discipline. These re-imaginings have involved exploring a range of new topics, re-configuring relationships to other academic disciplines and expanding the methodological and theoretical foundations of their research (e.g., Hansen, 2012; Scranton and Fridenson, 2013; Wadhwani and Bucheli, 2014; de Jong, Higgins and Driel, 2015; Decker, Kipping and Wadhwani, 2015). Business history, it is fair to conclude, is in an inventive mood, bursting with multiple futures and paths forward. Yet, little of this creative energy has been devoted to re-interpretations of business history's past. Even in a so-called "post-Chandlerian" era, the historiography of business history remains framed in reference to Chandler's work if not in Chandlerian terms and topics (Hausman, 2003; see e.g., Hannah, 1999; Friedman and Jones, 2011; Scranton and Fridenson, 2013). The very designation "post-Chandlerian" implies that in terms of periodization the field's history can and should be divided neatly into the era of "the founder", who supposedly lifted the study of business history out of purely narrative accounts of heroic if not always ethical entrepreneurs (McCraw, 1988), and the current epoch, in which both his disciples and his detractors have strayed into new lands.

To some extent, the neat Chandlerian/post-Chandlerian periodization that is often used to characterize the history of the discipline does provide a useful short hand for establishing one's position vis-à-vis the field's historiographical traditions. It designates the distinction between a moment when many business historians were indeed particularly focused on the rise of large industrial firms and the managerial hierarchies which controlled them and the period when other forms of organization, including small and medium sized enterprise, family businesses, business groups and networked organizations became subjects of growing interest (Jones and Zeitlin, 2007). It also signals a broadening of interest in business history beyond organizational form, to institutions, entrepreneurship and the cultural, social and political foundations of enterprise (Scranton and Fridenson, 2013; Yeager, 2015; Lipartito, 2016). In this regard, the conventional periodization of the historiography of business history is somewhat meaningful.

We nevertheless contend that the conventional historiographical account distorts the discipline and its development in fundamental ways and stifles business historians' engagement with their own intellectual past. Scholarly studies of the history of business and entrepreneurship long predate Chandler, and developed decades before the formal designation of "business history" as an identifiable area of research. These studies were much broader in scope than the Chandlerian focus on organizational form and hierarchies. Even around the height of Chandler's influence, historical studies of business often flourished in related disciplines, such as sociology, economics and management studies, with less of a myopic focus on organizational form and control. And, perhaps most notably, beyond the United States and to some extent Western Europe, business history developed both before Chandler and took on very different trajectories of intellectual development, even at the height of his influence.

Taking a longer-term view of the historiography of business history and considering alternative paths – both from disciplinary and geographical perspectives and including the roads not travelled – matters for more than simple antiquarian and/or comparative reasons. Revisiting and revising business history's past and multiple paths is inseparable from how we imagine and write its future. It allows those aiming to explore and extend its methodological, epistemological and theoretical boundaries to draw on a richer and more eclectic set of intellectual traditions than is commonly recognized. Ignoring this intellectual past, in contrast, not only tends to exaggerate the novelty of some of the recent developments in business history, it also deprives business historians of the opportunity to engage with and build on these interesting intellectual and international traditions and debates. In this chapter, we therefore seek to outline a revisionist historiography of business history that moves beyond Chandler and, ultimately, a US-centric account of the development of the discipline. In doing so, we do not seek to discount Chandler's contributions, nor his significance in the development of the discipline. Rather, we believe that incorporating the longer and more complex past and its multiple national and disciplinary paths into the discipline's historiography is essential to enriching its future.

The main structure of the chapter is chronological, subdivided into three periods: World War II, the second half of the twentieth century and the early twenty-first century. And while the second period is already quite well covered by others (e.g., Hausman, 2003), we also suggest revisions to the conventional account here. Within each of the three periods, we look at developments in a number of selected countries, focusing, in addition to the United States, on Germany, the United Kingdom and Japan and the involvement of various academic disciplines and intellectual traditions in researching the history of business, including economics (and economic history), history, sociology and management studies. The choice of these geographies and disciplines was driven mainly by: (i) hindsight regarding the roles they played in the development of what we understand as business history today; (ii) their ability to clearly illustrate our main concern regarding the need for an examination of long-term developments and multiple paths; and (iii) the availability of sufficient information covering developments in these countries and the interactions of these disciplines with our own. Our chapter should be understood as a call for further investigations into the varied histories of business history in other parts of the world and its ongoing or emerging relationships with other disciplines – always in the interest of enriching our research and enhancing our future impact.

Histories of business before "business history"

Most conventional accounts trace the origins of business history to the Harvard Business School (HBS), and notably the creation of the Isidor Straus Chair in Business History in 1927 and its first holder, N. S. B. Gras, who worked to establish business history as an independent field of research and teaching focused on the firm (e.g., Larson, 1947; Hausman, 2003). But, as this section shows, while HBS was indeed where "business history" as a term was coined, the roots of modern histories of business lay in the deeper past, and particularly in the emergence of "historical schools of economics" in Germany and the UK in the nineteenth century. Understanding these deeper origins is crucial for grasping both the diversity of topical, methodological and theoretical concerns that has characterized historical research on business enterprise, as well as comprehending its divergent paths of development around the world.

The historical schools and the origins of business history

Historical economics arose in Germany and the UK as a critique of the classical, and later neoclassical, schools of economics, and their use of abstract, theoretical terms to describe economic processes. While the "old" historical school shared with classical economists a quest for "laws" albeit "historical" ones, a younger generation of historical economists, such as Gustav von Schmoller in Germany and William Cunningham in the UK, saw the study of history as a more promising path for understanding economic processes (Schumpeter, 1954a, pp. 807–24, 1954b, pp. 152–201; Gay, 1941, pp. 9–14). These historical economists – and their successors, such as Max Weber and Werner Sombart – distinguished themselves not only from classical economics, but also from other prominent intellectual movements that aimed to understand change and economic process in historical terms. Thus, unlike Hegelian thought and Marxism they eschewed *a priori* metaphysical claims about historical dialectics and – given their emphasis on human agency – were skeptical of a predominantly materialist basis for historical change.

These historical schools anticipated modern business history in the range and nature of the subject matter with which it was concerned. The most commonly recognized of these in business historiography today is the concern for understanding the evolution of organizational forms and the nature of the authority that allowed for such variations in organization and control – a topic perhaps most closely associated with Max Weber's work (Weber, 1978). But historical economists also engaged a wide range of other intellectual concerns that continue to resonate in business history today. Historical economics was particularly concerned with institutions, for instance, in shaping the role, productivity and competitiveness of business (Hodgson, 2004). They also emphasized the importance of the agency and entrepreneurship of business people, in part as a critique of mainstream economics' reference to abstract factors of production (Wadhwani, 2010). Historical economics was interested in dynamic and evolutionary processes within capitalism, rather than the static or equilibrating processes that had been the focus of classical and neoclassical economics, tracking how institutions, firms and entrepreneurship interacted over time. In particular, historical economists viewed change in capitalism as proceeding through a series of stages, as forms of economic relations changed over time (see, for an overview, Schumpeter, 1954b, pp. 176–180).

In addition to the range of research that concerned historical schools of economics, two other aspects of their approach to historical research would shape the subsequent development of business history in lasting ways. One of these pertained to the role of methodology and theory in the research process. Many business historians are familiar with the dispute about methodology or *Methodenstreit* between Gustav von Schmoller and Carl Menger in the late nineteenth century, and the claims of the former that the methodological path forward was through painstaking inductive research and the production of detailed monographs that could – one day in the future – allow for broader theoretical claims (Peukert, 2001).

However, while the *Methodenstreit* is often interpreted as both the starting and end point of the historical engagement with methods and theory, historical economists and then early business historians actually continued to grapple explicitly with questions of methods and theory as they considered how to conduct research in meaningful ways. As Schumpeter (1954a) pointed out, the generation of historical economists who followed Schmoller embraced a form of theorizing from history through the use of "ideal types", an approach that would influence the emerging discipline of business history proper in the decades to come.

The other aspect of historical economics that would shape the development of business history was a belief in the practical value of historical knowledge for decision making in the present. The historical use of concrete evidence and specific, contextualized situations, historians argued, made historical economics a much more practical field than the abstractions provided by classical and neoclassical economics. Schmoller, in particular, saw history as a *practical* guide for policymakers in the present, an approach that provided concrete examples of decisions made by leaders in the past as examples from which leaders in the present could learn.

Independence and isolation: From economic to business history in the US

One place where the historical schools had an immediate and significant influence was the United States. Through the international flow of scholars and ideas, the historical schools first shaped the growth of institutional thinking and historical reasoning in economics, sociology, political science and law (Herbst, 1965). Among those who received their doctoral education with Schmoller was Edwin F. Gay who then obtained a position in economic history at Harvard and, more importantly, became the first dean of the Harvard Business School in 1908 (Cruikshank, 1987). But it was his successor, Wallace B. Donham, Dean from 1919 until 1942, who saw the study of past situations as a valuable source of insight for businessmen – one that also coincided with the case method of teaching he had introduced at HBS. Donham therefore endorsed the creation of a Business Historical Society in 1925, approved the inclusion of business history first as part of the Business Policy course in 1927, then as a separate elective course in 1928, and, in 1927, convinced the Straus brothers, who owned Macy's department store, to endow a chair in business history in memory of their late father Isidor (Cruickshank, 1987, pp. 112, 157–62).

The appointment of N. S. B. Gras as the first chairholder demonstrates the enduring influence of the German historical school on the development of business history (Anon., 1956; Boothman, 2001). A student of Gay's and deeply influenced by European, especially German, studies on economic history, Gras had researched commodity prices and tried to sketch out what he had seen as the stages of economic development over the course of millennia. At HBS, however, Gras and a coterie of research associates focused on developing detailed internal firm-level histories (Hausman, 2003, pp. 86–7). These were partially meant to provide teaching material for what had now become a full course in business history. In 1939, Gras published *Business and Capitalism: An Introduction to Business History* and a *Casebook in American Business History*, the latter together with Henrietta M. Larson, who had joined HBS as a research associate in 1926, became the schools' first female faculty member in 1939 and the first woman to become a full professor there in 1961, shortly before her retirement. She was instrumental in establishing business history at Harvard, including as editor of the *Bulletin of the Business Historical Society* between 1938 and 1953, the year it turned into the *Business History Review* (Yeager, 2001).

Gras and his group at HBS also drove forward the development of "business history" as a separate academic discipline, distinct from economic history. In developing his research agenda, Gras eschewed the calls from the younger generation of historical economists and sociologists for the identification and analysis of "ideal types", insisting instead on the production of detailed monographs, patterned on Schmoller's research program. Their research was in some ways methodologically novel in embracing the use of internal company records and telling the story of business development from what was essentially the perspective of senior management (Anon., 1956, p. 358; Boothman, 2001). But Gras' attempts to build business history as a separate discipline met with limited success in the US. Few other American universities embraced research and teaching in business history, with a 1948 survey putting the number of the latter at only fifteen (Holton, 1949).

More importantly, due to the rather narrow scope, methods and epistemic goals chosen by Gras and his singular focus on studying the dynamics of firms based on their internal records, early business historians cut themselves off from dialogue with related disciplines – including economics, sociology and history – at a moment in the interwar period when scholars, and the American public in general, were skeptical about the motives and power of firms and entrepreneurs. As a consequence, complained the University of Chicago's Richard Wohl (quoted in Boothman, 2001, p. 71), the new discipline managed to "divorce it[self] from the main body of American economic history". Indeed, while "business history" as a term was coined in the US, a quarter century of efforts by Gras and his colleagues to fortify its disciplinary walls had left the new field isolated. This was in stark contrast to the paths of development elsewhere.

Integration with economic history and sociology almost everywhere else

The main reason for the emergence of business history as a separate – and ultimately more isolated – discipline in the United States was its unique context in terms of the development of business education during the first half of the twentieth century (Engwall et al., 2016). The US was the only country that saw a widespread development of university-based business schools, where company case studies, developed first at Harvard, proved a useful method of teaching. The rather different organizational settings elsewhere left little room for the emergence of business history as a separate discipline, instead leaving it to often flourish as an important topic within (socio)economic history, which had become increasingly institutionalized in the 1920s.

In the UK, the development of separate higher education for business remained marginal, confined to departments of commerce in a few universities and entirely absent from the ancient ones at Cambridge and Oxford, hence offering no foundation for the creation of business history as a separate discipline. But having been one of the pioneers of historical economics, economic history flourished in the country and became deeply embedded in economics departments. An Economic History Society was formed in 1926 and began publishing the *Economic History Review* in 1927. It is here where broadly conceived histories of business thrived, including studies of institutions, ethics, entrepreneurship and business people (Ashley, 1927; Harte, 1971).

In Japan, scholars who had studied historical economics in Germany returned to establish the economics departments at the universities of Tokyo and Kyoto in 1919. In Kyoto, Japan's first economic history periodical was launched in 1929 and an Institute for Research in the Economic History of Japan was established in 1933. The first nationwide association, the Socio-Economic History Society, was established in Tokyo in 1930, and empirical research on business and industries flourished within its confines (Saito, 2015). There was little effort to separate business history from socio-economics. Rather, the study of business and economic history was fundamentally shaped by the need to account for what scholars and policymakers saw as the country's economic backwardness and the desire to understand the institutional foundations for modernization and economic development. Not surprisingly then, the historical schools of economics, and German historicism in particular, played a formative role in shaping its development, albeit with very different objectives than they did in the US (Schwentker, 1998; Roth, 1999; Yanagisawa, 2001).

Ironically, in Germany, which had served as the cradle of education for the first generation of American and Japanese economic and business historians, historical studies of business and economics went into precipitous decline. While originating outside universities at the turn of the twentieth century, education for business quickly developed a scientific approach akin to the predominant *Wissenschaft* tradition in the country's universities, where it became incorporated as business economics or *Betriebswirtschaftslehre* (BWL) during the interwar period (Engwall et al., 2016). In this context, historical case studies as they were being developed and used in the US, were not seen as sufficiently scientific. Historical economics did retain some intellectual influence within the faculties of national economics or *Volkswirtschaftslehre* (VWL), but here the focus was on the role of the state rather than on firms and entrepreneurs. And while the Historical School à la Weber and Sombart had a promising legacy in German economic sociology in the early twentieth century, the academic environment for such thought was decimated following the seizure of power by the Nazis in 1933.

Business history in the second half of the twentieth century

In the conventional account, Chandler's work comes to eventually define business history and it's concerns in the post-World War II era, and particularly after the 1960s (Hausman, 2003). His research is often understood as a triumph of what history can offer to the study of management and organizations. But, as this section shows, it was never as successful or all-encompassing as some have made it out to be. In some ways, it actually isolated business history as a discipline even more than under Gras. Moreover, it was not the only, or at times even the most vibrant intellectual movement within historical studies of business. And, beyond the US, business history continued to flourish in non-Chandlerian terms and with distinctly non-Chandlerian concerns.

The scientistic turn in management studies and the marginalization of business history

Beginning in the late 1950s and early 1960s business schools in the US increasingly emulated the hypothesis-testing natural science model to enhance their own legitimacy within the academic system of higher education, turning to established scientific disciplines in their recruitment of faculty and in research (Engwall et al., 2016). These developments did not escape the attention of business historians, as is apparent from a 1962 special issue of the *Business History Review*. In particular, Glover (1962, pp. 71–73) highlighted the increasing importance of the social sciences and their methods within business schools, portraying these developments as an opportunity for business history to "provide an enormous deposit of fact against which a myriad hypotheses can be tested". He therefore advocated "a synthesis of skills and interest" in the sense that historians could "teach the other social scientists something about methods of research in historical sources", while forced though "to become more expert and more like specialists in the social sciences".

The prime example for such a "synthesis of skills and interest" that would emerge at the time was the early work of Alfred Chandler, who had spent his initial career at MIT and John Hopkins (McCraw, 1988). In his 1962 book *Strategy and Structure*, he explicitly aimed to provide social scientists with empirical data to develop generalizations and theories. The study explored the organizational changes in the largest US firms, combining a large-scale, but statistically simple survey with four in-depth case studies (GM, DuPont, Standard Oil and Sears Roebuck), showing how four pioneering firms had, independently of each other, developed a decentralized structure, later called the multidivisional or M-from, to accommodate their growth and diversification. Chandler's book prompted a large-scale empirical research effort on the M-form, initially at the Harvard Business School, where he himself was appointed to the Straus chair in 1970, with follow-up studies stretching to the present day and including empirical testing of the so-called M-form hypothesis formulated by economist Oliver Williamson (for an overview, see Kipping and Westerhuis, 2012). Chandler's 1962 study also influenced additional, sometimes even contradictory schools of thought in the emerging and diversifying field of organizational studies (Üsdiken and Kipping, 2014) and, to this day, he is considered one of the classic examples for comparative, theory-building management research (e.g., Eisenhardt, 1991).

Chandler's work, and in particular his subsequent study of the emergence of the visible hand of management in US business (Chandler, 1977; John, 1997), also shaped business history, focusing its research interest on large-scale organizations – albeit without ultimately spurring the kind of interaction with social science methodology and theories advocated by Glover (1962). The "synthesis" that prevailed instead among business historians was the one formulated by Louis Galambos (1970, 1983). Intellectually, it claimed a Weberian heritage, which had also influenced Chandler via Talcott Parsons; methodologically, it proposed using the "traditional tools of historical thought", albeit without making those very explicit; and in terms of content it focused on "large-scale, national, formal organizations […] characterized by a bureaucratic structure of authority" (Galambos, 1970, pp. 279–280). But while this "organizational synthesis" provided some unified direction to business history, it led to an increasing separation from developments in management, which had now fully embarked on studying contemporary organizations with natural science methods.

Thus, what seemed like an opportunity for close cooperation in the early 1960s quickly turned into a chasm, as management and business history moved in opposite directions. Moreover, there were few institutional overlaps since the scholarly associations and publications of business history developed outside organization and management studies (see Kipping and Üsdiken, 2007; Üsdiken and Kipping, 2014 for details). As a result, business history came to be identified in the US as a narrow sub-discipline, separated by its particular object of analysis, the nature of the company sources it valorized, and the strong premise that the problems of coordination and control represented *the* central concern to be explained in the history of business. At its extreme in the 1970s and 1980s, business history invented its own narrow historiography that began – and often ended – with Chandler.

Entrepreneurial history as a stymied alternative in the US

However, the claim that an organizational synthesis prevailed in business history in the post-war period is at best incomplete, including for the United States. Even at HBS, there was no consensus that the internal development of firms should be the only, or even the primary focus in historical studies of business. Indeed, in the 1950s and early 1960s, the more dynamic research agenda pertaining to the history of business was "entrepreneurial history", which emerged to some extent as an alternative path to Gras' program in business history (Wadhwani, 2010). Inspired and explicitly supported by Schumpeter, and organized by HBS economic historian Arthur Cole, entrepreneurial history sought to keep "business and businessmen [...] continually in the foreground" while incorporating the broader social and economic setting in which they were both embedded and which they shaped, thus taking a more socially embedded view of business history. Entrepreneurial history was also far less reticent of engaging in theory, eschewing the position taken by Gras – and inspired by Schmoller – that historical research needed to focus on painstaking and detailed archival research as its paramount task. In laying out the agenda for research at the intersection of history and entrepreneurship, Schumpeter (1951, p. 259) suggested the need for "an incessant give and take between historical and theoretical analysis".

Entrepreneurial history, and the Research Center in Entrepreneurial History (1948–58) at HBS in particular, was a diverse, interdisciplinary hothouse of ideas, evidence, theory and debate. The strongest camp was made up of institutionalists, including Thomas Cochran, David Landes and Douglas North. The institutionalists looked for the ways in which both legal rules and cultural norms shaped the supply of entrepreneurship and the impact on economic growth. They tended to consider national institutions in particular, which led to investigations into so-called national types of entrepreneurial behavior – a tendency that still persists in a recent volume co-edited by Landes, Mokyr and Baumol (2010). Others, including Arthur Cole (1959), were interested in entrepreneurial processes and their relationship to industrial change, which was probably the agenda closest to what Schumpeter (1949) had imagined. The wide array of disciplines engaged in entrepreneurial history in the 1950s and 1960s, including psychology, sociology, economics and history, meant that the field was a broad and diverse camp that included the cross-disciplinary flow of ideas, often quite speculative, and debates, sometimes quite heated (Jones and Wadhwani, 2007).

Ironically, the interest in "entrepreneurial history" went into decline in the 1960s and 1970s, just as popular interest in entrepreneurship was on the rise. The reasons for this decline were complex, but were at least partly attributable to the growing influence of both Chandler in business history and cliometrics in economic history in the US (Jones and Wadhwani, 2007). *Explorations in Entrepreneurial History*, which had been the first scholarly journal in any discipline devoted to entrepreneurship, was, in 1969, converted to *Explorations in Economic History*, a venue for the growing interest in cliometrics.

From Marx to Chandler? The post-WWII emergence of business history around the world

Outside the US, business history had by and large remained embedded within (socio) economic history and, generally, addressed broader research questions. But since the 1950s it also gradually, and at different paces, came to develop its own identity and organizations. Chandlerian ideas had some influence over these developments, in particular in contexts where Marxist ideas held some sway within economic history. But, as they did in the earlier period, institutional factors, namely the developments in national business education fields, played a more important role in determining what kind of business history eventually gained traction.

In postwar Japan, business history emerged rapidly in the 1950s as a sub-discipline of socio-economic history with its own identity well before Chandler (Mishima, 1961). Socio-economic scholarship in the period was dominated by Marxism, which hued closely to materialist dialectics as the explanation for historical change. In economic history, the primary school of thought coalesced around the ideas of Otsuka Hisao, a professor at the University of Tokyo and one of the most influential intellectuals in postwar Japan. The "Otsuka School" combined Marxist economics and a Weberian view on society and ethics to explain the origins of "modernity" in the West and the "backwardness" of Japanese society. It focused, in particular, on the early modern era – where Otsuka held a negative view on the economic and social role of pre-modern merchants and commerce in Japan – and the formation of national economies, applying a Weberian methodology of ideal types to examine societies in comparative-historical perspective (Otsuka, 1982; Kondo, 1993). Within this academic context, business history emerged as an alternative approach, shaped to some extent by the methods of Gras and Larson, but more so by the ideas behind "entrepreneurial history" in the US. Economic historians with an antipathy to orthodox Marxism and ones dissatisfied with the stylized approach of the "Otsuka School" were attracted to business and entrepreneurial history (Keieishi Gakkai, 2014, pp. 6–10). The emerging sub-discipline was free from the highly negative views on Japanese tradition and the role of merchants held by the Otsuka School, and it attracted scholars with more optimistic assessments of postwar Japanese business and society, especially ones from the Kansai region, the center of merchant culture in Japan.

Interest in business history was propelled by the rapid institutionalization of educational programs on the topic, which led to massive job creation in the 1960s and 1970s. In 1964, the Business History Society of Japan (BHSJ) was founded and enrolled close to 350 members within two years; it started publishing its own journal, the *Japan Business History Review*, in 1965. The growing interest in business history also coincided with the massive expansion of university education, especially the establishment of departments of management. By capitalizing on these opportunities, the first generation of Japanese business historians successfully convinced the Ministry of Education to make business history courses mandatory in management education. Since the creation of positions in business history preceded the training of business historians, economic historians employing a variety of approaches were recruited, ensuring that the subject remained broad and interdisciplinary (Keieishi Gakkai, 2014). Historical studies of European and American business, as well as comparative research, formed a conspicuous feature of Japanese business history in the subsequent decades (Kobayashi, 1978).

Though the introduction of Chandlerian thought into this mix beginning in the mid-1960s did have an important impact, business history already had strong momentum and its own identity in the country. For some of the "core" members of the BHSJ, Chandler's systematic work renewed and intensified their identity as business historians, but the discipline itself retained its broader perspective on both topics and methodologies (Keieishi Gakkai, 1985, 2014; Kudo, 2003). Moreover, due to the late and limited expansion of cliometrics in Japanese economic history, and the slow pace at which scientization proceeded in management studies in the country, an extensive overlap between business history, economic history and management studies persisted. More than half the members of the BHSJ retained a double affiliation with the Socio-Economic History Society, and approximately 20–30% did so with management related associations.

Since the turn of the twenty-first century, however, the discipline has faced a growing crisis of relevance due to the very nature of its original foundations. The need to understand "economic backwardness" and economic development processes became less broadly relevant, as Japan grew into a rich country afflicted with the problems of a mature economy rather than one struggling to catch up. And the emphasis on specialization and on painstaking archival work in the Schmoller tradition made the situation worse, as scholars were rewarded for increasingly focused and narrow studies with little theoretical and conceptual basis for comparison (Kurosawa, 2014).

In Europe, during the late 1960s and 1970s, Chandler's views regarding the importance of technological progress, the role of organization in creating economies of scale, and the emergence of big business as "an act of economic rationality" also appealed to "many left-leaning scholars" often inspired by Marxist ideas (Amatori, 2015). Some of them took a kind of pilgrimage to HBS, which had, once again, become a center for a "pure", self-contained – in other words, isolated – business history focusing on big business. Upon their return, these scholars translated Chandler's books and/or conducted and fomented replication studies. But while they might have dominated business history research and teaching in certain universities, the extant and evolving institutional frameworks proved ultimately more powerful in determining the development of business history across Europe.

Thus, in the UK, business history gained its own eponymous journal in 1958, and a first chair was created at the University of Glasgow in 1959, followed by Liverpool. Most of those studying the history of business remained based in economics and economic history departments though, where a large number of scholars produced studies examining a variety of issues, such as entrepreneurship, organizational innovations, decision-making processes, relationships between business and politics and industrial development from the view of micro-level entities (Yonekawa, 1973). They positioned their work as a branch of economic history (e.g., Barker et al., 1960; Payne, 1967). The dynamics changed beginning in the late 1970s, when economics and economic history were increasingly affected by the cliometric revolution and became less hospitable for business historians, while the number of management departments and business schools began to grow. At least initially, the latter were often populated by (economic) sociologists, less keen on hypothesis testing and more favorable towards business historians and (comparative) case studies.

An important vehicle for the promotion of a separate identity and a hub attracting those conducting business historical research both in the UK and also from other countries was the Business History Unit (BHU), established by the London School of Economics and Imperial College in 1978 (Jones and Sluyterman, 2007, p. 114). While initially home to a group of Chandlerian scholars, it soon developed a broader research agenda and several of its members eventually moved on to other universities, establishing active groups of business historians there. By the end of the 1980s, the number of self-identified business historians had grown to an extent that warranted the establishment of a separate Association of Business Historians (ABH). Today, while economic history departments have all but vanished, business history in the UK is a rather vibrant discipline well embedded within the broader management education field (Kurosawa, 2014).

It is ironic that given the formative influence of Schmoller and the German Historical School and given the strong tradition of support for archives and historical research, it was in Germany where business history struggled the most to develop in the post-WWII era. The decimation of many academic centers, and of sociology in particular, during the Nazi period had gutted what had once been the intellectual home for histories of business and entrepreneurship. The studies that were conducted, often with the (financial) support of firms and local chambers of commerce, remained largely descriptive. The historian Wilhelm Treue did establish a journal, *Tradition: Zeitschrift für Firmengeschichte und Unternehmerbiographie*, in 1956. But the discipline struggled to develop its academic independence and move beyond basic narrative descriptions. Universities provided little support, with positions identified specifically as "business history" largely non-existent (Yonekawa, 1973, p. 173; Schröter, 2003).

Lacking university-based resources, business historians depended on organized support from companies, which themselves had an interest and agenda in shaping their public image. The first association, the Society for Enterprise History or *Gesellschaft für Unternehmensgeschichte*

(GUG), was founded in 1976 based on an initiative from the think tank of the German employers and business federations in order to support the archival, historical, and public relations work of German industry, publishing its own journal, the *Zeitschrift für Unternehmensgeschichte*, since 1977. Representatives from companies, usually the large ones, dominate the GUG board, with academics confined to an advisory council. It was not until 1991 that a dissenting group of academic historians founded a working party for critical enterprise and industry history or *Arbeitskreis für kritische Unternhemens- und Industriegeschichte* (AKKU), to promote a more critical historical perspective on business and enterprise in Germany (Schröter, 2000) and, more recently, transdisciplinary research. Overall, academic research in business history has grown stronger, particularly employing political and social analyses of the development of firms and industries, but institutional support from the universities remains weak.

The hidden continuity of recent changes

In the last two decades, business historians have moved in a number of seemingly new directions, engaging interdisciplinary frontiers and exploring new theoretical and methodological avenues. In light of business history's origins and multiple paths of development, however, these efforts seem less of a stark break from the past and more in line with what the discipline has long done, as can be seen in recent engagements between business history and the disciplines of management, history and economics.

Rejoining roads? Management and business history

Despite the marginalization of business history within most business schools in the US due to the "scientization" of management research, some topics remained open for historical approaches (Kipping and Üsdiken, 2007). This was notably the case of studies on multinational enterprise and international business, where Chandler's work also resonated; but even here, the reference to history and its importance tended to be little more than lip service (Khanna and Jones, 2006). Since the 1980s, however, a new interest in history arose within organization and management studies.

On the one hand, this was due to novel research questions, which required historical data and new theoretical constructs where past events or processes became part of the theories themselves (Kipping and Üsdiken, 2014). While these research programs proved popular and increased in visibility and while there were explicit calls for taking history more seriously, the number of management scholars using archival sources and making references to historical studies has grown only slowly. Business historians have not yet taken full advantage of this openness by attempting to make contributions to these research programs, despite opportunities being available in a number of special issues of leading management journals – opportunities predominantly exploited by management scholars themselves, based on their familiarity with the requirements for publishing in such journals. The already noted reticence of most business historians to make broader generalizations, let alone build theories, probably explains the slow pace of engagement. So far, repeated calls for bridging the continuing gap (e.g., Kipping and Üsdiken, 2007; Wadhwani and Bucheli, 2014) have only partially been heeded.

On the other hand, history more generally became part of an effort to broaden the methodological, epistemological and ontological base of management studies due to a growing dissatisfaction with the dominant science paradigm (for details, see Üsdiken and Kipping,

2014). In the US, Zald (1993, p. 514), for instance, argued for a return to the "philosophical, philological, historical and hermeneutic traditions" of the discipline – traditions, on which business history had also drawn originally as we have shown above. In Europe where these traditions had originated, Kieser (1994), not surprisingly, pointed to Weber as an example for the benefits of combining sociology and history, suggesting historical cases as a way to develop and apply "ideal types" or generate new hypotheses. Others have gone even further, arguing that organization studies as a whole need an "historic turn" (Clark and Rowlinson, 2004; see also Rowlinson, Hassard and Decker, 2014). In essence, they suggest making the "narrative" central, not in the sense of its critical, even formal analysis but as a way "to stress [...] complexity, uniqueness and contingency" (p. 343) – here, most business historians would concur – while ultimately also, in a postmodern sense, accepting its subjectivity and value per se beyond any objectivist truth claims – and here, most business historians would not concur (for an exception, see Hansen, 2012).

Unlike the above mentioned research programs in organization and management theory, these suggestions have found some resonance though, leading to an emerging strand of scholarly work now widely referred to as "uses of the past." It brings together business historians and management scholars and looks at how (business) organizations draw on "narratives" in the broadest sense, ranging from company histories to artefacts, to legitimize their existence and actions. Led by scholars interested in strategy and organizational identity, this stream of research has examined how history is "constitutive" (Wadhwani and Bucheli, 2014), i.e. shapes how actors view themselves, their choices and behavior (e.g., Mordhorst, 2008; Suddaby et al., 2010). Relatedly, there has been some recourse to Foucault's particular approach to history among management scholars, but this perspective has thus far gained little traction among business historians (for an exception, see McKinlay, 2013).

Business history and economic theory and methods

There have also been notable developments at the intersection of business history and economics or economic history. As we have seen, the barriers between these two disciplines have never been sharp in some national contexts, like Japan and the UK, where socio-economic history and economic history respectively have long been "big tents", which included narrative business and entrepreneurial history. But efforts have also been under way at this intersection and in contexts, like the US, where the distinction has often been sharper – including work at both the theoretical and methodological frontiers of the disciplines. Theoretically, Lamoreaux, Raff and Temin (2003) in the US and Casson (1997) in the UK, among others, have done much to incorporate economic theories of information asymmetry into business and entrepreneurial history. Methodologically, de Jong et al. (2015) have recently promoted quantification and hypothesis development and testing as an important path forward for "new" business history, as an analog to "new", i.e. cliometric, economic history.

Business history in history

One discipline with which business historians have rather infrequently engaged is mainstream history. In the US, this can partly be attributed to business history's once-isolationist stance and elsewhere to its primary engagement with economic history and sociology. To some extent though, this has also been due to mainstream history's limited interest in studying business as a central institution of modern societies (see also Hausman, 2003). Preferences in academic history for political and then social and cultural narratives have often gone hand in hand with a lack of careful analysis of the rise of business institutions, though there have been notable new left and Marxist historians who produced important critical explanations of the rise of big business (e.g., Kolko, 1963; Sklar, 1988). In the last two decades, however, mainstream academic historians have more consistently engaged with business history.

In part, this engagement has been promoted and prompted by scholars interested in introducing a greater range of historical topics to business history (Scranton and Fridenson, 2013). But it has also been shaped by the efforts to apply the kind of social and cultural analysis that has predominated in mainstream history to business history. Thus, the analysis of class, race, and especially of gender has become more central to business history research (e.g., Kwolek-Folland, 1998), as has the analysis of language, narrative and culture (e.g., Lipartito, 1995; Laird, 2009; Hansen, 2012). Most recently, in the US, the engagement between mainstream history and business history has mainly taken place under the "history of capitalism" label (Interchange, 2014). Though still an intellectual movement in development, historians of capitalism often describe their research as encompassing and integrating bottom up and top down history, incorporating labor and business, as well as class, race, gender and culture into their analysis of capitalism as an evolving system. Of particular note in this regard, have been the largely successful efforts to incorporate the history of slavery as an important topic within business history.

Implications and conclusion

In this chapter, we have developed an alternative to the linear narrative of business history as originating with N.S.B. Gras, maturing with Alfred Chandler, and entering a "post-Chandlerian" period, marked by the "discovery" of new organizational forms and topics, in the present. We have instead shown that academic histories of business trace their roots to the development of nineteenth-century historical schools of economic thought. Drawing back the origins of the field allowed us not only to see the deeper, common beginnings of historical reasoning and research about business, but also to trace the multiple paths through which it spread and took root – or failed to do so – around the world. We found that several factors shaped divergences in these paths of development. The intellectual contexts and academic *raison d'être* for the emergence of business history, for instance, differed in various parts of the world; its foundations as a tool for business education in the United States, for instance, differed from its purposes in Japan as a lens for understanding the relative strength of Western enterprises and capitalism. Its patterns of institutionalization in higher education and its relationship to the "storytelling" activities of firms also varied. And, its relationship to related disciplines, including economics, sociology, management studies and history differed from place to place and evolved over time, with business history in the US traditionally occupying an unusually isolationist position.

The complex lineage of business history, we find, suggests that the discipline has been more open, diverse and protean than has often been recognized. The history of business history, in other words, resists purist or originalist claims about the "essence" of the discipline and its "legitimate" practices. In different historical places and periods, it has held widely varying positions on the role of theory, sometimes embracing Schmoller's skepticism of abstraction, while at other times engaging in bolder Weberian conceptualization. Its "legitimate sources" and interpretive methodologies have likewise varied; in the narrow confines of post-WWII HBS, for instance, the Gras-and-Larson methods of mining company archives and narrating organizational development was challenged by entrepreneurial history's more sweeping interpretations about the social and cultural embeddedness of economic actors. Even business history's basic objects of study have varied from place to place and changed over time. Thus, while the term "business" in "business history" has sometimes referred to the study of firms and their internal management, as it did with Chandler, it has also commonly been used to refer to entrepreneurial processes, to business cultures or practices, and to institutions or whole business systems.

Its own history thus suggests that business history cannot truly be characterized as a discipline or sub-discipline, but rather as a shifting and evolving community or, more accurately, communities of scholars with diverse backgrounds, who find a home – sometimes permanently, sometimes temporarily – by converging on topics of common and pressing interest, such as the emergence and development of big business, the role of entrepreneurship in economic change, the causes of progress and "backwardness" in business systems or, more recently, the uses of history by organizations. To use a geographical metaphor, business history has been a kind of "borderlands" or a frontier, where scholars of different backgrounds go to trade in ideas and approaches not readily available within disciplinary cores. In this sense, business history has not *one* specific "home discipline" – not economics, not sociology, not management studies, not history.

This diversity and malleability, we believe, is an important source of business history's originality and its ability to respond to questions facing societies, economies and organizations – a condition to be protected and nurtured. But it has also historically been business history's central existential problem. As "foreigners" in all disciplines, business historians have often struggled to find institutional and organizational homes. No discipline is considered "incomplete" without business history and no academic institution must have it in order to survive or succeed. As the German case makes abundantly clear, a strong intellectual tradition is no guarantor of success or even survival. Where it has survived – in economics departments, like in the UK and Japan; business departments or schools, to some extent in the US, but more so in Japan, several European countries and more recently, Canada; and in a few history departments, again in the US – business historians have had to *make* a place for themselves with some institutional ingenuity and collective effort. Attending to these institutional challenges, our overview shows, is no small feat and represents an ongoing existential threat that each generation of business historians must face anew.

The historiography of business history also should make us cautious about espousing any "orthodoxy" of whatever denomination and weary of any efforts to promote, if not impose, lists of worthwhile topics or specific methodologies. As long as business historians maintain the openness and willingness for dialogue that has characterized their discipline for most of its past, new opportunities will arise, as is happening at the moment with "history of capitalism" and "uses of the past" and as might still happen with some of the promising research programs in management and organization theory. The most imminent danger it seems is the shortage of organizational homes, in particular now that business history is largely marginalized in US business schools and far from the mainstream in economics and history departments and no longer mandatory in Japan. But even today, there are encouraging indicators, for instance with undergraduate business programs returning to some liberal arts focus, where (business) history should be able to claim a more prominent role as it already does in certain business schools. As Winston Churchill famously remarked, the future is unknowable, but the past should give us hope. While he did not refer to business history, he could have.

Note

1 Names are in alphabetical order. All authors contributed equally to the chapter.

References

Amatori, F. (2015). 'Alfred Chandler's Second Industrial Revolution'. *The American Interest*, *11*(1), 1–10.

Anon. (1956). 'Norman Scott Brien Gras, 1884–1956'. *Business History Review*, *30*(4), 357–60.

Ashley, W. (1927). 'The Place of Economic History in University Studies'. *Economic History Review*, *1*(1), 1–11.

Barker, T. C., Campbell, R. H. & Mathias, P. (1960). *Business History*. London: Historical Association.

Boothman, B. E. C. (2001). 'A Theme Worthy of Epic Treatment: N.S.B. Gras and the Emergence of American Business History'. *Journal of Macromarketing*, *21*(1), 61–73.

Casson, M. (1997). 'Institutional Economics and Business History: A Way Forward?' *Business History*, *39*(4), 151–171.

Chandler, A. D. Jr. (1962). *Strategy and Structure. Chapters in the history of the industrial enterprise.* Cambridge, MA: MIT Press.

Chandler, A. D. Jr. (1977). *The Visible Hand: The Managerial Revolution in American Business*. Cambridge, MA: The Belknap Press Harvard University Press.

Clark, P. & Rowlinson, M. (2004). 'The Treatment of History in Organisation Studies: Towards an "Historic Turn?"' *Business History*, *46*(3), 331–52.

Cole, A. H. (1959). *Business Enterprise in its Social Setting*. Cambridge, MA: Harvard University Press.

Cruikshank, J. L. (1987). *A Delicate Experiment: The Harvard Business School 1908–1945*. Boston, MA: Harvard Business School Press.

de Jong, A., Higgins, D. H. & van Driel, H. (2015). 'Towards a New Business History?' *Business History*, *57*(1), 5–29.

Decker, S., Kipping, M. & Wadhwani, R. D. (2015). 'New Business Histories! Plurality in Business History Research Methods'. *Business History*, *57*(1), 30–40.

Eisenhardt, K. M. (1991). 'Better Stories and Better Constructs: The Case for Rigor and Comparative Logic'. *Academy of Management Review*, *16*(3), 620–7.

Engwall, L., Kipping, M. & Üsdiken, B. (2016). *Defining Management: Business Schools, Consultants, Media*. New York, NY: Routledge.

Friedman, W. & Jones, G. (2011). 'Business History: Time for Debate'. *Business History Review*, *85*(1), 1–8.

Galambos, L. (1970). 'The Emerging Organizational Synthesis in Modern American History'. *Business History Review*, *44*(3), 279–90.

Galambos, L. (1983). 'Technology, Political Economy, and Professionalization: Central Themes of the Organizational Synthesis'. *Business History Review*, *57*(4), 471–93.

Gay, E. F. (1941). 'The Tasks of Economic History'. *Journal of Economic History*, 1(Supplement), 9–16.

Glover (1962). 'Comment' (in F. Redlich, 'Approaches to Business History'). *Business History Review*, *36*(1), 70–75.

Gras, N. S. B. (1939). *Business and Capitalism: An Introduction to Business History*. New York, NY: F.S. Crofts & Co.

Gras, N. S. B. & Larson, H. M. (1939). *Casebook in American Business History*. New York, NY: F.S. Crofts & Co.

Hannah, L. (1999). 'Marshall's "Trees" and the Global "Forest": Were "Giant Redwoods" Different?' In N. Lamoreaux, D. M. G. Raff and P. Temin (eds.), *Learning by Doing in Markets, Firms and Countries*. Chicago, IL: University of Chicago Press, 253–93.

Hansen, P. H. (2012). 'Business History: A Cultural and Narrative Approach'. *Business History Review*, *86*(4), 693–717.

Harte, N. B. (1971). *The Study of Economic History: Collected inaugural lectures, 1893–1970*. London: Cass.

Hausman, W. J. (2003). 'Business History in the United States at the End of the Twentieth Century.' In F. Amatori and G. Jones (eds.), *Business History around the World*. Cambridge, MA: Cambridge University Press, 83–110.

Herbst, J. (1965). *The German Historical School in American Scholarship: A Study in the Transfer of Culture*. New York, NY: Cornell University Press.

Hodgson, G. M. (2004). *The Evolution of Institutional Economics: Agency, Structure, and Darwinism in American Institutionalism*. London: Routledge.

Holton, H. (1949). 'Survey of the Teaching of Business History'. *Bulletin of the Business Historical Society*, *23*(2), 96–103.

Interchange: The History of Capitalism (2014). *Journal of American History*, *101*(2), 503–36.

John, R. R. (1997). 'Elaborations, Revisions, Dissents: Alfred D. Chandler, Jr.'s "The Visible Hand" after Twenty Years'. *Business History Review, 71*(2), 151–200.

Jones G. & Khanna, T. (2006) 'Bringing History (back) into International Business'. *Journal of International Business Studies, 37*(4), 453–68.

Jones, G. & Sluyterman, K. (2003). 'British and Dutch Business History'. In. F. Amatori and G. Jones (eds.), *Business History around the World*. New York, NY: Cambridge University Press, 111–45.

Jones, G. & Wadhwani, R. D. (eds.) (2007). *Entrepreneurship and Global Capitalism*. Cheltenham: Edward Elgar.

Jones, G. & Zeitlin, J. (eds.) (2007). *The Oxford Handbook of Business History*. Oxford: Oxford University Press.

Keieishi Gakkai (1985). *Keiei Shigaku no Nijūnen: Kaiko to Tenbō* [BHSJ (1985). 20 Years History of Business History Studies: Retrospection and Future Perspective]. Tokyo: University of Tokyo Press.

Keieishi Gakkai (2014). *Keieishi no Ayumiwo Kiku* [BHSJ (2014). Interviews: History of Business History Studies]. Commemorative Publication for the 50th Anniversary of the Business History Society of Japan. Tokyo: Bunshindo.

Kieser, A. (1994). 'Why Organization Theory Needs Historical Analyses – And How This Should Be Performed'. *Organization Science, 5*(4), 608–20.

Kipping, M. & Üsdiken, B. (2007). 'Business History and Management Studies'. In G. Jones and J. Zeitlin (eds.), *The Oxford Handbook of Business History*. Oxford: Oxford University Press, 96–119.

Kipping, M. & Üsdiken, B. (2014). 'History in Organization and Management Theory: More Than Meets the Eye'. *Academy of Management Annals, 8*(1), 535–88.

Kipping, M. & Westerhuis, G. (2012). 'Strategy, Ideology and Structure: The political processes of introducing the M-form in two Dutch banks'. *Advances in Strategic Management*, 29, 187–237.

Kobayashi, K. (1978). 'Recent Trends in Business History in Japan'. *Business and Economic History*, 7, 62–70.

Kolko, G. (2008). *Triumph of Conservatism*. New York, NY: Simon and Schuster.

Kondo, M. (1993). 'Otsuka Hisao and Comparative Economic History Research in Japan'. *Japanese Studies, 13*(3), 73–8.

Kudo, A. (2003). 'The State of Business History in Japan: Cross-National Comparison and International Relations'. In F. Amatori. and G. Jones (eds.), *Business History around the World*. New York, NY: Cambridge University Press, 271–97.

Kurosawa, T. (2014). 'Sekai no Keieishi Kanren Gakkai no Sousetsu- Hattenshi to Kokusaika: Kadai to Senryaku [History and Strategy of Business History Research Associations around the World]'. *Keieishigaku (Japan Business History Review), 49*(1), 23–50.

Kwolek-Folland, A. (1998). *Incorporating Women: A history of Women and Business in the United States*. New York, NY: Palgrave.

Laird, P. W. (2009). *Pull: Networking and Success Since Benjamin Franklin*. Cambridge, MA: Harvard University Press.

Lamoreaux, N., Raff, D. M. G. & Temin, P. (2003). 'Beyond Markets and Hierarchies: Toward a New Synthesis of American Business History'. *American Historical Review 108*(2), 404–33.

Landes, D. S., Mokyr, J. & Baumol. W. J. (eds.) (2010). *The Invention of Enterprise: Entrepreneurship from Ancient Mesopotamia to Modern Times*. Princeton: Princeton University Press.

Larson, H. M. (1947). 'Business History: Retrospect and Prospect'. *Bulletin of the Business Historical Society, 21*(6), 173–99.

Lipartito, K. (1995). 'Culture and the Practice of Business History'. *Business and Economic History, 24*(2), 1–42.

Lipartito, K. (2016). 'Reassembling the Economic: New Departures in Historical Materialism.' *The American Historical Review, 121*(1): 101–139.

McCraw, T. K. (ed.) (1988). *The Essential Alfred Chandler. Essays Toward a Historical Theory of Big Business*. Boston, MA: Harvard Business School Press.

McKinlay, A. (2013). 'Following Foucault into the Archives: Clerks, Careers and Cartoons'. *Management & Organizational History, 8*(2), 137–154.

Mishima, Y. (1961). *Keiei Shigaku no Tenkai* [Historiography of Business History]. Kyoto: Minerva.

Mordhorst, M. (2008). 'From Counterfactual History to Counter-Narrative History'. *Management & Organizational History, 3*(1), 5–26.

Otsuka, H. (1982). *The Spirit of Capitalism: The Max Weber Thesis in an Economic Historical Perspective*. Tokyo: Iwanami Shoten.

Peukert, H. (2001). 'The Schmoller Renaissance'. *History of Political Economy, 33*(1), 71–116.

Payne, P. L. (1967). *Studies in Scottish Business History*. London: Cass.

Roth, G. (1999). 'Max Weber at Home and in Japan: On the Troubled Genesis and Successful Reception of His Work'. *International Journal of Politics, Culture, and Society, 12*(3), 515–525.

Rowlinson, M., Hassard, J. & Decker, S. (2014). 'Research strategies for organizational history: A dialogue between historical theory and organization theory'. *Academy of Management Review, 39*(3), 250–274.

Saito, O. (2015). 'A very brief history of Japan's Economic and Social History Research', XVIIth World Economic History Congress, Kyoto, Japan, 3–7 August. http://www.wehc2015.org/pdf/History_of_economic_and_social_history_in_Japan.pdf.

Schröter, H. G. (2000). 'Die Institutionalisierung der Unternehmensgeschichte im deutschen Sprachraum'. *Zeitschrift für Unternehmensgeschichte, 45*(1), 30–48.

Schröter, H. G. (2003). 'Business History in German-Speaking States at the End of the Century: Achievements and Gaps'. In F. Amatori, F. and G. Jones (eds.), *Business History around the World*. New York, NY: Cambridge University Press, 170–91.

Schumpeter, J. A. (1949). 'Economic Theory and Entrepreneurial History'. *Change and the Entrepreneur*. Cambridge, MA: Harvard University Press.

Schumpeter, J. A. (1951). 'Economic Theory and Entrepreneurial History'. In Clemence, R. V. (ed.). *Essays on Economic Topics of Joseph Schumpeter*. Port Washington, NY: Kennikat Press.

Schumpeter, J. A. (1954a). *History of Economic Analysis* (edited from manuscript by E. B. Schumpeter). New York, NY: Oxford University Press.

Schumpeter, J. A. (1954b). *Economic Doctrine and Method: An Historical Sketch* (translated by Aris, A. from the German *Epochen der Dogmen- und Methodengeschichte*). New York, NY: Oxford University Press.

Schwentker, W. (1998). *Max Weber in Japan. Eine Untersuchung zur Wirkungsgeschichte 1905–1995*. Tübingen: Mohr Siebeck.

Scranton, P. & Fridenson, P. (2013). *Reimagining Business History*. Baltimore, MD: Johns Hopkins University Press.

Sklar, M. J. (1988). *The corporate reconstruction of American capitalism, 1890–1916: The market, the law, and politics*. New York, NY: Cambridge University Press.

Suddaby, R., Foster, W. M. & Trank, C. Q. (2010). 'Rhetorical History as a Source of Competitive Advantage'. In, J. A. C. Baum and J. Lampel, J. (eds.). *The Globalization of Strategy Research*, Bingley: Emerald, 147–73.

Üsdiken, B. & Kipping, M. (2014). 'History and Organization Studies: A Long-Term View'. In M. Bucheli and R. D. Wadhwani (eds.), *Organization in Time: History, Theory, Methods*. New York, NY: Oxford University Press, 33–55.

Wadhwani, R. D. (2010). 'Historical Reasoning and the Development of Entrepreneurship Theory'. In H. Landstrom and F. Lohrke (eds.), *The Historical Foundations of Entrepreneurship Research*. Cheltenham: Edward Elgar, 343–362.

Wadhwani, R. D. & Bucheli, M. (2014). 'The Future of the Past in Management and Organization Studies'. In M. Bucheli and R. D. Wadhwani (eds.), *Organizations in Time: History, Theory, Methods*. Oxford: Oxford University Press, 3–32.

Weber, M. (1978). *Economy and Society: An Outline of Interpretative Sociology* (edited by G. Roth and C. Wittich) (Translation of *Wirtschaft und Gesellschaft:Grundriss der verstehenden Soziologie*, 4th German edition, 1954). Berkeley, CA: University of California Press.

Yanagisawa, O. (2001). 'The Impact of German Economic Thought on Japanese Economist before World War II'. In Y. Shionoya (ed.), *The German Historical School*. New York, NY: Routledge, 173–87.

Yeager, M. (2001). 'Mavericks and Mavens of Business History: Miriam Beard and Henrietta Larson'. *Enterprise & Society, 2*(4), 687–768.

Yeager, M. (215). 'Women Change Everything'. *Enterprise & Society, 16*(4): 744–69.

Yonekawa, S. (1973). *Keiei Shigaku: Seitan, Genjō, Tenbō* [Business History: Origins, Recent Studies, and Future Perspective]. Tokyo: Toyo Keizai Shinposha.

Zald, M. N (1993). 'Organization Studies as a Scientific and Humanistic Enterprise: Toward a Reconceptualization of the Foundations of the Field'. *Organization Science, 4*(4), 513–28.

4

A citation analysis of business history and related disciplines

Abe de Jong, David Higgins and Hugo van Driel

Introduction

This chapter describes citation patterns which have emerged from our analysis of business history appearing in key academic journals and monographs. Articles and books relate to each other via citations of earlier works. A common justification for citation analyses is that referencing reveals the extent to which academic work influences other scholars inside and outside a particular discipline. The analysis of referencing has multiple goals, including: determining the most-cited works in a field, and describing citation practices in a discipline and citation relations between disciplines.

In this chapter we use citation analysis to provide an overview of the most-cited articles and books in the field of business history. This overview can be used as a reading list for scholars interested in the key publications in business history, but without a clear idea as to where to start in the vast and diverse field of research generated by this discipline. Additionally, this broad review will provide an indication of 'impact' within and outside the discipline. We also relate citations in business history to other disciplines. This achieves two objectives. First, by tracing references to other disciplines and the references made in other fields to business history, the inter-disciplinarity of business history becomes more visible. Second, our investigation permits a comparison of citation practices in business history to similar practices in cognate fields.

To the best of our knowledge there exists only one published citation analysis of publications in business history (Eloranta, Ojala and Valtonen, 2010), and an unpublished follow-up study by the same authors (Valtonen, Ojala and Eloranta, 2013).[1] They list the top-10 articles cited from *Business History* and *Business History Review* between 1990 and 2000. One important observation made by these authors is that the substance of an article has more influence on the chance of being cited than the theory or the methodology employed (Valtonen, Ojala and Eloranta, 2013). Our contribution extends this earlier work by including book citations and by distinguishing more systemically and quantitatively citations of business history articles within and outside the discipline and by assessing in more detail the type of influence of these articles. However, a caveat needs to be added: our approach is more limited because we only include articles from Web of Science, not Google Scholar.

In Section 2, we first describe the framework of our citation analyses and introduce the tables and figures used. In Section 3 we focus on business history and in Section 4 we describe the relations between business history and related disciplines. Section 5 presents our conclusions.

Citation analysis for business history

Using citation impact analysis we analyse publications with the largest impact on business history.[2] As of March 2015, information from the Web of Science (WoS) was derived for all articles in the three leading English language journals in the field: *Business History, Business History Review* and *Enterprise & Society*. Our investigation commences in 2000 for the first two journals, and 2004 for the last. Starting the analysis in 2000 gives a current perspective on the field and sufficient observations for a robust outcome (E&S is only added in 2004 to WoS). Our results complement the work of Eloranta, Ojala and Valtonen (2010) and Valtonen, Ojala and Eloranta (2013) on the 1990s. We begin with references listed in articles published by these journals. To investigate the differences in impact of the type of publication a distinction is made between references to publications in WoS sources, non-WoS-journal articles, books or book chapters and WoS-journal articles published before 1980. Next, we collect the citations of articles appearing in the three business history journals defined above. We thus compile a data base with all business history journal articles (defined as published articles in the three main outlets), references in these articles (WoS journals and otherwise) and citations of the articles (only WoS journals). The limitations of this data base are that the emphasis is on journal publications, especially WoS journals, and that the definition of 'business history' is simply based on outlet.

Table 4.1 presents the ten most cited articles published and cited in the three business history journals over the period of 2000 to March 2015. In Table 4.2 we include citations from all WoS-journals (and exclude the three business history journals). We present the ten articles most-cited by the business history journals that were not published in a business history journal, but in another WoS journal. Generally, the latter articles have more citations than the business history articles listed in Table 4.1. Because the WoS universe is limited, we list the top-20 non-WoS publications most cited in the three leading business history journals (Table 4.3). The majority of these works are books. In order to compare the results from previous tables, we provide in Table 4.4 a combined top 50 of the most influential works for business historians, measured by citations in the three leading business history journals. Again, most of the citations in this Table are to books. Table 4.5 presents the top 20 most-cited articles published in the three business history journals, *excluding* citations within these journals. This Table shows that articles with a relatively low citation impact in business history journals appear; none reached the top 10 of intra-field citations presented in Table 4.1.

The remaining Tables and Figures illustrate citation practices in business history vis-à-vis related disciplines. Figure 4.1 shows the citation-based relations between a selective set of journals, using the *VOSviewer* (see www.vosviewer.com). The size of the balloons depict the number of articles in the network. Figure 4.2 is similar, but includes the direction of the citations, using *Gephi* (see www.gephi.org). Table 4.6 presents the 'incoming' and 'outgoing' citations to and from business history journal articles within a selection of relevant WoS journals.

Table 4.1 Top 10 most-cited business history journal articles published and cited in the three business history journals

Rank	No. of cit.	Author(s)	Year	Title	Journal
1	22	Hannah, L.	2007	'The "divorce" of ownership from control from 1900 onwards: re-calibrating imagined global trends'.	*Business History*
2	18	Toms, S. and Wilson, J.	2003	'Scale, scope and accountability: towards a new paradigm of British business history'.	*Business History*
3	18	Wilkins, M.	1992	'The neglected intangible asset – the influence of the trade mark on the rise of the modern corporation'.	*Business History*
4	16	John, R.	1997	'Elaborations, revisions, dissents: Alfred D. Chandler, Jr.'s, the visible hand after twenty years'.	*Business History Review*
5	16	Toms, S. M. and Wright, M.	2002	'Corporate governance, strategy and structure in British business history, 1950–2000'.	*Business History*
6	16	Jones, G. and Rose, M.	1993	'Family capitalism'.	*Business History*
7	15	Church, R.	1993	'The family firm in industrial-capitalism – international perspectives on hypotheses and history'.	*Business History*
8	14	Casson, M.	1997	'Institutional economics and business history: a way forward?'	*Business History*
9	13	Toms, S. and Wright, M.	2005	'Divergence and convergence within Anglo-American corporate governance systems: evidence from the US and UK, 1950–2000'.	*Business History*
10	13	Hannah, L.	2007	'Pioneering modern corporate governance: a view from London in 1900'.	*Enterprise & Society*

Source: CWTS, April 2015.

Which business history matters for business historians?

In this section we discuss the most influential business history publications within the dis-cipline. Citations in business history journals are low (Table 4.1). This confirms the earlier findings of Valtonen, Ojala and Eloranta (2013) for the period 1990–2000: business histo-rians do not tend to refer frequently to other articles published in the three business history journals (a practice which we from now on will call intra-field citations). Providing an expla-nation for this observation is difficult. One possibility is that business historians traditionally do not fully-embed their research within the existing literature. Moreover, they may often write on specific empirical issues, such as a case study of a specific firm or practice, for which there will usually only be a few (possibly none) citable articles published in the business his-tory journals. It is clear that journal articles in business history have meagre influence on the

Table 4.2 Top 10 non-business history journal articles most-cited by the three business history journals

Rank	No. of cit.	Authors	Year	Title	Journal
1	35	Granovetter, M.	1985	'Economic action and social structure – the problem of embeddedness'.	*American Journal of Sociology*
2	30	Lamoreaux, N., Raff, D. and Temin, P.	2003	'Beyond markets and hierarchies: toward a new synthesis of American business history'.	*American Historical Review*
3	27	Church, R.	1999	'New perspectives on the history of products, firms, marketing, and consumers in Britain and the United States since the mid-nineteenth century'.	*Economic History Review*
4	24	Rajan., R. and Zingales, L.	2003	'The great reversals: the politics of financial development in the twentieth century'.	*Journal of Financial Economics*
5	22	Wilkins, M.	1988	'The freestanding company, 1870–1914 – an important type of British foreign direct investment'.	*Economic History Review*
6	20	La Porta, R., Lopez-de-Silanes, F., Shleifer, A. and Vishny, R.	1998	'Law and finance'.	*Journal of Political Economy*
7	20	La Porta, R., Lopez-de-Silanes, F. and Shleifer, A.	1999	'Corporate ownership around the world'.	*Journal of Finance*
8	18	Jones, G. and Khanna, T.	2006	'Bringing history (back) into international business'.	*Journal of International Business Studies*
9	18	Sabel, C. and Zeitlin, J.	1985	'Historical alternatives to mass production – politics, markets, and technology in 19th-century industrialization'.	*Past & Present*
10	14	David, P.	1985	'Clio and the economics of QWERTY'.	*American Economic Review*

Source: CWTS, April 2015.

field, with no single article in the top 30, and only three in the top 50, of the most frequently cited publications in the three business history journals (see Table 4.4). Here, business history seems to differ fundamentally from other fields such as economics, organization studies and management science where intra-field citations to and from other journal articles show a much higher density (see Figure 4.2).

Books on business history receive far more citations than publications from other fields, including economic history and management science. Unsurprisingly, perhaps, the three

Table 4.3 Top 20 most-cited studies (outside WoS universe) in the three business history journals

Rank	No. of citations	Authors	Year	Title
1	162	Chandler, A.	1990	*Scale and Scope*
2	130	Chandler, A.	1977	*The Visible Hand*
3	61	Chandler, A.	1962	*Strategy and Structure*
4	43	Jones, G.	2005	*Multinationals and Global Capitalism*
5	43	Jones, G.	2000	*Merchants to Multinationals*
6	40	North, D.	1990	*Institutions, Institutional Change and Economic Performance*
7	37	Jones, G.	1996	*The Evolution of International Business*
8	32	Wilkins, M.	1974	*The Maturing of Multinational Enterprise*
9	31	Scranton, P.	1997	*Endless Novelty*
10	31	Nelson, R. and S. Winter	1982	*An Evolutionary Theory of Economic Change*
11	30	Williamson, O.	1985	*The Economic Institutions of Capitalism*
12	29	Laird, P.	1998	*Advertising Progress*
13	29	Berle, A. and Means, G.	1932	*The Modern Corporation and Private Property*
14	29	Hall, P. and D. Soskice	2001	*Varieties of Capitalism*
15	28	Gerschenkron, A.	1962	*Economic Backwardness in Historical Perspective*
16	28	Williamson, O.	1975	*Markets and Hierarchies*
17	28	Wilson, J.	1995	*British Business History, 1720–1994*
18	28	Penrose, E.	1959	*The Theory of the Growth of the Firm*
19	27	Piore, M. and Sabel, C.	1984	*The Second Industrial Divide*
20	24	Wilkins, M.	1970	*The Emergence of Multinational Enterprise*

Source: CWTS, April 2015.

Table 4.4 Top 50 most-cited publications in the three business history journals

Rank	No. of cit.	Authors	Year	Title	Journal
1	162	Chandler, A.	1990	*Scale and Scope*	
2	130	Chandler, A.	1977	*The Visible Hand*	
3	61	Chandler, A.	1962	*Strategy and Structure*	
4	43	Jones, G.	2005	*Multinationals and Global Capitalism*	
5	43	Jones, G.	2000	*Merchants to Multinationals*	
6	40	North, D.	1990	*Institutions, Institutional Change and Economic Performance*	
7	37	Jones, G.	1996	*The Evolution of International Business*	
8	35	Granovetter, M.	1985	'Economic action and social structure – the problem of embeddedness'.	*American Journal of Sociology*
9	32	Wilkins, M.	1974	*The Maturing of Multinational Enterprise*	
10	31	Scranton, P.	1997	*Endless Novelty*	

Rank	No. of cit.	Authors	Year	Title	Journal
11	31	Nelson, R. and S. Winter	1982	An Evolutionary Theory of Economic Change	
12	30	Williamson, O.	1985	The Economic Institutions of Capitalism	
13	30	Lamoreaux, N., Raff, D. and Temin, P.	2003	'Beyond markets and hierarchies: toward a new synthesis of American business history'.	American Historical Review
14	29	Laird, P.	1998	Advertising Progress	
15	29	Berle, A. and Means, G.	1932	The Modern Corporation and Private Property	
16	29	Hall, P. and D. Soskice	2001	Varieties of Capitalism	
17	28	Gerschenkron, A.	1962	Economic Backwardness in Historical Perspective	
18	28	Williamson, O.	1975	Markets and Hierarchies	
19	28	Wilson, J.	1995	British Business History, 1720–1994	
20	28	Penrose, E.	1959	The Theory of the Growth of the Firm	
21	27	Piore, M. and Sable, C.	1984	The Second Industrial Divide	
22	27	Church, R.	1999	'New perspectives on the history of products, firms, marketing, and consumers in Britain and the United States since the mid-nineteenth century'.	Economic History Review
23	24	Wilkins, M.	1970	The Emergence of Multinational Enterprise	
24	24	Chandler, A.	2001	Inventing the Electronic Century	
25	24	Rajan, R. and Zingales, L.	2003	'The great reversals: the politics of financial development in the twentieth century'.	Journal of Financial Economics
26	23	Strasser, S.	1989	Satisfaction Guaranteed	
27	23	Colli, A.	2003	The History of Family Business	
28	23	Whittington, R. and Meyer, M.	2000	The European Corporation	
29	23	Friedman, W.	2004	Birth of a Salesman	
30	23	Wilkins, M. and Schröter, H.	1998	The Free Standing Company	
31	22	Hannah, L.	2007	'The "divorce" of ownership from control from 1900 onwards: re-calibrating imagined global trends'.	Business History
32	22	Jones, G.	1993	British Multinational Banking	
33	22	Marchand, R.	1985	Advertising the American Dream	
34	22	Cohen, L.	2003	Consumers' Republic	
35	22	Wilkins, M.	1988	'The freestanding company, 1870–1914 – an important type of British foreign direct-investment'.	Economic History Review

(Continued)

Rank	No. of cit.	Authors	Year	Title	Journal
36	21	Hannah, L.	1983	*The Rise of the Corporate Economy*	
37	21	Coase, R.	1937	'The nature of the firm'.	*Economica*
38	20	Hughes, T.	1983	*Networks of Power*	
39	20	Wilkins, M.	1989	The History of Foreign Investment	
40	20	Hounshell, D.	1984	*From the American System to Mass Production*	
41	20	La Porta, R., Lopez-de-Silanes, F., Shleifer, A. and Vishny, R.	1998	'Law and finance'.	*Journal of Political Economy*
42	20	La Porta, R., Lopez-de-Silanes, F. and Shleifer, A.	1999	'Corporate ownership around the world'.	*Journal of Finance*
43	19	Colli, A., Perez, P. and Rose, M.	2003	'National determinants of family firm development'.	*Enterprise & Society*
44	19	Wilkins, M.	1989	*The History of Foreign Investment*	
45	19	Jones, G.	2005	*Renewing Unilever*	
46	19	Lazonick, W.	1991	*Business Organisation*	
47	19	Wilson, J. and Popp, A.	2003	*Industrial Clusters*	
48	18	Toms, S. and Wilson, J.	2003	'Scale, scope and accountability: towards a new paradigm of British business history'.	*Business History*
49	18	Wilkins, M.	1992	'The neglected intangible asset – the influence of the trade mark on the rise of the modern corporation'.	*Business History*
50	18	Casson, M.	1999	'The economics of the family firm'.	*Scandinavian Economic History Review*

Source: CWTS, April 2015.

well-known books by Alfred Chandler top the list (Valtonen, Ojala and Eloranta (2013) counted 12,000 references to this trilogy in Google Scholar by May 2009), with books by a later occupant of his chair at Harvard, Geoffrey Jones, taking three of the following four places. There can be little doubt that the books just noted made a considerable impact on business history but, once again, explaining the higher citation rate for books is not straightforward. Part of the explanation might be simple: the higher word limit of books (around 100 to 150 thousand), gives authors more scope to set out bigger agendas and to comprehensively address major and multi-faceted themes, which would be impossible in a typical journal article of approximately 10,000 words.

Despite the differences that exist between the citation scores for business history journals and business history monographs, our tables indicate particular themes which have been featured prominently. The dominant themes are those associated with the growth of 'big' firms which have many shared characteristics: they are publicly quoted, which has stimulated debates on corporate governance and the extent to which ownership is separated from control

(Berle and Means, 1932; Hannah, 2007a, 2007b). These firms have complex management structures, promoting analysis of the limitations to managerial control and the role of transaction costs within firms (Penrose, 1959; Williamson, 1975, 1985). Many of the biggest firms subsequently evolved into multinationals – which has stimulated in-depth research (Jones, 1993, 2000, 2005), and fostered investigation into foreign direct investment (Wilkins, 1988). Finally, aligned with the growth of 'big' companies, was the extensive national and multinational marketing of brands and the emergence of a consumer society (Cohen, 2003; Laird, 1998; Marchand, 1985; Wilkins, 1992).

However, the importance and relevance of the 'typical' American model of fully-vertically integrated companies was challenged. Family firms – the antithesis of the Chandlerian firm – have also featured prominently in business history debates. The former, which rarely have a public quotation, face different survival problems compared to large companies (Casson, 1999; Colli, Perez and Rose, 2003; Jones and Rose, 1993). In the 1980s, extensive corporate restructuring prompted scholars to examine the success of alternative models of capitalism, including 'flexible specialisation' (Piore and Sable, 1984). Some of the insights from this last work were subsequently applied to analysis of industrial and regional clusters (Wilson and Popp, 2003).

Interdisciplinarity in business history

Outside influences

In this section we describe the most important non-business historical works used in business history, and class these as outside influences. The top ten WoS extra-field citations (Table 4.2) have articles from various fields, both within and outside. The subjects of these articles are more varied than the publications included in Tables 4.1 and 4.3. Some are reviews and only one is purely theoretical (the article by Granovetter ranked no. 1). However, in combination, Tables 4.2, 4.3 and 4.4 show that several theoretical contributions and models in other fields are widely referred to in business history articles. This demonstrates the eclectic nature of the discipline.

The most important influence probably comes from the related disciplines of economic history and institutional economics. For example, in his 1990 book, *Institutions, Institutional Change and Economic Performance*, the Nobel Prize-winning historian, Douglas North, had a path-breaking influence on how we think about institutions and economic change. Consider also Gerschenkron's (1962) publication, *Economic Backwardness in Historical Perspective*, and Williamson's (1975, 1985) analyses of transaction costs to explain hierarchical versus market organization. To these authors could be added Nelson and Winter's (1982) contributions to the economics of evolutionary change and David's (1985) examination of path dependence in technological and economic change. Finally, economists and legal scholars writing on corporate governance have had an important influence on business historians. Beginning with Berle and Means' (1932) explanation of the divergent interests of professional managers and shareholders, several financial economists have examined the effects of governance laws and practices on firm performance (see La Porta et al., 1998, 1999). From a different perspective, sociology has provided important insights for business historians. Consider, especially, Granovetter's (1985) argument that social embeddedness constrains economic activities. More recently, the economic-sociology approach of Hall and Soskice (2001) has helped business historians understand different varieties of capitalism.

The influence of business history on other disciplines

Table 4.5 presents the top 20 most-cited articles published in the three business history journals, using WoS, but excluding references *within* these journals. Interestingly, articles with a relatively low citation impact in business history journals now appear. None of them reached the top 10 intra-field citations presented in Table 4.1.

Table 4.5 Top 20 most-cited business history journal articles outside the three business history journals

Rank	No. of cit.	Authors	Year	Title	Journal
1	128	Cusumano, M., Mylonadis, Y. and Rosenbloom, R.	1992	'Strategic manoeuvring and mass-market dynamics – the triumph of vhs over beta'.	*Business History Review*
2	71	Christensen, C.	1993	'The rigid disk-drive industry – a history of commercial and technological turbulence'.	*Business History Review*
3	61	Langlois, R.	1992	'External economies and economic progress – the case of the microcomputer industry'.	*Business History Review*
4	55	Helper, S.	1991	'Strategy and irreversibility in supplier relations – the case of the United States automobile industry'.	*Business History Review*
5	42	Galambos, L. and Sturchio, J.	1998	'Pharmaceutical firms and the transition to biotechnology: a study in strategic innovation'.	*Business History Review*
6	33	Sull, D.	1999	'The dynamics of standing still: firestone tire & rubber and the radial revolution'.	*Business History Review*
7	32	Kipping, M.	1999	'American management consulting companies in western Europe, 1920 to 1990: products, reputation, and relationships'.	*Business History Review*
8	32	Haigh, T.	2001	'Inventing information systems: the systems men and the computer, 1950–1968'.	*Business History Review*
9	28	Ghemawat, P.	2002	'Competition and business strategy in historical perspective'.	*Business History Review*
10	28	Sabel, C. and Zeitlin, J.	2004	'Neither modularity nor relational contracting: inter-firm collaboration in the new economy'.	*Enterprise & Society*
11	28	Dutton, J., Thomas, A. and Butler, J.	1984	'The history of progress functions as a managerial technology'.	*Business History Review*

Rank	No. of cit.	Authors	Year	Title	Journal
12	26	Chesbrough, H.	2002	'Graceful exits and missed opportunities: Xerox's management of its technology spin-off organizations'.	*Business History Review*
13	26	Chandler, A.	1994	'The competitive performance of United States industrial-enterprises since the World War II'.	*Business History Review*
14	25	Clark, P. and Rowlinson, M.	2004	'The treatment of history in organisation studies: towards an "historic turn"?'	*Business History*
15	25	Leslie, S. and Kargon, R.	1996	'Selling Silicon Valley: Frederick Terman's model for regional advantage'.	*Business History Review*
16	24	Folkman, P., Froud, J., Johal, S. and Williams, K.	2007	'Working for themselves? capital market intermediaries and present day capitalism'.	*Business History*
17	21	Usdiken, B. and Kieser, A.	2004	'Introduction: history in organisation studies'.	*Business History*
18	21	Langlois, R.	2004	'Chandler in a larger frame: markets, transaction costs, and organizational form in history'.	*Enterprise & Society*
19	20	Galambos, L.	1983	'Technology, political-economy, and professionalization – central themes of the organizational synthesis'.	*Business History Review*
20	19	Guinnane, T., Harris, R., Lamoreaux, N. M. and Rosenthal, J.	2007	'Putting the corporation in its place'.	*Enterprise & Society*

Source: CWTS, April 2015.

Clearly, the articles that matter most to business historians are different from the articles that are relevant to other disciplines. Unlike the publications of business historians listed in Tables 4.1 and 4.3, which mainly focus on ownership and governance as a theme, or large corporations in specific countries, the first eight articles in Table 4.5 are all concerned with the evolution of specific industries and technologies, especially in information technology and consumer electronics (in total, six of the top-20 publications deal with these subjects). Lower on the list we mainly find general and conceptual studies, including reviews.

Employing a different methodology, by combining WoS and Google Scholar, Eloranta, Ojala and Valtonen (2010) compiled a list of the most-cited articles published in *Business History* and *Business History Review*, between 1990 and 2000 (see their Tables 4.5 and 4.6). Their top-five *Business History Review* articles are identical with ours, albeit in a slightly different order. According to their lists, articles from *Business History Review* receive considerably more citations than those in *Business History*-which accords with our Table 4.5 (impact outside the field). However, this does not mean that the latter has had less impact than the former outside the field: the outgoing citations for *Business History* are higher than those for *Business History Review* (see Table 4.6). Apparently, the outgoing citations from *Business History* are more evenly distributed across the set of articles.

In an earlier publication (de Jong, Higgins and van Driel, 2015) we argued that theory-informed business history, using an explicit methodology aimed at testing hypotheses and generalization, would advance the discipline. The majority of the relevant top 10 articles with the largest impact outside business history do not fulfil these requirements.[3] All of the top 10 articles are qualitative case studies; only one employs analytical statistics (comparable to the 11% we assessed for all articles published in the three business history journals *Business History, Business History Review* and *Enterprise and Society* in 2012, see de Jong, Higgins and van Driel, 2015 for the figures presented in this paragraph). In general, the top 10 articles lack an explicit and focused research question informed by theory which could be reformulated into a hypothesis (in line with the low 11% score for the 2012 articles earlier assessed by us). The two exceptions are Christensen (1993) who asked why incumbent integrated firms became less successful at introducing new technologies in the rigid disk drive industry than start-ups between 1973 and 1989, while distinguishing five types of firms and several categorizations of types of innovation, and Helper who enquired, "why the automakers found it profitable to give up monopsony power over their outside suppliers" (1991, p. 738) elaborating upon a voice or exit perspective. Sull posed an explicit "why" question too, but it is an open empirical question ("why rubber industry leader *Firestone Tire & Rubber* failed to respond effectively to new technology and foreign competition", 1999, abstract, p. 430), and only after 25 pages did he introduce, define and apply a central theoretical concept, "punctuated equilibrium", followed by his own term "active inertia" in the conclusion. Similarly, Dutton, Thomas and Butler formulate an empirical "where, how, and when" question on the emergence of the progress function as a managerial technology (1984, p. 204), but only on the final page of their article do they discuss "experience effects" referred to by other studies. Two other articles from the top 10 have no explicit and focused question, but include theoretical concepts central to their analysis. The first, by Cusumano, Mylonadis and Rosenbloom (1992) contains briefly defined theoretical concepts (such as first mover advantages, bandwagon effects, network externalities and positive feedback) without an explicit framework linking these concepts as the basis for an explicit central research question.[4] The second, by Langlois (1992), seems to use (not necessarily similar) concepts of "external capabilities" and "external economies" indiscriminately, without giving extensive definitions. After a long description, it is only at the end of the article that the author provides a conclusion of the importance of "external economies" (basically understood as reliance on external suppliers-outsourcing-in following a modular approach). Finally, Chesbrough makes explicit operationalization of the term "technology spin-off firm" (2002, p. 810), which describes the phenomenon studied, but is not a concept that is (or could be) part of his causal mechanism. The remaining three articles do not contain formally-defined theoretical concepts at all relevant to the main analysis. The outcome that 70% of the articles formally define concepts is considerably higher than calculated for the business history articles published in 2012 (38%). The use of theory-in the sense of relating variables or concepts according to a mechanism or causality explanation-is low: 20% (Christensen and Helper) compared to the score of 39% for the 2012 articles. Furthermore, only one of the top-10 articles includes a (somewhat elaborated) explanation of their methodology (Chesbrough, 2002, p. 810; typically, partly in a footnote),[5] which is a lower percentage than we assessed for the 2012 business history journal articles (32%).

Overall, the top 10 articles in Table 4.5 are not more explicit in using theory and adopting a formal methodology compared to the general pattern for articles published in the three business history journals in 2012. The top 10 articles are atypical for business history in other respects. Only two cite unpublished material from archives. On the other hand, seven use author interviews as a source. Our earlier contents analysis of the leading business history journals published in 2012, assessed the share of archive-based articles as 83%; oral history was used in only 10% of the articles (de Jong, Higgins and van Driel, 2015, p. 11). One explanation of this divergence from the outcome of our study of the articles published in 2012, is the focus of several of the top 10 articles on relatively recent periods, often having particular relevance to the electronics industry. The identity of the authors may have played a role, too: as a feature already signaled by Eloranta, Ojala and Valtonen (2010, p. 85), the large majority of the writers of the top 10 articles (13 out of 15) originated from outside business history (departments or units).

The focus on specific technologies and industries by authors originating from outside business history may explain why their articles have received higher citations outside business history compared to the average article published in major business history journals. Information technology and related industries, in addition to the car and pharmaceutical industries are likely to be popular subjects in other disciplines. Valtonen, Ojala and Eloranta (2013) found that "substance/novel finding" rather than theory, methodology or level of quantification, determined the number of citations of business history articles (without exactly quantitatively distinguishing intra-and extra-field impact). To be more specific: their citation analysis of the top 10 most-cited articles published in *Business History* and *Business History Review* found that only 11% of the cited articles focused on method or theory, while 40% concerned "substance/novel finding". The remaining 49% mainly contained "a "list-type" of citations to previous literature, with no particular focus" (Valtonen, Olaja and Eloranta, 2013, pp. 6–7).

To obtain insights into the factors that make particular business history articles more appealing to other disciplines we make more inductive distinctions, avoiding the (large) category of "other". From the 128 WoS articles quoting the business history article listed as number one in Table 4.5 (Cusumano, Mylonadis and Rosenbloom, 1992, in the remainder of this paragraph referred to as Cusumano et al.), we sampled the top-20 which themselves generated the highest number of citations in WoS.[6] Of these articles, only one mentions Cusumano et al. as an example of a historical case-study[7] and another one refers to Cusumano et al. as an empirical source (Helfat and Raubitscheck, 2000). The remaining 18 articles all cite Cusumano et al. as an illustration of theoretical aspects of innovation and standardisation, in various ways (the terms used are incremental changes, strategic maneuvering, first mover effects, transaction costs, dominant designs/standards, path dependence and network externalities, networks of innovation, licensing, customer expectations, open innovation and coordinating problems. It should be noted that Cusumano et al. themselves do not use some of the concepts listed). Eleven of these 18 articles do not contain any details of the video-cassette standards battle described by Cusumano et al.; the remaining seven articles, with one exception (Suarez and Utterback, 1995), devote but a few sentences on the case itself. In sum, in regard to the most quoted business history article outside the field, unlike Valtonen, Ojala and Eloranta (2013), we conclude that the application of "theory" (or perhaps more precisely "theoretical concepts") matters more than "content" (our "translation" of the category "substance/novel finding" used by Valtonen, Ojala and Eloranta, 2013), in triggering citations of business history articles outside the field.

In contrast, the most cited business history article within the three business history journals (Hannah, 2007a) is quoted mainly as an *empirical* source. Seventeen of the 22 citing articles refer to Hannah's general thesis of an earlier divorce of ownership and control among large British firms compared to US ones (which derives its importance from opposing

Chandler's view that Britain suffered from "personal capitalism" (Chandler, 1990)), or – to a lesser degree – to more specific facts on corporate governance and stock exchange rules in the two countries involved.[8] In other words, while the specific empirical subject of Cusumano, Mylonadis and Rosenbloom (1992) certainly matters, we conclude that this business history article most cited outside the discipline has a more general theoretical appeal than the one most cited within the discipline. Interestingly, it should be noted that the business history article generating the most extra-field citations has been cited only four times by one of the three business history journals, which emphasises the different citation patterns within and outside the discipline of business history.

This comparison is centred on the two articles most cited inside and outside the discipline of business history, and ignores the fact that some of the top 10 articles cited outside business history do not contain any formally defined theoretical concepts. Within this subset, the article by Galambos and Sturchio (1998) on the change-over of pharmaceutical firms to biotechnology is not only the most cited, but also one of the two articles from the list co-authored by a business historian. We find that 18 out of the top 20 articles quoting Galambos and Sturchio are on the pharmaceutical industry, biotech sector and/or life sciences (the other two deal with affiliated empirical subjects of nanotechnology and industrial R&D).[9] This provides a strong indication that citations of this article concern references to empirical content ("substance") rather than theoretical concepts. Seven of the articles citing Galambos and Sturchio contain central theoretical concepts used, but not formally defined by Galambos and Sturchio, that is, (strategic) alliances and (organizational) capabilities. These two concepts are not part of some explanatory mechanism, but are simply used for describing the events covered. We note that some citing articles connect theoretical concepts to Galambos and Sturchio, that is, herd behaviour, complementary assets and heuristics, which are not used by Galambos and Sturchio themselves. Similar to the quotations of Cusumano, Mylonadis and Rosenbloom (1992) for empirical purposes, 18 of the 20 citing articles devote only one or two sentences to Galambos and Sturchio, sentences sometimes referring to other sources, too. Unlike in the case of Cusumano, Mylonadis and Rosenbloom (1992), however, 17 of the 20 citing articles mention empirical details derived from Galambos and Sturchio. Compared to the intra-field use of Hannah's article, these extra-field references to Galambos and Sturchio are more varied in nature and are less concentrated on one central empirical finding. Next to applying certain theoretical concepts, focusing on a certain industry characterized by high technological dynamism in recent decades may also be a fruitful strategy to create impact outside business history.

Cross-disciplinary citation pattern

In Section 3 of this chapter we noted the low number of intra-field citations within business history articles. Figure 4.2 shows that this pattern distinguishes business history (and also economic history) journals from those in economics, organization and management studies, where intra-field citation is much more intensive (Figures 4.1 and 4.2, as well as Table 4.6, exclusively include citation patterns within a selective set of WoS journals). Still, this does not mean that business history journals have a strong interdisciplinary orientation: 42% of the incoming citations and 72% of the outgoing citations in the three business history journals are intra-field (see Table 4.6). This tendency also becomes visible in Table 4.2, which has the ten articles most cited in business history journals that were not published in a business history journal, but another journal in the WoS universe. Although the most-cited articles have more cites than the business history articles in Table 4.1, the tenth article still has only 14 citations.

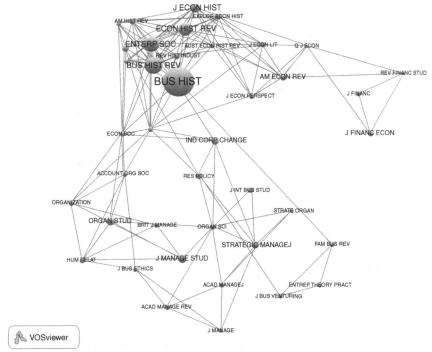

Figure 4.1 Citation relations for the three business history journals
Source: CWTS, April 2015.

In comparison, the top 20 non-WoS publications most cited by business history articles, which are all books, have much higher scores (see Table 4.3). In sum, publishing articles in business history is characterized by low citations from WoS journals within and outside the discipline.

Finally, we conducted a bi-directional citation analysis on the WoS universe for the three business history journals in order to trace those journals with the strongest connections to business history. Figure 4.1 shows that business history is most closely related to economic history, where the *Economic History Review* and the *Journal of Economic History* have the strongest ties with business history. The analysis shows that we were correct to classify *Industrial and Corporate Change* as a non-business history journal. Next, the economics journals *American Economic Review* and the *Journal of Economic Literature* are relevant, as well as three finance journals (*The Journal of Finance*, *Review of Financial Studies* and *Journal of Financial Economics*). Furthermore, there are ties with management and organization journals, especially *Organization Studies, Strategic Management Journal* and *Journal of Management Studies*. *Business History Review* (and, to a much lesser degree, *Enterprise & Society*), is much more balanced in incoming and outgoing citations than *Business History* (see Table 4.6). It appears that authors of articles appearing in the latter are more inclined to cite from journals outside history than the former: 45% of all incoming citations, compared to 33% for *Business History Review* and 29% for *Enterprise & Society* (calculated from Table 4.6), suggesting a more interdisciplinary and theoretical orientation of *Business History*. Remarkably, however, compared to *Business History* (23% and 11%), *Business History Review* (34% and 19%) and *Enterprise & Society* (34% and 17%) have a higher share of outgoing citations outside the field of business history and outside history respectively (calculated from Table 4.6). Table 4.5 shows an overrepresentation of *Business History Review* in the list of articles with the largest extra-field impact as discussed in section 4.2.

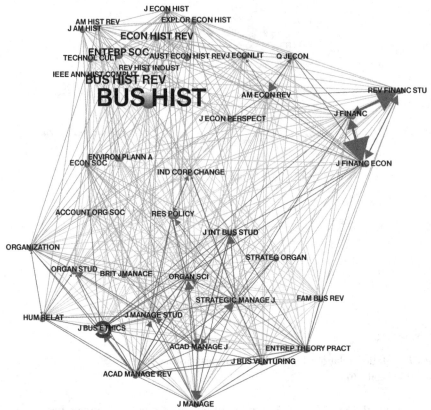

Figure 4.2 Citation directions for the three business history journals
Source: CWTS, April 2015.

Table 4.6 Incoming and outgoing citations of the three business history journals from and to a selective set of WoS journals

	All			Intra-Field Only			Outside History Journals		
	Incoming	Outgoing	Out/In	Incoming	Outgoing	Out/In	Incoming	Outgoing	Out/In
BH	2.060	1.012	0.49	857	776	0.91	937	108	0.12
BHR	536	469	0.88	234	308	1.32	179	87	0.49
E&S	509	324	0.64	207	214	1.03	150	55	0.37
Total	3.105	1.805	0.58	1.298	1.298	1.00	1.266	250	0.20

Note: Calculated from CWTS data, April 2015. The journals involved are those contained in Figures 4.1 and 4.2, covering only part of all incoming and outgoing citations from and to articles published in WoS journals.

Conclusions

Business historians cite relatively few articles from their peers and tend to refer more to books, both from business history (in particular on big corporations and governance) and other fields (for diverse theory, illustrating the eclectic nature of business history writing). We suggest that the low intra-field citation rate of journal articles is not easily explained.

Nonetheless, one feature is clear: subject matter has a direct bearing on intra-field citations and this is most pronounced for studies on the evolution of the corporate economy and cognate subjects. The top business history article in terms of intra-field citations, on corporate governance (Hannah, 2007a) is almost exclusively cited for its empirical findings. Choice of substance also seems to matter for extra-field impact as the business history articles generating the most extra-field citations are about the development of specific industries and technologies in recent decades. However, the business history article most cited extra-field, on consumer electronics (Cusumano, Mylonadis and Rosenbloom, 1992), is mainly quoted for theoretical concepts. Still the top 10 of articles with the largest impact on journals from other disciplines, although mainly written by non-business historians, are not particularly methodologically advanced compared to an average business history article. It makes sense anyhow for business historians searching extra-field impact to focus on industries which in recent decades have shown high technological dynamism, as is shown by the many extra-field citations to the article on the pharmaceutical industry including no formally defined theoretical concepts (Galambos and Sturchio, 1998).

Notes

1 In a more limited sense, Lamoureux, Raff and Temin (2008) assessed the extent to which the economics literature was cited in three business history journals at five year intervals between 1960 and 2000 (*Business History*, *Business History Review* and *Business and Economic History*, the latter only between 1965 and 1995).

2 The analysis has been conducted by Ludo Waltman of CWTS (Leiden University, the Netherlands). Please note that the CWTS algorithm applied to WoS sources results in a more comprehensive set of citing studies than the WoS online-version used by university libraries. Still, due to errors in the literature references made by citing authors, the CWTS-method may underreport citations to certain articles, too.

3 See Table 4.5. For the following analysis, article no. 9 is excluded as being a 'history of ideas' and article no. 10 is excluded because it is a literature review. In their place, articles numbered 11 and 12 are included in the top 10.

4 Sometimes even very obvious references to the theoretical literature are missing. Cusumano, Mylonadis and Rosenbloom (1992) do not refer to Paul David's famous article on QWERTY keyboard (1985) as an illustration of path dependence in the selection of technological standards. Similarly, Haigh (2001), at the time of publication a Ph.D. candidate in a History and Sociology of Science Department, neglects to consider the sociological literature on professionalization which is highly relevant for his article. His study is about "the frustrated hopes of 1950s corporate "systems men" (represented by the Systems and Procedures Association) to establish themselves as powerful "generalist" staff experts in administrative techniques." (Haigh, 2001, p. 15). In addition, some of the top 10 articles discuss insights from theoretical and empirical literature only in the footnotes.

5 It should be noted that some of the articles pay explicit attention to their source base (e.g., Kipping, 1999, p. 194–195).

6 From the formal top 20, we omitted two articles which include Cusumano et al. in their literature list, but does not refer to it in the text. Probably, in these articles references were skipped during the reviewing process, without removing the reference in the list. Instead, we added numbers 21 and 22.

7 This happens in a somewhat derogatory way, as the companion to an observation that "The common belief that historical research is unscientific may explain the limited number of articles that apply this method in marketing". This sentence is immediately followed by a footnote explaining that "Several historians have presented their research on marketing topics in journals such as *Business History Review* and *Journal of Economic History* And books" (Golder, 2000, p. 156), suggesting a low status of these journals and referring to Cusumano, Mylonadis and Rosenbloom as "historians", which their affiliation mentioned in the article does not indicate.

8 Three of these 17 articles are (co-)authored by Hannah himself.

9 Again, one of the top 20 citing articles according to WoS does not contain any reference to Galambos and Sturchio's article; we added no. 21 from the list to our sample (all excluding intra-field citations).

References

Publications included in the tables

Berle, A. & Means, G. (1932). *The Modern Corporation and Private Property*. London: Transaction Publishers.

Casson, M. (1997). "Institutional Economics and Business History: A Way Forward?" *Business History, 39*(4), 151–171.

Casson, M. (1999). "The Economics of the Family Firm". *Scandinavian Economic History Review, 47*(1), 10–23.

Chandler, A., Jr. (1962). *Strategy and Structure: Chapters in the History of the Industrial Enterprise*. Cambridge: MIT Press.

Chandler, A., Jr. (1974). *The Visible Hand: The Managerial Revolution in American Business*. Cambridge: Harvard University Press.

Chandler, A., Jr. (1990). *Scale and Scope: The Dynamics of Industrial Capitalism*. Cambridge: Belknap Press.

Chandler, A., Jr. (1994). "The Competitive Performance of U.S. Industrial Enterprises since the Second World War". *Business History Review, 68*(1), 1–72.

Chandler, A., Jr. (2001). *Inventing the Electronic Century*. Cambridge: Harvard University Press.

Chesbrough, H. (2002). "Graceful Exits and Missed Opportunities: Xerox's Management of Its Technology Spin-off Organizations". *Business History Review, 76*(4), 803–837.

Christensen, C. (1993). "The Rigid Disk Drive Industry: A History of Commercial and Technological Turbulence". *Business History Review, 67*(4), 531–588.

Church, R. (1993). "The Family Firm in Industrial Capitalism: International Perspectives on Hypotheses and History". *Business History, 35*(4), 17–43.

Church, R. (1999). "New Perspectives on the Story of Products, Firms, Marketing and Consumers in Britain and the United States Since the Mid- nineteenth Century". *Economic History Review, 52*(3), 405–435.

Clark, P. & Rowlinson, M. (2004). "The Treatment of History in Organisation Studies: Towards an Historic Turn". *Business History, 46*(3), 331–352.

Coase, R. (1937). "The Nature of the Firm". *Economica* 4, 386–405.

Cohen, L. (2003). *A Consumers' Republic*. New York: Knopf.

Colli, A. (2003). *The History of Family Business, 1850–2000*. Cambridge: Cambridge University Press.

Colli, A., Perez, P. & Rose, M. (2003). "National Determinants of Family Firm Development? Family Firms in Britain, Spain and Italy in the Nineteenth and Twentieth Centuries". *Enterprise & Society, 4*(1), 28–64.

Cusumano, M., Mylonadis, Y. & Rosenbloom, R. (1992). "Strategic Manoeuvring and Mass-Market Dynamics: The Triumph of VHS over Beta". *Business History Review, 66*(1), 51–94.

David, P. (1985). "Clio and the Economics of QWERTY". *American Economic Review (Papers and Proceedings), 75*(2), 332–337.

Dutton, J., Thomas, A. & Butler, J. (1984). "The History of Progress Functions as a Managerial Technology". *Business History Review, 58*(2), 204–233.

Folkman, P., Froud, J., Johal, S. & Williams, K. (2007). "Working for Themselves? Capital Market Intermediaries and Present Day Capitalism". *Business History, 49*(4), 552–572.

Friedman, W. (2004). *Birth of a Salesman*. Cambridge: Harvard University Press.

Galambos, L. (1983). "Technology, Political Economy, and Professionalization: Central Themes of the Organizational Synthesis". *Business History Review, 57*(4), 471–493.

Galambos, L. & Sturchio, J. (1998). "Pharmaceutical Firms and the Transition to Biotechnology: A Study in Strategic Innovation". *Business History Review, 72*(2), 250–278.

Gerschenkron, A. (1962). *Economic Backwardness in Historical Perspective*. Cambridge: Harvard University Press.

Ghemawat, P. (2002). "Competition and Business Strategy in Historical Perspective". *Business History Review, 76*(1), 37–74.

Granovetter, M. (1985). "Economic Action and Social Structure: The Problem of Embeddedness". *American Journal of Sociology, 91*(3), 481–510.

Guinnane, T., Harris, R., Lamoreaux, N. & Rosenthal, J. (2007). "Putting the Corporation in its Place". *Enterprise & Society, 8*(3), 687–729.

Haigh, T. (2001). "Inventing Information Systems: The Systems Men and the Computer, 1950–1968". *Business History Review, 75*(1), 15–61.

Hall, P. & Soskice, D. (2001). *Varieties of Capitalism: the Institutional Foundations of Comparative Advantage*. Oxford: Oxford University Press.

Hannah, L. (1983). *The Rise of the Corporate Economy*. London: Methuen.

Hannah, L. (2007a). "The Divorce of Ownership from Control from 1900 Onwards: Recalibrating Imagined Global Trends'. *Business History, 49*(4), 404–438.

Hannah, L. (2007b). "Pioneering Modern Corporate Governance: A View from London in 1900". *Enterprise & Society, 8*(3), 642–686.

Helper, S. (1991). "Strategy and Irreversibility in Supplier Relations: The Case of the U.S. Automobile Industry". *Business History Review, 65*(4), 781–824.

Hounshell, D. (1984). *From the American System to Mass Production, 1800–1932*. Baltimore: Johns Hopkins University Press.

Hughes, T. (1983). *Networks of Power*. Baltimore: Johns Hopkins Press.

John, R. (1997). "Elaborations, Revisions, Dissents: Alfred D. Chandler Jr.'s, 'The visible hand' after Twenty Years". *Business History Review, 71*(2) 151–200.

Jones, G. (1993). *British Multinational Banking, 1830–1990*. Oxford: Clarendon Press.

Jones, G. (1996). *The Evolution of International Business*. London: Routledge.

Jones, G. (2000). *Merchants to Multinationals: British Trading Companies in the Nineteenth and Twentieth Centuries*. Oxford: Oxford University Press.

Jones, G. (2005). *Multinationals and Global Capitalism: From the Nineteenth to the Twenty First Century*. Oxford: Oxford University Press.

Jones, G. (2005). *Renewing Unilever: Transformation and Tradition*. Oxford: Oxford University Press.

Jones, G. & Khanna, T. (2006). "Bringing History (back) Into International Business". *Journal of International Business, 37*(4), 453–468.

Jones, G. & Rose, M. (1993). "Family capitalism". *Business History, 35*(4), 1–16.

Kipping, M. (1999). "American Management Consulting Companies in Western Europe, 1920 to 1990: Products, Reputation, and Relationships". *Business History Review, 73*(2), 190–220.

La Porta, R., Lopez-de-Silanes, F., Shleifer, A. & Vishny, R. (1998). "Law and Finance". *Journal of Political Economy, 106*(6), 1113–1155.

La Porta, R., Lopez-de-Silanes, F. & Shleifer, A. (1999). "Corporate Ownership Around the World". *Journal of Finance, 99*(54), 471–517.

Laird, P. (1998). *Advertising Progress: American Business and the Rise of Consumer Marketing*. Baltimore: Johns Hopkins University Press.

Lamoreaux, N., Raff, D. & Temin, P. (2003). "Beyond Markets and Hierarchies: Toward a New Synthesis of American Business History". *American Historical Review, 108*(2), 404–433.

Langlois, R. (1992). "External Economies and Economic Progress: The Case of the Microcomputer Industry". *Business History Review, 66*(1), 1–50.

Langlois, R. (2004). "Chandler in a Larger Frame: Markets, Transaction Costs, and Organizational Form in History". *Enterprise & Society, 5*(3), 355–375.

Lazonick, W. (1991). *Business Organisation and the Myth of the Market Economy*. Cambridge: Cambridge University Press.

Leslie, S. & Kargon, R. (1996). "Selling Silicon Valley: Frederick Terman's Model for Regional Advantage". *Business History Review, 70*(4), 435–472.

Marchand, R. (1985). *Advertising the American Dream*. Berkeley: University of California Press.

Nelson, R. & Winter, S. (1982). *An Evolutionary Theory of Economic Change*. Cambridge: Harvard University Press.

North, D. (1990). *Institutions, Institutional Change and Economic Performance*. Cambridge: Cambridge University Press.

Penrose, E. (1959). *The Theory of the Growth of the Firm*. Oxford: Oxford University Press.

Piore, M. & Sabel, C. (1984). *The Second Industrial Divide: Possibilities for Prosperity*. New York: Basic Books.

Rajan, R. & Zingales, L. (2003). "The Great Reversals: The Politics of Financial Development in the Twentieth Century". *Journal of Financial Economics, 69*(1), 5–50.

Sabel, C. & Zeitlin, J. (1985). "Historical Alternatives to Mass Production: Politics, Markets and Technology in Nineteenth Century Industrialisation". *Past & Present, 108,* 133–176.

Sabel, C. & Zeitlin, J. (2004). "Neither Modularity nor Relational Contracting: Inter-Firm Collaboration in the New Economy". *Enterprise & Society, 5*(3), 388–403.

Scranton, P. (1997). *Endless Novelty: Speciality Production and American Industrialisation, 1865–1925.* Princeton: Princeton University Press.

Strasser, S. (1989). *Satisfaction Guarantee; The Making of the American Mass Market.* Washington: Smithsonian Institute Press.

Sull, D. (1999). "The Dynamics of Standing Still: Firestone Tire & Rubber and the Radial Revolution". *Business History Review, 73*(3), 430–464.

Toms, S. & Wilson, J. (2003). "Scale, Scope and Accountability: Towards a New Paradigm of Business History'. *Business History, 45*(4), 1–23.

Toms, S. & Wright, M. (2002). "Corporate Governance, Strategy and Structure in British Business History, 1950–2000". *Business History, 44*(3), 91–124.

Toms, S. & Wright, M. (2005). "Divergence and Convergence Within Anglo-American Corporate Governance Systems: Evidence from the US and UK, 1950–2000". *Business History, 47*(2), 267–295.

Usdiken, B. & Kieser, A. (2004). "Introduction: History in Organisation Studies". *Business History, 46*(3), 321–330.

Whittington, R. & Meyer, M. (2000). *The European Corporation.* Oxford: Oxford University Press.

Wilkins, M. (1970). *The Emergence of Multinational Enterprise.* Cambridge: Harvard University Press.

Wilkins, M. (1974). *The Maturing of Multinational Enterprise.* Cambridge: Harvard University Press.

Wilkins, M. (1988). "The Free-Standing Company, 1870–1914: An Important Type of British Foreign Direct Investment". *Economic History Review, 41*(2), 259–282.

Wilkins, M. (1989). *The History of Foreign Investment in the United States 1914–1945.* Cambridge: Harvard University Press.

Wilkins, M. (1992). "The Neglected Intangible Asset: The Influence of the Trademark on the Rise of the Modern Corporation". *Business History, 34*(1), 166–95.

Wilkins, M. & Schröter, H. (1998). *The Free-Standing Company in the World Economy, 1830–1996.* Oxford: Oxford University Press.

Williamson, O. (1975). *Markets and Hierarchies; Analysis and Antitrust Implications.* New York: The Free Press.

Williamson, O. (1985). *The Economic Institutions of Capitalism.* London: The Free Press.

Wilson, J. (1995). *British Business History, 1720–1994.* Manchester: Manchester University Press.

Wilson, J. & Popp, A. (2003). *Industrial Clusters and Regional Business Networks in England, 1750–1970.* Aldershot: Ashgate.

Other publications cited in the text

de Jong, A., Higgins, D. M. & van Driel, H. (2015). "Towards a New Business History?" *Business History, 57*(1), 5–29.

Eloranta, J., Ojala, J. & Valtonen, H. (2010). "Quantitative Methods in Business History: An Impossible Equation?" *Management & Organizational History, 5*(1), 79–107.

Golder, P. N. (2000). "Historical Method in Marketing Research with New Evidence on Long-Term Market Share Stability." *Journal of Marketing Research, 37*(2), 156–172.

Helfat, C. E. & Raubitschek. R. S. (2010). "Product sequencing: co-evolution of knowledge, capabilities and products." *Strategic Management Journal, 21*(10–11), 961–979.

Lamoreaux, N., Raff, D. & Temin, P. (2008). 'Economic Theory and Business History', in G. Jones and J. Zeitlin, eds. *The Oxford Handbook of Business History.* Oxford, Oxford University Press, 40–45.

Suárez, F. F. & Utterback, J. M. (1995). "Dominant Designs and the Survival of Firms." *Strategic Management Journal, 16*(6), 415–430.

Valtonen, H., Ojala, J. & Eloranta, J. (2013). "What Makes 'interesting' Business History. Evaluation of the Most Cited Recent Business History Journal Articles." Unpublished working paper.

Part II
Business ownership

5

Personal capitalism

Andrea Colli

Introduction

This chapter will deal with the nature, diffusion and persistence of personal capitalism around the world in the long run. Its main purpose is to discuss the main features of the concept of personal capitalism, and to analyse how, and why, different forms of concentrated ownership in the hands of individuals (and sometimes of their relatives) is common both to developing and developed countries, constituting probably the most diffused form of ownership in the world.

This overall persistence compels us to reconsider the idea of personal capitalism as a transitory stage. Apart from the (non-trivial) issue of defining the boundaries of the concept itself, a primary goal of this chapter is thus to deal with the institutional conditions allowing the owners to maintain a strict control over their companies even during the process of corporate growth, and with a limited investment of personal resources. Personal capitalism can instead be considered a peculiar form of ownership and management which challenges the consolidated idea of a unidirectional evolution of corporate organizations towards the realm of what is defined, also in this Companion, "managerial capitalism".

An implicit assumption in this chapter is that the legal form of ownership, the level of its concentration and the nature of ultimate owners are not only the result of dynamics related to the process of dimensional growth of corporate organizations, but are also the product of a certain institutional environment. In its turn, the institutional environment can be seen as the product of constraints derived both from culture and history. In emphasizing these issues, this chapter shows a close connection with the bulk of literature known for exploring the theme of the differences among capitalist systems. The degree of diffusion of personal capitalism varies, in fact, across different areas according to different institutional conditions which can – at least conditionally – make concentrated ownership efficient.

As we will see in the following paragraphs, personal capitalism is in general considered as a transitory stage or condition both in the life cycle of single enterprises (the micro level), and in the process of development of national economies (macro level). According to the classic business history approach, the evolution of modern capitalism can thus be seen as a process in which progressively small, individual and family business evolved into large companies – necessarily no longer controlled by individuals and less and less by families– which concentrate the vast majority of production, investments and assets of the economy. If this interpretation holds largely true in many cases, as noted above the personal and/or family "dimension" is still a relevant component in the corporate landscape of developed countries, notably among large or even very large companies. According to the data made available by the research in the fields of corporate governance and corporate finance, the share of the largest companies in different economies under the control of individuals and/or families oscillates around one third, with sharp variations across different countries (see for instance La Porta, Lopez-De Silanes and Shleifer, 1999; Faccio and Lang, 2002).

Personal ownership is a very broad concept. It includes corporate typologies ranging from the individual workshop to more sophisticated organizational structures, including joint stock companies and other private forms of ownership. It is thus important to understand better the intimate nature of personal ownership, providing a tentative taxonomy of the various possible typologies included in this category. In this respect, business history provides an almost infinite variety of possible examples, enormously enriching the whole framework of analysis.

Given the nature and aims of this Companion, the chapter will be based on the existing literature in the field and on secondary sources. The aim is to provide a clear-cut analysis of the nature and structure of personal capitalism, its process of development and its relevance in the process of industrialization. This will mostly be done through the comparative and longitudinal methodological approach that characterizes business history research.

Defining personal capitalism

So, what is personal capitalism? When one moves from what is intuitive – that is, personal capitalism as something that has to do with the individual dimension of running a business – to something more analytical, problems start to arise. For instance, a search of a definition of personal capitalism in the main encyclopaedic dictionaries will generate some disappointment. Definitions of capitalism are of course countless; State capitalism is always included in dictionaries and encyclopaedias, and the same happens in the case of other declinations of capitalism, as for instance "family capitalism", a concept which is of course closely related to that of personal capitalism – being however not exactly synonymous. Another well scrutinized declination of capitalism is, of course, "managerial" capitalism, always present in the main knowledge repositories and companions, including the one in which this entry is included. This imbalance is, by the way, mirrored in other indicators. A nice exercise is, for instance, to look at the results of a search with the N-gram quotations in Google Books. "State capitalism" is by far the most frequent quotation in books present in the Google Books database from 1800 to 2000, followed by "managerial capitalism" (whose recurrence starts during the Sixties) and then by "family capitalism", and "entrepreneurial capitalism". The less frequently cited is – maybe surprisingly–"personal capitalism", appearing for the first time (in the database) in a publication back in 1907.

Such an unequal distribution of cites is of course the outcome of many concurrent factors, among which academic path dependence and conformism, or also, more modestly, the presence of more appealing terms – in the case of "personal capitalism", a quasi-synonym as "entrepreneurship", for instance. It however cannot be excluded that it is also the relative vagueness of the term, which discourages its use. A look at the (few) definitions available confirms this impression. A definition of "personal capitalism" can, for instance, be retrieved (maybe a bit paradoxically) in the entry "Capitalism, managerial" in the very popular online

Encyclopedia.com.[1] Here "personal capitalism" is described as "built on competitive interaction among small firms within industries", something extremely close to the view of the firm, which is condensed into the well-known theoretical apparatus of neoclassic Marshallian economics. Small firms in settings characterized by perfect or quasi-perfect competition are, thus, identified with the domain of personal capitalism, while large firms and oligopolies are associated with managerial control. A more structured and dynamic vision of personal capitalism is still the one provided by Alfred Chandler in his bestseller *Scale and Scope*, who, discussing the historical evolution of three different capitalist models (the North-American, the British and the German), labels the British as "personal" (Chandler, 1990, p. 235 ff.), offering in the same section a clear explanation of the choice. Chandler put Britain right at the opposite of the US model, the epitome of managerial control over the corporation. By the First World War Britain had lost its leadership among the world capitalist countries, and her original sin was basically the failure – or maybe unwillingness – to transform the intimate structure of companies in capital intensive industries, which "remained personally managed", in the sense that British entrepreneurs tended to rely on "smaller management teams", maintaining key positions both in the top but also in the middle management of their enterprises – an attitude that in America had vanished already by the interwar period (Chandler, 1990, p. 240). To be precise, under the label "personal" Chandler put both the enterprises run without the support of extensive managerial hierarchies and those in which professional managers were recruited externally but the founders and their heirs maintained a relevant influence, both as executives and as relevant block holders. According to the influential American business historian, under the category of "personal capitalism" should thus be included "firms managed by individuals or by small numbers of associates, often members of founders' families, assisted by only a few salaried managers" (Chandler, 1990, p. 236).

Independently from his own vision of "personal capitalism" as basically detrimental for a firm's (and therefore for an economic system's) competitiveness, in Chandler's vision are thus condensed two (plus one) relevant and constitutive components of personal capitalism. First, the dimension of ownership and governance: the realm of personal capitalism is one in which ownership is concentrated in the hands of a single person or of a few individuals. Second, the dimension of management: personal capitalism refers to firms characterized by the involvement of owners in management positions, despite the (more or less moderate) involvement of professionals. The third (less structural) aspect in Chandler's perspective is the inclusion of the family dimension in the picture. Personal capitalism is apparently including, in his writings, both the entrepreneurial dimension, but also the very variegated kaleidoscope of family business. As we will discuss in the following section, however, this is probably not accurate, being family firms characterized by a set of peculiar aspects and problem only partially shared by those run by individuals. Family capitalism is not, in sum, a perfect synonymous of personal capitalism, and should be better seen as a possible outcome of a transformation process which may or may not take place.

One point in Chandler's analysis is, however, clear. Personal capitalism is considered more a stage, rather than a permanent status, of course for companies doomed to acquire a critical dimension in order to benefit of economies of scale and scope. As a stage, it is a necessary step, but also something which needs sooner or later to be substituted by other forms of governance, ownership and management. Problems arise when, and if, the transformation does not take place. In *Scale and Scope* (p. 240) Chandler mentions three stages in the evolution of the governance of large firms. The first one is the phase of the "personal enterprise", when founders operate without the presence of real managerial hierarchies. The second is the stage of "the entrepreneurial or family-controlled enterprise", characterized by the presence of founders,

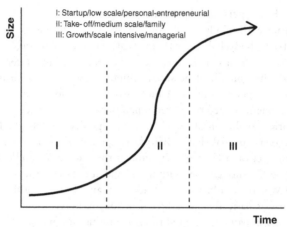

I: Startup/low scale/personal-entrepreneurial
II: Take- off/medium scale/family
III: Growth/scale intensive/managerial

Figure 5.1 A three stage model of governance

of their relatives and also of an extensive managerial hierarchy. This phase paves the way to the managerial form, "in which the executives in the administrative hierarchy have no connection with the founders or their families and have little or no equity in the company". The transition between personal to family and from family to managerial capitalism is considered as a stage process of evolution – a framework which Chandler had become increasingly familiar when he joined Harvard Business School, the "temple" of executive education, during the 1960s – and a consequence of the impact of technological change on the intimate structure of the firm. In contemporary words it is easy to identify the three stages with other concepts, as for instance start-up, fast growth and maturity, or with different levels in the scale of production (low, medium, high – see Figure 5.1). In this model, personal capitalism is thus a status, which appears during stages 1 and in the first part of stage 2, but is totally absent in stage 3.

Personal capitalism: the bad and the good

As widely known, the vision of personal capitalism that emerges from Chandler's writings is not particularly optimistic. To be clear, it is full of pejorative connotations, being in his vision, as said above, that the origin of British industrial decline was at the beginning of the twentieth century. Personal capitalism is thus identified with negative attitudes as nepotism, which was detrimental to professionalization and managerialization of large companies – a behaviour, of course, not limited to British entrepreneurs. Sentences as "in the United States nepotism had a pejorative connotation. In Britain it was an accepted way of life" (Chandler, 1990, p. 292) clearly synthetize Chandler's opinion about personal capitalism British-style (perhaps luckily, the book doesn't have chapters on France, Spain and of course Italy). To go back to a personal and individualistic management style was a sin probably even more unforgivable, as the treatment that Chandler gives to Henry Ford in his writings easily shows. Personally managed firms are, in sum, lacking of the fundamental virtue common instead to those run by managers, that is the capability of coordinating complex and extended hierarchies and processes typical of the modern, large organizations. This thesis has been further developed in detail by some of the main business historians who followed, more or less closely, Chandler's footsteps in analysing the evolution of modern capitalism, as for instance Hannah (1983) and Lazonick (1991).

It is interesting to note how Chandler's perspective on personal capitalism is still quite popular, even if in different contexts and relatively to other typologies of capitalism. In the case of Asian business systems, for instance, many commentators stress the pervasiveness of "personal capitalism" among large and very large companies as a distinctive feature of an institutional environment in which the involvement of relatives prevails over the appointment of professionals external to the family in top management positions. In some countries, as Malaysia, this leads to situations clearly sub-optimal, where "owners-entrepreneurs exercise little managerial control over their subsidiaries, and rarely manage their enterprises according to a strategic plan, preferring instead to engage in opportunistic investments to buy and sell business units according to purely financial criteria". This already gloomy framework is further worsened by the fact that "personalism in the corporation is nurtured and sustained in the political domain" (Carney and Andriesse, 2014, p. 145).

Personalism is also considered to be a "soft spot" when other aspects of the modern enterprise are considered, for instance propensity to undertake risky investments, a behaviour more common to managers, and due to a structure of incentives different from that of wealth preservation (Fama and Jensen, 1983). On top of this, the necessity of maintaining a close control over the firm may, according to some research, have consequences on the availability of sufficient capital and financial resources. Majority shareholders are in fact reluctant to raise resources on the capital market fearing an excessive loss of control, while minority shareholders may be reluctant to invest further capital fearing expropriation practices by controlling owners (Carney and Gedajlovic, 2001, p. 347). Personally managed firms tend thus to be undercapitalized, either to ante pone unrelated diversification strategies to others in order to attain a convenient degree of risk, something which many commentators see as negative for the development and transmission of capabilities inside the organization. On the top of this, personalism is generally associated with high levels of path dependence and conservatisms, something that can be detrimental in fast-changing environments (see for a nice exemplification Popp, 2000).

Of course, not everybody is happy with these views. It is not a case that a large section of "post-Chandlerian" business history emphasizes instead the virtues of family and personal capitalism (e.g., Church, 1993; Lloyd-Jones and Lewis, 1994; Colli, 2003) but also of entrepreneurial capitalism (see for instance Langlois, 1996; Acs, 2003; and of course Baumol, Litan and Schrann, 2009 – especially Chapter 4). These various declinations of personalistic attitudes are depicted as the good side of capitalism, opposing the bad side – in which normally both crony capitalism and also financial capitalism is included. Understandably, these views have been further strengthened during negative economic cycles, when managers, bankers and financiers have been blamed by the public opinion for their selfish end extractive behaviour, opposite to that of creative entrepreneurs running their own business with an ultimately positive outcome for the society. As in the case, very much celebrated by the literature of family firms, the incentives' system in personally managed firms based on wealth preservation, very long-term orientation and parsimony (Carney and Gedajlovic, 2001, p. 346) goes in the direction normally associated with the stability of society. The identification between ownership and control is also drastically reducing the intensity of agency problems which are at the opposite the normal situation in managerial companies, and absorb a vast amount of resources for keeping them under control.

The good and the bad of centralized management and personalistic attitudes are thus quite evident and widely debated in the available literature in various fields, being this subject rather interdisciplinary.

Andrea Colli

Personal capitalism as an evolutionary process

The stage model depicted in Figure 5.1 can be further analysed looking more in depth at the possible evolution of ownership and governance forms in the course of the life cycle of an enterprise. In Figure 5.2 the various possible patterns are schematized. Of course the process can be seen as a dynamic one, i.e., taking place over time but also as something influenced by external elements as for instance technology (impacting on the scale and capital intensity of production processes), institutional and/or legal arrangements (allowing more or less impersonal forms of ownership, or introducing/eliminating mechanisms enhancing the control of dominant shareholders) and the nature and "thickness" of the financial markets.

The personalistic/individual stage is, here, (I admit, quite arbitrarily) seen as characterizing the start-up phase, and coincides, in the most standard version, with a status of pure individual authority and control over the business. This holds also in case of small start-ups of a few associates, being however here the standard example the one provided by the entrepreneurial small workshop of artisanal nature. This can be, of course, a permanent status enduring for the whole life of the enterprise – and probably the most common and diffused, no matter if the firm remains small, or becomes large (path #1). A founder can maintain a close grip on the enterprise without any intention of transmitting it to relatives (dynastic motive), or of leaving its control to managerial hierarchies. In most cases, the life cycle of the enterprise coincides with that of the founder/entrepreneur, while in some others the alternative is the sale of the business. Examples are of course countless. As purely descriptive exemplification, let me mention the origins of my mother institution, Bocconi University, which was founded in 1903 with the generous endowment of a brilliant entrepreneur in mass distribution, Ferdinando Bocconi, and named after one of his sons, Luigi, who had died very young some years before. Luigi was the last of three, and was expected to be the one going to run the family business, while his brothers were either unable or uninterested. His death transformed completely the process from one characterized by a dynastic process to another of a completely different nature. In 1917 Ferdinando sold the business to another entrepreneur, Senatore Borletti, which changed completely its name (which became La Rinascente) and its strategy (Amatori, 2008a). In other cases, the absence of heirs is at the basis of the decision to sell, as in the case of US Steel, at the time of the sale (1901) probably the largest company in the world, still run in a very centralized and personal way by its founder, Andrew Carnegie.

The alternative to this path is depicted by path #2, which shows the transformation of personal capitalism in case of absence of the purpose of transmitting the firm to the following generation. If the founder has the willingness to keep the company alive without involving any of the relatives, (s)he may opt for the transmission to managers already active inside the company, involving them as quasi-relatives in business, even distributing to them portions of the company's shares. A couple of interesting historical examples are that of the early history of the German steelmaker August Thyssen, who, in front of the deterioration of kinship relations inside the family, strengthened the links with managers transforming, de facto, the company into a community of professionals (Fear, 1997), and the one of the Boucicaut family. At the death of Aristide, the founder of the first modern department store (Au Bon Marchè) in Paris, his wife ran the business for some years, strengthening progressively the relationships with the community of professional managers who considered themselves as part of a single extended family (Miller, 1994). In this case, one may also suggest a sort of new model of "open personal firm", even if this term has not been until now introduced in the literature.

62

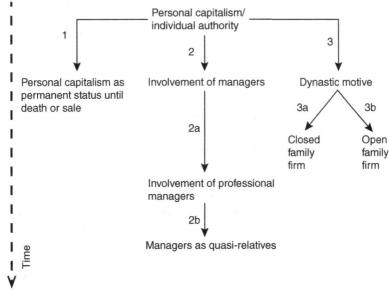

Figure 5.2 The transformation of personal capitalism

The possibility and willingness of transmitting the business to the following generations opens different directions to the evolution of personal capitalism. A first pattern is the replication of the personalistic attitudes of the founder inside the family firm. In this model, all or almost all the strategic roles inside the firm are in the hands of the founder and of his/her relatives. After the death of the entrepreneur, the firm remains a closed partnership among family members, characterized by an almost perfect identification between the family and the firm itself (pattern #3). This can be seen, and actually de facto is, one of the stages of the life cycle of the firm, as suggested by Chandler (see above). It can, however, be seen as a permanent status, particularly when families are able to find inside themselves the necessary human resources able to run the business (#3a). Of course, this pattern of evolution coincides with the transformation of the purely personalistic attitudes of the founder into a larger body characterized by a sort of collective authority, which derives from kinship ties. In particular, family members tend to present themselves as a cohesive group that tends to act as a single individual, maybe under the leadership of one member more charismatic than others. An interesting exemplification is provided by the story of another well-known Italian brand, Benetton. Founded in the mid-1950s, the company has been since the beginning run by four siblings, each one in charge of a strategic area of activity. Even if the most popular among the public is Luciano – actually a charismatic leader who had first the entrepreneurial idea – the three others have been, since the beginning, running the business relatively behind the scenes, behaving in a really cohesive way and without recurring to professional managers in leading positions. The "closed" family firm (Casson, 2000) can thus, in some way, be seen as a version of personal capitalism in which the centralization of authority in the hands of a single individual is mitigated by the division of labour and of managing responsibilities among relatives. The two forms of personal capitalism share the absence of professional management and by the coincidence of ownership and control, and, in principle, by a very low degree of agency problems.

As widely debated in the family business research, another possible pattern (#3b) of evolution is the process of opening a closed family firm. An "open" family firm (Casson, 2000) is thus a firm in which the founder and the family maintains a close control over ownership stakes and some involvement in management roles, leaving however a large part of strategic decisions to professional managers. In the case of open family firms, the internal distribution of power between family and non-family members is the result of a delicate and dynamic process, which may show significant variation in the long run. A nice exemplification of this process is the history of one of the symbols of Italian family capitalism, that is the Agnelli family and Fiat, the automotive company which the family has been controlling for over a century. Founded by Giovanni Agnelli in 1899, the company rapidly became one of the largest in Italy. After the First World War, Fiat already was at the top of the ranking of Italian companies in terms of turnover and had become a vertically integrated group. The management style of the founder was a mix between personal charisma and the ability to rely on a small nucleus of capable managers, however his intent was clearly dynastic, that is to transmit the leadership to his son Edoardo. It is maybe hazardous to define Fiat, at this point, as a sort of open family firm, but this is probably not too distant from what it actually was. Edoardo, however, died in a plane crash in 1935; his sons were thus too young to take any active role in the company. When the founder died, in 1945, the leadership was thus put in the hands of the managing director, who had previously covered the role of CFO, Vittorio Valletta.

Valletta was a capable manager, who had in the interwar period consolidated his authority inside Fiat and had been able to build an efficient and cohesive cohort of managers supporting his leadership. Notwithstanding this, his leadership style was characterised by very high levels of personalism and centralization, but also by the sincere willingness to serve the family's interests, something very close to the present concept of "stewardship". Without owning a single share of Fiat, he claimed to act "in loco parentis", that is basically as the temporary substitute of the father of the future leaders, the two brothers Giovanni and Umberto Agnelli, to whom he actually handed over the company in 1966, after having expanded and consolidated it during the miraculous decades following the Second World War (Amatori, 2008b). The two brothers' leadership, however, was much less characterised by personalism and centralization. Thanks also to the active role of American consulting firms (and of the leader of an influent Italian merchant bank, Mediobanca), the degree of delegation and professionalization rose steadily during the Seventies and Eighties, when Fiat could have been quite correctly defined as an "open" family firm. A similar case is the one of the German Bertelsmann family, which was able to increase the degree of authority decentralization after the 1950s, something which led to a very much successful process of international growth after the 1980s (Berghoff, 2013).

The realm of personal capitalism

The Fiat-Agnelli example is not only useful in clarifying the concept of the open family firm, but also shows in an effective way the delicate balance between personalistic attitudes and the necessity of granting the necessary freedom to the management. It is however also indicative of the fact that the boundaries of personal capitalism are blurry, and are probably to be seen coinciding more with management styles than with aspects related to ownership. As noted by Chandler and by others, personal capitalism includes two analytic dimensions, that quite obvious of ownership and the other, the degree of centralization of the authority in the hands of an individual. However, as discussed above, personalistic attitudes are not limited to founders and individuals, and may be extended to include the centralization of authority characteristic of closed family firms but also, to a certain extent, the attitude of managers, even without any formal ownership in the company. The identification, in sum,

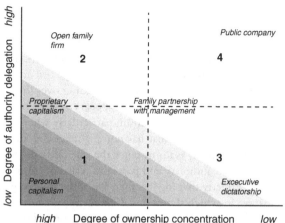

Figure 5.3 The domain of personal capitalism

of personal capitalism with ownership *and* control concentration in the hands of a single individual is clearly reductive, and has probably to be expanded to include other sections of the continuum between individual ownership and control and a form of capitalism fully managerial, characterised by the complete separation of ownership and control.

Figure 5.3 tentatively schematizes what could be defined as the domain of personal capitalism, simply elaborating on the two dimensions of concentrated and dispersed ownership, and of the centralization/decentralization of authority.

Bottom left (quadrant 1) represents the area of maximum degree of ownership and control concentration, which naturally coincide with personal/entrepreneurial capitalism. In this area are thus included the companies in the early stage of activity, those characterised by artisanal structures but also larger ones still under the control of their founders. Historically, this area is coinciding with the phase that preceded the genesis of modern management (Pollard, 1965), in which the overlapping between ownership and control was almost complete.

Top left quadrant 2 coincides with structures characterised by high ownership concentration, as for instance family firms, but also by a very high decentralization of authority to professionals and by extended managerial hierarchies. The pattern from quadrant 1 to 2 is basically what above has been described as the progressive opening of family firms to professional management, for instance, where ownership remains highly concentrated in the hands of family members and/or founders who however give up managerial responsibilities almost fully to professionals. In quadrant 2, however, one can find other typologies of enterprise less intuitive. For instance, a case of high concentration of ownership but dispersion of control is represented by investment holdings stably controlling subsidiaries in very diverse fields, and employ professional managers leaving them freedom of action (as by the way happens, with much shorter time – horizons, in the case of private equity firms). At the end of the 1980s the already mentioned Benetton family started a process of unrelated diversification from the core business creating a holding which started to acquire relative or full majority stakes in companies in mass retailing (Autogrill), and in infrastructures as motorways and airports. Notably, almost all these companies, formerly state-owned, were put on sale during the privatization process of the 1990s. At the moment of their acquisition, most of them kept intact the managerial structures and hierarchies already present before the privatization wave. In this case, the concentrated ownership of a family holding coexisted with the dispersion of control. Can this still be considered as personal capitalism?

The answer is neither immediate nor straightforward. If one looks at ownership, yes, no if one considers control.

Bottom right (quadrant 3) is the area of minimum concentration of ownership, but in which personalism still dominates. Apparently this is an area that should be probably empty; how is it possible to find personalism where ownership is dispersed and nobody has enough administrative rights to make his/her power prevail, deciding over the strategy and the tactics of the enterprise? At a closer look, however, it appears evident how cases of very high ownership dispersion can coexist with personalism, particularly when ownership dispersion is the final stage of a process of growth that has not challenged at all the authority of the founding family. Cases are abundant, as for instance the one of the Italian Pirelli, where the family enjoyed an unchallenged authority and power in terms of control occupying the top management positions but directly owning less than 5% of the share capital. In this area one can also include companies in which the personal authority of controlling owner is maintained in a situation of ownership dispersion thanks to the presence of control enhancing mechanisms as for instance dual class shares.

A recent example is provided by the listing of Google in 2004. The use of dual class shares, which de facto perpetuate the full authority of the three founders, coexists with high ownership dispersion. Beyond the reasons put forward in order to motivate the existence of such a mechanism in Google, the outcome is again a high degree of the founders' personal control in front of ownership dispersion. In this quadrant I am also including those cases of public companies governed by some charismatic manager with a very high degree of personalistic centralization. One may include in this group, for instance, companies as Jack Welch's General Electric during the Eighties, or today's FCA under the strong grip of Sergio Marchionne. The term that better describes these situations of personal capitalism without ownership is probably that of "executive dictatorship".

Moving upward in quadrant 4, one finds the area of maximum ownership dispersion and authority decentralization, which characterizes the standard model of managerial capitalism-which is however analysed in another chapter of this Companion and thus falls outside the scope of this chapter.

Figure 5.3 also depicts some intermediate situations, some of which are worth analysing more in depth. At the centre of the matrix one can place federations of family members, or family partnerships, that is family firms in which blocks of ownership are divided among relatives which simultaneously occupy top management positions. Situations like the one described above are very common in companies characterised by the dynastic motive and evolving from pure personal/entrepreneurial firms to family firms. As for other categories, examples are countless: a significant one is that of the US chemical giant Dupont, which for most of the twentieth century and in the course of its global expansion a federation of relatives owned more or less relevant stakes of the company (Lombardi, 2014). Of course, these kinds of quasi-personal and quasi-managerial firms are most likely to evolve into public companies run by managers, in particular when the company is listed allowing relatives not interested in the business to liquidate their stakes. However, it is also not possible to exclude the opposite pattern, when in a family partnership one member liquidates the others becoming, again, the sole owner and controller of the company.

Another interesting case of an intermediate category of firms that nicely locates between quadrant 1 and 2 in Figure 5.3 is the one described in detail by Quail (2000), in reference to the British case before the First World War – something which can however can be easily extended to other national cases, and to more recent historical periods. According to this author, the governance of most of the largest British firms before the Great War was characterised by "proprietorial" attitudes. In these joint-stock companies, often generated by the aggregation of smaller (personal or family owned) companies, the shareholders who composed the Board of Directors tended to manage directly most of the firm's function, through an extensive use of committees and recurring only seldom to professional management. According to Quail, this generalised attitude led, in general, to inefficient management practices, and to permanent damages in the organizational capabilities of British firms.

The grey area in which falls the combination of sufficient ownership concentration and enough polarization of authority can be considered, broadly speaking, as the domain of various varieties and typologies of personal capitalism. The figure shows also the different intensity of personalism starting from bottom left.

Three determinants: technology, institutions and culture

Personal capitalism as defined in the previous sections is of course dependent on a number of factors, which can both incentivize its diffusion and persistence, or *au contraire* push for an evolution in the direction of the top-right area in Figure 5.3. For sake of clarity, I have grouped the main determinants under the three broad categories of a) technology and technological change, b) institutions (in which one can include regulation and legislation) and c) culture, which coincide with the prevailing attitudes towards the way of running a business.

a) Technology and technological change

Technology and technological change has been traditionally considered as the main driver in the process of transition between forms of concentrated ownership and control towards more complex organization and governance structures. The transition from preindustrial forms of manufacturing to those of the first, and of the second industrial revolution has been, according to business historians, largely determined by changes in the technology of production, which basically allowed firms to enjoy economies of scale and scope. The pure enlargement of the volume of production compels founders and owners to start a process of delegation of authority, and to follow the pattern described in Figures 5.1 and 5.2. This process is generally seen as non-reversible and monotonic. A reversal of the process, as in the above mentioned case of Henry Ford, who in the interwar period took his company again private and significantly reduced the level of power delegation, is normally taken as a clear example of how dangerous is to leave the pattern of modernization in scale intensive industries turning back to the "old way" of doing things. Technology has been however recently seen also as the driver of the "fragmentation" process of the large, vertically integrated corporation (Langlois, 2003). Technology, in this case mainly communication and transportation technology, reduces the need of coordination and of control, allowing at the same time the dispersion of the production chain into a web of network relations among smaller and flexible production units. Putting it boldly, if production technology has been, for a certain period, at the basis of the decline of personal capitalism in some industries, communication and transportation technologies have been at the basis of the rebirth of personal capitalism in the same industries. They are in fact allowing a reduction in the level of vertical integration, the subsequent fragmentation of the production process into smaller units that are characterised by simpler organizational structures, and are thus easily manageable by individuals or very small groups of people. Similar structures can be, and could be in the past, found in industrial districts, regional agglomerations of small firms, each one characterised by personalistic organizational structures, clustering together around the production of a single or a few range of goods. Industrial districts and the local condensation of entrepreneurial creativity have been much celebrated in the past (e.g., Becattini, 2004; Piore and Sabel, 1984; Sabel and Zeitlin, 1997) as systems able to conjugate efficiency and "human" dimension in modern capitalism. Again, it is easy to see a virtuous connection between personal capitalism and creativity in the historical development of some high-tech industries characterised by the clustering of interconnected capabilities, as in the case of Silicon Valley (Saxenian, 1996). Historians such as Phil Scranton have been quite vocal in stressing the close connection between specialty production industries and personal capitalism (Scranton, 1983, 1997).

b) Institutions

Institutional arrangements are equally relevant in framing the conditions for the presence and persistence of personal capitalism. Both their absence, and/or presence can efficiently condition the process of growth and organizational evolution of firms, as well as their intimate governance processes. For instance, rules governing inheritance transmission, or regulating the process of inheritance partition, heavily influence the possibility of transmitting the enterprise to one single leader, or to many, starting therefore a process of authority dilution. It is widely recognized how, for instance, the legislation about inheritance tax has a key role in incentivizing or hindering the dynastic motive. A very high inheritance tax incentivizes the listing of enterprises and is therefore weakening, in general, the diffusion and persistence of personal and/or family orientations (Colli, Fernandez and Rose, 2003). Research on the evolution of the capitalist enterprise in Britain and Continental Europe (Wilson, 1995) shows quite well how the regulation of joint-stock companies had some effect on the propensity of entrepreneurs to open their capital to a larger constituency, therefore accepting some interference also in the enterprise's management. Another example of institutional influence is the above-mentioned legislation concerning control-enhancing mechanisms, and in particular dual-class shares, allowing the founders and owners to raise financial resources maintaining intact their voting power. In some "mature" economies, the enduring pervasiveness of personal and family capitalism is clearly connected to the availability of such mechanisms, as evident for instance in the case of the Swedish Wallenberg family, able to exert a close control, for decades, on a vast business empire thanks also to the issuing of multiple voting shares. Legislation provides the best example of institutional impact over the persistence of family capitalism, but there are other cases of institutional influence on the probability of the persistence of personal capitalism. A quite often mentioned one refers to the nature and structure of financial markets. Basically, the argument on which it is based reads that the more efficient in terms of efficiency and "thickness" a financial market is, the higher the incentives are for entrepreneurs to collect resources on these markets. This is of course accelerating the process of transition of personal capitalism to more impersonal forms of management. Inefficient financial markets tend to be consistent with the persistence of centralized ownership and control, also because lenders tend to prefer to interface with personal owners than with professional managers. Of course, this argument is very consistent with the bulk of academic literature in corporate finance that explains the diffusion of personal and above all family capitalism in environments characterised by a low level of efficiency and transparency of financial markets (La Porta, Lopez-De Silanes and Shleifer, 1999).

c) Culture

A third cluster of elements, which contribute to explain the nature and persistence of personal capitalism are those related to culture. While of course the impact of technological change and of legislation can to some extent be quantified and measured through more or less sophisticated econometric techniques, cultural elements are of a much more problematic analysis. Anyway, scholars analysing personal capitalism and personalistic attitudes in business have often stressed the role of culture, intended more specifically as the role assigned to business in the society. For instance, in social settings in which stability, long-term orientation and social commitment are appreciated as founding values of the society, personal and family capitalism are considered as a form of ownership and management particularly suitable in order to promote and maintain the status quo. A good example of this attitude is, for instance, the debate about the role of *Mittelstand* in the course of German industrial and economic history. Hartmut Berghoff (2006) has variously stressed the importance of the personal/family dimension (in his view, the two are synonyms). The Mittelstand is a general category of medium and small firms, characterised by the presence of six main elements as the role of the founder and the family, long term orientation, emotional attachment (what is today known under the umbrella-concept of socioemotional wealth; see Berrone, Cruz and Gomez-Meija, 2012), generational continuity (or dynastic motive), patriarchial culture and informality and independence (Berghoff, 2006, p. 272 ff.). Needless to say, top management positions are all shared in the family, giving outsiders little or no space at all. In his article the author describes the evolution of this model after the 1970s, in front of the process of globalization, but he is quite clear about the fact that this model coincided with a more general orientation of the German society towards values of moderation, long-term orientation, concreteness. Quoting Gary Herrigel (1996), the author underlines how the Mittelstand is a product of a specific institutional environment that in its turn has been generated by a specific business culture. Explicitly, this model of capitalism largely based upon personal committed authority was since the beginning perfectly fitting in the nation of "Sozialmarktwirtschaft", the social market economy built upon a compromise between market forces and social imperatives.

Culture could work in favour of the persistence of personalistic attitudes even when, in principle, both technological change and law were not putting obstacles to a full transition to managerial capitalism. According to Quail (2000, p. 4), in late nineteenth-century Britain "there was no reason in law (…) why delegations to management should not have been extensive. The praxis of the period, however, was generally considerably more restrictive".

Personal capitalism around the world

The presence (or absence) of technological, institutional and cultural incentives to the persistence of personal capitalism and various forms of concentrated control over the business activity explains the different degree of diffusion of personal capitalism across different countries in the world, both in space and time. Of course, it is quite reasonable to expect a higher diffusion of personal capitalism in countries at the early stage of their process of industrial development, even if, as demonstrated above, the diffusion of high-tech industries often coincides with a new wave of entrepreneurial and personal capitalism. Industrial maturity *should* coincide with less personal capitalism, as well as a high level of efficiency of capital markets. In the very end, this is the explanation put forward by a large bulk of literature in the fields of corporate governance and corporate finance. According to the path-breaking research by

La Porta and colleagues (La Porta, Lopez-De Silanes and Shleifer, 1999), for instance, the high level of diffusion of concentrated ownership in the hands of individuals and families is ultimately motivated by the degree of efficiency of local capital markets which allow the persistence of concentrated control, or, put in another way, incentivize owners to keep a firm control on their companies since they can easily extract high benefices from control. Personal/family control among the largest businesses is thus very high in Central and South America, Asia and in several European countries. According to similar research, such a situation of entrenchment is ultimately undermining the efficiency of those economies in which personalistic attitudes persist among large firms (Morck, Wolfenzon and Yeung, 2004).

The argument against personal capitalism as an ownership/management arrangement ultimately damaging the efficiency of firms and of entire economic systems, however, is partially weakened by the fact that, as stressed above, the presence of concentrated ownership strengthened by the creative use of control enhancing mechanisms often does *not* coincide with centralization of control. In cases as those mentioned above, as for instance the one very symbolic of Bertelsmann, are able to offer a unique (yet fragile) blend of personal/family and managerial capitalism (Berghoff, 2013). The coexistence between patient, long-term oriented family ownership and professional management in key decisional roles can thus be seen more as an efficient solution and an effective management model.

Conclusion

Personal capitalism is probably the most diffused form of ownership and management today, as it was for sure in the past. Business historians come, sooner or later in their research, in close contact of issues related to personal ownership, centralized authority and management of firms, both if they focus on the history of single companies examining the stages of their evolution and also when they look at the evolutionary processes of economies. The mainstream literature in business history has tended, and still largely tends, to consider personal capitalism at best as a (necessary) stage in the evolution of the enterprise, a stage which, at least in core industries, was necessarily going to be substituted by more decentralized forms of control (managerial hierarchies) and of ownership (public companies). After all, this was the lesson which one could derive from the story of the surpass in the world industrial leadership by the US, symbol of managerial capitalism, and the UK, considered to be the realm of the most reactionary and conservative personal capitalism, unable and unwilling to adapt to the compulsory changes in ownership and control models introduced by the Second Industrial Revolution. More recently, business historians started to adopt a more cautious and inclusive approach, partially also due to a general reconsideration of models of industrialization different from those based on the large, managerial public company. The influence of areas of research as those of entrepreneurial studies, and of family business, has clearly introduced a less negative view of concentrated forms of ownership and control in relation to economic development. Personal capitalism has thus started to be considered not only as a stage to be quickly surpassed, but as a managerial model in itself.

This new focus on personal capitalism has highlighted the complexity, or better the inclusiveness of the concept. In this chapter I have thus tried to schematize both the "varieties" of personal capitalism and the process of their generation. At the same time, introducing the two dimensions of ownership and of authority I tried also to suggest a more inclusive definition of personal capitalism not limited to the identification between full ownership and control in the hands of one or a few individuals.

This chapter also suggests some reflections on two other relevant aspects. The first concerns the determinants of the persistence and diffusion of personal capitalism in space and over time. For sake of brevity, I focused on three large domains: that of technology, that of institutional arrangements and the more "blurry" one of culture. All them play a relevant role, of course with a high degree of "endogeneity effects". The second aspect concerns the diffusion of personal capitalism, and above all its persistence in economies which are considered as "developed", thus characterised by more sophisticated forms of ownership and management. The available literature, particularly in the field of finance, tends to consider this as the result of a distortion in capital markets. A more equilibrated view would instead look at the fact that concentrated ownership may coexist with professional management, a coupling that can ultimately be generating very positive outcomes.

Note

1 "Capitalism, Managerial." International Encyclopedia of the Social Sciences. 2008. *Encyclopedia. com.* (September 17, 2015). http://www.encyclopedia.com/doc/1G2-3045300278.html.

References

Acs, Z. (2003). "Entrepreneurial Capitalism: If America Leads will Europe Follow?" *Journal of Small Business and Enterprise Development, 10*(1), 113–117.

Amatori, F. (2008a). "Managers and Owners in an Italian Department Store: La Rinascente from 1920 to 1970", in Susanna Fellman, Antti Kuustera and Eero Vaara (eds), *Historical Perspectives on Corporate Governance. Reflections on Ownership, Participation and Different Modes of Organizing.* The Finnish Society for Science and Letters, Helsinki, 139–154.

Amatori, F. (2008b). "Big and Small in the History of Industrial Italy", *Rivista di Storia Economica*, n.s. 24(2), 207–224.

Becattini, G. (2004). *Industrial districts: a new approach to industrial change.* Cheltenham: Elgar.

Berghoff, H. (2006). "The End of Family Business? The Mittelstand and German Capitalism in Transition, 1949–2000", *Business History Review, 80,* 263–295.

Berrone, C. & Gomez-Mejia (2012). Pascual Berrone, Cristina Cruz and Luis Gomez-Mejia, "Socio-emotional Wealth in Family Firms: Theoretical Dimensions, Assessment Approaches, and Agenda for Future Research", *Family Business Review, 25*(3), 258–279.

Carney, M. & Andriesse, E. (2014). "Malaysia: Personal Capitalism" in Michael A. Witt and Gordon Redding (eds.), *The Oxford Handbook of Asian Business Systems,* 144–168.

Carney, M. & Gedajlovic, E. (2001). "Corporate Governance and Firm Capabilities: A Comparison of Managerial, Alliance, and Personal Capitalisms", *Asia Pacific Journal of Management, 18,* 335–354.

Casson, M. (2000). "The Family Firm: An Analysis of the Dynastic Motive" in *Enterprise and Leadership.* Cheltenham: Elgar, ch. 8.

Church, R. (1993). "The Family Firm in Industrial Capitalism: International Perspectives on Hypotheses and History", *Business History, 35*(4), 17–43.

Colli, A. (2003). *The History of Family Business, 1850–2000.* Cambridge: Cambridge University Press.

Colli, A., Fernandez, P. & Rose, M. (2003). "National Determinants of Family Firm Development? Family Firms in Britain, Spain, and Italy in the Nineteenth and Twentieth Centuries", *Enterprise and Society, 4*(1), 28–64.

Faccio, M. & Lang, L. H. P. (2002). "The Ultimate Ownership of Western European Corporations", *Journal of Financial Economics, 65,* 365–395.

Fama, E. & Jensen, M. (1983). "Separation of Ownership and Control", *Journal of Law and Economics, 26*(2), 301–325.

Fear, J. (1997). "August Thyssen and German Steel", in Thomas Mc Craw (ed.), *Creating Modern Capitalism. How Entrepreneurs, Companies and Countries Triumphed in Three Industrial Revolutions.* Cambridge: Harvard University Press, 185–226.

Hannah, L. (1983). *The Rise of the Corporate Economy: The British Experience*. London: Methuen.

Herrigel, G. (1996). *Industrial Constructions. The Sources of German Industrial Power*. Cambridge: Cambridge University Press.

La Porta, R. Lopez-De-Silanes, F. and Shleifer, F. (1999). "Corporate Ownership Around the World", *The Journal of Finance, 56*(2), 471–517.

Langlois, R. (1996). "Schumpeter and Personal Capitalism" *Economics Working Papers*, Paper 199605, University of Connecticut, http://digitalcommons.uconn.edu/econ_wpapers/199605.

Langlois, R. (2003). "The Vanishing Hand: the Changing Dynamics of Industrial Capitalism", *Industrial and Corporate Change, 12*(2), 351–385.

Lazonick, W. (1991). *Business Organization and the Myth of the Market Economy*. New York: Cambridge University Press.

Lloyd-Jones, R. & Lewis, M. J. (1994). "Personal Capitalism and British Industrial Decline: The Personally Managed Firm and Business Strategy in Sheffield, 1880–1920", *Business History Review, 68*(3), 364–411.

Lombardi, L. (2014). *When DuPont Went Global. How the DuPont Family Built a Multinational Empire (1910–1967)*, PhD Dissertation, University of Geneva.

Miller, M. (1994). *The Bon Marché: Burgeois Culture and the Department Store, 1869–1920*. Princeton: Princeton University Press.

Piore, M. & Sabel, C. (1984). *The Second Industrial Divide: Possibilities for Prosperity*. New York: Basic Books.

Pollard, S. (1965). *The Genesis of Modern Management: A Study of the Industrial Revolution in Great Britain*. Cambridge: Harvard University Press.

Popp, A. (2000). "Specialty Production, Personal Capitalism and Auditors' Reports: Mintons Ltd., c.1870–1900", *Accounting, Business & Financial History, 10*(3), 347–369.

Quail, J. (2000). "The Proprietorial Theory of the Firm", *Journal of Industrial History, 3*(1), 1–28.

Sabel, C. & Zeitlin, J. (1997). (eds), *World of Possibilities. Fexibility and Mass Production in Western Industrialization*. New York: Cambridge University Press.

Saxenian, A. L. (1996). *Regional Advantage. Culture and Competition in Silicon Valley and Route 128*. Cambridge: Harvard University Press.

Scranton, P. (1983). *Proprietary Capitalism: The Textile Manufacture at Philadelphia 1800–1885*. New York: Cambridge University Press.

Scranton, P. (1997). *Endless Novelty: Specialty Production and American Industrialization, 1865–1925*. Princeton: Princeton University Press.

Wilson, J. (1995). *British Business History 1720–1995*. Manchester: Manchester University Press.

6

Managerial capitalism 2.0

John Quail

"Managerial" capitalism is a name for the economic system of North America and Western Europe in the mid-twentieth century, a system in which production is concentrated in in the hands of large joint-stock companies. In many sectors of economic activity the classical entrepreneur has virtually disappeared... As a result (so a substantial body of writers have suggested), entrepreneurship in the modern corporation has been taken over by transcendent management, whose functions differ in kind from those of the traditional subordinate or "mere manager". These people, it is argued, can wield considerable power without necessarily holding equity, sharing profits or carrying risks.

—(Marris, 1967, p. 1)

Introduction

For a number of decades after World War Two 'managerial capitalism' became in the US, and to a significant but lesser extent in the UK, a term of approbation for a new social order understood to combine a social landscape of giant corporations dominated by professional management with economic efficiency, social responsibility and general affluence. This explicitly 'linked American plenty with American management' (Locke, 1996, p. 4). It was a positive variant of a longer established, often dystopian, view of bureaucratically-run modern mass society and as long as the general affluence persisted the US managerial model remained exemplary. Google N-grams show that the term 'managerial capitalism' became a meme in the 1950s, peaked in the early 1990s and then declined. This profile represents the rising then declining sustainability of both the concept and US management's reputation as competition, particularly Japanese competition, and a resurgent domestic financial capitalism brought widespread economic uncertainty and the collapse of the American management mystique (Locke, 1996).

So the term 'Managerial Capitalism' has utility in describing a recognisable phase in the development of the capitalist corporation in the 'Anglo-Saxon' economies, arguably a point when it reached maturity but also a period when the phenomenon was considered newly socially significant. However, capitalism has remained to this day no less managerial in the sense that its institutions are controlled by administrative hierarchies. Capitalism was also managerial well before the phrase gained significance: the large US corporation was overwhelmingly controlled by its managers rather that its beneficial owners, the shareholders, by 1930 (Berle and Means, 1932). Moreover the separation of ownership and control which has been described as 'the quintessence of managerialism' (Nichols, 1969) goes back to well before the First World War for the UK – earlier in fact than the US (Foreman-Peck and Hannah, 2012). Indeed the very nature of the Corporation lies in some measure of separation of owners and operators from its beginnings.

The discussion in this paper has been limited to the Anglo-Saxon economies because of distinctive differences between them and other economies, particularly the different dynamic between financial capital and non-financial corporations, and the role of the state. Above all, though, the hegemonic ideological construction that led to the assumption that the professional managers of capitalist corporations acting in their own interests would thereby act in the interest of the citizenry as a whole seems to have only been possible in the Anglo-Saxon economies. Elsewhere capitalism may have been managerial but it wasn't Managerial Capitalism.

By definition, in order for managerial capitalism to exist corporations must be sovereign bureaucracies, free to define their aims. Orderly structures composed of a wide range of appropriately skilled personnel using effective control techniques must be in place to realise these aims. The highest tier of management must be the governing body. The processes whereby this situation came to be were contingent, largely the unforeseen consequences of activities carried out for other purposes (Roe, 1994; Roy, 1997). The process was also unpredictably constrained or enabled, in the US particularly, by an activist state (Fligstein, 1990). It was emphatically not an unfolding endogenous expression of administrative/managerial logic. There was no necessary sequence, no pre-determined teleological end point (Quail, 2008a).

US corporations grew in size and power from the end of the nineteenth century to the 1920s through a series of spectacular merger waves, fuelled largely by increasing access to finance capital. The process required greatly reduced legal restraints on the activities and geographical scope of corporations, ends that were achieved by legal assaults at both State and Federal level. The managerial and governance structures which lie at the heart of Chandler's narrative of 'the managerial revolution in American business' (Chandler, 1977) were first imposed by investment banks or ownership interests, notably by J P Morgan, in order to impose order and control on ragged and malfunctioning amalgamations to ensure that the investments the bank had mobilised paid out. They used the centralised functional departmental structure which 'became and still remains today a standard way of organizing a modern integrated industrial enterprise' (Chandler, 1977, p. 433). The banker's presence was tenacious and long term though temporarily reduced to cadet status by New Deal legislation in the 1930s and early 1940s (Simon, 1998; Herman, 1981). This left managers with hegemonic power in corporations with a high degree of autonomy and centralised control. The multi-divisional structure, routinely assumed to be synonymous with managerial capitalism, was an adaptation of the centralised functional departmental structure designed to preserve owner-control as corporations became larger and more complex. The early, and only retrospectively iconic, linked cases of DuPont and General Motors are examples of proprietorial, not managerial, interests in action. The wide adoption of this structure did serve the purposes of centralised managerial power, however, particularly after World War Two as corporations increasingly adopted financialised strategies (Fligstein, 1990; Lazonick, 1990).

In the UK huge amalgamation waves also took place over the same period and for similar reasons. Their organisational course was different however. The absence of hegemonic investment banks left a different and continuing tradition of self-perpetuating boards and board committees of non-executive directors occupying the space held by top management in the US. The holding company structure, the preferred form, allowed nested hierarchies of subsidiaries and sub-subsidiaries which preserved the director/manager split. It was not until the end of World War Two that boards of directors began to be significantly transformed by the accession of full time functional executive directors, beginning with finance directors (Matthews, Anderson and Edwards, 1998). Managing directors morphed into full time CEOs. The process appears to have reached critical mass only in the 1970s (Quail, 1999).

Having been assembled to ensure survival through some degree of market control, the large amalgamated US or UK corporation was faced with significant problems of internal control. Issues of planning, costing, accounting, transparent administrative structures and information flows were interlinked and required systems of budgetary control to manage them. Such systems allow coordinated planning across functions, task allocation and targets cascaded down functional hierarchies, out-turn information in sufficient detail to account for variances and use of this information to rebalance subsequent budgets. This iterative process establishes a feedback loop without which learning and optimum control is impossible. Budgetary control, therefore, rather than return on capital employed – an investor metric which on its own gives no clue as to causes and remedies – is the true measure of both ordered corporate structures and adequate measures of corporate control (Quail, 2008b; Quail, 1997; Chandler and Redlich, 1961).

Particularly in the US, the 25 years after World War Two were marked by a combination of circumstances which gave the managerial large corporations a very good press. These were years of growing prosperity. Popular suspicions of big business for a variety of reasons not least its gross incapacity in the 1930s and the consequent New Deal rescue and control regime were mitigated by the successes of war production. The Cold War both contributed to prosperity through a permanent arms economy and a confluence of political rhetoric and corporate PR contrasting 'Soviet totalitarianism' with 'free enterprise'. In order to combat advocates of the 'creeping socialism' of the social democratic mixed economies in western Europe and persisting New Deal attitudes at home, US corporations jointly and severally developed forms of welfare capitalism accompanied by well-funded propaganda. This presented the professionally managed corporation as a new socially responsible phenomenon leaving behind the robber barons and feral business tycoons of the past. 'Managerial Capitalism' as a concept could therefore acquire a complex set of meanings by association and ascription, helped in no small measure by the Chandlerian school of business history. The explanation for the blossoming usage then fade-out of the phrase 'managerial capitalism' is that the substantial ideological deck cargo carried by the term had limited sustainability. 'Managerial capitalism' emerged as a sustainable description of current realities as the long post-World War Two Western boom took off and suffered a delayed action decline as the boom disintegrated, the Cold War ended, and new financialised and global competitive realities showed their teeth.

In what follows we will consider the processes that created the giant corporation, their eventual domination by professional management, the development of organisational structures and control technique that made it possible, the origins and content of the ideological framework that constructed managerial capitalism and the real world processes that dismembered it.

The corporation

The corporation is a creation of the state and the course of its development is written in law however pragmatic and crisis driven its development might be (Gelderblom, de Jong and Jonker, 2013). US and UK corporate law has common origins in the English law of the late seventeenth and early eighteenth century. The practice in the two countries drifted apart for a number of reasons, one being the rural and developmental eighteenth century economy of the US whose primary needs were for local infrastructure and better communications. Corporate charters for these purposes appear to have been fairly readily granted, firstly by Colony Governors and then State legislatures. Companies like the Bank of England or the East India Company had Governors and Deputy Governors who ran their corporations with wide powers subject to oversight of diminishing power over time by courts of proprietors. This structure was adopted by larger earlier US corporations like the Bank of North America (1781), the Bank of the United States (1791) (O'Donnell, 1952) and the Massachusetts Society for Useful Manufactures (1791) (Davis, 1917). In the UK by comparison the speculative mania in the early eighteenth century that collapsed in 1720 brought with it the Bubble Act that forbade the formation of joint stock companies without (expensive and difficult) Parliamentary approval and remained in force until 1825. While the Bubble Act supposedly applied to the American colonies it appears to have been simply ignored.

The Bubble Act did not stop large numbers of UK quasi-corporate bodies operating under legal flags of convenience such as trusts or deeds of settlement, though their legal status remained essentially that of large unlimited partnerships and the proprietors were legally 'liable to their last shilling and acre', as one Chief Justice put it (Cottrell, 1980, pp. 39–40). Certain common features developed in the governance of UK companies. While routine day-to-day tasks were carried out by management, endemic corruption, embezzlement and conflict between managers and boards left no inclination to delegate wide powers to managers. Instead as they grew companies increasingly appointed sub-committees of the board to oversee different aspects of the business. By 1844–9, 63% of all new companies and 75% of large ones stipulated them. Furthermore, despite democratic intentions in governing instruments, director's appointments had become appropriated by boards on which longevity of membership became the norm (Freeman, Pearson and Taylor, 2012). Significantly, too, an increasing proportion of UK companies up to 1844 stipulated that directors were not to have an office of profit – a salaried job – or have contracts with the company. Freeman, Pearson and Taylor explain the genealogy of this as a congruence of company and public/political arrangements with shifting public opinion driving increasing attempts to prevent jobbery and private interest. The strict separation of director and manager roles was enshrined in Table A in the Companies Acts from 1862 and combined with the development of director's departmental subcommittees established the dominant modus operandi of UK capitalism until World War Two and after (Quail, 2000).

By contrast the US practice of readily available incorporation which led to standard forms of charter and a greater acceptance of strong managerial roles led to a very different outcome. In the years up to 1830, governance practice as set out in incorporation charters varied considerably, with examples of control by shareholder general meetings, boards subject to varying degrees of shareholder control or strong managerial centralisation. An increasing volume of applications to state legislatures for incorporation led to moves towards standardisation. In Massachusetts for example, the 1830 Manufacturing Corporations Act introduced 'a comprehensive code for manufacturing corporations. Its most important provisions' included the requirements to 'choose a president, clerk, treasurer, and three directors, the method of choice not being stated' (Dodd, 1954, p. 233). Earlier legislation had not mentioned presidents specifically. Subsequent legislation spread this formula to insurance and railroad companies and other sectors. The introduction of general incorporation statutes in other US states followed a similar pattern: an increased volume of applications for incorporation by special charter led to standardisation and generally followed a similar formula to Massachusetts (Hurst, 1970).

There were practical reasons why a strong constant controlling management presence was essential for US business corporations. The barely legally restrained entrepreneurial capitalism of the United States that emerged after the Civil War led to every variety of underhand expediency in desperate struggles for survival, profit and dominance. This constant warfare meant that a premium was placed on constant attention and speedy decision-taking with little time for consultation leading more or less inevitably to individual dominance of a corporation's affairs. *The Economist* (1893, cited in Campbell, 1938, pp. 127–8) while condemning 'the virtually despotic power possessed by too many American railway officials' with directors apparently unable to apply 'a drag on a reckless president,' nevertheless admitted that 'unfortunately, it is not easy to discover a remedy... since an American railway is in nine cases out of ten essentially a fighting organism'.

The de facto tendency towards increased autonomy of US management within the firm was complemented by formal legal developments lessening the power of shareholders (Dodd, 1934; Roy, 1997; Hurst, 1970). This further diminished with the increase in size and complexity of corporations as result of the late nineteenth century amalgamation wave and the liberalisation of state incorporation charters that made it possible. Of particular importance was New Jersey's legalising of one corporation's acquisition of the stock of another in the period 1888–1893. At the national level too, as a result of litigation involving many separate individual corporations in the latter part of the nineteenth century, 'drastic change set in toward removing regulatory emphasis from the general incorporation acts, with a high premium on giving the greatest freedom and vigor to central management' (Hurst, 1970, p. 57).

But while the principles of corporate autonomy and one-man management were triumphant in the individual corporation, the business system was moving into crisis in the later nineteenth century. The US cut-throat competitive economy (combined, particularly on railroads, with predatory insider speculation) plunged repeatedly into recession leading to widespread insolvency in the 1890s, pre-World War One and again in the 1920s. This led to amalgamation waves which were essentially attempts to control competition. Between 1895 and 1904, 157 substantial combinations took place with more than 1800 firms disappearing. While the pace of consolidation never reached the same level again, the process continued with over 1600 firms disappearing into combinations in the period of 1905–1920 with a new peak of activity in 1924–29 (Lamoreaux, 1985; Nelson, 1959).

How have the motives for, and the outcomes of, these mergers been interpreted? At the time there appears to have been a broad Progressive consensus that they were attempts at monopoly to be resisted (Brandeis, 1913). A later account quietly registers this in passing but emphasises the organisational opportunities they represented: 'mergers were rarely successful until managerial hierarchies were created – that is until production was consolidated and its administration centralized and until the firm had its own marketing and purchasing organisations' (Chandler, 1977, p. 338). Any implication that this happened through a conscious search for efficiency rather than being forced by crisis or external actors, or that efficiency paid off better than market control is highly questionable: 'mergers producing high concentration can bring substantial monopoly power gains that may persist more or less indefinitely, whether administrative and technical overhaul takes place or not' (Du Boff and Herman, 1980, p. 98). Official reports show that concentration was not accompanied by any significant operational economies. Economic performance if anything declined: despite the increasing number of large corporations those reporting net income in excess of $100,000 increased only marginally from 1918 to 1926 and declined in the same period for the largest single category, manufacturing. The advantages of size actually appeared to lie in increased market share giving greater marketing dominance and access to capital (Thorp, 1929).

There was a busy political response to the merger waves but the existence of the large corporation was not threatened as long as monopoly was not at issue. That the State could and would act was clear: Theodore Roosevelt used the Sherman Act of 1890 to break up Standard Oil in 1911. The focus of most political attention, however, was on the 'Money Trust', the investment bankers and their satellites who not only financed numbers of large amalgamated companies but were represented on their Boards, Executive and Finance Committees. A succession of Acts were passed prior to World War One and under the New Deal and steadily reduced, but did not entirely end the investment bankers' influence (Simon, 1998; Herman, 1981). In one key respect, however, the lasting influence of the bankers has been seriously under-emphasised: their role in the creation of modern corporate structures. This will be considered in the next section.

The origins and development of orderly management structures

The US merger waves of the late nineteenth and early twentieth century produced some very large corporations: by 1919, 65 were managing more than 50 establishments, 10 more than 60 and 2 more than 100 (Thorp, 1924). These were combinations of strong egos as well as economic units (Tarbell, 1925, Chapter 6). There is persistent evidence that the operating principle of making only the minimum necessary changes was general with only a minority of firms like the Pennsylvania Railroad engaging in unforced organisational change. Amalgamations tended to preserve both the contours of the amalgamating firms and substantial powers of previous owners over 'their' firms. The more economically successful the corporation, the less likely was any restructure, as with US Steel, Western Union and Standard Oil (Du Boff and Herman, 1980).

Even faced with deteriorating outcomes and significant elements of external *force majeure*, change could be reluctant and slow. A representative example is International Harvester. The agricultural machinery industry was intensely competitive. While various attempts at a protective merger over ten years failed, finally, this time with the participation of J P Morgan, five firms, some 90% of the industry's capacity, were amalgamated in 1902. It took a further four years of disappointing results before J P Morgan, for all its power, could force dismemberment of the founding companies and the formation of a unified administration structure on the new company (Kramer, 1964; Chandler 1977). In the pursuit of efficient corporate management structures in the firms they controlled, J P Morgan appeared to be unique among US investment bankers (Carosso, 1970). Their strategic approach had evolved from practical problem-solving in a logical and explicit way (Hannah, 2011; Carosso, 1987; Corey, 1930). The firm mobilised European funds for US investment. If these investments did not succeed the bank took control of the company seeking order and efficiency. Power was centralised in a voting trust, swingeing capital reconstruction was accompanied by reorganisation of boards and the imposition of executive and finance committees whose members Morgan chose. Management was centralised and, as evidence gathered by Chandler shows, the centralised functional departmental structure that 'became and still remains today a standard way of organizing a modern integrated industrial enterprise' was imposed (Chandler, 1977, p. 433).

Morgan held 72 directorships 'in 47 of the largest corporations in the country' in 1911 (Brandeis, 1913, p. 32). Given that amalgamations up to 1919 produced 65 companies combining more than 50 firms, which we may take as a proxy for 'large', this indicates huge influence. With the caveat that quasi-monopoly profits reduced the urgency of reorganisation, it does not seem improbable that a large number of these companies acquired centralised functional departmental structures. Furthermore, J P Morgan as the leader of a working alliance including their controlled trust companies, the First National and National City Banks of New York cumulatively held 341 directorships in 112 corporations with a total capitalisation of $22.2 billion (Brandeis, 1913). We can reasonably assume, given the bank's standing and its successful record of company reorganisation, some pressure to follow a similar organisational course in a further 47 corporations.

The approach of Morgan stands out particularly when compared to an apparent widespread indifference to organisational questions elsewhere. Dennison noted in 1929 that despite frequent mergers there was an absence of published material on structural organisation and reorganisation (Dennison, 1929). In the early 1930s, Urwick wrote that the large amalgamated companies had no real appreciation of the organisational issues facing them (Urwick, 1933). A 1941 survey of 31 unnamed 'leading industrial corporations' found a variety of hybrid structural and governance forms which for 'many companies is a result of tradition, merger or unplanned growth' while only a few companies had 'given the attention and study it deserves' to 'a sound and clean-cut plan of top-management organization'. 'In many companies' the responsibilities and functions of the board, general and operating management levels are 'indistinct and confused'. The situation was changing slowly and many companies 'have found or are beginning to find that as their businesses expand in extent or diversity' these arrangements are inadequate. A 'definite urge and trend towards decentralization of management' is noted so if any trend was observable' it is perhaps (*sic*) in the direction of the product-division plan... This structure presents 'a special problems of co-ordination... with respect to policies, practices and costs... generally accomplished by setting up central staff agencies to exercise overriding *functional* direction, supervision and control...' (Holden, Fish and Smith, 1941, pp. 30, 15–16, 30–35). Divisions can be held accountable on a profit-and-loss basis. Of the 31 companies surveyed, 16 used budgetary control in some form but no detail is given on actual practice.

So by 1941 only a minority of very large companies had moved towards a product-division structure and those that had, had apparently applied a centralised functionally departmental structure to control the divisions. This account, based on an extensive contemporary survey, contradicts Chandler's claim that 'by 1917... the majority of mergers used an organizational form similar to that devised at these two innovating enterprises' namely DuPont and General Motors (Chandler, 1977, p. 417). Holden, Fish and Smith's account is supported by a composite time series of US M-forms which shows 2 in existence by 1929 and 9 by 1939 (Fligstein, 1985, Table 2). The M-form only became general after World War Two though difficulties remained: a 1947 survey of 130 US companies showed advances in administrative structure and technique. However, decentralisation was limited by 'the high degree of functional control exercised by one or more executives of major rank at the home office' (Hopf, 1947, pp. 402–3). It also found that roles of policy determination and execution were still too often combined at the top leading to confusion and insupportable workloads.

There are two issues here. Why the apparent widespread indifference to organisational questions in the interwar years, and why the apparent upturn in interest at the beginning of the 1940s? A persuasive answer lies in Fligstein's model of shifting concepts of market control and the concomitant optimal organisational structures required. The model is rich and detailed and what follows is a simplified version. He proposes four historic stages of corporate quests for dominance within a wider landscape of shifting legal constraints and specific competitive environments. A first phase of predatory competition from 1870 to the 1890s ended in systemic over production and the merger waves on either side of the First

World War. A second phase, the manufacturing concept of control, followed during the interwar years. Here manufacturing scale and efficiency led to oligopolistic market dominance allowing price leadership and price stability. This required large integrated firms. A third phase emerged in the Depression and burst into bloom in the post-World War Two years: the marketing concept of control. This gained advantage through product differentiation and diversification, frequent model change and advertising. The ensuing problems of integrated central functional control across increasingly diverse activities favoured the adoption of the multidivisional firm controlled through budgets. A fourth and current stage, the finance concept of control originated in antitrust action against corporate concentration in product lines. Combined with diversification this produced unrelated product conglomerates with strategies of acquisition and de-merger based on strictly financial return on investment criteria (Fligstein, 1990, pp. 20–32).

This schema suggests that except in a few cases there was simply no need for multidivisional structures in the interwar years. Not surprisingly then, there was very little mention of the DuPont/General Motors structure in interwar literature. It appears necessary to avoid magical thinking about the multidivisional form. Of the two earliest examples, General Motors was a collection of companies assembled by a megalomaniac entrepreneur who fortuitously stripped his subsidiaries of corporate status before going bankrupt, leaving the large investors DuPont and J P Morgan in charge of the now multi-divisional firm over which a standard Morgan central governance structure was placed. The DuPont company structure evolved from a similarly Morgan-style central control and functional structure in a series of steps designed to retain family control as the firm's hierarchy lengthened. The DuPont's had direct experience of J P Morgan's approach through the bank's acquisition of a steel company, in which they held stock and had management roles, to form Federal Steel (Chandler and Salibury, 1971). The issue, to state the obvious, was central control. It seems apparent from the Holden, Fish and Smith survey and Hopf's comments that post World War Two central micromanagement and central functional control in divisional structures still frequently vitiated any decentralisation. Johnson and Kaplan cite Oliver Williamson's hypothesis that 'the multidivisional enterprise has the capacity to exact stricter compliance with owner's goals than the capital market can exact from top managers of independent vertically integrated firms'. They go on to say, 'It does this in large part because top managers can scan complete and timely information about subordinates' performance. Providing this information is the major contribution of management accounting to the multidivisional firm's superior performance' (Johnson and Kaplan, 1987, p. 113). The theme is developed by Solomons who notes: 'By its system of budgets, more than by any other means, top management maintains control of its divisions while allowing them a large amount of freedom in the day-to-day… conduct of their operations' (Solomons, 1965, p. 233). Dearden (1962 cited in Solomons, 1965, p. 233) says that this 'requires a more sophisticated and expensive budgeting and planning system to overcome the problems of communication, co-ordination and evaluation that profit decentralization creates'. A 1958 survey of over 400 US companies found that 89% had 'a formal budget or profit planning program' (Sord and Welsch, 1958, p. 35). This suggests that divisional control by the corporate centre had shifted from central functional control of practice to central control of performance through sanctioned budgets and analysed performance over 15 years or so. This is again confirmation that the M-form is a lengthened hierarchy to accommodate increased size and diversity with strong central control whose mode shifts over time.

Developments in the UK, in the absence of external forces, tended to preserve proprietorial power and proprietorial structures that enabled it. The forces that had moulded centralised management structures in the US, particularly pro-active investment bankers, were absent. The UK's director's committee structure as a response to corporate diversity or complexity was general. This governance structure had serious consequences. It meant that management was in departmental silos, the heads of departments were co-equal, co-ordination being the prerogative of the board. But boards were generally part-time. So coordination was weak. The information that boards needed to exercise power might be forthcoming in some cases – costing for example – but in many cases its use by boards was limited, not least because of ignorance or incapacity. So control technique was weak and under-developed. This structure continued until well after World War Two. Its larger consequences were lack of adaptability and innovation, defensive amalgamation and cartels; amalgamations generally resulted in loose holding companies with nested subsidiaries and sub-subsidiaries, and under-development of managerial capacity and control technique. There were points of light such as Unilever but as a whole it was dysfunctional (Quail, 2000).

Channon remarks that the tardy adoption of new forms of company and the reluctance to abandon loose holding company structures 'reflects the relatively "amateur" British approach to management which was still more bound up with an elitist class system rather than a meritocratic professionalism' (Channon, 1978, p. 274; Quail, 1998). This social closure was greater because the operating environment for UK business had been protected or advantaged for 30 years or so. Changes in business structure challenged deeply entrenched privilege and were resisted until crisis made them inevitable. The 1960s marked the beginning of that crisis. Poor performance and sharpening external competition combined with loose and barely controlled structures found many large UK manufacturing companies apparently incapable of finding solutions to organisation and performance problems themselves. Many turned to US consultants who advocated the adoption of the multidivisional form (McKenna, 2006a, Chapter 7). Channon suggests that 13% of the top 100 manufacturing companies were multi-divisional by 1950. By 1960 this had risen to 30% and by 1970 to 72% (Channon, 1973). Caution is needed, however: British companies 'widely adopted the multidivisional structure ... as the organisational form best suited to manage the diversified enterprise. However ... many of the internal characteristics of [these] corporations ... reflected prior structural forms'. These characteristics included incomplete divisionalisation with blurred policy making and authority lines. Budgetary control was present in many cases but had usually only been recently introduced and was limited and unsophisticated apart from a minority of high-technology firms. This was even more the case for financial planning and the macro-control of divisions through such measures as return on capital. There was rarely 'a level of general managers within the central office to supervise the activities of divisions' (Channon, 1973, pp. 213, 209).

Things improved, however. A survey in 1982 of a sample of the top 500 UK firms found 80% of the companies were multidivisional. It also found evidence of increased sophistication and ease among large UK corporations in dealing with organisational complexities whereby already divisionalised firms undertook fundamental organisational change, frequently without consultants (Hill and Pickering, 1986). A 1985 study of 16 large UK companies found levels of organisational understanding and mastery of control technique that would have been extremely rare ten or fifteen years earlier (Gould and Campbell, 1987). So by the mid-1980s large UK enterprise had become comfortable with the multidivisional form, able to adjust it to specific requirements and deploy the necessary accounting and other control techniques. For the first time there was a large market for a professionalised managerial workforce which was met by a rapid increase from the mid-1980s in the numbers of undergraduate and post-graduate management degree courses (Quail, 1992).

Ideological components of 'managerial capitalism'

The rise of the large corporation and oligopolistic concentration combined with the steady separation of ownership and control in the US had implications that were starkly set out by Berle and Means in 1932. The 'wealth of innumerable individuals has been concentrated into huge aggregates... whereby control over this wealth has been surrendered to a unified direction. The power attendant upon such concentration has brought forth princes of industry, whose position in the community is yet to be defined'. The old relationship of property ownership to control had been broken, raising questions both of the motives of the new princes and how the proceeds of industry would be distributed. Managerial control continued to advance, corporations grew bigger and their power increased while ownership became dispersed 'and the corporate system is thereby more securely established. This system bids fair to be as all-embracing as was the feudal system in its time' (Berle and Means, 1933, pp. 2, 9). The issues were not entirely new – similar ideas were current in the Progressive Era – but the sheer weight of evidence, the sharpness of the analysis and the sense of foreboding that marked the book caused a sensation.

The political consequences were long term. Berle became a member of Franklin Roosevelt's advisory 'Brain Trust' which, among other things, contemplated corporate reform. Apparently reasoning that the loss of ownership control was irreversible, it remained politically possible to ensure a competitive economy through control of monopoly. Active anti-trust activity became a strong institutional force after World War Two. Corporate counter-arguments stressing the benign necessity of the giant oligopolistic corporation's ability to produce goods and services at a price affordable to the common man rather fell on stony ground in the New Deal years but blossomed after World War Two 'as employers stepped forward to shape national social and economic policies'. The most visible manifestations were national political battles, but equally important though less noisily 'corporate leaders constructed and sold a specific vision of the reciprocal relationship of businesses and citizens [where] corporate leaders claimed the right to control America's economic destiny without significant interference from unions or the state while acknowledging their responsibility to make the benefits of industrial capitalism available to all. Economic growth rather than the redistribution of income... would allow business to uphold its end of the bargain'. Nationally 'business organizations ... orchestrated multimillion dollar public relations campaigns that relied on newspapers, magazines, radio, and later television to re-educate the public in the principles and benefits of the American economic system' (Fones-Wolf, 1994, pp. 5–6).

As to the content of these campaigns, a study by Sutton et al. found 'a pervasive divergence between adherents of what we call the *classical* and the *managerial* strands in the creed...'. The classical strand describes 'a decentralized, private, competitive capitalism, in which the forces of supply and demand, operating through the price mechanism, regulate the economy in detail and in aggregate'. The managerial strand differs 'in the emphasis it places on the role of professional managers in the large business firm who consciously direct economic forces for the common good [and] emphasizes the fundamental transformation of the last fifty years [seeing] in the present economic system a radical break with the past' (Sutton et al., 1956, pp. 9, 33–34). The primary manifesto of the managerial strand was *USA, The Permanent Revolution* by the editors of *Fortune*, the business magazine (*Fortune* was in the habit of employing former Trotskyists and the title was surely a borrowed one: an English translation of Leon Trotsky's *The Permanent Revolution* was published in New York in 1931). 'Fifty years ago' they said, 'American capitalism seemed to be what Marx predicted it would be and what all the muckrakers said it was – the inhuman offspring of greed and irresponsibility, committed by its master, Wall Street, to a long life of monopoly [but there] has occurred a great transformation, of which the world as a whole is as yet unaware … '.

Their thesis was that Wall Street no longer controlled large non-financial corporations. Because the main motivation of the managers who ran these corporations was long run survival and growth, social responsibility was a necessary part of that aim augmented by the ethics of modern professional management. While managers had to make profits they had to think in the long term and consequently 'maintain an *equitable and working balance* among the claims of stockholders, employees, customers, and the public at large'. Large corporations increasingly provided health insurance, maternity leave and pensions. They increasingly ensured continuity of employment by ironing out production peaks and troughs. They ensured common interests with employees by profit sharing and bonuses. So 'a manager is a trustee not only for the owner but for society as a whole. Such is the Transformation of American Capitalism. In all the world there is no more hopeful economic phenomenon' (The editors of *Fortune*, 1956, pp. 62–63, 72–74, 82).

This thesis was widely cited and discussed. The socio-economic academic analysis of the concept of managerial capitalism and its implications was wide-ranging but ultimately, however, without consensus. There *were* many large oligopolistic corporations run by managers with no discernible control by shareholders. The economic and political power they wielded or could wield *was* huge. How was it actually wielded? To what extent were such actions dangerous or benign? Were there any constraints on managerial power and if so, what? To what extent should their power and actions be directed or moderated by the democratic state, by their employees, by the communities within which they operated or even perhaps the shareholders? The boundary between the public and the private sector was becoming more vague with corporations contracted by the state to carry out its functions. Was there, or should there be, a convergence of private and public corporate status? A well-regarded collection of essays edited by Mason covers this ground and more and ends with more questions than answers and no obvious synthesis. Mason concluded that '[w]hat we need is a twentieth-century Hobbes or Locke to bring some order into our thinking about the corporation and its role in society' (Mason, 1959, p. 19). Was such a synthesis even possible? Perhaps not: Robin Marris introducing a 1974 collection of papers, *The Corporate Society*, which he had intended to weld 'into some kind of grand synthesis' wrote that while the contributions were 'original, helpful and stimulating… I cannot pretend to have even begun to achieve a synthesis' (Marris, 1974, p. vii). Later writers like Herman see a capitalist continuum rather than a historic break. Capitalism in 1981 was managerialist, indeed increasingly so, but it was still capitalist: the managerial corporation's drive to greater size and higher profits was no different than an owner-dominated one, with attitudes and practices to match. The details might change but the key dynamic remained that of corporation and state and the power balance between them (Herman, 1981).

There is however one scholar whose account of 'the managerial revolution in American business' has remained as citable as ever and has probably kept the idea in circulation: Alfred Chandler. His narrative has permeated a range of works well outside business history in a way no other business historian has come near to managing. His work emerged in a period in US history typified by McCarthyite Cold War paranoia and a university climate dominated by witch hunts of 'disloyal' and 'un-American' academics (Lazersfeld and Thielens, 1958; Diamond, 1992; Schrecker, 1986; Wang, 1999). An anti-liberal, anti-Progressive pro-business revisionist school of business history was in the ascendant (Galambos, 1970; Hofstadter, 1968) and 'from 1948 onward, among historians as among other academics and intellectuals, there was an accelerating abandonment of dissidence, a rapid accommodation to the new postwar political culture' (Novick, 1998, p. 323). Chandler's work essentially ignores this context producing a new synthesis of a number of disparate contemporary themes which undoubtedly suited the quietist spirit of the times. These themes included the mantle of the entrepreneur ascribed to top corporate managers by the Center for Entrepreneurial History at Harvard in which Chandler became involved (Cole, 1946). The concept of strategy came from his time as research assistant to John McDonald the ghost writer of Alfred Sloan's Memoirs (McDonald, 2002; McKenna, 2006b). A joint paper with Fritz Redlich applied German rigour to the analysis of corporate hierarchies (Chandler and Redlich, 1961). The importance of decentralisation/divisionalisation came from Drucker (Chandler, 1956). Finally the centrality of the use of archives and the study of the administration of the business unit came from the practise of the group of academic business historians at Harvard (Larson, 1947).

The synthesis was extremely attractive. It provided an explanation of the development of the corporation in terms of strategic adaptive top managerial responses in first-mover firms to changing market conditions. The necessary rise of the professional manager came because the resulting administrative complexity was too taxing for proprietors. Variations in organisational response by different sectors are explained by the relative complexity of the administration required to deal efficiently with their particular markets. In other words, competition is the spur and efficiency is the result. This chimed with both the traditional and the managerial strands of the corporate creed. The market was there, competition was there, but so too was the managerial prince, legitimised and heroic. There is however a curious disconnect between the introductions and conclusions of *Strategy and Structure* and *The Visible Hand* and the historical material between them. As we have seen there is much material that can point to radically different conclusions than those derived. There is much that is omitted that would muddy the picture considerably, not least the unpredictably crisis-prone economy, the sporadically hostile state, the sheer messiness of history that can make far-sighted strategic planning a liability when opposed by a combination of attention to new or apparently weak signals and opportunism. But the model remains, is still taught, and so in a small way the high summer of managerial capitalism lives on in an autumnal Chandlerian glow.

Afterword

At the heart of the optimistic idea of managerial capitalism lay some idea of arriving at a period of stability – stable employment, stable prospects – combined with gently rising prosperity for all. Capitalism, however, does not go in for stability. The managerial corporation, it turned out, was no less enthusiastic for growth and profit than an owner-controlled one. As we have seen, Fligstein's model of strategies for market control moves from a 'marketing concept of control' to a 'finance concept of control' in the post-World War Two period. The marketing concept relied on product diversification, model changes, market research and in the process becomes more difficult to manage. Functional micromanagement did not work. Separate profit centres with day-to-day autonomy, central budgetary control and the multidivisional structure became necessary. Continuing diversification, most easily managed through mergers, meant acquiring unfamiliar businesses whose performance was most easily judged on financial criteria. Fligstein argues that the Celler-Kefauver Act passed into law in 1950 designed to prevent market concentration and preserve a competitive economy discouraged mergers in general but particularly horizontal and vertical mergers further encouraging unrelated mergers. Problems of integration were greatly increased and financial performance measures almost inevitably became the sole measure of divisional performance. The 'finance concept of control' made a virtue of this necessity and brought to prominence corporate leaders with financial backgrounds who pursued conglomerate mergers in what became named the market in control. Products or divisions which failed to meet financial performance criteria were sold rather than overhauled. Acquisitions were made purely on the basis of profitability rather than strategic fit. The spectacular growth rates of these firms were difficult to ignore and the model they provided became a dominant one (Fligstein, 1990).

This model was made viable by developments in finance capitalism. The declaration by the more enthusiastic proponents of the managerial revolution that Wall Street no longer had power over non-financial businesses did not remain valid for long after World War Two. A boom in debt and equity issues began in the 1950s, with institutional investors purchasing large blocks of securities, brought some re-concentration of ownership. The emergence of venture capital funds after World War Two had, by the end of the 1960s, brought a situation 'very reminiscent of pre-depression financial capitalism'. Long term linkages became established between various financial institutions – including commercial banks, trust bankers and underwriters – and corporations requiring funds (Calomiris and Ramirez, 1996, p. 162).

The boards of large US corporations had substantial financial institutional representation in the 1970s though the non-financial corporations were dominant. Herman shows that in 1975, 20% of the top 200 US non-financial corporations were significantly influenced by financial institutions and 79% had one or more financial institution representatives on their board. The agenda for the finance interests was creditworthiness and profit growth and, 'Its natural tendency is to affiliate with "profit machines" and managements that know how to guide them and then to give them free reign. If these managements see the future as requiring a stream of acquisitions, financial institutions will compete to finance them'. In other words, a well-funded systematic takeover mechanism had been institutionalised. At this stage the chief actors were 'large, cash-rich firms [seeking] out well-managed and profitable companies in areas of potential growth [demonstrating] the vulnerability of small companies [and] the dominance of large corporations as purchasers'. Meanwhile there was a 'lack of evidence of profitability enhancement as a consequence of acquisitions' (Herman, 1981, pp. 159, 161, 100).

The stage was set for a series of developments which were marked by non-financial corporate instability, significant damage caused by lack of competitiveness as the US (and the UK) were confronted by international competition and an increasingly rampant finance capitalism. Finance in the 1980s became the driving force, the flywheel of the world economy (Drucker, 1989). Lazonick argues that the opportunistic and short-termist conglomerate mergers and demergers of the 1960s and 1970s undermined organisational capability and long term strategic investment, activities at the heart of the virtuous vision for managerial capitalism (Lazonick, 1990). The new breed of corporate leaders driven by stock price and short term profitability were (and indeed still are) in no position to change things. The increasingly frenetic and uncontrolled international financial system sharply and readably described by Susan Strange in *Casino Capitalism* and *Mad Money* has introduced growing inequality, a systemic economic instability and has undermined the power of nation states to control it. The aftereffects of the global crisis of 2007–8 are still with us and pundits are predicting the next crisis in two to three years. From an age marked by the return of the Robber Barons, post-World War Two assertions of the arrival of a transcendent managerial capitalism appear to be simply confabulation.

References

Berle, A. A. & Means, G. C. (1932). *The Modern Corporation and Private Property*. New York: Macmillan, 1932.

Brandeis, L. D. (1913). *Other People's Money and How The Bankers Use It*. New York: McLure.

Calomiris, C. W. & Ramirez, C. D. (1996). 'Financing the American Corporation: The Changing Menu of Financial Relationships' in Carl Kaysan (Ed) *The American Corporation Today*. Oxford: Oxford University Press, 128–186.

Campbell, E. G. (1938). *The Reorganization of the American Railroad System, 1893–1900*. New York: Columbia University Press.

Carosso, V. P. (1970). *Investment Banking In America*. Cambridge: Harvard University Press.

Carosso, V. P. (1987). *The Morgans*. Cambridge: Harvard University Press.

Chandler, A. D. (1956). 'Management Decentralization: An Historical Analysis', *Business History Review, 30*, 111–174.

Chandler, A. D. (1977). *The Visible Hand The Managerial Revolution in American Business*. Cambridge: Belknap.

Chandler, A. D. & Redlich, F. (1961). 'Recent Developments in American Business Administration and Their Conceptualization', *Business History Review, 35*(1), 1–27.

Chandler, A. D. & Salisbury, S. (1971). *Pierre S. DuPont and the Making of the Modern Corporation*. New York: Harper and Row.

Channon, D. (1973). *The Strategy and Structure of British Enterprise*. London: Macmillan.

Channon, D. (1978). *The Service Industries: Strategy, Structure and Financial Performance*. London: Palgrave Macmillan.

Cole, A. (1946). 'An Approach to the Study of Entrepreneurship', *Journal of Economic History, 6* (supplement), 1–15.

Corey, L. (1930). *The House of Morgan*. New York: AMS Press.

Cottrell, P. L. (1980). *Industrial Finance 1830–1914*. London: Methuen.

Davis, J. S. (1917). 'The "S.U.M.": The First New Jersey Business Corporation' in J S Davis, *Essays in the Earlier History of American Corporations*. Cambridge: Harvard University Press, 349–522.

Dearden, J. (1962). 'Mirage of Profit Decentralization' in *Harvard Business Review, 40*(6), 140–154.

Dennison, H. (1929). 'Management' in *Recent Economic Changes in the United States: Report of the Committee on Recent Economic Changes of the Presidents Committee on Unemployment*. New York: McGraw Hill.

Diamond, S. (1992). *Compromised Campus*. New York: Oxford University Press.

Dodd, E. M. (1954). *American Corporations Until 1860*. Cambridge: Harvard University Press.

Drucker, P. (1989). *The New Realities: In Government and Politics, in Economy and Business, in Society and in World View*. New York: Harper Row.

Du Boff, R. B. & Herman, E. S. (1980). 'Alfred Chandler's New Business History: A Review', *Politics and Society, 10*(1), 87–110.

The editors of *Fortune* (1956). *USA, The Permanent Revolution*. Cambridge: Harvard University Press.

Fligstein, N. (1985). 'The Spread of the Multidivisional Form Among Large Firms 1919–1974', *American Sociological Review, 50*(3), 377–391.

Fligstein, N. (1990). *The Transformation of Corporate Control*. Cambridge: Harvard University Press.

Fones-Wolf, E. A. (1994). *Selling Free Enterprise – The Business Assault on Labor and Liberalism, 1945–60*. Chicago: University of Illinois Press, 1994.

Foreman-Peck, J. & Hannah, L. (2012). 'Extreme Divorce: the managerial revolution in UK companies before 1914', *Economic History Review, 65*(4), 1217–1238.

Freeman, M., Pearson, R. & Taylor, J. (2012). *Shareholder Democracies? Corporate Governance in Britain and Ireland before 1850*. Chicago: University of Chicago Press.

Galambos, L. (1970). 'The Emerging Organizational Synthesis in Modern American History', *Business History Review, 44*(3), 279–290.

Gelderblom, O., de Jong, A. & Jonker, J. (2013). 'The Formative Years of the Dutch Corporation: The Dutch East India Company, 1602–1623', *Journal of Economic History,73*(4), 1050–1076.

Gould, M. & Campbell, A. (1987). *Strategies and Styles: The Role of the Centre in Managing Diversified Corporations*. Oxford: Wiley-Blackwell.

Hannah, L. (2011). 'J. P. Morgan in London and New York before 1914', *Business History Review, 85*, 113–140.

Herman, E. S. (1981). *Corporate Control, Corporate Power*. Cambridge: Cambridge University Press.

Hill, C. W. L. & Pickering, J. F. (1986). 'Divisionalisation, Decentralisation and Performance of Large United Kingdom Companies', *Journal of Management Studies, 23,* 26–50.

Hofstadter, R. (1968). *The Progressive Historians.* New York: Knopf.

Holden, P. E., Fish, L. S. & Smith, H. L. (1941). *Top Management Organization and Control.* Stanford: Stanford University Press.

Hopf, H. A. (1947). *Evolution in Organisation During the Past Decade.* Paper delivered to the Eighth International Management Congress, Stockholm, July 1947. Reprinted in *Papers on Management by Harry Arthur Hopf Volume 1.* Easton (US): Hive Publishing Co, 1973.

Hurst, J. W. (1970). *The Legitimacy of the Business Corporation in the Law of the United States 1780 – 1970.* Charlottesville: University Press of Virginia.

Johnson, H. T. & Kaplan, R. S. (1987). *Relevance Lost – The Rise and Fall of Management Accounting.* Boston: Harvard Business School Press.

Kramer, H. M. (1964). 'Harvesters and High Finance: Formation of the International Harvester Company', *Business History Review, 38*(3), 283–301.

Lamoreaux, N. R. (1985). *The Great Merger Movement in American Business.* Cambridge: Cambridge University Press.

Larson, H. M. (1947) 'The Business History Foundation Inc', *Bulletin of the Business Historical Society, 21*(3), 51–54.

Lazarsfeld, P. F. & Wagner Thielens, W. (1958). *The Academic Mind – Social Scientists in a Time of Crisis.* Illinois: Free Press of Glencoe.

Lazonick, W. (1990). 'Organizational Capabilities in American Industry: The Rise and Decline of Managerial Capitalism', *Business and Economic History,* Second Series, *19,* 35–54.

Locke, L. L. (1996). *The Collapse of the American Management Mystique.* Oxford: Oxford University Press.

Marris, R. (1967). *The Economic Theory of 'Managerial' Capitalism,* London: Macmillan.

Marris, R. (Ed) (1974). *The Corporate Society.* London: Macmillan.

Mason, E. S. (Ed) (1959). *The Corporation in Modern Society.* Cambridge: Harvard University Press.

Matthews, D., Anderson, M. & Edwards, J. R. (1998). *The Priesthood of Industry – The Rise of the Professional Accountant in British Management.* Oxford: Oxford University Press.

McDonald, J. (2002). *A Ghost's Memoir.* Cambridge: MIT Press.

McKenna, C. D. (2006a). *The World's Newest Profession.* Cambridge: Cambridge University Press.

McKenna, C. D. (2006b). 'Writing the Ghost Writer Back In: Alfred Sloan, Alfred Chandler, John McDonald and the Intellectual Origins of Corporate Strategy', *Management and Organizational History, 1*(2), 107–126.

Nelson, R. L. (1959). *Merger Movements in American Industry 1895–1956.* Princeton: Princeton University Press.

Nichols, T. (1969). *Ownership, Control and Ideology.* London: George Allen.

Novick, P. (1988). *That Noble Dream.* Cambridge: Cambridge University Press.

O'Donnell, C. (1952). 'Origins of the Corporate Executive', *Bulletin of the Business Historical Society, 26*(2), 55–72.

Quail, J. (1997). 'More Peculiarities of the British: Budgetary Control in US and UK Business to 1939', *Business and Economic History, 26*(2), 617–631.

Quail, J. (1998). 'From Personal Patronage to Public School Privilege' in Alan Kidd and David Nicholas (Eds) *The Making of the British Middle Class.* Stroud: Sutton.

Quail, J. (1999). 'Mapping the Managerial Revolution in the UK – Definitions, Dating and Demonstrations' in *Business History, Theory and Practice – Proceedings of the Conference on Business History & Theory July 1999, Glasgow.* Glasgow: Centre for Business History in Scotland, 222–235.

Quail, J. (2000). 'The Proprietorial Theory of the Firm and its Consequences', *Journal of Industrial History, 3*(1), 1–28.

Quail, J. (2008a). 'Becoming Fully Functional: The Conceptual Struggle for a New Structure for the Giant Corporation in the US and UK in the First Half of the Twentieth Century.' *Business History, 50*(2), 127–146.

Quail, J. (2008b). 'The historic significance of Return on Capital Employed in the development of financial control of the multi-unit enterprise', paper presented to the Accounting and Business History Conference. Cardiff University 11–12 Sept.

Roe, M. J. (1994). *Strong Managers, Weak Owners.* New Jersey: Princeton University Press.

Roy, W. G. (1997). *Socializing Capital.* New Jersey: Princeton University Press.

Schrecker, E. W. (1986). *No Ivory Tower.* New York: Oxford University Press.

Simon, M. S. (1998). 'The Rise and Fall of Bank Control in the United States 1890–1939', *American Economic Review*, *88*(5), 1077–93.

Solomons, D. (1965). *Divisional Performance: Measurement and Control*. Homewood: Richard D Irwin.

Sord, B. H. & Welsch, G. A. (1958). *Business Budgeting*. New York: Controllership Foundation.

Strange, S. (1986). *Casino Capitalism*. Oxford: Basil Blackwell.

Strange, S. (1998). *Mad Money*. Manchester: Manchester University Press.

Sutton, F. X., Harris, S. E., Kaysen, C. & Tobin, J. (1956). *The American Business Creed*. Cambridge: Harvard University Press.

Tarbell, I. M. (1925). *The Life of Elbert H Gary*. New York: Appleton.

Thorp, W. L. (1924). *The Integration of Industrial Operation*. Washington: Bureau of the Census.

Thorp, W. L. (1929). 'The Changing Structure of Industry' in *Recent Economic Changes in the United States: Report of the Committee on Recent Economic Changes of the President's Conference on Unemployment*. New York: McGraw Hill.

Urwick, L. (1933). *Management of Tomorrow*. London: Nisbet.

Wang, J. (1999). *American Science in an Age of Anxiety*. Chapel Hill: University of North Carolina Press.

Wilson, J. F. (1991). *Lighting the Town*. Liverpool: Paul Capman.

7

The past, present and future of banking history

Christopher L. Colvin

Introduction

Banking history as a field of inquiry is the historical study of banks and other financial inter-mediaries, of bankers and financiers and of the business of banking and the banking of business. Often considered a subfield of business history, scholars who self-identify as banking historians traditionally craft context-rich descriptions of the operations of a single bank or a country's entire banking sector, or write historical narratives recounting an important chain of events at some critical juncture in the history of that bank or sector. Banking historians usually rely on qualitative archival evidence and public sources written by key decision-makers and outside observers, contemporary to the events being described. This scholarly tradition tends to be idiographic in nature, focusing on contingency and agency.

My aim here is to broaden the definition of banking history to include a wider set of subject matters and epistemological traditions. In particular, I am keen for banking historians to acknowledge and draw on social science approaches to history that are more nomothetic in nature, that theorise and generalise. I attempt to do this by cataloguing and describing all journal articles published since the year 2000 that in some way involve the history of banking. I include articles that many banking historians may themselves not identify as constituting banking history, but nevertheless in my view touch on the history of banks, bankers and banking in important ways. By systematically categorising *all* scholarly banking histories along several dimensions, this essay serves as a map on which banking historians can plot where their work fits in the broader research universe, and identify research niches that are rife for scholarly exploration in the decades to come.

In a recent exchange on the future of business history between de Jong et al. (2015) and Decker et al. (2015), the latter warn that business history should not uncritically adopt the epistemological approach of the New Economic History. They advocate instead for a plurality in research methods. I agree with such sentiment, but wish to augment their conclusions by pushing explicitly for a greater mutual understanding among scholars who use different research approaches to write histories of banks, bankers and banking. Echoing the argument put forward in Rowlinson et al. (2014), theories from the social sciences can be very useful in the construction of narratives that explain singular events, while narratives themselves can be analysed by social scientist as data to inform generalisations. By working together or at least in tandem, there is potential for both idiographic and nomothetic banking histories to have a greater impact on other fields of study – a greater potential for our research to matter.

This essay proceeds as follows. Section 2 discusses the broader history of the field of banking history in the twentieth century, and how it relates to other fields of study. Section 3 analyses my database of 247 banking history-related articles published in international journals between 2000 and 2014, which I believe represents the entire population of English-language academic banking history research output disseminated in the twenty-first century. Finally, Section 4 concludes by highlighting different exemplar works of banking history published since 2000, and by speculating on the future direction of the field.

Banking history in historiographical context

Banking and financial history are usually taken together as a single field of study (Turner, 2016). After all, banks and bankers operate in financial markets, and bank loans are a substitute for capital market financing. For the purpose of this essay, however, I consider banks in isolation. Aside from being the scope requested of me by the editors of this handbook, there is good economic justification for treating banks differently: unlike capital market financing, bank financing requires financial intermediation; while buyers and sellers of financial instruments transact with (almost) no go-between, the business of banking exists exactly because buyers and sellers cannot easily meet in the marketplace and require a mediator to act on their behalf. Any transaction is instead internalised within the firm, which can exploit information asymmetries to match the demand and supply of money, usually at a profit (for relevant economic theory see, e.g., Freixas and Rochet, 2008).

Implicitly or explicitly, banking historians grapple with important questions that have the potential to contribute to the social sciences more broadly. Perhaps core among these is optimising the industrial organisation of banking to ensure both economic growth *and* stability. Should banks finance their activities by taking deposits, by borrowing from other financial institutions or from transacting on financial markets? Should they lend freely, demand strict guarantees or not lend at all? Should they confine themselves to some defined geographic market, or expand nationally or even internationally? Should they be owned by a small group of controlling shareholders, or disperse their ownership widely and employ professional managers? Which among these best ensures banks can withstand the bankruptcy of their customers, their rivals or their sovereign? Which choice best ensures that the society banks serve can prosper rather than decline? Does this answer depend on whether our unit of analysis is a specific bank, a class of banks, a country's financial system or its entire economy? Are economic growth and stability even compatible objectives?

In terms of their impact on the field, probably the two most important works of banking history-related scholarship are Alexander Gerschenkron's 1962 book of essays entitled *Economic Backwardness in Historical Perspective*, and a monograph by Milton Friedman and Anna J. Schwartz published in 1963 entitled *A Monetary History of the United States, 1867–1960*. The former, cited 8,188 times since publication according to Google Scholar, argues that universal banks acted as the key financial and entrepreneurial institutions that facilitated industrialisation in countries – particularly Germany – that had missed the Industrial Revolution. The latter, cited 6,698 times, documents the various bank failures of the US Great Depression and argues that these panics helped to transmit and amplify the Depression across America. The former contribution set off generations of economic and business historians thinking about the relationship between banking and industrial advancement; the latter about the role of banks in economic disasters. Each of these genre-defining works is discussed in relation to the banking history research agendas they helped to inspire.

Gerschenkron, an Austrian-trained Harvard-based economist, put banking business organisations central stage in a post-Smith, post-Marx, post-Rostow stage theory of economic development, and helped to initiate new historical research on the optimal organisation of banking businesses, in Germany but also elsewhere (e.g., Cameron, 1967, 1972; Sylla, 1969). Gerschenkron's contribution was important in that he provided both a "grand theory" of industrial development and a more nuanced view on its sensitivity and specificity as a result of his work being inherently historical and comparative in nature. By examining the long run of history, and by comparing Britain's industrialisation path with those of France, Germany and Russia, Gerschenkron identified features in the financial systems of late industrialisers that were absent in industrial leaders. The close coordination between Germany's leading banks and the industrial sectors that they helped to finance functioned, according to Gerschenkron, as a substitute for factors like the endowment of natural resources and the pattern of foreign trade that had already made Britain an economic success in an earlier epoch. In short, universal banking – sometimes called mixed banking – substituted for the usual economic prerequisites for Industrial Revolution. While the linking of universal banking with Germany's industrialisation was not new in the German-language literature when he published his book in 1962, Gerschenkron did make an important contribution aside from merely popularising the idea of a banking-growth-nexus in English: he theorised that these were specific substitutes that worked for Germany in the late-nineteenth century, but that other sets of substitutes may be more conducive to industrialisation at other times and in other places. For example, in the case of Russia, Gerschenkron specified that the crucial substitute was the state and its military interests.

Gerschenkron's characterisation of Germany's banking sector, and therefore also the banking-industrialisation relationship that follows, has not gone unchallenged. Goldsmith (1969), an alternative to Gerschenkron's German-centric model of financial development, can be read as a general criticism of the idea that Germany's performance can be attributed to its financial structure. While Tilly (1967) and Chandler (1990) were perhaps a little more supportive, the work of Ogilvie and Edwards (1996) and Fohlin (1999), among others, has resulted in a fundamental reassessment, not only of the view that Germany had a bank-based economy, but also that universal banks even had very much influence over the direction of the industries they invested in. This more recent banking history scholarship has demonstrated that the industrial organisation of Germany's banking sector had a lot more in common with that of Britain than Gerschenkron would perhaps have liked. Despite these revisions, Gerschenkron's overall contribution to banking history scholarship still stands: there is no one path to industrialisation that all countries have followed, or can follow in the future. It is up to banking historians to specify when, where and why banking organisations – and financial markets more broadly – have been good for growth, and when, where and why they have not. A good example of work that has taken such lessons to heart is that of Capie and his various co-authors (1995, 1999) on banking and industry in Britain.

While Gerschenkron inspired historical inquiry into banking and industrialisation, the work of Friedman and Schwartz opened up a debate on the causes and consequences of banking crises. Their work proved highly influential in policy spheres and helped to win Friedman the Sveriges Riksbank Prize in Economic Sciences – the "Economics Nobel" – in 1976 'for his achievements in the fields of consumption analysis, monetary history and theory and for his demonstration of the complexity of stabilization policy'. The 1963 monograph is not strictly a work of banking history; it documents a long span of US monetary development, in which banks play a key role as the suppliers of money. At the book's core is a chapter on what the authors call the Great Contraction, and at the centre of that is a section on bank failures in the 1930s. The decisions made by, and the relationship between, key players in high finance and officials at the Federal Reserve come under particular scrutiny. It is this context-rich historical narrative of banks, bankers and banking that makes *A Monetary History* a work of banking as well as monetary history, of the history of the institutions that create money alongside the story of the money they created. The links drawn between the money supply and banking stability, and the role of monetary policy in particular, have proven to be highly influential in subsequent monetary and banking history scholarship, such as that of Capie and Webber (1985) for the case of Britain. And the context-rich chronological narrative methodological approach they adopted forms part of a long tradition of such banking history scholarship: Jones (1993), Jonker (1996) and Wicker (1996) are important examples.

The role of banks in depressions is a topic that financial historians have pursued with some vigour, perhaps none so vigorously as Charles Kindleberger. His *Manias, Panics, and Crashes* was first published in 1978, and is currently in its sixth edition – published posthumously as Kindleberger and Aliber (2011). His contribution to banking history is placing the US banking crises of the 1930s into a broader international context. Like Friedman and Schwartz, Kindleberger's particular focus has been on central banking and the role of the lender-of-last-resort. But unlike Friedman and Schwartz, he blames the Depression on a failure of US leadership in the world economy. He provided subsequent scholars with a general recipe for panics, and a list of suspects for their culprits. For him, and much in common with the view of Hyman Minsky, speculative bubbles are endogenous to financial markets, and banking crises are just one manifestation of a general pattern of fragility inherent in finance.

Three important developments occurred in late twentieth-century banking history-related research. All stemmed from US academia. Together these have in my view significantly changed the nature of the field of banking history. The three developments are: (1) the adoption of ideas from the New Economic History, or cliometrics; (2) the use of banking's past by financial economists and macroeconomists; and (3) the historical nature of economic enquiry into financial regulation. Most profound of these was the cliometric turn. Instead of developing discursive narratives, US-based academics started to explicitly use economic theory and econometric techniques to explain both the banking-industry relationship, and the causes and consequences banking crises. This better addressed issues of causality and made historical enquiry falsifiable – and so compatible with other social sciences. Some influential cliometric banking enquiry includes: works by White (1986) and Calomiris (1991), who develop quantitative counterfactuals in order to measure the impact of the Glass-Steagall Act on the industrial organisation of US banking; by Lamoreaux (1994), who uses corporate governance theories to better understand the strategies of bankers during America's industrialisation; by Guinnane (1994), who uses information economics to explain the successes and failures of cooperatively-owned banks; by Grossman (1994), who pitches macroeconomic and microeconomic explanations against one another to ascertain why banking stability differed across countries during the 1930s; and by Bordo et al. (1994), whose historical comparisons of the industrial organisation of US and Canadian banking explains their wildly different exposure to financial crises.

In parallel with these cliometric contributions have been works of macroeconomics and financial economics that have used banking history as a research laboratory. The first set of contributions employs the Great Depression, and sometimes other crises, as the core motivation for theoretical insights into the transmission of economic disasters. The main exponent of this is Bernanke (1983), who links the failure of financial institutions with the costs of credit intermediation and the protracted nature of the Depression. In so doing, Bernanke revises the Friedman and Schwartz monetary channel to include additional ways in which banks can affect the real economy. On the financial economics side are works that explicitly test microeconomic theories using various banking crises across the centuries, such as Calomiris and Gorton's (1991) quantitative re-evaluation of Diamond and Dybvig's (1984) random withdrawal risk bank run model.

Enquiry into the relationship between the law and banking business has necessitated economists to look into banking's past, both to generate and test theory. A particular interest has been so-called "free banking", a term that can mean a range of different things: in the US context free banking refers to the lower barriers for new entrants into banking markets in force between 1837 and 1864, while in the Scottish case it refers to the period of 1716 to 1845 when banks were not subject to any special regulation and could issue their own paper money. This scholarship relates both to questions on banking and industrialisation, and banking crises. Examples include the debate between Rolnick and Weber (1983) and Rockoff (1985) on the case of antebellum US banking, and between White (1984, 1995) and Carr and Mathewson (1988) for nineteenth-century Britain.

In summary, then, and taking banking history as distinct from financial history, the field has been dominated in the second half of the twentieth century by two questions: (1) the role of banks in industrialisation; and (2) the causes and consequences of banking crises. Germany has remained the core inspiration in the former; the US Great Depression has retained its position in the latter. Important developments have included a move towards a more social scientific approach to history. But while the field became more nomothetic in its method of enquiry, idiographic narrative histories remained a significant component of the historiography well into the 1990s – especially in universities located in Europe where the tradition of commissioned histories persisted.

Banking history in the new millennium

Important monographs and edited volumes have been published in the field of banking history since 2000. In particular, the world financial crisis that started in 2008 has meant that banking history research has found itself new audiences and is perceived to have the potential for generating significant policy impact. This is especially the case where similarities or differences between banking's past and present may lead to the better isolation of the causal mechanisms behind crises. Examples of important English-language book-based contributions published in the new millennium include: Bodenhorn (2000) and Wright (2001) on the deep historical origins of the US banking system; Temin and Voth (2013) on the early origins of banking in Britain and its role in the Industrial Revolution; Forsyth and Verdier (2001) and Fohlin's (2007) fundamental reassessment of the Gerschenkron thesis; Grossman (2010) and Cassis's (2011) comparative banking histories that cover the development of modern commercial banking, and the crises experienced by them, in different countries; Hannah and Ackrill (2001) and Jones's (2012) histories of the emergence and performance of banking multinationals; Murphy (2009) and Capie (2010) on the earliest and much more recent roles of the Bank of England in coordinating the British economy; and Calomiris and Huber (2014) and Turner (2014) post-crisis political economies of the causes of banking instability in the long run.

Looking at book-based research does not provide the full picture, however. For a start, their scholarly influence cannot yet easily be gauged, simply because they have been published too recently. Furthermore, an "Americanisation" of publication strategies has resulted in a move away from producing books for reasons of career progression, (inter-) national recognition and the generation of research funding. Books have become the preserve of mid- or late-career scholars who already have an established body of work published in the form of journal articles, and so focusing on books runs the risk of missing new trends in the field. Instead, then, my analysis looks at journal articles. Of course, a focus solely on this output does itself bring limitations to the ensuing analysis, especially if book-based research is systematically different to journal-based output in terms of subject matter or epistemological approach. But changing publication strategies aside, the lead-time for producing a journal article is generally shorter than that of a monograph, and so tracking journal output across time probably better reflects "real-time" trends in the field. Even if the negation of book-based research from this quantitative literature review systematically biases results in some way, it remains interesting nonetheless because the career objectives of most early career banking historians is to exclusively publish journal articles. And it is these early career banking historians who will be writing the monographs of the future.

The bibliometric content analysis that follows relies on a systematic classification of all articles involving banks, bankers or the business of banking as their main subject of analysis and which have appeared in the core journals of the fields of economic and business history between the years 2000 and 2014. These articles are 227 in number and were published in *Financial History Review, Business History, Business History Review, Enterprise & Society, Journal of Economic History, Explorations in Economic History, Economic History Review* or *European Review of Economic History*. In addition, I have catalogued all banking history-related research that has been published in important journals in economics and finance that have a tradition of disseminating historical analysis. These are 20 articles in number and appeared in *American Economic Review, Economic Journal, Journal of Finance, Journal of Money, Credit & Banking* or *Journal of Law & Economics*.

Each article in the database is classified according to type of research, topic of inquiry, time and place of research subject and geographic region of researchers. By type of research, I classified articles by research question, scholarly approach and principal evidence used. By topic of inquiry, I adopted eight broad topics that together encompass the entire field of banking history. By time and place of research subject, I used the standard classification popularised by the *Journal of Economic Literature*, which has a category on financial markets and institutions in economic history (N2). This has eight sub-categories that designate the principal regions of the world and, for Europe and North America, the historical time period under analysis (either pre- or post-1913). By geographic region of researchers, I located the corresponding author – or where this is not noted the most senior author – to the UK and Ireland, Continental Europe, North America or the rest of the World.

More specifically, in terms of type of research, I classified an article's research question as being motivated by material typically thought of as constituting business history, economic history, social history or financial history. By business history, I refer to research concerning the structure and operations of banking business; economic history to questions about the impact of banking on the wider economy, or the impact of the wider economy on banking; social history to questions that are primarily motivated by the social attributes and socialisation of bankers and other financial professionals; and financial economics to research employing historical banking data to answer puzzles in financial economics, as opposed to research that is primarily motivated by a historical question.

By scholarly approach, I divided articles into works that were primarily descriptive in nature, which do not have as their central aim to understand causation and do not employ theory in their analysis; and analytical, where causation is a key concern of the article and theory, broadly defined, is drawn upon either explicitly or implicitly. Principal evidence was judged to be qualitative, by which I mean textual or archival; quantitative, which refers to financial or other statistics; or mixed, where both types of evidence were used together and both were necessary to make the argument of the article.

By topic of research, I assigned the literature into eight broad categories based on an examination of their content. In cases where articles include content relevant to multiple categories, I have chosen, what is in my judgement, to be the principal one. The discussion in the previous section focused on two main content themes within banking history scholarship: (1) banking and industrialisation; and (2) banking crises. While such simple delimitation largely still holds, the categorisation used here is designed to be more nuanced and overlapping, reflecting the fact that it is not yet possible to tell which topic will turn out to have the most significant and lasting impact. Each topic is explained as follows: by alternative banking, I refer to works studying the history of savings banks, cooperatively-owned banks, not-for-profit banks or other non-traditional financial intermediaries. By bankers and employees, I refer to works that have as their unit of analysis the individuals rather than the institutions or organisations they manage or work for. By central banking I refer to articles that discuss either the *de facto* or *de jure* lender-of-last-resort. Growth and industrialisation refers to works that look at the impact of banking on the industrial economy. The category industrial organisation refers to scholarship that examines the structure, strategy and performance of banks – including issues surrounding ownership and control, and competition. Internationalisation refers to research that looks at how banking business operates across national boundaries. Panics and crises refer to the role of banks in causing and propagating financial crises. Finally, rules and institutions refer to works that analyse the legal environment in which banks operate.

The results of this exercise are displayed in a series of tables, which collate: journal of publication and region of principal author by type of research (Table 7.1); topic of inquiry and time and place of research subject by type of research (Table 7.2); number of authors and region of corresponding author by journal of publication (Table 7.3); and topic of inquiry and time and place of research subject by journal of publication (Table 7.4). Each table reports the number of articles in each category, and the percentage of the total number of articles in all categories.

A number of interesting patterns emerge, a few of which are perhaps surprising. In terms of journal of publication, the research question focus of each journal is broadly in line with expectations. One finding of note is that *Financial History Review* is more focused on publishing research that pursues questions motivated in economic history rather than business history. Most articles classified are analytical in terms of scholarly approach, with the exception of *Financial History Review*, which has an even split between descriptive and analytical, and *Enterprise & Society*, which is almost entirely descriptive. Much in line with their reputations, *Financial History Review*, *Business History*, *Business History Review* and *Enterprise & Society* all predominantly rely on qualitative or mixed evidence, while the other journals mainly publish work that exploits quantitative evidence.

The region of residence of articles' principal authors shows strong geographic concentration by both research question and the principal evidence used. While banking historians in the UK and Ireland are overwhelmingly writing in the business history tradition, scholarship in North America is predominantly economic history in nature. While researchers in the UK and Ireland and Continental Europe use qualitative or mixed evidence, those based in

Table 7.1 Journal of publication and region of principal author, by type of research, 2000–2014

Category	Research Question								Scholarly Approach				Principal Evidence					
	Business History		Economic History		Social History		Financial Economics		Descriptive		Analytical		Qualitative		Quantitative		Mixed	
	No.	%	No.	%	No.	%	No.	%	No.	%	No.	%	No.	%	No.	%	No.	%
All Articles	84	34	105	43	23	9	35	14	54	22	193	78	84	34	118	48	45	18
By Journal of Publication																		
Financial History Review	10	18	31	55	4	7	11	20	24	43	32	57	32	57	12	21	12	21
Business History	31	65	6	13	8	17	3	6	9	19	39	81	23	48	15	31	10	21
Business History Review	12	67	5	28	1	6	0	0	5	28	13	72	12	67	1	6	5	28
Enterprise & Society	7	39	4	22	7	39	0	0	12	67	6	33	11	61	1	6	6	33
Journal of Economic History	10	29	23	68	0	0	1	3	1	3	33	97	3	9	27	79	4	12
Explorations in Economic History	5	19	18	67	0	0	4	15	0	0	27	100	0	0	24	89	3	11
Economic History Review	6	43	4	29	3	21	1	7	2	14	12	86	2	14	9	64	3	21
European Review of Economic History	3	25	6	50	0	0	3	25	0	0	12	100	0	0	10	83	2	17
Other*	0	0	8	40	0	0	12	60	1	5	19	95	1	5	19	95	0	0
By Region of Principal Author																		
UK & Ireland	40	53	20	26	7	9	9	12	20	26	56	74	34	45	30	39	12	16
Continental Europe	19	31	27	44	5	8	11	18	13	21	49	79	24	39	27	44	11	18
North America	16	19	47	55	7	8	15	18	15	18	70	82	19	22	51	60	15	18
Rest of World	8	40	9	45	3	15	0	0	4	20	16	80	5	25	9	45	6	30

Notes: * Other = American Economic Review, Economic Journal, Journal of Finance, Journal of Money, Credit & Banking, or Journal of Law & Economics.

Table 7.2 Topic, time and place of inquiry, by type of research, 2000–2014

Category	Research Question								Scholarly Approach				Principal Evidence					
	Business History		Economic History		Social History		Financial Economics		Descriptive		Analytical		Qualitative		Quantitative		Mixed	
	No.	%	No.	%	No.	%	No.	%	No.	%	No.	%	No.	%	No.	%	No.	%
All Articles	84	34	105	43	23	9	35	14	54	22	193	78	84	34	118	48	45	18
By Topic of Inquiry																		
Alternative Banking	7	33	11	52	2	10	1	5	4	19	17	81	7	33	5	24	9	43
Bankers and Employees	7	30	2	9	13	57	1	4	9	39	14	61	12	52	8	35	3	13
Central Banking	4	17	17	71	1	4	2	8	6	25	18	75	8	33	10	42	6	25
Growth and Industrialisation	7	28	15	60	0	0	3	12	4	16	21	84	5	20	14	56	6	24
Industrial Organisation	25	53	13	28	1	2	8	17	7	15	40	85	9	19	31	66	7	15
Internationalisation	7	54	5	38	1	8	0	0	5	38	8	62	9	69	1	8	3	23
Panics and Crises	13	28	19	41	1	2	13	28	5	11	41	89	12	26	27	59	7	15
Rules and Institutions	14	29	23	48	4	8	7	15	14	29	34	71	22	46	22	46	4	8
By Time and Place of Inquiry																		
General, International, or Comparative	9	35	9	35	1	4	7	27	4	15	22	85	15	58	9	35	2	8
US & Canada, pre-1913	12	28	25	58	1	2	6	14	5	12	39	91	10	23	28	65	6	14
US & Canada, post-1913	3	12	15	58	3	12	6	23	6	23	21	81	7	27	17	65	3	12
Europe, pre-1913	26	35	27	36	9	12	13	17	17	23	58	77	22	29	35	47	18	24
Europe, post-1913	21	50	15	36	4	10	3	7	15	36	28	67	23	55	15	36	5	12
Asia, including Middle East	5	42	6	50	1	8	0	0	3	25	9	75	2	17	8	67	2	17
Latin America & Caribbean	3	33	6	67	1	11	0	0	2	22	8	89	2	22	4	44	4	44
Africa & Oceania	5	50	2	20	3	30	0	0	2	20	8	80	3	30	2	20	5	50

Notes: The JEL classification system used to distinguishing time and place of inquiry was developed for use in the *Journal of Economic Literature.* Top-category N = Economic History. Category N2 = Financial Markets and Institutions. Sub-category N20 = General, International, or Comparative; N21 = US & Canada, pre-1913; N22 = US & Canada, post-1913; N23 = Europe, pre-1913; N24 = Europe, post-1913; N25 = Asia, including Middle East; N26 = Latin America & Caribbean; N27 = Africa & Oceania.

Table 7.3 Number of authors and region of corresponding author, by journal of publication, 2000–2014

Category	FHR		BH		BHR		E&S		JEH		EEH		EHR		EREH		Other	
	No.	%	No.	%	No.	%	No.	%	No.	%	No.	%	No.	%	No.	%	No.	%
All Articles	55	22	48	19	18	7	17	7	34	14	27	11	14	6	12	5	20	8
By Number of Authors																		
1	38	26	29	20	15	10	13	9	19	13	16	11	7	5	6	4	3	2
2	18	22	12	15	2	2	5	6	12	15	6	7	7	9	5	6	15	18
3	0	0	5	33	1	7	0	0	3	20	3	20	0	0	1	7	2	13
4	0	0	2	50	0	0	0	0	0	0	2	50	0	0	0	0	0	0
By Region of Corresponding Author																		
UK & Ireland	20	26	24	32	3	4	5	7	3	4	7	9	9	12	3	4	3	4
Continental Europe	20	32	13	21	2	3	3	5	10	16	4	6	2	3	7	11	1	2
North America	11	13	6	7	11	13	6	7	19	22	14	16	3	4	1	1	15	18
Rest of World	4	20	5	25	2	10	3	15	2	10	2	10	0	0	1	5	1	5

Notes: Journals abbreviated as follows: FHR = Financial History Review; BH = Business History; BHR = Business History Review; E&S = Enterprise & Society; JEH = Journal of Economic History; EEH = Explorations in Economic History; EHR = Economic History Review; EREH = European Review of Economic History; Other = American Economic Review, Economic Journal, Journal of Finance, Journal of Money, Credit & Banking, or Journal of Law & Economics.

Table 7.4 Topic, time and place of inquiry, by journal of publication, 2000–2014

Category	FHR No.	FHR %	BH No.	BH %	BHR No.	BHR %	E&S No.	E&S %	JEH No.	JEH %	EEH No.	EEH %	EHR No.	EHR %	EREH No.	EREH %	Other No.	Other %
All Articles	55	22	48	19	18	7	17	7	34	14	27	11	14	6	12	5	20	8
By Topic of Inquiry																		
Alternative Banking	8	38	5	24	3	14	2	10	1	5	0	0	1	5	1	5	0	0
Bankers and Employees	5	22	9	39	3	13	2	9	0	0	3	13	1	4	0	0	0	0
Central Banking	8	33	0	0	1	4	0	0	3	13	6	25	2	8	3	13	1	4
Growth and Industrialisation	7	28	3	12	1	4	2	8	4	16	4	16	1	4	0	0	3	12
Industrial Organisation	9	19	12	26	3	6	2	4	5	11	4	9	5	11	4	9	3	6
Internationalisation	4	31	6	46	0	0	1	8	0	0	0	0	0	0	2	15	0	0
Panics and Crises	10	22	7	15	3	7	2	4	10	22	6	13	1	2	0	0	7	15
Rules and Institutions	5	10	6	13	4	8	7	15	11	23	4	8	3	6	2	4	6	13
By Time and Place of Inquiry																		
General, International, or Comparative	12	46	4	15	3	12	0	0	0	0	2	8	0	0	2	8	3	12
US & Canada, pre-1913	5	12	2	5	7	16	0	0	17	40	9	21	0	0	0	0	4	9
US & Canada, post-1913	1	4	2	8	1	4	4	15	6	23	4	15	0	0	0	0	9	35
Europe, pre-1913	23	31	18	24	2	3	2	3	4	5	8	11	11	15	4	5	3	4
Europe, post-1913	9	21	15	36	2	5	6	14	2	5	1	2	3	7	5	12	0	0
Asia, including Middle East	3	25	2	17	0	0	3	25	1	8	2	17	0	0	0	0	1	8
Latin America & Caribbean	1	14	1	14	1	14	2	29	4	57	0	0	0	0	1	14	0	0
Africa & Oceania	2	20	4	40	2	20	1	10	0	0	1	10	0	0	0	0	0	0

Notes: See note under Table 7.3 for journal abbreviations.

North America are more quantitative in nature. There is no obvious pattern of scholarly approach by region; scholars in the UK and Ireland are a little more ready to write descriptive pieces, but the overall division appears similar to that elsewhere.

Particularly popular topics of inquiry concern the industrial organisation of banking sectors, financial panics and crises, and the rules and institutions that govern banks. Of these, the majority of industrial organisation articles are written in the business history tradition, while there are more scholars taking an economic history perspective in the latter two topics of inquiry. Growth and industrialisation are a particular focus of economic history articles, and bankers and their employees is something found predominantly in social history articles. Pre-1913 Europe is by some margin the most popular time and place of research subject, followed by post-1913 Europe. Research on both pre- and post-1913 US and Canada is written mostly in the economic history tradition, while work on both pre- and post-1913 Europe is more evenly spread between economic and business history research questions. While comparative articles rely on qualitative evidence, work on the US and Canada relies heavily on quantitative evidence. There are very few published articles on areas of the world outside Europe and the US and Canada.

In terms of the number of authors per article, there are more solo-authored than multi-authored articles in the field of banking history overall. There are, however, interesting differences between the relative proportion of author numbers in each of the journals catalogued. Banking history-related articles published in economics and finance journals are nearly all multi-author and publications in the business history journals appear to involve comparatively more collaborations than in the economic history journals. In terms of the region of residence of articles' corresponding authors, their location correlates highly with the country of a journal's sponsoring professional society and the location of its principal editorial staff. So while *Financial History Review*, *Business History* and *European Review of Economic History* predominantly publish works from the UK and Ireland and Continental Europe, *Business History Review*, *Journal of Economic History* and *Explorations in Economic History* are more North America focused. An interesting exception is *Enterprise & Society*, which publishes works from both sides of the Atlantic in equal measure.

The journals catalogued in this exercise clearly attract submissions and/or choose to publish papers addressing rather narrow topics of inquiry. Only *Financial History Review* publishes evenly across all topic categories. While *Business History* focuses on the industrial organisation of banking and published nothing relating to central banking, *Explorations in Economic History* focuses on central banking and panics and crashes, but publishes nothing on the internationalisation of banking business. Just as journals have a geographic concentration in their authors, a geographic focus is also evident in their topic of inquiry. Again, this is correlated with the location of a journal's sponsoring professional society or editorial staff.

In terms of trends in publication, Figures 7.1 and 7.2 plot the number of publications by region of corresponding author and by topic of research across the full period of analysis. While the scholarly output of academics based in the UK and Ireland and Continental Europe increases following the 2008 crisis, an uptake in North America starts earlier, in 2005. There is no discernible trend in publications from authors located in the Rest of the World. In terms of the topic of research, there is no clear trend other than in publications concerning panics and crashes, and rules and institutions. It is perhaps too early to tell whether the 2008 crisis has acted as a new impetus for research. There does appear to be one interesting temporary shift between 2010 and 2012: away from publishing work on central banking and growth and industrialisation, and towards alternative banking and bankers and employees.

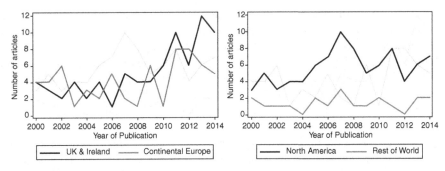

Figure 7.1 Number of banking history-related articles by region of corresponding author, 2000–2014

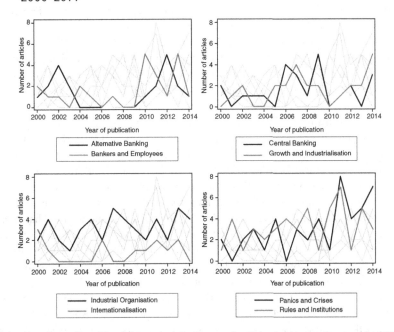

Figure 7.2 Number of banking history-related journal articles by topic of research, 2000–2014

The future of banking's past

This chapter takes a very broad definition of banking history scholarship, one that includes works that "traditional" banking historians may fail to recognise as constituting banking history. This new definition has allowed me to examine patterns of publication within the population of journal-based scholarship involving the history of banks, bankers and the business of banking, rather than focusing on some narrowly defined epistemological approach or research topic within this field. So, what can banking historians learn from the last 15 years of banking history-related journal output? And, can we discern what will likely be the influential research agendas of the future?

In terms of their research impact on the most recent generation of scholarship, banking history's intellectual giants clearly remain Gerschenkron, and Friedman and Schwartz, the first of which ignited a long research agenda on the relationship between banking and industrialisation, the second on the causes and consequences of banking crises. By my reading, researchers exploring these questions have in the last decade drawn more explicitly on ideas from microeconomics, and specifically from theory on the industrial organisation of banking markets. Indeed, it is these more nomothetic works that attempt to identify causal channels that I think will have the greatest impact on the field of banking history in the years to come. Examples range from Fohlin (2001) and Burhop (2006), who have continued Gerschenkron's focus on the role of banks in Germany's industrialisation; to Mitchener and Wheelock (2013) and Jaremski (2014), who have turned their attention to the bank-industry-nexus in the US case. Meanwhile, on the topic of banking crises and stability, Guinnane (2003) has continued his research agenda on the institutional features which made Germany's cooperative banks so stable, while Carlson and Mitchener (2006) have exploited differences in banking rules between US states in the early twentieth century to understand the competition-stability relationship. Researches on crises that are rooted in macroeconomics still feature: Accominotti (2009) and Sylla (2009) look at crisis management by central banks in France and the US, while Ramirez and Shively (2012) have work that further illuminates the link between banking failures and economic depressions in history.

A number of research areas have in my view shown great potential for generating an impact on the field of economics in the wake of the 2008 financial crisis. A renewed interest in the identity, behaviour and influence of the shareholders of banks includes work on nineteenth-century Britain by Turner (2009) on the quality of bank shareholders following the introduction of limited liability banking, Acheson and Turner (2011) on the financial motivations of those bank investors and Grossman and Imai (2013) on the effect of contingent shareholder capital on bank risk-taking incentives. A focus on corporate governance continues with the work of Battilossi (2009) on the governance failures of universal banks in interwar Italy, and Deloof et al. (2010) on the dividend policy of Belgian firms that were connected with universal banks. While much of this work is quantitative in nature, my own work in Colvin (2014) and Colvin and McLaughlin (2014) demonstrates that qualitative sources can also be used to construct nomothetic hypothesis-driven banking histories.

Questions concerning the origins of banking remain in my view an open area for research; while Temin and Voth (2006) and Newton (2010) have gotten us closer to an answer for the case of joint-stock banks, and Samy (2007) and McLaughlin (2014) on mortgage and savings banks, I would like to see more work on other types of banking organisations, and crucially for countries outside the Anglosphere. Indeed, works like Austin and Uche (2007) on banking collusion in colonial Africa and Maurer and Haber (2007) on related lending in Gold Standard-era Mexico aside, there is still precious little being published on banking history topics concerning geographies outside Europe and North America. Banking histories remain, in my estimation, an untapped evidence base for researchers in other scientific fields; works like that of Bátiz-Lazo and Wardley (2007), who use the experience of banks to write a history of technology, and Seltzer (2013), who uses historical banking records to examine important questions in labour economics, remain rare. And banking histories have a great potential to contribute to understanding broader social and cultural phenomena; the work of Hansen (2012), who analyses narratives of financial crises to trace societal enforcement of norms and values, provides scholars with an approach.

It is, of course, too early to judge what specific research output from the last decade will be most influential for future scholarship; citation analysis is not credible for very recent literature. The above are simply my own personal highlights, which are no doubt a function of my own academic training and interests. But after collecting and analysing 15 years of banking history research, what has become abundantly clear to me is that whether, and how, this output will come to influence future scholarship will depend in no insignificant part on the publication outlet decision-making process, both by submitting authors and receiving editors. My bibliometric content analysis confirms that banking history in the new millennium has remained heterogeneous in terms of epistemological approach and research subject and it shows that the journals banking historians publish in tend to specialise. Highly-focused journal outlets are not necessarily a problem; indeed, Smithian specialisation may improve research quantity and quality. But it is important that scholars remain aware of research output published in *all* our important journals; banking historians can ill afford to focus solely on the traditional business history outlets.

Despite the field's heterogeneity, a few generalisations can be made: (1) economic and business history questions, and analytical rather than descriptive approaches, now predominate in the field of banking history; (2) North American and European banking history topics clearly still dominate, and scholars (understandably) still tend to write about the banking history of their own part of the world; (3) although works covering panics and crashes, and also rules and institutions, have increased in popularity across the last decade, the impact of recent financial turmoil on research agendas is likely not yet fully realised; (4) while there is sufficient intellectual and physical space in the various journals frequented by banking historians for all types of research, it probably pays off for scholars to specialise and target their output to specific venues; and (5) reading the tables and figures constructed for this essay suggests that there are untapped combinations of methodologies and subjects that are rife for exploitation. This last point can be more easily achieved if scholars on both sides of the Atlantic Ocean form closer collaborative partnerships; while North American scholars can re-incorporate contingency and agency into their analysis with the help of their European colleagues, Europeans can learn to theorise and generalise from Americans.

Acknowledgement

This essay was conceived while I was visiting the University of California, Davis, and I thank Greg Clark in particular for his hospitality. Comments from Matthias Blum, Abe de Jong, Eoin McLaughlin and John Turner on an earlier draft are greatly appreciated. Thanks also to Matthew McCracken for research assistance, and to my PhD students Stuart Henderson and Nikita Lychakov for their unique perspective on the text.

References

Accominotti, O. (2009). 'The Sterling Trap: Foreign Reserves Management at the Bank of France, 1928–1936', *European Review of Economic History*, *13*(3), 349–376.

Acheson, G. G. & Turner, J. D. (2011). 'Investor Behaviour in a Nascent Capital Market: Scottish Bank Shareholders in the Nineteenth Century', *Economic History Review*, *64*(1), 188–213.

Ackrill, M. & Hannah, L. (2001). *Barclays: The Business of Banking, 1690–1996*. Cambridge: Cambridge University Press.

Austin, G. & Uche, C. U. (2007). 'Collusion and Competition in Colonial Economies: Banking in British West Africa, 1916–1960', *Business History Review*, *81*(1), 1–26.

Bátiz-Lazo, B. & Wardley, P. (2007). 'Banking on Change: Information Systems and Technologies in UK High Street Banking, 1919–1969', *Financial History Review*, *14*(2), 177–205.

Battilossi, S. (2009). 'Did Governance Fail Universal Banks? Moral Hazard, Risk Taking, and Banking Crises in Interwar Italy', *Economic History Review*, *62*(S1), 101–134.

Bernanke, B. S. (1983). 'Nonmonetary Effects of the Financial Crisis in the Propagation of the Great Depression', *American Economic Review*, *73*(3), 257–276.

Bodenhorn, H. (2000). *A History of Banking in Antebellum America*. New York: Cambridge University Press.

Bordo, M. D., Rockoff, H., & Redish, A. (1994). 'The U.S. Banking System from a Northern Exposure: Stability versus Efficiency', *The Journal of Economic History*, *54*(2), 325–341.

Burhop, C. (2006). 'Did Banks Cause the German Industrialization?', *Explorations in Economic History*, *43*(1), 39–63.

Calomiris, C. W. (1995). 'The Costs of Rejecting Universal Banking: American Finance in the German Mirror, 1870–1914', in: Naomi Lamoreaux and Daniel Raff (eds.), *The Coordination of Economic Activity Within and Between Firms* (257–321). Chicago: University of Chicago Press.

Calomiris, C. W. & Gorton, G. (1991). 'The Origins of Banking Panics: Models, Facts, and Bank Regulation', in: R. Glenn Hubbard (ed.), *Financial Markets and Financial Crises* (109–173). Chicago: University of Chicago Press.

Calomiris, C. W. & Huber, S. H. (2014). *Fragile by Design*. Princeton: Princeton University Press.

Cameron, R. (ed.) (1967). *Banking in the Early Stages of Industrialization: A Study in Comparative Economic History*. New York: Oxford University Press.

Cameron, R. (ed.) (1972). *Banking and Economic Development: Some Lessons of History*. New York: Oxford University Press.

Capie, F. H. (2010). *The Bank of England: 1950 to 1979*. Cambridge: Cambridge University Press,

Capie, F. H. & Collins, M. (1999). 'Banks, Industry and Finance, 1880–1914', *Business History*, *41*(1), 37–62.

Capie, F. H. & Mills, T. C. (1995). 'British Bank Conservatism in the Late 19th-Century', *Explorations in Economic History*, *32*(3), 409–420.

Capie, F. H. & Webber, A. (1985). *A Monetary History of the United Kingdom*. London: Allen & Unwin.

Carlson, M. & Mitchener, K. J. (2006). 'Branch Banking, Bank Competition, and Financial Stability', *Journal of Money, Credit, and Banking*, *38*(5), 1293–1328.

Carr, J. L. & Mathewson, G. F. (1988). 'Unlimited Liability as a Barrier to Entry', *Journal of Political Economy*, *96*(4), 766–784.

Cassis, Y. (2011). *Crises and Opportunities, 1890–2010: The Shaping of Modern Finance*. Oxford: Oxford University Press.

Chandler, A. D., Jr. (1990). *Scale and Scope: The Dynamics of Industrial Capitalism*. Cambridge (MA): Harvard University Press.

Colvin, C. L. (2014). 'Interlocking Directorates and Conflicts of Interest: The Rotterdamsche Bankvereeniging, Müller & Co. and the Dutch Financial Crisis of the 1920s', *Business History*, *56*(2), 314–334.

Colvin, C. L. & McLaughlin, E. (2014). 'Raiffeisenism Abroad: Why did German Cooperative Banking Fail in Ireland but Prosper in the Netherlands?', *Economic History Review*, *67*(2), 492–516.

Decker, S., Kipping, M., & Wadhwani, R. D. (2015). 'New Business Histories! Plurality in Business History Research Methods', *Business History*, *57*(1), 30–40.

de Jong, A., Higgins, D. M., and van Driel, H. (2015). 'Towards a New Business History?', *Business History*, *57*(1), 5–29.

Deloof, M., Roggeman, A., & Overfelt, W. V. (2010). 'Bank Affiliations and Corporate Dividend Policy in Pre-World War I Belgium', *Business History*, *52*(4), 590–616.

Diamond, D. & Dybvig, P. (1983). 'Bank Runs, Liquidity, and Deposit Insurance', *Journal of Political Economy*, *91*(3), 401–419.

Edwards, J. & Ogilvie, S. (1996). 'Universal Banks and German Industrialization: A Re-Appraisal', *Economic History Review*, *49*(3), 427–446.

Fohlin, C. (1999). 'Universal Banking in Pre-World War I Germany: Model or Myth?', *Explorations in Economic History*, *36*(4), 305–343.

Fohlin, C. (2001). 'The Balancing Act of German Universal Banks and English Deposit Banks, 1880–1913', *Business History*, *43*(1), 1–24.

Fohlin, C. (2007). *Finance Capitalism and Germany's Rise to Industrial Power*. New York: Cambridge University Press.

Forsyth, D. J. & Verdier, D. (eds.) (2003). *The Origins of National Financial Systems: London: Alexander Gerschenkron Reconsidered*. Routledge.

Freixas, X. & Rochet, J. C. (2008). *Microeconomics of Banking*, 2nd edition. Cambridge: MIT Press.

Friedman, M. & Schwartz, A. J. (1963). *A Monetary History of the United States, 1867–1960*. Princeton: Princeton University Press.

Gerschenkron, A. (1962). *Economic Backwardness in Historical Perspective: A Book of Essays*. Cambridge: The Belknap Press of Harvard University Press.

Goldsmith, R. W. (1969). *Financial Structure and Development*. New Haven: Yale University Press.

Grossman, R. S. (1994). 'The Shoe That Didn't Drop: Explaining Banking Stability During the Great Depression', *The Journal of Economic History*, *54*(4), 654–682.

Grossman, R. S. (2010). *Unsettled Account: The Evolution of Banking in the Industrialized World Since 1800*. Princeton: Princeton University Press.

Grossman, R. S. & Imai, M. (2013). 'Contingent Capital and Bank Risk-Taking among British Banks before the First World War', *Economic History Review*, *66*(1), 132–155.

Guinnane, T. (1994). 'A Failed Institutional Transplant: Raiffeisen's Credit Cooperatives in Ireland, 1894–1914', *Explorations in Economic History*, *31*(1), 38–61.

Guinnane, T. W. (2003). 'A 'Friend and Advisor': External Auditing and Confidence in Germany's Credit Cooperatives, 1889–1914', *Business History Review*, *77*(2), 235–264.

Hansen, P. H. (2012). 'Making Sense of Financial Crisis and Scandal: A Danish Bank Failure in the First Era of Finance Capitalism', *Enterprise & Society*, *13*(3), 672–706.

Jaremski, M. (2014). 'National Banking's Role in U.S. Industrialization, 1850–1900', *The Journal of Economic History*, *74*(1), 109–140.

Jones, G. G. (1993). *British Multinational Banking 1830–1990*. Oxford: Clarendon Press.

Jones, G. G. (ed.) (2012). *Banks as Multinationals*. London: Routledge.

Jonker, J. (1996). *Merchants, Bankers, Middlemen: The Amsterdam Money Market during the First Half of the 19th Century*. Amsterdam: NEHA.

Kindleberger, C. P. (1978). *Manias, Panics, and Crashes: A History of Financial Crises*. New York: Basic Books.

Kindleberger, C. P. & Aliber, R. Z. (2011). *Manias, Panics, and Crashes: A History of Financial Crises*, 6th Edition. London: Palgrave Macmillan.

Lamoreaux, N. R. (1994). *Insider Lending: Banks, Personal Connections and Economic Development in Industrial New England*. New York: Cambridge University Press.

Maurer, N. & Haber, S. (2007). 'Related Lending and Economic Performance: Evidence from Mexico', *The Journal of Economic History*, *67*(3), 551–581.

McLaughlin, E. (2014). '"Profligacy in the Encouragement of Thrift": Savings Banks in Ireland, 1817–1914', *Business History*, *56*(4), 569–591.

Mitchener, K. J. & Wheelock, D. C. (2013). 'Does the Structure of Banking Markets Affect Economic Growth? Evidence from U.S. State Banking Markets', *Explorations in Economic History*, *50*(2), 161–178.

Murphy, A. L. (2009). *The Origins of English Financial Markets: Investment and Speculation Before the South Sea Bubble*. Cambridge: Cambridge University Press.

Newton, L. (2010). 'The Birth of Joint-Stock Banking: England and New England Compared', *Business History Review*, *84*(1), 27–52.

Ramirez, C. D. & Shively, P. A. (2012). 'The Effect of Bank Failures on Economic Activity: Evidence from U.S. States in the Early 20th Century', *Journal of Money, Credit, and Banking*, *44*(2–3), 433–455.

Rockoff, H. (1985). 'New Evidence on the Free Banking Era in the United States', *American Economic Review*, *75*(4), 886–89.

Rolnick, A. J. & Weber, W. E. (1983). 'New Evidence on the Free Banking Era', *American Economic Review*, *73*(5), 1080–1091.

Rowlinson, M., Hassard, J., & Decker, S. (2014). 'Research Strategies for Organizational History: A Dialogue between Historical Theory and Organizational Theory', *Academy of Management Review*, *39*(3), 250–274.

Samy, L. (2012). 'Extending Home Ownership Before the First World War: The Case of the Co-operative Permanent Building Society, 1884–1913' *Economic History Review*, *65*(1), 168–193.

Seltzer, A. (2013). 'The Impact of Female Employment on Male Salaries and Careers: Evidence from the English Banking Industry, 1890–1941', *Economic History Review*, *66*(4), 1039–1062.

Sylla, R. (1969). 'Federal Policy, Banking Market Structure, and Capital Mobilization in the United States, 1863–1913', *The Journal of Economic History*, *29*(4), 657–686.

Sylla, R. (2009). 'Alexander Hamilton, Central Banker: Crisis Management During the U.S. Financial Panic of 1792', *Business History Review*, *82*(S1), 61–86.

Temin, P. & Voth, H-J. (2006). 'Banking as an Emerging Technology: Hoare's Bank, 1702–1742', *Financial History Review*, *13*(2), 149–178.

Temin, P. & Voth, H-J. (2013). *Prometheus Shackled: Goldsmith Banks and England's Financial Revolution after 1700*. New York: Oxford University Press.

Tilly, R. (1967). 'Germany, 1815–1870', in Rondo Cameron (ed.), *Banking in the Early Stages of Industrialization: A Study in Comparative Economic History* (151–182). New York: Oxford University Press.

Turner, J. D. (2009). 'Wider Share Ownership?: Investors in English and Welsh Bank Shares in the Nineteenth Century', *Economic History Review*, 62(S1), 167–192.

Turner, J. D. (2014). *Banking in Crisis: The Rise and Fall of British Banking Stability, 1800 to the Present.* Cambridge: Cambridge University Press.

Turner, J. D. (2016). 'Financial History and Financial Economics', QUCEH Working Paper No. 14–03. Forthcoming in: Youssef Cassis, Richard S. Grossman and Catherine Schenk (eds.). *Oxford Handbook of Banking and Financial History*, Oxford: Oxford University Press.

White, E. N. (1986). 'Before the Glass Steagall Act: An Analysis of the Investment Banking Activities of National Banks', *Explorations in Economic History*, 23(1), 33–55.

White, L. H. (1984). *Free Banking in Britain: Theory, Experience and Debate, 1800–1845.* New York: Cambridge University Press.

White, L. H. (1995). *Free Banking in Britain: Theory, Experience and Debate, 1800–1845*, 2nd edition. London: Institute of Economic Affairs.

Wicker, E. (1996). *The Banking Panics of the Great Depression.* New York: Cambridge University Press.

Wright, R. (2001). *Origins of Commercial Banking in America, 1750–1800.* Lanham: Rowman & Littlefield.

8

Stock markets and financial capitalism

Andrew Smith and Kevin D. Tennent

This chapter examines the historical relationship between corporate governance and finance by examining the historical development of financial capitalism and the stock market, with a view to demonstrating the contemporary relevance of business-historical research on this topic. In recent years, academics, policymakers and businesspeople have debated the complex relationship between financialization, corporate governance and the ideology of shareholder value (Westlake, 2013, pp. 326–343). Many academics blame financialization and the rise of shareholder value ideology for a range of ills that include the post-1980 stagnation in US median living standards, the wave of scandals that prompted the passage of the Sarbanes-Oxley Act, and the Global Financial Crisis of 2007–9 (Dore, 2008; Lazonick, 2011). The intensification of cross-border M&A activity involving countries with very different corporate governance systems, such as the famously ill-fated DaimlerChrysler merger, also focused attention on comparative corporate governance (Gilson, 2001; Martynova and Renneboog, 2011; Sudarsanam and Broadhurst, 2012). The ongoing battles over corporate governance are intense because the right to control a sizeable proportion of GDP is at stake (Gourevitch and Shinn, 2005). In sum, corporate governance is one of the major issues confronting our time.

History matters. The thesis of this chapter is that research by business historians is highly relevant to the aforementioned present-day debates. This chapter will introduce readers to key themes and debates in the historical literature on corporate governance. We recognize that there is some value in the existing quasi-historical research of corporate governance, such as the work of Morck and Steier (2007). However, this chapter argues that it is important that qualitative and archive-focused scholars who work in the intellectual tradition associated with the late Alfred Chandler engage with a topic that has hitherto been dominated by scholars from the disciplines of economics and finance. These scholars have dabbled in the history of corporate governance without adopting the research methods associated with any of the main variants of business history. It would be hard to provide an example of a typical business-historical case study, since business historians fall into a number of camps, including Chandlerian, anti-Chandlerian and post-Chandlerian (Decker, Kipping and Wadhwani, 2015; de Jong and Higgins, 2015; Kipping and Üsdiken, 2015). However, the business-historians are united by a commitment to a research process that involves starting in the past, immersion in corporate archives and other primary sources, and then working towards the present (Rowlinson, Hassard and Decker, 2013). This research method contrasts with the positivistic and aprioristic approach of economists and finance scholars (Coleman, 1987). This chapter is, in part, a call to arms to business historians to enrich the topics of corporate governance and financialization by publishing more research on the evolution of corporate governance over the last five centuries.

Background

Financialization

The meaning of the term "financialization" is contested. The most straightforward definition revolves around the percentage of GDP represented by financial services. In a barter economy, financial services are non-existent (Palley, 2007). As towns and commerce emerge, an identifiable financial-services sector develops in the form of goldsmiths, moneylenders and the like. With further development, finance's share of GDP increases to significant levels. Among mainstream social scientists, there is a near-consensus that a financial sector of *some size* is essential for the functioning of a modern economy (Levine, 1997; Rajan and Zingales, 2001; cf. Graeber, 2014). There are, nonetheless, lively debates about whether a perpetual increase in the percentage of GDP represented by finance is normative. Although every OECD country is demonstrably more financialized than the world's poorest nations, the advanced capitalist countries differ somewhat in the percentage of total economic activity generated by financial services (see Figure 8.1 and Table 8.1). These differences suggest that modest variations in the level of financialization are compatible with high living standards, urbanization and development. Moreover, the degree of financialization has not increased in a linear fashion: Rajan and Zingales found that the economies of Britain and the United States were highly financialized on the eve of the First World War and that they did not return to this high level of financialization until the 1980s (Rajan and Zingales, 2003). The intervening period saw massive improvements in human welfare in the two countries. Kedrosky and Stangler (2011) report that the United States experienced massive de-financialization between the early 1930s and the mid-1940s.

Some of the most forceful academic critics of today's (allegedly) excessive degree of financialization are on the left of the political spectrum (Lin and Tomaskovic-Devey, 2013;

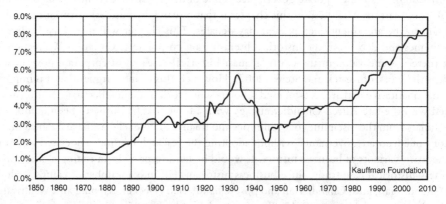

Figure 8.1 Financial sector as share of GDP, United States, 1850–2009
Source: Kedrosky and Stangler (2011), Figure 1.

Table 8.1 Financial intermediation as a percentage of GDP

Financial intermediation; real estate, renting, and business activities

	2000	*2012 or latest year*
Australia	28.1	30.7
Canada	25.0	..
France	27.5	30.4
Germany	26.2	27.2
Japan	15.9	17.0
Switzerland	21.3	20.3
United Kingdom	25.4	31.3
United States	31.7	34.2
Euro area	24.7	26.9
EU 28	24.2	26.2
China	8.3	11.1
Indonesia	8.3	7.2
Russian Federation	4.6	16.2
South Africa	18.6	21.5

Source: OECD Factbook 2014: Economic, Environmental and Social Statistics.

Kus, 2013). Krippner (2005), who defines financialization as a "pattern of accumulation in which profit making occurs increasingly through financial channels rather than through trade and commodity production", believes that the (excessive) financialization of the US economy since the late 1970s has contributed to de-industrialization, increasing inequality, and other serious social problems. Epstein (2005) associates excessive levels of financialization to the ideology of shareholder value and to the worldwide diffusion of the Anglo-American fixation of equity markets. The last chief executive of the UK's now defunct Financial Services Authority (Turner, 2012), has concluded that much of the money-making activity in the financial services sector is socially parasitical. Libertarian critics of financialization believe that finance's share of GDP is unnaturally large due to unwise government meddling with market forces, such as the implicit government guarantees of the 'Too Big to Fail' Banks. Classical liberalism is compatible with the critique of financialization offered by Johnson and Kwak (2011), which is grounded in a belief in the superiority of true (i.e., free-market) capitalism over the existing financial system, in which a cocktail of subsidies and regulations produces socialized losses and privatized profits. Others fear that financialization has distorted the allocation of human capital towards financial services and away from other sectors (Kneer, 2013).

The social function of securities markets

Stock markets evolved over time as securities and the need for complex financing of ventures grew. Michie (2006, pp. 17–19) traces the evolution of the modern securities market back to the trading city states of Venice, Genoa, and Florence in medieval Italy, where proto-securities markets can be identified from the twelfth century. A notable innovation came in 1171–2 when war-torn Venice imposed an indefinite forced loan upon its wealthiest inhabitants, introducing a 5% annual interest rate in return, to be paid until the state could afford to repay the loan. These bonds carried a low value at first but in time the Venetian government realised it could raise higher loans if its repayments were more reliable; between 1262 and 1379 Venice never missed an interest payment. A secondary market in bonds was thus created, and over the next few hundred years the scope expanded to include marine insurance and bills of exchange. By the beginning of early modern times, and the exploration of the Americas, the focus had begun to shift to the Low Countries, traders from Italy transferring their practices to the Place de la Bourse in Bruges in the late fifteenth century (Michie, 2006, pp. 22–23). It was in this region that the first recognisable joint-stock companies would evolve during the seventeenth and eighteenth centuries (see below) and the stock market would take on the role as a place for secondary trading of corporate securities. The joint-stock company idea spread to England shortly afterwards and along with it the idea of a stock market spread to London, with traders specialising in trading on their own account (stock jobbers) and traders who traded on the account of others (stock brokers). The establishment of a formal institution with regulatory powers followed in 1801 when the Committee of the London Stock Exchange established a 'subscription room' in order to impose rules of trading and remove defaulting traders (Michie, 1999, pp. 35–37). As the corporate economy grew the institution of the stock exchange provided the infrastructure for the evolution of firms with a widely diversified shareholding, making possible private organization on a mass scale. Moreover, stock exchanges became icons of capitalism and the physical sites where financialization and competing philosophies of corporate governance interacted.

Shareholder value ideology

Shareholder value ideology holds that the sole function of a company is to benefit its shareholders. This philosophy of corporate governance is shared by most of the executives, institutional investors, legislators, judges, business academics, lawyers and business journalists who collectively shape the systems of corporate governance in the English-speaking countries. A rival theory of the firm holds that managers ought to take the interests of a wide range of non-shareholder stakeholders such as workers into account (Charreaux and Desbrières, 2001; O'Sullivan, 2000; Beyer and Hoppner, 2003; Lazonick, 2011). Between the 1920s and the 1970s, Germany developed an elaborate system of co-determination that embodied a variant of the stakeholder model. In the late 1990s, some management and legal academics concluded that all corporate governance systems would soon converge towards the Anglo-American model. Adapting the words of Francis Fukuyama (1989), Hansmann and Kraakman (2011) announced the "end of history" in corporate governance. Such predictions were just plain wrong: as of 2015, companies in France, Germany and Japan continue to practice stakeholder theories of corporate governance. Few companies in these countries, even those with listings on US exchanges, have adopted a US-style shareholder-value orientation (Fiss and Zajac, 2004; Tuschke and Luber, 2012, p. 75).

Stout (2012) and Lazonick (2011) argue that the ethos of shareholder value has caused US firms to be callous in their treatment of non-shareholder stakeholders. They also charge that it promotes short-term thinking and thus undermines necessary corporate investment in worker training and R&D. An increasing number of American business academics and even corporate leaders whose political sympathies are not with the left are critical of the ideology of shareholder value. Jack Welch, the former head of GE, recently called shareholder value "the dumbest idea in the world". His change of heart on this issue is striking since he was a leading implementer of the ideology of shareholder value in the 1980s and 1990s (Martin,

2011, pp. 29–32). Martin Wolf, a *Financial Times* columnist, has been scathing in his denunciations of managers' exclusive focus on shareholder value (Wolf, 2014).

The LLSV paradigm

A team of economists in the United States developed the law and finance hypothesis or paradigm in the late 1990s. La Porta, Lopez-de-Silanes, Shleifer and Vishny (LLSV) argued that the degree of legal protection afforded to outsider shareholders determines both the dispersal of share ownership and the overall efficiency of a country's capital markets. Taking the institutions of the present-day United States as normative, they argue for the diffusion of share ownership, the separation of management and ownership, and giving shareholders strong legal rights over corporate managers. This arrangement would, in their view, promote an active market for corporate control. LLSV argue that legal systems derived from England tend to have better investor protection than countries with other legal traditions, such as those derived from the Napoleonic Code (La Porta, Lopez-De-Silanes, Shleifer and Vishny, 1997; La Porta, Lopez-De-Silanes, Shleifer and Vishny, 1999; La Porta, Lopez-De-Silanes, Shleifer and Vishny, 2000).

Non-historians have criticized the LLSV paradigm on a variety of grounds. Some economists argued that LLSV exaggerate the importance of the law on corporate ownership patterns (Coffee, 2001; Holderness, 2014) or that the categorization of countries into legal families is an unsophisticated method of comparing the amount of legal protection for shareholders (McLean, Zhang and Zhao, 2012). Despite a barrage of such criticisms, the key chapters by LLSV remain extremely influential in both academe and policymaking (Siems and Deakin, 2010). For this reason, it is vitally important for business historians to ascertain whether the claims made by LLSV are, in fact, historically accurate.

Financialization: historical evolution

Many academic critics of financialization regard the process as both socially destructive and without historical precedent. Popular unease with financialization may, in part, be a function of perceived novelty. Financialization, however, is not new and capitalist countries have experienced cycles of financialization and de-financialization over the course of the twentieth century. In recent years, historians interested in the emergence of the corporation have developed our knowledge of the long pre-history of corporate finance. Until recently, most business historians have associated the rise of the corporation and the birth of financialization with north-western Europe in the period just before the Industrial Revolution. Newer research has established that institutions resembling the modern joint-stock company existed long before that time.

Quasi-corporate forms can be traced back as far as the Roman Republic, when Roman citizens bidding for government leases formed partnerships known as *Societates Publicanorum* (Malmendier, 2005). During the period of the Republic, the Roman state guided economic activity but gave leases for various forms of public work – from building aqueducts to supplying the army, and also for tax farming. These *societates* were formed by *publicani*, who specialised in government leaseholding in order to raise capital, which would later be reimbursed by the state. Scholars have seen parallels to more modern corporate forms in the *societates* – certainly, over time the principle of continuity was introduced so that the partnership was not wound up or reconstituted on the death of a partner. There was also a secondary market in shares. But there was certainly not yet any idea of corporate personality or limited liability in Roman law – the contracts were actually let by the government to a nominated representative of the partnership known as the *manceps* who took on personal liability for the contract. It is also dubious as to how far these arrangements represent financial capitalism in the sense that the state rather than the market defined the need for the leases, and essentially these contracts represented a way of keeping the Roman Republic's debt, and risk, 'off the balance sheet'. Augustus, the first Roman Emperor, restricted the role of the *societates* to tax farming, and the Empire gradually internalised all of the functions previously performed by them; certainly, if the *societates* were a form of financial capitalism Roman civilization did not rely upon these corporate forms to survive. The subsequent fall of the Empire and the Dark Ages gave little known opportunity for financial capitalism. The medieval period from c. 1150 saw the rise of the Hanseatic League of merchants, certainly a mass organization devoted to the principle of gain from trade. Although a loose confederation of cities, the League became financially dominant enough in the twelfth and thirteenth centuries to assume some of the characteristics of a state, setting up trading colonies known as Kontors and even went to war with Denmark in the 1360s (Kirby and Kirby, 2015). In spite of this supranational legal personality there was no centralised form of governance and the capital was contributed by individual merchants who did not share profits; the purpose was to create a sort of cartel to reduce transaction costs by facilitating exchange. The league gradually declined and its last formal meeting was held in 1669, but some of its attributes, such as the involvement of individual merchants, carried over into newer mercantile ventures.

It is generally agreed that the first recognisably modern corporation was the Dutch East India Company, or *Vereenigde Oost-Indische Compagnie* (VOC), which was chartered in 1602 (Gelderblom, and Jonker, 2004; Gelderblom, de Jong and Jonker, 2013). By 1795, the VOC had sent 4,785 ships totalling 3.4 million tons to Asia (De Vries, 2003, pp. 40–41, 46). The VOC's capital structure helped it to establish a permanent infrastructure of docks, forts, ports and trading posts along the sea routes to Asia. The creation of the VOC allowed investors to pool the high risks associated with fragile wooden sailing ships and maritime warfare. Smaller investors also had the additional reassurance that the VOC's directors retained unlimited liability for most of the company's debt obligations.

Diffusion of the corporate form to other countries

The corporate form represented by the VOC also appeared in England (Michie, 1999, p. 15). In England, an East India Company (EIC) was formed in 1600. Before the political revolution of 1688–9, there were a mere 15 joint-stock companies in England. After the so-called Glorious Revolution, the number of companies in England increased dramatically. This was due, in part, to liberalised registration, as power had decisively shifted towards parliament, which now provided the principal source of authority for incorporation (Freeman, Pearson and Taylor, 2012, pp. 20–21). Investors and company promoters took advantage of the new political constitution, and as many as 150 new joint-stock companies were formed by 1695 (Freeman, Pearson and Taylor, 2012, p. 17). Small investors were re-assured by corporate constitutions that mandated proportional weighting to increase the power of smaller investors and reduce the domination of larger, insider shareholders (Scott, 1910, pp. 340–341). Incorporation became far more difficult in 1720, when the Bubble Act was passed at the urging of the directors of the South Sea Company, who sought to prevent competing firms from crowding out the company's capital, thus pushing the prices of their own shares higher (Freeman, Pearson and Taylor, 2013, p. 21) Many business historians argue that the Bubble Act, which remained in force until 1825, retarded the growth of the joint-stock company in England, and thus slowed the rise of the corporate economy (Campbell, 1967; Patterson and Reiffen, 1990, pp. 44–45; Mirowski, 1991; Freeman, Pearson and Taylor, 2012, pp. 23–25).

The longevity of the Bubble Act in 1720 was, in part, a function of widespread unease about financialization and related phenomena such as the rise of banks, the stock exchange and the emergence of a class of city-dwellers who made their living from finance rather than so-called "honest toil". Perhaps the most vociferous critic of financialization was Viscount Bolingbroke, who equated it with the corruption of Walpole's Whig Party (Kramnick, 1992, pp. 60–61). Suspicion of finance was deeply rooted in the civic republican tradition, an influential political philosophy with roots in classical antiquity. Civic republicans regarded farmers, particularly small holders, as the repository of all social virtues and demonized cities, commerce and, in particular, finance (Pocock, 2009, pp. 437, 447, 529, 538). This tradition informed the thinking of the American Revolutionaries, who thought that the corruption inherent in commercialization had destroyed British liberty, and shaped the agrarian, anti-urban ideologies of the philosopher Jean-Jacques Rousseau (LaFreniere, 1990) and US President Thomas Jefferson (Banning, 1986). The existence of these critics of financialization in the eighteenth and nineteenth centuries suggest that the worldview of twenty-first century critics of financialization has deep historical roots.

Many French people expressed hostility to finance in the aftermath of the financial crisis associated with a Scottish adventurer named John Law, who created that *Compagnie d'Occident* in 1717. In 1716, Law had established a French central bank to reduce the French Crown's, reliance on Genevan lenders and short-term instruments known as *Billets d'Etat*. Both the bank and company were intended to purchase these assets, in the case of the company converting it into equity. Law succeeded in creating a financial boom based on liquidity, and briefly demonstrated how a secondary market in shares might work, but an attempt in 1720 to cool the market destroyed confidence in the experiment (Murphy, 2005, pp. 191–195). Just as the collapse of the South Sea Bubble in Britain resulted in a backlash against financialization in that country, many French people came to oppose financialization. Physiocracy, a school of economic thought that emerged in France in the aftermath of the 1720 crisis, was hostile to finance, which it regarded as a socially parasitical activity (Meek, 2013, pp. 18–22).

Anti-finance sentiment was also widespread in the United States during its founding period, which is ironic given that Wall Street later emerged as a global financial centre and a powerful force in US politics. After the ratification of the US Constitution in 1789, many companies were formed: the 1790s witnessed 247 incorporations, and by 1860 the states had chartered at least 22,000 limited-liability firms (Sylla and Wright, 2013, pp. 653–654). The emergence of banks and a corporate economy in the early republic divided Americans and contributed to the development a two-party system. A central bank, the Bank of the United States, was created at the urging of New York's Alexander Hamilton and other nationalists. Hamilton, who was a leader of the emerging Federalist Party, championed financial development and the growth of commerce, cities and long-distance trade. The supporters of Thomas Jefferson, in contrast sought to preserve the United States as an agrarian nation of virtuous farmers who were uncontaminated by the sophisticated financial institutions they associated with the hated British monarchy. Jefferson reported that the merchants of New York were, unfortunately, attempting to introduce English-style financial institutions into the United States: "Too many of these stock jobbers & king-jobbers have come into our legislature, or rather too many of our legislature have become stock jobbers & king-jobbers" (Jefferson to Lafayette, 16 June 1792).

In the aftermath of the Panic of 1792, Wall Street's very first financial crisis, Americans debated the desirability of financialization (Sylla, Wright and Cowen, 2009). Despite the opposition of many Jeffersonians to the development of corporations and financial institutions, the process continued. Many firms continued to be incorporated through the passage of special charters by the state legislature, but an increasing number of states passed general incorporation laws, a revolutionary development. Such a system was established first in New York State, in 1811, for manufacturing corporations only, but was adopted more widely, some 24 states having introduced general incorporation laws by 1860. By that year, there were at least 4,263 registered corporations in the United States (Sylla, Wright and Cowen, 2009, p. 654). Perpetual succession, which allows corporations to continue to operate despite changes in ownership, was important in facilitating a more active secondary market in shares, and likely encouraged the separation of ownership from control (Moss, 2002, p. 56; Wright, 2002; Hansmann, Kraakman and Squire, 2006). Later, President Andrew Jackson (1829–1837), a leading spokesman for the civic republican tradition, prevented the re-chartering of the Bank of the United States, then the country's central bank (Hammond, 1957, p. 449). Ironically, Jackson's move may have encouraged further financialization as it led to the proliferation of banks.

The railway age and globalisation: financial capitalism broadens

The advent of railways, steamships and telegraphs caused business organizations to become more complex and capital-intensive. These technologies required new governance structures that were characterised by the separation of ownership and control, corporate personality and limited liability (Gourvish, 1980, p. 128; McCartney and Arnold, 2002, 2003; Chandler, 1954; Sudrià and Pascual, 1999; Bryer, 1991). The expansion of the railways brought new investors into the corporate equity market, and led to the creation of new stock exchanges (Reed, 1975, pp. 120–186). The London Stock Exchange listed overseas-registered as well as British companies, which further increased the distance between shareholders and managers. Company registration in Britain was made more attractive by the 1856 and 1862 Companies Acts, which introduced full limited liability into British corporate governance for the first time. A limited liability company could now be created without requiring any sort of charter or special Act of Parliament (Armstrong and Jones, 1987, pp. 5–6; Coles, 1908, pp. 142–146). The Acts led to a considerable expansion of financial capitalism as they enabled the expansion of limited liability companies. The most widely held company by 1911 was the Midland Railway with some 79,400 shareholders, while the mean number of shareholders for a London listed company was around 6,000 (Foreman-Peck and Hannah, 2012, p. 1223). Continental countries copied Britain's example: in 1867, France dramatically simplified the procedure for creating a limited-liability company (Murphy, 2005, pp. 202–203). Germany followed suit, introducing a new incorporation law from 1870 (Herrigel, pp. 474–475). The success of the UK model inspired a variety of common and civil law countries to play catch-up with regards to corporate governance laws.

Many contemporaries felt very ambivalent, even hostile, to the rise of the corporate economy. This ambivalence about financialization was present even in Britain, the cockpit of the world's financial system. As the business historian Ranald Michie has demonstrated in his study of contemporary fiction, Victorian and Edwardian Britons were ambivalent about financialization (Michie, 2009). Hostility towards finance became even more widespread in Western countries in the aftermath of financial crises such as those of 1907 and 1929. In other words, the anti-financier sentiment that was very much in evidence after the 2008 financial crisis has many historical precedents.

Contributions of business historians

Shareholder value ideology

Today, academics associate the ideology of shareholder value with the English-speaking countries, while firms in continental Europe and Japan are said to operate on the basis of various stakeholder theories of corporate governance. This global pattern is actually quite new: as Stout, Heilbron, Verheul, Quak and Lazonick have demonstrated, the orientation towards shareholder value is not one of the essential or enduring differences between Anglo-American and continental European variants of capitalism. Lynn Stout argues that between the 1930s and the 1970s, a stakeholder model of corporate governance informed how most US corporations were run. She shows that Adolf Berle and Gardiner Means outlined this model in their massively influential 1932 book *The Modern Corporation and Public Property*, which appeared near the nadir of the Great Depression. The vision of management as a sacred trust espoused by Berle and Means dethroned capital and suggested that society's interests would be best served by ceding control to public-spirited salaried experts trained in business schools. The variant of stakeholder theory outlined in Berle and Means's book helped to confer legitimacy on American business during its existential crisis in the 1930s. It also, according to Stout, laid the foundations for several decades of equitable growth and rapid technological innovation (Stout, 2013). Rakesh Khurana argues that the managerialist philosophy of Berle and Means dominated business-school education in the United States until the 1970s, when it was replaced by the anti-manager free-market ideology associated with the University of Chicago (Khurana, 2007, pp. 296–8).

Lazonick and O'Sullivan (2000) argue that the ideology of shareholder value was developed in the late 1970s, partially as a response to the post-1973 economic slowdown and the resulting drop in corporate profitability. In their narrative, academics such as Milton Friedman and Eugene Fama of Chicago and Michael Jensen and William Meckling of Rochester, promoted the idea that the sole purpose of a company is to maximize shareholder value, as did the non-academic authors who coined and then popularized the phrase "corporate governance" in the mid-1970s. Institutional investors (e.g., pension funds) gave added force to these ideas by depicting the managers of the conglomerates of the 1960s as self-interested individuals who were appropriating resources that rightfully belonged to shareholders. Moreover, the increasing trend towards paying top executives primarily in stock options contributed to a shift in the orientation of senior managers towards shareholder value. However, Lazonick and O'Sullivan argue that it was only in the 1980s that the ideology of shareholder value became dominant in corporate America.

Their view of when the ideology of shareholder value became dominant in the United States is largely congruent with more recent research by Heilbron, Verheul and Quak (2014). These scholars, however, date the rise of shareholder value ideology with somewhat greater precision than Lazonick and O'Sullivan: according to Heilbron, Verheul and Quak, the ideology of shareholder value became hegemonic in the United States in the period between the recession of 1981–1982 and the foundation of the Council of Institutional Investors in 1985. A somewhat different chronology is provided by Stout, who regards the bear market of 1973–4 as the crucial turning point away from "managerialism" and towards a renewed emphasis on shareholder value. She sees the publication in 1976 of Jensen and Meckling's influential chapter on the theory of the firm as the crucial watershed (2013, p. 1173). Although Stout disagrees with Heilbron, Verheul and Quak about the precise timing, she shares their view that shareholder value ideology was promoted by an alliance of interest groups and the intellectuals in business schools. Khurana (2007, pp. 296–8) dates the adoption of share-holder value ideology to a somewhat later period than that identified by these scholars. He notes that as late as 1990, the American Business Roundtable condemned the view that "only the interests of shareholders should be considered by directors". By 1997, this organization had repudiated the managerialist ideals of Bearle and Means by expressing the view that " the paramount duty of management and of boards of directors is to the corporation's stockholder" and that it would be wrong for directors to attempt to "balance the interests of other stakeholders" with those of shareholders (Khurana, 2007, pp. 320–1). Although there are clearly some minor disagreements about when precisely shareholder value ideology became dominant in the United States, it is clear that this process was relatively recent. The take-home lesson for scholars of comparative capitalism from this historical research is that it would be wrong to view shareholder-value ideology as a permanent or intrinsic feature of the American variant of capitalism.

The LLSV paradigm

In the last decade, historians have continued to develop our understanding of the history of corporate governance. In testing the LLSV paradigm against the historical record of different countries, business historians have discovered severe problems with it, as Musacchio and Turner observe (2013). Let us review the business-historical evidence against the LLSV paradigm. The modern corporation, which traces its legal roots back to Rome, was born in a civil-law country: the Netherlands and only spread later to common-law jurisdictions such as England and the United States (Hansmann, Kraakman and Squire, 2006). The LLSV paradigm indicates that common-law jurisdictions are more hospitable to the emergence of a market for corporate securities. LLSV also argue that corporate governance structures in which shareholders have legal power over directors is important for the development of active corporate equity markets. However, while the corporate governance system of the VOC, the first major joint-stock company, deprived shareholders of any say over board composition, VOC securities nevertheless proved popular with Dutch investors (Van Lent and Sgourev, 2013).

Additional problems with the LLSV paradigm become evident when we look at the nineteenth century. The 1856 and 1862 Companies Acts in Britain provided shareholders with few of the legal protections that LLSV regard as essential for the creation of a large and liquid capital market (Armstrong and Jones, 1987, pp. 5–6; Maltby, 1998, p. 11; Acheson et al., 2010, p. 7). Nevertheless, Britain's market for corporate equities flourished in this period. Despite the absence of significant legal protections for shareholders in pre-1914 England and Wales, share ownership was highly dispersed (Campbell and Turner, 2011). In their critique of the historical accuracy of LLSV, Musacchio and Turner note that "ownership dispersion occurred before" legislators increased the legal protection afforded to "shareholders protections" in some countries, which is actually the opposite of what the LLSV paradigm would predict. They note that the "separation of ownership and control in corporations was commonplace in some economies in the nineteenth century" even these countries had weak shareholder protection laws (2013, p. 528). The British parliament did not introduce effective legal protections for shareholders until the twentieth century (Cheffins, 2001), a historical epoch that not coincidentally saw the rejection more generally of the ideology of laissez-faire and then the creation of a welfare state (Clarke, 1997, pp. 57–8; Campbell and Turner, 2011, p. 574).

The experience of the United States in the nineteenth century also calls the LLSV paradigm into question. Prior to the New Deal, the laws governing financial reporting and accounting standards in US corporations were weak. Professional management remained rare and corporations had relatively few independent directors. In a study of companies registered in New York State in the 1820s, Hilt (2008, pp. 651–653) found that ownership was frequently separated from control: ownership of corporate equities was geographically dispersed and a large proportion of corporate equity was owned by outsiders unconnected to the managers. He also found that New York State gave shareholders little protection. He concludes that shareholding was dispersed despite the weakness of legal protections for shareholders. Hilt's research, like that of the aforementioned British business historians, therefore, undermines the LLSV paradigm.

LLSV's view that civil law legal systems discourage widespread equity ownership compared to common-law systems is also incompatible with business-historical research on Germany, a civil-law jurisdiction. On the eve of the First World War, Germany had a well-developed stock market despite the country's civil law system: "by the start of World War I, the Berlin market ranked among the top in the world, lagging only London in overall size and liquidity" (Fohlin, 2007, p. 627). Moreover, total stock market capitalisation as a percentage of GDP was higher in Germany (44%) than in the United States (39%) in 1913 (Rajan and Zingales, 2003, p. 15), which is the precise opposite of what the LLSV paradigm would predict.

Further evidence to refute the LLSV paradigm can be found in Japan, which modernized after 1868 by selectively borrowing institutions from various Western countries. Stock market capitalisation relative to GDP was quite high, despite the alleged defects of the legal system, which was based on that of Germany. For instance, stock market capitalisation in Japan was 49% of GDP in 1913, while it was 39% in the United States, which already had an elaborate system of corporate law based on generations of Anglo-American jurisprudence (Franks, Mayer and Miyajima, 2014).

Directions for additional research

The foregoing survey of the secondary literature has made it clear that a number of scholars associated with the business history community have made important contributions to our understanding of the topic of corporate governance. However, it is also clear that much work remains to be done by business historians.

First, business historians have devoted insufficient attention to how corporate governance was influenced by the process of de-financialization that many Western countries experienced after 1914. The process in the United States, which was particularly rapid between the 1929 Wall Street Crash and the end of the Second World War, is evident in Figure 8.1. Historians trained in archival research need to delve beneath the statistics and engage in qualitative research on the experience of specific companies, stock exchanges and other organizations. This period is important, as it saw the rise of managerialist capitalism and what was arguably capitalism's greatest existential crisis. Finance was unable to prevent and resist the growth of fascism in central and southern Europe, while more liberal regimes, such as that in the US, sought to channel its power through legislation such as the Securities Exchange Act of 1934. Janice M. Traflet's study of the NYSE's efforts to promote mass shareholding during the early Cold War period (2013) illustrates how archival research can underpin a deeper understanding of the social and political history of financialization.

Second, business historians need to invest resources in studying the international diffusion of the ideology of shareholder value in the 1980s and 1990s. Researching this topic will, of course, involve building on the aforementioned research on the genesis of this ideology in the United States in the 1970s and 1980s. Business historians can use intensive primary source research to enrich our understanding of the process that has been described by Heilbron, Verheul and Quak in broad brushstrokes. The diffusion of the US ideology of shareholder value to the other English-speaking countries and the failure of this ideology to take root in societies such as Germany also requires additional investigation. This research will likely involve large multinationals which straddle these cultural systems. Research on this topic will doubtless require business historians to engage with literature on comparative legal history, political science and comparative capitalism. In particular, there will be opportunities for co-authorship between business historians and scholars based in law schools.

Third, the history of corporate governance in emerging markets remains a massively under-researched topic, notwithstanding the existence of some interesting research on corporate governance in pre-1949 China (Köll, 1998; Thomas, 2001). For instance, the standard work on the business history of India, which is an emerging market of some importance, does not deal with the issue of corporate governance in a sustained fashion (Tripathi and Jumani, 2007). Business historians should prioritize research on the histories of corporate governance and financialization in both the so-called BRIC countries and in the smaller emerging markets. Emerging markets have industrialised while relying upon family or so-called praetorian capitalism (Jhatial et al., 2014), with less well-developed equity markets, and a high tendency towards information asymmetry. Clearly, the separation of ownership and control has occurred in these environments, yet some of these organisations have now grown large enough to acquire firms operating in the supposedly more optimal shareholder-value oriented Anglo-American system.

Fourth, gender has recently emerged as an important research topic for non-historical corporate governance scholars. There is growing evidence that firms with female representation on their boards tends to outperform firms with all all-male boards. This evidence has been used to justify the 2003 gender quota law for company boards in Norway and the proposals for similar laws in other countries (Machold et al., 2013, p. 106). Although business historians have done important work on gender in corporate governance, such as Maltby and Rutterford's study of women shareholders in Victorian Britain (2006), far more historical research in this area is required. It remains unclear whether or how the shifting gender balance of boards in the last few decades has affected the strategy of firms. Business historians can remedy this lacuna and many others related to our understanding of corporate governance.

Fifth, the relationship between secularization and competing visions of the company needs to be explored in greater detail. Khurana argues that the managerialist philosophy that animated American business reformers and educators in the first seven decades of the twentieth century was deeply rooted in the social reform ideas of liberal Protestantism, an ideology that informed the creation of the Wharton and Harvard business schools and the move to make management into a profession similar to medicine and the law (2007, pp. 296–8). Khurana implies that the subsequent decline of liberal Protestantism paved the way for the less romantic worldview espoused by Chicago-trained academics after the 1970s. Khurana, it should be noted, was a part of an abortive movement to create an oath for MBAs in which future managers would pledge to consider the public interest (Bennett, 2010). Historians need to investigate Khurana's historical argument and to see whether it also applies to the other post-Christian nations that have undergone secularization as well societies with very different religious traditions. Understanding the cultural and religious roots of management ideas and practices in different societies may help us to implement the reforms desired by Khurana and other reformers.

By adopting a comprehensive approach to the history of corporate governance that integrates the research of cultural, social, intellectual and even gender historians, business historians will deepen our understanding of the rise, fall and rise again of shareholder value ideology. Such research will be useful to the present because it will engage with a wide range of financial, cultural, political and ethical issues. By eschewing monocausal explanations and by providing thick description based on archival materials, business historians will help to refine our understanding of how the world's principal corporate governance systems evolved.

References

Acheson, G. G., Hickson, C. R. & Turner, J. D. (2010). "Does limited liability matter? Evidence from nineteenth-century British banking". *Review of Law & Economics, 6*(2), 247–273.

Armstrong, J. & Jones, S. (1987). *Business Documents: Their Origins, Sources and Uses in Historical Research.* London: Mansell Publishing.

Banning, L. (1986). "Jeffersonian ideology revisited: liberal and classical ideas in the new American republic". *The William and Mary Quarterly: A Magazine of Early American History and Culture,* 4–19.

Bennett, D. (2010). "Executive honor: can an 'MBA oath' fix what's wrong with business?" *Boston Globe,* May 16, 2010.

Berle, A. A. & Means, G. (1932). *The Modern Corporation and Private Property.* New York: Commerce Clearing House.

Beyer, J. & Hoppner, M. (2003). "The disintegration of organised capitalism: German corporate governance in the 1990s". *West European Politics, 26*(4), 179–198.

Bryer, R. A. (1991). "Accounting for the "railway mania" of 1845—A great railway swindle?" *Accounting, Organizations and Society, 16*(5), 439–486.

Campbell, G. & Turner, J. D. (2011). "Substitutes for legal protection: corporate governance and dividends in Victorian Britain". *The Economic History Review, 64*(2), 571–597.

Campbell, R. H. (1967). "The law and the joint-stock company in Scotland". *Studies in Scottish Business History, 136.*

Chandler, A. D. (1954). "Patterns of American Railroad Finance, 1830–50". *Business History Review, 28*(03), 248–263.

Charreaux, G. & Desbrières, P. (2001). "Corporate governance: stakeholder value versus shareholder value". *Journal of Management and Governance, 5*(2), 107–128.

Cheffins, B. R. (2000). "Does law matter?: the separation of ownership and control in the United Kingdom". *ERSC Centre for Business Research, University of Cambridge, Working Chapter,* (172).

Clarke, P. F. (1996). *Hope and Glory: Britain 1900–1990* (Vol. 9). London: Penguin (Non-Classics).

Coffee, J. C. (2001). "The rise of dispersed ownership: the roles of law and the state in the separation of ownership and control". *Yale Law Journal,* 1–82.

Coleman, D.C. (1987). "The uses and abuses of business history". *Business History, 29*(2), 141–156.

Coles, A. (1908). "The Secretary to a Joint-Stock Company", in Blain, H. E. (ed) *Pitman's Secretary's Handbook: A Practical Guide to the Work and Duties in Connection with the position of Secretary to a Joint-Stock Company, Public Institution, Member of Parliament, etc.* London: Sir Isaac Pitman & Sons Ltd.

Dari-Mattiacci, G., Gelderblom, O., Jonker, J. & Perotti, E. C. (2013). "The emergence of the corporate form". *Amsterdam Law School Research Chapter,* (2013–11).

Decker, S., Kipping, M. & Wadhwani, R. D. (2015). "New business histories! Plurality in business history research methods". *Business History, 57*(1), 30–40.

de Jong, A. & Higgins, D. M. (2015). "New business history?" *Business History, 57*(1), 1–4.

de Jong, A. & Roell, A. (2005). "Financing and control in the Netherlands: a historical perspective", in *A History of Corporate Governance around the World: Family Business Groups to Professional Managers* (467–516). Chicago: University of Chicago Press.

De Vries, J. (2003). "Connecting Europe and Asia: A Quantitative Analysis of the Cape-Route Trade, 1497–1795", in *Global Connections and Monetary History, 1470–1800,* O' Flynn, D., Giraldez, A. and Von Glahn, R. (eds). Aldershot: Ashgate.

Dore, R. (2008). "Financialization of the global economy". *Industrial and Corporate Change, 17*(6), 1097–1112.

Epstein, G.A. ed. (2005). *Financialization and the World Economy.* Cheltenham: Edward Elgar Publishing.

Fiss, P.C. & Zajac, E. J. (2004). "The diffusion of ideas over contested terrain: the (non) adoption of a shareholder value orientation among German firms". *Administrative Science Quarterly, 49*(4), 501–534.

Fohlin, C. (2007). "Does civil law tradition and universal banking crowd out securities markets? pre-World War I Germany as a counter-example". *Enterprise and Society, 8*, 602–641.

Foreman-Peck, J. & Hannah, L. (2012). "Extreme divorce: the managerial revolution in UK companies before 1914". *The Economic History Review, 65*(4), 1217–1238.

Franks, J., Mayer, C. & Miyajima, H. (2014). "The Ownership of Japanese Corporations in the 20th Century". *Review of Financial Studies*, hhu018.

Freeman, M., Pearson, R. & Taylor, J. (2012). *"Shareholder Democracies?: Corporate Governance in Britain and Ireland Before 1850"*. Chicago: University of Chicago Press.

Fukuyama, F. (1989). "The end of history". *The National Interest, 16*(4).

Gelderblom, O., de Jong, A. & Jonker, J. (2013). "The formative years of the modern corporation: the Dutch East India company, 1602–1623". *The Journal of Economic History, 73*(4), 1050–1076.

Gelderblom, O. & Jonker, J. (2004). "Completing a financial revolution: the finance of the Dutch East India trade and the rise of the Amsterdam capital market, 1595–1612". *The Journal of Economic History, 64*(3), 641–672.

Gilson, R.J. (2001). "Globalizing corporate governance: convergence of form or function". *The American Journal of Comparative Law*, 329–357.

Gourevitch, P. A. & Shinn, J. (2005). *Political Power and Corporate Control: The New Global Politics of Corporate Governance*. Princeton: Princeton University Press.

Gourvish, T. R. (1980). *Railways and the British economy, 1830–1914*. London: Macmillan Pub Ltd.

Graeber, D. (2014). *Debt-Updated and Expanded: The First 5,000 Years*. New York: Melville House.

Hammond, B. (1991). *Banks and Politics in America from the Revolution to the Civil War*. Princeton: Princeton University Press.

Hansmann, H. & Kraakman, R. (2001). "The end of history for corporate law". *Georgetown Law Journal, 89*, 439.

Hansmann, H., Kraakman, R. & Squire, R. (2006). "Law and the rise of the firm". *Harvard Law Review*, 1333–1403.

Heilbron, J., Verheul, J. & Quak, S. (2014). "The origins and early diffusion of "shareholder value" in the United States". *Theory and Society, 43*(1), 1–22.

Herrigel, G. (2008). "Corporate governance: history without historians". *Handbook of Business History*, 470–497.

Hilt, E. (2008). "When did ownership separate from control? corporate governance in the early nineteenth century". *Journal of Economic History, 68*(03), 645–685.

Holderness, C. G. (2014). "Law and ownership re-examined". *Critical Finance Review, 5* (2016), 41–83.

Jefferson, T. (1792). Letter of 16 June 1792 in *The Writings of Thomas Jefferson*, Writings, ed. HA Washington (Washington, 1853), 3: 450.

Jhatial, A. A., Cornelius, N. & Wallace, J. (2014). "Rhetorics and realities of management practices in Pakistan: Colonial, post-colonial and post-9/11 influences". *Business History, 56*(3), 456–484.

Johnson, S. & Kwak, J. (2011). *13 Bankers: The Wall Street Takeover and the Next Financial Meltdown*. New York: Random House LLC.

Kedrosky, P. & Stangler, D. (2011). "Financialization and its Entrepreneurial Consequences". *Kauffman Foundation Working Chapter*.

Khurana, R. (2007). *From Higher Aims to Hired Hands: The Social Transformation of American Business Schools and the Unfulfilled Promise of Management as a Profession*. Princeton: Princeton University Press.

Kipping, M. & Üsdiken, B. (2015). "Turning how and where?", in Kerr, C. (ed.) *The Routledge Companion to Management and Organizational History*, 372–379. London: Routledge.

Kirby, E. & Kirby S. L. (2015). *An Examination of Medieval Trade: Interorganizational Relationships and the Hanseatic League*, Academy of Management Conference, Submission 12300.

Kneer, C. (2013). *The Absorption of Talent into Finance: Evidence from US Banking Deregulation*. No. 391. Netherlands Central Bank, Research Department.

Köll, E. (1998). "Controlling modern business in China: the Da Sheng enterprise, 1895–1926". *Journal of Asian Business, 14*, 41–56.

Kramnick, I. (1992). *Bolingbroke and His Circle: The Politics of Nostalgia in the Age of Walpole*. Ithaca: Cornell University Press.

Krippner, G.R. (2005). "The financialization of the American economy". *Socio-Economic Review, 3*(2), 173–208.

Kus, B. (2013). "Financialization and income inequality in OECD nations: 1995–2007". *The Economic and Social Review, 43*(4), 477–495.

La Porta, R., Lopez-de-Silanes, F., Shleifer, A. & Vishny, R. W. (1997). "Legal determinants of external finance". *Journal of Finance*, 1131–1150.

La Porta, R., Lopez-de-Silanes, F., Shleifer, A. & Vishny, R. (2000). "Investor protection and corporate governance". *Journal of Financial Economics, 58*(1), 3–27.

LaFreniere, G. F. (1990). "Rousseau and the European roots of environmentalism". *Environmental History Review*, 41–72.

Lazonick, W. (2011). "From Innovation to Financialization: how Shareholder Value Ideology is Destroying the US Economy", in Wolson, M. H. and G. A. Epstein (eds) *The Handbook of the Political Economy of Financial Crises*, 491–511. Oxford: Oxford University Press.

Lazonick, W. & O'Sullivan, M. (2000). "Maximizing shareholder value: a new ideology for corporate governance". *Economy and Society, 29*(1), 13–35.

Levine, R. (1997). "Financial development and economic growth: views and agenda". *Journal of Economic Literature*, 688–726.

Lin, K.-H. & Tomaskovic-Devey, D. (2013). "Financialization and US income inequality, 1970–2008". *American Journal of Sociology, 118*(5), 1284–1329.

Lythe, S. G. E. & Butt, J. (1975). *An economic history of Scotland, 1100–1939* (19). Glasgow and London: Blackie.

Machold, S., Huse, M., Hansen, K. & Brogi, M. (eds.) (2013). *Getting Women on to Corporate Boards: A Snowball Starting in Norway*. Cheltenham: Edward Elgar Publishing, 2013.

Malmendier, U. (2005). 'Roman Shares' in Goetzmann W. N. and Rouwenhorst, K. G. (eds), *The Origins of Value: The Financial Innovations that Created Modern Capital Markets*. Oxford: Oxford University Press.

Maltby, J. (1998). "UK joint stock companies legislation 1844–1900: accounting publicity and 'mercantile caution'". *Accounting History, 3*(1), 9–32.

Maltby, J. & Rutterford. J. (2006). "'She possessed her own fortune': women investors from the late nineteenth century to the early twentieth century". *Business History, 48*(2), 220–253.

Martin, R. L. (2011). *Fixing the Game: Bubbles, Crashes, and What Capitalism can Learn from the NFL* Cambridge: Harvard Business Press.

Martynova, M. & Renneboog, L. (2011). "Evidence on the international evolution and convergence of corporate governance regulations". *Journal of Corporate Finance, 17*(5), 1531–1557.

McCartney, S. & Arnold, A. J. (2002). "Financial reporting in the context of crisis: reconsidering the impact of the 'mania' on early railway accounting". *European Accounting Review, 11*(2), 401–417.

McCartney, S. & Arnold, A. J. (2003). "The railway mania of 1845–1847: Market irrationality or collusive swindle based on accounting distortions?" *Accounting, Auditing & Accountability Journal, 16*(5), 821–852.

McLean, R. D., Zhang, T. & Zhao, M. (2012). "Why does the law matter? Investor protection and its effects on investment, finance, and growth". *The Journal of Finance, 67*(1), 313–350.

Meek, R. L. (2013). *Economics of Physiocracy*. London: Routledge.

Michie, R. C. (2006). *The Global Securities Market: A History*. Oxford: Oxford University Press.

Michie, R. C. (1999). *The London Stock Exchange: A History*. Oxford: Oxford University Press.

Michie, R. C. (2009). *Guilty Money: The City of London in Victorian and Edwardian Culture, 1815–1914*. London: Pickering & Chatto.

Mirowski, P. (1985). *The Birth of The Business Cycle*. New York: Garland.

Morck, R.K. & Steier, L. (2007). The Global History of Corporate Governance: An Introduction. In Morck, ed. *A History of Corporate Governance Around the World: Family Business Groups to Professional Managers*. Chicago: University of Chicago Press.

Moss, D. A. (2002). *When All Else Fails: Government as the Ultimate Risk Manager*. Cambridge: Harvard University Press.

Murphy, A. (2005). "Corporate ownership in France: the importance of history". In *A History of Corporate Governance Around the World: Family Business Groups to Professional Managers* (185–222). Chicago: University of Chicago Press.

Musacchio, A. (2008). "Laws versus contracts: shareholder protections and ownership concentration in Brazil, 1890–1950". *Business History Review, 82*(3), 445–473.

121

Musacchio, A. & Turner, J. D. (2013). "Does the law and finance hypothesis pass the test of history?" *Business History*, *55*(4), 524–542.

O'Sullivan, M. (2000). *Contests for Corporate Control: Corporate Governance and Economic Performance in the United States and Germany*. Oxford: Oxford University Press.

Palley, T.I. (200). *Financialization: What It Is and Why It Matters*. No. 525. Working chapters, The Levy Economics Institute.

Patterson, M. & Reiffen, D. (1990). "The effect of the Bubble Act on the market for joint stock shares". *The Journal of Economic History*, *50*(01), 163–171.

Pocock, J. G. A. (2009). *The Machiavellian Moment: Florentine Political Thought and the Atlantic Republican Tradition*. Princeton: Princeton University Press.

Porta, R., Lopez-de-Silanes, F., & Shleifer, A. (1999). "Corporate ownership around the world". *The Journal of Finance*, *54*(2), 471–517.

Rajan, R. G. & Zingales. L. (2001). "Financial systems, industrial structure, and growth". *Oxford Review of Economic Policy*, *17*(4), 467–482.

Rajan, R. G. & Zingales, L. (2003). "The great reversals: the politics of financial development in the twentieth century". *Journal of Financial Economics*, *69*(1), 5–50.

Reed, M. C. (1975). *Investment in Railways in Britain, 1820–1844: A Study in the Development of the Capital Market*. Oxford: Oxford University Press.

Rowlinson, M., Hassard, J. & Decker, S. (2013). "Strategies for Organizational History: a Dialogue Between Historical Theory and Organization Theory". *Academy of Management Review*, amr-2012.

Scott, W. R. (1912). *The Constitution and Finance of English, Scottish and Irish Joint-Stock Companies to 1720* (Vol. 1). Cambridge: Cambridge University Press.

Siems, M. & Deakin, S. (2010). "Comparative law and finance: past, present, and future research". *Journal of Institutional and Theoretical Economics JITE*, *166*(1), 120–140.

Stout, L. A. (2012). "On the rise of shareholder primacy, signs of its fall, and the return of managerialism (in the closet)". *Seattle University Law Review 36*, 1169.

Stout, L. A. (2012). *The Shareholder Value Myth: How Putting Shareholders First Harms Investors, Corporations, and the Public*. Oakland: Berrett-Koehler Publishers.

Sudarsanam, S. & Broadhurst, T. (2012) "Corporate governance convergence in Germany through shareholder activism: impact of the Deutsche Boerse bid for London Stock Exchange". *Journal of Management & Governance*, *16*(2), 235–268.

Sudrià, C. & Pascual, P. (1999). "Financing a railway mania: capital formation and the demand for money in Catalonia, 1840–66". *Financial History Review*, *6*(2), 127–145.

Sylla, R. & Wright, R. E. (2013). "Corporation formation in the antebellum United States in comparative context". *Business History*, *55*(4), 653–669.

Sylla, R., Wright, R. E. & Cowen, D. J. (2009). "Alexander Hamilton, central banker: crisis management during the US financial panic of 1792". *Business History Review*, *83*(1), 61–86.

Thomas, W. A. (2011). *Western Capitalism in China: A History of the Shanghai Stock Exchange*. Aldershot: Ashgate.

Traflet, J. M. (2013). *A Nation of Small Shareholders: Marketing Wall Street After World War II*. Baltimore: Johns Hopkins University Press.

Tripathi, D. & Jumani, J. (2007). *The Concise Oxford History of Indian Business*. New Delhi: Oxford University Press.

Turner, A. (2012). *Economics After the Crisis: Objectives and Means*. Cambridge: MIT Press.

Tuschke, A. & Luber, M. (2012). "Corporate Governance in Germany: Converging Towards Shareholder Value-Orientation or Not So Much?" *The Convergence of Corporate Governance: Promise and Prospects*, 75.

Van Lent, W. & Sgourev, S. V. (2013). "Local Elites versus Dominant Shareholders: Dividend Smoothing at the Dutch East India Company". In *Academy of Management Proceedings* (Vol. 2013, No. 1, p. 15592). Academy of Management.

Westlake, S. (2013). "Rebalancing act: rationales and policies for sectoral economic rebalancing". *Oxford Review of Economic Policy*, *29*(2), 326–343.

Wolf, M. (2014). "The Folly of Shareholder Value". *Financial Times*, 26 August.

Wright, R. E. (2002). *The Wealth of Nations Rediscovered: Integration and Expansion in American Financial Markets, 1780–1850*. Cambridge: Cambridge University Press.

9

The 'third sector'

Co-operatives, mutual, charities and social enterprises

Anthony Webster

A dictionary of business history written in the 1980s would almost certainly have been a briefer and less diverse volume than the present. By then, notions of what were considered valid business organisational models were characterised by a degree of certainty and restricted scope which seems refreshingly obsolete a quarter of a century later. At the height of the 'neo-liberal' revolution sweeping the Anglo-American world at that time, economists and business analysts seemed to share the conviction that at base all business models by definition shared one key ingredient: the paramountcy of the profit motive as the key driver and *raison d'être* for all business activity. In this context the profit motive was solely about the enrichment of individuals or corporate bodies; the pursuit of wealth for its own sake. Other models, in which either the profit motive was entirely absent, or in which profit was to be used for purposes other than individual or corporate enrichment which trumped the pure profit motive, were implicitly regarded as either inferior or in some way invalid. Business was about individuals enriching themselves, and any motive which superseded this reason for being involved in business threatened business integrity by diluting the discipline of market fundamentals. This was one reason why, over a period of a quarter of a century or so, business models based on collective rather than individual and corporate interests faded from economics and business literature (Kalmi, 2007). This questioning of the legitimacy of mutual and collective models of business organisation was given legal force by new legislation in the UK and in many Western economies designed to allow mutual organisations such as building societies to be converted into mainstream 'investor-led' public limited companies, usually with the help of substantial financial incentives for members or owners of mutual organisations.

But since the 1980s, 'non-traditional' forms of business enterprise such as co-operatives, mutuals and other forms of social enterprise have begun to reinstate themselves as 'legitimate' components of the world of business enterprise, not least as a result of an intellectual and political backlash against the more hubristic claims of neo-liberalism. A series of governance scandals starting in the 1990s, including Enron in 2001, and culminating in the massive banking crisis of 2008, demonstrated that the 'investor-led' model might not, after all, be the paragon of corporate business virtue its proponents had claimed. In addition, increasing parsimony in the provision of state services (and contraction after 2008), and perceived shortcomings in some of the investor-led organisations which took over state provision, prompted a reassessment of the potential usefulness of alternative models of business, including co-operatives and other forms of social enterprise. Earlier assumptions about the supposed inadequacy of mutual models were also challenged by the fate of many of the British building societies demutualized in the 1990s; many of which either succumbed to corporate takeovers or were pivotal in the debacle of 2008, such as Northern Rock. These developments, and the devastating consequences of the 2008 crisis in terms of massive state spending cuts and retreat from service provision, exacerbated other maturing concerns about longer term declining social and political participation in western societies, and the need to create a sense of dynamic and participatory citizenship. Widening wealth disparities and a general perception that western societies were atomising, with fractured family and communal ties, declining electoral turnouts and a plethora of serious social problems emerging as a result, all contributed to a new urgency to seek ways of stimulating popular socio-economic and political engagement and a renewed sense of social solidarity. Even erstwhile sceptics of the value of mutualism, such as the British Conservative Party, by 2010 had come full circle and now supported the promotion of alternative business models in certain circumstances. This was symbolized not only by David Cameron's championing of the 'Big Society', in which a range of voluntary organisations, co-operatives, mutuals and social enterprises were to be summoned into existence to fill the gap left by a retreating state, but by the establishment of Big Society Capital in 2012 to provide social investment, and a range of other initiatives to strengthen the 'social economy' (Social Investment, 2014). This was buttressed by the Social Value Act, which required public sector service procurers to consider the social effects of their decisions. By 2014, the Coalition government boasted that there were 180,000 social enterprises in the UK, constituting 15% of all SMEs and contributing £55 billion annually to the national economy. Moreover, these enterprises were now lauded for the record in reaching and assisting particularly deprived communities. Parallel moves were apparent in the wider European context. Faced with widespread retrenchment in state spending across the continent after 2008, the EU prioritised 'Social Innovation' as a key response, with a strong emphasis on promoting social enterprise as a key component.

Confusion over the value – and even the identity – of the non-state, 'non private profit/investor led' sector of the economy is thus nothing new. As shown, it partly stems from ideological doubts about the sector, and these are not confined to the neo-liberal right. Both revolutionary and gradualist state socialists have long regarded charities, co-operative, mutual and the voluntary sector as a whole as potentially problematic. Such organisations are frequently regarded as trespassing on roles which are seen as the primary duty and responsibility of the state, for which the state can be held democratically accountable. Another source of confusion is the sheer diversity of different types of non-mainstream enterprises which are not solely concerned with individual gain or under the control of the state. These include charities, voluntary organisations, a wide variety of co-operatives, mutuals and various kinds of socially oriented businesses with varying structures of ownership and governance. The net result has been the tendency to lump these organisations/enterprises under one or several disputed umbrella categories. A popular term which has emerged is 'The Third Sector', chosen to distinguish these organisations from the state and the private sector of the economy principally concerned with personal or corporate enrichment through profitable business activity. Thus, in 2006, the UK government established an 'Office for the Third Sector', and a Centre for Third Sector Research two years later (Ridley-Duff and Bull, 2011). Similar initiatives to promote third sector organisation provision of services which the state can no longer afford have been evident in other countries over the last decade. In Sweden, for example, increased financial pressures on state resources have prompted the sanctioning of 'second welfare' insurances policies for workers to 'top up' state benefits. Since 2007 this has prompted a startling shift of welfare employment from the state to private and third sector organisations, with public sector welfare employment contracting from 975,000 in 2007 to 938,000 in 2013; while private and co-operative employment in the sector has risen from 148,000 to 175,000 (Maino and Ferrera, 2014). In Germany, a small number of third sector organisations have become managing agents for key services – notably in the management of some schools in Hamburg (Maino and Ferrera, 2014). In France, a similar approach has stimulated a growing third sector, creating 500,000 jobs since 2006 (Maino and Ferrera, 2013).

It is perhaps indicative of a lack of consensus that the UK coalition government changed the name to 'Office for the Third Sector' from 'Office for Civil Society' in 2010 (Civil Society News, 2010). This is the term preferred by the UK National Council for Voluntary Organisations, who see it as a better description of the motives and direction of the sector, and its concern with promoting wider public good and engaging a broad mass of the population (NCVO annual report and accounts, 2013/14). But a baffling plethora of alternative terms are used – voluntary sector, 'not-for-profit sector' (frequently challenged as many organisations with a social purpose actively seek profit to sustain and expand their activities) or 'social enterprises', a term equally regarded as unsatisfactorily vague. It is important to reach beyond the debate about terminology and to identify the constituent parts of the sector, explaining the differences between them and charting their historical development. For this purpose, the chapter will address the development of charities/voluntary organisations, co-operatives and mutual and other forms of 'social enterprise' as sub-categories.

Charities, voluntary organisations and 'social enterprises'

Charitable organisations may be defined as ones whose major purpose is to provide assistance to those in need, such as the poor or the physically disabled. They were probably the earliest manifestations of this sector, and many are linked to the growth of major religious movements and institutions, including Judaism, Christianity, Hinduism, Buddhism and Islam. For example, from the early Middle Ages a range of charitable organisations sprang up under the auspices of the Catholic Church, including many religious orders such as the *Knights Hospitaller,* an order originally dedicated to the care of the sick, but which evolved into a military order. There were many instances of abbeys and churches providing relief for the poor from monies collected from parishioners for this purpose. Thus emerged the principle of charitable giving, especially by the wealthy, and the establishment of institutions to administer charitable relief. In Europe, charitable organisation was probably most advanced by the seventeenth century in the Netherlands, with an extraordinary concentration of local charities led by local dignitaries. The sheer efficiency and scale of charitable operations in the Dutch Republic has attracted substantial interest from historians (Van Voss and Van Leeuwen, 2010). The United States also enjoys its own well established tradition of charity and philanthropy, dating back to before the revolution, and historians have shown how here, as in Europe, the boundaries between public and private provisions for the needy were complex and interwoven. Historians have also noted the role of charity in the USA in opening new vistas for those disadvantaged for reasons of ethnicity and gender, helping to forge a new democratic political culture (Friedman and McGarvie, 2002). Recent work on worldwide charitable initiatives, including Meji Japan, Tukey, Sudan, Lebanon, imperial and early Republican China and the Islamic world in general, demonstrates that charities were indeed a global historical phenomenon (Brown and Pierce, 2013). In England, at the beginning of the seventeenth century, legislation was passed in the UK to regulate charities, in certain important ways that have continued to determine charity organisation. The Charitable Uses Act of 1601 defined charities as organisations with the primary purpose of advancing some aspect of public good or community benefit, such as education, promotion of religion or the relief of poverty. From this developed certain central concepts which have shaped charities down to and including 2006; especially the role of key actors in the operation of the organisation. The governance body in a charity is the Board of Trustees, individuals who determine the policy and direction of the charity without benefitting personally from the role in any way. If the charity's work is quite extensive, it will also have employees who carry out the work of the charity, and a guiding principle has always been that employees are barred from trusteeship in the charity to avoid a conflict of interest. A third key group are those who benefit from the work of the charity, and while historically they were barred from trusteeship on grounds of conflicting interest, recent legislative changes now permit this in cases where conflicted interests are openly avoided.

Charities, of course, may or may not operate as businesses. At its simplest, a charity's role may only involve the collection and disbursement of funds, and it may not operate as a revenue earning or generating concern. But many do, in effect, trade for a profit as a way of covering costs and of generating funds which can then be used for charitable purposes. A classic example of a trading charity is Oxfam, founded in 1942 to relieve hunger in war-torn Europe, and evolving into a global relief charity by the end of the decade (History of Oxfam, 2015). It opened its first Oxfam shop in 1948, and today is designated as a not-for-profit limited liability company. It combines fundraising and revenue-generating business to pay for a global operation employing over 5,000 people, with £89 million of its total income of £389.1 million in 2013/14 coming from its trading activities (Oxfam Annual Report and Accounts, 2013/14). For such commercially oriented charities, there are now a variety of legal models under UK law. These include Companies limited by shares or guarantee, Community Interest Companies or Charitable Incorporated Organisations. Which is chosen generally reflects the specific circumstances of the charity involved, and its business model. Of these the least preferred option tends to be company limited by shares, which, though having the advantages of being able to raise equity finance, are rarely eligible for either grants or charitable status. But companies limited by guarantee are frequently preferred by charities, as they are able to secure grants and charitable status. More recently, charities have had the option to become Community Interest Companies by shares or guarantee, the principal advantage of which is a lock on the assets of the Company which prevent their transfer into uses which are not for the good of the community (an 'asset lock'). Another relatively recent option is that of Charitable Incorporated Organisation (CIO). Since the Charities Act of 2011, charities have had the option of applying to the Charity Commission for this status, with the advantage of fewer administrative burdens than having to also register as a Company with Companies House (Guardian, 21 January 2013).

These new forms of legal status have helped stimulate a wide range of new business organisations with a social mission. They have been given the generic name of 'social enterprises', signifying organisations which trade and seek to make a profit, but with the express purpose of using that profit to improve or extend the provision of social benefit, which is the *raison d'être* of the organisation, rather than the enrichment of enterprise's owners. The benefits to society may vary, but the essential model of a business organisation trading for profits ear-marked for improving the social benefits offered by that organisation is the commonly accepted definition of social enterprise (Why Social Enterprise? 2012). The financial crisis of

2008 and its aftermath gave an additional boost to the social enterprise sector, especially in the wake of the public expenditure cuts implemented by the Coalition government between 2010 and 2015. A policy of contracting services out created new opportunities for social enterprises, while the Public Sector (Social Value) Act of 2012, required local authorities and other public bodies to consider the social impact of their service commissioning policies, rather than just price – a provision which promises to expand opportunities for social enterprises. To facilitate the growth of the social enterprise sector, a range of new funding bodies – some government financed – have been created, including Big Society Capital and Key Fund. In addition, there has been a flourishing of a variety of 'umbrella organisations' to help support social enterprise expansion, such as Social Enterprise UK, as part of a much wider initiative to promote this new sector. Charities increasingly have been tempted down the social enterprise route, as state and other sources of grant funding have dried up (Why Social Enterprise? 2012). Growth in the sector has been significant, and by the end of 2012, it was estimated that there were some 68,000 social enterprises contributing £24 billion to the British economy (Why Social Enterprise? 2012). As shown above, growth since then has been considerable. There is an especially strong interest in the potential for this model to reach out to the poorest communities in Britain and other societies – not only to alleviate poverty and inequality, but also to secure more active engagement in civil society within increasingly isolated communities. For all of these reasons, social enterprises, including the many charitable organisations which have gone down this route, are seen as an essential component in a modern business environment, offering the possibility of greater dissemination of wealth, more creative wealth creation able to overcome lack of capital as a barrier to entrepreneurial aspirations, greater social and political engagement by alienated communities and, consequently, greater social stability within which capitalism as a system can thrive. Certainly it is clear that the shareholder-led 'one-size fits all' model of business organisation which so dominated economic and political thinking in the 1980s, has now made space for social enterprises and other charitably driven business models. Of course such types of enterprise are not new; and perhaps one of the most historically significant categories of enterprise which has frequently centre-staged their social mission has been the co-operatives and mutuals.

Co-operatives and mutuals

Co-operatives and mutual businesses share one important common organisational feature: they are both democratic membership organisations which operate on the basis of one member on vote (House of Commons Communities and Local Government Committee, 2012). These notions of membership and member democracy distinguish them from many social enterprises, which are not necessarily run on the basis of member democracy. A key difference between the two is that since 1995 most co-operatives subscribe to an internationally defined statement of values and identity, which define a co-operative as:

> "an autonomous association of persons united voluntarily to meet their common economic, social, and cultural needs and aspirations through a jointly-owned and democratically-controlled enterprise" (Co-operative identity, values and principles, 2012).

In practice this subscribes to the notion not only of open membership, but also to wider social goals as well as economic objectives. Historically, co-operatives have tended to be more emphatically identified with wider values of social solidarity and a commitment to wider social ends than just the interests of its members than mutuals – central and dominant though these tend to be in the case of many co-operatives. Mutuals have, however, played an important role globally – especially in such fields as financial self-help, insurance and securing mortgage finance for homes.

Mutuals: friendly societies and building societies

Friendly societies in Britain emerged during the industrial revolution, when the state providing few benefits or support for the poor. While friendly societies subsequently became an international phenomenon, they seem initially to have been a product of the social insecurities generated by industrialisation in Britain. By joining and paying a subscription fee, members of a friendly society would be able to secure benefits such as sick pay during ill health, funds to pay for doctors or even a pension. As late as the 1940s, there were approximately 14 million members of Friendly Societies in Britain, though since the emergence of the modern welfare state these numbers dropped dramatically. By 2013 there were approximately still 2090 Friendly Societies operating in Britain (Friendly Societies, 2015). An example of one of the oldest and most successful is the Foresters Friendly Society, formed in 1834, and still offering financial investment packages and advice to its members in 2015 (Foresters Friendly Society, 2015). A similar example is the Shepherds Friendly Society formed in 1826, and also still offering range of financial services to its members (Shepherds Friendly Society, 2015).

Even more significant, however, were the Building Societies, which emerged in the eighteenth century. These were societies which arranged loans for members to buy their own houses. The first recorded building society was Richard Ketley's Society which was established in Birmingham in 1775. By 1825, there were over 250 building societies in existence across Britain; such was the demand for their services (History of Building Societies, 2015). But these were on the whole, limited and temporary organisations, formed to meet the needs of a fixed group of members, and only receiving funds from members who expressly wished to borrow from the society. But from the mid-1840s permanent building societies, which accepted deposits from non-home buyers also emerged. The first such society was the Metropolitan Equitable, but by 1860 there were at least 2,750 building societies nationally. The societies remained a crucial part of the housing and financial markets, playing an especially important role in the substantial expansion of home ownership in the 1950s to 1990s period. But a major financial reform was introduced in the Building Societies Act of 1986, which amongst other things made it easier for building societies to change their status by vote of their members, to become banks or PLCs. It facilitated a phenomenon which became known as demutualization, in which they were converted into mainstream banks. The numbers opting for this gathered pace in the late 1990s, as major societies such as the Cheltenham and Gloucester, Halifax, Bradford and Bingley and Northern Rock all opted to become PLC banks. Only a relatively small number, including Britannia and the Nationwide, chose to retain their building society status. Significantly, most of these converted building societies did not retail their independent identities, many being taken over by larger banks in subsequent years. Some, like Northern Rock, found themselves at the centre of the highly speculative investment practices which led to the great financial crash in 2008. As a result, many observers have been quite critical of demutualization, arguing that it contributed to a near financial 'monoculture' in which similar investor-led financial institutions tended to make the same errors of imprudent investment. It has been pointed out that some of this behaviour also crept into the remaining building societies, which felt that they had to engage in riskier activity in order to deliver more attractive member rewards in an effort to stave off possible moves by the latter towards PLC status. The Kelly Review into the near failure of the Co-operative Bank noted for example the high risk nature of much of Britannia's loan book, when the former merged with it in 2009 (Kelly Report, 2014). Regardless of what became an international trend in demutualization, many observers are now quite concerned about how many of these have played out. Increasingly the benefits of diversity in the financial market place are receiving supportive press from academics and politicians – irrespective of major embarrassments such as the Co-operative Bank crisis of 2013 (Battilani and Schröter, 2012).

Consumer co-operatives in Britain and elsewhere

The history of this sector is intertwined with the growth and development of economies in the modern period, especially in the wake of industrialisation. Britain is widely accepted to have seen the earliest development of co-operatives in their modern forms, though collective enterprise was not, of course, a uniquely British phenomenon. Co-operation in Britain is frequently associated with the Rochdale Pioneers, who founded a celebrated consumer co-operative in 1844. This is because the model they devised proved to be spectacularly successful. By 1900 there were over 1200 local consumer co-operatives across Britain based on the 'Rochdale model', with millions of members. But before exploring this phenomenon, a wider examination of the development of co-operation and mutualism is necessary, as earlier experiments and failures shaped the strategies of the Rochdale model and contributed to its success.

Economic and social change in Britain during the eighteenth and nineteenth centuries prompted a range of self-help and co-operative initiatives. Large numbers of people were ejected from the land by new forms of agricultural organisation (enclosures), swelling the population of rapidly growing towns and cities and providing workers for new industries. Social relations changed dramatically, with a breakdown of traditional ties and obligations between social groups. Thompson described the disintegration of the 'Moral Economy' of urban and rural life (Thompson, 1971). The social contract, by which the lower ranks of society gave their obedience to their social 'betters' in exchange for paternalistic attention to their welfare, broke down under the onslaught of new market-driven economic and social relationships. The growing incidence of bread riots resulted from the refusal of grocers, millers and the authorities to enforce price limits which had been formerly enforced by tradition and custom. Randall argues that the violent resistance offered by working people throughout the eighteenth century stemmed from this breakdown of social relations (Randall, 1991, 2006). The formation of co-operatives in the early nineteenth century was part of this wider collective response by the poor and dispossessed to agricultural and industrial change, urbanization and the emerging hegemony of the market. Bamfield shows mutual self-help organizations had been emerging before the early nineteenth century, in contrast to earlier assessments by Cole and Birchall (Bamfield, 1998; Birchall, 1994; Cole, 1944). He shows that they were both more widespread, and some were far more durable, than has been previously assumed. In particular, he shows that many were in response to the bread riots cited by Thompson. A variety of mutual societies emerged, engaged in milling, baking and retailing bread – some 38 in areas where food rioting had been a major problem in the period (Birchall, 1994). A key factor in the emergence of these and early co-operatives was a strong sense of communal solidarity – frequently based on common employment; especially in new industries such as mining, railway employment and cotton, where trade union organisation and militancy were also strongly evident (Purvis, 1990; Walton, 1996).

Snell shows that another factor in the rise of co-operatives and mutuals was a response to the loss of village ties by urbanising rural workers, desperate to forge new support networks (Snell, 2012). This partly explains why the 'communitarian' ideas of co-operation publicised by leaders such as Robert Owen and Dr William King, were so attractive. Owen (1771–1858) was a cotton mill manager in Manchester and later in Scotland, where he created the New Lanark experiment which came to be seen as one of the earliest experiments in co-operation. He became a prominent socialist leader and was involved in a number of attempts to create co-operative communities in Britain and the USA–none of them lasting long. Dr William King (1786–1865) was a physician who became interested in co-operation in the late 1820s, and established the *Co-operator*, a journal which promoted co-operation in the 1830s. These 'co-operative intellectuals' regarded co-operative businesses as a means of funding self-sufficient 'co-operative communities' (Birchall, 1994). They wanted to acquire land upon which these co-operative communities would become self-sufficient, an aim which appealed to those who had recently lost ties with their rural homes. Co-operatives and mutuals were also, of course, a highly practical response to the day to day but serious difficulties posed by life in a time of rapid change. Food supplies to the towns and cities were uncertain and unregulated in terms of safety and quality; indeed, there was a lag between urban growth and the provision of adequate food retailing, allowing a wide range of nefarious retailing practices (Blackman, 1963, 1967). There was ample scope for unscrupulous traders to defraud consumers in price and quality (Scola, 1992). Such was the wider context which eventually gave birth to the Rochdale Pioneers in 1844. As mentioned, there was also a strong middle class intellectual movement, horrified by the hardships and squalor of unfettered industrialisation, which saw co-operation as the route to a more humane and ordered society. In addition to Owen and King were Christian Socialists such as John M. F. Ludlow, Frederick D. Maurice, Charles Kingsley, Thomas Hughes and Edward Vansittart Neale who were appalled by what they saw as the anti-Christian amorality of capitalist industrial society. They were instrumental in promoting the establishment of worker co-operatives in the 1850s, but principally in facilitating legal changes in that decade which placed co-operatives on a sounder legal footing (Bonner, 1961).

But there is no doubt that the Rochdale Pioneers consumer co-operative represented a sea-change in the fortunes of co-operatives, the vast majority of which up till 1844 had failed, usually within a few years of their creation. The reason for its success was the organisational structures and principles enshrined in its rules – often referred to as the 'Rochdale model'. Central to the model was democracy based on one member one vote, regardless of the number of shares held in the co-operative. Officers and managers were elected on the basis and held accountable to the membership at regular general meetings of the membership. A second key principle, open membership, admitted all who could pay the membership subscription, irrespective of creed or gender. This facilitated a large critical mass of members and overcame limited capital resources. This openness was underpinned by a third principle of political and religious neutrality, designed to removal ideological obstacles to membership. The fourth principle, that only fixed and limited interest would be paid on share and loan capital, sought to balance the need to reward investors, whilst also maximising the funds available for reinvestment in the business. But probably the most important principle was the distribution of surplus on purchase. The more a member bought from the co-operative store, the more he or she received in dividend – a compelling incentive to shop exclusively at the Co-op store. Dividends could be accumulated in the society as savings, an important facility for working class people unwelcome in contemporary banks. But the Rochdale model, at least in its initial manifestation, shunned trade on credit on the grounds that this rendered the society vulnerable to bad debts, and encouraged shiftlessness among working class members and consumers. Added to this, a commitment to sell unadulterated goods cemented faith in the co-operative stores, while the principle to support education of members provided members with a route to self-improvement and economic betterment at a time when there was no state provision of education. The principles proved successful at building membership and retaining their loyalty. They were also easily replicated in other locations, and this in part accounts for the flourishing of consumer co-operation in Britain over the next 100 years. Consumer co-operatives proved not only financially rewarding to members, but also became the focus of many working class communities, as they became not only hubs of economic activity, but also social recreation and cultural entertainment (Gurney, 1996; Robertson, 2010).

Nor was consumer co-operation solely a British phenomenon. In fact, it spurred imitators all over Europe. In Sweden consumer co-operative sprang up in the late nineteenth century, in an environment where a scattered and sparse population often faced difficulties in accessing provisions and other day to day essentials. In this context, consumer co-operative societies flourished rapidly, and by the early 1900s it had its own leadership and wholesaling organisation, the *Kooperativa Förbundet* (KF) (Friberg, 2005; Friberg, Vorberg-Rugh, Webster and Wilson, 2012). Indeed, across the Scandinavian countries consumer co-operation not only flourished, but actually fared rather better than in Britain and many other locations (Ekberg, 2008). Consumer co-operatives also flourished in Italy, Germany, and Austria and across Europe generally, as well as emerging in other parts of the world, especially in the British Empire (Zamagni, 2012).

Until the period after the Second World War, British consumer co-operation remained in rude health, expanding its operations, the number of societies and membership. In 1863 many societies came together to form the Co-operative Wholesale Society (CWS), a secondary co-operative the members of which were the hundreds of co-operative societies across England and Wales. A few years later a similar wholesale society was established in Scotland (SCWS). In both instances the injection of society capital in membership subscription created large and wealthy organisations, able to fund extensive commercial infrastructure and production facilities. An important stimulant to CWS growth and efficiency was the fact that co-operative societies were not compelled to source their supplies from the wholesales, an arrangement which forced the latter to be as efficient and competitive as possible. By 1900 both organisations owned factories, warehouses and infrastructure to supply the hundreds of co-operative society member societies across the country. CWS also owned its own shipping fleet, banking department (which evolved into the modern Co-operative Bank) and operated overseas branches as far afield as New York, Copenhagen, Hamburg and Sydney. It even came to own tea plantations in India. By the early 1950s co-operative societies commanded about 25% of the domestic British retail market; but thereafter the movement plunged into steep decline. This resulted from the geographical disintegration of working class communities during the period of post war high growth and reconstruction, declining engagement with collective entities such as co-operatives and the emergence of powerful retail PLCs such as Sainsbury's, Tesco's and others, with the capital and centralised control to adjust to the rapidly changing retail market place. In consequence, between the mid-950s and the late 1980s, the share of the retail market enjoyed by British consumer co-operatives shrank to less than 5%, in spite of major attempts at internal reform within the movement. CWS saw the numbers of co-operatives fall to about 200 by the mid-1980s due to mergers or absorption into CWS or CRS (Co-operative Retail Service), a sub department of CWS set up in the 1930s to assist co-operative societies in trouble. By the 1970s, the CRS had effectively achieved a substantial measure of independence from CWS and was becoming effectively a rival centre of authority and commercial power in the movement. Matters were compounded by the failure of the SCWS bank in the early 1970s, resulting in the merger of CWS and SCWS in 1973. By the end of the 1980s the future looked grim indeed.

But the 1990s saw the beginnings of major restructuring and revival in the movement. The recovery began in the wake of the financial crisis of the early 1990s, following the financial crisis of that period. Partly by building a reputation for 'ethical' banking, the co-operative bank emerged in the 1990s and early 2000s as the most profitable CWS operation, largely underpinning a wider recovery of the organisation during that period. The formation of the Co-operative Retail Trading Group (CRTG) in 1993, under which CWS purchased for, rather than sold to, co-operative societies, also contributed to the recovery. But it was the abortive attempt by the City *Lanica* consortium to take over CWS in 1997 which galvanised the movement to first resist this move and then to empower the CWS CEO, Graham Melmoth, to implement the most far reaching reforms in the structure of the movement in its history. It resulted (following the report of a special co-operative commission in 2001) in the creation of the Co-operative Group encompassing CRS, the Co-operative Insurance Society (CIS) and the Co-operative Bank, the fortunes of which seemed to go from strength to strength in the following decade. There were a flurry of mergers between some of the larger remaining regional retail societies and the Group, culminating in the merger with one of the biggest, United, in 2007. By 2010, only a score or so of societies existed which were independent of the Group. During that period, retail market shares modestly recovered (largely due to a policy of concentration on convenience stores), and ambitious plans were set in train to grow the organisation through mergers – on the retail wing by an effective takeover of Somerfields, and in banking by a merger with the Britannia Building Society, both in 2009 (Wilson, Webster and Vorberg-Rugh, 2013).

The revival was brought to an abrupt end by the near failure of the co-operative bank in 2013, stemming almost directly from inheritance of bad debts from the Britannia takeover and well catalogued failings of governance and management both within the bank and the Group more generally (Kelly, 2014; Myners, 2014). The fallout of the crisis was very severe indeed, as the group was forced to meet much of the bank's shortfall. The outcome was to effectively surrender control of the bank by the Group to creditors and a selloff of major businesses to fund the exorbitant cost the banks troubles have imposed upon it. While the more recent problems of the Co-operative Group are undoubtedly due to gross mismanagement, it is important to acknowledge that the longer term decline of British consumer co-operatives reflect wider social and commercial trends which have afflicted consumer co-operation elsewhere in Europe, which saw the complete failure of consumer co-operation in countries such as Austria, Germany and France (Krampfer, 2012). Similar problems such as declining membership and participation – effectively the atrophying of co-operative culture – also played a central role in consumer co-operative decline. Exceptions to this trend are to be found in Norway and Finland, partly due to skilful adaptation to a more competitive climate, and partly because private competition does not seem to have been as intense (Ekberg, 2009, 2012). There are also examples of more specialised forms of consumer co-operatives, where the market is unable to supply consumer with essential goods or services. A notable example is to be found in the USA, where remote rural communities have struggled to secure electricity supplies, and formed their own co-operatives to meet the need. Many of these flowered during the 1930s, and in 2012 there were 900 such co-operatives operating across the USA under the auspices of the National Rural Electrification Co-operative Association (NRECA), an umbrella organisation for the industry. Accounting for 12% of electricity sales in the USA, these co-operatives supply 42 million people in 47 states (NRECA, 2015). But notwithstanding impressive success stories such as this, consumer co-operation certainly faces a tougher future in the developed world than was the case in its early twentieth century heyday.

Worker and producer co-operatives

A second tradition in co-operation is co-operatives established by those who work for the business – either by taking over an existing business or by setting up their own. Such co-operatives certainly emerged in Britain from the middle of the nineteenth century, particularly encouraged by such Christian Socialist organisations as the Society for Promoting Working Men's Association, which sought to help working men establish their own worker co-operatives (Cole, 1944). There were indeed numerous worker co-operatives established in Britain in the nineteenth century, notably in textiles, mining and engineering. But compared to the pattern of consumer co-operative growth, worker co-operatives made relatively modest progress. There were success stories. The Hebden Bridge Fustian Manufacturing Society, established in 1870, successfully operated its own mill until it was sold to CWS in 1918. But this was only possible because of the willingness of consumer co-operative societies to invest in it, taking a share of the profits in the process (Hebden Bridge Fustian Manufacturing Society, 2014). Recent research suggests that co-operatives in the textile industry on the whole fared well in terms of efficiency compared to their private competitors; though few survived for long (Toms, 2012). The consumer movement's attitude towards worker and producer co-operatives was initially quite sympathetic, with the CWS seeking to become a major purchaser of producer/worker co-operative output. But many of these co-operatives (especially in mining) ran into serious trouble in the 1870s, with the CWS being forced to take a number of them over. The result was a series of catastrophic losses on these businesses in the early 1880s, which left a legacy of hostility and doubt within the consumer movement towards worker co-operatives (Wilson, Webster and Vorberg-Rugh, 2013). This undoubtedly contributed to the relatively limited development of worker co-operation in Britain during this period.

But worker co-operatives fared better elsewhere in Europe, notably in Italy, Spain and France, where numbers of worker co-operatives run into the thousands. Confirming Toms' findings, recent research into these continental variants suggests that in terms of efficiency and productivity, these co-operatives compare well with the private sector, and often in the face of legal disadvantages (Perotin, 2012). Perhaps the most celebrated of these worker co-operatives is the mighty Mondragón Group of the Spanish Basque Country, which consists of a range of mutually supporting worker and other co-operatives which dominate the economic life of the region. Astonishingly, this grew out of the superficially least promising period of Spanish history, under Franco's dictatorship, which generally reacted to autonomous workers' initiatives with savage repression. What protected Mondragón were the patronage of the Roman Catholic Church and the inspirational leadership of its founding father, the priest José Mariá Arizmendiarrieta, who remained a force within the movement until his death in 1976 (Molina and Walton, 2011). The worker co-operative model has not only attracted blue collar or industrial workers. It has been a preferred model for some white collar professionals, especially architects and town planners. One of the most successful such co-operatives has been the Co-operative of Architects and Engineers in Reggio Emilia (CAIRE) founded in 1952, which has maintained a significant presence in the world of architecture and urban planning in this region of Italy ever since (CAIRE, 2015; Maccaferri, 2011).

The term 'producer co-operative' is also employed in respect of co-operatives created not by employees, but by businesses which collaborate in order to overcome common obstacles. Among the most common of these globally are agricultural co-operatives, whose members are farmers, who combine to access services which otherwise would not be available, such as marketing infrastructure and organisation. Some of the most long-standing of these are found in the USA. For example, Sun Maid USA is a raisin producer's marketing co-operative, which processes and sells raisins. Established originally in 1912, in 2012 Sun Maid processed 200,000 tons of raisins per year, or one third of the raisins in the USA, yielding revenues of $360 million. It is the largest processor of dried fruit in the world, supplying some 60 countries (Sun Maid, 2015). In Britain, a good example of a similar farmer co-operative is Anglia Farmers, formed in 2003 in Norfolk. Its main activity is in the purchase of equipment on behalf of its 3,500 members who farm over a million hectares (Anglia Farmers, 2015). With a buying power of £250 million, the co-operative buys about a tenth of total UK farming input purchases. In the USA, some of these large agricultural co-operatives have become increasingly sophisticated, as capital demands for modernising operation have grown more challenging. Some have adopted elements of ordinary shareholding for some participants, with mainstream shareholder rights, alongside traditional co-operative membership. These hybridised 'new generation co-operatives' have become the subject of much study, especially in respect of the extent to which co-operative values and practices are diluted as a result (Chaddad and Cook, 2012).

Credit unions

In parallel with the development of 'Rochdale model' consumer co-operation in Britain and elsewhere, mainland Europe saw the development of a different co-operative form designed to address the capital shortages of small scale businesses in both rural and urban contexts. During the nineteenth century this tradition emerged in the 1860s in Germany through the ideas of Friedrich Raiffeissen, the leader of the rural credit union movement. At the same time Hermann Schulze-Delitzsch established a parallel credit union movement to handicraft workers and artisans. Both movements stressed self-help in securing funding for the co-operative. These credit unions were member organisations in which funds were pooled in order to lend to members, enabling them to acquire essential capital equipment, or to tide over difficult periods when cash flow was tight while income for sales was awaited. The credit union movement became international, and indeed the British Empire deliberately promoted credit unions in India, Burma and other less developed colonies in an effort to alleviate the worst forms of hardship (Rhodes, 2012; Webster, 2013). Credit Unions remain central in helping poorer members of the community across both the developed and less developed world. Perhaps the best example is the Canadian co-operative group *Desjardins*, which is composed of 481 caisses (credit unions) representing 5.6 million members and clients, with assets of $200 billion (Desjardins, 2015). The social benefits are represented not just by the loans to members and businesses, but by the large sums given to social and community projects ($81 billion in 2011). In Britain in recent years, credit unions have been championed by many social commentators a preferable alternative to pay-day lenders whose practices have at times been called into question.

Conclusion

Whereas in the 1980s a neo-liberal consensus among economists tended to assume that the development of business structures was converging on models which approximated to the investor-led, shareholder-value dominated PLC, there is now a tendency to see the virtues and resilience of a variety of ownership and organisational models which allow space for businesses which cherish a wider range of objectives than the interests of individual and corporate shareholders. Of course in a turbulent economic environment, it remains to be seen if this new consensus lasts longer than previous ones.

In terms of academic work on the Third Sector, there are a number of quite glaring areas for further research. First of all, the global burgeoning of the new social enterprise sector has outstripped research into the enormous variety of forms, organisational types and economic sectors. Given the centre-stage shift of the sector into public sector service delivery, there is an urgent need to assess what works and what does not. The same point applies to the charity sector, which is increasingly seen in many states as an important co-deliverer with the public sector of key social services.

Second, the performance and growth potential of social enterprises, charities and co-operatives cannot be ascertained in a vacuum – they have to contend with a wide variety of economic, political and institutional contexts not all of which are supportive of the 'Third Sector'. Again, given the growing importance of the Third Sector for the state, not only in delivering services, but in participating in policies of regional regeneration and the alleviation of deprivation, this is a field of research which badly needs to be developed. What kind of local, state and civil society institutions and frameworks are required for the Third Sector to flourish and play its full role in economic and social policies? A case in point is the increasingly important role the state expects the sector to play in contracting to deliver services previously provided by public sector bodies. In Britain the Social Value Act of 2012 encourages the public sector to have an eye on wider social benefits when contracting out services, a piece of legislation which is widely seen as being potentially beneficial for the Third Sector. But already it is clear that public sector organisations have bidding processes which tend to favour larger and well established organisations rather than smaller and embryonic ones. This is hardly conducive to developing a flourishing Third Sector in which dynamic and fast growing organisations are able to galvanise the sector and stimulate growth. What kind of institutional adjustments andarrangements are needed in order to nurture a dynamic Third Sector able to deliver what is increasingly expected of it?

A third – and very old-question for the sector, which is related to the last point is funding for start-up, innovation and the scaling up of operations. It is true that some state financial provision has exists for this, notably in Britain under the 'Big society' initiative. There is also a plethora of bodies with funds to lend or give grants to Third Sector organisations. But quantity of funding remains a problem for many, as well as the short term nature of many grants. Small and emergent social enterprises and Third Sector organisations frequently face a bewildering array of alternatives – many of which do not offer 'best fit' for the organisation's needs. The topic for more research is therefore how best to provide financial support for the sector and to encourage a culture of investment and responsible business management. Are there successful models at work, what are they and how might they be adapted to a range of circumstances?

Finally, the co-operative sector merits a special comment. The decline and revival of co-operation in the last 50 years or so has been described, and certainly there remains massive scope for research into why and how some models of co-operation have thrived while others have withered. Again this research has to focus as much upon institutional, cultural and social factors as upon the organisation of the co-operatives themselves. But with its traditions of participation and member democracy, the co-operative movement's shifting fortunes and the reasons for this, merit further investigation for other reasons. As Western societies experience declining levels of social and political engagement among their citizens, and problems of inequality escalate, the need for new strategies to spread wealth, to democratically energise populations and revitalise civil society become ever more pressing. Co-operative enterprises have always sought to reconcile the demands of wealth creation with the principles of widening democratic participation and the promotion of greater equality. Much new research needs to focus upon how co-operative cultures and behaviours can be fostered and nurtured, and examples of success can inform much of modern practice here. The task is pressing, if the twenty first century is to become one which will be remembered for thriving democracy, shared values and prosperity for all.

References

Anglia Farmers (2015). www.angliafarmers.co.uk, accessed April 2015.

Bamfield, J. (1998) "Consumer-owned flour and bread societies in the eighteenth and early nineteenth centuries" *Business History, 40*(4), 16–36.

Battilani, P. & Schröter, H. G. (2012). "Demutualization and its problems" in Battilani, P. & Schröter, H. G. (eds), *The Co-operative Business Movement, 1950 to the present.* Cambridge, Cambridge University Press, 150–174.

Birchall, J. (1994). *Co-op: The People's Business,* Manchester, Manchester University Press, 4–5; 20–21.

Blackman, J. (1963). "The Food Supply of an Industrial Town: A Study of Sheffield's Public Markets 1780–1900" *Business History, 5*(2), 83–97; 94.

Blackman, J. (1967). "The Development of the Retail Grocery Trade in the Nineteenth Century" *Business History, 9*(2), 110–117; 111.

Bonner, A. (1961). *British Co-operation,* Manchester, Co-operative Union, 66–67.

Brown, R. A. & Pierce, J. (eds.) (2013). *Charities in the Non-Western World: The Development and Regulation of Indigenous and Islamic Charities,* New York, Routledge.

CAIRE (2015). http://www.cairepro.it/en/, accessed April 2015.

Chaddad, F. & Cook, M. L. (2012). "Legal frameworks and property rights in US agricultural co-operatives: the hybridization of co-operative structures" in Battilani, P. & Schröter, H. G. (eds), *The Co-operative Business Movement, 1950 to the present.* Cambridge, Cambridge University Press. 175–194.

Cole, G. D. H. (1944). *A Century of Co-operation.* Manchester; Co-operative Union, 13–16.

Co-operative identity, values and principles (2012). *International Co-operative Alliance,* 2012, http://2012.coop/en/whatco-op/co-operative-identity-values-principles accessed April 2015.

Civil Society News (2010). http://www.civilsociety.co.uk/governance/news/content/6618/office_for_civil_society_to_replace_office_for_the_third_sector, accessed April 2015.

Desjardins (2015). www.desjardins.com/en/a_propos accessed April 2015.

Ekberg, E. (2008). *Consumer Co-operatives and the Transformation of Modern Food Retailing: A comparative study of the Norwegian and British consumer co-operatives.* Oslo, Acta Humaniora.

Ekberg, E. (2009). "Consumer co-operation and the transformation of modern food retailing: the British and Norwegian consumer co-operative movement in comparison, 1950–2002" in Black, L. & Robertson, N. (eds.), *Consumerism and the Co-operative Movement in Modern British History.* Manchester, Manchester University Press, 51–68.

Ekberg, E. "Organization: Top Down or Bottom Up? The organizational development of consumer co-operatives" in Battilani, P. & Schröter H. G. (eds.), *The Co-operative Business Movement, 1950 to the Present.* Cambridge, Cambridge University Press, 222–242.

Foresters Friendly Society (2015). http://www.forestersfriendlysociety.co.uk/about-us/why-foresters/, accessed April 2015.

Friberg, K. (2005). *The Workings of Co-operation: A Comparative Study of Consumer Co-operative Organisation in Britain and Sweden 1860–1970.* Växjö, Växjö University Press.

Friberg, K., Vorberg-Rugh, R., Webster, A. & Wilson, J. F. (2012). "The Politics of Commercial Dynamics: Co-operative Adaptations to Post-war Consumerism in the United Kingdom, and Sweden" in Battilani, P. & Schröter H. G. (eds.), *The Co-operative Business Movement, 1950 to the Present.* Cambridge, Cambridge University Press, 243–262.

Friedman, L. J. & McGarvie, M. D. (eds.) (2002). *Charity, Philanthropy and Civility in American History.* Cambridge, Cambridge University Press, especially. Friedman, L. J. "Philanthropy in America: Historicism and its Discontents" 1–22.

Friendly Societies (2015). http://www.friendlysocieties.co.uk/history.htm accessed April 2015.

Guardian 21 January 2013.

Gurney, P. (1996). *Co-operative Culture and the Politics of Consumption in England, 1870–1930.* Manchester, Manchester University Press.

Hebden Bridge Fustian Manufacturing Society (2014). http://www.archive.coop/hive/the-workers-who-ran-their-own-mill accessed April 2015.

History of Building Societies (2015). https://www.bsa.org.uk/information/consumer-factsheets/general/the-history-of-building-societies accessed April 2015.

History of Oxfam (2015). http://www.oxfam.org.uk/what-we-do/about-us/history-of-oxfam accessed April 2015.

House of Commons Communities and Local Government Committee (2012). *Mutual and cooperative approaches to delivering local services.* Fifth Report of Session 2012–13, 21 November 2012, 7.

Kalmi, P. (2007) "The Disappearance of Co-operatives from Economics Textbooks" *Cambridge Journal of Economics, 31*(4), 625–647.

Kelly Report (2014). Sir Chris Kelly, 'Failings in Management and Governance: Report of the Independent Review into the events leading to the Co-operative Bank's capital shortfall" (30 April 2014) http://www.co-operative.coop/PageFiles/989442031/kelly-review.pdf accessed April 2015.

Krampfer, P. (2012). "Why Co-operatives Fail: Case Studies from Europe, Japan and the United States, 1950–2010" in Battilani, P. & Schröter, H. G. (eds.), *The Co-operative Business Movement, 1950 to the Present.* Cambridge, Cambridge University Press, 126–149; especially 132–137.

Maccaferri, M. (2011). "'A co-operative of intellectuals': the encounter between co-operative values and urban planning. An Italian case study" in Webster, A., Shaw, L., Walton, J. K., Brown A. & Stewart, D. (eds.), *The Hidden Alternative: Co-operative Values, Past, Present and Future,* Manchester, Manchester University Press, 251–265.

Maino, F. & Ferrera, M. (eds.), "First Report on Second Welfare in Italy" (November 2013) 13–15 at http://secondowelfare.it/edt/file/FIRST_REPORT_ON_SECOND_WELFARE_IN_ITALY_EXTRACT.pdf. accessed April 2015.

Maino, F. & Ferrera, M. (eds.) (2014). "Social Innovation beyond the state: Italy's secondo welfare in a European perspective" (2014) 11 http://secondowelfare.it/allegati/ferrera_maino_wp2_2014_2wel.pdf accessed April 2015.

Molina, F. & Walton, J. K. (2011). "An alternative co-operative tradition: the Basque co-operatives of Mondragón" in Webster, A., Shaw, L., Walton, J.K., Brown A. & Stewart, D. (eds.), *The Hidden Alternative: Co-operative Values, Past, Present and Future.* Manchester, Manchester University Press, 226–250.

Myners, P. (Lord) (2014). "The Co-operative Group: report of the independent governance review" (7 May 2014) at: http://www.co-operative.coop/Corporate/PDFs/Myners/Report_of_the_Independent_Governance_Review.pdf accessed April 2015.

National Rural Electrification Co-operative Association (NRECA) (2015). www.nreca.coop & www.nreca.coop/programs/CRN/ accessed April 2015.

NCVO annual report and accounts (2013/14). https://www.ncvo.org.uk/images/documents/about_us/annual-reports/ncvo-annual-report-2013-2014.pdf accessed April 2015.

Oxfam Annual Report and Accounts (2013/14). http://www.oxfam.org.uk/~/media/Files/OGB/What%20we%20do/About%20us/Plans%20reports%20and%20policies/6182_Oxfam_ARA_web_final.ashx accessed April 2015 accessed April 2015.

Perotin, V. (2012). "The performance of workers' co-operatives" Battilani, P. & Schröter, H. G. (eds.), *The Co-operative Business Movement, 1950 to the Present.* Cambridge, Cambridge University Press, 195–221.

Purvis, M. (1990). "The Development of Co-operative Retailing in England and Wales, 1851–1901: A Geographical Study" *Journal of Historical Geography, 16*(3), 314–331.

Randall, A. (1991). *Before the Luddites: Custom, Community and Machinery in the English Woollen Industry, 1776–1809.* Cambridge, Cambridge University Press.

Randall, A. (2006). *Riotous Assemblies: Popular Protest in Hanoverian England.* Oxford, Oxford University Press.

Rhodes, R. (2012). *Empire and Co-operation: How the British Empire Used Co-operatives in Its Development Strategies 1900–1970.* London, John Donald Short Run Press.

Ridley-Duff, R. & Bull, M. (2011). *Understanding Social Enterprise: Theory and Practice.* London, Sage, 11.

Robertson, N. (2010) *The Co-operative Movement and Communities in Britain: Minding their own Business.* Farnham, Ashgate.

Scola, R. (1992) *Feeding the City: The Food Supply of Manchester 1770–1870.* Manchester, Manchester University Press.

Shepherds Friendly Society (2015). https://www.shepherdsfriendly.co.uk/ accessed April 2015.

Snell, K. D. M. (2012). "Belonging and Community: Understandings of 'Home' and 'Friends' among the English Poor, 1750–1850" *Economic History Review, 65*(1), 1–25.

'Social investment: Brief background note on UK government's approach' (2014). https://www.gov. uk/government/uploads/system/uploads/attachment_data/file/353044/CO_Social_investment_ background_one-pager_July_2014.pdf accessed April 2015.

Sun Maid (2015). www.sunmaid.com; http://www.agmrc.org/business_development/strategy_and_ analysis/analysis/sun-maid-growers-ofcalifornia/ accessed April 2015.

Thompson, E. P. (1971). "The Moral Economy of the English Crowd in the Eighteenth Century" *Past and Present, 50*(1), 76–136.

Toms, S. (2012). "Producer Co-Operatives and Economic Efficiency: Evidence from the Nineteenth Century Cotton Textile Industry" *Business History, 54*(6), 855–882.

Van Voss, L. H. & Van Leeuwen, H. D. (2010). "Charity in the Dutch Republic: An Introduction" in *Continuity and Change, 27*(2), 175–197.

Walton, J. K. (1996). "The Making of a Mass Movement: The Growth of Co-operative Membership in Lancashire 1870–1914" in Lancaster, B. & Maguire, P. *Towards the Co-operative Commonwealth: Essays in the History of Co-operation.* Manchester, Co-operative College and History Workshop Trust, 17–28.

Webster, A. (2013). "Co-operatives and The State In Burma/Myanmar 1900–2012: A Case Study of Failed Top-Down Co-Operative Development Models?" in Brown, R. A. & Pierce, J. (eds.), *Charities in the Non-Western World: The Development and Regulation of Indigenous and Islamic Charities.* New York, Routledge, 65–87.

Why Social Enterprise? A Guide for Charities (2012). Social Enterprise UK http://www.socialenterprise. org.uk/uploads/editor/files/Why_Social_Enterprise.pdf; pp. 5–6 accessed April 2015.

Wilson, J. F. Webster, A. & Vorberg-Rugh, R. (2013). *Building Co-operation: A Business History of the Co-operative Group, 1863–2013.* Oxford, Oxford University Press, 80.

Zamagni, V. (2012). "A World of Variations: Sectors and forms" in Battilani, P. & Schröter, H. G. (eds.), *The Co-operative Business Movement, 1950 to the Present.* Cambridge, Cambridge University Press, 63–82; esp. 71–74.

Part III
International varieties
of capitalism

10

African business history

Gareth Austin

Business history as a discipline has focussed on the firm, in the sense of an organization totally dedicated to business: unlike a household or individual, however economically active. Firms collectively have been dominant in the economies of North America and Western Europe for over two centuries, so it is no surprise that the study of business history originated and flourished there. In the historiography of Sub-Saharan Africa much has been written about the inputs, outputs, networks and culture of business, but much less about firms as such, especially individual firms: their strategies, structures, profitability and impacts. It would be easy to take this simply as proof that African business history is still a young field with much catching-up still to do. This is partly true. It is only forty years since A. G. Hopkins could report that business history had 'no following in African studies' (Hopkins, 1976a, p. 29), and there remain areas of neglect, though an aim of this essay is to illustrate the fact that much has been achieved by now (for the latest survey, see Verhoef, 2014).

But catching-up is only part of the story, because the lower profile of the firm in the historiography of African business also reflects historical reality: compared to the heartlands of the profession of business history, firms have been, and to a lesser extent still are, significantly less dominant in the history of extra-subsistence production and exchange south of the Sahara, especially outside the former settler colonies. A classic example of entrepreneurs transforming the productivity and production functions of African economies was the adoption of cocoa farming in late-nineteenth-century southern Ghana and south-west Nigeria. This required risk-taking and long-term investment, in an unfamiliar kind of capital good: a recently-introduced exotic tree which took several years to begin to yield. In Nigeria the introduction was the work of Creole merchants who had accumulated capital in the export-import trade (Hopkins, 1978). Their enterprises could perhaps be described as sole-owner firms, but those who followed their example, as cocoa-farming spread, were mostly relatively small-scale farmers whose economic enterprise, though often extending to the hiring of some labour, was not sharply distinguished from their family commitments. In Ghana, the cocoa take-off was the work of migrant cocoa farmers: Polly Hill described 'the migrant farmer as a "capitalist", whose primary concern has been the continued expansion of his business' (Hill, 1997, p. 3). Despite this orientation, one could question how far their enterprises were structurally organized as firms. In terms of transforming economic policies, again, the decisions of millions of unregistered sole traders remain potentially decisive. For instance, since the independence of most African countries around 1960, there has been a single continent-wide watershed in policy: the replacement of state-led development policies by market-oriented ones, which in most of Africa happened in the 1980s. While this is often attributed to pressure from the international financial institutions, in many countries what obliged governments to accept 'Structural Adjustment' was a fiscal crisis resulting from multitudes of small-scale producers and traders bypassing official markets in reaction against severe price controls (see, for example Azarya and Chazan, 1987).

Thus, another aim of this chapter is to make a case that business historians need to give more systematic attention to entrepreneurs whose businesses form only part – though a large and literally vital part – of their wider individual and household activities, without becoming formally or definitively specialized. Their response to Coase's (1937) fundamental question, why do firms exist, was not to form a firm; though in some cases the distinction is blurred, which itself reflects the less than dominant status of the firm in most African economies historically, and in some cases even up to the present. In Africa non-firm and quasi-firm businesses have been and remain a key part of the environment within which firms work, and studying them can offer insights into problems of general interest for business history, such as the transition (or not) from a less specialized business enterprise to a firm.

The discussion below is organized in four sections. The first focusses on non-firm businesses, the second on firms. Both will consider primary sources, the growth of the literature and highlight some of the themes that have emerged. The third section considers the evolution of business-government relations, always a fundamental issue, not least in Africa. The fourth is devoted to the crucial question of why business enterprises in Africa have often not become large enough to be restructured as firms, and why relatively few indigenous firms have tended to start small and grow big. In this context we will focus upon entry thresholds, asymmetric competition and the rarity of trans-generational survival of firms, in the changing settings of the last three centuries.

Business beyond the firm

For the post-independence period, and so far even for the colonial era, interviews have been the most important source for studies of African enterprises that are not firms in the sense of being separable from the other commitments of the individual or household. While surveys have been part of this, probably the most rewarding method for historical research is the in-depth interview, in which entrepreneurs – and employees (Van den Bersselaar, 2011a) – talk about their lives in business. Oral sources have been supplemented by a range of written ones including newspapers, private papers and photographs, government and academic reports and surveys, papers from government archives, civil court records and funeral notices. The further back the historian goes, the more oral testimonies (of the entrepreneurs themselves, or those who remember them) necessarily give way to reliance on written sources, where they exist. For the pre-colonial period these come mostly from European visitors, many of them merchants.

The study of African entrepreneurship in all its forms got a strong start from the atmosphere of decolonization that surrounded the beginnings of the continuous professional study of African history, across much of the continent in the late 1950s and early 1960s. A major theme was the uncovering of African agency in African history. This was epitomized in Hill's work on 'Ghanaian capitalist cocoa-farmers' and her 'plea for indigenous economics' (requiring qualitative field observation) (Hill, 1997 [1963], 1966, 1970). In East

Africa, it helped motivate research on the African side of the Indian Ocean trade of the pre-colonial era, underlining that the Swahili-speaking towns and trading culture of the coast were a joint African-Arab product, rather than essentially an import (this and other elements are blended in Sherrif, 1987, albeit by then overlaid by an infusion of Dependency theory).

One of the most influential formulations to emerge from the study of African business in the post-independence period was Abner Cohen's (1971) model of an ethnic trading diaspora. As an anthropologist, Cohen's particular example of what he defined as an 'ethnic group in dispersal' (Cohen, 1971, p. 267n) was Hausa merchants from northern Nigeria in the majority-Christian, Yoruba-speaking southwest of Nigeria. He argued that the diaspora served as a 'moral community', creating trust and ensuring that contracts were fulfilled (Cohen 1971, p. 267), more cheaply and reliably than through resort to an external judicial process.[1]

Cohen's idea had most impact among historians of precolonial Africa, notably Philip Curtin (1975), who highlighted the role of other Muslim trading diasporas, in this case in the long-distance trade of Senegambia, crossing political and ethnic boundaries and spanning hundreds of kilometres. Curtin (1984) went on to apply the concept on a global scale. Paul Lovejoy (1980, 1986) extended Curtin's approach with books of his own on two of the major precolonial long-distance trades of West Africa-especially northern Nigeria and its neighbours-in kola nuts and salt.[2] In a related article, Lovejoy (1973) also reinforced the historical plausibility of the interpretation of the trading diaspora as, precisely, a tool of commerce. Specifically, he documented how three different Hausa-speaking Muslim immigrant communities differentiated themselves from each other and from co-religionists and fellow Hausas in general, not only by endogamy but – at least in the case of the Kambarin Beriberi, which he studied in detail – also by cultivating a different tradition of origin and adopting distinctive face and body markings. Whatever the motive, such bonding and differentiation presumably strengthened commercial cooperation within the group.

Recent years have seen several major studies of the cultures of external trades before colonization, especially the slave trades from West and West-Central Africa, and across the Sahara. Ugo Nwokeji (2010) re-examined the major non-Muslim ethnic trading diaspora in West Africa, that of the Aro, today an Igbo sub-group, who dominated the trade in the hinterland of the Bight of Biafra: a geographically small region that was one of the largest suppliers of slaves to the Atlantic trade. Nwokeji combined Aro oral traditions with the quantitative record of slave embarkations available from European sources to develop a more detailed account of the chronology of Aro trade since the seventeenth century than is offered in the still very important earlier works (notably Dike, 1956; Northrup, 1978). In particular, he focussed upon cultural shifts and patterns associated with the establishment of the Aro trading diaspora, which contributed to shaping the content of the trade (for example, the gender distribution of the slaves sold to the European ship-captains). Toby Green (2012) went back to the early centuries of the Atlantic trade, going beyond the analysis of diasporas as such to highlight the formation of Afro-European 'cultural communities' which enabled the trade to operate on the huge scale that it eventually did. Roquinaldo Ferreira (2012) also examines cross-cultural exchange, this time in what became the Lusophone world of Angola and Brazil, adopting a more multi-biographical approach. Finally, there is the remarkable scholarship of Ghislaine Lydon, whose *On Trans-Saharan Trails* (2009) is an astonishingly comprehensive history of the trans-Saharan trade – not only in slaves, but in much else besides – in cultural, social and economic terms, with incisive discussions of the organization of trade and how the problems of contracting were tackled.

Another notion coined by an anthropologist in the early 1970s, one which has been even more influential than that of the ethnic trading diaspora, was Keith Hart's (1973) concept of the 'informal sector', which may be defined as comprising unregulated, untaxed, usually small-scale private enterprises, the majority of them not 'firms' in the strict sense. The term has framed a flow of new work ever since. The vitality in research reflects the vitality of the subject. The informal sector expanded further when parallel markets mushroomed in reaction to growing state regulations in the 1970s and early 1980s, sometimes offering opportunities for entrepreneurship and capital accumulation even amid such an extreme case of dysfunctional government as Mobutu's Zaire (MacGaffey, 1987). It continued to attract scholarly attention after economic liberalization, partly because of the question of how informal enterprise should be regarded: as a refuge from, or even a disguised form of, unemployment in the ever-more precarious labour markets of the last thirty years, or a source of innovation with the potential to transform the economy. A characteristic of the more complex and dynamic informal sectors is the tendency for industrial clusters to emerge, whether focussed on car parts in Suame, Kumasi (Ghana, from the 1970s), machine-making in Gikomba, Nairobi (where it spread during 1975–95), or shoe and garment manufacture in Aba (southeastern Nigeria), which expanded dramatically while formal-sector manufacturing shrank following economic liberalization in the later 1980s (respectively, Dawson, 1991; King, 1996, pp. 88–111; Meagher, 2010, pp. 56–61). While most of this work has been by economic anthropologists, the potential for historical studies, over several decades and spanning the colonial/independence divide, is illustrated by Rajiv Ball's work on small-scale industry in Ghana (Ball, 1997). From a business history perspective, the existing literature is full of insight and information, and should inspire studies of individual enterprises in detail over many years, as they sought not only to survive but to grow in the face of (usually) government neglect and highly unstable macroeconomic environments.

An important strand in the literature on (mostly) non-firm businesses has focussed on female entrepreneurs in the late precolonial and early colonial periods. For the nineteenth century, Toyin Falola (1991) documented Yoruba-speaking southwest Nigeria as a region within which the numerous trading caravans were 'usually dominated by women', in contrast to the very long-distance trade of Africa which, requiring months away from obligations to spouses and children, was a male domain (Falola, 1991, pp. 114–15, quote at p. 114). In terms of innovation and strategy, Colleen Kriger's study of women weavers in the Igbo town of Akwete, southeast Nigeria, shows them responding to the exogenous transition from the Atlantic slave trade to the export of palm oil by switching from a policy of competing with imports on price to competing with them on quality. To this end, they invented a new type of cloth, aimed at attracting the custom of newly enriched palm oil exporters. They also reduced labour costs, apparently through broader looms, and by specializing fully in weaving, while buying imported yarn instead of spinning their own. Weaving moved from a part-time, seasonal occupation of some women in Akwete to a full-time occupation of most women in the town (Kriger, 2006, pp. 49–51), making it likely that some of the businesses crossed the border from personal or family business to firm.

Finally in this section, it is worth reiterating that the categories of 'firm' and 'non-firm' business enterprises are not always easy to distinguish. The institution of the 'canoe house' in the eastern Niger Delta during the last few centuries of the precolonial era was simultaneously a trading, military and local government unit. Nimi Wariboko (1998) reviewed the historiography in the framework of transactions cost and internalization theory: why business people replace market exchange with hierarchy by internalizing transactions which would otherwise be made between independent buyers and sellers. Wariboko interpreted the canoe house as an institution that aimed at continuity of employment so as to overcome incentive problems which arose because individuals acquired skills that were not easily transferable without loss of value to both worker and employer, and because of difficulties in measuring individuals' productivity (see also Wariboko, 1997).

The firm in African history

Since the age of the chartered companies who conducted so much of the Atlantic slave trade (see, for instance Law, 1993), firms have been much more visible in government records and newspapers than smaller, less specialized enterprises. Big companies were also more likely to have the resources to generate and preserve their own papers, and to consider putting at least selections of them in the public domain. As with non-firm enterprises, for recent years companies can also be researched through interviews with their owners and employees, and the company may be both easier to find and better able to track down their retired staff. But these optimistic remarks require qualification, and not only because, like governments, firms tend to impose a lengthy moratorium before opening files to researchers. There are two specific problems in accessing papers of firms operating in Africa. One is political: firms with a colonial or, in the case of South Africa, apartheid-era background may be either nervous about opening their records to what they expect to be hostile investigation, or may conceivably try to anticipate this risk by exposing just a carefully selected part of their files, designed to portray themselves at their most liberal (Decker, 2013, p. 165). The other problem is a lack of interest by management in the history of their own organizations, a problem which seems to be particularly severe in Africa. The Lagos Chamber of Commerce, for example, suffered the destruction of its earlier records by fire in 1946 (Hopkins, 1965). But the apparent non-survival of most of the Chamber's subsequent papers (with exceptions such as board minutes) is presumably by its own choice.[3]

Still, there are positive examples too, such as the two major construction firms in Nigeria who opened their records to Hanaan Marwah, helping her create a time series of actual investment in construction in the country for 1976–85, in the post-colonial period, to contrast with the much higher official figures – the discrepancy being a rough index of the scale of corruption in the award of public contracts during the oil boom (Marwah, 2014). Companies' own records apart, other valuable sources include interviews, commercial directories (notably Allister Macmillan's *Red Book of West Africa* of 1920, which has photographs and brief descriptions of leading African as well as expatriate businessmen), official company registration lists (which provided a starting point for the local study of African firms in Jos, central Nigeria, by S. U. Fwatshak [2011]) and stock exchange records (as with the Brussels stock exchange, whose records enabled Frans Buelens and Stefaan Marysse [2009] to provide for the case of Belgian companies operating in the Belgian Congo the first rigorous time-series of the profitability of companies in tropical Africa). There are also rare studies of both expatriate and indigenous firms in a specific sector, using company and government records plus oral testimonies (Bosteen, 1993).

The majority of research on the history of firms has been on expatriate companies. Yet even on this topic scholarship made only a gradual start, partly because of the priority which, in the aftermath of Independence, Africanist historians gave to 'the history of Africans in their own continent' (Hopkins, 1976a, 29). Hence, until the 1970s company histories in Africa were almost all written either by enthusiastic insiders, and/or were commissioned (Hopkins, 1976a, 1976b, pp. 267–71). Over the last four decades there has been a gradual but still very insufficient accumulation of monographic business histories of individual firms or groups of firms in Africa, in addition to more plentiful thematic studies of how groups of firms obtained labour or capital, cooperated with each other and/or pursued their interests with government. This accumulation surely owes something to the stimulus, over the years, of Hopkins's survey articles (1976a, 1976b, 1987), a special issue of the journal *African Economic History* on 'Business empires in Equatorial Africa' (Clarence-Smith, 1983), and of something close to a special issue of the *Business History Review* (spring 2007). But already in 1980, Nicola Swainson's *The Development of Corporate Capitalism in Kenya 1918–1977* used several case-studies of individual multinationals investing in the country, in developing a careful analysis that reshaped understandings of the economics of decolonization in Kenya.

Over the last four decades a number of scholars have written full-length studies of individual major companies, all of whom could be described as originally expatriate, though in some cases they became domesticated. This includes David Fieldhouse (1995) on the United Africa Company, which examined the history of the largest import-export firm in colonial Africa, through to its struggle to cope with decolonization and its eventual absorption into its parent company, Unilever. The most important firm in South African (and southern African) history, Anglo-American (which became the majority shareholder in the De Beers diamond company in 1926), was valuably examined from a Marxist perspective by Duncan Innes (1984), in the context of the general political economy of South Africa under segregation and apartheid, but without access to the company's archives.[4] The latter have been used, in part, by some more recent works, but, despite a useful popular overview of De Beers (Kanfer, 2000), the Anglo group has yet to receive a comprehensive, long-term business history treatment (despite, for example, a business history of the early years of De Beers: Newbury, 1987). Chibuike Uche has researched the history of British banks in colonial Nigeria (Uche, 1996, 1998, 1999; also Austin and Uche, 2007). The story of Ashanti Goldfields Corporation as a stand-alone company, from its creation in 1897 until its takeover in 2004 by the South African company Anglo Gold (constituting the former gold interests of Anglo American), is the subject of a full-scale business history by Ayowa Afrifa-Taylor (2006).[5] There have also been studies of companies or groups of companies who operated partly, though mostly not primarily, in Africa, notably Geoffrey Jones on British multinationals (1993, 2000). The improvement in the situation since the 1970s owes much to the opening and cataloguing of many company archives, such as Cadbury, Barclays DCO and the United Africa Company. Conversely, the remaining gaps partly reflect continued denial of access to archives, for example in the case of the Liberian operations of Firestone, the US rubber company that has dominated the modern economic history of the country.[6] There are some questions that cannot be properly answered without internal company records. On the other hand, despite being unable to locate company papers, Ian Phimister (1994) made a remarkable study of the history of labour relations on the Wankie colliery in what is now Zimbabwe, using government records supplemented by private papers of individuals, plus interviews with former colliery employees. It would be fair to say that research on expatriate firms has focussed on the colonial and, increasingly, the post-colonial periods, but important contributions on their involvement in earlier trades have continued, for example Jelmer Vos' (2010) use of the papers of the largest Dutch private slave-trading company to reconstruct aspects of the slave trade from West Africa.

Asian diasporas have been a major feature of African business history, from Arab (especially Omani) and Gujarati involvement on the precolonial east coast; through the growth of the Levantine and Indian business presence in West and East Africa respectively, during the colonial period; to the establishment and rapid expansion of Chinese entrepreneurship across most of Africa, mainly from the 1990s onwards. Traditionally rather neglected, their business histories have been explored more fully in recent years, for example by Xerxes Malki (2008) on the Lebanese in Ghana, and Gijsbert Oonk (2009, 2013) on the Indians in

East Africa. For post-colonial Kenya, David Himbara (1994) made an important intervention in the debate about the developmental potential of its indigenous capitalist class, arguing that the most dynamic constituent of Kenyan capitalism, notably in manufacturing, was the community of Indian descent.

The newest of the big Asian commercial diasporas in Africa is the Chinese. Though there were precedents, the great growth of investment by Chinese firms, and settlement of Chinese citizens, began only in the 1990s. Amid the excitement and hysteria that Chinese involvement has provoked in some Western and African media, a particularly well-researched study of the management objectives of Chinese enterprises is Ching Kwan Lee (2014) on Chinese mining and construction firms in Zambia. From interviews with Chinese managers as well as observation of firms' behaviour, she shows that the big mining company owned by the Chinese government (NFCA, a subsidiary of the China Nonferrous-Metal Mining Company) does indeed have somewhat different objectives from the private, London stock-exchange-listed multinationals with which it is competing on the Copperbelt. In the context of a liberal economic regime locally and globally, all the mining companies shifted the terms on which they employ workers from regular and relatively long-term, to casual and precarious. But when copper prices fell two-thirds in a matter of months in response to the Western financial crisis of 2008, NFCA alone adopted a '"Three Nos" policy: no layoffs, no production reduction, no salary cuts' (Lee, 2014, p. 38). Thirty per cent of the Zambian miners lost their jobs, but none of these were NFCA workers. The management were explicit that they pursue profit: but, compared to their international rivals, they do so with a longer term in view, including with interests in stability of output, and in cultivating their relationship with the host government.

There has been a gradual accumulation of studies of firms founded by black Africans, especially in West Africa, which had arguably the broadest traditions of indigenous entrepreneurship before colonization and, relatedly, largely avoided settler colonialism. Pioneering studies by Raymond Dumett and Stephen Baier demonstrated the potential of analytical commercial biographies of colonial-era West African merchants whose enterprises were clearly firms in the sense defined above: Dumett (1973, 1985, 2013) on John Sarbah and other Gold Coast merchants of the late nineteenth century, and Baier (1980) on Al-Hajj Muktar, a prominent Zinder merchant in the early to mid-twentieth century. Both studies used their subjects' own papers. Alusine Jalloh and Toyin Falola's collection *Black Business and Economic Power* (2002) offered a range of critical surveys of broader issues. Jalloh (1999) himself has studied in detail the Muslim Fula merchants who have been very prominent in the economy of colonial and post-colonial Sierra Leone. Uche (2010) has provided the first comprehensive overview of the indigenous banking movement in colonial Nigeria. Tom Forrest's *The Advance of African Capital* (1994) injected some optimism and the use of local sources into what had become an increasingly pessimistic (Schatz, 1984) international conversation about the deficiencies of the Nigerian economy. Forrest profiled the larger entrepreneurs and firms of the Nigeria of the later 1980s and early 1990s, set in the context of developments since 1900. He highlighted conglomerates employing several thousand people, the recent growth of manufacturing in the southeast and elsewhere in the country, and the emergence of M. K. O. Abiola, who had become the best-known tycoon in tropical Africa.[7]

Born in 1937, Abiola reputedly started his first business at the age of nine, selling firewood. After a first-class degree in accountancy at Glasgow University he returned to Nigeria and developed a range of interests including, most conspicuously, telecoms (for ITT and on his own account) and newspapers. His career was notable partly for his skillful use of government contacts (Forrest, 1994, pp. 98–102), but this was also to pave the way to a tragic end. After the military government of the day announced it was stepping down and called a presidential election for 1993, Abiola won a party nomination and is widely thought to have won the election. The military annulled the results, however, and after proclaiming victory Abiola was arrested in 1994 and died in prison four years later.

Fwatshak's (2011) book on African entrepreneurship in Jos, from the beginning of the colonial period to the end of the oil boom, is pioneering in being a case-study of a particular locality, carried out in empirical depth and well-situated in the relevant historical and contemporary debates. Even by West African standards, Nigeria, with its precolonial history of particularly strong commitment to production for the market, and especially with the militantly non-settler policy followed by the colonial administration (see below) offered a relatively encouraging environment for black enterprise. Apartheid South Africa was the opposite, yet even there, black African businesses developed, notably in the townships.

Business and the state

Given the fundamental shifts in the political setting of business entailed by the European partition of Africa (1879-c.1905), decolonization (south of the Sahara, 1957–75) and the fall of white minority rule in Rhodesia (Zimbabwe) and South Africa (1979–80 and 1994 respectively), the changing relationships between firms and the state is a particularly salient theme in African business history, and has been the subject of a number of important studies in recent decades.

The role of European firms in motivating the Scramble for Africa was emphasised in the literatures on West and South Africa, in particular. For West Africa, Hopkins argued that, faced with a 'crisis in the economy of legitimate commerce' that had followed the decline and abolition of the Atlantic slave trade, British, French and German merchants petitioned their respective governments, especially via their chambers of commerce back home, appealing for annexations to reduce the costs and risks they faced in doing business in the region (Hopkins, 1973, pp. 124–66; see further Hynes, 1979). In South Africa, the economic interpretation of the British war of conquest in 1898–1901 against the two Boer republics, the Transvaal and the Orange Free state, highlighted the struggle for control over African labour between the (foreign-owned) mining companies and the Afrikaner governments, and the white farmers the latter represented. Both theses have provoked controversy (on South Africa, among a large literature, see for example Marks and Atmore, 1979; Porter, 1990), and ultimately metropolitan decision-makers presumably decided whether the interests of 'their' firms in Africa were worth fighting for (Cain and Hopkins, 2002). The debate continues, with an important new contribution on the attitude of the City of London towards South African gold in prospect (Phimister, forthcoming).

In the early twentieth century the regimes establishing or consolidating settler economies reserved much or, in the case of South Africa, most of the land for whites, and sought by such dispossession to oblige black Africans to sell their labour rather than their produce in order to obtain cash. By the 1930s the governments of Southern Rhodesia (Zimbabwe) and Kenya accepted that African production for the market was not going to disappear, and decided to tax it instead. Even with that concession, it must be emphasised that the governments of settler (South Africa, Southern Rhodesia), semi-settler (Northern Rhodesia, Kenya) and plantation-concessionaire colonies (in equatorial Africa and much of Angola and Mozambique) did much to hinder, if not make impossible, the emergence of specialized firms owned by black Africans. The other colonial economies developed around export agriculture under African ownership. Nigeria was the extreme case, where the colonial administration excluded Europeans from acquiring land (including rejecting applications from Lever to establish a huge oil palm plantation there; eventually, the company found a welcome in the Belgian Congo). Yet even in Nigeria and the rest of British West Africa, the colonial administrations tolerated European monopolies and cartels in the import-export trade, shipping and banking, thereby restricting the scope for African enterprise.

There was a colonial scramble *out* of Africa in the late 1950s and early 1960s, Portugal apart. If one accepts the views that business interests were important in the decisions to colonize at least some major areas of Africa, it comes as a surprise to read that the British government, at both colonial and metropolitan level, paid very little attention to the pleas of British companies in the later 1940s and 1950s that the government do more to protect their interests, whether in relation to the timing of decolonization or to the security of foreign investments after independence. Yet this is what emerges from the well-documented research of Sarah Stockwell (2000) on Ghana, and to a large extent also that of Robert Tignor (1998) on Nigeria and Kenya. The latter colony was a partial exception, but much of the interest the government showed there in the views of British businesses was simply because the financial secretary in Kenya for much of the 1950s was a settler himself. In the French case, Jacques Marseille (2005) has made a well-known argument that French private enterprise had increasingly lost interest in the colonies, focussing instead on markets in industrialized economies. Marseille, however, has relatively little to say about France's colonies in tropical Africa, compared to his coverage of Indochina for example, and it seems unlikely that French companies in Sub-Saharan Africa were any more sanguine about the process of decolonization that their anxious, but largely ignored, British counterparts. As independence approached, and in the years that followed, European firms had no choice but to adapt if they were to remain in Africa, for instance by Africanization of management (Fieldhouse, 1995; Decker, 2005). For the case of British firms in West Africa, Decker (2007, 2014) has explored further areas of adaptation, notably in advertising strategies (see further, Van den Bersselaar, 2011b) and even the architecture of their premises (see also Murillo, 2011).

On the whole, the growth of government intervention from the 1930s Depression (in the case of colonies) and the Second World War until the introduction of Structural Adjustment in the 1980s probably did more to restrict than enlarge the scope for the emergence of medium and large-scale African firms in non-settler colonies. Private European merchants gave way to government marketing boards with statutory export monopolies of the major cash-crops. When independence came, governments varied as to whether they allowed private firms, African or foreign, to participate in the buying of produce directly from the farmers, as licensed buying agents. For instance, Nigeria did so, whereas Ghana did not – the first president, Kwame Nkrumah, saw no place for African private enterprise beyond the small scale. By contrast, the rule of Kenya's first president, Jomo Kenyatta, saw the emergence of sizeable private African firms enjoying the patronage and support of the state. This phenomenon stimulated a lively debate at the time among Dependency and Marxist scholars about whether Kenya and perhaps a few other former colonies in Africa had embarked on a path of national capitalist development, breaking away from neo-colonial dependence on the West (Leys, 1978; Kitching, 1985; Berman and Leys, 1994). However, Kenyatta's successor, Daniel Arap Moi, systematically dismantled his predecessor's clientage network, in the process demonstrating the political vulnerability of indigenous as well as foreign businesses even in a country with an exceptionally strong record of formal political stability (no successful coup d'états).

Post-colonial government policies towards foreign business varied greatly, from Senegal's provision of tariff protection to foreign investors in manufacturing, from the 1950s until the beginning of the 1980s (Boone, 1992), to Nigeria's indigenization policy in the 1970s. The latter involved excluding foreigners from small-scale business activity, and requiring Nigerian equity participation in large firms (Biersteker, 1987; Uche, 2012). According to Fwatshak's study of Jos, the Nigerian legal monopoly of small business did indeed help 'private entrepreneurs in Jos and in Nigeria generally' (Fwatshak, 2011, p. 191). In 1979 Nigeria nationalized British Petroleum's Nigerian subsidiaries. Although officially presented as a foreign policy response to the UK's proposal that oil supplies be resumed to apartheid South Africa, Ann Genova (2010) argues plausibly that the move was actually the culmination of a cumulative policy of promoting indigenous capitalism. Further steps in this direction became much harder under the economic liberalization that swept Africa in the 1980s, including Nigeria in 1986.

Ironically, while Structural Adjustment was unquestionably pro-market, it was not necessarily pro-business. Handley commented of Ghana and Zambia that 'despite the adoption of two of the most rigorous neo-liberal reform programs on the continent', governments remained uninterested in talking to business associations; business contacts with the state were limited to individual businesspeople entering clientage relations with members of the government (Handley, 2008, p. 244). Handley thought that South Africa and Mauritius were different, in that while in both cases the state elite was ethnically different from the business elite, both states 'had created a more or less market-driven context in which business could operate' (Handley, 2008, p. 243). Since the time she wrote, however, at least to a superficial eye, South Africa seems to have become more patrimonial.

More than a generation on from the Nigerian indigenization policy, the Black Economic Empowerment policy in South Africa is aimed at achieving the same for black entrepreneurs and shareholders there. Ironically or not, there is a partial precedent in the *volkscapitalisme* movement in white-ruled South Africa, which sought to extend Afrikaner participation in the ownership of the economy beyond its traditional base in agriculture, to services and even mining and manufacturing. After the National Party's victory in the 1948 election, the government obliged, notably by transferring public accounts and deposits to Afrikaner finance companies, and awarding contracts preferentially to Afrikaner firms (O'Meara, 1983; Lipton, 1986; Verhoef, 2009).

As Grietjie Verhoef (2014, pp. 17–19) has shown, this story has an important contemporary sequel, significant for what is shows about (at least originally) nationalist companies, 'empowerment' programmes and the contemporary international presence of African corporations. In the context of the end of apartheid and the commercial globalization of the 1990s and early 2000s, the largest Afrikaner life assurance company, SANLAN (founded in 1918), adopted an internationalisation strategy from 1995. After initial setbacks, this achieved some success by 2010, notably in other African markets and with South African clients in Britain (Verhoef, 2016). Most strikingly, another of the original Afrikaner nationalist enterprises, Nasionale Pers (founded in 1915) transformed itself from a South African newspaper group into a giant of electronic media, internet services and e-commerce in several continents. According to Verhoef (2014, p. 18), as of 2014 Naspers (it changed its name in 1997) was 'the largest emerging market company' in the world, with a market capitalization of around US $37 billion, still based in South Africa and listed on the Johannesburg Stock Exchange. Nasionale Pers was also the founder of MTN, in 1994, which has become a leading cellphone network in much of Africa and parts of the Middle East. MTN is now 72.1% owned by the Johannesburg-listed firm M-Cell – which itself is 62.5% owned by a black empowerment group, Johnnic (Verhoef, 2014, p. 18).

The structure of competition and constraints upon the formation and growth of firms

The vast majority of indigenous enterprises in Africa today are small firms or not firms in the strict sense at all. This is not necessarily surprising in relatively poor economies whose main productive activities often afford few opportunities for advantages of scale in production. But a historical perspective may enable us to refine and qualify such generalizations.

The obstacles to the formation and growth of firms during the last two or three centuries before the European partition of Africa might appear overwhelming: lack of scale economies in agriculture, land abundance which might make it physically unnecessary as well as expensive to substitute trade for self-sufficiency, a multiplicity of often small polities creating borders and tolls to disrupt long-distance trade, the risk of capture by slave raiders in many areas, the lack of legal protection of investors' capital and the cost of transport in a continent in much of which sleeping sickness prevented the use of large animals in transport and arable agriculture. In such settings, it is actually remarkable that there was so much extra subsistence production and trade, especially in West Africa, where the acquisition of saleable goods was often essential for marriage, prestige and statecraft. An older literature maintained that kingdoms such as Dahomey and Asante imposed actual or virtual state monopolies of export-import trade, but this view is rejected by more recent research (Law, 1977; Austin, 1996). And as we have seen, indigenous institutions such as the canoe house of the Niger Delta and, much more widely, the ethnic-cum-religious trading diaspora enabled problems of cooperation and contracting to be handled successfully. It has also to be recognised that slave trading offered opportunities for firm formation, because the nature of the trade entailed a high capital entry threshold (Hopkins, 1973, pp. 125–6; Evans and Richardson, 1995). The work of Lovejoy and Richardson (1999, 2005) has explored how the credit given by European ship-captains to their African trading partners was guaranteed, in nearby port-states in the Niger Delta: by a hostage system in one case, and – more successfully – by royal guarantee in another.

At the same time, the slave trade inflicted a kind of 'double Dutch' disease on the economies which supplied it, diverting investors from peaceful occupations and making the pursuit of the latter often dangerous (Austin, forthcoming; also Inikori, 2007). And while the ethnic-cum-religious diasporas made trade possible on a scale and over distances on which it would otherwise have been impossible, their monopolies over specific routes and their deliberate exclusiveness presumably constituted barriers to new entrants (Austin, 2002, p. 125).

The transition from the export of slaves to exporting cash crops, which effectively began with British withdrawal from the slave trade in 1807, but began in East Africa effectively only in the 1870s, enabled small producers and traders to enter the maritime export trade (Hopkins, 1973; Law, 1995). The coming of the steamship, with services between Europe and West Africa starting in the 1850s, lowered entry barriers to the import-export trade in West Africa (Lynn, 1997). The result was an influx of smaller European firms plus African traders. The latter enjoyed two or three decades of success, peaking around 1885 according to Dumett for the case of the Gold Coast. During this period they had a large share of the market, and, as in the case of John Sarbah, opened networks of stores which extended the availability of manufactured imports to African customers, and worked to open new sources of supply of agricultural exports (Dumett, 1973). By the end of the nineteenth and into the twentieth century, however, the relative and absolute position of independent African import-export traders seems to have been declining. They were hit by an adverse trend in the barter terms of trade and increasing competition from European merchants. The latter, encouraged by their governments' partition of Africa, began to establish their own branches in the interior, and readily resorted to merger and takeover when faced with adverse market conditions. In some colonies African fortunes were also reduced by the colonial demonetization of existing currencies, as well as the (often very gradual) ending of slavery. The decline of African middlemen is attested in important studies on the British colonies of West Africa (notably Nwabughuogu, 1982; Olukoju, 2002; Akyeampong, 2014), and most comprehensively for the French colonies (Goerg, 1980; Barry and Harding, 1992; Harding and Kipre, 1992; Gandah Nabi, 2013). The latter works also show, however, that some African merchants survived as independent operators, while others retained a degree of autonomy even while being reduced to agents of large European companies. For example, Laurence Marfaing (1991) shows for Senegal that, by 1930, African traders had adapted to French rule, rather than being in danger of disappearance.

In 1978 Hopkins summarized the asymmetric nature of competition even in the non-settler colonies of tropical Africa in the following hypothesis, which still requires further research on both sides of the divide that it describes:

> the profit maximising model may well prove a better fit with respect to the indigenous inhabitants of the colonies than with respect to the expatriate firms operating there. Colonial subjects found themselves competing strongly, both within colonies (because of low entry costs in typical trading and agricultural activities) and between them (because cross-elasticities of demand affected many colonial products which were substitutes or near-substitutes). There was little or no slack in indigenous enterprise. The expatriate firms, on the other hand, operated a system of market-sharing agreements within colonies and to some extent between them, and they were responsible for very few innovations, at least in tropical Africa, during the colonial period.
>
> *(Hopkins, 1978, p. 95)*

Shipping and banking tended to be controlled by cartels of European firms (Olukoju, 1992, 2001–2; Austin and Uche, 2007), while in the 1900s to 1930s the export-import trade was characterized by concentration of ownership (culminating in the formation of the United Africa Company, the largest trading firm in tropical Africa, in 1929) and intermittent formation of price agreements ('pools') among the European firms. In Nigeria, the colonial government excluded Europeans from agriculture, but among Africans competition was intense the entry barriers were minimal, as they were also in the lower rungs of trading. In certain circumstances, African middlemen were able to exploit information asymmetries to extract rents from European produce-buyers when the world price changed while they were in the process of buying on credit (Austin, 2005, pp. 366–73, 535–6). But these were examples of what the economic anthropologist Jane Guyer (2004) has called 'marginal gains'. The big picture was that although in non-settler colonies, like Nigeria, Senegal and Uganda, African peasants and small capitalists were able to produce crops for export, in stark contrast to their coercive exclusion from export agriculture in settler economies: even in non-settler colonies it was extremely difficult for African businesses to accumulate capital on a large scale.

Meanwhile, in the settler economies, especially South Africa and Southern Rhodesia (now Zimbabwe), black Africans were literally denied the economic space in which to build up businesses and accumulate wealth (though a small minority eventually succeeded, even so). Moreover, in these economies, the biggest business opportunities were ones with a high capital-entry threshold and significant scale economies: especially deep mining. Early goldrushes whose actors included individual prospectors gave way to a rapid concentration of ownership, culminating in the formation of giant individual firms, such as Anglo-American and De Beers, the establishment of monopsonistic labour-recruitment agencies for the mines and, in the case of De Beers, a policy of striving to establish and uphold a monopoly in the market for diamonds.

In the larger agricultural-exporting colonies, in particular, Africans protested against European cartelization of commerce. In southern Ghana, from 1908 to 1938, African producers and traders combined in a series of a series of organized cocoa 'hold-ups': refusals to sell beans to European firms until the latter not only raised the producer price but dissolved the latest 'pool' by which they had fixed the price (Miles, 1978). In Nigeria, the duopoly of Barclays and the Bank of British West Africa was challenged by the formation of a series of indigenous banks. The first was launched in 1929, and by independence in 1960, a total of 29 had been founded of which six survived (Uche, 2010). The founder of the first of these banks was a Ghanaian, Winifried Tete-Ansá, at a time when Africans were prohibited from forming banks in Ghana. In a book he published himself in New York in 1930, Tete-Ansá accused 'foreign corporations, mostly European' of 'attempting to monopolize the marketing by creating a vicious barrier between the producers and the consumers abroad through organized systems of banking and trading which practically deny those facilities required in an international exchange of commodities' (Tete-Ansá, 1930, p. 63). The solution, he argued, was for Africans to adopt European business structures, especially the limited liability company (Hopkins, 1966).

The harshly asymmetric structure of competition in the colonial period was to a great extent continued after independence, in the shape of the 'formal' versus 'informal' distinction: the former now featuring state corporations as well as foreign-owned firms. The boundary was broken down to an extent by state-enforced sales of shares by foreign firms to national citizens, and, with economic liberalization, by privatization of many state (or 'parastatal') corporations, and perhaps also by the modest proliferation of stock exchanges in Africa, small though they remain outside Johannesburg. But it remains the case that relatively very few African businesses start small and grow big, or even outlive their founders. Are the historic causes of this limited to the structure of competition, pre-emption by the state, and the general instability of economic life? The Nigerian nationalist and future prime minister, Nnamdi Azikiwe, in a book published in 1937, criticised what he saw as the preference of African businessmen for working alone, rather than pooling financial resources. One-man businesses 'will work out temporarily, but [a] time will come when that one man will face problems which require many heads to solve' (Azikiwe, 1937/1968, p. 132). 'Because of this' single-handedness, and in contrast to European firms, 'the average African business liquidates with the death of the owner' (Azikiwe, 1937/1968, p. 133). The latter issue has been highlighted in recent historiographical surveys (Iliffe, 1983, pp. 73–5; Kennedy, 1988; Austin, 2002, pp. 121–2). Ayodeji Olukoju (2013) undertook specific research on this, by surveying/reviewing the biographies of a number of Yoruba business men and women. While he confirmed the effect of adverse pressures from the environments in which businesspeople operated, his conclusions emphasised cultural constraints. For example, few in his sample had 'had a clear succession plan within or outside the lineage' (Olukoju, 2013, p. 228); and acrimonious disputes among heirs often 'effectively destroyed their legacies' (Olukoju, 2013, p. 228). This study is particularly interesting because Nigeria, specifically including both the Hausa and Yoruba-speaking areas, has been seen as the home of the main exceptions to the general African pattern of firms not outliving their founders (Iliffe, 1983, pp. 74–5).

Conclusions

The last forty years has seen a gradual accumulation and diversification of research on business in Africa. While the majority of it has focussed on European and white South African enterprise, a substantial amount has been on black African business, informal and formal, and on various Asian business communities in Africa. Much of the work highlights and explores, in a range of ways, certain enduring themes: the importance of state interventions in delineating the scope for indigenous and foreign business, the persistence of non-firm and quasi-firm enterprises as a key part of African economies, the gradual spread but also continuing struggles of black African firms, the asymmetric structure of competition in colonial and, to a large though perhaps diminishing extent, post-colonial economies. Three priorities for future scholarship should surely be the search for and protection of the records of companies and individual business people and employees; further research on black African businesses, in all periods of African history; and the interpretative challenge of integrating firm and non-firm business in the study of business history: in Africa, and globally.

Finally, the proliferation of business and management courses in Africa since economic liberalization in the 1980s, often taught in new private universities, raises the hope that the study of management in Africa will include recognition of the value of business history for current and future managers and entrepreneurs. At the time of writing, however, this has yet to occur.

Notes

1 There is a parallel to the later work of Avner Greif (1989) on Jewish trading diasporas on both sides of the Mediterranean, though the latter formulated his arguments in formal economic terms, as did Janet Landa (1994) in her theoretical exploration of much the same idea.
2 On kola, see also Abaka, 2005.
3 As one of my graduate students, Damilola Adebayo, discovered in 2015.
4 I am grateful to Mariusz Lukasiewicz for discussing the sources with me.
5 As the main supervisor, I declare an interest, but Verhoef (2015, 15) describes it as 'perhaps the first quality business history on an African firm this century'.
6 Even as of early 2016, a colleague's request for access (not even specifically for the purpose of a business history, but for what these archives would reveal about the general economic history of Liberia) was rejected only a few months ago.
7 A position perhaps currently occupied by his compatriot Aliko Dangote (Akinyoade and Uche, 2016).

References

Abaka, E. (2005). *Kola is God's Gift: Agricultural Production, Export Initiatives and the Kola Industry of Asante and the Gold Coast c.1820–1950*. Oxford: James Currey.
Afrifa-Taylor, A. (2006). 'An Economic History of the Ashanti Goldfields Corporation, 1895–2004: Land, Labour, Capital and Enterprise', PhD dissertation, London School of Economics.
Akinyoade, A., & Uche, C. (2016). Dangote Cement: An African Success Story? Leiden: African Studies Centre Working Paper Number 131.
Akyeampong, E. (2014). 'Commerce, credit, and mobility in late nineteenth-century Gold Coast: changing dynamics in Euro-African trade', in Emmanuel Akyeampong, Robert H. Bates, Nathan Nunn and James A. Robinson (eds), *Africa's Development in Historical Perspective*. New York: Cambridge University Press, 231–63.
Austin, G. (1996). '"No elders were present": commoners and private ownership in Asante, 1807–96', *Journal of African History, 37*(1), 1–30.
Austin, G. (2002). 'African business in nineteenth century West Africa', in Alusine Jalloh and Toyin Falola (eds), *Black Business and Economic Power*. Rochester: University of Rochester Press, 114–44.
Austin, G. (2005). *Labour, Land and Capital in Ghana: From Slavery to Free Labour in Asante, 1807–1956*. Rochester: Rochester University Press.
Austin, G. & Uche, C. U. (2007). 'Collusion and competition in colonial economies: banking in British West Africa, 1916–1960', *Business History Review, 81* (Spring), 1–26.
Azarya, V. & Chazan, N. (1987). 'Disengagement from the state in Africa: reflections on the experience of Ghana and Guinea', *Comparative Studies in Society and History, 29*(1), 106–31.
Azikiwe, N. (1968 [1937]). *Renascent Africa*. London: reprinted by Frank Cass.
Baier, S. (1980). 'A commercial biography', *An Economic History of Central Niger*. Oxford: Oxford University Press, 192–206.

Ball, R. (1997). 'The State and the Development of Small-Scale Industry in Ghana since c.1945', PhD dissertation. London School of Economics.

Barry, B. & Harding, L. (1992). *Commerce et Commerçants en Afrique de l'Ouest: Le Sénégal*. Paris: L'Harmattan.

Berman, B. J. & Leys, C. (eds) (1994). *African Capitalists in African Development*. Boulder: Lynne Reiner.

Biersteker, T. J. (1987). *Multinationals, the State and Control of the Nigerian Economy*. Princeton: Princeton University Press.

Boone, C. (1992). *Merchant Capital and the Roots of State Power in Senegal, 1930–1985*. New York: Cambridge University Press.

Bosteen, L. B. (1993). 'Processed Food Marketing in Ivory Coast, 1956–1990: Distribution Techniques and Foreign Domination in a Developing Economy'. PhD dissertation, London School of Economics.

Buelens, F. & Marysse, S. (2009). 'Returns on investments during the colonial era: the case of the Belgian Congo', *Economic History Review, 62*(S1), 135–66.

Cain, P. J. & Hopkins, A. G. (2002). *British Imperialism, 1688–2000*, 2nd edition. London: Longman.

Clarence-Smith, W. G. (1983). 'Business empires in Equatorial Africa', special issue of *African Economic History*.

Coase, R. H. (1937). 'The nature of the firm', *Economica*, n.s. *4*(16), 386–405.

Cohen, A. (1971). 'Cultural strategies in the organization of trading diasporas' in Claude Meillassoux (ed.), *The Development of Indigenous Trade and Markets in West Africa*. London: Oxford University Press for the International African Institute, 266–81.

Curtin, P. D. (1975). *Economic Change in Precolonial Africa: Senegambia in the Era of the Slave Trade*. Madison: University of Wisconsin Press.

Curtin, P. D. (1984). *Cross-Cultural Trade in World History*. Cambridge: Cambridge University Press.

Dawson, J. (1991). 'Development of small-scale industry in Ghana: a case study of Kumasi', in Henk Thomas, Francisco Uribe-Echevarría and Henny Romijn (eds), *Small-scale Production: Strategies for Industrial Restructuring*. London: Intermediate Technology Publications, 173–207.

Decker, S. (2005). 'Decolonising Barclays Bank DCO? Corporate Africanisation in Nigeria, 1945–69', *Journal of Imperial and Commonwealth History, 33*(3), 419–40.

Decker, S. (2007). 'Corporate legitimacy and advertising: British companies and the rhetoric of development in West Africa, 1950–1970', *Business History Review, 81* (spring), 59–86.

Decker, S. (2013). 'The silence of the archives: business history, post-colonialism and archival ethnography', *Management & Organizational History, 8*(2), 155–73.

Decker, S. (2014). 'Solid intentions: an archival ethnography of corporate architecture and organizational remembering', *Organization, 21*(4), 514–42.

Dike, K. O. (2011 [1956]). *Trade and Politics in the Niger Delta, 1830–1885*, 2nd edition. Ibadan: Bookcraft, with a foreword by Gareth Austin; first edition by Oxford University Press.

Dumett, R. E. (1973). 'John Sarbah, the Elder, and African mercantile entrepreneurship in the late nineteenth century', *Journal of African History, 14*(4), 653–79.

Dumett, R. E. (1985). 'African merchants of the Gold Coast, 1860–1905: dynamics of indigenous entrepreneurship', *Comparative Studies in Society and History*, 25, 661–93.

Dumett, R. E. (2013). *Imperialism, Economic Development and Social Change in West Africa*. Durham: Carolina University Press.

Evans, E. W. & Richardson, D. (1995). 'Hunting for rents: the economics of slaving in pre-colonial Africa', *Economic History Review, 48*, 665–86.

Falola, T. (1991). 'The Yoruba caravan system of the nineteenth century', *International Journal of African Historical Studies, 24*(1), 111–32.

Ferreira, R. (2012). *Cross-Cultural Exchange in the Atlantic World: Angola and Brazil during the Era of the Slave Trade*. Cambridge: Cambridge University Press.

Fieldhouse, D. K. (1995). *Merchant Capital and Economic Decolonisation: The United Africa Company, 1929–1987*. Oxford: Oxford University Press.

Forrest, T. (1994). *The Advance of African Capital: The Growth of Nigerian Private Enterprise*. Edinburgh: Edinburgh University Press.

Fwatshak, S. U. (2011). *African Entrepreneurship in Jos, Central Nigeria, 1902–1985*. Durham: Carolina Academic Press.

Gandah Nabi, H. (2013). *Commerçants et Entrepreneurs du Niger, (1922–2006)*. Paris: L'Harmattan.

Genova, A. (2010). 'Nigeria's nationalization of British Petroleum', *International Journal of African Historical Studies, 43*(1), 115–36.

Goerg, O. (1980). 'La destruction d'un reseau d'échange précolonial: l'exemple de la Guinée', *Journal of African History, 21*(4), 467–84.

Green, T. (2012). *The Rise of the Trans-Atlantic Slave Trade in Western Africa, 1300–1589.* Cambridge: Cambridge University Press.

Greif, A. (1989). 'Reputation and coalitions in medieval trade: evidence on the Maghribi traders', *Journal of Economic History, 49*(4), 857–82.

Guyer, J. I. (2004). *Marginal Gains: Monetary Transactions in Atlantic Africa.* Chicago: Chicago University Press.

Handley, A. (2008). *Business and the State in Africa: Economic Policy-Making in the Neo-Liberal Era.* New York: Cambridge University Press.

Harding, L. & Kipre, P. (1992). *Commerce et Commerçants en Afrique de l'Ouest: La Côte d'Ivoire.* Paris: L'Harmattan.

Hart, K. (1973). 'Informal income opportunities and urban employment in Ghana', *Journal of Modern African Studies, 11*(1), 61–89.

Hill, P. (1966). 'A plea for indigenous economics: the West African example', *Economic Development and Cultural Change, 15*(1), 10–20, reprinted in Hill, *Studies in Rural Capitalism in West Africa.* Cambridge: Cambridge University Press, 1970.

Hill, P. (1970). 'Ghanaian capitalist cocoa-farmers', in Hill, *Studies in Rural Capitalism in West Africa.* Cambridge: Cambridge University Press, 21–9.

Hill, P. (1997 [1963]), *The Migrant Cocoa-Farmers of Southern Ghana,* 2nd edition. Hamburg: LIT, with new introduction by Gareth Austin; first edition by Cambridge University Press.

Himbara, D. (1994). *Kenyan Capitalists, the State, and Development.* Boulder: Lynne Reiner.

Hopkins, A. G. (1965). 'The Lagos Chamber of Commerce, 1888–1903', *Journal of the Historical Society of Nigeria, 3*(2), 241–8.

Hopkins, A. G. (1966). 'Economic aspects of political movements in Nigeria and the Gold Coast, 1918–39', *Journal of African History, 7*(1), 133–152.

Hopkins, A. G. (1973). *An Economic History of West Africa.* London: Longman.

Hopkins, A. G. (1976a). 'Imperial business in Africa': Part I, 'Sources', *Journal of African History, 17*(1), 29–48.

Hopkins, A. G. (1976b). 'Imperial business in Africa': Part II, 'Interpretations', *Journal of African History, 17*(2), 267–90.

Hopkins, A. G. (1978). 'Innovation in a colonial context: African origins of the Nigerian cocoa-farming industry, 1880–1920', in Clive Dewey and A. G. Hopkins (eds), *The Imperial Impact.* London: Athlone Press for University of London, 83–96, 341–2.

Hopkins, A. G. (1987). 'Big business in African studies', *Journal of African History, 28*, 93–102.

Hynes, W. G. (1979). *The Economics of Empire: Britain, Africa and the New Imperialism.* London: Longman.

Iliffe, J. (1983). *The Emergence of African Capitalism.* London: Macmillan.

Inikori, J. E. (2007). 'Africa and the globalization process: western Africa, 1450–1850', *Journal of Global History, 2*(1), 63–86.

Innes, D. (1984). *Anglo American and the Rise of Modern South Africa.* New York: Monthly Review Press.

Jalloh, A. (1999). *African Entrepreneurship: Muslim Fula Merchants in Sierra Leone.* Trenton: Africa World Press.

Jalloh, A. & Falola, T. eds, (2002). *Black Business and Economic Power.* Rochester: University of Rochester Press.

Jones, G. (1993). *British Multinational Banking, 1830–1990.* Oxford: Oxford University Press.

Jones, G. (2000). *Merchants to Multinationals: British Trading Companies in the Nineteenth and Twentieth Centuries.* Oxford: Oxford University Press.

Kanfer, S. (2000). *The Last Empire: De Beers, Diamonds, and the World.* Houndmills: Macmillan.

Kennedy, P. (1988). 'Entrepreneurial endeavour, business success and social origins', in his *African Capitalism: the Struggle for Ascendency.* Cambridge: Cambridge University Press, 158–83.

King, K. (1996). *Jua Kali Kenya: Change and Development in an Informal Economy, 1970–95.* London: James Currey.

Kitching, G. (1985). 'Politics, Method and Evidence in the "Kenya Debate"', in Henry Bernstein and Bonnie K. Campbell (eds), *Contradictions of Accumulation in Africa.* Sage: Beverly Hills, 115–49.

Kriger, C. E. (2006). *Cloth in West African History.* Lanham: AltaMira Press.

Landa, J. T. (1994). *Trust, Ethnicity and Identity: Beyond the New Institutional Economics of Ethnic Trading Networks, Contract Law, and Gift-Exchange.* Ann Arbor: University of Michigan Press.

Law, R. (1977). 'Royal monopoly and private enterprise in the Atlantic trade: the case of Dahomey', *Journal of African History, 18*(4), 555–77.

Law, R. (1993). 'The Royal African Company of England's West African correspondence, 1681–1699', *History in Africa, 20,* 173–84.

Law, Robin, ed. (1995), *From Slave Trade to 'Legitimate' Commerce: the Commercial Transition in Nineteenth-century West Africa.* Cambridge: Cambridge University Press.

Lee, C. K. (2014). 'The spectre of Global China', *New Left Review, 89,* 28–65.

Leys, C. (1978). 'Capital accumulation, class formation and dependency: the significance of the Kenyan case', *Socialist Register 1978,* 241–66.

Lipton, M. (1986). *Capitalism and Apartheid: South Africa, 1910–1986,* 2nd edition. London: Wildwood House.

Lovejoy, P. E. (1973). 'The Kambarin Beriberi: the formation of a specialized group of Hausa kola traders in the nineteenth century', *Journal of African History, 14*(4), 633–51.

Lovejoy, P. E. (1980). *Caravans of Kola: the Hausa Kola Trade 1700–1900.* Zaria: Ahmadu Bello University Press.

Lovejoy, P. E. (1986). *Salt of the Desert Sun: a History of Salt Production and Trade in the Central Sudan.* Cambridge: Cambridge University Press.

Lovejoy, P. E. & Richardson, D. (1999). 'Trust, pawnship, and Atlantic history: the institutional foundations of the Old Calabar slave trade', *American Historical Review, 104*(2), 333–55.

Lovejoy, P. E. & Richardson, D. (2005). '"This horrid hole": royal authority, commerce and credit at Bonny 1690–1840', *Journal of African History, 44*(3), 363–92.

Lynn, M. (1997). *Commerce and Economic Change in West Africa: The Palm Oil Trade in the Nineteenth Century.* Cambridge: Cambridge University Press.

Lydon, G. (2009). *On Trans-Saharan Trails: Islamic Law, Trade Networks, and Cross-Cultural Exchange in Nineteenth-Century Western Africa.* New York: Cambridge University Press.

MacGaffey, J. (1987). *Entrepreneurs and Parasites: the Struggle for Indigenous Capitalism in Zaire.* Cambridge: Cambridge University Press.

Macmillan, A. (compiler and ed., 1920). *The Red Book of West Africa.* London: Frank Cass.

Maegher, K. (2010). *Identity Economics: Social Networks and the Informal Economy in Nigeria.* Oxford: James Currey.

Malki, I. X. (2008). 'The Alienated Stranger: A Political and Economic History of the Lebanese in Ghana, c.1925–1992'. D.Phil dissertation, University of Oxford.

Marfaing, L. (1991). *L'Évolution du Commerce au Sénégal 1820–1930.* Paris: L'Harmattan.

Marks, S. & Trapido, S. (1979). 'Lord Milner and the South African state', *History Workshop Journal, 8,* 50–80.

Marseille, J. (2005). *Empire Colonial et Capitalisme Français: Histoire d'un Divorce,* 2nd edition. Paris: Albin Michel.

Marwah, H. (2014). 'What explains slow sub-Saharan African growth? Revisiting oil boom-era investment and productivity in Nigeria's national accounts, 1976–85', *Economic History Review, 67*(4), 993–1011.

Miles, J. (1978). 'Rural protest in the Gold Coast: the cocoa hold-ups, 1908–1938', in Clive Dewey and A. G. Hopkins (eds), *The Imperial Impact: Studies in the Economic History of Africa and India.* London: University of London and Athlone Press, 152–70, 353–7.

Murillo, B. (2011). '"The devil we know": Gold Coast consumers, local employees, and the United Africa Company, 1940–1960', *Enterprise and Society, 12*(2), 317–55.

Newbury, C. (1987). 'Technology, capital, and consolidation: the performance of De Beers Mining Company Limited, 1880–1889', *Business History Review, 61*(1), 1–42.

Northrup, D. (1978). *Trade Without Rulers: Pre-colonial Economic Development in South-Eastern Nigeria.* Oxford: Oxford University Press.

Nwabughuogu, A. I. (1982). 'From wealthy entrepreneurs to petty traders: the decline of African middlemen in eastern Nigeria, 1900–1950', *Journal of African History, 23,* 365–79.

Nwokeji, G. U. (2010). *The Slave Trade and Culture in the Bight of Biafra.* Cambridge: Cambridge University Press.

Olukoju, A. (1992). 'Elder Dempster and the shipping trade of Nigeria during the First World War', *Journal of African History, 33*(2), 255–71.

Olukoju, A. (2001–2). '"Getting too great a grip": European shipping lines and British West African lighterage services in the 1930s', *Afrika Zamani, 9&10,* 19–40.

Olukoju, A. (2002). 'The impact of British colonialism on the development of African business in colonial Nigeria', in Alusine Jalloh and Toyin Falola (eds), *Black Business and Economic Power,* 176–98.

Olukoju, A. (2013). 'Accumulation and conspicuous consumption: the proverty of entrepreneurship in Western Nigeria, ca. 1850–1930', in Emmanuel Akyeampong, Robert H. Bates, Nathan Nunn and James A. Robinson, eds, *Africa's Development in Historical Perspective*, New York: Cambridge University Press, 208–30.

O'Meara, D. (1983). *Volkscapitalisme: Class, Capital and Ideology in the Development of Afrikaner Nationalism, 1934–1948*. Cambridge: Cambridge University Press.

Oonk, G. (2009). *The Kaarimjee Jivanjee Family: Merchants Princes of East Africa 1800–2000*. Amsterdam: Pallas.

Oonk, G. (2013). *Settled Strangers: Asian Business Elites in East Africa 1800–2000*. New Delhi: Sage.

Phimister, I. (1994). *Wangi Kolia: Coal, Capital and Labour in Colonial Zimbabwe 1894–1954*. Harare: Baobab.

Phimister, I. (forthcoming). 'Brokers and Boers: the City of London and the coming of war in South Africa, 1895–1899'.

Porter, A. (1990). 'The South African War (1899–1902): context and motive reconsidered', *Journal of African History, 31*(1), 43–57.

Schatz, S. P. (1984). 'Pirate capitalism and inert economy in Nigeria', *Journal of Modern African Studies, 22*, 45–57.

Sheriff, A. (1987). *Slaves, Spices and Ivory in Zanzibar*. London: James Currey.

Stockwell, S. (2000). *The Business of Decolonization: British Business Strategies in the Gold Coast*. Oxford: Oxford University Press.

Swainson, N. (1980). *The Development of Corporate Capitalism in Kenya 1918–1977*. London: Heinemann.

Tete-Ansá, W. (1930). *Africa at Work*. New York: self-published.

Tignor, R. (1998). *Capitalism and Nationalism at the End of Empire: State and Business in Decolonizing Egypt, Nigeria, and Kenya, 1945–1963*. Princeton: Princeton University Press.

Uche, C. (1996). 'Credit discrimination controversy in British West Africa: Evidence from Barclays Bank DCO', *African Review of Money, Finance and Banking, 20*, 87–106.

Uche, C. (1998). 'Accounting and control in Barclays Bank (DCO): the lending to Africans episode', *Accounting, Business and Financial History, 8*(3), 239–60.

Uche, C. (1999). 'Foreign banks, Africans, and credit in colonial Nigeria, c.1890–1912', *Economic History Review, 52*(4), 669–91.

Uche, C. (2010). 'Indigenous banks in colonial Nigeria', *International Journal of African Historical Studies, 43*(3), 467–87.

Uche, C. (2012). 'British government, British businesses, and the indigenization exercise in post-independence Nigeria', *Business History Review, 86*(4), 745–71.

Van den Bersselaar, D. (2011a). '"Doorway to success"? Reconstructing African careers in European business from company house magazines and oral history interviews', *History in Africa, 38*, 257–94.

Van den Bersselaar, D. (2011b). 'Who belongs to the "Star People"? Negotiating beer and gin advertisements in West Africa (1949–1975)', *Journal of African History, 52*(3), 385–408.

Verhoef, G. (2009). 'Savings for life to build the economy for the people: the emergence of Afrikaner corporate conglomerates in South Africa 1918–2000', *South African Journal of Economic History, 24*(1), 118–63.

Verhoef, G. (2014). 'Business history in Africa: the state of the art', *South African Economic History Annual, 3*, 10–20.

Verhoef, G. (2016). '"Not to bet the farm": SANLAM and internationalisation, 1995–2010', *Business History* (published early online).

Vos, J. (2010). 'The slave trade from the Windward Coast: the case of the Dutch, 1740–1805', *History in Africa, 38*, 29–51.

Wariboko, N. (1997). *The Mind of African Strategists: A Study of Kalabari Management Practice*. Rutherford: Farleigh Dickenson University Press.

Wariboko, N. (1998). 'A theory of the canoe house corporation', *African Economic History, 26*, 141–72.

11

Australia

Settler capitalism *sans doctrines*

Simon Ville and David Merrett

Introduction

Capitalism, or the system of business, varies between countries since it is the product of both local conditions and the transmission of ideas and practices from abroad. Attempts to generalise about capitalism are therefore fraught with difficulties. The isomorphic notion that business systems in all countries would gradually converge to a single preferred best practice overlooks the uniqueness of locality.[1] The varieties of capitalism (VoC) literature distinguished two different business systems, liberal market economies and coordinated market economies.[2] While this provided pluralism with no convergence, many countries do not fit easily or solely into either camp. There are further complications both with dynamics-over time aspects of a nation's business system can change[3], and geographic unit there may be heterogeneity at the sub- or supra- national level such as one country two capitalisms.

For several reasons, Australia was assumed to be a late adopter of best practice as embodied in American competitive managerial capitalism.[4] The growth of a professional managerial class was slow to supersede family business in many firms and, as we will see below, competitive rivalry was often muted. Australia was defined as a *liberal market economy* in the VoC literature although with very little specific analysis or empirical detail. In fact, Australian business has shown institutional elements from both main varieties of capitalism, for example the prevalence of collaborative inter-firm behaviour fits the *coordinated market economy*. Both literatures, best practice and VoC, have been widely criticised[5] and it is fair to say provide no more guidance for understanding and generalising about Australian business than they do for many other nations.

In this chapter we delve into the experience of Australian enterprise since about the middle of the nineteenth century when forms of capitalism began to emerge from the limitations of the prior convict economy. Our focus is on capitalist forms established by British settlers rather than indigenous enterprise. There have existed particular elements in the local operating environment and transmissions from overseas which blend into a distinctive set of Australian practices. Taken together, these set of practices, we argue, form a distinctive brand of business in Australia that we refer to as *Settler capitalism sans doctrines*.[6]

Influences

Legacies and transmissions

Australia was bequeathed capitalism by Britain. This provided the security of the dominant world power, the stable political and commercial institutions of the most advanced economy, and access to plentiful and complementary export markets and sources of labour and capital as the Australian colonies began to expand. Besides the broad developmental benefits of a parliamentary democracy, an independent judicial system and a free press, embryonic businesses were able to draw upon commercial law regulations that included enforceable property rights in factor and goods markets, and rules relating to the conduct of businesses and employment of workers. Finally, part of this package of institutions was the entrepreneurial ethos of the 'workshop of the world'.[7]

Importantly, these institutions and values were gradually modified and adapted to suit local Australian conditions. Having had capitalism thrust upon them, Australians never uncritically accepted its logical outcome – wealth distributed solely through the mechanism of the market. Australia shunned the Dickensian world populated by the rich, an anxious petty bourgeoisie and a desperate under-class. Under pressure from changing local and overseas imperatives, a contested narrative of capitalism plays out through Australia's history – the free market versus the redistributive role of government. Land reform, public ownership, progressive taxation, competition law, social security and assistance to those suffering losses from drought, fire and flood tempered the notion of an unfettered market and offered a safety net to the 'losers'.

The sources of international transmissions gradually shifted in the twentieth century, or at least diversified, as America, Japan and then China increasingly entered the picture. Australian capitalism again responded to these impulses, reshaped and modified business methods balancing local needs with overseas ideas and practices. McLean has reminded us of Australia's close synchronicity in economic vicissitudes with other major nations.[8] In spite of the tyranny of distance, or maybe the perils of proximity in recent decades, Australia has become increasingly integrated into the wider international economy on which it draws for sources of labour, capital, innovation and manufacturing goods, supplying in return the products of its resource-based industries to the world.

Environmental forces

In spite of the institutional legacy, the British settlement of Australia in 1788 as a convict colony was not a propitious starting point for modern enterprise. Even when some of the constraints of the convict period, such as unfree labour and legal limitations on forms of enterprise and overseas trade, began to atrophy by the mid-nineteenth century, the business challenges were still immense.

The populations of each of the Australian colonies were small and scattered. Their capitals were remote from one another and much more so from the main foreign centres of economic activity and population concentrations. Small and remote populations impacted adversely on both factor and product markets. Labour and capital were in short supply, and export markets far off. Distance and poor communications also presented challenges of internal corporate control for the more geographically diverse enterprises.

Domestic population expansion, by natural increase and immigration, and improved connections to the outside world through many advances in transport and communications in the course of the nineteenth and twentieth centuries have done much to mitigate the constraints of erstwhile limited internal and external markets. The economic rise of the Asian giants has brought major economies closer to Australia's door. The multiculturalisation of Australia, of which this was part, challenged the largely Anglicised nature of enterprise.

Each colony emerged as a separate political entity through the nineteenth century, particularly as a result of the granting of self-government in the 1850s. The sense of regional particularism translated into economic life as colony-based changes to land tenure laws and mining leases widened access to resources. The nature and availability of productive natural resources also varied between colonies. Such distinctiveness remained a feature of Australian development with the conversion of colonies into states at Federation in 1901.

The climate and terrain were unfamiliar to early British settlers and survival itself was a day to day battle. It was a common struggle against an apparently harsh and alien environment where ideologies and belief systems, including doctrinaire forms of religion, played second fiddle to practical secular needs at work and play. Australia lacked the powerful influence of religion among its earliest settlers that the Puritan ideals of the earliest British settlers had carried to the American colonies. The church was instead viewed, in secular fashion, for its educative role and as 'a source of stability, civilisation and public good'.[9] Equally, attitudes to politics veered towards the pragmatic in most cases with ideology never occupying the central place it did in Europe. Political conflict, as it evolved in Australia, focussed on practical matters with ideology largely an opportunistic handmaiden of such needs. Nonetheless, a tacit sense of egalitarianism ran through these developments even though it was rarely rationalised as an underpinning ideology. Observant visitors, including Anthony Trollope, D. H. Lawrence and Mark Twain, observed the elevation of secular and practical forms of behaviour over political ideology or religious doctrine.

The natural resource riches were rarely understood by the earliest generations beyond basic fishing and hunting. This began to change as settlers acclimatised and embraced the business opportunities provided by the natural environment. Australia gradually built a modern wealthy economy based upon a set of primary industries that regularly reinvented themselves in new products – wool from the 1840s, a variety of mineral discoveries from the 1850s, thence to wheat production, dairying and an ever widening set of resource-based industries in the twentieth century.[10] Somewhat surprisingly, though, Australia soon developed as a highly urbanised nation since these industries required long and complex supply chains to bring the product to market; many of the nodes on these chains were set in an urban environment and involved labour intensive service providers – transport from rail to ship, insurance, marketing, storage, loading and overseas shipment.

Some distinguishing features of Australian capitalism

This pattern of local conditions and international influences shaped the exceptionalism of Australian capitalism in several important respects. Small local markets required firms to maximise available economies of scale either internally, through aggressively horizontal expansion, or externally, by cooperation to share scarce resources of capital and information. Moreover, the small scale of economy and society and its relative cultural homogeneity, for at least the first century of British settlement, facilitated a range of structured inter-firm relationships at low transaction costs such as business groups and industry associations. Both strategies, however, also led to anti-competitive behaviour through concentration and collusion.

Government's important ongoing role included addressing these sources of anti-competitive behaviour. They also responded to sources of market imperfections facing small remote colonial economies by connecting firms with, and sometimes protecting them from, external factor and product markets. They funded, built and operated costly infrastructure that was unlikely to be provided privately in a small economy, and offered advice to firms on how best to exploit their resource rich environment.

While governments played an important role in attracting foreign labour and capital, overseas multinationals found an attractive home in Australia, especially in the manufacturing sector where few local firms had the scale or technological connections to compete with them. The influence of multinationals stretched to helping shape business cultures and organisational structures in Australia.[11]

The economic focus on primary industries further shaped the nature of Australian capitalism including its international connection through exporting. Manufacturing firms were less common among the largest enterprises than in industrialising nations like USA, Japan and Britain. Mining companies, pastoral financiers and other service industries supporting those sectors were among the largest and most influential corporations in Australia. Mostly, they were capital intensive, highly innovative and spread along complex international supply chains requiring careful coordination but prone to unstable export markets.

The distinctive regional elements of Australian capitalism had more to do with differences in the natural environment than in political particularism. Those states to the west and north (Western Australia, South Australia and Queensland) suited more to mining than pastoralism and agriculture experienced greater uncertainty due to the risks associated with prospecting and unstable export markets. This may have attracted more risk taking forms of entrepreneurship although unpredictable rainfall also periodically unsteadied grain and wool markets in the south-east with reverberatory effects for local consumer industries.[12]

Organisational and governance structures continued for a long time to embody personal systems associated with family and trusted employees to counter the risks of opportunism in remote environments with poor communications. While big business dominated the corporate landscape to a degree uncommon elsewhere, even the largest firms were minnows compared with those of other nations such as USA where scale drove changes in firm strategy and structure. Inter-firm relationships and structures also mattered for the reasons we saw above.

In the following section we will analyse how these distinctive elements of Australian capitalism played out in practice and shifted over time.

Phases of capitalist development

Foundations of a settler corporate economy (c. 1850–1900)

By the middle of the nineteenth century the embryonic Australian colonies had begun to break from the shackles of the convict economy where opportunities for conducting business were limited and the few successful firms had to diversify across a wide range of products and services to survive.[13] Rapid mid-century expansion – economic, demographic and geographic – provided opportunities and challenges that began to shape the long-term pattern of business enterprise in Australia.

Central to the early stages of growth were the resource industries, which flexed their muscles with the pastoral boom beginning in the 1830s and the gold rushes from the 1850s. The production and trade in raw and processed wool spawned a long supply chain of specialist firms in transport, marketing, finance and equipment. Each deployed their own proprietary knowledge base in the service of a heterogeneous commodity. Central to the supply chain were the stock and station agents who conducted livestock and property auctions, consigned wool to London markets and facilitated rural finance. They were the conduit between the farmer and the national and international commodity and financial markets.[14] The gold rushes, beginning in Victoria in the 1850s, spurred corporate growth and specialisation, initially through small individual prospectors and partnerships.

These industries motivated the first wave of internationalisation of business – rapid increases in resource exports, investment and the development of regular overseas shipping routes. The earliest British multinationals began to arrive primarily based in resource-related enterprise such as land ownership, mining, commodity trading and service industries particularly banking, stock and station agency, utilities and transport. Many took the form of 'free-standing companies', whose operations were largely based outside Britain but drew finance, business connections and entrepreneurial expertise from a physical presence in the City of London. British banks, for example, arrived to help fund the wool trade to London, notably the Bank of Australasia (1835), the Union Bank (1837), the Bank of South Australia (1851), the English, Scottish and Australian Bank (1853) and the London Chartered Bank of Australia (1853).

These developments raised incomes, and produced a larger, more skilled and mobile workforce, an improved supply of good quality entrepreneurs and the early stages of a domestic capital market. Larger, more specialized firms emerged as strategies shifted from scale to scope economies in response to expanded markets. New industries came into being, others subdivided into specialisations. Specialist financiers proliferated—savings banks, building societies, friendly societies, insurance, investment and land companies—tailored to serve a widening range of funding needs. Retailing, stockbroking and ship owning were among other service industries affected by the growth of scale and specialization in business.[15] Manufacturing industries emerged as domestic demand rose to the minimum scale often required and the urban concentration of the growing population, particularly in Sydney and Melbourne, meant larger, denser markets. Food, drink, tobacco, clothing and textiles drew upon the rising population, building materials on urbanization and metals and machinery from the need to service and repair engineering equipment in transport, mining and pastoralism. However, this is a gradual story. Most industries remained atomistic in structure, and firms were located at just one or several sites. The average factory employed only 17 people by 1891 and factory production mostly relied on minimal technology and resembled an agglomeration of individual workshops.[16]

The emerging shape of modern capitalist enterprise in Australia not only took its form from new opportunities but also from the fresh challenges that expansion drew forth, particularly capital shortfalls, operations control and refocussed entrepreneurial values. Continued expansion in mining required large injections of capital as shafts deepened and more equipment such as rock crushing batteries were needed. Mining dominated the incorporated enterprises that flowed from the new company legislation of the 1860s and 1870s. Once the most apparent sources of ores had been quickly exploited, prospecting became far more risky. While the general incorporation Acts (1864 in Victoria and 1874 in New South Wales) closely followed British legislation, the higher risk environment of Australian mining necessitated a more specific measure. The local innovation of 'no liability' companies, beginning in Victoria in 1871, where partly paid shares imposed no further liability on investors, reflected the high risks and stakes faced. Most likely this only helped to fuel a get rich quick mentality that was reflected in the appearance of 1,000 companies in Bendigo alone by the end of that year.[17] Most remained small, and many were speculative ventures, until the Broken Hill boom of 1887–8 that attracted significant inter-colonial investment.[18] The West Australian gold rushes of the 1890s, that left many ghost towns in their wake, repeated this pattern of behaviour by investors.

An appetite for risk permeated other areas of enterprise, such as during the Melbourne land boom of the 1880s when speculative, indeed fraudulent, behaviour reached epidemic proportions. This created agency problems between lenders and borrowers and buyers and sellers. For banks it deepened the control risks associated with serving disparate pastoral and mining communities. Internal controls were tightened in the wake of the 1893 bank collapses – decision-making became more centralised and 'inspectors' paid more regular visits to the branches. Although increasing numbers of firms took advantage of the general incorporation laws to raise funds and claim limited liability, concerns about agency limited the locus of ownership in many cases to family, friends and business associates. Shipowner and trader Burns Philp offered shares to branch managers and followed this up with regular branch inspections. Wool broker Dalgety addressed managerial opportunism by making important branch appointments from among experienced and well-known staff in its Melbourne head office. In a small, relatively homogeneous society, personal associations and contacts were easier to develop and maintain. Personal capitalism, viewed as a source of inefficiency in the Chandlerian framework, was thus a rational response to the operating environment.

The value of personal connection came more clearly to the fore as an element of Australian capitalism in the final decade or so of the nineteenth century when the booming economy of previous decades began to run out of steam and firms faced a deadly cocktail of financial crisis, drought and industrial conflict. The economic uncertainty encouraged industry and firm level cooperation. The rise of large scale trade unions in the 1870s and 1880s had prompted the formation of employer unions to address industrial issues in Victoria (1885), South Australia (1887) and New South Wales (1888) (Matthews, 1983, pp. 116–20). The 1890s industrial unrest and strikes of shearers, maritime workers and miners encouraged greater cooperation among regional employers' associations leading to the creation of national bodies – the Australian Chamber of Commerce, the Associated Chambers of Manufactures (1908) and the Australian Council of Employers Federations – that could more effectively negotiate with trade unions and lobby governments. At the same time, the rich vein of social capital running through Australian society moderated the natural competitive corporate instincts and facilitated such coordinated strategies.

Many firms reverted to cooperative behaviour in industries that produced staple homogeneous goods or services for which product differentiation and output reductions were not promising strategies in times of reduced demand: agreements mitigated the risk of price wars. By the end of the century, inter-firm agreements had spread widely including the brick, confectionery, sugar, tobacco, dried fruit, fresh produce, mineral oil, coal, beer and shipping industries.[19] Their size, formality and entry barriers varied between industries and over time. Cooperation also had constructive motives in building markets and strengthening supply chains. The repatriation of the wool market from London to Australia provided strong economic stimuli for the export ports of Sydney, Melbourne, Adelaide and Brisbane with the arrival of overseas buyers, the establishment of auction rooms and of display warehouses. Associations of wool brokers were established at each of the regional centres in the 1890s to coordinate cooperation.

The distinctive role of government in the corporate economy began to take shape in this period. We saw above the particular forms of legislation that assisted the funding needs of mining, but government adopted further measures to address failures in the market for public infrastructure in a small economy by attracting overseas funds on the collateral of state revenue raising. Besides funding, Australian entrepreneurs lacked experience operating large scale enterprise. Thus, as part of this 'colonial socialism' movement, colonial government also owned and operated natural monopoly enterprises in critical network industries, particularly the railways and postal services. The New South Wales Government Railways (1855) and Victorian Railways (1859) assumed control of railway building and operation in their respective colonies over the following decades with similar experiences elsewhere.[20] Their capitalization and labour force towered over private enterprise. By 1900 New South Wales Government Railways employed over 14,000 workers at a time when most large enterprises would have counted their workforce in hundreds (Railways Commissioners, 1900, p. 24). By 1910 the asset value of Victorian Railways was nearly six times the largest private non-financial firm, Dalgety.[21] Colonial postal and telegraph departments were similarly huge enterprises that stretched over vast areas and counted many hundreds of branch offices. By 1891 Victoria had 1,729 post offices in its network and New South Wales had 1,384 (*Year Book of Australia*, 1912, p. 755). When the state offices merged in 1901 the new federal Post Master General employed nearly 16,000 workers across some 7,400 offices.[22]

Big business and multinational enterprise (c.1901–70)

Government network monopolies continued to outsize the largest private enterprises for most of the twentieth century: it was not until the 1980s that BHP had become larger than any government corporation. Nonetheless, a series of factors together shaped the growth of the size and geographical reach of leading firms after Federation: improvements in transport and communications; developments in scale-based production technologies; the expansion of domestic capital markets; the growth of per capita incomes and with it a consumer society; and the tariff protection of some infant industries. Federation brought nation building strategies that helped to drive the growth of large scale enterprise particularly by access to larger more unified inter-state domestic markets and through external trade protection. Domestic capital markets strengthened by the 1920s and 1930s, stimulated by the opportunities to adopt foreign innovation and to cash in on the growth of consumer society as reflected in rising expenditures on household durables. While many of these benefits flowed to a burgeoning manufacturing sector, resource firms continued to play a distinctive role.

All of these factors contributed to the emergence of big business in Australia, both domestic and multinational. The growth of large scale enterprise has been analysed in detail elsewhere.[23] A number of distinguishing features, though, should be briefly noted. The largest firms were more commonly found in, or supporting, resource industries than elsewhere with Dalgety (pastoral agent), Colonial Sugar Refiners, BHP (mining) and Burns Philp (South Seas trader and plantation owner) persistently among the very largest firms for much of the century. British Tobacco and Shell were examples of the importance of multinationals in this group. Some of these firms were also characterised by their longevity at the top of the list of the largest firms. To prosper these 'corporate leaders' needed to be adaptive and agile, responding to changes in their environment. In the early decades of the twentieth century, successful large firms aggressively pursued horizontal growth to leverage economies of scale by capturing share in small markets and exploiting new mass production technologies. In some cases diversification, with the promise of economies of scope, followed. This was especially the case for resource-based firms conscious of the need to pursue growth opportunities away from crowded resource markets into expanding manufacturing sectors such as building materials (CSR) and fabricated steel products (BHP).

Australia's firms were minnows compared with the largest in countries such as USA or Britain. This may help to explain why they were slow to adopt modern governance and organisational structures associated with the divorce of ownership from control and the development of systematic managerial hierarchies. In many cases, the founding families continued to exert ownership and management influence into the post-World War Two era. There was little evidence of hierarchies of salaried managers outside banks, pastoral companies or mines. There were no educational programs to train managers, and the universities and schools of mines generated only limited numbers of professional engineers, industrial chemists, metallurgists and the like.[24] In the early 1950s a study of the largest 102 companies in Australia, including financial institutions and subsidiaries of foreign firms, indicated that founding families were able to control the majority of those companies through their positions on boards and through stockholdings. Only a third of domestic companies could be identified as management controlled.[25]

At the same time, it is striking that big business was actually more dominant domestically than in these other nations. The smallness of the local market and the presence of foreign multinationals are a big part of the reasons for this dominance, which has led to the coining of the term *Big End of Town*. The epithet has also been taken to imply that the largest firms tended to keep themselves apart from the main stream of corporate Australia and perhaps even that they colluded together. Given the degree of concentration and that some were controlled from abroad or survived in the elite list for a long period of time, lends credence to concerns about their exclusivity. It also helps to explain the belated changes to governance systems.

The continuing influence of key business families in running several leading corporations, sometimes as part of a formal or informal business group, pointed in the same direction. A literature on Australian groups and business families implies insidious forms of control exercised by elite groups of entrepreneurs and their families. Books, often running to multiple editions, with titles like *Who owns Australia*; *The 60 rich families who own Australia*; and *The Controllers* are, on one level, polemical attacks on the wealthy. They reveal much about interlocking directorates, share ownership and business influence exercised by individuals across groups of firms. One particularly intriguing piece of research by Rawling produced a complex network diagram for 1939 entitled 'Seventy-nine men and some of the companies they control'. More specifically, he described the 'Kingdom of 360 Collins Street'. Seven leading mining companies, including the Collins House group, occupied this building. Thirty men occupied the 63 directorate seats on their boards, 14 sitting on more than one of these companies. Many of these directors held shares in, or sat on the board of, companies from other sectors including brewing, finance, pastoral agency, textiles, paper, vehicle production, chemicals, glass, rubber, packaging, engineering and transport. In a similar vein, Campbell identified key groups of families in Melbourne, Sydney and Adelaide who were intertwined through business (shareholdings and directorships), intermarriage, social ties (religion, clubs), attending the same schools and living within the same residential areas. Thus, for example, the 'Main Sydney Group' consisted of 10 families who between them held directorships in 40 companies with a total paid up capital of A$155m that spanned a wide range of industries including sugar, banking, insurance, beer, gas, textiles, chemicals, finance, industrial, pastoral, rubber and coal.

In spite of this colourful literature, the 'robber baron' tag never stuck in Australia. Campbell's work for example, which drew upon American writings, had little leverage beyond the Communist Party. Until the 1960s there was no push for the type of anti-trust legislation adopted by American governments since the turn of the twentieth century. Australia's Industries Preservation Act (1910) soon became a dead letter. As part of the ongoing contested narrative, business broadly defined created a story of pioneering, nation building and job creating enterprise—business of whatever size and hue was contributing to 'progress'.

Another aspect of disputation was the multinational. They continued to play a central role in the Australian corporate economy in the twentieth century: on average, multinationals constituted about a quarter of the top 100 non-financial firms. The opportunity to jump tariff barriers, tap into an expanding market with good levels of per capita income and utilise a trained, educated workforce were now more appealing than the search for natural resources that had driven the free-standing companies of the nineteenth century. As a result, multinationals clustered in manufacturing rather than primary and increasing numbers, especially from the 1920s, arrived from the United States as the principal industrial nation. By the post-World War Two era increasing numbers of Japanese firms also arrived on the landscape. Multinationals often occupied a central position in industries associated with progressive scientific, administrative, managerial and technical capabilities that were transferred to Australia. By the 1960s several expanding Australian industries were dominated by global firms such as Shell, BP, Mobil, Esso (oil refining), Ford, General-Motors Holden, Toyota (vehicle production) and Nestlé and Unilever (food processing).

While local competitors, suppliers and customers benefitted from spillover effects from multinationals, their presence also raised the ire of some contemporaries. It was argued that they suffocated the ability of some local firms, lacking scale and experience, to establish themselves. This may explain, in part, the paucity of Australian firms internationalising before about the 1980s. However, there were other factors including the smallness of the local market as a launching pad for international expansion and high wages compared with many newly industrialising nations. Australia's comparative advantage, as we have seen, lay predominantly with resource industries for whom exporting was often the preferred mode of internationalisation. The contentious issue of transfer pricing, wherein 'adjusted' internal costs facilitated tax minimisation, and the influence of international business on government macroeconomic policy were also hotly debated.

Competition, de-regulation, modern business practices (c.1970–)

The post-Federation policy environment that had focussed for decades on the broad objective of growth moderated only by egalitarian values underwent several phases of change after World War Two. Government in Australia, as elsewhere, took centre stage after 1945, seeking to extend state ownership and pulling their Keynesian instruments of macroeconomic policy in pursuit of full employment, growth with low inflation and external balance. However, by the 1970s, protection, regulation, state enterprise, subsidies and centralised wage determination were viewed as among the main culprits for a decline in international competitiveness alleged by national inquiries and international bodies including the OECD. The decline in economic performance in the 1960s and 1970s—slowing growth combined with stagflation—further motivated a re-evaluation of economic and business conventional wisdom. Borland has described the fundamental changes in policy from the 1970s designed to shift from growth to efficiency in firms and markets particularly through the introduction of competition policy, tariff reduction, financial deregulation and privatisation.[26] How has this affected the nature of enterprise in Australia? Certainly new opportunities were presented to business from deregulating financial and exchange markets and aligning wages more closely with productivity. Competition policy, privatisation and tariff reductions, promised increased efficiency by exposing and driving out lazy monopolists and colluding associations.

There was a dramatic upsurge in the number of Australian firms establishing overseas in the 1980s. Major firms, including, miners, builders, retailers and transport firms, ventured overseas. These included Newscorp, Lend Lease, Fosters, CSR, WMC, BHP and AMP.

Only a handful of manufacturers made the move, mostly restricting their advances within the south Pacific region. Many of these ventures ended unsuccessfully with forced divestments from later in the 1990s. The advantages accruing from the changed conditions in the local market, it seems, rarely translated beneficially into overseas expansion. Merrett has observed that these firms were novices at internationalisation and had diversified rather than built up core strengths in particular products and industries that could be leveraged to effect in overseas markets.[27] Successful exceptions such as CSL (plasma products) and Cochlear (hearing devices) have focussed on a specific research intensive product and built alliances to assist the development of overseas marketing and production.

The deregulation of financial and exchange markets and the close policy scrutiny of market share in particular industries may have contributed to the rise of large diversified business groups in the 1980s. This conglomeration 'fad', though, also drew upon trends in overseas markets in Europe and North America. Prominent examples included Adsteam, Elders IXL and Bond Corporation. There were plenty of others! Many sought ambitious and over-reaching expansion, appropriately captured in the title of Trevor Sykes account, *The Bold Riders*.[28] Their rise and fall was dramatic – by the turn of the twenty-first century most had disappeared from the landscape of Australian corporate leadership with the dismantling of the groups. 'Charismatic' entrepreneurs controlled most groups—Alan Bond (Bond Corporation), John Elliott (Elders IXL) and John Spalvins (Adsteam). They controlled large sections of the economy in the 1980s including all beer production, the largest pastoral companies, the second largest retail chain and a similarly substantial presence in industrials, food, textiles, property, mortgages and car dealers.

Researchers have been highly critical of the impact of most of the groups, arguing that they destroyed far more wealth than they created. Between them they lost an estimated A$16bn and inflicted serious damage on many Australian corporate icons. The prudential standards of banks, non-executive directors, lawyers, accountants and brokers have all been brought into question. Politicians accepted 'donations' and many journalists feared libel cases or merely held these groups in misplaced admiration. Tax payers, shareholders and bank customers paid a heavy price for years to come.[29] The verdict on these groups has focussed on their speculative nature driven by pragmatic entrepreneurial practices, subsequently revealed as unethical if not illegal and earning for this generation of entrepreneurs the epithet, 'corporate raiders'. There was a failure to nurture the skills, culture, strategy and structure that underpin the long-term success of business groups. They overestimated their ability to manage effectively across a diverse range of industries and hold together a large group.

The microeconomic reforms, by leading to greater openness and enhanced competition, also helped to modernise business practices in Australia in a manner not dissimilar to some of the precepts of the liberal market economy described in the VoC literature – competitive market arrangements, anti-trust policies, formal education and enterprise level wage bargaining. Business practices in general moved towards modern best practices with the spread of human resource planning, marketing strategies and management accounting tools. Organisational structures also matured – the separation of ownership from control in more cases, and the development of rational hierarchies supported by enhanced management training.

All of this might suggest that the distinctive local flavour of Australian capitalism, drawing heavily on the local operating environment and enriched with international influences, has atrophied in recent decades by converging to an international model particularly associated with so-called liberal market economies of the Anglo-Saxon world. This would overstate the case significantly. Many of the local defining characteristics have persisted. Resource-based industries continue to play an important role in shaping the business community as indicated by their role in the sustained secular boom in the 1990s that far outstripped the performance of most economies. Large scale enterprise, both foreign and domestic, continues to cast a long shadow over the competitive structure of markets. Relationships among firms continue to be negotiated as much through networks and associations as the competitive location of the marketplace. Governments have largely forsaken their operational role in network industries but directional policies supported by the work of research entities, such as the Productivity Commission, continue to have a major influence on the future direction of business.

Was there a distinctive variety of Australian capitalism? Pragmatism over ideology

When French socialist writer Albert Métin visited Australia in 1899 he was impressed at the advanced social development (for example in the franchise, education and social security) that had been achieved through practical and empirical, rather than theoretical or ideological impulses, which he described in his book *Le Socialisme sans Doctrines*.[30] The intervention of government in the economy and society was not driven by ideology or philosophy in contrast to Socialist France. Instead, socialism *sans doctrine* followed what was pragmatically needed.

Similarly, Australian enterprise was not predominantly the product of a particular ideology but rather the response to conditions in the local environment and a range of overseas influences. Australian enterprise, with the exception of the convict and wartime eras, was capitalist in nature, in its pursuit of profit, but this included, nonetheless, an important role for government as we have seen. Intervention, however, was not borne of ideological underpinnings as had been the case of government economic intervention in France. Nor, despite the broad institutional inheritance from Britain, was Australian capitalism the product of Smithian laissez-faire and free trade policies that had permeated the UK and found nineteenth-century expression in the Manchester School beliefs of Richard Cobden and John Bright that the private market would bring benefits to all.

Strategies of firms and their structures were therefore largely the product of the pragmatic and practical requirements of a settler society. A 'here and now' response was called for in the battle against unfamiliar, often undeveloped and remote, surroundings faced by new settlers. As we have seen, the extent and nature of central intervention in the free market and redistribution of its riches was continually debated and adjusted in response to the changing needs of the Australian economy and society. This has led us to deploy the epithet "settler capitalism sans doctrine". Like some other settler societies, this educed entrepreneurial responses that included government intervention to resolve market failures, the influential hand of multinationals, cooperative behaviour to engage common threats and opportunities and the embracing of an economically beneficent natural environment.

Can we be more specific – has the flavour of Australian capitalism differed from that of other, similar, settler societies? We might expect the degree of convergence to be greatest with similar British colonies such as New Zealand given the role of the imperial power. The precise nature and timing of British influence, though, varied between countries, and indeed among states/colonies within Australia, as did the nature of the natural environment that settlers faced. Moreover, though British practices, institutions and personnel were important, local adaptations to particular Australian conditions occurred such as differences in corporations' law and lending practices. Cooperative behaviour among firms on the other hand, arguably had more of a Continental European coordinated market economy edge to it than British individualist capitalism.

Another way of looking for quintessential elements to Australian capitalism is through the lens of entrepreneurship. We know that Australian business for most of the last two centuries has relied heavily upon entrepreneurs operating family-controlled firms and cooperating with other business leaders. Individual and collective character traits matter. There is a growing historical and psychological literature that seeks to identify behavioural traits common to particular societies. Two common themes for Australia have been 'larrikinism' and 'mateship'. A larrikin is associated with someone who is considered irreverent, challenging of conventional wisdom and sceptical of hierarchy. Mateship addresses the idea of close, reliable friendships particularly to help each other out in hard times. The origins of both of these values have been variously associated with the convict past, the challenges of working in the bush or behaviours, 'nourished throughout our history'.[31] While often the caricature of a larrikin has been a low life figure, maybe a youth, almost a social outcast, Bellanta in her recent history notes, "the first larrikins hankered after small-time capitalist enterprise".[32] This link to the world of business also emerges from Dyrenfurth's very recent history of mateship.[33] While erstwhile associated with worker solidarity, he shows that the first Australians to call each other 'mate' were business partners.

Understanding the origins of such personality traits is beyond the scope of this chapter. However, their association with challenging authority, conventional wisdom and through cooperation with others can be related to a corporate culture that favoured shared risk-taking adaptiveness, and inventiveness. All these are quite positive attributes of entrepreneurship although each has its dark side especially when cooperation becomes anti-competitive collusion and risk-taking becomes risky business. As we have briefly highlighted in this chapter, the history of Australian enterprise has been a narrative of both inspired risk-taking and ignominious backsliding.

Notes

1 The extensive body of work of Alfred Chandler and some of his followers is the best example of isomorphism in business history.
2 Hall and Soskice, *Varieties of Capitalism*. Some hybrids have also been introduced.
3 Fellman, Iversen and Sjogren, *Creating Nordic Capitalism*.
4 Chandler, *Scale and Scope*.
5 For example, Chambers, *The Workshop of the World;* Ward, *The Australian Legend*.
6 For an account of the Australian Labour Party's brief flirtation with socialism see Frank Farrell, 'Socialism, Internationalism, and the Australian labour Movement, *Labour/Le Travail*, 15 (Spring 1985), 125–44. http://www.lltjournal.ca/index.php/llt/article/viewFile/2459/2862.
7 Chambers, *The Workshop of the World*.
8 MClean, *Growth in a Small Open Economy: An Historical View*, ibid., pp. 7–10.
9 Watson, *The Bush*, p. 415.
10 Ville and Wicken, *The Dynamics of Resource-Based Economic Development*.
11 Brash, *American Investment in Australian Industry*.
12 A detailed account of historic economic data by colony/state is provided in W. A. Sinclair, 'Annual Estimates of Gross Domestic Product: Australian Colonies/States 1861–1976/77'(2009), http://arrow.monash.edu.au/hdl/1959.1/88855.
13 Ville, *Business Development in Colonial Australia*.
14 Ville, *The Rural Entrepreneurs*.
15 Ville, *Business Development in Colonial Australia*, pp. 28–9. Keneley, *The Service Economy*.
16 Butlin, *Investment in Australian Economic Development, 1861–1900*, p. 207.
17 Blainey, *The Rush That Never Ended*, pp. 75–6.
18 Blainey, *The Rise of Broken Hill*, p. 30.
19 Wilkinson, *The Trust Movement in Australia*.
20 Ergas and Pincus, *Infrastructure and Colonial Socialism*.

21 Fleming, Merrett and Ville, *The Big End of Town*, p. 14.

22 Moyal, *Clear across Australia*, p. 88.

23 Fleming, Merrett and Ville, *The Big End of Town*; Merrett, Big Business and Foreign Firms.

24 Edelstein, 'Professional Engineers in Australia', AEHR, September 1988; Schedvin *Shaping Science and Industry.*

25 Wheelwright, *Ownership and Control of Australian Companies*, pp. 4, 119.

26 Borland, *Microeconomic reform.*

27 Merrett, Big Business and Foreign Firms.

28 Sykes, *The Bold Riders.*

29 Sykes, *Bold Riders,* ch. 17.

30 Metin, *Le Socialisme sans Doctrines.*

31 Crawford, *Australia*, p. 152; Ward, *The Australian Legend*; Watson, *The Bush.*

32 Bellanta, *Larrikins: A History*, p. xviii.

33 Dyrenfurth, *Mateship.*

References

Bellanta, M. (2012). *Larrikins: A History.* St Lucia, Queensland: University of Queensland Press.

Blainey, G. (1963). *The Rush That Never Ended: A History of Australian Mining.* Melbourne: Melbourne University Press.

Blainey, G. (1968). *The Rise of Broken Hill.* Melbourne: MacMillan.

Borland, J. (2015). Microeconomic reform. In: S. Ville and G. Withers, eds. *The Cambridge Economic History of Australia.* Melbourne: Cambridge University Press, 419–37.

Brash, D. T. (1966). *American Investment in Australian Industry.* Canberra: Canberra Australian National University Press.

Butlin, N. G. (1964). *Investment in Australian Economic Development, 1861–1900.* Cambridge: Cambridge University Press.

Chambers, J. D. (1961). *The Workshop of the World: British Economic History from 1820 to 1880.* London: Oxford University Press.

Chandler, A. D. J. (1990). *Scale and Scope: The Dynamics of Industrial Capitalism.* Cambridge: Belknap Press of Harvard University Press.

Crawford, R. M. (1952). *Australia.* London: Hutchinson University Library.

Dyrenfurth, N. (2015). *Mateship: A very Australian History.* Brunswick: Scribe.

Edelstein, M. (1988). Professional Engineers in Australia-Institutional Response in a Developing-Economy, 1860–1980. *Australian Economic History Review 28* (2), 8–32

Ergas, H. & Pincus, J. J. (2015). Infrastructure and Colonial Socialism. In: S. Ville and G. Withers, eds. *The Cambridge Economic History of Australia.* Melbourne: Cambridge University Press, 222–44.

Fellman, S., Iversen, M. J. & Sjogren, H. eds. (2008). *Creating Nordic Capitalism: The Development of a Competitive Periphery.* Basingstoke: Palgrave Macmillan.

Fleming, G. A., Merrett, D. & Ville, S. P. (2004). *The Big End of Town: Big Business and Corporate Leadership in Twentieth-Century Australia.* New York: Cambridge University Press.

Hall, P. A. & Soskice, D. (eds.) (2001). *Varieties of Capitalism. The Institutional Foundations of Comparative Advantage.* Oxford: Oxford University Press.

Keneley, M. J. (2015). The service economy. In: S. Ville and G. Withers, eds. *The Cambridge Economic History of Australia.* Melbourne: Cambridge University Press.

McLean, I. (1989). Growth in a small open economy: an historical view. In: B.J. Chapman, eds. *Australian Economic Growth: Essays in Honour of Fred H. Gruen.* Melbourne: Macmillan.

Merrett, D. (2015). Big business and foreign firms. In: S. Ville and G. Withers, eds. *The Cambridge Economic History of Australia.* Melbourne: Cambridge University Press.

Metin, A. (1901). Le Socialisme sans Doctrines. Boulevard St Germain, https://archive.org/search. php?query=publisher%3A%22F.+Alcan%22 F. Alcan.

Moyal, A. (1984). *Clear across Australia: A History of Telecommunications.* Melbourne: Nelson.

Schedvin, C. B. (1987). *Shaping Science and Industry. A History of Australia's Council for Scientific and Industrial Research 1926–49.* Sydney: Allen & Unwin.

Sykes, T. (1994). *The Bold Riders: Behind Australia's Corporate Collapses.* St. Leonards: Allen & Unwin.

Ville, S. (1998). Business Development in Colonial Australia. *Australian Economic History Review*, *38*(1), 16–41.

Ville, S. & Wicken, O. (2013). The Dynamics of Resource-Based Economic Development: Evidence from Australia and Norway. *Industrial and Corporate Change, 22*, 1341–71.

Ville, S. P. (2000). *The Rural Entrepreneurs: A History of the Stock and Station Agent Industry in Australia and New Zealand*. Oakleigh: Cambridge University Press.

Ward, R. (1958). *The Australian Legend*. Melbourne: Oxford University Press.

Watson, D. (2014). *The Bush. Travels in the Heart of Australia*. Melbourne: Penguin.

Wheelwright, E. L. (1957). *Ownership and Control of Australian Companies. A Study of 102 of the Largest Pulic Companies Incorporated in Australia*. Sydney: The Law Book Company of Australasia.

Wilkinson, H. L. (1914). *The Trust Movement in Australia*. Sydney: Critchley Parker Pty Ltd.

12

Enterprise in the Soviet and Soviet-Type-Economies

Martin Kragh[1]

The economic history of the recent past reminds us that in the mid-twentieth century, one third of the world's population lived under communist regimes, stretching across a landmass from Berlin to Canton. The main institutions of the Soviet economy were established by Vladimir Lenin and Joseph Stalin in the 1920s and early 1930s: nationalization of industry, collectivization of agriculture and centralized state control over the economy. Allocation of resources in the Soviet economy was the exclusive purview of higher authorities, whose commands – in Soviet parlance "plan targets" – were legally binding; and enterprise management, at least in theory, was assumed to respond exclusively to the commands of the central planners. As communist regimes spread across the globe in the post-World War II era, so did the main institutions of the Soviet-Type-Economy. Although the experience of Soviet-Type-Economies, with the exception of North Korea and Cuba, can now be written in the past tense, its legacies in terms of industrial structure, economic geography, institutions and possibly behavioral patterns, have continued to be felt in the post-transition eras.

Business historians have provided several studies of enterprise in a number of totalitarian regimes of the twentieth century, i.e., Germany under Adolf Hitler, Spain under Francisco Franco and Nicaragua under the Somoza dynasty (Bucheli, 2008; Jones and Lubinski, 2012). All totalitarian regimes have in common the extreme politicization of economic activity. One important distinction between right-wing totalitarian regimes and those established by communist rule is that the former never abolished the institution of private property, even when they introduced restrictions on ownership and managerial structure (although there were important exceptions, such as the Nazi German expropriation of property held by Jews).[2] Right-wing dictators and autocrats have often also sought cooperation (through concessions or direct investment) with foreign multinational firms as a means to forge political alliances and modernize their domestic economies. Communist regimes, in contrast, have striven for self-sufficiency and kept to a minimum any "dependency" on their capitalist rivals, even when they engaged with the outside world (with the main exception being China since 1979).

Contrary to the expectations of Karl Marx and other socialist intellectuals in the nineteenth century, the communist revolution did not originate in the most advanced capitalist states of Europe, but in Russia. On 7 November, 1917, the Bolsheviks overthrew the Kerensky Provisional Government which had succeeded that of the Tsar, and set about imposing on society their visions for the economic, political and military modernization of the Soviet Union. During World War II, the Red Army defeated Nazi Germany and her allies, and the Soviet model was exported to Eastern Europe and China. The purpose of this essay is to provide a historical background and comparative analysis of the Soviet and Soviet-Type-Economies which emerged in the twentieth century, with particular reference to the enterprise level.

Background

Following the geopolitical fragmentation of two world wars, the communist club expanded in concentric circles. From the creation of the Union of Soviet Socialist Republics (USSR) in 1922, de facto Soviet territory was expanded during World War II to also include Estonia, Latvia, Lithuania, Moldova and eastern Poland and Finland. With the backing of Soviet authorities, communists assumed power in Albania, Bulgaria, Czechoslovakia, East Germany, Hungary, Poland and Romania. Communist regimes were established also in Yugoslavia, North Vietnam, North Korea, Mongolia, China, Cuba, Laos and Cambodia; and in the wake of anti-imperialist movements in Asia, the Middle East and Africa, the Soviet Union gained adherents as an attractive alternative to colonial and semi-colonial models of economic and political development (Applebaum, 2013; Frieden and Rogowski, 2014). For the purposes of this essay I will focus mainly on the Soviet Union, and to a lesser extent Eastern Europe and China, although it means excluding the experience of Soviet-Type-Economies in, for example, India, Ethiopia and Syria.

Communist regimes by the mid-twentieth century had in common two important themes. Firstly, virtually all of them had been created following a period of war or political calamity, and none of their leaders had been elected by popular mandate. As a result, the usurpation of power by communist parties was often followed by military hostilities (inherited or self-created). Secondly, countries where communist regimes were established tended to be comparatively poor: Eastern Europe was poorer than Western Europe, and China was poorer than India or Japan (Harrison, 2012). Some members of the communist club, however, had been more economically developed than others prior to communist rule (primarily Czechoslovakia, which had also been a democracy, and East Germany), and all countries had a relatively congenial environment for enterprise and so were capable of attracting foreign direct investment and government loans; institutions such as stock markets, joint-stock companies and private property existed virtually everywhere in Europe (Teichova, 1997). In no communist regime was development therefore ever started entirely from scratch, something which is true even for China.

Economic policy and industrial structure

There are many criteria for distinguishing between different economic systems, and between varieties within the individual systems. As the characteristics and varieties of market economies are covered elsewhere in this volume, I will merely state the most useful distinction for our purposes: the market economy is a system in which the market mechanism performs the chief task of coordinating the activities of individual economic units. A command economy, in contrast, is one where the producers (firms and households) employ resources primarily by virtue of directives from higher authorities, directives which cannot easily be ignored under the threat of punishment. In a command economy – what I refer to in this essay as the Soviet-Type-Economy – the manager of a firm executes commands as his or her principal mode of behavior (Grossman, 1963). But while command is the dominant mode, this does not preclude the presence of other elements such as markets and customary behavior (Temin, 1980). In order to understand more fully the functioning of Soviet-Type-Economies, and their varieties, it is necessary to analyze how the three different modes interacted over time.[3]

Communist regimes are often described as both monolithic and politically stable. This is a statement in need of qualification. Although the emphasis here is the history of the Soviet-Type-Economies, their functioning cannot be separated from the fact that all of them have materialized in countries that were also dictatorships. As a result, Soviet-Type-Economies have been highly sensitive to the ideals of their political leaders. In the 1920s, Stalin altered his position on economic policy more than once before securing his undisputed personal rule by 1929. After Stalin's death in 1953, his successors would never again resort to the levels of repression reached in the 1930s and 1940s, and experiments were made to introduce more market elements. Mao Zedong repeatedly changed economic policies in accordance with the changes in his own revolutionary ideals or personal whims and wishes, and in contrast to both the Soviet Union and China, North Korea remains the only communist regime to maintain a hereditary succession of power. So, even though the main institutions of Soviet-Type-Economies have typically remained stable (in the former Soviet bloc, until 1989–91), policies have shifted between different countries as well as over time.

Communist regimes have historically defended their policies in the abstract as the most efficient means to reach a "higher" development phase characterized by abundance rather than scarcity of goods. Under Stalin and Mao, this aim would in practice entail decisions to shift resources from consumption to accumulation and defense through forced savings and surpluses extracted from collectivized agriculture. The importance of defense and security in Soviet strategic thinking in the 1920s and 1930s, rather than visionary socialist ideals, has been reemphasized by recent scholarship (Davies, 2008; Kontorovich, 1986; Simonov, 1996). In fact, Communist Party leaders never made their larger security concerns a secret. In 1931, Stalin (1949, pp. 40–41) remarked how the Soviet Union was "fifty or a hundred years behind the advanced countries. We must make good this distance in ten years. Either we do it, or they crush us". These sentiments were later echoed by Mao in 1965, who explained that "we have begun to build steel, armaments, machinery, chemicals, petroleum and railroad base areas, so that if war breaks out we have nothing to fear".[4]

What differentiated leaders in communist regimes from those in capitalist countries in the 1950s was not their belief in heavy industry as a key to modernization as such, but rather their view on industrialization as a means to achieve primarily defense and security related objectives (objectives which, however, would have been readily recognized by Sergei Witte or Otto von Bismarck, and nationalist governments in Japan and pre-revolutionary China). Both Stalin and Mao sought to secure their regimes from foreign and domestic threats. Translated into economic policy, this threat perception motivated the construction of a railway grid linking previously isolated parts of the Soviet Union and China, respectively; the exploitation of ferrous and non-ferrous metals and minerals; the erection of hydroelectric dams and coal power plants; and the construction of modern manufacturing enterprises. The manufacturing enterprises built included metal forming plants capable of producing missiles, sputniks, and airplanes and factories with the capacity to mass produce heavy machinery, trucks, tanks, chemicals and modern armaments.

Drawing on the Dexter-Rodionov database, Figure 12.1 details the annual number of Soviet defense plants from 1917 to 1991 for seven important branches – armaments (artillery, infantry, naval), munitions (ammunition, explosives, chemical agents), shipbuilding, radio electronics (radio, radar, air defense systems, telephone, electronic components), aerospace (aircraft, missiles, space), armored vehicles and atomic weapons. These seven branches were few in comparison to the total number of enterprises in the Soviet economy (in 1988, there were in total 47,000 industrial enterprises in the Soviet Union), but they were significant in terms of size, strategic import and employment. Looking at the dynamics, two interesting phenomena of the Soviet economy stand out. Firstly, the rapid expansion of basic defense industry beginning in the 1930s – especially regarding armaments, munitions, shipbuilding and armored vehicles – an expansion which accelerated through World War II. Secondly, the subsequent stability of aforementioned industries in the post-war arms race complemented with the massive build-up of new branches. By 1991, of the 5,060 defense firms in our sample, 2,030 were in radio electronics, a branch which together with atomic weapons had expanded the most since 1945. Why radio electronics in the post-war period became the largest branch in terms of establishments can be explained by deliberate policy: Soviet planners tended to make electronic firms small by Soviet standards (1,000–3,000 workers), and the firms were widely scattered across a large territory (perhaps for security and mobilization reasons).[5] But radios and communication equipment had also been in short supply during World War II, so it is possible that the changing composition of defense industry in the post-war period reflected a sense of urgency.

Defense considerations do not only explain the industrial priorities, but also the geographical allocation and size of new industrial plants. In Tsarist Russia, industries had been built around Saint Petersburg, Moscow, and the western districts of the empire. Soviet planning, in contrast, paid less consideration to factors such as distance to markets or costs of transportation. Under Stalin, construction of large enterprises was shifted to the Urals and western Siberia, where production was more secure in the event of invasion, although pre-existing industrial capacity would remain in the western parts of the country until the large scale evacuations during World War II (Coal and German, 1961; Kumo, 2004). Under Mao's

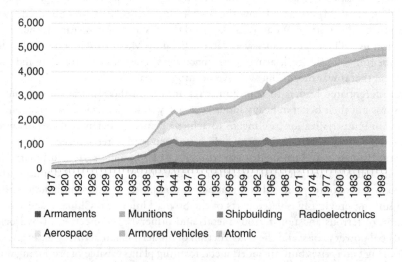

Figure 12.1 Annual number of Soviet defense plants by industries, 1917–1991
Source: Adapted from Dexter and Rodionov (2015).

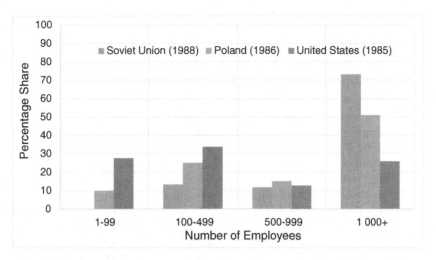

Figure 12.2 Size distribution of industrial enterprises in the Soviet Union, Poland and the United States (share of employees)

Source: Adapted from Fischer (1994, p. 241). The percentage share of Soviet industrial enterprises with less than 100 employees was only 1.8%, for which reason it is not visible in the figure.

"Third Front" program in the 1960s, the industrial center of gravity was transferred even more dramatically from the coastal enclaves to the inland regions or the north-east (Naughton, 1994).

Because of a preference for "gigantism", size distribution of industrial enterprises in both the Soviet and Chinese economies was also highly biased towards large firms (Yudanov, 1997, 398), with very few industrial firms operating with less than 100 employees – a noticeable contrast to the size distribution normally observed in market economies. As illustrated by Figure 12.2, industrial enterprises with more than 1,000 employees constituted 51% of all enterprises in Poland (year 1986) and 73.3% in the USSR (year 1988), but only 25.8% in the US (year 1985). At the other end of the spectrum, only 1.8% and 10% of the Soviet and Polish industrial enterprises, respectively, had fewer than 100 employees, whereas the corresponding figure for the US economy was 27.6%. Services provided by small and medium-sized firms in market economies were simply absent, or internalized in larger Soviet-Type firms.

Enterprise

Soviet-Type enterprises do not possess any of the features we associate with normal corporate governance in market economies. Firms do not engage in strategic planning, spending decisions or marketing, nor do they fully control related activities such as logistics or personnel capabilities. All real powers of ownership are exercised by the government through a multilevel bureaucratic hierarchy. Because managers do not make any strategic decisions, or influence the pricing of its products, they are not held accountable for the firm's eventual profits (which are taken by the government) or losses (which are made up by the government). The primary role of the manager is to fulfill the plan targets that he or she had been assigned, with the enterprises operating under soft budget constraints. The term "soft budget constraint" was coined by Kornai (1980) in his study of the Hungarian Soviet-Type-Economy, and has since been applied to phenomena arising also in the more decentralized market economic systems. In the apt formulation of Maskin (1996, p. 126), a soft budget-constraint "pertains wherever a funding source – e.g., a bank or government – finds it impossible to keep an enterprise to a fixed budget, i.e., whenever the enterprise can extract ex post a bigger subsidy or loan than would have been considered efficient ex ante".

In contrast, a perfectly hard budget-constraint exists when a company has to finance all of its activities in a given time period from its own income. In market economies with normal financing regimes, access to outside funding relaxes the hard budget constraint without removing the incentives for efficient risk management and cost-benefit analysis. In the Soviet-Type-Economies, differences in state priorities could influence the severity of the budget constraint. Soviet defense industry, because of its high priority, was allocated the best available material inputs and provided with funding for comparatively favorable conditions of employment and recruitment. It was also a sector characterized by excess capacity and stock-piling of resources for war (including, besides armaments and other military hardware, non-ferrous metals and oil which technically belonged to the civilian sector), creating bottlenecks and hold-ups in other sectors in the economy. Lower priority sectors were deprived of the funding necessary to maintain equal standards of production quality and terms of employment. This structural feature of the soft budget constraint conditioned Soviet economic development for six decades, causing significant structural distortions in the allocation of resources (Cooper, 2013).

The soft budget constraint of Soviet-Type firms at the macro level created behavioral patterns at the micro level which deviated from behavior normally regarded as desirable in market economic systems. We can observe these deviations in a number of important situations, such as behavior regarding the role of money and credit, use of informal negotiations over resources, and patterns of organization of production – phenomena which in various degrees contradicted command as the dominant mode of behavior. Our knowledge about these behavioral patterns in the Soviet economy heralds from the pioneering work of Berliner (1957), Granick (1954) and Fainsod (1958). Archive based studies in the last two decades have provided more details (Ellman, 2008), and we now also possess a better understanding of the Chinese experience. An analysis of the enterprise level provides a vision of how the three modes of behavior outlined above – command, market and customary – interacted in the allocation of resources.

Money and credit

According to theory of socialist planning, money and finances were not supposed to matter for the allocation of resources, and national currencies were only financial expressions of physical transactions. Money, in the Soviet-Type-Economy, was "passive", and its role was restricted in a very narrow sense – i.e., the monitoring by financial authorities (with the exception of household wages, which were paid in cash). In contrast to a market economy, where the financial ability determines allocation of resources and not the other way around, plan targets determined what amount of financial resources were allocated to Soviet enterprises. Archival research on the Stalin era, however, suggests that money and credit did play an active role in at least two important ways. Firstly, enterprises had the discretionary ability to hoard money and petition for a softening of their soft budget constraints, preferably for cash. Secondly, enterprises could expand the size of outstanding debt through the horizontal issuing of credit outside of plan.

How Soviet enterprises in practice could circumvent their budget constraints has been shown by Gregory and Tikhonov (2000). To simplify, firm A had to perform its delivery plans to firm B in accordance with command regardless of B's solvency. If B was financially restrained, some ministry would always guarantee that A received the value of its deliveries regardless (or A was compensated indirectly, through for example subsidies or tax reliefs). In order to manage the increases in subsequent debt arrears, the State Bank – i.e., Gosbank – reluctantly became a de facto Lender of Last Resort for every industrial enterprise in the country. Intermittently, accumulated debts were simply cleared from the books. There was no other way around a universal soft budget constraint, a behavioral pattern which inevitably gave rise to moral hazard. Bank money was siphoned into cash and hoarded by enterprises for similar reasons. Cash was used in transactions outside the formal plan, and siphoning became so widespread it created inflationary pressures (Kim, 2002; Harrison and Kim, 2006).[6]

Shortages

One of the most distinctive features of the Soviet-Type-Economies was the chronic deficit of input supplies, a shortage which not necessarily was a consequence of a deficit in the aggregate production of the inputs. The problem of shortages, unavoidable in economies characterized by soft budget constraints, was addressed primarily through customary behavior such as queuing or informal networks, with the exact behavioral pattern depending on the situation. Shortages were most keenly felt among households. Whereas insiders (the *nomenklatura*, high-ranking officials, managers of large enterprises) could bypass queues and waiting-lists, outsiders were requested to patiently adapt. The supply of ordinary consumption goods such as meat, soap, light bulbs and radio sets was rationed for the majority population, who also had to wait several years for access to an apartment or a car. The shortages were not arbitrary, nor were they historical legacies from a distant past or an outcome of comparative underdevelopment. Shortages were system-related: per capita density of trade in 1931 in the USSR was less than one-fifth of Russia's prerevolutionary average (Hessler, 2004, p. 195).[7] Shortages, in other words, occurred because command took systematic precedence over the market for the allocation of resources.

Enterprise managers were also confronted with shortage restraints: resources had to be constantly negotiated, inputs were often insufficient or of the wrong quality, and workers had to be kept from withdrawing effort or leaving their workplace (Kragh, 2011). The shortage problem was exacerbated by the aforementioned tendency of Soviet-Type-Economies to favor large industrial establishments (the "gigantism"-syndrome). When forced industrialization was introduced in the Soviet Union under Stalin (in 1929) and in China under Mao (in 1952), 80% of their respective populations lived in the countryside. In contrast to growth patterns under market conditions, Soviet-Type industrialization in both countries saved on factors of production that were in relatively abundant supply, such as labor; whereas demand was raised per unit of output for factors that were in very short supply, such as capital (and in particular imported capital goods), skilled labor, managerial and technological know-how, processed raw materials and transport (Smolinski, 1962, p. 145). In the long run, economic growth would somewhat remedy these distortions. In the short run, large and capital intensive establishments exacerbated the shortage problem, even if it was believed to simplify economic planning.

Firms in the light industries faced comparatively harder budget restraints than the high-priority heavy and defense industries. The phenomenon of shortages and delays, consequently, may therefore be illustrated by looking at the industries producing shoes, furniture, clothes, consumer electronics and kitchen supplies, and how the construction of light industries was subject to delays. According to a Soviet government report for the years 1959–1962,

Table 12.1 Completion of important construction projects in Soviet Light Industry, 1959–1962

	Number of Firms under Construction			
	1959	1960	1961	1962
Number of new construction projects	102 (100%)	127 (100%)	135 (100%)	152 (100%)
Completed	25 (25%)	39 (31%)	19 (14%)	37 (24%)
Non-Completed, of which:	77 (75%)	88 (69%)	116 (86%)	115 (76%)
Completion level: < 50%	8 (10%)	9 (10%)	24 (21%)	23 (20%)
Completion level: 50–75%	19 (25%)	17 (19%)	32 (27%)	40 (35%)
Completion level: 75–99%	50 (65%)	62 (71%)	60 (52%)	52 (45%)

Source: The Russian State Archive of the Economy (RGAE), f. 1562, op. 337, d. 6431, l. 117.

"construction of different important firms in light industry is implemented unsatisfactory. The allocation of capital investments is incomplete, and concentrated on the wrong projects".[8] Certain projects commenced already in 1951, the report complained, had been completed by only 40% some 12 years later. Table 12.1 illustrates the discrepancy between plan goals and actual outcome in light industry. Of the circa 100–150 new construction projects started each year from 1959 to 1962, 10–20% were completed by less than 50%. Another 20–35% of the projects were completed by only 75%. The number of non-completed investments in light industry accumulated over time, resulting in capital waste (Sanchez, 2010).

Informal networks

Market-like enclaves of various kinds existed in all Soviet-Type-Economies and complemented command as the dominant mode of behavior. The role of market transactions in the allocation of resources was sometimes perfectly legal (as in the sale of agricultural surpluses at peasant markets), sometimes informal but tolerated by authorities (as in enterprise negotiations outside of plan) and sometimes illegal (as in theft, "speculation", or self-enrichment schemes). The combination of highly aggregated plan targets on the one hand (plans which were not sufficiently detailed to provide enterprises with operative guidelines), and shortages of inputs on the other hand, meant that actual resource allocation was often achieved through market or customary modes of behavior. Behavioral patterns including informal networks, patronage and collusion, have therefore been inherent features of Soviet-Type-Economies in order to solve structural restraints which could otherwise not have been easily overcome.

Since communist regimes criminalized a range of activities which in a market economy would be deemed legal, the notion of illegal economic activity needs to be qualified. Soviet authorities criminalized (or restricted through law, taxation or regulations) property ownership, currency exchange, reselling of goods, foreign trade, labor and travel opportunities – phenomena which are typically intrinsic to normal market economies. In China during the Cultural Revolution, law had virtually ceased to function as an institution. However, other types of scams which existed in the Soviet-Type-Economies – such as false invoicing, theft of public property for private use or the buying and selling of public office – would be serious crimes in any legal system. These types of economic activities, according to Grossman (1994), grew in importance in the last two decades of Soviet rule, causing growth-retarding corruption throughout the political system.[9] In China, law was rehabilitated after the death of Mao, followed by renewed campaigns against economic crime (Townsend, 1987).

Recent scholarship has emphasized the similarities between the Chinese and Soviet practices of *guanxi* and *blat* – two idioms denoting the flexible use of personal networks to solve various sorts of problems (Ledeneva, 2008; Yang, 2002). Most commonly, the idioms have denoted behavior such as the exchange of favors and gifts, or the cultivation of personal relations and mutual dependence. In the Soviet-Type-Economies, informal and personal networks were important for enterprise managers in the bargaining process for plan target reductions or the procurement of resources subject to shortage. The individuals managing these types of relations between enterprises were referred to as "supply agents", or *caigouyuan* and *tolkachi* in their respective Chinese and Soviet institutional contexts. Soviet authorities were aware of and tolerated informal horizontal transactions, provided the purpose of the action was plan fulfillment rather than personal self-enrichment (Belova and Gregory, 2002).

Foreign enterprise and trade

The Soviet economy benefitted in its early stages from foreign enterprise in at least three ways, some of them coercive, others through the market. Firstly, the legacy of foreign investment in Tsarist Russia before 1917 was a source of gratis capital stock in the Soviet industrialization plans. The Bolsheviks had initially renamed all nationalized industries – so that Putilov was now "Red Putilovets"; Browley Brothers, "Red Proletariat"; Ludwig Nobel Machine Factory, "Russkii Diesel"; and J.P. Goujon's Metal Factory, "Serp i Molot" (the "Sickle and Hammer")–or concealed their identity with a numbering system (for secrecy reasons or convenience). But the factories by and large remained the same. In fact, one paradoxical tendency of Soviet-Type-Economies has been to preserve plants and their machinery for long stretches of time, whereas firms in market economies have replaced their technologies through phases of creative destruction within much shorter time horizons. In the Soviet economy, new technologies often complemented, rather than replaced, existing capital stock. When the Swedish representative of ASEA (now ABB) in the early 1980s visited a Yaroslavl factory of electric machines delivered by the company six decades earlier, he could observe how all of the original equipment was still in use (Berglund, Dunbäck and Ericson, 1996).

Secondly, Soviet planners and engineers learned how to efficiently adapt new technologies. By the mid-1920s, somewhere around 100 foreign firms had remained in the Soviet Union as concessionaires (Heywood, 2000), providing stimuli to the revival of the Soviet economy which had collapsed during the revolution and civil war. Among the concessionaires were important industry leaders such as SKF, AEG, Westinghouse (Metropolitan Vickers) and Brown-Boveri. Siemens established an office in Moscow in 1928, whose task it was to provide technical input and advanced technology to high-profile projects such as the Moscow subway the Istra dam (Feldenkirchen, 2004). Beginning during the more isolated political climate of the first Five-Year Plan (1929–32), import and adaptation of foreign technologies substituted for concessions which by then had been almost universally suspended. For example, the Red Putilovets tractor was based on the Fordson model, the GAZ-AA truck a licensed copy of the Ford AA and the T-40 tank a developed version of the American Christie. Several large projects, such as the Dnepr dam, was built using American General Electric turbines, and the oil industry in Baku was rebuilt using aggregates, pipes and special tubes from Standard Oil and Vickers (Shpotov, 2005).[10]

Lastly, Soviet authorities claimed as war reparation properties and whole factories in East Germany, Hungary, Romania and Poland in 1945. Out of 17,024 medium and large factories identified by Soviet authorities in East Germany, more than 4,500 were dismantled and transferred to Soviet territory. Some of these factories had been industry leaders before the war, such as the Zeiss Jena optical factory (subsequently the Kiev camera works). Through the Council of Mutual Economic Assistance (CMEA), Eastern European satellite states were also required to sell resources to the Soviet Union at artificially low (administrative) prices, and Soviet authorities took a 50% stake of many large firms. Poland provided Soviet industry with coal at prices well below world market prices, but the Soviet Union, in turn, also reciprocated the favor for a number of other goods (Sanchez, 2014).

Communist bloc trade was based on a two-pronged principle in the post-World War II period. On the one hand were Soviet-Type-Economies participants with the advanced Western nations on the global market, where nations normally enter as price-takers. Whatever plan authorities wanted to charge for their goods, price setting could not deviate substantially from world market equilibrium. This was in particular true in export of grains, where there are many sellers, and oil and gas, which in the 1970s emerged as Moscow's key source of foreign reserves income (Gaddy and Ickes, 2005). On the other hand, most Soviet-Type trade was with countries in the communist bloc, where exchange was conducted under different institutional circumstances. A foreign trade monopoly transacted all imports and exports bilaterally, almost never multilaterally, and all currencies involved – unless an agreement was made to use hard currency – were inconvertible (Holzman, 1968).[11]

In contrast to the Soviet government, China did not formally nationalize foreign properties *sensu strictu*, but created instead a regulatory climate (restrictions, predatory taxes and fixed prices) which in practice amounted to de facto, if not de jure, nationalization (Thompson, 1979). The major exception was the factories in Manchuria, including railways and heavy industry, expropriated from Japan by the Soviet Army in 1945. This district had large economic significance: Manchuria possesses rich deposits of coal and iron ore; before and during the war, industries there had produced the bulk of China's electric power, iron and cement, and more than half of industrial output value. As a result of Moscow's interventions, the seeds for a Soviet-Type-Economy in China were therefore in the ground well before the People's Republic was created in 1949 (Kirby, 2006). China's first Five-Year plan (1953–57) embodied 156 large industrial projects, all of them built on blueprints and technology from the Soviet Union or Eastern Europe. Payment was often in kind: in the early 1950s China received five tons of steel products in exchange for one ton of frozen pork, and a steel-pipe factory for 10,000 tons of tobacco (Mah, 1964).

Legacies of the Soviet-Type-Economies

Virtually all former Soviet-Type-Economies today possess the formal institutions of a modern market economy, with rules and legislation to regulate private property, finance, trade and business activity, and enterprises applying normal corporate governance procedures in their business operations. However, legacies of command continue to influence and restrain economic policies and opportunities in several post-Soviet countries. These legacies may be observed in at least three dimensions: industrial structure and economic geography, institutions and possibly behavioral patterns (Ericson, 2014).

The structural legacy of Soviet-Type industrialization is the most visible. All communist regimes where possible created vertically integrated companies in the oil, gas, electricity, banking, engineering and steel sectors, sectors which in the post-Soviet era have been resistant to reform. Certain countries, however, have witnessed more dramatic reform than others, a variation which to some extent can be explained with reference to the varieties in command which existed already in the communist era. China's hierarchical structure was more decentralized than its Soviet precursor. The number of products directly under the central plan in China was relatively small, only 791 in 1979, whereas in the USSR at the same time, central planning allocated more than 12 million products (Qian and Xu, 1993). As a result, China's transition away from command towards market has been less restrained by structural legacies of centralization or bureaucratic inertia (Jefferson and Rawski, 1994).

If evaluated by cost effectiveness, factories, power stations, railroads and whole cities in the Soviet-Type-Economies, were from the beginning built in the wrong ways. Military and ideological considerations, rather than careful economic and engineering analysis, decided construction of industry. Two hallmarks of Stalinist construction, the Dnepr Dam and the Magnitogorsk steel plant ("the world's largest"), illustrate the dilemma. Since the level of water in the Dnepr River is inadequate during winter, and the topography is too flat, the Dnepr hydroelectric plant had to be complemented from the beginning with thermal power (i.e. coal). Magnitogorsk, on the contrary, was located in an area with iron ore but no coal (and initially no sufficient infrastructure, or labor force reserves). As a result, coal has had to be hauled in at high costs of transportation (Graham, 2013, pp. 50–51). In 2000, a Russian government report estimated there were 467 cities and 332 smaller towns dependent on one large enterprise for their survival – so called mono-towns – of which about half relied on state support for their survival (World Bank, 2010).

One of the most significant institutional legacies of the Soviet-Type-Economies was the absence of legislation and established practices to regulate markets and business activity – institutions which in Russia had not existed for over seven decades. In this institutional vacuum, conditions for rent seeking and opportunistic behavior were ripe in the 1990s when state resources were privatized and markets liberalized, resulting in high levels of ownership concentration and corruption (Guriev and Rachinsky, 2005). The richest "one percent" of the Russian population controlled 71% of the country's stock market capital in 2012, higher than in India (49%) and the US (37%) (Guriev and Tsivinskii, 2012). However, the market reforms which made possible the oligarchs also abolished Soviet legacies such as shortages and queuing, and created opportunities for whole new sectors to emerge (retail, banking, services, real estate, IT). Also in China, privatization of state enterprises and liberalization of trade and foreign direct investments in 1997 reduced some of the last barriers left from the Mao Zedong era (Zhu, 2012). In countries such as Estonia, Latvia, Lithuania and Poland, private property was restituted in the 1990s and market reforms abolished legacies of Soviet planning.

Economic reform in several post-Soviet economies has been a bifurcated process. Starting in 2003, a decade of disinvestment from state enterprises in Russia was reversed. Under President Vladimir Putin, new "commanding heights" – primarily in the extractive and banking sectors – have come under almost complete state control (de facto or de jure). The strengthening of the state in the economy has been an element of a behavioral pattern officially referred to as the strengthening of Putin's "power vertical" (*vertikal' vlasti*); the same pattern under President Hu Jintao and Premier Wen Jiabao has been captured by the phrase *guojin mintui* ("the state advances, the private sector retreats"). The intertwining of government and industry has created a regimented market structure. In both Russia and China (and other post-Soviet states), state-owned firms and politically connected private firms have been able to reap significant pecuniary and regulatory benefits, while also being subjected to the "policy burden" (whereby the managers of the firm are made to fulfill both economic and political, non-profit oriented, objectives) (Johansson and Feng, 2013). Command elements, in other words, have to various degrees remained or reemerged in post-Soviet economies (with notable exception the countries that are now EU-members).

Acknowledgements

Earlier drafts of this paper were presented at the Uppsala Centre for Russian and Eurasian Studies (UCRS), Uppsala University, on 10 February, 2015 and at the Institute for Economic and Business History Research (EHFF), Stockholm School of Economics, on 9 December, 2014. In particular, I thank Mark Harrison, Anders Johansson, Erik Lakomaa, Håkan Lindgren and Steve Nafziger for generous comments. All the usual disclaimers apply.

Notes

1 Contact: Martin.Kragh@ui.se; Swedish Institute of International Affairs (UI); Box 27035; SE-102 51 Stockholm; Sweden. Bio: Martin Kragh is head of Russia and Eurasia Programme at the Swedish Institute of International Affairs and a researcher at Uppsala Centre for Russian and Eurasian Studies.

2 Nazi Germany also confiscated private property in occupied territories, and in Germany proper, during World War II. Hitler also confiscated property of resisters, such as the business of Hugo Junkers.

3 By focusing only on economies where command was the dominant mode of behaviour, I exclude other mixed economies such as the New Deal in the USA, or the Swedish welfare state system, where markets and private ownership were never rejected. I also exclude other state-oriented economies, such as Egypt under Muhammad-Ali in the nineteenth century, or Japan after 1868 and the Meiji restoration.

4 Translation by Naughton (1988, p. 351). There exists alternative translations, see "Directives After Hearing The Reports Of Ku Mu And Yu Ch'iu-li On Planning Work", at http://www.marxists.org/reference/archive/mao/selected-works/volume-9/mswv9_39.htm (accessed 2014-11-25).

5 This paragraph relies on the author's comments from Mark Harrison and Julian Cooper.

6 At the macro level Soviet authorities issued mandatory bonds to the population, on which they subsequently defaulted, and the ruble was redenominated twice (in 1947 and 1961) in order to reduce cash holdings of households (each time by 90%). These monetary imbalances would persist until 1991, when dramatic price adjustments and hyperinflation followed the disintegration of the Soviet system (Nakamura, 2011).

7 Shortages may occur in any economy where command takes precedence over market, the most notable example being housing shortages in cities applying strict rent controls and/or other regulatory restrictions on the market.

8 RGAE, f. 1562, op. 337, d. 6431, l. 117.

9 Grossman's intuition has later been substantiated by empirical research, arguing that rent-seeking activities in the 1970s increased *pari passu* a decline in economic growth (Harrison and Kim, 2006).

10 The concession sector in the Soviet economy was completely abolished in 1937 by decision of the Soviet government. Technology transfers continued throughout the Soviet era. During World War II, the US government provided lend-lease, and in the post-war period normal imports coexisted with larger turnkey projects. Under such arrangements, the plant contractor undertook all facets of the production process, from design and procurement to installs, training of staff and continuous maintenance and service. Two such well-known arrangements were the Fiat based car factory in Tolyatti on the Volga River built in 1966, and the synthetic-fiber complex built at Mogilev by the British Polyspinners Consortium in 1964.

11 Technically speaking, exchange rates in Soviet-Type-Economies were disequilibrium rates, in the sense that they failed to: (1) generate without controls a balance on the international current accounts, or (2) reflect in any meaningful way the relative domestic purchasing power of the respective currencies on internationally traded goods (Chao and Mah, 1964).

References

Applebaum, A. (2012). *Iron Curtain: The Crushing of Eastern Europe, 1944–1956*. London: Penguin UK.

Belova, E. & Gregory, P. (2002). Dictator, Loyal, and Opportunistic Agents: The Soviet archives on creating the Soviet economic system, *Public Choice, 113*(3/4), 265–286.

Berglund, L., Dunbäck, J. & Ericson, L. (1996). *ASEA/ABBs etableringsprocess i Ryssland 1958–1996 – En fallstudie*. Uppsala University: Department of Business Studies.

Berliner, J. (1957). *Factory and Manager in the USSR*. Cambridge: Cambridge University Press.

Bucheli, M. (2008). Multinational Corporations, Totalitarian Regimes and Economic Nationalism: United Fruit Company in Central America, 1899–1975, *Business History, 50*, 433–454.

Chao, K. & Mah, F-H. (1964). A Study of the Rouble-Yuan Exchange Rate, *China Quarterly, 17*, 192–204.

Cooper, J. (2013). From USSR to Russia. The fate of the military economy. In: *Handbook of the Economics and Political Economy of Transition*, eds. Paul Hare & Gerard Turley. London & New York: Routledge, 98–107.

Davies, R. W. (2008). Planning for Mobilization: The 1930s. In: Mark Harrison (ed.). *Guns and Rubles. The Defense Industry in the Stalinist State*. New Haven & London: Yale University Press.

Dexter, K. & Rodionov, I. (2015). The Factories, Research and Design Establishments of the Soviet Defence Industry: A Guide. Volume 16, The University of Warwick: Department of Economics.

Ellman, M. (2008). The Political Economy of Stalinism in the Light of the Archival Revolution, *Journal of Institutional Economics, 4*, 99–125.

Ericson, R. (2013). Command Economy and Its Legacy. In: Michael Alexeev & Shlomo Weber (eds). *The Oxford Handbook of the Russian Economy*. New York: Oxford University Press, 51–85.

Fainsod, M. (1958). *Smolensk under Soviet Rule*. London: Macmillan & Co.

Feldenkirchen, W. (2004). Siemens in Eastern Europe. In: *European Business, Dictatorship, and Political Risk, 1920–1945*, eds. Christopher Kobrak & Per Hansen. New York: Berghahn Books, 122–145.

Fischer, S. (1994). Russia and the Soviet Union Then and Now. In: *The Transition in Eastern Europe, Volume 1*, eds. Oliver Blanchard, Kenneth Frost & Jeffrey Sachs. Chicago: Chicago University Press, 221–258.

Gaddy, C. & Ickes, B. (2005). Resource Rents and the Russian Economy, *Eurasian Geography and Economics, 46*(8), 559–583.

Germuska, P. (2010). Military Industry versus Military-Related Firms in Socialist Hungary: Disintegration and Integration of Military Production during the 1950s and Early 1960s, *Enterprise & Society, 11*(2), 316–349.

Graham, L. (2013). *Lonely Ideas. Can Russia Compete?* Cambridge: MIT Press.

Granick, D. (1957). *Management of the Industrial Firm in the USSR*. New York: Columbia University Press.

Gregory, P. & Tikhonov, A. (2000). Central Planning and Unintended Consequences: Creating the Soviet Financial System, 1930–1939, *Journal of Economic History, 60*(4), 1017–1040.

Grossman, G. (1963). Notes for a Theory of the Command Economy, *Soviet Studies, 15*(2), 101–123.

Grossman, G. (1994). What Was – Is, Will Be – the Command Economy?, *MOCT-MOST, 4*(5), 5–22.

Guriev, S. & Rachinsky, A. (2005). The Role of Oligarchs in Russian Capitalism, *Journal of Economic Perspectives, 19*(1), 131–150.

Guriev, S. & Tsivinskii, O. (2012). Rossiia – lider po neravenstvu raspredeleniia bogatstva, *Vedomosti*, November 6, 2012.

Harrison, M. (2011). Forging Success: Soviet Managers and Accounting Fraud, 1943 to 1962, *Journal of Comparative Economics, 39*(1), 43–64.

Harrison, M. (2014). Communism and Economic Modernization. In: *The Oxford Handbook in the History of Communism*, Ed. Stephen A. Smith. Oxford: Oxford University Press, 387–406.

Harrison, M. & Kim, B-Y. (2006). Plans, Prices, and Corruption: The Soviet Firm under Partial Centralization, 1930 to 1990, *Journal of Economic History, 66*(1), 1–44.

Heywood, A. (2000). Soviet Economic Concessions Policy and Industrial Development in the 1920s: The Case of the Moscow Railway Repair Factory, *Europe-Asia Studies, 52*(3), 549–569.

Holzman, F. (1968). The Ruble Exchange Rate and Soviet Foreign Trade Pricing Policies, 1929–1961, *American Economic Review, 58*(4), 803–825.

Johansson, A. & Feng, X. (2013). The State Advances, the Private Sector Retreats: Firm Effects of China's Great Stimulus Program, Stockholm School of Economics Asia Working Paper No. 25, August 2013.

Jones, G. & Lubinski, C. (2012). Managing Political Risk in Global Business: Beiersdorf 1914–1990, *Enterprise & Society, 13*(1), 85–119.

Kim, B-Y. (2002). Causes of Repressed Inflation in the Soviet Consumer Market, 1965–1989: Retail Price Subsidies, the Siphoning Effect, and the Budget Deficit, *Economic History Review, 55*(1), 105–127.

Kontorovich, V. (1986). What Do Bosses in Command Economies Do? Working Paper. Princeton Junction: Command Economies Research, Inc.

Kornai, J. (1980). *Economics of Shortage*. Amsterdam: North Holland Publishing.

Kragh, M. (2011). Stalinist Labour Coercion during World War II: An Economic Approach, *Europe-Asia Studies*, 63(7), 1253–1273.

Kumo, K. (2004). Soviet Industrial Location: A Re-examination, *Europe-Asia Studies*, 56(4), 595–613.

Ledeneva, A. (2008). "Blat" and "Guanxi": Informal Practices in Russia and China, *Comparative Studies in Society and History*, 50(1), 118–144.

Mah, F-H. (1964). The Terms of Sino-Soviet Trade, *China Quarterly*, 17, 174–191.

Maskin, E. (1996). Theories of the Soft Budget Constraint, *Japan and the World Economy*, 8, 125–133.

Nakamura, Y. (2011). Did the Soviet Command Economy Command Money? A Quantitative Analysis, *Europe-Asia Studies*, 63(7), 1133–1156.

Naughton, B. (1988). The Third Front: Defense Industrialization in the Chinese Interior, *China Quarterly*, 115, 351–86.

Naughton, B. (1994). What is Distinctive about China's Economic Transition? State Enterprise Reform and Overall System Transformation, *Journal of Comparative Economics*, 18(3), 470–490.

Naughton, B. (2007). *The Chinese Economy. Transitions and Growth*. Cambridge: MIT Press.

Sanchez-Sibony, O. (2010). Soviet Industry in the World Spotlight: The Domestic Dilemmas of Soviet Foreign Economic Relations, 1955–1965, *Europe-Asia Studies*, 62(9), 1555–1578.

Sanchez-Sibony, O. (2014). Capitalism's Fellow Traveler: The Soviet Union, Bretton Woods, and the Cold War, *Comparative Studies in Society and History*, 56(2), 290–319.

Shpotov, B. M. (2005). Uchastie amerikanskikh promyshlennikh kompanii v sovetskoi industrial-izatsii, 1928–1933 gg. In: L. Epifanova (ed.), *Ekonomicheskaia istoriia. Ezhegodnik 2005*, Moscow: Rosspen, 2005, 172–198.

Simonov, N. (1996). *Voenno-promyshlennyi kompleks SSSR v 1920–1950–e gody*. Moscow: Rosspen.

Smolinski, L. (1962). The Scale of Soviet Industrial Establishments, *American Economic Review*, 52(2), 138–148.

Stalin, J. (1949). The Tasks of Business Executives. In *Works*, Vol. 13, Moscow: Foreign Languages Publishing House, 40–41.

Teichova, A. (ed.) (1997). *Central Europe in the Twentieth Century. An Economic History Perspective*. Aldershot: Ashgate.

Temin, P. (1980). Modes of Behavior, *Journal of Economic Behavior and Organization*, 1(2), 175–195.

Thompson, T. (1979). *China's Nationalization of Foreign Firms: The Politics of Hostage Capitalism, 1949–57*. Baltimore: School of Law, University of Maryland.

Townsend, D. (1987). The Concept of Law in Post-Mao China: A Case Study of Economic Crime. *Stanford Journal of International Law*, 24(1), 227–258.

World Bank (2010). *Russian Economic Report*, No. 17, www.worldbank.org.ru.

Yang, M. M-h. (2002). The Resilience of *Guanxi* and Its New Deployments: A Critique of some New *Guanxi* Scholarship, *The China Quarterly*, 170, 459–476.

Yudanov, A. (1997). "USSR: Large enterprises in the USSR – the functional disorder". In *Big Business*, eds. Chandler, Amatori and Hikino.

13

The history of business in Latin America

Rory M. Miller

Introduction

Writing in 2009 on the Latin American 'variety of capitalism', which he termed 'hierarchical market capitalism', Ben Ross Schneider identified four defining features of business structures in the early twenty first century: diversified business groups; multinational corporations (MNCs); atomistic labour relations; and low skills. The relative lack of research on business history, he observed, meant that we knew much more about the political activities of domestic business and its relations with multinational corporations than the ways in which 'local capitalists built and organised their firms' (Schneider, 2009, p. 555).

In some ways this criticism seemed slightly unfair, in the light of a wave of research undertaken during the previous twenty years and summarised in various historiographical essays (Miller, 1999; Szmrecsanyi and Topik, 2004; Barbero, 2008; Dávila, 2013). However, there were still many obstacles to understanding the development, organisation, management and operations of business in Latin America. First, geographical coverage was uneven, with research much more advanced in Mexico, Colombia and Argentina and less on Peru, Chile and, surprisingly, Brazil. Second, research agendas within Latin America had often focused on questions that reflected local debates: the nature (or lack) of domestic entrepreneurship, and the existence (or not) of a 'national' bourgeoisie. Third, research on foreign investment had also emphasised particular issues, especially business-government relations and questions of imperialism and dependency, rather than the structure, organisation and management of firms (Miller, 2011). Much had appeared only in Spanish, presenting a further problem for monolingual Anglophone readers.

Historians would agree with Schneider on the importance of diversified or family business groups and international firms as two key elements in the structure of Latin American business since independence in the early nineteenth century. However, his analysis largely ignored the role of state-owned enterprises (SOEs), which diminished significantly after neoliberalism and privatisation became the dominant policy paradigm following the debt crisis of the 1980s. This contrasted with the influential work of Peter Evans (1979) on Brazil thirty years earlier. Evans likened the structure of contemporary Brazilian capitalism to a tripod, whose legs were MNCs, SOEs and the large business groups that dominated the domestic private sector.

The interplay among these three sets of actors has been dynamic, with marked variations among countries and over time, and the relative importance of each has been subject to advances and reversals. Since Schneider wrote, SOEs have regained significance in countries like Argentina and Bolivia. Understanding the history of business in Latin America requires, therefore, some appreciation of the phases of the region's economic history and policy-making, since these framed the environment within which the three key elements developed and interacted.

The economic background

Conventionally, historians of Latin America distinguish four phases in the region's economic history, though the demarcation between them is fuzzy and varies according to country (Bulmer-Thomas, 1994; Thorp, 1998; Bértola and Ocampo, 2012). First, independence (between 1810 and 1825) opened the formerly mercantilist economies of the Spanish colonies and Portuguese Brazil to global trade and foreign merchants, though the impact this had during the following half-century forms the subject of intense debate. Resource endowments (minerals, land, labour), state capacity, political conflicts and European demands for particular foodstuffs and raw materials together determined how quickly individual countries and regions resumed the growth that had characterised many areas immediately before independence. The transition from colonial legal and labour systems and institutions was often slow; transport and transaction costs remained high; government revenues depended heavily on overseas trade; and volatility, uncertainty and risk characterised the business environment. From around the 1870s, however, growth based on rapidly increasing exports, foreign investment and, in some places, immigration from Europe, became widespread, and this era of *desarrollo hacia afuera* (development towards the outside) forms the second phase. In the larger and wealthier countries of the region, especially Mexico and Brazil, the resulting development of domestic markets stimulated modern light manufacturing industries. The third phase, import-substituting industrialisation (ISI), took hold during the Depression of the 1930s, when governments adopted emergency measures to confront shortages of tax revenues and foreign exchange arising from the collapse of exports and traditional foreign investment. Over time, these short-term solutions coalesced into long-term strategies. During the 1960s and 1970s government policies deliberately stimulated the growth of capital-intensive industries such as automobile manufacturing, steel and petrochemicals, as well as the nationalisation of foreign interests in resource extraction and services. However, these developments came at the cost of increasing dependence on foreign technology and capital. The debt crisis of 1982, and the hyperinflation that often followed, introduced the most recent phase of Latin America's economic history, a shift towards the neoliberal policies that John Williamson (1990) labelled the 'Washington Consensus'. With the emphasis now on low tariffs, freedom of trade and capital movements, and privatisation, these measures radically altered the environment for business again.

This summary highlights the volatility of the Latin American economic environment. An abrupt curtailment of demand for exports or the supply of foreign investment, together with changes in government policy which, in the later ISI period, often led to alternating bouts of inflation and recession, created threats to the survival of enterprises founded during periods of growth. Urban property and, until the agrarian reforms of the 1960s, rural landholding normally offered the least risky investments in such circumstances, and also provided security for borrowers to gain access to scarce credit facilities. In the case of foreign firms, a continuing undercurrent of economic nationalism might also hinder operations, though the same desire for 'national' development and state intervention could offer opportunities for local business through concessions on tariffs and the provision of credit, subsidies and preferences. Both foreign investors and local entrepreneurs needed good connections with government. As Carlos Dávila (2013, p. 113) has written: 'Entrepreneurs finesse their profit-seeking behaviour to adapt to contextual political changes and accumulate the political capital needed to operate in many Latin American environments'. It is hardly surprising, perhaps, that many business historians, according to Tamás Szmrecsanyi and Steven Topik (2004, p. 183), focused on 'the politics of business more than on the economics of enterprise', especially as 'the personalist and family-based culture of firms left few company records available to historians'.

Business groups

'Large-scale Argentine capitalism is, and has been, structured on the basis of the family', write María Inés Barbero and Andrea Lluch (2015, p. 220). This statement holds for every country in the region. While the nature of each is unique, family business groups have dominated the domestic private sector since the nineteenth century.

What are their main characteristics? First, the most successful groups have exhibited a remarkable degree of longevity, spanning three or four generations. The Edwards and Matte groups in Chile date back to the early nineteenth century, while the most successful recent Peruvian groups, the Romeros and Brescias, have also operated for over a hundred years (Martínez, 2015; Monsalve, 2015). Second, groups have often diversified across business sectors, though with considerable variations over time and space. The well-known Matarazzo group in mid-twentieth century Brazil, for example, which had begun in the 1890s, possessed interests in sugar refining, milling, food oils, soap and textiles, sectors typical of early manufacturing growth. In the 1960s it employed 30,000 people in over a hundred different firms linked by a family holding company (Musacchio, 2008; della Costa et al., 2015). Growth and diversification did not mean a loss of family control, which could be maintained through holding companies and different legal classes of shareholdings. Third, as some of these surnames suggest, immigrants from Europe, accumulating capital in trade and then diversifying into production, founded many groups. In northern Mexico (and Cuba), Spanish-born capitalists developed many new enterprises (Cerutti, 1999). Elsewhere, in Brazil, Argentina and Peru, Italian surnames frequently appear in twentieth-century lists of leading businessmen, while later immigrants from the Ottoman empire (often known collectively as *turcos*) also became important at regional level. In Chile, Pascual Baburizza, a Croat migrant, became a dominant figure in the nitrate trade in the 1920s before moving into tin-mining and rural landholding (Torres-Dujisín, 2003). The descendants of one of Baburizza's Croat managers, Andrónico Luksic, later became the leading family business group in Chile, with a London Stock Exchange listing for Antofagasta Holdings, a leading copper-mining company, as well as extensive other interests (Schneider, 2008; Martínez, 2015). Fourth, diversification into finance (banking and insurance), through shareholdings and directorships, often helped further expansion. In the Peruvian case the Banco Italiano (later renamed the Banco de Crédito), founded in 1889, financed many immigrant businessmen. The Banco Popular was central to the Prado family's diverse industrial investments, and the Banco del Perú y Londres closely linked with leading coastal landowners and some mining interests (Quiroz, 1989; Quiroz, 1993). In Argentina, the Tornquist family group had a bank at its centre (Barbero and Lluch, 2015). Many of the large Mexican business groups in the mid-twentieth century, before bank nationalisation in 1982, also possessed close links with leading financial institutions through cross-shareholdings and interlocking directorships (Hamilton, 1982; Del Angel, 2015).

Explanations for the dominance of business groups in Latin America, rather than the broad share ownership and sectoral focus characteristic of Anglo-American capitalism, have varied. Nathaniel Leff (1978), in an influential article, ascribed their growth to scarce and imperfectly marketed entrepreneurial, managerial and financial resources, and hence the need to internalise these assets. Though focusing less on Latin America, Tarun Khannu and Krishna Palepu (1997) also emphasise institutional voids – in product, capital and labour markets, as well as government regulation – for the continued importance of business groups in emerging markets. Mauro Guillén (2000), concentrating on the ISI era, argues that the importance of business groups stems from their capacity to mediate between host governments and foreign investors in closed economies with high levels of state intervention and regulation. Such an analysis, however, ignores the long history of diversified family business groups within Latin America, and their continuity through different phases of economic history.

That is not to argue that business groups do not decline and fail. Iberian inheritance laws, which favoured equal distribution of property among children, posed a threat to continuity, although the use of holding companies and, as Mario Cerutti (2015) indicates for the case of northern Mexico, extensive intermarriage might alleviate this. Financial crisis and mismanagement caused the demise of many groups. The Mauá empire in Brazil, an early example of diversification, collapsed in 1878 due to financial and political miscalculations (Graham, 1968). Neither Matarazzo in Brazil nor SIAM di Tella in Argentina, two of the largest and most dynamic family groups during the ISI period, proved able to survive the volatile and inflationary conditions of the 1960s, though the agony of the latter lasted years (Rougier and Schvarzer, 2006). Leading Chilean groups of the 1970s, such as Cruzat-Larraín and Jorge Vial's Banco Hipotecario group, suffered badly in the financial crisis of 1982 due to excessive US dollar borrowings (Martínez, 2015). Like any other firm, family-based groups depend on their senior managers' ability to guard against excessive risk, anticipate economic crisis and respond quickly to changed circumstances.

Thus the leading groups in each country may have changed, but the importance of this structure has continued into the twenty first century. Indeed, one might argue that a well-managed diversified business group is better situated to withstand abrupt changes of policy or sudden crisis than a single-sector focused firm. During the neoliberal era groups from several countries have grown and internationalised to become *multilatinas*, in this way reducing their exposure to the risk of operating in a single country. The survival of diversified family business groups through the abrupt shift in policy in the 1980s, and their subsequent international expansion, have thus become key areas for research.

On the first, Schneider (2008) notes that while many groups lost ground as a result of sudden policy changes (especially in Argentina where economic and policy volatility were particularly marked), others responded flexibly to the new environment, incorporating professional managers, investing in management education for the next generation and taking advantage of financial opening to issue ADRs (American Depositary Receipts) to raise capital in the United States without ceding voting control. Their local advantages, such as networks, market knowledge and access to governments, many of which consulted leading businessmen regularly on economic matters, also proved crucial. Many of the new *multilatinas* expanded across borders in low-technology sectors with few requirements for research and development and fewer economies of scale. Central American groups provide a good example, with international investments in construction, wholesale and retail distribution and tourism, at times in joint ventures or franchise arrangements with multinational firms (Bull, 2013). In contrast to diversified business groups concentrating on domestic or regional markets, however, many of the largest *multilatinas* have grown on the basis of sectoral specialisation, most obviously Carlos Slim's Grupo Carso in telecommunications, Cemex in construction materials, Vale in minerals or Chilean retailers like Ripley and Falabella. Initially, at least, they followed standard international business theory predictions, by investing first in neighbouring markets, where linguistic and cultural similarities meant that psychic proximity gave them advantages over US or European multinationals. However, the largest groups like Cemex, through acquisitions backed by international finance, have grown much more aggressively. The 2014 *América Economía* rankings (by sales) show that the ten largest non-financial *multilatinas* each operated, on average, in 25 countries, while confirming their focus in low-technology businesses (*América Economía*, 2014).

Multinational firms

The opening of Latin American economies during the independence era stimulated an immediate influx of foreign merchants importing goods from Europe and North America, in particular textiles. Though the British tended to dominate numerically until late in the century, French, German and US merchant houses were also widespread. Normally merchants organised themselves as linked partnerships, often with a parent house in a European port like Liverpool or Hamburg and associates in South America. Most did not survive long: partners died or disagreed, while the length of communications lines and unpredictability both of demand and politics (and hence wars, blockades and forced loans) also created enormous instability. In other cases, foreign merchants gradually became naturalised, like the Boultons in Venezuela. However, some international partnerships lasted for generations, such as the London house of Antony Gibbs & Sons, the dominant merchants first in the Peruvian guano trade and then in the Chilean nitrate industry, the New York firm of W.R. Grace & Co. or the Liverpool-based partnerships of Graham Rowe and Duncan Fox (Greenhill and Miller, 1998; Clayton, 1985).

From the 1860s foreign investors taking advantage of new opportunities began to gain in significance compared with merchants; by 1913, Latin America accounted for roughly a quarter of Britain's overseas investments, but only one-tenth of its export trade (Miller, 1993). In the 1920s the United States replaced Britain as the major source of new investment. Both portfolio and direct investment were important. In the case of the former, national, provincial and municipal governments all issued bonds overseas to finance budget deficits and public works until the Depression. During crises, especially, merchant banks such as Rothschilds might obtain significant influences over public finance, since they were central to debt restructuring, as in Argentina after 1890 or Brazil in 1897 or the 1920s (Marichal, 1989).

Direct investment took two different forms, with free-standing companies dominant before 1914, and multinational enterprises thereafter. A 'free-standing company', a term invented by Mira Wilkins (1988), normally possessed only a small office in a financial centre like the City of London or New York, holding the bulk of its assets in one country overseas. As other authors have noted, individual firms might form part of 'investment groups', such as the nitrate enterprises controlled by Gibbs or Grace (Chapman, 1986; Jones, 1997).

Most foreign-owned railways in Latin America fit the definition of 'free-standing companies' well, as do many mining enterprises and public utilities before the early twentieth century. Multinational companies, in contrast, expanded overseas from a substantive home base, usually in search of resources or markets, and normally operated in several different countries. Early twentieth-century examples include the United Fruit Company, integrating production and railway transport in various Central American countries with shipping and distribution in the United States; the Guggenheims' American Smelting and Refining Company which invested in Mexico, Chile and Peru; or international petroleum companies such as Standard Oil of New Jersey and Royal Dutch Shell which, between them, dominated the industry in several countries by 1930. After World War I, mergers and acquisitions of free-standing companies strengthened the role of multinational firms. This happened, for example, in public utilities: International Telephone and Telegraph (ITT) and American and Foreign Power, initially a subsidiary of General Electric, both acquired a long list of Latin American subsidiaries in the 1920s (O'Brien, 1996; Lanciotti and Saes, 2015). British banks, some of which dated back to the 1860s, merged into the Bank of London and South America in 1923, which operated in several countries and acquired the remaining British independent, the Anglo South American Bank, in 1936 (Joslin, 1963).

In manufacturing, multinational companies' investments in major markets like Argentina and Brazil predated the First World War. One of the early British multinationals, J. & P. Coats, established sales offices and manufacturing facilities in Brazil and Mexico, while British American Tobacco (BAT) also entered South American markets before 1914. International competition in particular consumer goods industries, local preferences for foreign products and the expansion and integration of markets due to foreign trade and investment all stimulated the growth of market-seeking investments by firms that had the financial resources to support initial losses and acquire rivals. This trend accelerated in the 1920s, when both Ford and General Motors established assembly plants in Argentina and Brazil. Multinationals providing professional services, such as J. Walter Thompson and the large accountancy firms, accompanied the manufacturing companies (Woodward, 2002; Moreno, 2004); foreign banks were already there. The Depression stimulated new investments as governments in need of revenue raised import tariffs, sometimes with a deliberately protectionist intent, and imposed exchange controls, making it difficult for exporters from the United States and Europe to repatriate earnings. After World War II protectionism, through tariffs, import restrictions and foreign exchange controls, became much more deliberate. The automobile, heavy vehicle and machinery sectors were particular targets for governments attempting to stimulate the growth of more technologically complex industries, with the result that Brazil in 1956, Argentina in 1959 and Mexico in 1962 all introduced legislation requiring motor companies to manufacture locally. They also stipulated high levels of local content, leading other firms in the multinationals' supply chains, such as electrical, glass and tyre manufacturers, to invest as well (Jenkins, 1984).

Whatever their form and their source, foreign direct investments in Latin America for much of the twentieth century had similar motives for expansion, similar forms of organisation and created similar problems for host societies and governments. Multinational companies sought at least one of three things: resources for processing or export (minerals, oil, meat, tropical agricultural products); markets for services which employed foreign technology and expertise (electricity, telephones, railways); or consumer markets where they could exploit the 'allure of the foreign' (Orlove, 1997; Bauer, 2001). Their brands, their technology, their access to cheap capital and credit and superior management resources all gave them advantages. Industrial firms often started with sales offices followed by secondary manufacture (vehicle assembly from imported parts, for example, or the mixing and packing of pharmaceuticals), and then invested in primary manufacture and developed local supply chains and distribution networks. As well as making 'greenfield' investments, multinationals also purchased existing firms; acquisitions in low-technology industries like soap and household goods, foodstuffs and sewing thread eliminated local competition. From the late 1950s, however, joint ventures (JVs) with Latin American business groups became more common, partly because this improved the multinationals' access to government and business lobbies. JVs also took care of local distribution and limited the amount of capital that the multinational needed to transfer, an important consideration during periods of high inflation and exchange depreciation. Thus, Unilever expanded in Argentina and Brazil in the interwar period by building new factories, acquired its major competitor in Brazil in 1960, and used JVs to establish its brands in Chile, Peru and Colombia.

During the ISI period multinationals normally relied on a multi-domestic structure, with general managers in each country to organise operations and access politicians, lawyers and financial institutions. Attempts at regional management did not work well, given the economic barriers and political jealousies between states. Until the 1950s most MNCs filled senior roles with expatriates, creating national and linguistic divisions between senior management and the bulk of their white-collar and manual workforce. While local shortcomings in literacy, numeracy and technical education might partly explain this, it also reflected ethnic biases. As authors like Thomas O'Brien (1996), Thomas Klubock (1998) and Julio Moreno (2004) have shown, many US business leaders believed that Latin Americans were inherently uneducated, immoral and lazy, and thus regarded themselves as 'missionaries' encouraging the adoption of US business norms and behaviour. European managers often shared such attitudes of moral superiority, if not the missionary intent, but the employment of expatriates also reflected a need to control subsidiaries in alien cultural environments and supply the technical and managerial skills that enterprises like railways, public utilities and manufacturing firms required. British companies, for example, recruited potential managers and engineers direct from school or comparable enterprises in the United Kingdom and posted them abroad on three-year contracts, socialising them into the firm and into expatriate culture, and making benefits like home leave and pensions dependent on their behaviour (Jones, 1993).

Latin Americans were ambivalent about the role of foreign business from the beginning, creating an undercurrent of economic nationalism that sometimes seriously threatened the interests of multinational firms. One particular problem with the mining and oil firms, railways and public utilities was that they generally operated under specific concessions and contracts, giving considerable scope for disputes over issues like tax avoidance, and in the case of the railways and utilities, their tariffs and the quality of their services. Mining and oil firms suffered from the problem that Raymond Vernon (1971) defined as the 'obsolescing bargain', where governments, often themselves under pressure from nationalist media and opposition politicians, attempted to alter the terms of generous concessions granted by their predecessors, for example in Venezuela after the death of President Gómez in 1935 (Philip, 1982). Many transport and public utility companies enjoyed the right to import supplies duty-free, which did little to stimulate local industries, and to adjust charges if local currencies depreciated. This caused particular problems in the 1930s, when suburban railways and tramways confronted intense competition from road transport. Given the rapid growth of Latin American cities in the twentieth century, utility companies could often not keep up with demand unless they made significant profits they could reinvest, but requests for tariff increases frequently met with the response that they should forego dividends and remedy poor services (Lanciotti and Saes, 2014). These long-running disputes resulted in a wave of nationalisations of transport, utility and petroleum companies, commencing with the foreign oil firms in Mexico in 1938, followed by the British-owned railways in Argentina and Uruguay in 1948.

Foreign industrial firms faced far fewer threats of this kind, partly because host countries needed the capital and technology they provided. However, the combination of import licences, exchange controls, inflation, regulation of prices and local content requirements made life increasingly difficult for them during the ISI period. From the early 1960s, especially, manufacturing multinationals came under increasing pressure from nationalist academics and politicians on a number of grounds: accusations of transfer pricing and excessive royalties payments, most notoriously perhaps by pharmaceuticals companies; balance of payments problems caused by their greater propensity to import; their preference for borrowing locally rather than importing capital; the inappropriateness of 'First World' technology for less developed countries; lack of employment generation; and their unwillingness to transfer higher value-added activities such as research and development expenditures to Latin America. In retrospect, while governments in East Asia adopted deliberate policies to learn from multinationals and eventually diminish dependence upon them, in Latin America governments tended to blame rather than learn. Moreover, the failure of regional market integration until the 1990s made for inefficient production, since the companies could not take advantage of economies of scale. Even relatively small markets like Peru and Chile had tens of car and truck plants. However, very few multinational manufacturing companies were expropriated, except in Cuba and (briefly) Chile, and most learned to survive and grow in a difficult environment.

State-owned enterprise

The ideological attack on state-owned enterprises (SOEs) that has transformed the world since the 1980s coincided with the aftermath of the 1982 debt crisis in Latin America and brought about extensive privatisations throughout the region. Sometimes this trend was voluntary, as in Mexico after 1988 or Peru after 1990; elsewhere, as in Argentina, it was the price paid for economic stabilisation and new inflows of capital. However, some important SOEs did remain under public ownership, for example CODELCO, the Chilean state copper company, and, in Brazil, BNDES, the national development bank and Petrobrás, the state oil company. Such SOEs were central to national economies. Elsewhere, for ideological or practical reasons, renationalisation has occurred. Both the Bolivian and Argentine governments annulled water concessions granted to foreign companies in the 1990s. Bolivia suddenly expropriated hydrocarbons firms in 2006, while six years later Argentina renationalised YPF, the former state oil company that a Spanish multinational, Repsol, had acquired following privatisation.

While North American and European free market advocates may condemn such interventions, state-owned enterprise has a long tradition in Latin America. It has not always been unsuccessful, although there are some striking examples of long-term failure to generate surpluses for investment or serve customers adequately, such as PEMEX (the Mexican state oil company) or Aerolíneas Argentinas. The problem for historians is that here, even more than for family business groups, access to archives and oral sources has been difficult, and the ideological implications of research more acute.

State intervention was fundamental to the successful nineteenth-century export boom, for example to underwrite the construction of railways, one of the most critical technologies that transformed Latin America. The cost and risk of building trunk lines far exceeded the capacity of local investors, who could earn 12–24% annually on short-term loans. In order to attract foreign investment, therefore, governments frequently offered profit guarantees, often 7% on capital invested (Lewis, 1983). Even this did not suffice to build lines that were political projects rather than those with strong economic potential. In Argentina, British firms eventually dominated the ownership of railways in the pampa, but by 1914 the state constructed, owned and operated almost 6,000 kilometres of track in marginal zones. In Chile, British firms dominated the north but the government controlled the network on which business in the centre depended (Palermo, 2006; Oppenheimer, 1982). In Mexico the federal government took a majority shareholding in the national railways, until then primarily US-owned, early in the twentieth century, while in both Brazil and Peru foreign companies exploited state-owned railways under long-term leases. Where governments maintained their credit on foreign stock exchanges, they could often raise money relatively cheaply; those that defaulted, however, saw the progress brought by the steam locomotive delayed, since neither the private sector nor the state had sufficient resources.

The marked economic presence of the state in Latin American economies in fact dated back to colonial times. The Spanish government reserved and farmed out important monopolies, most importantly tobacco, but also essential items like salt. In mining it retained ownership of the subsoil, granting concessions to private miners in return for royalties. This legislative framework separating ownership of the surface from the subsoil predominated into the twentieth century. The same principle applied to oil in its early stages, though in the course of the 1920s many countries passed specific petroleum legislation. State control over the oil industry increased, both upstream and downstream. In Argentina, a chance oil strike by government engineers in 1907 led to the formation of YPF (Yacimientos Petrolíferos Fiscales) in 1922. YPF developed rapidly as a production, refining and distribution enterprise under a military officer, General Enrique Mosconi, although he never succeeded in his intention of excluding foreign multinationals completely (Solberg, 1982). Both in Chile and Uruguay, which had no oil deposits, the state established refineries in the 1930s, in part to keep a check on the prices charged by multinationals for gasoline, kerosene and fuel oil.

Like oil, several business sectors became subject to increased state control in the twentieth century. Different levels of government (federal or national, provincial, municipal) became heavily involved in granting contracts and regulating business, in particular in areas like transport, public utilities, banking and insurance. In the latter case, both Peru and Uruguay established reserve and investment requirements that effectively excluded foreign companies and favoured local groups. Much depended on specific local circumstances and the particular business–state conflicts that occurred. Following the Baring Crisis in 1890, the Argentine government found itself forced to take charge of water and sanitary works in Buenos Aires, forming Obras Sanitarias. Immediately after World War II several governments took control of foreign-owned assets in transport and public utilities, particularly in Argentina, Uruguay and Brazil. For the most part these nationalisations were not contentious: many concessions would shortly expire; several firms did not have the resources to finance new investment and/or provide better services when government controls and market competition made it difficult to raise tariffs; and governments had the resources to pay compensation. A further intense period of nationalisation occurred in the 1960s and 1970s (Sigmund, 1980). This encompassed most of the remaining transport and utility firms across the region, US mining interests in Peru and Chile (though never Mexico) and foreign-owned petroleum assets in Bolivia, Peru and, most importantly, Venezuela in 1975 (Mexico had already expropriated foreign oil companies in 1938 and paid compensation during the war). By then state-directed development and public-sector firms had become commonplace.

Alongside the recovery of foreign-owned concessions, which were often essential to their development projects and required considerable new investment, governments also established SOEs to advance industries regarded as 'strategic'. The long-term loan facilities offered by the World Bank, the Inter-American Development Bank and even the US Export-Import Bank underpinned many of these public-sector projects. Brazil, where Getúlio Vargas's administration established the Companhía Siderúrgica Nacional (CSN) in 1941 to build a steel plant at Volta Redonda (Dinius, 2010), offers a good example. Exercising control of basic industries such as steel and energy was central to the developmentalist ideas of nationalists and the military. After returning to power in 1951, Vargas established both BNDES and Petrobrás; Eletrobrás (a state electricity company) followed in 1962 during the administration of João Goulart, his former vice president. The military government that overthrew Goulart in 1964 retained, and indeed expanded, all these corporations. In Argentina the post-war Peronist government assembled expropriated German firms into the Dirección Nacional de Industrias del Estado (DINIE) in 1948, encompassing industries ranging from textiles to pharmaceuticals, steel and machinery; by then the military also possessed almost twenty enterprises of its own under the umbrella of Fabricaciones Militares (Belini and Rougier, 2008). A radical military government in Peru in the early 1970s likewise formed a series of SOEs to take over and develop key sectors of the economy, such as Centromín and Mineroperú for mining, Pescaperú for fishing and Petroperú for oil exploration, production and distribution, many on the basis of expropriated foreign assets.

State intervention in banking and finance was often central to ideas of national development, as the foundation of BNDES illustrates. Other governments, besides Brazil's, formed development banks and corporations. Mexico's Nacional Financiera dates back to 1934 and Chile's CORFO (Corporación de Fomento) to 1939. In some cases, governments created banks to finance particular sectors such as Argentina's Banco Industrial, reformed into BANADI (Banco Nacional de Desarrollo Industrial) in 1970. Rather than simply making loans, the Banco Industrial acquired minority shareholdings in hundreds of private-sector firms. In Peru, the military government of 1968–75 established a development corporation, COFIDE, as well as separate banks for industry, agriculture and mining, and expropriated Chase Manhattan's Banco Continental. The state-owned Banco de la Nación became a key institution for ordinary consumers transacting business with the state.

The Peruvian case, however, illustrates many of the problems resulting from state intervention. Apart from the difficulties of recruiting adequately trained and experienced managers for the new SOEs, they also found it difficult to raise investment capital, and the 'Peruvian experiment' quickly became an economic morass (Thorp and Bertram, 1978). Throughout the region state-owned enterprise became increasingly difficult to defend and justify in business terms. Apart from inefficiencies, as anyone who tried to obtain a telephone landline in Lima or Buenos Aires in the 1970s and 1980s would recognise, governments used SOEs for their own purposes. In some cases, especially as inflation worsened, SOEs found it impossible to obtain permission to raise prices sufficiently to cover costs, in effect subsidising popular consumption through low prices for gasoline or public transport and utilities like energy and water. This meant that they failed to generate surpluses for reinvestment, exacerbating problems of poor service and inefficiency. In other cases, politicians or labour unions 'captured' an SOE's management, distorting strategies and often making it impossible to reduce staff numbers. The nationalised railways in Argentina and PEMEX, the state-owned oil company in Mexico, provide two notorious examples. Twenty years after nationalisation, a report on Argentina's railways pointed out, first, deterioration due to lack of new investment (3,400 of the 3,770 steam locomotives were over 30 years old, and a third of the newer diesel locomotives were under repair), and second, that up to 50,000 of the 150,000 staff, already reduced from over 200,000 at the beginning of the 1960s, were superfluous (*Primera Plana*, 10 August 1965). PEMEX became dominated by powerful trade union leaders affiliated to the party that controlled Mexico between 1929 and 2000. This brought a high degree of industrial peace, but at the cost of lack of management control, high levels of corruption and government interference in key decisions (Philip, 1982; Teichman, 1996). As inflation worsened in many Latin American countries in the 1970s and 1980s, all SOEs faced similar problems to the private sector in terms of price-setting and cost-accounting, but fell behind in developing techniques to deal with this. By the end of the 1980s SOEs throughout Latin America faced serious financial problems, and for many in the political elite, the domestic business community and the international financial institutions, privatisation supported by foreign investment appeared the obvious solution.

This is not to argue that all SOEs were equally poorly managed, as a contrast between Argentina and Brazil illustrates. In Argentina four decades of political and economic instability, marked by dysfunctional governments and trade union militancy, meant that few SOEs remained solvent. By 1976 the Argentine state controlled or participated in almost 800 firms; the most visible such as the railways, Aerolíneas Argentinas and YPF had gained a reputation for poor management, overstaffing and unprofitability. The development banks' investment portfolios contained hundreds of distressed firms. Attempts at reform changed little. In 1989 a hundred SOEs accounted for 87% of the federal government deficit (Belini and Rougier, 2008, p. 41; Baer and Montes-Rojas, 2008). In the case of Brazil, however, BNDES provided considerable long-term funding for both MNCs and the private sector, and its technocrats gained a high reputation for competence (and autonomy from the state). One historian concludes that it was never 'a financial black hole that protect[ed] unproductive industry and bail[ed] out large conglomerates', and officials adapted successfully to changes in government development strategy and a frequently volatile financial environment (Von Mettenheim, 2010, p. 171). Other SOEs in Brazil also gained good reputations for professional autonomy and technical innovation. Petrobrás became a world leader in deepwater oil exploration, developing complex technologies of its own (Dantas and Bell, 2009). Embraer, founded in 1969, used a strategy of alliances with foreign suppliers to produce commuter and trainer aircraft for the domestic and export markets; at the time of privatisation in 1994 it had already begun the design programme that would make it one of the two leading global manufacturers of regional jets (Goldstein, 2002).

Both internal and external forces thus brought about the wave of privatisations in Latin America that began in Chile after the military coup of 1973, and intensified following the debt crisis. Internal pressures came in the form of the drain on government finances arising from SOEs' deficits, as well as from the domestic private sector; externally, international financial institutions advised countries facing problems of debt and inflation to liberalise their economies.

Scholars have raised questions about the prices that governments received for public assets, and the extent to which they succeeded in regulating privatised companies thereafter, especially since firms such as utilities and transport companies were 'natural monopolies'. The Argentine case has been especially subject to criticism (Baer and Montes-Rojas, 2008). Inadequate regulation of commercial banks, together with the liberalisation of capital flows, caused major crises when national currencies fell sharply in Chile in 1982 and Mexico in 1994/95 due to their accumulation of dollar-denominated debt. Privatisation also altered the balance among domestic business groups, multinationals and SOEs, as multinationals bought control of SOEs and, given renewed international confidence in Latin America in the 1990s, invested in new ventures. Spanish firms such as Repsol, energy companies like Iberdrola and two banks, Santander and BBVA, were especially prominent. The criticisms and conflicts that then arose, especially in countries like Argentina, Bolivia, Ecuador and Venezuela, which all elected left-wing governments, have a strangely familiar air to any historian of foreign business in the late nineteenth and early twentieth centuries.

Concluding comments

Latin America had its own 'variety of capitalism' in terms of the roles and the interplay of three sets of actors: domestic business groups, most of them family-based and many of them diversified across business sectors; multinational firms, almost always welcomed by the elite but also the subject of popular distrust; and SOEs, which dominated the business environment between the 1960s and 1980s. The relative significance and interaction of these three elements differed over time and among countries. Colombia, for example, never received the degree of foreign investment that other countries did, and local business groups remained extremely powerful. Although stock markets in the major countries enjoyed a brief florescence in the early twentieth century, for the most part investment depended on retaining profits within the family firm and access to local financial institutions, but without the direct involvement of banks in business management, in contrast, for example, to Germany. The state in Latin America also played a very different role from the technocratic states of East Asia. Lack of continuity in economic policies, macroeconomic volatility and weak legal institutions made informal networks and trust of prime importance to business success. For both domestic business groups and multinational firms, access to politicians was often critical: the former needed to shape policies in their own interests, while the latter had to protect themselves against labour militancy and nationalist demands for the rewriting or rescinding of concessions.

Ironically, perhaps, the shifting balance among the state, foreign investors and domestic firms in the late twentieth century helped to boost business history in many countries, as the nationalistic ISI model disintegrated and intellectual antagonism towards the private sector diminished. The expansion of business schools employing historians also contributed, together with the interest of North American and European scholars. This resulted in a plethora of case studies published as articles and monographs, and a new generation of young historians with strong research capabilities, who began to transform the field. Special issues of international journals, and institutional support from North American and Spanish foundations, as well as national research councils, helped to bring their work to the attention of a broader audience. One problem, though, was that very few family groups and SOEs permitted access to their archives; when historians did obtain such material the harvest could be very rich. However, other sources such as the specialist daily and weekly press, government publications, contemporary reports, congressional debates and oral history have all helped to shed light on the past. The formation of international networks under the leadership of senior figures like Mario Cerutti, Carlos Dávila and María Inés Barbero also stretched the horizons of those whose perspective would otherwise have been limited to their own country. The future is bright, even if much of the past still remains obscure.

References

América Economía (2014). *Ránking 100 multilatinas 2014*: available at http://rankings.americaeconomia. com/multilatinas-2014/ranking/ accessed 24 August 2015.

Baer, W. & Montes-Rojas, G. (2008). 'From Privatization to Re-Nationalization: What Went Wrong with Privatizations in Argentina', *Oxford Development Studies, 36*(3), 323–37.

Barbero, M. I. (2008). 'Business History in Latin America: A Historiographical Perspective', *Business History Review, 53*(2), 555–75.

Barbero, M. I. & Lluch, A. (2015). 'El capitalismo familiar en Argentina: modelos y dinámicas a largo plazo', in Fernández Pérez and Lluch (eds), *Familias empresariales y grandes empresas familiares*, 219–46.

Bauer, A. J. (2001). *Goods, Power, History: Latin America's Material Culture*. Cambridge: Cambridge University Press.

Belini, C. & Rougier, M. (2008). *El estado empresario en la industria argentina: conformación y crisis*. Buenos Aires: Manantial.

Bértola, L. & Ocampo, J. A. (2012). *The Economic Development of Latin America since Independence*. New York: Oxford University Press.

Bull, B. (2013). 'Diversified Business Groups and the Transnationalisation of the Salvadorean Economy', *Journal of Latin American Studies, 45*(2), 265–95.

Bulmer-Thomas, V. (1994). *The Economic History of Latin America since Independence*. Cambridge: Cambridge University Press.

Cerutti, M. (1992). *Burguesía, capitales e industria en el norte de México: Monterrey y su ámbito regional, 1850–1910*. Mexico City: Alianza.

Cerutti, M. (1999). 'Regional Studies and Business History in Mexico since 1975', in Dávila, Carlos and Miller, Rory (eds.), *Business History in Latin America: The Experience of Seven Countries*. Liverpool: Liverpool University Press, 116–27.

Chapman, S. D. (1986). 'British-Based Investment Groups before 1914', *Economic History Review, 38*(2), 230–51.

Clayton, L. A. (1985). *Grace. W.R. Grace & Co.: The Formative Years*. Ottawa: Jamieson Books.

Dantas, E. & Bell, M. (2009). 'Latecomer Firms and the Emergence and Development of Knowledge Networks: The Case of Petrobras in Brazil', *Research Policy, 38*(5), 829–44.

Dávila, C. (2013). 'The Current State of Business History in Latin America', *Australian Economic History Review, 53*(2), 109–20.

Del Angel, G. A. (2016). 'The Nexus between Business Groups and Banks: Mexico, 1932–1982', *Business History, 58*(1), 111–128.

Della Costa, A. et al. (2015). 'Empresas y grupos empresariales brasileños en perspectiva histórica', in Fernández Pérez and Lluch (eds.), *Familias empresariales y grandes empresas familiares*, 189–217.

Dinius, O. (2010). *Brazil's Steel City: Developmentalism, Strategic Power and Industrial Relations in Volta Redonda, 1941–1964*. Stanford: Stanford University Press.

Evans, P. B. (1979). *Dependent Development: The Alliance of Multinational, State and Local Capital in Brazil*. Princeton: Princeton University Press.

Fernández Pérez, P. & Lluch, A. (eds.) (2015). *Familias empresariales y grandes empresas familiares en América Latina y España: una visión de largo plazo*. Bilbao: Fundación BBVA.

Goldstein, A. (2002). 'Embraer: From National Champion to Global Player', *CEPAL Review, 77*, 97–116.

Graham, R. S. (1968). *Britain and the Onset of Modernization in Brazil, 1850–1914*. Cambridge: Cambridge University Press.

Greenhill, R. & Miller, R. (1998). 'British Trading Companies in South America after 1914', in Jones, Geoffrey (ed.), *The Multinational Traders*. London: Routledge. 102–27.

Hamilton, N. (1982). *The Limits of State Autonomy: Post-Revolutionary Mexico*. Princeton: Princeton University Press.

Jenkins, R. (1984). *Transnational Corporations and Industrial Transformation in Latin America*. London: Macmillan.

Jones, C. (1997). 'Institutional Forms of British Foreign Direct Investment in South America', *Business History, 39*(2), 21–41.

Jones, G. (1993). *British Multinational Banking, 1830–1990*. Oxford: Clarendon Press.

Jones, G. (2005). *Renewing Unilever: Transformation and Tradition*. Oxford: Oxford University Press.

Joslin, D. (1963). *A Century of Banking in Latin America: The Bank of London and South America Limited, 1862–1962*. London: Oxford University Press.

Khannu, T. & Palepu, K. (1997). 'Why Focused Strategies May Be Wrong for Emerging Markets', *Harvard Business Review, 75*(4), 41–51.

Klubock, T. M. (1998). *Contested Communities: Class, Gender, and Politics in Chile's El Teniente Copper Mine, 1904–1951*. Durham: Duke University Press.

Lanciotti, N. & Saes, A. M. (2015). 'American and Foreign Power in Argentina and Brazil, 1926–65', *Australian Economic History Review, 54*(2), 120–44.

Leff, N. H. (1978). 'Industrial Organization and Entrepreneurship in the Developing Countries: The Economic Groups', *Economic Development and Cultural Change, 26*(4), 661–75.

Lewis, C. M. (1983). 'The Financing of Railway Development in Latin America, 1850–1914', *Ibero-Amerikanisches Archiv, 9*(3/4), 255–78.

Marichal, C. (1989). *A Century of Debt Crises in Latin America: From Independence to the Great Depression, 1820–1930*. Princeton: Princeton University Press.

Martínez Echezárraga, J. (2015). 'Grandes familias empresariales en Chile: sus características y aportes al país, 1830–2012', in Fernández Pérez and Lluch (eds.), *Familias empresariales y grandes empresas familiares*, 409–36.

Miller, R. (1993). *Britain and Latin America in the Nineteenth and Twentieth Centuries*. London: Longman.

Miller, R. (1999). 'Business History in Latin America: An Introduction', in Dávila, Carlos and Miller, Rory (eds.), *Business History in Latin America: The Experience of Seven Countries*. Liverpool: Liverpool University Press, 1–16.

Miller, R. (2011). *Foreign Firms and Business History in Latin America*. Bogotá: Universidad de los Andes.

Monsalve Zanatti, M. (2015). 'Evolución de la gran empresa familiar peruana, 1890–2012', in Fernández Pérez and Lluch (eds.), *Familias empresariales y grandes empresas familiares*, 381–408.

Moreno, J. (2004). 'J. Walter Thompson, the Good Neighbor Policy, and Lessons in Mexican Business Culture, 1920–1950', *Enterprise & Society, 5*(2), 254–80.

Musacchio, A. (2008). 'Laws versus Contracts: Shareholder Protections and Ownership Concentration in Brazil, 1890–1950', *Business History Review, 82*(3), 445–73.

O'Brien, T. F. (1996). *The Revolutionary Mission: American Enterprise in Latin America, 1900–1945*. Cambridge: Cambridge University Press.

Oppenheimer, R. (1982). 'National Capital and National Development: Financing Chile's Central Valley Railroads', *Business History Review, 56*(1), 54–75.

Orlove, B. (ed.) (1997). *The Allure of the Foreign: Imported Goods in Postcolonial Latin America*. Ann Arbor: University of Michigan Press.

Palermo, S. A. (2006). 'Del Parlamento al Ministerio de Obras Públicas: la construcción de los ferrocarriles del estado en Argentina, 1862–1916', *Desarrollo Económico, 46*(187), 215–43.

Philip, G. (1982). *Oil and Politics in Latin America: Nationalist Movements and State Companies*. Cambridge: Cambridge University Press.

Quiroz, A. (1989). *Banqueros en conflicto: estructura financiera y economía peruana, 1884–1930*. Lima: Instituto de Estudios Peruanos.

Quiroz, A. (1993). *Domestic and Foreign Finance in Modern Peru, 1850–1950: Financing Visions of Development*. Basingstoke: Macmillan.

Rougier, M. & Schvarzer, J. (2006). *Las grandes empresas no mueren de pie: el (o)caso de SIAM*. Buenos Aires: Grupo Norma.

Schneider, B. R. (2008). 'Economic Liberalization and Corporate Governance: The Resilience of Business Groups in Latin America', *Comparative Politics, 40*(4), 379–97.

Schneider, B. R. (2009). 'Hierarchical Market Economies and Varieties of Capitalism in Latin America', *Journal of Latin American Studies, 41*(3), 553–75.

Sigmund, P. (1980). *Multinationals in Latin America: The Politics of Nationalisation*. Madison: University of Wisconsin Press.

Solberg, C. (1982). 'Entrepreneurship in Public Enterprise: General Enrique Mosconi and the Argentine Petroleum Industry', *Business History Review, 56*(3), 380–99.

Szrmecsanyi, T. & Topik, S. (2004). 'Business History in Latin America', *Enterprise & Society, 5*(2), 179–186.

Teichman, J. (1996). *Privatization and Political Change in Mexico*. Pittsburgh: University of Pittsburgh Press.

Thorp, R. (1998). *Progress, Poverty and Exclusion: An Economic History of Latin America in the 20th Century.* Washington: Inter-American Development Bank.

Thorp, R. & Bertram, G. (1978). *Peru, 1890–1977: Growth and Policy in an Open Economy.* Basingstoke: Macmillan.

Topik, S. (1987). *The Political Economy of the Brazilian State, 1889–1930.* Austin: University of Texas Press.

Vernon, R. (1971). *Sovereignty at Bay: The Multinational Spread of US Enterprises.* New York: Basic Books.

Von Mettenheim, K. (2010). *Federal Banking in Brazil.* London: Pickering & Chatto.

Wilkins, M. (1988). 'The Free-Standing Company, 1870–1914: An Important Type of British Foreign Direct Investment', *Economic History Review, 41*(2), 259–82.

Williamson, J. (ed.) (1990). *Latin American Adjustment: How Much Has Happened.* Washington: Institute for International Economics.

Woodward, J. (2002). 'Marketing Modernity: The J. Walter Thompson Company and North American Advertising in Brazil, 1929–1939', *Hispanic American Historical Review, 82*(2), 257–90.

14

North American capitalism

Mark R. Wilson

Introduction

North America is often understood as the region of the world in which capitalism has flourished most fully. Even during the colonial era, economic historians and sociologists have suggested, North America served as "capitalism's promised land" (Atack, 2014). The early United States, in the eyes of European observers, including Alexis de Tocqueville and Werner Sombart, seemed to be exceptional for its fluid markets for consumer goods and labor, as well as its avoidance of strong socialist movements. By the twentieth century, as the historian Victoria de Grazia has explained it, the United States was a global capitalist hegemon, "the premier consumer society", remarkable above all for its ability to create and export a system of mass-market capitalism (De Grazia, 2005). North America has been identified as the leading center of "liberal market economy", a variety of capitalism featuring modest levels of regulation of business, flexible labor markets (with weak unions), high levels of poverty and inequality and a privileging of capitalists (investors) over employees and other stakeholders (Hall and Soskice, 2001; Rosser and Rosser, 2004; Thelen, 2004; Jacoby, 2005).

These macro-historical, sociological accounts of North American capitalism differ slightly from those that may be more familiar to students of business and business history. According to Alfred D. Chandler, Jr., the leading historian of big business, the United States was the pioneer in the development of a "competitive managerial capitalism". This was distinct from the "personal capitalism" that endured in Great Britain, and the "cooperative managerial capitalism" that developed in Germany. For Chandler, Britain's "personal capitalism" was clearly inferior, because it failed to take advantage of the benefits that came from large investments and professional management. Germany, on the other hand, did succeed in developing large modern firms, but these were less competitive with one another than their US counterparts, in part because U.S. law was more hostile to cartels (Chandler, 1990). Over the past several decades, business historians have backed away from Chandler's focus on the rise of the large industrial corporation, by stressing the vulnerabilities of big business and the enduring vitality of smaller firms and flexible networks (Lamoreaux, Raff and Temin, 2003). This post-Chandlerian business history appears to point the way to a less exceptionalist account of North American capitalism. However, its elaboration awaits more comparative business history scholarship.

All of these grand generalizations about North American capitalism, whether they be Chandlerian or macro-historical, deserve closer scrutiny and elaboration. One question we may ask at the outset about "North American capitalism" is the extent to which that label refers only to the United States and its predecessor colonies. Mexico, despite its recent participation in NAFTA, the important trade agreement with Canada and the USA that has been in place since the end of the twentieth century, is normally studied as part of Latin America. Furthermore, Mexico and Canada were both economic midgets, in comparison to the United States, for the better part of the nineteenth and twentieth centuries. Unlike other continental capitalisms, in other words, "North American capitalism" is one in which the various national cases are most highly imbalanced. This essay, written by a historian of the United States, deals with this problem by including Mexico and Canada, albeit in a limited and selective way.

As it surveys the subject of North American capitalism, broadly defined, this chronologically organized essay emphasizes four major themes. The first of these is a warning against the overstatement of American exceptionalism. From the beginning through the present day, North American capitalism has included plenty of regulation, trade unionism, state enterprise and other challenges to the "liberal market economy". Indeed, as the historical sociologist Monica Prasad has suggested, it could be argued that Americans have a very strong political tradition of sharp criticisms of free-market capitalism and willingness to turn to government interventions (Prasad, 2006; Novak, 2008; Prasad, 2012). The shape and influence of these critiques and interventions have varied significantly over time. Given this complexity, would-be generalizers should be cautious about making assumptions about trans-historical continuities, and consensus.

Keeping that warning against exceptionalism in mind, this essay points to three aspects of North American capitalism that may be relatively distinctive. One is the influence of federalism: non-national political authorities, most notably the various state governments, have enjoyed comparably large amounts of authority over economic policy. The results have been complex, but one of the net long-run effects, at least in the United States, seems to have been that business firms have enjoyed more opportunities to escape heavy regulation (Scheiber, 1975). Federalism seems to have promoted the proliferation of corporations, the decentralization of banking, the fluidity of labor markets, the relative weakness of unions and other important manifestations commonly associated with "liberal market capitalism" (Mann, 1993; Yarmie, 2003; Dunlavy and Welskopp, 2007; Bordo, Redish and Rockoff, 2015).

A second special characteristic of North American capitalism—in the United States and Canada, at least—has been the relatively widespread ownership of property, the flexibility and fluidity of real estate markets and the ubiquity of small-proprietor enterprises (including family farms). Although the family farming has declined over the last century, real property ownership and small-scale enterprise should be seen as an important and enduring feature of capitalism in North America, across four centuries. Thus, although many scholars and business historians have traditionally emphasized North America's special status as the birthplace of modern "big business", we should also understand it as a place overflowing with smaller enterprises, a home to a more popular capitalism.

That claim about the breadth of property ownership and small-scale enterprise needs to be complemented, and partially contradicted, with the observation that North American capitalism has been distinctive for its heavy reliance on slavery and, more broadly, its high tolerance of extreme inequalities. As many historians have suggested over the last half-century, American slave owners of the eighteenth and nineteenth centuries should be understood not as feudal throwbacks, but as innovative capitalists. Given the importance of slavery in its long-run history, North American capitalism should be understood as having been reliant on cruelty, racism and violence. Although this evil has been reformed over the last half century, it is worth asking how this historical foundation may have also influenced more recent developments.

The age of merchant capital, sixteenth to nineteenth centuries: a dynamic imperial periphery, prosperous but cruel

By the early eighteenth century, capitalism was well-established across North America. Europeans were investing in a variety of profit-seeking enterprises, including silver mines in Mexico, sugar plantations in Jamaica, tobacco farms in Virginia, fur trading posts in Canada and fishing and whaling operations in New England. The output of these enterprises was shipped all around the Atlantic world by sophisticated European merchants, who also developed a massive trade in slaves. For more than three centuries, these merchants, based in London and other European cities, were the top overseers of North American capitalism. But already, during this colonial era, North America could claim to rank as the region of the world in which capitalism operated most freely. It offered some exceptional economic opportunities to European men, along with plenty of instability, inequality and—especially for hundreds of thousands of Africans—terrible cruelty and violence.

Was there capitalism in North America before the arrival of Europeans? Most scholars answer this question in the negative. Certainly, there was plenty of sophisticated agriculture, town-building and long-distance trade (Calloway, 2003). However, the economies of most Native American societies, in comparison to their European counterparts, provided fewer formal rights to private property, and fewer stable mechanisms for private investments in enterprise and the accumulation of money profits. Many historians, writing of interactions between Native Americans and Europeans during this period, emphasize a clash of economic cultures, in which grasping Europeans encounter aboriginal peoples whose approach to economics is more focused on sustainability, hospitality, gift-giving, cooperation and reciprocity (White, 1983; Taylor, 2006; Hämäläinen, 2008). Other scholars have down-played this alleged clash, by pointing to evidence of the sophistication of Atzec markets and merchants (Hassig, 1985), or the apparently "industrious" attitudes of Indian fur traders in colonial Canada (Carlos and Lewis, 2010). But even when Native Americans did accommodate themselves to capitalist markets, this was in the context of an unequal exchange, which became more unequal over time, as Europeans gained more ability to dominate via organized violence (Isenberg, 2000; Knight, 2002).

The first Europeans to build North American capitalism were the Spanish. According to many historians and economists, the variety of capitalism they developed in New Spain was an impure, inferior one. That is, colonial administration and economic institution building in New Spain is often characterized as full of unfree labor, corruption, rent-seeking, excessive taxation and overregulation (Semo, 1993; Salvucci, 2010). New Spain was home to plenty of profit-seeking capitalists, who included merchants and mine operators, as well as the original conquistadors. But the massive holdings of the Spanish crown, as well as those of the Church, limited private property ownership. Because many indigenous people were bound to estates, labor markets and agricultural enterprise in New Spain were more feudal than they would become in the rest of colonial North America. Mobility was restricted; guilds were powerful. Meanwhile, Spanish mercantilism was far more burdensome than was British (or French) mercantilism. According to many economic historians, all of these barriers to the flourishing of capitalism, along with some geographical factors, help to explain why per-capita income in New Spain was only about half that in British North America by the end of the eighteenth century (Coatsworth, 1978; Coatsworth, 1993; Easterbrook, 1990; Maddison, 2007; Robinson, 2009).

This comparison with New Spain helps us to appreciate the importance of capitalism in British North America. To be sure, as students of American history know well, the British colonies were full of servants and slaves; the burdens imposed by imperial administrators, if not massive, became heavy enough to inspire revolt and revolution. Still, capitalism flourished in British North America, in various forms: mercantile, plantation and small-scale proprietary. Capitalism fueled not just the expansion of slavery, but the broader growth of economic inequalities in the British colonies. And clashes among capitalists—especially between colonial merchants and planters and their metropolitan creditors and rivals—helped to spark the war that gave rise to the United States.

As we survey the economic history of North America in the seventeenth and eighteenth centuries, three things stand out. First, chattel slavery was becoming increasingly important, especially in the Chesapeake region. Second, despite the rise of slavery, there was an abundance of small-scale proprietary agricultural enterprise—family farming—which seems to have been highly productive and substantially (and increasingly) oriented toward markets, rather than subsistence. Finally, the abundant credit supplied by European merchants helped many colonists to attain world-class living standards, as well as significant debts.

The development of capitalism in British North America was perhaps most dramatic in Virginia, where thousands of tobacco planters, using slave labor and abundant credit from British merchants, amassed small fortunes. For much of the seventeenth century, tobacco planters who wanted labor turned to indentured servants, most of them from Britain. But by the turn of the eighteenth century, they relied increasingly on African slaves. Thus North American capitalism, from its early days, became entangled with extreme, reprehensible inequalities and systematic oppression and violence. By the mid-eighteenth century, Virginia was dominated by the gentry: a handful of families who owned several thousands of acres of land, along with dozens or hundreds of slaves. Their large purchases of land and slaves, along with their comfortable living conditions, were facilitated by the credit extended by English and Scottish merchants. By the 1760s, this credit had become generous enough that even smaller planters had considerable ability to borrow. The massive indebtedness of Chesapeake planters (such as George Washington) became obvious in the early 1770s, during a credit crunch that helped to fuel the American Revolution (Price, 1954; Kulikoff, 1986; Holton 1999).

As the abundance of credit in eighteenth-century Virginia suggests, it seems that North American capitalism has long been characterized by relatively high levels of borrowing (and debt), which have allowed remarkable amounts of personal and household consumption. Such a view of colonial America is certainly suggested by the historian T. H. Breen, who has described the mid-eighteenth century colonies as awash in consumer goods (Breen, 2004). This expansion of consumer capitalism was enjoyed by a relatively wide swath of the population, by global standards. But it also highlighted growing inequalities, which were present not just in the countryside, but in the growing port cities, such as Philadelphia, New York and Baltimore. These cities and others would continue to be home to a large population of working poor, long after the Revolution (Smith, 1990; Rockman, 2009).

Outside the cities, and north of the Chesapeake, there were hundreds of thousands of family farms, on which parents and children, more than slaves, servants or employees, did most of the work (Chandler, 1977; McCusker and Menard, 1991; Vickers, 1994; Egnal, 1998). Here was small-scale proprietary capitalism, less dependent on British credit, which slowly but surely was helping to make North America one of the world's richest regions. These family farmers, combining African, Native American and European techniques, were innovative and productive. Many of them went well beyond bare subsistence farming, by selling surplus at market. Their market sales increased over time, as transportation costs fell. This growth of real markets was accompanied by a cultural transformation, at least in New England, which saw the pursuit of profit become more legitimate, by the later eighteenth century, than it had been a few generations before (Bushman, 1967; Innes, 1988; Rothenberg, 1992; Menard, 2006).

Family farmers, like the operators of larger plantations, needed land. This resource was abundant in colonial North America, but after the seventeenth century, it was rarely free. Instead, colonists, as they fought wars with Native Americans and each other for control of territory, built well-developed real estate markets. In this environment, land speculation became one of the most important, and popular, of all enterprises. According to the eminent historian Bernard Bailyn, "land speculation was everyone's work". In other words, while it was true that the biggest land deals were struck by elites, including the Chesapeake gentry and royal governors and their friends, forms of land speculation on a smaller scale were practiced by large numbers of small farmers, many of them with humble origins (Bailyn, 1988, p. 66; see also Holton, 1999; Taylor, 2006).

So, by the eve of the Revolutionary War, North American capitalism featured mass participation in market sales and real estate transactions. This popular agrarian capitalism coexisted with far more inegalitarian forms, which saw some merchants, tobacco planters and fur traders enjoy fantastic gains, in contrast to the hardscrabble lives lived by common laborers, sailors, servants and slaves.

New national economies in the nineteenth century: expanding agrarian and industrial capitalisms

Between the 1780s and the 1860s, North America changed from a region of European colonies to one of new independent nations. Here the obvious leader was the United States, which by the end of the nineteenth century would rank as the world's largest national economy. This period saw considerable industrialization, particularly in the United States, which started to develop a globally competitive manufacturing sector, thanks in part to its use of tariffs and incorporation laws. But capitalist agriculture also expanded, both in its plantation-slave labor forms (now used especially for cotton) and in its small-proprietor, free-labor forms (which produced huge amounts of wheat and other crops). Agrarian and industrial capitalism were both fueled by a growing financial sector, which in the United States during this period came to be highly decentralized, and by a rapidly improving transport and communications system, built by a combination of public and private enterprises.

Given the record of the expansion of agrarian capitalism in the colonial era (see above), it is hard to embrace the idea that the early nineteenth-century United States experienced a "market revolution". Historians have spilled lots of ink debating this subject; no doubt they will continue to do so, in part because it is so difficult to measure the thoughts of average Americans about the legitimacy of capitalism, or to determine when exactly a nation crosses the threshold into becoming a true "market society" (Sellers, 1991; Zakim and Kornblith, 2012). Still, we should probably reject any claims of a sudden "market revolution" in earlier nineteenth century North America, in favor of an emphasis on longer-run continuities, and on how changing transport and communications technologies facilitated market exchange (Rothenberg, 1992; Howe, 2007).

The expansion of agrarian capitalism in nineteenth century North America included developments in the South, where the continent's new premier export crop, cotton, was produced mostly by slaves. Economic historians have long regarded Southern plantations as rationally managed, efficient and profitable capitalist enterprises (Fogel and Engerman, 1974). More recently, a new generation of historians has done even more to portray Southern slaveholders as modern capitalists, by documenting their reliance on mercantile and bank credit, and their substantial accumulations of wealth, built on the backs of their slaves. These slaves and slaveholders were key players in global networks of commodity production, trade and consumption, which in the case of cotton, came to involve millions of people around the world (Beckert, 2014; Baptist, 2014).

Although cotton was indeed central to the early nineteenth century North American and global economies, we should not forget that the agricultural sector continued to con- tain plenty of "family capitalism" and free-labor enterprises, including huge numbers of small-scale farms (Clark, 2012; Blackmar, 2012). By the early twentieth century, when over a quarter of the US labor force worked in agriculture and half the population still lived in rural settings, about three-quarters of rural household heads in the United States were landowners (in Canada, also home to thousands of small-scale wheat farmers, the situation was similar). In Mexico, by contrast, only about 2% of rural residents owned land (Enger- man and Sokoloff, 2012). Such figures suggest the enduring importance of small-proprietor enterprise in the northern part of North America, even in the later nineteenth century, when independent family farming was becoming harder to sustain (Bogue, 1955; Levy, 2012). Most Northern farmers were better off than their counterparts in the post-Civil War South, where many recently freed slaves, along with many poorer white farmers, were never able to acquire any land at all, as they found themselves deep in debt, stuck in tenant farming and sharecropping (Ransom, 1989; Woodman, 1995).

The expansion of small-proprietor farming in the United States and Canada, as well as much larger agricultural operations, was made possible by massive consolidations of national territory, which was quickly converted by settlers into millions of acres of arable land. After the revolution, western lands, formerly controlled by the British Crown and a handful of co- lonial elites, were confiscated and privatized. Starting in the 1790s, and continuing into the nineteenth century, Europeans and Americans bought and sold millions of acres of western lands (Gates, 1960; Nettels, 1962). The available acreage expanded dramatically over time, especially in the United States, which used the Louisiana Purchase, and then the Mexican War, to triple its territory. By aggressively surveying and selling this territory, and by provid- ing the military force necessary to seize and hold it, the US government helped to promote settler capitalism (Wilson, 2008).

Government was also important in the making of the so-called transportation revolution, which facilitated North America's rapid economic growth. Here is an example that suggests that the historical development of North American capitalism relied on something more that "liberal market" arrangements. The national, state and local governments invested heavily in public goods, including canals, railroads, postal services and public schools (Goodrich, 1960; John, 1995; Larson, 2001; Long and Ferrie, 2013). This public enterprise was complemented by private investment, which became larger over time, most notably in the case of railroads. But even some later nineteenth century railroad companies used substantial public subsidies, especially in the form of land grants (White, 2011).

Railroad and canal companies were among the growing numbers of enterprises in nineteenth century America that were organized not as family businesses or partnerships, but as government-chartered limited liability corporations. By 1817, the new states in the United States had already provided charters to more than two thousand corporations. Thousands more were created later in the century, after many states—often competing with one another—passed general incorporation laws that made it easier to set up such firms. The ubiquity of corporations, promoted by federalism, was a distinctive characteristic of North American capitalism since 1800 (Nettels, 1962; Wright, 2012).

One of the industries in which corporations were common was banking. Here again, we should be struck by the extent to which North American capitalism, even in its corporate varieties, promoted the proliferation of large numbers of smaller enterprises. The United States already had 89 banks by 1811 (Nettels, 1962); a century later, it was home to about 30,000 banks, far more than in any other part of the world (McCraw, 1997; Haber, 2012). This growth and decentralization of the American financial sector was promoted by federalism, as well as a democratic political culture. As President Jackson's successful war against the Second Bank of the United States suggested, many Americans disliked the idea of a single dominant bank, but were happy to use smaller local banks that could provide them with mortgages and business loans. Some historians have emphasized the economic benefits of this fast-developing financial sector, which was far more robust and sophisticated than anything that developed in Canada or Mexico (Haber, 1991; Perkins, 1994; Sylla, 2006). But the decentralized US banking sector failed to do much to protect Americans, throughout the nineteenth century and into the twentieth, from regular and brutal "panics" (recessions). Among the worst of these periodic crises, before the Great Depression, were those that started in the years 1819, 1837, 1857, 1873, 1893 and 1907. Perhaps North American capitalism would have been more stable, and more humane, over the long run, if the United States had established more of a Canadian-style financial industry, with smaller numbers of larger banks, more diversified and more heavily regulated (Bordo, Redish and Rockoff, 2015).

Corporate capitalism also spread, albeit slowly and unevenly, in the manufacturing sector. In fact, for much of the nineteenth century, most American manufacturers were still dependent on merchants, for financing as well as marketing (Porter and Livesay, 1971; Chandler, 1977). However, North America did see the rise of industrial capitalism, which in the early nineteenth century developed most dramatically in New England, where successful merchant families invested some of their profits into substantial textile mills (Dalzell, 1987). Faced with stiff competition from larger, better-established British producers, the New England companies were aided by tariffs. This was an important aspect of North American capitalism during the long nineteenth century: government-imposed tariffs, championed by the Whig and Republican parties, helped to build up a competitive American manufacturing sector (Bensel, 2000).

In the early New England textile industry, most of the wage workers were young women. Their involvement raises the larger question of the kinds of economic opportunities that North American capitalism has offered members of politically and socially subordinated groups, such as women, African-Americans and immigrants. Until the later nineteenth century, the vast majority of women and African Americans were making giant contributions to the growth of the North American capitalist economy, albeit through labor that was unpaid. Still, many tens of thousands of women, and free African-Americans of both sexes, worked for wages. Some even rose to the ranks of true capitalists, by becoming successful entrepreneurs. For women, entrepreneurship was somewhat easier in fields understood as requiring their special skills and knowledge, such as millinery, dressmaking and cosmetics (Gamber, 1997; Peiss, 1998). For African-American men, the rise of Jim Crow segregation in the later nineteenth century limited opportunities to compete in wider fields, but could also create some new possibilities for at least small-scale entrepreneurship, in fields such as insurance, undertaking and dentistry (Walker, 2009; Weems, 1996). Meanwhile, small-proprietor capitalism was practiced by many immigrants, whose numbers swelled in the late nineteenth century, as millions of southern and eastern Europeans moved to North America (Godley, 2001), and again in the late twentieth century, when Asians and Mexicans were the most numerous migrants (Light and Bonacich, 1988). All this activity reminds us again of the centrality of small-scale entrepreneurship to North American capitalism, even in an age that saw the rapid rise of "big business".

Later nineteenth to later twentieth centuries: The rise of big business, economic empire and stabilizing regulation

The period from the 1880s through the 1960s may be understood as the golden age of American "big business", a label most often used to refer to large, multi-departmental industrial corporations, led by professional managers. The development of these enterprises was well-documented by Alfred Chandler, who started his investigations of them in the 1950s, the heyday of American big business and US economic power. Thanks in part to the work of Chandler, we understand the big industrial corporation as one of the most important components of North American capitalism. This is reasonable enough, but we should add three additional observations about North American capitalism during the long twentieth century. First, small-scale enterprise, often overlooked by those who focus on the story of the rise of big business, did not disappear. Second, this was the era during which North American capitalists, commanding more and more wealth and market power, came to have much more influence abroad. Finally, the rise of big business helped to fuel an era of progressive reform, in which governmental regulation and organized labor became much more powerful.

As we have seen, there were plenty of corporations in mid-nineteenth century America. However, between the American Civil War and World War I, the sizes of the largest American firms jumped. Rather suddenly, there were many industrial corporations with tens or even hundreds of millions of dollars in invested capital; some of them employed tens of thousands of workers. These enterprises, following a model that had been pioneered by the nineteenth-century railroads, were led by teams of professional managers, rather than by their owners. Some raised capital from the public, in growing markets for industrial securities, centered in New York; others relied on re-invested profits, or on capital supplied by the large banks, such as J. P. Morgan. In many manufacturing and processing industries, by the early twentieth century, just one or two firms, or a handful, dominated the market. Some of the leaders of North America's biggest industrial enterprises, including John D. Rockefeller and Andrew Carnegie, became some of the world's wealthiest and best-known capitalists. Equally important, during the twentieth century, some of the most successful of the large multidivisional, professionally-managed American industrial corporations, such as General Motors, provided models of organization that would be widely (if unevenly) emulated, in North America and around the world (Chandler, 1962, 1977, 1990).

One of the most controversial questions in the field of business history, in recent years, has been about how to explain the rise of these giant enterprises. Chandler's influential account stressed the importance of technology and the size of the US domestic market, as well as innovations in marketing and organization. Over the last quarter-century, Chandler has been challenged by many scholars, who have pointed to the importance of American law, which could serve to favor large firms over small. These critics suggested that big business was less efficient than Chandler suggested (Berk, 1994; Roy, 1997). Similar conclusions were suggested by those who pointed to the continuing vitality of smaller, more flexible firms (Scranton, 1997). Other scholars pointed to the importance of the severe economic recession of the 1890s and the hostility of American law to collusive cartels. The result was a legal and economic environment that encouraged mergers, creating a large number of monopolistic or oligopolistic industries (Lamoreaux, 1985; Dunlavy and Welskopp, 2007).

At the same moment that the mergers of the 1890s were creating many of the US industrial giants, the United States entered the global stage as an imperialist power. By the time of the Spanish-American War of 1898, the United States not only had a larger population than any European nation, but also had the world's most productive national agricultural and manufacturing sectors. Its size and output were being boosted further by the skills and labor power of millions of immigrants, most of them from eastern and southern Europe, many of whom were pulled to America by the promise of a share in capitalism's fruits. This growing economic might—which became even more disproportionate after Europe was impoverished by two giant world wars—allowed North American capitalism more ability to touch businesses and consumers in other parts of the world.

The new global reach of North American capitalism was evident even before the USA's emergence as a military imperial power. Before the later nineteenth century, North America's main role in the global economy was that of a commodity exporter (and importer of capital and labor). But by the late nineteenth century, North American companies and brands, many of them nourished in their early years by large domestic markets, became better known abroad. Some even set up important branches overseas. Some of the more successful American multinationals operating in the increasingly integrated world economy before World War I included Standard Oil, American Tobacco and Singer Sewing Machine (Wilkins, 1970; Gordon, 2012).

The growing economic influence of the United States was also evident within North America, as Yankees came to serve as an increasingly important source of foreign direct investment, as well the resident managers of important enterprises. In Canada, where British capital continued to be important, the dominance of the USA came relatively late: it was not until the early Cold War era that Canadians would decry their nation's "silent surrender" to US capital, which by that time owned about half of the Canadian mining, petroleum and large-scale manufacturing industries (Muirhead, 2007). By contrast, in Mexico, the influence of Yankee capitalists was far more obvious, at an earlier date. The regime of Porfirio Diaz, who ruled Mexico from 1876 to 1911, courted foreign capital, which helped to provide Mexico with some significant economic growth, after its many decades of stagnation. Individual US companies and investors, such as Edward Doheny and the Phelps Dodge Corporation, became especially important in the fields of railroad construction, mining and oil (O'Brien, 1996; Ansell, 1998; Kuntz Ficker, 2000). The involvement of Yankee capitalists was an important, and politically controversial, part of the broader operations of the Diaz regime, which offered Mexicans a more privatized and dynamic economy, albeit one in which few common people were able to share in the fruits of growth. The Diaz regime, even though it did institute some major regulations and reforms, became infamous for its reliance on "crony capitalism", in which small elite networks dominated both politics and economics (Haber, 1989, 2002). This highly inegalitarian style of capitalism, along with the highly visible participation of foreigners in it, was a main target of the leaders of the Mexican Revolution of the 1910s–1930s. Those revolutionaries offered Mexicans a much more regulated capitalism, via a new constitution that limited private property rights and promoted labor unions, as well as major land reform and the nationalization of the oil industry (Schneider, 2004).

The record of crony capitalism and revolutionary reform in Mexico offers some helpful comparative perspective on the development of capitalism in the early twentieth century United States. In that nation, there were also huge economic inequalities, thanks in part to the rise of big business; these had been made obvious in the extraordinarily violent labor-management clashes of the late nineteenth century, at Homestead, Haymarket, Pullman and elsewhere (Mann, 1993). But the United States, unlike Mexico and Russia, saw no radical revolution. This can be explained not only by American capitalism's continuing ability to offer relatively high opportunities for property ownership and small-scale entrepreneurship, but also by its overhauling and stabilization, via several decades' worth of progressive reforms. No less than Europeans, who provided them with models and ideas, Americans of this period tried, with some substantial success, to address what they regarded as capitalism's excesses and failures (Rodgers, 1998).

The progressive reform of North American capitalism in the early twentieth century owed a great deal to the practitioners of agrarian capitalism—the small farmers, many of whom gathered under the Populist banner, who protested the growing concentration of economic and political power. They went beyond merely demonizing big business, by calling for more government interventions—in education, transport and communications, as well as in agriculture—to create a fairer, more egalitarian capitalism (Postel, 2007; O'Donnell, 2015).

These reformers succeeded in transforming North American capitalism, into a version that was far more regulated, more stable and more egalitarian, than what it had been before. To be sure, some of the stabilization could be attributed to the rise in economic concentration in many industries, which some mid-twentieth century critics regarded as an important step in the direction of some sort of post-capitalist, more bureaucratized society (Brick, 2006). However, the reforms need to be understood as political achievements, won only because of the hard political work, at the grassroots and the halls of government, of farmers, workers, politicians and even lawyers and intellectuals. Especially in the 1910s and 1930s, these progressives and New Dealers managed to create a new kind of North American capitalism, which in many fields was no less stabilized and regulated than its counterparts abroad. New kinds of government regulation, added to older forms of regulation and government promotion of enterprise (Pisani, 1987), arose. Some of this reform was a direct response to the Great Depression, but much of it was begun earlier, in an era of persistent, if less horrific, macroeconomic crises. Progressives and New Dealers, broadly defined, installed the foundations of a progressive tax system; stabilized and regulated banks and securities markets, along with agriculture and transport, food and pharmaceuticals; offered social security; and even created new rules that helped unions to organize a large fraction of the labor force (Mehrotra, 2013; Carpenter, 2010; Dubofsky, 1994; Smith, 2013). To be sure, the USA developed a "divided welfare state", in which benefits were enjoyed disproportionately by white male union members working for larger private companies (Hacker, 2002; see also Klein, 2003). Still, this era saw a remarkable reversal of what had been a long-run trend in the direction of economic inequality. Instead, the North American capitalism of the mid-twentieth century was associated with what today is understood as a historically unusual "great compression" of wealth and income (Piketty, 2014).

Since the 1950s: globalization, deregulation, financialization and relative decline

As the previous discussion suggests, North America's status as archetypal home of the "liberal market economy" was not necessarily evident in the first half of the twentieth century, when in some respects American reformers were at least as successful as their counterparts abroad in building a style of capitalism that was more coordinated, and regulated. However, during the second half of that century, North American capitalism transformed again. After the 1970s, as the world economy became more integrated, North American capitalism was de-industrialized and—to use a term that has only recently become standard—financialized. It also became more hostile to labor unions, less regulated (in certain fields) and more inegalitarian. So, to a considerable extent, what some scholars take for granted as a trans-historical qualities of North American capitalism may be better understood as more recent developments, or else revivals of older ones.

Some important developments after 1945 merely expanded upon those that had already begun. Certainly this was true of the global reach of North American capitalism, which had been very substantial even before World War II (De Grazia, 2005). After 1945, with the United States a true hegemon, American companies and brands became even more powerful abroad. As many scholars have shown, the Americanization of the global economy was far from total; it involved plenty of resistance, negotiation and even some two-way exchange (Kipping and Bjarnar, 1998; Zeitlin and Herrigel, 2000; Moreno, 2003; Nolan, 2012). Still, it was surely during the Bretton Woods era of the 1950s-60s, when the US dollar was king, that North American capitalism—and US companies and brands in particular—had the greatest opportunities to reshape other regional capitalisms into something closer to its own image.

Since the 1970s, as the volume of global trade has skyrocketed, North America has been less dominant. This was obvious to average American consumers as they surveyed changes in the automobile market, where companies headquartered in Japan and Europe, such as Toyota and Volkswagen, became competitive with the formerly dominant Ford, Chrysler and G.M. Somewhat less obvious, but equally important, was the influence of globalization in the retail sector, where American consumers enjoyed even more abundant and cheaper products, many of them made in China, thanks to the new global supply chains forged by Walmart, the new industry leader and its rivals, which came to include online sellers, such as Amazon. As the historian Nelson Lichtenstein has argued, the rise of Walmart was one dramatic aspect of a broader shift of economic power away from manufacturers and back to merchants, as more goods became commodified (Lichtenstein, 2009, 2012).

The de-industrialization of North American capitalism in the late twentieth century involved not just the general decline of manufacturing relative to the retail and service sectors, but also the more specific phenomenon of so-called financialization. In fact, this term embraces at least two distinct meanings. On the one hand, it serves to suggest the expanding share of output and employment that was enjoyed by the banking and financial services sectors. This expansion coincided with the decline of manufacturing, which suffered not just from global competition, but from the choices of American policymakers (Stein, 2010). Those policymakers favored a partial deregulation of banking (along with other sectors), which helped to fuel more macroeconomic volatility, most obviously during the crisis of 2008–09.

But the term financialization was also used to describe a different aspect of the late-twentieth century transformation of North American capitalism: the growing emphasis, within firms, on maximizing short-run financial returns to investors. This new prioritizing of "shareholder value", understood by its practitioners as both rational and fair, has been criticized by many scholars, who have asked whether its focus on short-run profits may have degraded longer-run productivity and competitiveness (Fligstein, 1990; Dore, Lazonick and O'Sullivan, 1999; O'Sullivan, 2000; Lazonick, 2010). Financialization has also contributed to remarkable increases in inequalities of wealth and income, particularly in the United States (Piketty, 2014). Economic and social mobility, which had been greater in North America, both in myth and in fact, for much of modern history, was no longer particularly impressive in America (Long and Ferrie, 2013).

Despite all the evidence of the emergence of what some called a second Gilded Age, there remained important legacies, and new manifestations, of the more stabilized North American capitalism that had emerged in the early twentieth century. Even as many industries were deregulated (as in the fields of transport, utilities, telecommunications, banking, education and defense), some powerful new governmental enterprises and regulations emerged. Starting in the mid-1960s, under President Johnson's Great Society, the national government became a much larger provider of medical care, as well as old-age pensions. North America (like Japan) had sizeable welfare states, albeit somewhat less generous ones, particularly to the non-elderly, than those in Europe (Lynch, 2006; Lindert, 2014). Meanwhile, environmental regulation became far more important, even in the otherwise mostly deregulatory-minded USA, where a new Environmental Protection Agency, along with various new statutes, succeeded in altering the behavior of many business firms (Kagan, Gunningham and Thornton, 2003). Here was a success story of late twentieth century North American capitalism: many of the most toxic outputs that had accompanied industrialization were now being limited, and in some cases even cleaned up. This did not occur fast enough to stave off the growing global environmental crisis that had been fueled by decades of huge carbon emissions, but it did suggest that even at the center of "liberal market capitalism", it was possible for reformers to achieve important shifts in the direction of sustainability.

Meanwhile, North American capitalism, though de-industrialized and challenged from abroad, continued to feature some globally competitive industries and organizations. These included not just New York banks and hedge funds, management consultants and accountants, but also Hollywood studios, universities and even a few manufacturers. Perhaps the most celebrated of the late-twentieth century North American superstars were the firms of Silicon Valley. Some of its observers, including scholars of varieties of capitalism and celebrants of Silicon Valley's apparent origins in genius entrepreneurship and garage-based small-proprietor capitalism, have suggested that the quick rise of the high-tech American firms was consistent with free-market capitalism's tendency to foster disruptive, "radical innovation" (Hall and Soskice, 2001; Isaacson, 2011). Such a view fails to do enough to acknowledge the extent to which Silicon Valley firms had been nursed and subsidized by the US military, especially during the early Cold War (Lecuyer, 2006). This was one example of the many contributions of government to the stability and success of North American capitalism, even in the age of deregulation, when they were frequently overlooked and obscured (Block, 2008; Mettler, 2011).

Finally, North America in the late twentieth and early twenty first centuries surely saw something of a renaissance of smaller-scale and proprietary capitalism. In this most recent phase in the history of North American capitalism, there was still plenty of "big business"—including older giants such as DuPont and General Motors, along with new behemoths such as Walmart, Apple and Bank of America. However, the champions of smaller-scale capitalist enterprise could still find much to like in North America. This was true in high-tech manufacturing, where it was becoming increasingly clear, by the 1980s, that so-called Fordist styles of mass production might be outdone by efforts from smaller, leaner, more flexible firms (Lamoreaux, Raff and Temin, 2003; Brick, 2006).

Outside the manufacturing sector, there was a broader flourishing of small business, in a variety of forms. Notably, in the wake of the Civil Rights and second-wave feminist movements, African Americans and women, besides winning higher wages and more opportunities in firms controlled by white men, also enriched North American capitalism by becoming entrepreneurs, in much larger numbers than they had previously done (Wright, 2013; Kwolek-Folland, 1998; Reed, 2001). In the early twenty first century, any careful survey of North American capitalism would have to take account of its huge numbers of smaller firms, from restaurants and craft breweries, to "home office" service firms, to a remarkable variety and diversity of direct selling enterprises (Biggart, 1989; Williams and Bemiller, 2011).

This was evidently a more decentralized, and in many ways more entrepreneurial, capitalist economy than the one that had existed just a half century before. In many ways, it represented a triumph of the vision of the many vocal champions of a less regulated capitalism, who had never accepted the legitimacy of the progressive New Deal political economy. By the turn of the twenty first century, capitalism in North America, if not North American capitalism in the global arena, had become in many important ways more politically and culturally hegemonic than ever before. This victory appeared to offer North Americans more abundant opportunities for credit, consumption, property ownership and the accumulation of wealth; it also seemed to come with the price of less economic stability and social security.

Conclusion

North American capitalism has been celebrated, not without some reason, as a model of political economy with a solid record of achieving prosperity and growth. Even in the late colonial period, residents of British North America enjoyed relatively high standards of living. From 1800 to 2000, per capita income (in the United States) increased in real terms by a factor of about twenty. This prosperity, which was accompanied by some significant opportunities for average people to own property or otherwise enjoy previously unmatched levels of consumption and standards of living, was envied, and not just resented, by millions of people around the world. During the twentieth century, North American capitalism partially colonized much of the rest of the world, where mass consumption and American management and advertising techniques became more widely emulated, if not fully embraced or enjoyed.

As this essay has emphasized, we need to be careful about generalizing about North American capitalism. In fact, there were varieties of North American capitalism, in two senses. First, to the extent that it contained any core tendencies or characteristics at all, those could change substantially over time. The more regulated, stabilized North American capitalism of the mid-twentieth century was not the same animal as the more "liberal" North American capitalisms that seemed to prevail before, and after. This fact deserves more attention from students of business history, and social scientists more generally, who wrongly ascribe trans-historical qualities to more recent social forms.

We also should do more to recognize the extent to which varieties of North American capitalism have existed simultaneously, interacting uneasily with one another, at any given point in time. In the mid-nineteenth century, cotton and wheat production were both enormously important parts of North American capitalism. Yet one of these commodities was cultivated largely by chattel slaves, working under threat of the lash in relatively large agricultural enterprises, fueled with ample bank and mercantile credit. The proprietors of cotton plantations, some of whom enjoyed very large fortunes, were certainly capitalists.

But so too, in an important sense, were the predominant producers of wheat: small farms in the United States and Canada, which at the time were still owned and operated by families. This co-existence of very different scales and styles of capitalist enterprises endures to the present day.

The existence of such multiplicities and historical alternatives should lead us to realize that North American capitalism, like other regional forms, or even global capitalism, has always been, and remains, a work in progress. Its changing shape has been influenced not just by overwhelming tides of change from abroad, nor just by the ever-powerful forces of supply and demand, but also by political struggle. North American capitalism should, in the remainder of the twenty first century, be capable of evolving in ways that will provide today's North American children with ample social security and collective prosperity, as well as more opportunity for individual advancement. How much it will succeed in doing so may depend upon North Americans' willingness to weave together some of the many strands of capitalism that have been practiced on the continent, over the last several centuries.

References

Ansell, M. R. (1998). *Oil Baron of the Southwest: Edward L. Doheny and the Development of the Petroleum Industry in California and Mexico.* Columbus: Ohio State University Press.

Atack, J. (2014). "America: Capitalism's Promised Land", in *The Cambridge History of Capitalism, Volume I: The Rise of Capitalism: From Ancient Origins to 1848*, ed. Larry Neal and Jeffrey G. Williamson. New York: Cambridge University Press, 533–73.

Bailyn, B. (1988). *The Peopling of British North America: An Introduction.* New York: Vintage.

Baptist, E. E. (2014). *The Half Has Never Been Told: Slavery and the Making of American Capitalism.* New York: Basic Books.

Beckert, S. (2014). *Empire of Cotton: A Global History.* New York: Knopf.

Bensel, R. F. (2000). *The Political Economy of American Industrialization, 1877–1900.* New York: Cambridge University Press.

Berk, G. (1994). *Alternative Tracks: The Constitution of the American Industrial Order, 1865–1917.* Baltimore: Johns Hopkins University Press.

Biggart, N. W. (1989). *Charismatic Capitalism: Direct Selling Organizations in America.* Chicago: University of Chicago Press.

Blackmar, E. (2012). "Inheriting Property and Debt: From Family Security to Corporate Accumulation", in Zakim and Kornblith, 93–117.

Block, F. (2008). "Swimming Against the Current: The Rise of a Hidden Developmental State in the United States", *Politics & Society, 36*(2), 169–206.

Bogue, A. G. (1955). *Money at Interest: The Farm Mortgage on the Middle Border.* Ithaca: Cornell University Press.

Bordo, M. D., Redish, A. & Rockoff, H. (2015), "Why Didn't Canada Have a Banking Crisis in 2008 (or in 1930, or 1907, or…)?" *Economic History Review, 68*(1), 218–243.

Breen, T. H. (2004). *The Marketplace of Revolution: How Consumer Politics Shaped American Independence.* New York: Oxford.

Brick, H. (2006). *Transcending Capitalism: Visions of a New Society in Modern American Thought.* Ithaca: Cornell University Press.

Bushman, R. L. (1967). *From Puritan to Yankee: Character and the Social Order in Connecticut, 1690–1765.* Cambridge: Harvard University Press.

Calloway, C. G. (2003). *One Vast Winter Count: The Native American West Before Lewis and Clark.* Lincoln: University of Nebraska Press.

Carlos, A. & Lewis, F. (2010). *Commerce by a Frozen Sea: Native Americans and the European Fur Trade.* Philadelphia: University of Pennsylvania Press.

Carpenter, D. P. (2010). *Reputation and Power: Organizational Image and Pharmaceutial Regulation at the FDA.* Princeton: Princeton University Press.

Chandler, A. D., Jr. (1962). *Strategy and Structure: Chapters in the History of Industrial Enterprise.* Cambridge: MIT Press.

Chandler, A. D., Jr. (1977). *The Visible Hand: The Managerial Revolution in American Business.* Cambridge: Harvard University Press.

Chandler, A. D., Jr. (1990). *Scale and Scope: The Dynamics of Industrial Capitalism.* Cambridge: Harvard University Press.

Clark, C. (2012). "The Agrarian Context of American Capitalist Development". In *Capitalism Takes Command: The Social Transformation of Nineteenth-Century America*, ed. Michael Zakim and Gary J. Kornblith. Chicago: University of Chicago Press.

Coatsworth, J. H. (1978). "Obstacles to Economic Growth in Nineteenth-Century Mexico", *American Historical Review, 83*(1), 80–100.

Coatsworth, J. H. (1993). "Notes on the Comparative Economic History of Latin America and the United States", in Walther L. Bernecker and Hans Werner Tobler, *Development and Underdevelopment in America: Contrasts of Economic Growth in North and Latin America in Historical Perspective.* Berlin and New York: Walter de Gruyter, 10–30.

Dalzell, R. F. (1987). *Enterprising Elite: The Boston Associates and the World They Made.* Cambridge: Harvard University Press.

De Grazia, V. (2005). *Irresistible Empire: America's Advance through Twentieth-Century Europe.* Cambridge: Harvard University Press.

Dore, R., Lazonick, W. & O'Sullivan, M. (1999). "Varieties of Capitalism in the Twentieth Century". *Oxford Review of Economic Policy, 15*(4), 102–120.

Dubofsky, M. (1994). *The State and Labor in Modern America.* Chapel Hill: University of North Carolina Press.

Dunlavy, C. A. & Welskopp, T. (2007). "Myths and Particularities: Comparing U.S. and German Capitalism". *GHI Bulletin, 41*, 33–64.

Easterbrook, W. T. (1990). *North American Patterns of Growth and Development: The Continental Context.* Toronto: University of Toronto Press.

Egnal, M. (1998). *New World Economies: The Growth of the Thirteen Colonies and Early Canada.* New York: Oxford University Press.

Engerman, S. L. & Sokoloff, K. (2012). *Economic Development in the Americas since 1500: Endowments and Institutions.* New York: Cambridge University Press.

Fligstein, N. (1990). *The Transformation of Corporate Control.* Cambridge: Harvard University Press.

Fogel, R. W. & Engerman, S. L. (1974). *Time on the Cross: The Economics of American Negro Slavery.* Boston: Little, Brown.

Gamber, W. (1997). *The Female Economy: The Millinery and Dressmaking Trades, 1860–1930.* Urbana: University of Illinois Press.

Gates, P. W. (1960). *The Farmer's Age: Agriculture, 1815–1860.* New York: Harper & Row.

Godley, A. (2001). *Jewish Immigrant Entrepreneurship in New York and London, 1880–1914.* New York: Palgrave.

Goodrich, C. (1960). *Government Promotion of American Canals and Railroads, 1800–1890.* New York: Columbia University Press.

Gordon, A. (2012). *Fabricating Consumers: The Sewing Machine in Modern Japan.* Berkeley: University of California Press.

Haber, S. H. (1989). *Industry and Underdevelopment: The Industrialization of Mexico, 1890–1940.* Stanford: Stanford University Press.

Haber, S. H. (1991). "Industrial Concentration and the Capital Markets: A Comparative Study of Brazil, Mexico, and the United States, 1830–1930", *Journal of Economic History, 51*(3), 559–80.

Haber, S. H. (2002). "The Commitment Problem and Mexican Economic History", in Jeffrey L. Bortz and Haber, eds., *The Mexican Economy, 1870–1930: Essays on the Economic History of Institutions, Revolution, and Growth.* Stanford: Stanford University Press, 324–36.

Hacker, J. S. (2002). *The Divided Welfare State: The Battle over Public and Private Social Benefits in the United States.* New York: Cambridge University Press.

Hall, P. A. & Soskice, D. (2001). "An Introduction to Varieties of Capitalism", in Hall and Soskice, eds., *Varieties of Capitalism: The Institutional Foundations of Comparative Advantage.* New York: Oxford University Press.

Hämäläinen, P. (2008). *The Comanche Empire.* New Haven: Yale University Press.

Hassig, R. (1985). *Trade, Tribute, and Transportation: The Sixteenth-Century Political Economy of the Valley of Mexico.* Norman: University of Oklahoma Press.

Holton, W. (1999). *Forced Founders: Indians, Debtors, Slaves, & the Making of the American Revolution in Virginia*. Chapel Hill: University of North Carolina Press.

Howe, D. W. (2007). *What Hath God Wrought: The Transformation of America, 1815–1848*. New York: Oxford University Press.

Innes, S. (ed.) (1988). *Work and Labor in Early America*. Chapel Hill: University of North Carolina Press.

Isaacson, W. (2011). *Steve Jobs*. New York: Simon & Schuster.

Isenberg, A. C. (2000). *The Destruction of the Bison: An Environmental History, 1750–1920*. New York: Cambridge University Press.

Jacoby, S. M. (2005). *The Embedded Corporation: Corporate Governance and Employment Relations in Japan and the United States*. Princeton: Princeton University Press.

John, R. R. (1995). *Spreading the News: The American Postal System from Franklin to Morse*. Cambridge: Harvard University Press.

Kagan, R. A., Gunningham, N. & Thornton, D. (2003). "Explaining Corporate Performance: How Does Regulation Matter?" *Law and Society Review, 37*(1), 51–90.

Kipping, M. & Bjarnar, O. (eds.) (1998). *The Americanisation of European Business: The Marshall Plan and the Transfer of US Management Models*. London: Routledge.

Klein, J. (2003). *For All These Rights: Business, Labor, and the Shaping of America's Public-Private Welfare State*. Princeton: Princeton University Press.

Knight, A. (2002). *Mexico: From the Beginning to the Spanish Conquest*. New York: Cambridge University Press.

Kulikoff, A. (1986). *Tobacco and Slaves: The Development of Southern Cultures in the Chesapeake, 1680–1800*. Chapel Hill: University of North Carolina Press.

Kuntz Ficker, S. (2000). "Economic Backwardness and Firm Strategy: An American Railroad Corporation in Nineteenth-Century Mexico", *Hispanic American Historical Review, 80*(2), 267–298.

Kwolek-Folland, A. (1998). *Incorporating Women: A History of Women and Business in the United States*. New York: Twayne.

Lamoreaux, N. R. (1985). *The Great Merger Movement in American Business, 1895–1904*. New York: Cambridge University Press.

Lamoreaux, N. R., Raff, D. M. G. & Temin, P. (2003). "Beyond Markets and Hierarchies: Toward a New Synthesis of American Business History", *American Historical Review, 108*(2), 404–33.

Larson, J. L. (2001). *Internal Improvement: National Public Works and the Promise of Popular Government in the Early United States*. Chapel Hill: University of North Carolina Press.

Lazonick, W.. (2010). "Innovative Business Models and Varieties of Capitalism: Financialization of the U.S. Corporation". *Business History Review, 84*(4), 675–702.

Lécuyer, C. (2006). *Making Silicon Valley: Innovation and the Growth of High-Tech, 1930–1970*. Cambridge: MIT Press.

Levy, J. (2012). *Freaks of Fortune: The Emerging World of Capitalism and Risk in America*. Cambridge: Harvard University Press.

Lichtenstein, N. (2009). *The Retail Revolution: How Wal-Mart Created a Brave New World of Business*. New York: Metropolitan Books.

Lichtenstein, N. (2012). "The Return of Merchant Capitalism". *International Labor and Working-Class History, 81*, 8–27.

Light, I. H. & Bonacich, E. (1988). *Immigrant Entrepreneurs: Koreans in Los Angeles, 1965–1982*. Berkeley: University of California Press.

Lindert, P. (2014). "Private Welfare and the Welfare State". In *The Cambridge History of Capitalism*, volume 2, edited by Larry Neal and Jeffrey Williamson. New York: Cambridge University Press.

Long, J. & Ferrie, J. (2013). "Intergenerational Occupational Mobility in Great Britain and the United States since 1850", *American Economic Review, 103*(4), 1109–37.

Lynch, J. (2006). *Age in the Welfare State: The Origins of Social Spending on Pensioners, Workers, and Children*. New York: Cambridge University Press.

Maddison, A. (2007). *Contours of the World Economy, 1–2030 AD: Essays in Macro-Economic History*. New York: Oxford University Press.

Mann, M. (1993). *The Sources of Social Power*, Vol. II, *The Rise of Classes and Nation-States, 1760–1914*. New York: Cambridge University Press, 138–39.

McCraw, T. K. (1997). "American Capitalism", in McCraw, ed., *Creating Modern Capitalism: How Entrepreneurs, Companies, and Countries Triumphed in Three Industrial Revolutions*. Cambridge: Harvard University Press.

McCusker, J. J. & Menard, R. (1991). *The Economy of British North America, 1607–1789.* Chapel Hill: University of North Carolina Press.

Mehrotra, A. K. (2013). *Making the Modern American Fiscal State: Law, Politics, and the Rise of Progressive Taxation, 1877–1929.* New York: Cambridge University Press.

Menard, R. R. (2006). "Colonial America's Mestizo Agriculture", in Cathy Matson, ed., *The Economy of Early America: Historical Perspectives and New Directions.* University Park: Pennsylvania State University Press, 107–23.

Mettler, S. (2011). *The Submerged State: How Invisible Government Policies Undermine American Democracy.* Chicago: University of Chicago Press.

Moreno, J. (2003). *Yankee Don't Go Home: Mexican Nationalism, American Business Culture, and the Shaping of Modern Mexico, 1920–1950.* Chapel Hill: University of North Carolina Press.

Muirhead, B. (2007). *Dancing Around the Elephant: Creating a Prosperous Canada in an Era of American Dominance, 1957–1973.* Toronto: University of Toronto Press.

Nettels, C. P. (1962). *The Emergence of a National Economy, 1775–1815.* White Plains: ME Sharpe.

Nolan, M. (2012). *The Transatlantic Century: Europe and America, 1890–2010.* New York: Cambridge University Press.

Novak, W. J. (2008). "The Myth of the 'Weak' American State". *American Historical Review, 113*(3), 752–72.

O'Brien, T. F. (1996). *The Revolutionary Mission: American Enterprise in Latin America.* New York: Cambridge University Press.

O'Donnell, E. T. (2015). *Henry George and the Crisis of Inequality: Progress and Poverty in the Gilded Age.* New York: Columbia University Press.

O'Sullivan, M. (2000). *Contests for Corporate Control: Corporate Governance and Economic Performance in the United States and Germany.* New York: Oxford University Press.

Peiss, K. (1998). *Hope in a Jar: The Making of America's Beauty Culture.* New York: Metropolitan Books.

Perkins, E. J. (1994). *American Public Finance and Financial Services, 1700–1815.* Columbus: Ohio State University Press.

Piketty, T. (2014). *Capital in the Twenty-First Century*, trans. Arthur Goldhammer. Cambridge: Harvard University Press.

Pisani, D. J. (1987). "Promotion and Regulation: Constitutionalism and the American Economy". *Journal of American History, 74,* 740–68.

Porter, G. & Livesay, H. C. (1971). *Merchants and Manufacturers: Studies in the Changing Structure of Nineteenth-Century Marketing.* Baltimore: Johns Hopkins University Press.

Postel, C. (2007). *The Populist Vision.* New York: Oxford University Press.

Prasad, M. (2006). *The Politics of Free Markets: The Rise of Neoliberal Economic Policies in Britain, France, Germany, and the United States.* Chicago: University of Chicago Press.

Prasad, M. (2012). *The Land of Too Much: American Abundance and the Paradox of Poverty.* Cambridge: Harvard University Press.

Price, J. M. (1954). "The Rise of Glasgow in the Chesapeake Tobacco Trade, 1707–1775". *William & Mary Quarterly, 11*(2), 179–99.

Ransom, R. L. (1989). *Conflict and Compromise: The Political Economy of Slavery, Emancipation, and the American Civil War.* New York: Cambridge University Press.

Reed, K. A. (2001). *Managing our Margins: Women Entrepreneurs in Suburbia.* London: Routledge.

Robinson, J. A. (2009). "The Political Economy of Equality and Growth in Mexico: Lessons from the History of the United States", in Santiago Levy and Michael Walton, eds., *No Growth Without Equity? Inequality, Interests, and Competition in Mexico.* New York: Palgrave Macmillan and The World Bank, 87–107.

Rockman, S. (2009). *Scraping By: Wage Labor, Slavery and Survival in Early Baltimore.* Baltimore: Johns Hopkins University Press.

Rosser, J. B. & Rosser, M. V. (2004). *Comparative Economics in a Transforming World Economy.* Cambridge: MIT Press.

Rothenberg, W. B. (1992). *From Market-Places to a Market Economy: The Transformation of Rural Massachusetts, 1750–1850.* Chicago: University of Chicago Press.

Roy, W. G. (1997). *Socializing Capital: The Rise of the Large Industrial Corporation in America.* Princeton: Princeton University Press.

Salvucci, R. J. (2010). "Some Thoughts on the Economic History of Early Colonial Mexico", *History Compass, 8/7,* 626–35.

Scheiber, H. S (1975). "Federalism and the American Economic Order," *Law and Society Review*, 10, 57–118.

Schneider, B. R. (2004). *Business Politics and the State in Twentieth-Century Latin America*. New York: Cambridge University Press.

Scranton, P. (1997). *Endless Novelty: Specialty Production and American Industrialization, 1865–1925*. Princeton: Princeton University Press.

Sellers, C. (1991). *The Market Revolution: Jacksonian America, 1815–1846*. New York: Oxford University Press.

Semo, E. (1993). *The History of Capitalism in Mexico: Its Origins, 1521–1763*. Austin: University of Texas Press.

Smith, B. G. (1990). *The "Lower Sort": Philadelphia's Laboring People, 1750–1800*. Ithaca: Cornell University Press.

Smith, J. S. (2013). *A Concise History of the New Deal*. New York: Cambridge University Press.

Stein, J. (2010). *Pivotal Decade: How the United States Traded Factories for Finance in the Seventies*. New Haven: Yale University Press.

Sylla, R. (2006). "Political Economy of Financial Development: Canada and the United States in the Mirror of the Other", *Enterprise and Society*, 7(4), 653–65.

Taylor, A. (2006). *The Divided Ground: Indians, Settlers, and the Northern Borderland of the American Revolution*. New York: Knopf.

Thelen, K. (2004). *How Institutions Evolve: The Political Economy of Skills in Germany, Britain, the United States, and Japan*. New York: Cambridge University Press.

Vickers, D. (1994). *Farmers & Fishermen: Two Centuries of Work in Essex County, Massachusetts, 1630–1850*. Chapel Hill: University of North Carolina Press.

Walker, J. E. K. (2009). *The History of Black Business in America: Capitalism, Race, Entrepreneurship, Second Edition*. Chapel Hill: University of North Carolina Press.

Weems, R. E. (1996). *Black Business in the Black Metropolis: The Chicago Metropolitan Assurance Company, 1925–1985*. Bloomington: Indiana University Press.

White, R. (1983). *The Roots of Dependency: Subsistence, Environment, and Social Change Among the Choctaws, Pawnees, and Navajos*. Lincoln: University of Nebraska Press.

White, R. (2011). *Railroaded: The Transcontinentals and the Making of Modern America*. New York: Norton.

Wilkins, M. (1970). *The Emergence of Multinational Enterprise: American Business Abroad from the Colonial Era to 1914*. Cambridge: Harvard University Press.

Williams, L. S. & Bemiller, M. (2011). *Women at Work: Tupperware, Passion Parties, and Beyond*. Boulder: Lynne Rienner.

Wilson, M. R. (2008). "Law and the American State from Revolution to Civil War: Institutional Growth and Structural Change". In *The Cambridge History of Law in America: Volume 2 (1790–1920)*, ed. Christopher L. Tomlins and Michael Grossberg. New York: Cambridge University Press, 1–35, 697–705.

Woodman, H. L. (1995). *New South, New Law: The Legal Foundations of Credit and Labor Relations in the Postbellum Agricultural South*. Baton Rouge: Louisiana State University Press.

Wright, G. (2013). *Sharing the Prize: The Economics of the Civil Rights Revolution in the American South*. Cambridge: Harvard University Press.

Wright, R. E. (2012). "Capitalism and the Rise of the Corporation Nation". In *Capitalism Takes Command: The Social Transformation of Nineteenth-Century America*, ed. Michael Zakim and Gary J. Kornblith. Chicago: University of Chicago Press.

Yarmie, A. (2003). "Employers and Exceptionalism: A Cross-Border Comparison of Washington State and British Columbia, 1890–1935", *Pacific Historical Review*, 72(4), 561–615.

Zakim, M. & Kornblith, G. J. (2012). "Introduction: An American Revolutionary Tradition", in Zakim and Kornblith, eds., *Capitalism Takes Command: The Social Transformation of Nineteenth-Century America*. Chicago: University of Chicago Press, 1–12.

Zeitlin, J. & Herrigel, G. (eds.) (2000). *Americanization and Its Limits: Reworking US Technology and Management in Post-War Europe and Japan*. New York: Oxford University Press.

15

International varieties of capitalism

The case of Western Europe

Keetie Sluyterman and Gerarda Westerhuis

Introduction[1]

In the section on international varieties of capitalism, our chapter deals with Western Europe. This is a fairly loose concept, but it stands for a number of countries that were relatively prosperous thanks to international trading since the sixteenth century, and pioneered an industrial way of producing from the late eighteenth century onwards. Together these countries were dominant in the world economy until their role was taken over by the United States and the Soviet Union during the twentieth century. In this chapter on Western Europe the focus is inevitably on the large countries, Britain, France and Germany, but we also include the Mediterranean countries, Italy, Portugal and Spain, as well as the small countries, especially Belgium and the Netherlands. Obviously, we won't be able to discuss the business history of every one of the eight countries separately. Instead we will focus on three debates, on how (most of) these countries figured in those debates and on how business historians contributed to these debates. Debates tend to concentrate on countries being ahead or behind in their industrial development or economic growth more generally, on companies as first movers or slow starters and on processes of convergence versus persisting varieties. In this way, we intend to show common features in those three critical debates and at the same time highlight important business developments in Western Europe from the nineteenth century onwards.

First we will deal with the discussions about early and late industrialisation. While the UK was obviously the front runner in the First Industrial Revolution, and Belgium an early follower, historians in all other countries had agonising debates about why the Industrial Revolution in their country arrived so late. It is a debate about favourable (or unfavourable) circumstances, the presence or lack of entrepreneurship and the role of financial institutions and the state.

The second debate focuses on the rise of the large managerial enterprise, and is related to the Second Industrial Revolution. The debate is not just about who was first or second, but also about the way the various countries organised their business, and about the respective merits of those ways of organising. Companies in the US and Germany seemed to have taken the initiative in quite distinct ways, while those in other countries were behind or failing for various reasons. This debate is also about the rise of the managerial company, internal organisation, cartels and the persistence of family firms.

The third and more recent debate is about the institutional context of the various countries and the way companies select strategies that make the most of their national comparative institutional advantages. This 'varieties of capitalism' debate deals with the relevance of national institutions and with the question of convergence (or divergence) between national economies. It contrasts the merits of the coordinated market economy versus the liberal market economy, a debate contrasting the UK with 'continental' Europe, and northern versus southern Europe. This debate has clear links with the arrival of the Third Industrial Revolution and its impact on globalisation. As historians we are, of course, well aware that those Industrial Revolutions were in many ways 'evolutions', but they were nonetheless very important, and do mark stages in the development of the European economies.

Debate about early and late industrialising countries

A particularly important issue after the Second World War was the question of how to achieve economic growth. To learn more about processes of economic growth, history offered an interesting laboratory to test patterns and pace of development. Walt Rostow's *Stages of Economic Growth: A Non-Communist Manifesto* (1960) described how a country's economy could move from a traditional society to mass consumption through five stages. The essential stage was the third, when the growth in an economy accelerates and 'takes off into sustained growth'. His book motivated many economic historians to search for that particular period of economic acceleration that for most European countries was positioned in the nineteenth century.

At about the same time, Alexander Gerschenkron (1962) offered a different interpretation of the European patterns of industrialisation. He argued that countries that industrialised early would show a different pattern from countries that industrialised later, the so-called backward countries: 'In several very important respects the development of a backward country may, by the very virtue of its backwardness, tend to differ fundamentally from that of an advanced country' (Gerschenkron, 1962, quote 7). For Gerschenkron, Britain was obviously the first industrializing country, and thus the most advanced one. All other European countries were considered late-comers to a smaller or larger extent. They would follow a different path, depending on their relative backwardness. The process of industrialisation for late-comers would be faster (the 'big spurt'), as they could borrow technology from the earlier industrializing countries. Late-comers would also restrain consumption, place greater emphasis on the production of capital goods and use more large-scale production technology. The more backward a country, the larger the need for investment banks and their entrepreneurial support; countries that were even more backward would need a supportive state and pro-industry ideology.

To illustrate his generalisations, Gerschenkron contrasted Britain with Germany and Russia as he developed his 'German-Russian paradigm'. In Germany the industrialisation process took off in the mid-nineteenth century, the focus was less on textiles and more on producer goods, the scale of factories was larger than in Britain and mixed banks were particularly important. In the latecomer Russia the period of fast industrialisation was more concentrated than in Germany and in this country the state was of decisive importance.

Gerschenkron's ideas stimulated a lot of historical research. First of all, economists and economic historians tried to establish the pace of economic growth. Overall, it turned out that identifying a specific 'spurt' in the process of economic growth was difficult because, as calculations by Crafts, Leybourn and Mills demonstrated, 'discontinuities in trend growth in nineteenth-century Europe were less common and less dramatic than Gerschenkron imagined – or indeed than most of the historiography would suggest' (Crafts, Leybourne and Mills, 1991, p. 141). But without a great spurt, there was less need for large investments during a short period of time, and thus for a prominent role of investment banks. There was more agreement with the way Gerschenkron characterized the European countries as more or less backward compared to Britain. However, the choice for countries as the main unit of analysis was contested by Sydney Pollard, who argued in his 1981 study on European industrialisation that until 1870 not countries, but regions, were the relevant units of analysis. He identified Sambre Meuse and Scheldt Valley of Belgium and northern France, as well as the Ruhr region of Germany, as the regions of early industrialisation after Britain. These regions followed the British 'model' of industrialisation (Pollard, 1981).

While comparing Britain and Germany, Gerschenkron devoted only a few pages to that other large European country, France. Gerschenkron positioned it as later than Britain, but earlier than Germany. The fact that in France the innovative Credit Mobilier of the Pereire brothers was established in 1852 seemed to fit the theory that investment banks were more important for latecomers. However, the new bank was not a great success. Gerschenkron dealt with this problem by arguing that the Credit Mobilier encouraged the traditional banks, such as the Rothschilds, to embrace investments in railways and industrial projects (Gerschenkron, 1962). Others, including Maurice Lévy-Leboyer and Michel Lescure, were of the opinion that France was not that far behind Britain, and that therefore there was no 'backwardness' that required a more active participation of banks. As far as the state was concerned, not all its investments were really effective. For instance, the state overinvested in railways (Lévy-Leboyer and Lescure, 1991).

Gerschenkron devoted a separate chapter to explore Italy, seen as one of the later industrializers. Confirming his theory, the country used similar mixed banks as Germany. In fact, German banks played a role in Italian industrialisation. Gerschenkron did not consider the role of the Italian state particular prominent, but he conceded that the state was certainly active, though perhaps not always as constructive in creating economic growth as it might have been (Gerschenkron, 1962). Later historians put more emphasis on the role of the state, in particular as owners and managers of natural monopolies, including railways and mail and telegraph services (Sylla and Toniolo, 1991; Toninelli, 2004).

Spain and Portugal don't figure in Gerschenkron's study, but they would certainly have been seen as part of the backward countries in terms of industrialisation. Pollard argues that Spain and Portugal belonged to the most prosperous countries of Europe in 1830, but were far behind the European average in 1913. He blamed both Spain and Portugal for relying too long on their colonial empires, which they then, for the most part, lost during the course of the nineteenth century (Pollard, 1981). Some Spanish historians blamed the backwardness on the lack of tariff protection, but others pointed towards a lack of entrepreneurship (Tortella, 2000). The latter hypothesis stimulated business history research (Carreras, Tafunell and Torres, 2003).

The Netherlands is another country ignored by Gerschenkron. It fits uneasily in his generalisations, because it combined a relatively high income per head with a very late industrialisation. Historians engaged in a lengthy debate about the causes of the late industrialisation, some arguing for a lack of entrepreneurial initiatives, including entrepreneurial bankers, others underlining the unfavourable economic circumstances such as a lack of natural resources. High wages and obsolete technologies were also proposed as explanations for backwardness (Mokyr, 1976). As the debate unfolded, the question was raised if the Netherlands was 'backward', or just 'different' (Griffiths, 1996). Indeed, the Netherlands achieved economic growth through expansion of trade and services, and modernization of the agricultural sector. As such, it showed a distinct growth trajectory (Van Zanden and Van Riel, 2000). For such a balanced growth, industry banks were not really necessary, because self-financing and the roll over of short-term credit sufficed (Jonker, 1996).

Gerschenkron attached great importance to the role of banking for the process of industrialization. Inspired by Rudolf Hilferding's notion that large German universal banks dominated strategic decision making at the corporate level (Hilferding, 1910), Gerschenkron argued that in Germany banks had close relations with industry enabling them to provide firms with finance and entrepreneurship. His argument helped creating the popular contrast between the bank-led financial system of Germany and much of continental Europe and the market-led financial system of Britain and the US. However, recent research has questioned this contrast (Westerhuis, 2016). The contrast between bank-based and market-based systems seems to imply that universal banks are incompatible with active security markets. Analysing the German financial system before the First World War, Carolin Fohlin (2007), however, came to the conclusion that universal banks and active security markets could function very well at the same time in the same market. Comparing Germany and the US, Fear and Kobrak (2010) found that banks had different roles than Gerschenkron assumed. Following Feldman (2006), they argue that the real issue was not whether the financial system could promote economic growth, but if and how it could promote stability. They showed that before 1914 both German and US banks channelled capital to firms, created trust for distant investors and increased confidence in capital markets. These functions were far more important than being substitutes for entrepreneurship, as Gerschenkron stated. Based on these findings, Fear and Kobrak argued that the financial systems of both countries did not differ substantially in this period, because in both countries banks acted as 'special intermediaries' in corporate governance and stock exchanges.

To round off the discussion on early and late industrialisation, we can quote the conclusion of Richard Sylla and Gianni Toniolo: 'During the years that have elapsed since Gerschenkron formulated his hypotheses about European industrialization, many scholars have questioned and even rejected important elements of his work. But no analytical insights or grand syntheses comparable to Gerschenkron's have come in the wake of the critical work his seminal ideas stimulated' (Sylla and Toniolo, 1991, p. 5). This conclusion still stands 25 years on.

Rise of the large managerial enterprise

The backwardness debate focused entirely on Europe. In contrast, our second debate on national varieties started in the United States with business historian Alfred D. Chandler, Jr. from Harvard University. In three famous books, Chandler developed what we might call the 'Chandler paradigm' (Chandler, 1962, 1977, 1990). In short, Chandler argued that the modern industrial enterprise played a pivotal role in the transformation of Western economies. These economies had been rural, agrarian and commercial, but subsequently became industrial and urban. This transformation brought the most rapid economic growth in the history of mankind. The revolution in transport and communications supported larger, faster and more regular movements of raw materials and finished goods. A new group of entrepreneurs moved quickly to exploit these market opportunities, using the new technologies of the Second Industrial Revolution to achieve economies of scale and scope. In these large companies, ownership became separated from control. This led to the rise of a new type of company, the managerial enterprise, and a new type of business men, the salaried manager. Some industrial sectors and some countries took the lead, while others stayed behind or followed later. It is another story of 'first movers' and 'followers', but now focused on companies and only later on their combined effect on national economies.

In his first book *Strategy and Structure*, published in 1962, Chandler described the rise of the large manufacturing companies in the US as a new phenomenon. In his view the biggest challenge for these new institutions was finding ways of creating an effective organization. In response to this challenge the companies formed extensive managerial hierarchies. Moreover, their organizational structure had to follow the company strategy, which in practical terms meant that a diversification strategy demanded a multi-divisional organization. Between the 1840s and 1920s, big business became the most powerful institution in the American economy and its managers the most influential group of economic decision makers. In his next book, *The Visible Hand*, published in 1977, Chandler further elaborated on the rise of the modern business enterprise, which brought with it the rise of a new class of businessmen, the middle and top managers, who together formed the managerial hierarchy. With a reference to Adam Smith's invisible hand of the market, Chandler argued that the large managerial enterprise, consisting of many distinct operating units, subsumed functions of the market through horizontal and vertical integration, thus coordinating the activities of the economy and allocating its resources. In many sectors of the economy the visible hand of management replaced the invisible hand of market forces. He further argued that building a managerial hierarchy was essential to the success of big business, and the companies which succeeded in building this hierarchy were hard to beat, and as a consequence dominated their economies for decades. Companies that continued to rely on family ownership and leadership, and thus failed to create a managerial hierarchy, were unlikely to succeed, at least in the new technologically advanced type of industries. According to Chandler, the US in the last decades of the nineteenth century was the first country to exploit the new possibilities of modern transport and technological progress to create these large vertically integrated companies managed by a hierarchy of professional managers.

In these first two books, Chandler offered a set of generalizations for the US that proved eminently suitable for comparing countries. In the volume *Managerial Hierarchies*, edited by him and Herman Daems, the US was compared with three Western European countries: Germany, Britain and France. Following up on the discussions on early and late industrialization, the various authors focused on the question at what point in time the European countries followed the US example. It was another debate about 'early or late', in this case the early or late rise of the 'modern enterprise'. The volume concluded that Germany in the late nineteenth century, Britain in the 1920s and France after 1945 formed US style modern business enterprises with large managerial hierarchies (Chandler and Daems, 1980). Britain was later than the US in forming integrated companies, but according to Leslie Hannah (1980), the markets functioned so well that the companies had less incentives to integrate vertically than US firms. And as British companies were smaller than those in the US, there was less need for extensive managerial hierarchies. Jürgen Kocka (1980) concluded for Germany that the early rise of large bureaucratic companies in chemicals and electrical engineering was a consequence of the country's 'backwardness'. Its lack of well-functioning markets forced the companies to integrate, develop managerial hierarchies, and rely on industrial banks for their financing. Moreover, the country had a tradition of bureaucracy. Finally, according to Maurice Lévy-Leboyer (1980), France had smaller companies compared to Germany and Britain, and relied longer than Germany on holding companies and business groups, but might have developed managerial hierarchies in the interwar years if not for the negative impact of the 1930s depression and the Second World War. However, after World War Two, France displayed a similar growth of big business as the other European countries. The volume concluded that by the mid-1970s, the economies of all three West-European countries were dominated by 'modern industrial companies', characterized by vertical and horizontal integration and large managerial hierarchies. By that time, these companies had also diversified and developed multi-divisional organizations. European countries had finally caught up with the US.

Chandler made further country comparisons in 1980, when he contrasted the US with Britain, and in 1984, when he looked at the US, Britain, Germany and Japan (Chandler, 1980, 1984). A far more in-depth comparison followed in 1990 with *Scale and Scope*. The basis for the country appraisals were again his trademark long lists of largest companies in benchmark years. In this book, he took as a starting point the years 1913 (Germany), 1917 (US) and 1919 (UK) and then for all three countries 1930 and 1948. Key ingredients were again the development of a managerial hierarchy and the creation of the multidivisional organization structure. To create a successful (that is long-term) business, companies had to make a 'three pronged' investment in production facilities, in marketing and distribution and – most importantly – in management. Comparing the rise of big business in the US, Great Britain and Germany, Chandler moved from assessing individual companies to judging whole economies. He contrasted the American 'Competitive Managerial Capitalism' with the 'Cooperative Managerial Capitalism' in Germany and the 'Personal Capitalism' in Britain (Chandler, 1990).

Germany followed closely on America's heels in the late nineteenth century, organizing production in large companies supported by cartels and protection of the home market. However, Britain failed to grasp the opportunities of the new technological developments in chemicals and electrical engineering, because it failed to make the 'three-pronged investment' by relying too long on family firms and personal networks for doing business. In this book Chandler devoted more attention than in his earlier book to the role of founders, family members and bankers, in contrast with professional managers (Chandler, 1990).

The claim that Britain failed because of 'personal capitalism' was contested by British historians. One line of argument was that the performance of British business wasn't so bad. Comparing the economic performance of Britain, France and Germany in the long twentieth century, Youssef Cassis (1997) found Britain to be the undisputable leader in Europe until the 1950s, when the performance of all three countries started to converge. Peter Wardley (1991) underlined that Britain was able to build big business in the service sector. Geoffrey Jones (1997) also wondered how Britain's supposed failure could be reconciled with British success in building large international companies. British entrepreneurs must have had some organizational qualities to build and sustain these companies.

Another criticism of Chandler argues that Britain did not have more family firms than Germany or the US, and that in any case, family firms as institutions could function very effectively and that there was no convincing argument to blame the family firm for Britain's perceived underperformance. Family firms may have had more problems than managerial companies in finding family successors, but there was no proof its management was unprofessional. Neither is there proof, argued Roy Church (1990), that families were less inclined to reinvest profits into the business than hired managers. More generally, Chandler's introduction of the concept of 'personal capitalism' led to a renewed debate on the merits and drawbacks of family firms (Jones and Rose, 1993; Colli, 2003; Colli, Fernandez Pérez and Rose, 2003).

For German historians there were fewer reasons to question the conclusions of *Scale and Scope*, because Chandler was overwhelmingly positive about German business. He even saw the frequent use of cartels as a sign of good management. For that reason, his generalisations led to a renewed interest in the functioning of cartels (Schröter, 2013). But later historians also underlined that Germany had indeed a few very large companies in chemicals and electrical engineering before 1914, but was less prominent in later years as a consequence of the First World War, and had far fewer large companies in other sectors, such as food. Moreover, it had its fair share of family firms, and was not so different from Britain in that respect (Cassis, 1997).

Conspicuously absent from the debate was France, or perhaps one should say that the country was very much on the fringe. It was still included in 1980, but hardly any longer in 1984 and totally absent in the 1990 *Scale and Scope*. The country doesn't stand out in any way in this debate, and it was even categorized as 'follower' in the 1998 volume *Big Business and the Wealth of Nations* (Chandler, Amatori and Hikino, 1997). However, Youssef Cassis (1997) included France in his above mentioned study about European big business, comparing Britain, Germany and France. Indeed, France didn't have a few very large companies early on like Germany, nor did it have a similar broad spread of large companies as Britain, but it nonetheless developed numerous quite large companies in heavy industry as well as in the new technological industries during the interwar period. In particular, the growth in car manufacturing stood out. Michael Smith (1998) drew up a list of France's 100 largest industrial firms in 1913 and concluded that French firms were indeed smaller than US firms, but otherwise behaved not so very differently. They developed cutting-edge technology, were prepared to invest in state-of-the-art production facilities and hired professional managers.

A strong advocate of the Chandler paradigm, Franco Amatori (1997) positioned Italy in his framework. Though later than Britain and Germany, Italy also created companies in the new technologies such as electrical engineering, chemicals, car making, rubber and oil. However, the main actors were different. Following Gerschenkron's argument that late industrializing countries needed different institutions, Amatori looked at the role of banks and the state. While Gerschenkron concluded that banks were of prime importance in Italian industrialisation, Amatori reserved this role for the government. As far as banks played a role, they were part of government schemes. Amatori concluded that the best way to describe Italian capitalism was not 'personal' as in Britain, or 'cooperative' as in Germany and certainly not managerial as in the US, but as 'political'. Family managers had access to the political powers, and professional civil servants and family managers together created a system resembling a command economy. In building up the national industry, this system produced successes as well as failures.

Chandler's *Scale and Scope* inspired many business historians to draw up lists of the hundred largest industrial companies in their country. Albert Carreras and Xavier Tafunell (1997) created a database of the top 200 Spanish firms, measured in assets, over the period 1917–1990. Compared to the US, the UK and Germany, Spanish business was much more concentrated in transport equipment and weaker in machinery. The development of large Spanish companies displayed a remarkable lack of continuity. The autarkic policies of the 1940s and 1950s destroyed some companies and led to the establishment of many national companies that were not internationally competitive. Carreras and Tafunell see a painful misallocation of resources. While national companies were unable to compete in world markets, Spain experienced an influx of international companies that successfully competed with local enterprises. Therefore, foreign owned companies became typical of the Spanish top-hundred and leaders in export.

For the Netherlands, Erik Bloemen, Jan Kok and Jan Luiten van Zanden (1993) assembled a list of the 100 largest managerial companies from 1913 to 1990. They wanted to test Chandler's proposition that companies that were the first to make the three-pronged investment in production, marketing and management would be hard to challenge by newcomers, and therefore would remain on top for a long time. They found that the turn over in the Dutch top 100 was in fact substantial. While a small number of prominent companies remained on top for the whole period, many other companies disappeared, sometimes through mergers. The importance of the top 100 companies for the Dutch economy was relatively large, and increased until 1973, but diminished since, again challenging the supposed durability of first movers. Based on a list of top 100 companies in 1930, Keetie Sluyterman and Hélène Winkelman (1993) evaluated the importance of family firms, especially in the sector of the Second Industrial Revolution. They concluded that the Netherlands resembled Britain in the enduring influence of the family firm and personal relationships. It contrasted as a country with Germany in that cartels and agreements did become important only after 1930. Personal capitalism was not synonymous with failure. Many of the smaller Dutch firms competed successfully in foreign markets.

One of Chandler's important claims was that company structure should follow company strategy to remain efficient. In practice, this meant that companies with a diversification strategy were wise to select a multidivisional organisation structure. As early as the interwar years, American companies saw the benefits of the multidivisional organisation. European historians have been at pains to find organization charts that showed a similar choice for the multidivisional structure in the interwar period, but they didn't succeed, apart from German electrical company Siemens (Kocka, 1980). The problem was that European historians compared real life with Chandlerian generalizations and felt their companies wanting. But perhaps the American companies were not really so early in time so clearly structured as Chandler suggested. For instance, John Quail (2008) found that in the interwar period books on company organization discussed the issues in terms of 'staff' and 'line' command, not in terms of centralization and decentralization. He couldn't find much confirmation of the presence of the multidivisional organization form in the US before 1940.

The rapid growth of European firms in the 1950s and 1960s motivated Harvard Business School scholars to investigate the top 100 industrial firms of France, West-Germany, UK and Italy to find out whether strategy and organizational structure of these firms converged towards the American model of large, diversified and managerial corporations. They concluded that numerous large European companies had followed a diversification strategy, and that quite a few of them had indeed created a multidivisional structure, though not nearly as many as in the US. Instead, the loose, decentralized holding company remained popular in Europe (Dyas and Thanheiser, 1976). Some twenty years later, Whittington and Mayer extended this research to 1993, including France, West-Germany and the UK, leaving out Italy. They found that despite national differences, European business had wholeheartedly adopted the diversified, divisionalized form because it was more effective than alternatives: 'The engineering-oriented and bank-connected Germans are just as diversified as the financially driven British. The statist, hierarchical French are even more divisionalized than the federal Germans' (Whittington and Mayer, 2000, quote 219). The research project focused on largest countries, neglecting other European countries. Instead, Veronica Binda and Martin Iversen (2007) compared the growth strategies and ownership of 40 largest Spanish and Danish firms between 1973–2003. They found no convergence in diversification strategies nor in ownership structures. However, the largest companies had become more internationally oriented in 2003. In a comparable article Binda and Colli (2012) compared the transformation of ownership, strategies and structures of the top 50 Italian and Spanish firms. They found continuities in ownership and structure, but profound changes in strategies (diversification, internationalization), which they related to European integration among other things. Their article was published in a special issue of *Business History*, aimed to fill existing gaps in the SSOP (Strategy, Structure, Ownership and Performance) literature by including internationalization as a strategy, smaller countries, such as the Netherlands, Sweden and Denmark, and the service sector (i.e., banks) (Colli, de Jong and Iversen, 2012). A related strand of research on how the multidivisional corporation spread over Europe focuses on the role of consultants (Kipping, 1999; Kipping and Engwall, 2002). In another study, Kipping and Westerhuis (2014) showed how consultants, in particular McKinsey, played a decisive role in the spread of the multidivisional form in the European banking sector.

Can we say that, at the turn of the twenty first century, European companies have converged in strategy and structure? Is there a European enterprise, and if so, how is it different from a non-European enterprise? And what are the implications of the process of globalisation for the European enterprise? These questions were central in the study *The European Enterprise,* edited by Harm Schröter. He concludes: 'On balance, our search for European enterprise as a special type of firm has not met with overwhelming success' (Schröter, 2008, quote 296).

While Chandler saw many similarities between US and Germany, and created a contrast between US and Britain, the Varieties of Capitalism debate, to which we will turn next, underlines the huge differences between the US and Germany, and, in contrast, clubs the US and Britain together.

The 'varieties of capitalism' debate

For business historians it is no surprise that capitalism comes in many forms and shapes. Nonetheless, the discussions on early or late industrialisation, and on the rise of the managerial enterprise assumed that, even if trajectories of economic development might have been different, countries and companies would ultimately move towards a common future in the shape of the 'industrial society', 'modern enterprise', or 'modern capitalism'. For instance, in his comparative study *Creating Modern Capitalism,* Thomas McCraw (1997) looks at the United States as the most successful economy, the undisputed leader in productivity throughout three industrial revolutions, that set an example for other countries to follow in their own different ways in order to reach that ultimate goal: modern capitalism. In comparing varieties of capitalism he wanted to discover what elements are essential to any capitalist system and which are not. Two other business history studies comparing the US with some other countries were based predominantly on the Chandler generalisations (Blackford, 1998; Boyce and Ville, 2002). In contrast, the Varieties of Capitalism approach, advocated by political scientists and sociologists, starts from the supposition that national varieties of capitalism are path-dependent and that each country can be successful in its own way. Moreover, this literature has developed an extensive sets of criteria to compare national capitalisms.

Peter Hall and David Soskice (2001) set a landmark in the debates on different ways of organizing the national economy with their *Varieties of Capitalism.* In their introduction to that volume they brought together many strands of thought of the 1990s and made propositions that have framed the debate for the next decade. Their emphasis on the firm as the key actor in a capitalist economy makes their approach particularly interesting for business historians, though in practice the firm often disappears behind abstract discussions on institutions.

In creating their core competencies, firms have to deal with problems of coordination. For Hall and Soskice five areas (spheres) of coordination are crucial, three of which relate to firms and their workforce. These are the coordination between employers and employees about wages and labour conditions on group level (industrial relations), the coordination on the individual level between the firm and its employees and the coordination of the training and education of the labour force. The remaining two main areas of coordination are the relation between firms and their providers of capital (corporate governance) and the interactions between firms, their suppliers and their clients (inter-firm relations).

Building on Michel Albert's contrast between Anglo-Saxon and Rhineland capitalism, Hall and Soskice introduced the terms 'Liberal Market Economy' (LME) and 'Coordinated Market Economy' (CME). The United States served as the prime example of a LME and Germany stood for the CME. In both cases the firms use the market, but in LMEs they combine arm's length, competitive relations with formal contracts, while in CMEs they prefer networks and collaboration. Two mechanisms will give durability to the national type of capitalism. First, the characteristics of the five spheres are not distributed at random but display an internal logic: the so-called institutional complementarities. Second, companies will follow strategies that make the most of the institutional context in which they operate. In doing so, they will confirm and reinforce that context. Technological revolutions and liberalization in the international economy provide challenges for national economies. Firms, however, will react differently to those challenges in accordance to their national setting. There might be change, but there is no reason to expect convergence between LME and CME countries. Hall and Soskice do not argue that one type of capitalism is superior to the other. However, they do argue that the two types differ with regard to their capacity for innovation and their distribution of income and employment. In a later article, Peter Hall and Daniel Gingerich (2004) calculated that countries with complementary institutions had higher economic growth. Thus, pure LME or CME countries performed better than countries with combined LME and CME characteristics.

On the basis of the five spheres, Hall and Soskice are able to cluster the OECD countries. Six were classified as LMEs: USA, Britain, Australia, Canada, New Zealand and Ireland, all Anglophone countries. Ten were classified as CME: Germany, Japan, Switzerland, The Netherlands, Belgium, Sweden, Norway, Denmark, Finland and Austria. Another six countries, France, Italy, Spain, Portugal, Greece and Turkey were considered difficult to identify with one of the two categories. Tentatively, Hall and Soskice introduced a third type of capitalism, Mediterranean Market Economy (MME), characterized by a large agrarian sector and extensive state intervention (Hall and Soskice, 2001). Thus, Western European countries varied from LME to CME and even included countries categorized as MME.

In the categorization of the various capitalisms, some familiar criteria from earlier debates returned, notably the contrast between bank-based (Germany) and market-based (US and Britain) financial systems, and the German preference for cartels versus the US anti-cartel attitude. But there were also new elements not part of the earlier debates, such as job protection versus hire-and-fire systems and training on the job versus general schools.

The VoC approach has received mixed reactions from business historians. Gary Herrigel and Jonathan Zeitlin (2010) considered the VoC approach too static and too structuralist and preferred their own 'historical alternatives' perspective. Geoffrey Jones (2015) suggested that business historian should develop their own historically informed organisational frameworks. That would no doubt be very useful, but for the time being the VoC approach offers a framework and vocabulary shared by many social scientists that allow business historians good opportunities to participate in the debates. Some business historians, therefore, feel inspired by the conceptual work done by scholars from other disciplines. Rory Miller (2010) suggested that the VoC framework, and in particular the 'hierarchical market economy' model, offered South American business historians a useful concept for comparative studies, while Martin Iversen (2010) encouraged business historians to do more with the notion that institutional structure conditions corporate strategy. Other business historians contributed to the discussions on Western Europe, as will be shown below.

The VoC framework as presented by Hall and Soskice created much debate, and unleashed many efforts to develop the concept further. The most obvious point for discussion was the focus on only two models. Why not more? Indeed, over time, new models were developed for other parts of the world, including Eastern Europe (dependent market economies), South America (hierarchical market economies) and Asia (emerging market economies) (Amable, 2003; Allen, 2004; Whitley, 2007). In this chapter we limit ourselves to Western Europe because other countries are dealt with elsewhere in this volume. Hall and Soskice had already suggested a possible third model with the Mediterranean Market Economy that included France, Italy, Portugal and Spain. In this third model the state had a role to play, while in their original two LME and CME models the firm occupied a prime position. Discussing the transformation of French capitalism, Vivien Schmidt (2003) argued that Europe still deserved three models, but that French capitalism had evolved from 'state-led' to 'state-enhanced'. This she understood as a situation in which the state was still active, but not as prominent as before, while CEOs possessed a greater autonomy, and labour relations were more market-reliant.

Linked to the discussion of models was the discussion about positioning countries in the framework. Labelling brought up further questions. It appeared that countries did 'fit' the bill in some periods but not in others. Ronald Dore, William Lazonick and Mary O'Sullivan (1999) compared institutional changes in the US, Britain, Germany and Japan during the twentieth century and found that all four countries had changed. But it was not a story of a long and steady process of convergence. Instead, the four countries seemed to be heading for more convergence in the 1960s but then diverged again in the 1980s. The 1990s came with renewed convergence. The authors did not reach a firm conclusion but noticed a pattern of 'ebb and flow' still to be explained.

The VoC framework is intended for comparing countries but also lends itself very well for comparing one country over different time periods. Dutch business historians used this approach to highlight their country's changing capitalism during the twentieth century. They found that the Netherlands was indeed a coordinated market economy during much of the twentieth century, but displayed many liberal features at the start and the very end of that century (Sluyterman, 2010, 2015a). These changes were visible in many spheres, such as the power of shareholder and managers (Jong, Röell and Westerhuis, 2015), the intensity of collaboration between firms (Bouwens and Dankers, 2015) and development of the knowledge infrastructure (Davids and Lintsen, 2015). In labour relations, coordination continued throughout the century but the role of government became less prominent, with more negotiations directly between employers and employees (Nijhof and Van den Berg, 2015). The First World War and the economic crisis of the late 1970s and early 1980s were clear turning points in the prevalent ideas about the respective roles of government, business and employees, while institutional changes followed after 10 to 20 years (Sluyterman, 2015a).

Is it possible to reconcile change with the idea of institutional complementarities? The Dutch case suggests that there is indeed some logic in the way the coordinated economy gradually took shape. The organisation of labour found a response in the organisation of employers and once employers reached agreements on higher wages, they were bound to seek agreements on other costs and sources of income. We see how coordination in one area was followed by coordination in other areas: collective labour agreements were followed by cartel agreements, and in the 1930s both were supported by the government. However, the complementarities act as a double-edged sword. Less coordination in one area forced flexibility in other areas. This opposite movement took place from the 1980s onwards with less government, tougher measures against collusive behaviour of companies, more pressure from shareholders and more flexible and individual labour arrangements (Sluyterman, 2010, 2015a). Taking a more macro-economic approach, and looking at the business organisation, labour relations, the welfare state and government economic policy, Jeroen Touwen (2014a; 2014b) positioned developments in the Netherlands within the context of other OECD countries. He underlined how the Netherlands could be seen as a hybrid country, more liberal than Germany and more coordinated and regulated than the UK, but economically successful nonetheless.

The Dutch experiences were comparable to those of other countries (Sluyterman, 2015b). For instance, the book *Creating Nordic Capitalism* compares the development of capitalism in Denmark, Norway, Sweden and Finland from 1850 to the present. What becomes immediately clear, is that those four countries experienced an ebb and flow in the way they organised their economy similar to The Netherlands, moving from a liberal market economy in the mid-nineteenth century to a coordinated market economy in the mid-twentieth century and back (to a certain extent) to a more liberal economy after 1980. Though the broad movement was similar, the timing between the four Nordic countries differed, as well as their starting points in the nineteenth century (Fellman, Iversen, Sjögren and Thue, 2008).

As the twenty first century progressed, it became increasingly clear that national economies had been and were still changing (Crouch, 2005; Jackson and Deeg, 2006; Hancké, Rhodes and Thatcher, 2007). Most of that change entailed a move from a coordinated to a liberal market economy. For instance, calculations by Martin Schneider and Mihai Paunescu (2011) over the period 1990–2005 showed moves in a more liberal direction for a number of countries, including Denmark, Finland, The Netherlands, Sweden and to a lesser extent Italy and Spain, while Germany and France remained firmly within the CME category. To a certain extent this move towards a more liberal market economy can be explained by a shift in Western Europe from manufacturing to services. While the manufacturing industry with its huge investment in fixed capital requires a disciplined workforce, the service sector with its personal and individualistic approach can easily deal with more flexible working relations.

The late twentieth century witnessed an enormous increase in vertical specialization in contrast to Chandler's dominance of vertically integrated firms. Langlois (2003) argues that the multi-unit firms will remain important but that they become an increasingly smaller part of the business landscape characterized by a variety of markets and network forms. To explain these developments he introduces the *vanishing hand* theory, which states that the *visible hand* will eventually fade away and make place for a return to the *invisible hand* because specialization allows for market forces to coordinate more effectively. Thus, large, vertically-integrated firms broke up into more specialized firms due to the removal of technological and legal barriers to trade, such as outsourcing. Though business historians are still debating the extent and impact of the Third Industrial Revolution, it is clear that the new information technology offered many possibilities of networking and flexibility (Dosi and Galambos, 2012). Studying the Italian corporate network in the third half of the twentieth century,

Rinaldi and Vasta (2012) noticed a clear relation between the arrival of the Third Industrial Revolution and the weakening ties between the state-owned enterprises and the private sector. The new technologies also contributed to the globalisation of business.

The VoC debate started with the argument that globalisation does not necessarily mean that all countries will move towards the same organisation of their economy (Hall and Soskice, 2001). Although many differences remain, at the same time it is clear that many economies underwent changes in recent years and that these changes meant a move in a more liberal direction. Markets have become more important, companies seek to serve more exclusively the interest of shareholders, labour relations have become more flexible and welfare arrangements have become less generous. Governments act less directly, but are more involved indirectly in rule setting. This movement in the same direction is also stimulated by international agreements and standard setting in international organisation, such as international audit standards, which tend to be geared towards neo-liberal points of view. Multinational companies with their transnational networks acted as 'institutional entrepreneurs' in creating new institutional combinations (Morgan, Kristensen and Whitley, 2003; Crouch, 2005; Sluyterman and Wubs, 2015).

Financial systems and corporate governance formed key components in tracing national differences. In the 1980s and 1990s there was a focus on explaining differences between national corporate governance systems. Distinctions were made between market-, bank- and state-based financial systems, whereas corporate governance systems were characterized by dispersed versus concentrated ownership. The large owners were often banks, families or the state (see for example Morck, 2005). More recently, attention has shifted to the assumed convergence of systems towards the American shareholder value model. France and Germany are often considered as representative of the continental European model of corporate governance, but have transformed considerably. By focusing on the changing role of the stock market in both countries in particular since the 1990s, O'Sullivan (2003) shows that substantial changes took place in the national governance systems, and moreover, that changes in institutions of corporate governance were earlier and more profound in France than in Germany. Analysing the financing and corporate governance in a much smaller country, the Netherlands, Westerhuis and de Jong (2015) highlight a move towards a coordinated market economy after the Second World War, but a return to a more market-based system in recent years. They show that important actors in financing during the twentieth century were subsequently families, banks and institutional and international investors, whereas the state continued to play a marginal role during the whole century.

The VoC debate started with comparing and categorizing national institutional differences in the expectation that these differences were durable over long periods of time due to internal coherence. However, further research revealed more changes than had been anticipated, and most of these changes involved a move towards a more liberal market economy. Still, the European countries, including the Western European ones, continued to show many differences, as for instance the euro crisis in 2014 made abundantly clear (Hall, 2014). The VoC research has now reached a third stage that entails the inclusion of the BRIC countries in international comparisons, more emphasis on individual actors, more attention for the internalisation of economic activities and for the role of the state. It is a research agenda that requires an interdisciplinary approach, combining political economy, sociology, business and management studies and other disciplines (Kristensen and Morgan, 2012). Business historian are well positioned to be one of those 'other disciplines' contributing to the ongoing debate on varieties of capitalism.

Conclusion

In our chapter we looked at Western Europe from the perspective of three debates (on early or late industrialisation, on the rise of the managerial enterprise and on varieties of capitalism) and three industrial revolutions. Since the mid-nineteenth century Western Europe developed into a prosperous region that combined economic growth with social welfare.

The countries all became industrialised, but the process started at different points in time, and with different industrial sectors in the lead. The mix of industrial sectors continued to be different, throughout the twentieth century, with for instance Britain strong in services and Germany still forerunner in manufacturing. In due course, all countries had their share of large, managerial companies, but their organisation continued to differ, with for instance more family firms and government participation in southern than in northern Europe. National differences in the way companies were organised also continued. A typical 'European enterprise' is still hard to find. After the Second World War, all countries built up welfare states, but some were more generous than others. Just as one European company failed to develop, there was no generally agreed framework for collaboration between state, employer and employees.

The expansion of the service sector, the liberalisation of the financial markets and agreements in the European Union, all led to increasing liberalisation of the market economies, but not to complete convergence. In two debates (on the rise of the managerial enterprise and on the varieties of capitalism) the US figured prominently in the comparisons between Western European countries. Often, European countries were only indirectly (that is via the US) compared with each other. Moreover, European researchers often felt defensive about their countries, highlighting varieties rather than similarities. These varieties can be explained by formal and informal institutions that evolved historically and are therefore deeply rooted. As these institutions have developed historically and in close interaction, different families of institutional arrangements within Europe have emerged, including an Anglo-Saxon model, a Continental European model, a Scandinavian model and a Mediterranean model.

The three debates surveyed in this chapter each offered lasting insights. Gerschenkron's idea that latecomers develop differently because their situation has become differently as a consequence of the first movers remains valid. Chandler showed convincingly that the large manufacturing companies formed an important new institutions, and that an efficient organization with the help of an extensive managerial hierarchy is a significant factor in competitiveness, even though other forms of organization continue to be relevant. The VoC debate is still very much on-going. By now, the debate on Varieties of Capitalism encompasses the whole world, and these broader international comparisons offer historians more scope and new insights for comparing Western European capitalism. Comparing Western Europe with Asia rather than the US will offer an important way of shedding more light on the common features of Western European countries. Asian countries are in many respects so different from Europe that similarities within Europe will come forth more clearly through such a comparison.

What the three debates have in common is a fervent search for paths leading to more economic growth. None of the debates deals with the question whether or not economic growth as such is desirable. This might well be the key question for Western Europe in the coming years, in combination with the need to divide wealth more equally in national and international context. For that reason, business historians would do well to devote more time and energy to issues such as stagnation, sustainability and inequality.

Note

1 We would like to thank Jan Luiten van Zanden and Maarten Prak for their excellent comments on an earlier draft.

References

Allen, M. (2004).'The varieties of capitalism paradigm: not enough variety?', *Socio-Economic Review*, 2, 87–108.

Amable, B. (2003). *The Diversity of Modern Capitalism*. Oxford: Oxford University Press.

Amatori, F. (1997). 'Italy: the tormented rise of organizational capabilities between government and families', in: Alfred D. Chandler, Franco Amatori, Takashi Hikino (eds.), *Big Business and the Wealth of Nations*. Cambridge and New York: Cambridge University Press, 246–276.

Binda, V. & Colli, A. (2012). 'Changing big business in Italy and Spain, 1973–2003: strategic responses to a new context', *Business History*, 5(1), 14–39.

Binda, V. & Iversen, M. J. (2007). 'Towards a "managerial revolution" in European business? The transformation of Danish and Spanish big business, 1973–2003', *Business History, 49*(4), 506–530.

Blackford, M. G. (1998) *The Rise of Modern Business in Great Britain, the US and Japan*. University of North Carolina Press, second edition.

Bloemen, E., Kok, J. & Luiten van Zanden, J. (1993). *De top100 van industriële bedrijven in Nederland, 1913–1990*. The Hague: AWT.

Bouwens, B. & Dankers, J. (2015). 'Coordination and Varieties of Capitalism', in: Keetie Sluyterman (ed.), *Varieties of Capitalism and Business History: The Dutch Case*. New York and London: Routledge.

Boyce, G. & Ville, S. (2002). *Development of Modern Business*. London: Palgrave MacMillan.

Carreras, A. & Tafunell, X. (1997). 'Spain: big manufacturing firms between state and market, 1917–1990', in: Alfred D. Chandler, Franco Amatori and Takashi Hikino, *Big Business and the Wealth of Nations*. Cambridge and New York: Cambridge University Press, 277–304.

Carreras, A., Tafunell, X. & Torres, E. (2003). 'Business history in Spain', in: Franco Amatori and Geoffrey Jones (eds.), *Business History Around the World*. Cambridge: Cambridge University Press.

Cassis, Y. (1997). *Big Business: The European Experience in the Twentieth Century*. Oxford: Oxford University Press.

Chandler, A. D. (1962). *Strategy and Structure. Chapters in the History of the Industrial Enterprise*. Cambridge: MIT Press.

Chandler, A. D. (1977). *The Visible Hand. The Managerial Revolution in American Business*. Cambridge and London: Harvard University Press.

Chandler, A. D. (1980). 'The growth of the transnational industrial firm in the United States and the United Kingdom: a comparative analysis', *Economic History Review, 33*(3), 396–410.

Chandler, A. D. (1984). 'The emergence of managerial capitalism', *Business History Review, 58*(4), 473–503.

Chandler, A. D. (1990). *Scale and Scope. The Dynamics of Industrial Capitalism*. Cambridge and London: Harvard University Press.

Chandler, A. D. & Daems, H. (eds.) (1980). *Managerial Hierarchies. Comparative Perspectives on the Rise of the Modern Industrial Enterprise*. Cambridge and London: Harvard University Press.

Chandler, A. D., Amatori, F. & Hikino, T. (eds.) (1997). *Big Business and the Wealth of Nations*. Cambridge and New York, Cambridge University Press.

Church, R. (1990). 'The limitations of the personal capitalism paradigm', *Business History Review, 64*(4), 703–710.

Colli, A. (2003). *The History of Family Business 1850–2000*. Cambridge: Cambridge University Press.

Colli, A., Fernandez Pérez, P. & Rose, M. (2003). 'National determinants of family firm development? Family firms in Britain, Spain and Italy during the nineteenth and twentieth centuries', *Enterprise and Society, 4*(1), 28–64.

Colli, A., Jong, A de & Iversen, M. J. (eds.) (2012). 'Mapping European Corporations: Strategy, Structure, Ownership and Performance', special issue *Business History, 53*(1), 1–206.

Crafts, N. F. R., Leybourne, S. J. & Mills, T. C. (1991). 'Britain', in: Richard Sylla and Gianni Toniolo (eds.), *Patterns of European Industrialization: The Nineteenth Century*. London and New York: Routledge, 110–152.

Crouch, C. (2005). *Capitalist Diversity and Change. Recombinant Governance and Institutional Entrepreneurs.* Oxford: Oxford University Press.

David, T., Degen, B., Mach, A. & Studer, B. (2012). 'Die schweizerische Variante des Kapitalismus', in: Patrick Halbeisen, Margrit Müller and Béatrice Veyrassat (eds.), *Wirtschaftsgeschichte der Schweiz im 20.Jahrhundert.* Basel: Schwabe Verlag.

Davids, M. & Lintsen, H. (2015). 'The Dutch knowledge infrastructure and institutional change', in: Keetie Sluyterman (ed.), *Varieties of Capitalism and Business History: The Dutch Case.* New York and London: Routledge.

Dore, R., Lazonick, W. & O'Sullivan, M. (1999). 'Varieties of capitalism in the twentieth century', *Oxford Review of Economic Policy, 15*(4), 102–120.

Dosi, G. & Galambos, L. (eds.) (2012). *The Third Industrial Revolution in Global Business.* Cambridge: Cambridge University Press.

Dyas, G. P. & Thanheiser, H. (1976). *The Emerging European Enterprise: Strategy and Structure in French and German Industry.* Boulder: Westview Press.

Fear, J. & Kobrak, C. (2010). 'Banks on Board: German and American corporate governance, 1870–1914', *Business History Review, 84,* 703–736.

Feldman, G. D. (2006). 'Business history, comparative history, transnational history', in Gunilla Budde (ed.) *Transnationale Geschichte* (Göttingen), 254–264.

Fellman, S., Iversen, M. J., Sjögren, H. & Thue, L. (eds.) (2008). *Creating Nordic Capitaliam. The Business History of a Competitive Periphery.* Houndmills Basingstoke: Palgrave Macmillan.

Fohlin, C. (2007). 'Does civil law tradition and universal banking crowd out securities markets? Pre-World War I Germany as Counter-Example', *Enterprise and Society, 8*(3), 602–641.

Gerschenkron, A. (1962). *Economic Backwardness in Historical Perspective. A Book of Essays.* Cambridge: Belknap Press of Harvard University Press.

Griffiths, R. (1996). 'Backward, late or different?', in Jan Luiten van Zanden (ed.), *The Economic Development of the Netherlands since 1870.* Cheltenham: Elgar.

Hall, P. A. (2014). 'Varieties of capitalism and the Euro crisis', *West European Politics, 37*(6), 1223–1243.

Hall, P. A. & Gingerich, D. (2004). 'Varieties of capitalism and institutional complementarities in the macroeonomy', *MPIfG discussion paper* 04/05.

Hall, P. A. & Soskice, D. (eds.) (2001). 'An introduction to varieties of capitalism', in: Peter A. Hall and David Soskice (eds.) *Varieties of Capitalism. The Institutional Foundations of Comparative Advantage.* Oxford: Oxford University Press.

Hancké, R., Rhodes, M. & Thatcher, M. (eds.) (2007). *Beyond Varieties of Capitalism. Conflict, Contradictions, and Complementarities in the European Economy.* Oxford: Oxford University Press.

Hannah, L. (1980). 'Visible and invisible hands in Great Britain', in: Chandler, A.D. and H. Daems (eds.), *Managerial Hierarchies. Comparative Perspectives on The Rise of the Modern Industrial Enterprise.* Cambridge and London: Harvard University Press, 41–76.

Herrigel, G. & Zeitlin, J. (2010). 'Alternatives to Varieties of Capitalism', *Business History Review, 84,* 667–674.

Hilferding, R. (1910). *Das Finanzkapital. Eine Studie über die jüngste Entwicklung des Kapitalismus.* Frankfurt: Europäische Verlagsanstalt.

Iversen, M. J. (2010). 'The "Varieties of Capitalism" approach as an analytical tool for business historians', *Business History Review, 84,* 664–666.

Jackson, G. & Deeg, R. (2006). 'How many varieties of capitalism? Comparing the Comparative Institutional Analyses of Capitalist Diversity', *MPIfG Discussion Paper 2,* Köln 06/02.

Jones, G. (1997). 'Great Britain: Big business, management, and competitiveness in twentieth-century Britain', in: Alfred D. Chandler, Franco Amatori and Takashi Hikino (eds), *Big Business and the Wealth of Nations.* Cambridge and New York: Cambridge University Press, 102–138.

Jones, G. (2015). 'Review of Keetie Sluyterman (ed.), Varieties of Capitalism and Business History. The Dutch case', *Tijdschrift voor Sociale en Economische geschiedenis, 12*(3), 98–101.

Jones, G. & Rose, M. (eds.) (1993). *Family Capitalism.* London, Frank Cass, special issue *of Business History.*

Jong, A. de., Röell, A. & Westerhuis, G. (2015). The evolving role of shareholders in Dutch corporate governance, 1900–2010', in: Keetie Sluyterman (ed.), *Varieties of Capitalism and Business History: The Dutch Case.* New York and London: Routledge.

Jonker, J. (1996). *Merchants, Bankers, Middlemen. The Amsterdam Money Market During the First Half of the 19th Century.* Amsterdam: NEHA.

Kipping, M. (1999). 'American management consulting companies in Western Europe, 1920 to 1990: products, reputation, and relationships', *Business History Review, 73*, 190–220.

Kipping, M. & Engwall, L. (2002). *Management Consulting: The Emergence and Dynamics of a Knowledge Industry.* Oxford: University Press Oxford.

Kipping, M. & Westerhuis, G. (2014). 'The managerialization of banking: from blueprint to reality', *Management and Organizational History, 9*(4), 374–393.

Kocka, J. (1980). 'The rise of the modern industrial enterprise in Germany', in: Chandler and Daems (eds.), *Managerial Hierarchies. Comparative Perspectives on the Rise of the Modern Industrial Enterprise.* Cambridge and London: Harvard University Press, 77–116.

Kristensen, P. H. & Morgan, G. (2012). 'Theoretical contexts and conceptual frames for the study of twenty-first century capitalism', in: Glenn Morgan and Richard Whitley (eds.), *Capitalisms & Capitalism.* Oxford: Oxford University Press.

Langlois, R. N. (2003). 'The vanishing hand: the changing dynamics of industrial capitalism', *Industrial and Corporate Change, 12*(2), 351–385.

Lévy-Leboyer, M. (1980). 'The large corporation in Modern France', in: Chandler and Daems (eds.), *Managerial Hierarchies.Comparative Perspectives on the Rise of the Modern Industrial Enterprise.* Cambridge and London: Harvard University Press, 117–160.

Lévy-Leboyer, M. & Lescure, M. (1991). 'France', in: Richard Sylla and Gianni Toniolo (eds.), *Patterns of European Industrialization: The Nineteeth Century.* London and New York: Routledge, 153–174.

McCraw, T. K. (ed.) (1997). *Creating Modern Capitalism: How Entrepreneurs, Companies, and Countries Triumphed in Three Industrial Revolutions.* Cambridge: Harvard University Press.

Miller, R. (2010). 'Latin American business history and Varieties of Capitalism', *Business History Review, 84*, 653–657.

Mokyr, J. (1976). *Industrialization in the low countries, 1795–1850.* New Haven and London: Yale University Press.

Morck, R. K. (ed.) (2005). *A History of Corporate Governance Around the World. Family Business Groups to Professional Managers.* Chicago and London: The University of Chicago Press.

Morgan, G., Kristensen, P. H. & Whitley, R. (eds.) (2003). *The Multinational Firm: Organising Across Institutional and National Divides.* Oxford: Oxford University Press.

Pollard, S. (1981). *Peaceful Conquest: The Industrialization of Europe, 1760–1970.* Oxford: Oxford University Press.

Nijhof, E. & van den Berg, A. (2015). 'Variation of coordination: labour relations in the Netherlands', in: Keetie Sluyterman (ed.), *Varieties of Capitalism and Business History: The Dutch Case.* New York and London: Routledge.

O'Sullivan, M. (2003). 'The policital economy of comparative corporate governance', *Review of International Political Economy, 10*(1), 23–72.

Quail, J. (2008). 'Becoming fully functional: the conceptual struggle for a new structure for the giant corporation in the US and UK in the first half of the twentieth century', *Business History, 50*(2), 127–146.

Rinaldi, A. & Vasta, M. (2012). 'The Italian corporate network after the "Golden Age" (1972–1983): from centrality to marginalization of state-owned enterprises', *Enterprise and Society, 13*(2).

Rostow, W.W. (1960). *The Stages of Economic Growth: A Non-Communist Manifesto.* Cambridge University Press.

Schmidt, V. A. (2003). 'French capitalism transformed, yet still a third variety of capitalism', *Economy and Society, 32*(4), 526–554.

Schneider, M. R. & Paunescu, M. (2011). 'Changing varieties of capitalism and revealed comparative advantages from 1990 to 2005: A test of the Hall and Soskice claims', *Socio-Economic Review, 9*(1), 1–23.

Schröter, H. G. (ed.) (2008). *The European Enterprise. Historical Investigation into a Future Species.* Heidelberg: Springer.

Schröter, H. G. (2013). 'Cartels revisited. An overview over fresh questions, new methods, and surprising results', *Revue Économique*, 989–1010.

Sluyterman, K. (2010). 'Introduction: changing business systems in the Netherlands in the twentieth century', *Business History Review, 84*, 737–750.

Sluyterman, K. (ed.) (2015a), *Varieties of Capitalism and Business History: The Dutch Case.* New York and London: Routledge.

Sluyterman, K. (2015b). 'Dutch changing capitalism in international perspective', in: Keetie Sluyterman (ed.), *Varieties of Capitalism and Business History: The Dutch Case*. New York and London: Routledge.

Sluyterman, K. & Winkelman, H. (1993). 'The Dutch family firm confronted with Chandler's dynamics of industrial capitalism, 1890–1940', *Business History*, *35*(4), 152–183.

Sluyterman, K. & Wubs, B. (2015). 'Multinationals as agents of change', in: Keetie Sluyterman (ed.), *Varieties of Capitalism and Business History: The Dutch Case*. New York and London: Routledge.

Smith, M. S. (1998). 'Putting France in the Chandlerian Framework: France's 100 largest industrial firms in 1913', *Business History Review*, *72*, 46–85.

Sylla, R. & Toniolo, G. (eds.) (1991). *Patterns of European Industrialization: The Nineteenth Century*. London and New York: Routledge.

Toninelli, P. A. (2004). 'Between state and market. The parabola of Italian public enterprise in the 20th century', *Entreprises et histoire*, 37, 53–74.

Tortella, G. (2000). *The Development of Modern Spain. An Economic History of the Nineteenth and Twentieth Centuries*. Cambridge: Harvard University Press.

Touwen, J. (2014a). *Coordination in Transition. The Netherlands and the World Economy, 1950–2010*. Leiden, Boston: Brill.

Touwen, J. (2014b). 'The hybrid variety: lessons in non-market coordination from the business system in the Netherlands, 1950–2010', *Enterprise and Society*, *15*(4), 849–884.

Wardley, P. (1991). 'The anatomy of big business: aspects of corporate development in the twentieth century', *Business History, 33*(2), 268–296.

Westerhuis, G. (2016). 'Commercial banking. Changing interactions between banks, markets, industry, and state', in: Youssef Cassis, Richard S. Grossmand and Catherine Schenk (eds.), *The Oxford Handbook of Banking and Financial History*. Oxford: Oxford University Press, 110–132.

Westerhuis, G. & de Jong, A. (2015). *Over geld en macht. Financiering en corporate governance van het Nederlands bedrijfsleven*. Amsterdam: Boom publisher.

Whitley, R. (2007). *Business Systems and Organizational Capabilities: the Institutional Structuring of Competitive Competence*. Oxford: Oxford University Press.

Whittington, R. & Mayer, M. (2000). *The European Corporation. Strategy, Structure, and Social Science*. Oxford: Oxford University Press.

Zanden, J. L. V. & van Riel, A. (2000). *Nederland 1780–1914. Staat, instituties en economische ontwikkeling*. Amsterdam: Uitgeverij Balans.

Part IV
Institutions

16

Pre-modern and early modern

Catherine Casson and Mark Casson

Introduction

Pre-modern and early modern business history has traditionally received relatively little attention compared to the period from 1750 onwards. Most standard business history books begin their analysis with the start of the Industrial Revolution in the eighteenth century, and consider the rise and spread of methods of organisation such as factories and joint-stock companies (Wilson, 1995; Jones and Zeitlin, 2007). The Industrial Revolution is often promoted as the starting point for the rise of the large modern corporation, due to the influence of Chandler (Chandler, 1977). However, a focus on corporations can downplay the significance of individual enterprise in the foundation and direction of business.

The financial crisis of 2008 has resulted in an increased interest in the relationship between government, financial institutions and business. This has been reflected in the business history literature, with a new focus on the Glorious Revolution of 1688 and its consequences, most notably the creation of the Bank of England in 1694 (Coffman, 2013; Coffman, Leonard and Neal, 2013; Murphy, 2009; Paul, 2011). These contributions have been very helpful in drawing attention to the significance of the pre-Industrial Revolution period. This chapter will show, however, that it is possible to extend the study of business history back even earlier, namely to the medieval period (Casson and Casson, 2013, 2014; Witzel, 2012). For the purposes of this chapter, business history is defined as the study of the evolution of business enterprise from the earliest time to the present day, focusing on its institutional and historical context. This chapter deals with the first phase of this process, covering the period of 1200–1500 for pre-modern and 1500–1700 for early modern.

Limited opportunities and ineffective procedures are the main characteristics that have often been associated with the pre-modern economy (Postan, 1973). The period 1200–1500 is often presented to students as a series of disasters, both political and environmental, which limited economic growth. The medieval monarchy and medieval church are perceived as deterring enterprise, the medieval monarchy through its concern with maintaining a rigid social hierarchy, and the medieval church through its prohibition on the lending of money at interest (Hilton, 2003; Farber, 2006, pp. 14–15, 17, 26–27, 30; Hunt and Murray, 1999, pp. 242–43). Selfishness and greed, meanwhile, are often the characteristics associated with the economy of 1500–1750. Individuals who were successful in business during this period are frequently presented as ruthlessly seizing opportunities from others, both at home and overseas. There can be a perception that they were preoccupied with the financial return from their business, and had little engagement with their employees or the local community (Braddick, 1996).

Business in the pre-modern and early modern period, however, was much more so-phisticated than these stereotypes suggest (Dyer, 2005, pp. 7–45). Monks, monarchs and merchants were just some of the groups engaged in business enterprise. They often needed to be able to work together to gain access to credit, information and resources (Muldrew, 1998; Stobart, 2004). Networks developed through trade organisations and through kinship ties. The records of the Gild of Holy Trinity in Luton, southern England, which was active from 1474–1547, reveal that many members came from the local area and used the guild to cement local trade links. However, some members also came from as far afield as Canterbury, Coventry and Halifax and may have become members as a result of business connections made on long-distance wool and cloth trade routes (Tearle, 2012). For kinship ties, mean-while, the fifteenth century Italian silk merchant Gregorio Dati recorded the 'sponsors' and godparents of all of his children and his role as Guild Consul; similarly, the Cely family let-ters relating to the family wool business reveal the involvement of a close family friend who was godfather to Richard Cely (Greary, 2003; Amt, 2001, pp. 465–78). Collaboration with other stakeholders could also be important, for example over infrastructure investments in piped water supplies (Lee, 2014).

For those establishing businesses in the period 1250–1750 there were opportunities and challenges, which this section will now sign-post. The urban revolution of c. 1200 saw a growth in both the number of towns, especially in England, and also in the size of exist-ing towns. In some cases, the towns themselves were founded and operated as a business. Bridgwater in Somerset, England, was developed in 1199 by William Brewer, a royal admin-istrator who saw the commercial opportunities in the grants of land he received from grateful monarchs (Alsford, 2015d; Bruce, 1917). Brewer was granted permission for a market and fair to be held in Bridgwater, and was able to collect tolls from visiting traders and rents from inhabitants who came to live in the town. New settlers benefitted from freedom from having to pay tolls in many other towns. With the expansion in trade, central government permitted the delegation of authority to local institutions, such as town courts, so that swift redress could be provided for any problems that occurred during transactions, including broken contracts and faulty goods (Britnell, 1995).

The credit revolution of c.1300 provided an opportunity for the development of multi-national firms. Lucchese merchants were one of the earliest to recognise the advantages of arrangements that allowed funds to be advanced in local currency to a merchant who was exporting from some city and to be repaid later in a different local currency in the city to which the exports had been consigned (Blomquist, 1971; Hunt and Murray, 1999). Known as bills of exchange, these credit instruments facilitated trade without actually requiring the transfer of cash. Gradually credit networks expanded to cover cities in many countries. Bills of exchange helped medieval merchants to develop multinational firms. Francesco Datini set up one of the first examples of a holding company, which covered a trading route running from London to Beirut. Datini was in overall charge of all the different companies, while the day-to-day running of each company was delegated to a local manager. The different companies shared information with each other, providing an overall competitive advantage (Instituto Datini, 2015; Origo, 1957).

The years around 1540 are often associated with upheaval in England, and in particular with the dissolution of the monasteries. Following an influx of Spanish silver from Latin

America about the same time, inflation began to spread across Europe after many years of stable prices. Together, these developments are often viewed as leading to a rise in individualism in business, and contributing to a greater awareness of the economic principles relating to supply and demand. The dissolution of the English monasteries ended entrepreneurial endeavours for some groups, notably the monastic orders, but for others it provided a unique opportunity to expand their businesses. The disposal of monastic property after dissolution provided an opportunity to acquire new business premises, and instigated some of the first large scale factories that preceded those of the Victorians, as Jackson has shown (Jackson, 2008).

Similar slightly conflicting attitudes to business occurred in the Stuart commercial revolution of 1600. During this period, in order to make money, the English crown sold off more and more concessions and assets. The state relied on farming out customs and excise taxes to make money, and entrepreneurs often took up these opportunities, although their activities were criticised (Yamamoto, 2011). In one debate in parliament these entrepreneurs were described as 'blood suckers' who were allowed too much control over too many essential commodities, and a surviving woodcut shows a monopolist being humiliatingly paraded backwards on a horse through London (Braddick, 1998, p. 1, pp. 206–9). However this period also saw the revival of business networks, and their greater application to overseas trade. Chartered companies allowed merchants to pool capital to undertake ventures overseas which could not be funded by a single individual. These ventures were usually supported by a particular state, which granted a charter that provided the company with a monopoly on trade for a certain number of years (Carlos and Nicholas, 1988).

The Financial Revolution and the Agricultural Revolution are the final key developments pertinent to business in the pre-modern and early modern period. The Financial Revolution refers to developments in 1689 when Mary, the Protestant daughter of James II, and her Dutch husband William of Orange succeed to the throne. This ushered in a period of financial reforms, which were influenced by a combination of the institutional reforms occurring in Amsterdam during this period, a need to reform problems in the previous English system and a need for cash to fund the war with France (Gelderblom, 2003). The key features of the financial revolution were the development of new forms of taxes to fund the war; the foundation in 1694 of the Bank of England to administer revenue from taxes and use it to repay loans and the development in 1698 of the civil list, which asserted parliamentary control over the amount of money placed at the crown's disposal (Dickson, 1967).

The agricultural revolution of c.1700–1760 was characterised by increased agricultural productivity obtained through a greater cultivation of land, use of higher yielding crops and a movement towards new technology to cultivate and harvest the crops (Overton, 1996). It has been suggested that developments that improved soil quality were equally important because they ensured that increased production did not eventually lead to soil exhaustion. Jethro Tull is famous for the invention of the mechanical seed drill, which replaced hand labour and potentially allowed agricultural labourers to take-up other work, including manufacturing. However, Sayre has shown how Tull's own writings emphasise the main contribution of the drill as being its potential to place seed more accurately in the ground, which meant that there was less competition between plants for the soil's resources and the plants grown were therefore 'larger and more productive' (Sayre, 2010).

The activities of these earlier entrepreneurs are recorded in company records, the archives of national and local government and the personal correspondence and diaries of merchants in much the same way as those of their successors, as this chapter will demonstrate (Landes, Mokyr and Baumol, 2010).

Key themes

Business historians often organise their research by specific sectors, and it is possible to apply this approach to the pre-modern and early modern material also. For some sectors there is potential to extend existing scholarship back to earlier periods. Wine and beer are both areas that have been studied for the post 1750 period but it is possible to investigate both individual businesses and the overall structure of the industries from a much earlier date (Manuel Falsca, 2013; Gourvish and Wilson, 1985; Silva Lopes, 2002; Stanziani, 2009). The activities of merchants involved in the wine trade appear in the records of central government, due to their import activities; of local government, where local officials monitored the quality and quantity of the product, and in trade organisations, such as the Vintners Company (Alsford, 2015f; Francis, 1972; Kirkbridge Jones and Veale, 1971; Sellers, 1911, pp. 13–14, 39–40). In their study of the medieval wine trade, for example, Kirkbridge Jones and Veale were able to trace the operations of over 70 Gascon vintners, many of whom subsequently settled permanently in England, through the records of central and local government, including the Treaty Rolls, the Gascon Rolls and the customs accounts (Curry, Morgan and Spence, 2015; Kirkbridge Jones and Veale, 1971, pp. 70–92). For the ale and beer trades, meanwhile, the records of central government demonstrate the crown's concern with regulating the price of ale and beer, which were staple commodities in the Middle Ages (Alsford, 2015f). The activities of individual brewers can generally be traced through local government records, where the assize of ale was enforced, or records of the trade organisations. In 1422 in London, for example, the brewers of London recorded that the former mayor Richard Whittington had complained to the current mayor, Robert Chichele, that members of the brewers craft were selling ale at too high a price and failing to follow the regulations that Whittington had drawn-up in 1419/20 (Alsford, 2015c; Chambers and Daunt, 1931, pp. 140–42, 182–85). The brewers were ordered to pay £20 (around £10,000 in modern money) towards the rebuilding of the guildhall for failing to follow the regulations (Alsford, 2015c; Chambers and Daunt, 1931, pp. 140–42, 182–85).

Forms of business organisation are a topic that is addressed in current business history literature, and information on these is available for the pre-modern and early modern period. In the brewing sector the records prior to c. 1450 reveal the presence of large numbers of part-time female brewers who sold from home and operated alongside larger businesses, such as a sixty-seat tavern built in London in 1342 (Alsford, 2015e; Bennett, 1996; Rickert, Olson and Crow, 1948). The perishability of ale and high transport costs meant that there was little opportunity or incentive to develop larger scale brewing businesses with greater geographical coverage. However, the shift towards beer, which contained more preservatives, combined with improvements in land and river transport and better technical knowledge, provided opportunities to up-scale businesses and contributed to the rise of regional breweries (Mathias, 1993).

The pre-modern and modern wool and cloth trades, in contrast, are often considered to have many parallels to modern businesses in their methods of organisation (Bell, Brooks and Dryburgh, 2007; Jackson, 2008). The church was a key player in the medieval wool trade, due to its ownership of large amounts of land, which it had previously exploited for growing crops. The Cistercian order, whose monasteries were usually in rural locations, was noted for the quality of the wool provided by its houses. Wool was in such demand that arrangements were often made for the advance sale of it to groups of overseas merchants, using forward-contracts remarkably similar to those used in modern organised commodity markets. A surviving document of 1287, for example, records an agreement between the Abbot of Meaux, a Cistercian monastery near Hull, and merchants of Lucca in which the abbot and his monks were paid in advance agreement for 11 sacks of their better wool, which they were to press and pack into round bales and deliver to the port of Hull for export in two years' time (Bell, 2005).

The cloth trade, meanwhile, was one of the earliest industries to enter into factory production, a development attributed to the clothiers Jack and John Winchcombe. As early as the sixteenth century they operated premises in a former monastic building where, 'Within one room being large and long/There stood two hundred looms full strong/Two hundred men, the truth is so/Wrought these looms all in a row' (Deloney, no date). The use of a range of sources is key to the ability to trace the activities of the Winchcombe family, for they appear not only in the records of central government, through their role in supplying government departments and in lobbying for the wool trade, but also in a novel based on Jack's life that was published in 1597 (Davids, no date; Deloney, no date).

Industrial districts have attracted much attention from business historians of the modern period, and the potential exists to explore them in an earlier form (Wilson and Popp, 2003). In the pre-modern period some towns developed reputations for their production of specific commodities, meaning that the town itself served as the equivalent of an industrial district (Casson, 2012). 'Fur of Chester', 'ale of Ely' and 'tiles of Reading' are all town characteristics listed in an anonymous poem of the mid-thirteenth century (Rothwell, 1995, pp. 881–884). Studies by historians of individual towns are often categorised as urban history, but can also inform business history. Hull, for example, has been examined by Horrox in relation to its important overseas trading links in cloth, fish and wine (Horrox, 1978, 1983a, 1983b). Great Yarmouth was especially associated with herring, and many London merchants held premises there in order to better control the inland distribution of the fish (Saul, 1975). While urban specialisation often reflected the proximity of the town to certain natural resources, it also reflected the skills of the town's workers (Rosser, 1997). In medieval Leicester the merchant guild was the main institution which supervised businesses in the town. Individuals who repeatedly brought the town's reputation into disrepute suffered severe consequences, especially when their offences concerned the town's key export trade of wool (Dale, 1958). In 1254 in Leicester, Roger Aldith was charged for twice offending against the guild by making a blanket that was of good and bad warp mixed and by sewing good and bad cloth together in Lynn. He then committed a third offence for which he was expelled from the guild in 1258 (Bateson, 1899, pp. 68–69, 77). After his re-admittance the following year he reoffended, and was only excused from a very severe punishment on that occasion 'at the prayer of good men who very eagerly and zealously made petition for him' (Bateson, 1899, pp. 86–88).

Industrial specialisation between towns is also reflected, on a smaller scale, in industrial zoning within towns. 'In one single street, named the Strand, leading to St. Paul's, there are fifty-two goldsmith's shops, so rich and full of silver vessels, great and small, that in all the shops in Milan, Rome, Venice, and Florence put together I do not think there would be found so many of the magnificence that are to be seen in London' is a description provided by an anonymous visitor to London in c. 1500 (Amt, 2001). While we cannot be certain how these zones developed, it seems likely that social structures based around certain churches played a part (Rosser, 1994). In 1346, for example, the white tawyers, who were processors of animal hides in London, ordained that the trade would have a wax candle 'to burn before Our Lady in the church of All Hallows, near London Wall' (Amt, 2001, p. 315; Sharpe, 1905, p. 153; Riley, 1868, pp. 232–34). Sometimes zones were desirable because industries were noisy and hazardous. The articles of the spurriers of London from 1346, for example, record complaints by residents that spurries were working when drunk 'to the annoyance and sick of all their neighbourhood' and were also blowing up 'their fires so vigorously that their forges begin at once to blaze, to the great peril of themselves and of all the neighbourhood around' (Amt, 2001, p. 314; Rutledge, 2004; Sharpe, 1905, p. 128; Riley, 1868, pp. 226–28). This illustrates that juxtaposing industry and residential accommodation could be problematic. In Norwich, meanwhile, concerns about hygiene in c. 1500 meant that butchers were required to keep their premises on higher ground downstream of the city centre so that unpleasant smells (which during this period were associated with the transmission of disease) and waste did not reach the city centre (Rawcliffe, 2004, p. 309).

People, as well as places, can also be investigated for the pre-modern and early modern periods. Female business owners are usually considered in a separate category from men in business history because up until the nineteenth century there were legal limitations on the extent to which women could be involved in running a business (Holcombe, 1983; Staves, 1990). In addition, there were often informal constraints (education, pregnancy and child-care and time needed to perform domestic tasks) which affected opportunities for women to be employees. There has therefore been much debate about the autonomy that women were able to exercise in business in 1200–1750. However, the records show the presence of women in the brewing and textile manufacturing sectors from the pre-modern period (Lemire, 1997). In 1368, for example, the records of local and central government record complaints made by the London silkwomen against the Italian merchant Nicholas Sardouche. The silkwomen complained that he had damaged their livelihood by buying up silk before it reached the open market, raising the price significantly (Thomas, 1929, pp. 100–05). The London silkwomen were involved in turning silk into yarn, weaving small silk items (but not whole cloths) and manufacturing small silk objects, such as tassels. They did not have a formal trade organisation like many male artisans or merchants. Nonetheless, they appear to have operated along very similar lines to a formal guild, for example by taking on female apprentices for a seven year training period (Dale, 1933). Noble women and abbesses, meanwhile, had the opportunity to perform roles equivalent to contemporary managers, administering landed estates on behalf of their absent husbands during long periods of warfare or on behalf of a religious community (Coss, 1998, pp. 36–72; Leyser, 1995 pp. 142–189; Spear, 2005, pp. 91–114). Their activities are recorded in manorial records and in monastic records.

Labour relations between employees and employers are the subject of many entries in local government records. While the pre-modern and early modern period is often associated with exploitative labour relationships, there are many instances of attempts by local government to prevent exploitation. In London in 1417, for example, a widow named Thomasina March was reported to the local authorities for apprenticing Agnes Tikyhall to a wiredrawer named William Celler for a term of 14 years. William left London without properly training Agnes in the skills needed to make cards for teazling wool or cloth, although Agnes remained in the care of his wife Joan. Upon examination the court found that Agnes was too young to be legally apprenticed, and had taken the training under threat of a beating and wished to return to her father (Thomas, 1943, pp. 53–54). She was therefore cleared of any obligation to continue the apprenticeship. For the late sixteenth and early seventeenth centuries Wallis has shown that the mayor's court played an important role in helping apprentices to leave unsuitable placements when informal reconciliation had had no effect (Wallis, 2012). While business historians often take a top-down view of employer-employee relations, this material can provide a bottom-up perspective.

Review of the primary sources

Company archives have traditionally been used by business historians as their main source of evidence about business practices. Edith Penrose is often seen as the pioneer of this approach, as a result of her investigation into the Hercules Powder Company and how it coped with its excess capacity in staff and materials the aftermath of WWI (Penrose, 1960). Penrose's analysis of the company archive showed that the Hercules Powder Company used the expertise of its existing staff to develop new chemical products, and also found new ways to use its excess stock of explosives, such as using them to blow-up trees for papermaking. In doing so she questioned the prevailing view that growth in the market was more important than growth in the firm.

The significance of Penrose's contribution to the fields of both economics and business history was such that many of her successors have also sought to find detailed and complete company archives on which to base their research. This has caused some problems, however, since in their efforts to find suitable company archives, business historians have sometimes neglected other types of sources altogether. These other sources, such as government records, trade organisation records and the accounts of employees and customers, are crucial to establish the external environment in which the business operates. They also provide the opportunity to compare and contrast opinions on the business and its practices, as there is a risk that only a partial story is provided in an official company archive (Taylor, Bell and Cooke, 2009; McKinlay and Taylor, 2015).

Concerns about the incomplete survival of records and language barriers have often deterred business historians from extending their research into the pre-modern and early modern periods. For the period 1200–1500, business historians have tended to restrict themselves to investigating the Cairo Geniza archive, which shows how trading networks operated before the development of formal institutions, and the Datini archive, which covers the one of the first multinational companies (Istituto Datini, 2015; Princeton Geniza Project, 2014; Greif, 1989). Chartered trading companies have been the main archives consulted for the period 1500–1750. While these are seen by many as the closest equivalent to the modern business archive, a range of other documents also provide similar information on individual businesses, even if they do not immediately appear as such. The following sections outline some of the main groups of documents available.

Records of central and local government

Records of government can inform both on the parameters in which businesses were required to operate and on the attempts of business people to change those parameters. During the period 1200–1750 central government in England was based at Westminster and was responsible for a number of issues relating to business, including direct and indirect taxation, the quality of the currency and the quality and price of key export commodities (such as cloth and wool) and daily necessities (such as bread and ale) (Musson and Ormrod, 1999). Local government operated in towns and the countryside and, while variations in local circumstances occurred, it was generally responsible for enforcing royal regulations and creating new, town-specific, regulations in response to local concerns. In towns the office-holders were usually local merchants, who were often elected yearly by at least some of the town's population. In the countryside local government was usually operated by the local landowner.

Parliament was the main forum where communication between central and local government occurred, and its records are therefore of particular interest to business historians. The parliament rolls cover the period 1272–1509, after which they are replaced by the journals of the house of lords and the house of commons (Given-Wilson, 2005). Parliament rolls often focus on overseas trading, partly because of its connection to indirect taxation, the level of which was of interest to both the crown and mercantile representatives. However broader concerns are also recorded. In 1363, for example, it was recorded that 'great misfortunes have recently come, both to our lord the king, the great men and the commonalty as well as to others of the land' due to traders stockpiling many different types of goods and creating deliberate scarcities, in order to raise the price (Ormrod, 2005). As a result, parliament ordained that 'each merchant of the land shall be restricted to his own merchandise; that is to say, vintners to wine, wool merchants to wool, drapers to cloth, shoemakers to shoes, tailors to tailoring only' in order to prevent general traders creating scarcities in 'all manner of saleable merchandise' (Ormrod, 2005). Competition from overseas trade was also a concern in both pre-modern and early modern parliaments. In 1692, for example, a petition was presented by the pinmakers of London complaining that their trade was suffering 'through the deceitful making of pins, and the importation of foreign pins, the said manufacture is like to be lost, and many families, who comfortably subsisted, are impoverished and undone' (House of Commons Journal, 1692). The pinmakers asked permission to bring in a bill to prohibit the import of foreign pins, a request which was granted.

Local government records often allow biographies to be developed of some of the most important business people in pre-modern and early modern towns. Business people frequently held positions in local government and their political careers and the policies they implemented while in office can be examined in depth for a number of towns, including Exeter, Norwich, York and London (Alsford, 1982; Kermode, 1999; Nightingale, 1995). The career of Thomas de Melcheburn of Lynn, reconstructed by Alsford, is an example of the kind of information that can be obtained (Alsford, 2015a). Melcheburn was arguably 'one of the great merchant capitalists of 14th century England' but one of his first appearances in the records is in the local court in Lynn when he accused another resident of breaking into his house and stealing a belt and purse (Alsford, 1982; Parker, 1971). Ten years later Melcheburn was engaged in supplying food and drink to the English army, a position which led to opportunities in the royal customs service in the export trade to Norway. Yet local affairs in Lynn were still important to Melcheburn, he served as mayor in 1338, and in 1340 travelled to London on behalf of his fellow citizens to present evidence of Lynn's exception from a building tax. Sometimes national and local affairs could be combined, as when Melcheburn represented Lynn at a number of parliaments between 1330 and 1340. The varied career of Melcheburn and many of his contemporaries means that it is often helpful to use the records of central as well as local government to construct biographies. Liddy, for example, has shown that merchants in Bristol and York made an important contribution to national economic policy by tracing their activities through records of central and local government and reconstructing the careers in royal service and civic office of a number of individuals for the period 1350–1400 (Liddy, 2005, pp. 217–234). This approach can also provide information on owners of smaller local businesses. Kowaleski was able to draw conclusions about local businesses in Exeter during the fourteenth century using taxation records, national and local customs accounts and records of the local mayor's court (Kowaleski, 1995, pp. 371–395).

In the countryside, meanwhile, the dominant method of business organisation was the manor. On many manors one part of the land was allocated for the lord of the manor, and either managed directly by the lord or leased by him to others, and the other part was allocated to the peasants. In return for their use of the land the peasants were required to provide a monetary payment to the lord, or perform a service for him. Mills, fisheries and mineral deposits were some of the other resources that lords could exploit on their manors (Bailey, 2002, p. 3; Farmer, 1995; Stone, 2005). Lords were permitted, by the crown, to administer these rural 'businesses' through their own courts. Many of these court records survived and they illustrate attempts by lords to administer their businesses carefully. For example, according to the court rolls of Walsham-in-the-Willows, Suffolk in 1340, William Wodebite was fined 3 pence for failing to 'bundle enough of the lord's straw for the men, as he was ordered', while Robert Banlone was fined 3 pence for allowing the manor's oxen to damage the lord's wood (Bailey, 2002, pp. 202–3; Lock, 1998). Other examples indicate the extent to which the manor's business operations could intrude into the life of ordinary people, as in 1340 Agnes Fitte was fined 2 shillings 8 pence for giving birth 'outside wedlock' (Bailey, 2002, pp. 202–3). The extent to which the operation of the manor as a business was detrimental to the lives of the peasant population has been the subject of much discussion in the medieval literature (Muller, 2013; Schofield, 1998).

Rural businesses continued to be important in the period 1500–1700, although by this point the feudal ties between lords and peasants had been removed. For this period we can often learn about the operation of these businesses through detailed accounts kept by their owners. For example John Hermitage, a Gloucester farmer during the early 1500s, recorded in his account book his attempts to turn around the farm he inherited from his father by switching its focus from arable to sheep (Dyer, 2012). Sheep also occupied the attention of Henry Best, a farmer from the East Riding of Yorkshire who, in 1641, produced an extremely detailed farming book. Best was particularly aware of the importance of timing in his business and he offers advice on how to ensure that lambs arrive at the most profitable time—'have fat lambs to sell about St Hellen-masse, at which time they are rare, and very hard to come by; wherefore good, fat, and well-quartered lambs will usually (at that time of year) give nobles and seven shillings a piece' (Best, 1857, p. 3). Market schedules are also recorded in great detail by Best; 'in winter times our folks go to Beverley, they are never stirring above two hours before day, because they are soon enough if they get but thither by eleven of the clock; oats go always well of on Wednesdays and Saturdays in this place, if so be that the Tuesdays and Fridays be calm-days' (Best, 1857, p. 101). In contrast, the market at Malton 'is quickest about nine of the clock' (Best, 1857). Similarly transcribed and translated primary sources can usually be found in the published series of local history societies (British History Online, 2015; Local History Societies, 2015; Museum of English Rural Life, 2014).

Church records

William Langland, in his poem *Piers Plowman* criticised churchmen for 'having no pity on the poor' and stated that 'they behave like lords, their lands stretch so far' (Talbot Donaldson, 1990, pp. 97–99). Certainly the medieval church was involved in a range of business activities, including marketing pilgrimage centres, selling produce from monastic estates and speculating in property. Monastic accounts from Battle Abbey reveal some of these activities, for example in 1369–70 the Abbey generated revenue from a range of sources, including 55 shillings 'from 3 tuns of cider sold from garden produce' and 62s 2d 'from the entrails of cattle' (Searle and Ross, 1967, pp. 61, 63). We can even learn a little about employee-employer relations from the evidence, for example that year 28s 8d was spent by the Abbey on 'staff's presents on Christmas and Easter Days' (Searle and Ross, 1967, p. 63). As consumers monastic houses made 'rational and informed choices', assessing where the best prices for goods could be obtained and using local suppliers and their tenants for grain, livestock and fish, and going further afield for imported and manufactured items (Threlfall-Holmes, 2005).

Wills are a form of record which are often considered to bridge the gap between church records and local government records (Thrupp, 1962). Wills can appear in church records due to the bequests that were often made to religious institutions and because of their discussion of burial arrangements. The records of St Mary at Hill church, London, for example, contain for the year 1353 the will of a mercer named John of Causton and a brewer named John Nasyng and for 1428 the will of an ironmonger named Richard Gosselyn (Alsford, 2015b; Littlehales, 1905, pp. 1–21). However, wills were also often enrolled in the records of local government, because they frequently related to the disposal of property. The Southampton city custumal known as The Black Book, for example, records the will of William Soper, a merchant and mayor of Southampton, who stipulated that his house 'situated in Holy Roos parish in the town of Southampton' should be left to his wife Joan for the remainder of her life and should then go 'to the mayor then in office and the burgesses of the town of Southampton' (Alsford, 2015h; Wallis Chapman, 1912). This suggests that merchants valued their place in the community enough to wish for it to be remembered after their death.

Records of trade organisations

Local government records allow a range of urban and rural businesses to be examined, but it is also possible in some instances to explore individual sectors in more depth. In London, in particular, many trade organisations had their own courts which allowed them to create and enforce regulations relating to their trade. The records of the London goldsmiths court reveal a concern with skills training and with the quality of goods produced. In 1386, for example, court records reveal a concern about apprentices leaving their contracts early 'having learnt a little of the…craft' and then relocating to 'other cities…[where] they do work that is not proper and not up to the legal standard…to the great discredit to the people of the said mistery' (Jefferson, 2003, p. 219). The social and political role of trade organisations is also revealed through their own records. The Guild of Merchant Taylors of the Fraternity of St. John the Baptist in the City of London recorded the meeting that they held in 1607 to discuss a banquet that they were to host for King James I. The main aim of the meeting was 'to advise and consult how everything may be performed for the reputation and credit of the Company and to give his Majesty's best liking and contentment' (Clode, 1875, pp. 147–181). Matters under discussion included whether or not the lord mayor of London should be invited, as he was a member of the Clothworkers company rather than the Merchant Taylors company and therefore 'would do his endeavour to cross our Companie of that honour which we understand the Prince's Highness means to confer upon our Company' (Clode, 1875, pp. 147–181). The company was careful to tell the mayor, however, that the reason for his exclusion was that 'they feared that the company of noblemen and ladies would be so great that they could not possibly give his Lordship and worships that entertainment as would be fit for Citizens to give to their Magistrates, which was the cause they forbear to invite them at this time' (Clode, 1875, pp. 147–181).

Literary sources

Literary sources, such as manuals and poems, are the final category of evidence that can yield insights into pre-modern and early modern businesses (Davis, 2012). In many cases literary sources were intended to provide some sort of moral, and occasionally practical, guidance to business people. William Caxton's *Dialogues in English and French* published in c.1483 was an adaptation of an earlier dialogue book for language training. It was intended to have a practical purpose, with Caxton stating 'He who wishes to learn from this book/May well venture to transport/Merchandize from one country to another/and to familiarize himself with/Wares worth buying,/Or selling, so as to become rich./Study this book diligently,/For it will literally prove profitable' (Alsford, 2015g; Bradley, 1900, pp. 3–4, 25, 31–44, 46). However it also contains some small portraits of businesses that a merchant might commonly encounter, including Lewin the brewer who 'Brews much more ale/Than he can sell;/For he is renowned/For bad-quality drink./So he often has to/Give it to his pigs' (Alsford, 2015g; Bradley, 1900, pp. 3–4, 25, 31–44, 46). This concept of warning customers of dishonest business practices was reinforced in other contemporary work. Sebastian Brant's 'The Ship of Fools', produced in 1494 discussed some of the fraudulent practices used by merchants to make a quick profit, including 'Bad herrings smuggled by a bold/Shrewd merchant oft for fresh are sold' (Zeydel, 1944, pp. 327–330).

The impact of trade on society was discussed by Daniel Defoe in *The Complete English Tradesman* published in 1724 (Defoe, 1724; Weber, 1995). Defoe explored the social shift that was occurring as 'the ancient families worn out by time and family misfortunes' had their landed estates 'possessed by a new race of tradesmen, grown up into families of gentry, and established by the immense wealth gained, as I may say, behind the counter; that is, in the shop, the warehouse, and the counting-house' (Defoe, 1724; Weber, 1995, pp. 476–481). While Defoe is slightly mocking in his discussion of how these newly wealthy business people come 'every day to the herald's office to search for the coats of arms of their ancestors, in order to paint them upon their coaches, and...embroider them upon their furniture', he also emphasises the important contribution they make to English governance and the economy through their payment of taxes (Defoe, 1724; Weber, 1995, pp. 476–481). While care needs to be taken in using such sources, because they were not necessarily intended to be realistic accounts, they are often very informative on attitudes towards business.

Conclusion

This chapter has shown that pre-modern and early modern sources can inform on a number of themes that are of interest to business historians. The surviving records overturn popular conceptions of the pre-modern and early modern periods as unsophisticated. Instead, evidence from these periods can inform on a range of topics that are of interest to business historians. Scholarship on sectors such as brewing can begin at an earlier date. A range of forms of business organisation can be examined, from part-time workers with small businesses through to the development of factories and the establishment of multinationals. Early industrial districts can be identified and further insights can be made into the role of women and into labour relations.

Engagement with a variety of material is crucial for studying pre-modern and early modern business history, as there are few direct equivalents to the type of archive that business historians are most familiar with. Consultation of a range of material also allows all participants in business to be considered, from owner-managers to trade organisations and employees.

References

Useful overviews

Crick, J. & Van Houts, eds. (2011). *A Social History of England, 900–1200.* Cambridge: Cambridge University Press.

Dyer, C. (2003). *Making a Living in the Middle Ages: The People of Britain 850–1520.* London: Penguin.

Horrox, R. & Ormrod, W. M. (eds.) (2006). *A Social History of England, 1200–1500,* Cambridge: Cambridge University Press.

Kümin, B. (2009). *The European World 1500–1800: An Introduction to Early Modern History.* London: Routledge.

Thirsk, J. (1978). *Economic Policy and Projects: Development of a Consumer Society in Early Modern England.* Oxford: Clarendon Press.

Skills training

http://apps.nationalarchives.gov.uk/latin/beginners/Anonline tutorial that requires no prior knowledge of Latin and uses examples from the National Archives.

Collections of primary sources, general portals and guides

http://www.british-history.ac.uk/catalogue/primary-sources A range of published primary soruces, especially those relating to central government and towns. This site also provides a searchable bibliography of secondary work.

http://labyrinth.georgetown.edu/index.cfm This searchable database on resources for medieval history is provided by Georgetown University. It is organised thematically and covers topics such as archaeology.

http://legacy.fordham.edu/halsall/sbook.asp The Internet Medieval History Sourcebook is run by Fordham University and covers a range of topics from c.1 ACE–1500.

http://legacy.fordham.edu/halsall/mod/modsbook1.html The Internet Modern History Sourcebook is run by Fordham University and covers a range of topics from 1500–c.1900 covering a range of countries. Links are provided to other Internet Sourcebook, such as the Internet African History Sourcebook.

http://www.nationalarchives.gov.uk/education/ Online resources, mainly aimed at the under 16s but containing some useful images and clear analysis.

West, J. (1982). *Village Records,* Second edition, Chicester: Phillimore.

West, J. (1983). *Town Records.* Chicester: Phillimore.

Central government

Amt, E. (2001). *Medieval England 1000–1500 A Reader.* Letchworth: Broadview Press.

Myers, A. R. ed. (1969) *English Historical Documents volume 4.* London: Eyre and Spottiswoode.

Rothwell, H. (ed.) (1995). *English Historical Documents volume 3.* Second edition. London: Eyre and Spottiswoode.

There is a helpful overview of the range of central government records in England in the Political History up to 1800 section of the National Achives website http://www.nationalarchives.gov.uk/records/looking-for-subject/default.htm.

Local government: Towns

Kowaleski, M. (2008). *Medieval Towns: A Reader.* Toronto: University of Toronto Press.

Local government: Manors

Bailey, M. (2002). *The English Manor c. 1200-c.1500.* Manchester: Manchester University Press.

Church

Heale, M. (1999). *Monasticism in Late Medieval England, c.1300–1535*. Manchester: Manchester University Press.

Records of trade organisations and literary sources

The most accessible material for beginners can be found in the material in the general portals and guides section.

References

Alsford, S. (1982). 'The Men Behind the Masque: Office-holding in East-Anglian boroughs, 1272–1460' (Unpublished MPhil thesis, University of Leicester, 1982) [Online]. Available from: Medieval English Towns' http://users.trytel.com/~tristan/towns/mc2_pt1.html [Accessed 25/1/15].

Alsford, S. (ed.) (2015a). Biographies: Lynn Thomas Melcheburn [Online]. Available from: Medieval English Towns http://users.trytel.com/~tristan/towns/biography/biolynn.html#melcheburn [Accessed 25/1/15].

Alsford, S. (ed.) (2015b). Borough probate of wills and testaments[Online]. Available from: Medieval English Towns http://users.trytel.com/~tristan/towns/florilegium/lifecycle/lcdth05.html [Accessed 25/1/15].

Alsford, S. (ed.) (2015c). Charges against the brewers of London. [Online]. Available from: Medieval English Towns http://users.trytel.com/~tristan/towns/florilegium/economy/eccom13.html [Accessed 15/1/15].

Alsford, S. (ed.) (2015d). Constitutional provisions at Bridgwater. [Online]. Available from: Medieval English Towns http://users.trytel.com/~tristan/towns/florilegium/government/gvcons16.html [Accessed 15/1/15].

Alsford, S. (ed.) (2015e). Plans for building a tavern. [Online]. Available from: Medieval English Towns http://users.trytel.com/~tristan/towns/florilegium/community/cmfabr03.html [Accessed 15/1/15].

Alsford, S. (ed.) (2015f). Regulations as to the sale of wine. [Online]. Available from: Medieval English Towns http://users.trytel.com/~tristan/towns/florilegium/economy/eccom12.html [Accessed 15/1/15].

Alsford, S. (ed.) (2015g). The exercise and moral standards of trades and occupations. [Online]. Available from: Medieval English Towns http://users.trytel.com/~tristan/towns/florilegium/lifecycle/lcmen02.html#cap4 [Accessed 15/1/15].

Alsford, S. (ed.) (2015h). Wills of two Southampton mayors. [Online]. Available from: Medieval English Townshttp://users.trytel.com/~tristan/towns/florilegium/lifecycle/lcdth15.html#p35 [Accessed 15/1/15].

Amt, E. (2001). *Medieval England 1000–1500 A Reader*. Letchworth: Broadview Press.

Bailey, M. (2002). *The English Manor c. 1200–c.1500*. Manchester: Manchester University Press.

Bateson, M. (ed,) (1899). *Records of the Borough of Leicester being a series of extracts from the archives of the Corporation of Leicester*. Volume 1, Cambridge: Cambridge University Press.

Bell, A. R. (2005). 'Advance contracts for the sale of wool in medieval England: An underdeveloped and inefficient market?', ISMA Centre Discussion Papers in Finance DP 2005–01 February 2005 [Online]. Available from: http://www.icmacentre.ac.uk/papers/advance-contracts-for-the-sale-of-wool-in-medieval-england-an-undeveloped-and-inefficient-market [Accessed 7/1/15].

Bell, A. R., Brooks, C., Dryburgh, C., & Dryburgh, P. (2007). *The English Wool Market, c. 1230–1327*. Cambridge: Cambridge University Press.

Bennett, J. M. (1996). *Ale, Beer and Brewsters in England: Women's Work in a Changing World*. New York: Oxford University Press.

Best, H. (1857). *Rural Economy in Yorkshire in 1641, Being the Farming and Account Books of Henry Best of Elmswell, in the East Riding of the Country of York*. Volume 33, London and Edinburgh: The Surtees Society.

Blomquist, T. W. (1971). 'The Castracani Family of Thirteenth Century Lucca', *Speculum*, *46*, 459–76.

Braddick, M. J. (1996). *The Nerves of State: Taxation and the Financing of the English State, 1558–1714*. Manchester: Manchester University Press.

Bradley, H. (ed.) (1900). *Dialogues in French and English by William Caxton*. London: Early English Text Society.

Britnell, R. H. (1995). 'Commercialisation and Economic Development in England, 1000–1300' in Richard H. Britnell and Bruce M. S. Campbell, eds., *A Commercialising Economy: England 1096 to c. 1300*. Manchester: Manchester University Press, 7–26.

British History Online [Online]. Available from: http://www.british-history.ac.uk/catalogue/primary-sources [Accessed 20/1/15].

Bruce D., T. (1917). 'The Burgesses of Bridgwater in the Thirteenth Century', *Proceedings of the Somersetshire Archaeological and Natural History Society, 63*, 55–56.

Carlos, A. M. & Nicholas, S. (1988). '"Giants of an Earlier Capitalism": The Chartered Trading Companies as Modern Multinationals', *Business History Review, 62*(3), 398–419.

Casson, C. (2012). 'Reputation and Responsibility in Medieval English towns: Civic Concerns with the Regulation of Trade', *Urban History, 39*(03), 387–408.

Casson, M. & Casson, C. (2013). *The Entrepreneur in History: From Medieval Merchant to Modern Business Leader*. Basingstoke: Palgrave Macmillan.

Casson, M. & Casson. C. (2014). 'The History of Entrepreneurship: Medieval Origins of a Modern Phenomenon', *Business History, 56*(8), 1223–42.

Chambers, R. W. & Daunt, M. (eds.) (1931). *A Book of London English 1384–1425*. Oxford: Clarendon Press.

Chandler, A. (1977). *The Visible Hand: The Managerial Revolution in American Business*. Cambridge: Harvard University Press.

Clode, C. M. (ed.) (1875). *Memorials of the Guild of Merchant Taylors of the Fraternity of St. John the Baptist in the City of London* (London, 1875), 147–181 [Online]. Available from: https://www.british-history.ac.uk/no-series/taylors-guild-london/pp147–181 [Accessed 24/1/15].

Coffman, D'M. (2013). *Excise Taxation and the Origins of Public Debt*. Basingstoke: Palgrave Macmillan.

Coffman, D'M., Leonard, A. & Neal, L. (eds,) (2013). *Questioning Credible Commitment: Perspectives on the Rise of Financial Capitalism*. Cambridge: Cambridge University Press.

Coss, P. (1998). *The Lady in Medieval England 1000–1500*. Stroud: Sutton Publishing.

Crick, J. & Van Houts, E. (eds.) (2011). *A Social History of England, 900–1200*. Cambridge: Cambridge University Press.

Curry, A., Morgan, P. & Spence, P. (2015) [Online] The Gascon Rolls project 1317–1468. Available from: http://www.gasconrolls.org/en/ [Accessed 21/1/15].

Dale, M. K. (1933). 'The London Silkwomen of the Fifteenth Century', *The Economic History Review, 4*(3), 324–335.

Dale, M. K. (1958). 'Social and Economic History, 1066–1509', in R. A. McKinley, ed., *The Victoria History of the County of Leicester. Volume 4*, London: Oxford University Press, 31–54.

Davids, R. L. 'WINCHCOMBE, alias SMALLWOOD, John (1488/89-1557), of Newbury, Berks.,' [Online]. Available from: http://www.historyofparliamentonline.org/volume/1509-1558/member/winchcombe-john-148889-1557 [Accessed 7/1/15].

Davis, J. (2012). *Medieval Market Morality: Life, Law and Ethics in the English Marketplace, 1200–1500*. Cambridge: Cambridge University Press.

Defoe, D. (1724). *The Complete English Tradesman*. London, NS.

Deloney, T. (no date). *The Pleasant History of John Winchcomb in His Younger Years Called Jack of Newbury* [Online]. Available from: https://archive.org/details/pleasanthistory00delogoog' [Accessed 11/1/15].

Dickson, P. G. M. (1976). *The Financial Revolution in England: A Study in the Development of Public Credit 1688-1756*. London: Macmillan.

Dyer, C (2003). *Making a Living in the Middle Ages: The People of Britain 850–1520*. London: Penguin.

Dyer, C. (2005). *An Age of Transition: Economy and Society in England in the Later Middle Ages*. Oxford: Oxford University Press.

Dyer, C. (2012). *A Country Merchant: 1495–1520: Trading and Farming at the End of the Middle Ages*. Oxford: Oxford University Press.

Farber, L. (2006). *An Anatomy of Trade in Medieval Writing: Value, Consent and Community*. Ithaca and London: Cornell University Press.

Farmer, D. L. (1995). 'Woodland and Pasture sales on the Winchester Manors in the Thirteenth Century: Disposing of a Surplus, or Producing for the Market?', in Richard H. Britnell and Bruce

M. S. Campbell, eds, *A Commercialising Economy: England 1086–c. 1300*. Manchester: Manchester University Press, 102–131.

Francis, D. (1972). *The Wine Trade*. London: Adam and Charles Black.

Gelderblom, O. (2003). 'The Governance of Early Modern Trade: The Case of Henri Thijs, 1556–1611', *Enterprise and Society*, 4(4), 606–39.

Given-Wilson, C. (2005). 'General Introduction', in C. Given-Wilson et al. eds., *The Parliament Rolls of Medieval England*. [Online]. Available from: http://www.sd-editions.com/PROME [Accessed 31/12/05].

Gourvish, T. R. & Wilson, R. G. (1985). 'Profitability in the Brewing Industry, 1885–1914', *Business History*, 27(2), 146–165.

Greary, P. (2003) *Readings in Medieval History: The Later Middle Ages*. Volume 2, New York: Broadview Press.

Greif, A. (1989). 'Reputation and Coalitions in Medieval Trade: Evidence on the Maghribi Traders', *Journal of Economic History*, 49, 857–82.

Heale, M. (1999). *Monasticism in Late Medieval England, c.1300–1535*. Manchester: Manchester University Press.

Hilton, R. (2003). *Bond Men Made Free: Medieval Peasant Movements and the English Rising of 1381*. Second edition. Abingdon: Routledge.

Holcombe, L. (1983). *Wives and Property, Reform of Married Women's Property law in Nineteenth Century England*. Oxford: Martin Robertson.

Horrox, R. (1978). *The Changing Plan of Hull, 1290–1650*. Hull: Kingston-upon-Hull City Council.

Horrox, R. (ed.) (1983a). *Selected Rentals and Accounts of Medieval Hull, 1293–1528*. York: Yorkshire Archaeological Society Records Series, 141.

Horrox, R. (1983b). *The De La Poles of Hull*. Hull: East Yorkshire Local History Society.

Horrox, R. & Ormrod, W. M. (eds.) (2006). *A Social History of England, 1200–1500*. Cambridge: Cambridge University Press.

Hunt, E. S. & Murray, J. M. (1999). *A History of Business in Medieval Europe, 1200–1550*. Cambridge: Cambridge University Press.

The Internet Modern History Sourcebook [Online]. Available from: http://legacy.fordham.edu/halsall/mod/modsbook1.html' [Accessed 12/1/15].

Instituto Datini[Online] Available from: http://www.istitutodatini.it/schede/datini/home_e.htm [Accessed 21/1/15].

Jackson, C. (2008). 'Boom-time Freaks or Heroic Industrial Pioneers? Clothing Entrepreneurs in Sixteenth- and Early Seventeenth-Century Berkshire', *Textile History*, 39(2), 145–71.

Jefferson, L. (ed.) (2003). *Wardens' Accounts and Court Minute Books of the Goldsmiths' Mistery of London 1334–1446*. Woodbridge: Boydell and Brewer.

Jones, G. & Zeitlin, J. (eds.) (2007). *The Oxford Handbook of Business History*. Oxford: Oxford University Press.

Journal of the House of Commons (1802–1830) London: HMSO [Online]. Available from: http://www.british-history.ac.uk/search/series/commons-jrnl [Accessed 14/1/15].

Kermode, J. (1999). *Medieval Merchants: York, Beverley and Hull in the Later Middle Ages*, Second edition. Cambridge.

Kirkbridge Jones, M. & Veale, E. M. (1971). *Studies in the Medieval Wine Trade*. Oxford: Clarendon Press.

Kowaleski, M. (1995). *Local Markets and Regional Trade in Medieval Exeter*. Cambridge: Cambridge University Press.

Kowaleski, M. (2008). *Medieval Towns: A Reader*. Toronto: University of Toronto Press.

Kümin, B. (2009). *The European World 1500–1800: An Introduction to Early Modern History*. London: Routledge.

Labyrinth Medieval Site [Online]. Available from: http://labyrinth.georgetown.edu/index.cfm [Accessed 15/1/15].

Landes, D. S., Mokyr, J. & Baumol, W. J. (eds.) (2010). *The Invention of Enterprise: Entrepreneurship from Ancient Mesopotamia to Modern Times*. Princeton: Princeton University Press.

Lee, J. S. (2014). 'Piped Water Supplies Managed By Civic Bodies in Medieval English Towns', *Urban History*, 41(3), 369–93.

Lemire, B. (1997). *Dress, Culture and Commerce: The English Clothing Trade before the Factory, 1660–1800.* Basingstoke: Macmillan.

Leyser, H. (1995). *Medieval Women: A Social History of Women, 450–1500.* London: Weidenfeld and Nicolson.

Liddy, C. D. (2005). *War, Politics and Finance in Late Medieval English Towns.* Woodbridge: The Boydell Press.

Littlehales, H. (1905). *The Medieval Records of A London City Church St Mary At Hill, 1420–1559.* London, NS [Online]. Available from: http://www.british-history.ac.uk/early-eng-text-soc/vol128/pp. 1–21 [Accessed 24/1/15].

Lock, R. ed. (1998). *The Court Rolls of Walsham le Willows 1303–1350.* Suffolk Record Society, vol XLI: The Boydell Press.

Manuel Falsca, C. (2013). 'Creating Wine: The Emergence of a World Industry, 1840–1914', *Business History, 55*(2), 318–320.

Mathias, P. (1993). 'The Entrepreneur in Brewing', *South African Journal of Economic History, 8*(1), 19–35.

McKinlay, A. & Taylor, S. (2015). 'Narrating Histories of Women at Work: In and Out of the Archive' (working paper).

Muldrew, C. (1998). *The Economy of Obligation: The Culture of Credit and Social Relations in Early Modern England.* Basingstoke: Macmillan.

Muller, M. (2013). 'Peasant Women, Agency and Status in Mid-Thirteenth to Late Fourteenth-Century England: Some Reconsiderations' in C. Beattie and M. F. Stevens eds., *Married Women and the Law in Premodern Northwest Europe.* Woodbridge: Boydell and Brewer, 91–113.

Murphy, A. (2009). *The Origins of the English Financial Markets: Investment and Speculation before the South Sea Bubble.* Cambridge: Cambridge University Press, 2009.

Musson, A. & Ormrod, W. M. (1999). *The Evolution of English Justice: Law, Politics, and Society in the Fourteenth Century.* Basingstoke: Macmillan Press.

Myers, A. R. (ed.) (1969). *English Historical Documents volume 4.* London: Eyre and Spottiswoode.

National Archives Education [Online]. Available from: http://www.nationalarchives.gov.uk/education/ [Accessed 16/1/15].

National Archives Latin Training [Online]. Available from: http://apps.nationalarchives.gov.uk/latin/beginners/ [Accessed 16/1/15].

Nightingale, P. (1995). *A Medieval Mercantile Community: The Grocers' Company and the Politics and Trade of London, 1000–1485.* New Haven and London: Yale University Press.

Origo, I. (1957).*The Merchant of Prato Francesco di Marco Datini.* London.

Ormrod, W. M. (ed.) 'Edward III: Parliament of 1341, Text and Translation', in C. Given-Wilson et al. eds., *The Parliament Rolls of Medieval England* [Online]. Available from: http://www.sd-editions.com/PROME [Accessed 31/12/05].

Overton, M. (1996). *Agricultural Revolution in England: The Transformation the Agrarian Economy, 1500–1850.* Cambridge, Cambridge University Press.

Parker, V. (1971). *The Making of Kings Lynn.* London: Phillimore.

Paul, H. (2011). *The South Sea Bubble: An Economic History of its Origins and Consequences.* Abingdon: Routledge.

Penrose, E. T. (1960). 'The Growth of the Firm - A Case Study: The Hercules Powder Company', *The Business History Review, 34*(1), 1–23.

Postan, M. M. (1973). *Essays on Medieval Agriculture and General Problems of the Medieval Economy.* London: Cambridge University Press.

Princeton Geniza Project [Online]. Available from: http://etc.princeton.edu/genizaproject/ [Accessed 3/1/15].

Rawcliffe, C. (2004). 'Sickness and Health', in Carole Rawcliffe and Richard Wilson, eds., *Medieval Norwich.* London: Hambledon and London, 301–24.

Rickert, E., Olson, C. & Crow, M. (eds.) (1948). *Chaucer's World.* New York: Columbia University Press.

Riley, H. T. (ed.) (1868). *Memorials of London and London Life in the Thirteenth, Fourteenth and Fifteenth Centuries.* London: Longmans, Green and Co.

Rosser, G. (1994). 'Going to the Fraternity Feast: Commensality and Social Relations in Late Medieval England', *Journal of British Studies, 33*, 430–46.

Rosser, G. (1997). 'Crafts, Guilds and the Negotiation of Work in the Medieval Town', *Past and Present, 154*, 3–31.

Rothwell, H. (ed.) (1995). *English Historical Documents Volume 3*. Second edition. London: Eyre and Spottiswoode.

Rutledge, E. (2004). 'Norwich before the Black Death', in Carole Rawcliffe and Richard Wilson eds. *Medieval Norwich*. London: Hambledon and London, 157–88.

Saul, A. (1975). 'Great Yarmouth in the Fourteenth Century: A Study in Trade, Politics and Society' (Unpublished PhD thesis, University of Oxford).

Sayre, L. B. (2010). 'The Pre-history of Soil Science: Jethro Tull, the Invention of the Seed Drill, and the Foundations of Modern Agriculture', *Physics and Chemistry of the Earth, 35*, 851–59.

Schofield, P. R. (1998). 'Peasants and the Manor Court: Gossip and Litigation in a Suffolk Village at the Close of the Thirteenth Century', *Past and Present, 159*, 3–42.

Searle, E. & Ross, B. (eds.) (1967) *Accounts of the Cellarers of Battle Abbey 1275–1513*. Sydney: Sydney University Press.

Sellers, M. (ed.) (1911) *York Memorandum Book, Part I* (1376–1419). Surtees Society, Volume 120.

Sharpe, R. R. (ed.) (1905). *Calendar of Letter-Books Preserved Among the Archives of the Corporation of the City of London at the Guildhall Letter-book F c. 1337–1352*. London: Corporation of London.

Silva Lopes, T. (2002). 'Brands and the Evolution of Multinationals in Alcoholic Beverages', *Business History, 44*(3), 1–30.

Spear, V. (2005). *Leadership in Medieval English Nunneries*. Woodbridge: Boydell Press.

Stanziani, A. (2009). 'Information, Quality and Legal Rules: Wine Adulteration in Nineteenth Century France', *Business History, 51*(2), 268–91.

Staves, S. (1990). *Married Women's Separate Property in England 1660–1833*. Cambridge: Harvard University Press.

Stobart, J. (2004). 'Personal and Commercial Networks in a English Port: Chester in the Early Eighteenth Century', *Journal of Historical Geography, 30*(2), 277–293 reprinted in Casson, Mark and Catherine Casson (2013), *History of Entrepreneurship: Innovation and Risk-taking Volume 1*. Cheltenham: Edward Elgar, 531–47.

Stone, D. (2005). *Decision-making in Medieval Agriculture*. Oxford: Oxford University Press.

Talbot Donaldson, E. (ed.) (1990). *William Langland Piers Plowman An Alliterative Verse Translation*. New York and London: W. W. Norton and Company.

Taylor, S., Bell, E. & Cooke, B. (2009). 'Business History and the Historiographical Operation', *Management & Organizational History, 4*(2), 151–66.

Tearle, B. (ed.) (2012). *The Accounts of the Guild of the Holy Trinity, Luton 1526/7-1546/7*. The Bedfordshire Historical Record Society, Volume 91.

The Journal of the House of Commons: Volume 10, 1688–1693 [Online]. Available from: http://www.british-history.ac.uk/commons-jrnl/vol10 [Accessed 20/1/15].

Thirsk, J. (1978). *Economic Policy and Projects: Development of a Consumer Society in Early Modern England*. Oxford: Clarendon Press.

Thomas, A. (ed.) (1929). *Calendar of the Plea and Memoranda Rolls of the City of London*. Volume 2, London, Corporation of London.

Thomas, A. H. (ed.) (1943). *Calendar of the Plea and Memoranda Rolls of the City of London*. Volume 4, London: Corporation of London.

Threlfall-Holmes, M. (2005). *Monks and Markets: Durham Cathedral Priory 1460–1520*. Oxford: Oxford University Press.

Thrupp, S. (1962). *The Merchant Class of Medieval London 1300–1500*. Ann Arbour: The University of Michigan Press.

University of Reading's Museum of English Rural Life [Online]. Available from: http://www.reading.ac.uk/merl/collections/merl-library.aspx [Accessed 15/1/15].

Wallis, P. (2012). 'Labor, Law, and Training in Early Modern London: Apprenticeship and the City's Institutions', *The Journal of British Studies, 51*(4), 791–819.

Wallis Chapman, A.B. (ed.) (1912). *The Black Book of Southampton volume 2*. Southampton Record Society, Volume 14.

Weber, E. (ed.) (1995). *The Western Tradition: From the Ancient World to Louis XIV*. Lexington; D.C., Heath: Cengage Learning.

West, J. (1982). *Village Records*. Second edition. Chicester: Phillimore.

West, J. (1983). *Town Records*. Chicester: Phillimore.

Wilson, J. F. (1995). *British Business History 1720–1994*. Manchester and New York: Manchester University Press.

Wilson, J. F. & Popp, A. (eds.) (2003). *Industrial Clusters and Regional Business Networks in England, 1750–1970*. Aldershot: Ashgate.

Witzel, M. (2012). *A History of Management Thought*. London: Routledge.

Yamamoto, K. (2011). 'Piety, Profit and Public Service in the Financial Revolution', *English Historical Review*, 126(521), 806–34.

Zeydel, E. H. (ed.) (1944). *The Ship of Fools, by Sebastian Brant*. New York: NS.

17

Networks and clusters in business history

Emily Buchnea

Introduction

Analysis of business networks and clusters by historians has become a prominent strand of research in several areas of business history over the past two decades. While many business historians choose to unravel the complexities of business relationships of the past, not all have chosen to adopt the framework of social network analysis to examine the functioning and characteristics of these relationships. Therefore, this chapter examines the presence and use of network themes and analysis within business history while also highlighting areas where networks have been misinterpreted and areas which could benefit from further research. The frequent use of social network analysis in the fields of sociology and contemporary management/business studies allow business historians to view how network analysis can be employed in their own work. Further to this, by looking to these fields for research inspiration through an analytical framework, historians are able to create a theoretical fluency which Maclean et al. (2015) argue will add to the dual integrity of business historians' research.

Networks can be complex structures containing a multitude of actors and linkages. The reasons for the presence of actors in a network and bonds they create vary, making it incredibly difficult to isolate networks. Thus, before launching into a discussion of the uses and abuses of networks and clusters in business history, it is logical to start with a definition. A commonly used definition of networks as they relate to economic actions comes from Smith-Doerr and Powell (2005) who define networks as 'formal exchanges, either in the form of asset pooling or resource provision, between two or more parties that entail ongoing interaction in order to derive value from the exchange'. Even further simplification and broadness is provided by Mitchell (1973) who explains that a social network 'can be thought of as the actual set of links of all kinds amongst a set of individuals'. Sociologists argue that network analysis focuses on the ties that link people, groups, organizations and countries and that the main purpose of analysing a network is to isolate and interpret patterns in these ties (De Nooy et al., 2005). The scope of these definitions implies that almost any grouping of individuals or institutions can be defined as a network and presumably operate under similar network themes and characteristics.

Therefore, networks can be a useful framework for historians attempting to understand group behaviour and interactions of the past and can open a dialogue between business historians and scholars of contemporary business and management. For the study of historical business communities, industrial districts and international trade routes, the use of social network analysis tools has been exceedingly useful. However, some that study these areas still have yet to adopt this perspective and more worryingly, 'networks' has also now become a buzz word for many historians who will claim to be analysing a historical network without employing a theoretical framework. Questions about the network approach need to then be asked here: is a network approach always the best approach for studying business groups or organizations in history? Is it wrong to apply a modern sociological framework to communities of the past? What are the dangers?

Network analysis before business history

Social network analysis emerged within the field of sociology in the 1970s and quickly became a widely accepted method for studying individual relationships and group behaviour. Many of the early social network theorists were crucial in influencing economic/business perspectives on network functions. Granovetter's 1973 article in the *American Journal of Sociology* was instrumental in shaping the way in which sociologists viewed network operations. He stressed that the existence of dyadic or weak ties in a network allowed for the accumulation of diverse knowledge, increased mobility and opportunity for network expansion. Importantly, Granovetter (1985) later stressed that one must focus on business groups as a category of network, stating that repeated exchange can create networks of cooperation and collusion. Knowledge of each other's characteristics as business men and women helps to match/refer each other to outside business opportunities. The networks which existed amongst marketplaces, industrial districts and trading communities act as model case studies for these sociological theories. Also prominent in the early 1970s, Lodhi and Tilly's (1973) work on urban and migratory networks remains one of the most influential early examples of the adoption of social network analysis by historians. They argue that historians could use social network analysis as a way of situating individuals within larger societal changes (for example, social uprisings, mass migration and urban expansion). This concept thus can also be applied to business history and changes in the nature of local, national and transnational business over the centuries.

In the last few decades, sociologists and economists such as Burt (2004), Rauch (2001), Watts (1999), Podolny and Page (1998) and Coleman (1988) have continued to produce theoretical works that historians have found useful in explaining network formation and functioning, especially within the context of business/economic communities. The flexibility of this theoretical framework and its ability to allow historians to pinpoint behavioural patterns which may not be explicitly pronounced in archival sources, not to mention the potential for inter-disciplinary collaborations, makes it an ideal approach for some to adopt. Yet, many still remain reluctant to think of historical communities in such a way. Wetherall (1998) argues that historians have typically been slow to adopt social network analysis as a research method because of three distinct reasons. First, the field of historical social network analysis first studied by sociologists is still widely unfamiliar to historians; second, historians using quantitative data to study their subjects make up a rather small proportion of historians[1] and third, social network analysis often requires quite robust data which certain subject areas and indeed historical 'eras' may not permit. Since Wetherall published his article in the late 1990s, there has been significant advancement in the field of historical network analysis, and much of this has been the work of business/economic historians. Network and cluster analysis allows for a framework through which business networks and clusters in history can maintain their individual diversity while still identifying trends in business organization and operation.

That said, business historians studying networks and clusters inevitably turn to much of the non-historical literature listed above, principally because of the important theoretical framework that many of these scholars laid out but also because of a lack of an extensive theoretical literature from business historians on networks. Thus there is substantial scope here for business historians to make a theoretical mark since, in many ways, the study of business networks helps historians deepen their understanding of interactions and exchange in business communities. As Cookson (1997) argues, 'businesses need networks, for industrialists must connect with others in order to buy and sell, to find finance and partners, to recruit and train staff and to develop technology and discover technical information'. While the study of eminent firms or conglomerates has pervaded much of early business history, historians such as Cookson (1997), Haggerty (2010), Toms (2004), Casson and Cox (1993) and Rose (2015) have shown that understanding communities and organizational structures in which businesses and business people develop can be equally valuable to the history of business.

The historians above have each contributed networked perspectives on business history and given that businesses do not emerge in isolation, the application of social network theory to understanding the internal dynamics of business communities and businesses themselves is valid. That said, the emergence of research on historical business networks has tended to be concentrated in a number of key areas. Histories of oceanic trade and merchant firms have yielded a number of influential studies on networks (Haggerty, 2013; Lamikiz, 2013; McWatters and Lemarchand, 2013; Margazalli, 2015; Games, 2000). If one thinks of a network as a tangled web, a port-to-port physical trade on an international scale tends to fit most naturally within a network framework. Merchants operated in a low institutional environment where personal relationships ruled and therefore using a network approach allows historians to grasp the complexities of a business environment centred on high-risk ventures, slow communication and lack of formal governance.

Another area in which the study of business networks has featured prominently is in the history of the industrial North-West of England. Being an area of business/economic history which has received much attention, fresh perspectives which incorporate more nuanced theories are a welcomed rejuvenation of a tried and tested topic (Parsons and Rose, 2005; Toms, 2004; Rose, 2000). Other areas also taking a network approach include studies of board interlocks, finance and credit networks and the history of innovation and industrial districts. Studies which pick apart inter-organizational relationships and internal business networks in a range of industries still remain primarily the remit of pure business/management scholars and sociologists. That said, much of their work reveals the scope for application of network theory in business history and perhaps a move towards more theoretical fluency. The following sections of this chapter will explore some of the major themes and contexts of network studies and how they have been utilized in business history. From this, areas which could benefit from network studies can be highlighted as well as areas in which network theory has allowed for misinterpretations of history.

Key themes

Through historical network studies a number of key themes have been identified: trust, reputation, risk and knowledge or information; all four are essential to network formation and function. There are, of course, much more complex themes that emerge in network studies such as embeddedness, obligation, etc.; however, these initial four comprise the most basic attributes of networks and are often the first examined in historical business networks.

Trust is an intrinsic part of networked communities and, in business in particular, it is one of the core attributes of a transacting relationship. Fukuyama (1996) in his important work devoted to the concept argues, 'trust is the expectation that arises within a community of regular, honest, and cooperative behaviour, based on commonly shared norms, on the part of other members of the community...but while contract and self-interest are important sources of association, the most effective organizations are based on communities of shared ethical values' (1996, p. 26). In business, trust is required to establish a working relationship and although trust can come in different forms, the idea that an individual expects a business contact to behave in a particular way, one which will not bring harm to themselves or their business, is fundamental to every business relationship. Therefore, trust as it relates to the creation of networks becomes an important aspect of analysing historical business networks.

Business historians have analysed the concept of trust within the context of networks in several ways. In studies of international trading networks, trust was required in every business exchange (buying, selling, credit extension) because contacts were often located in distant locations, communication was slow and formal governance procedures were almost non-existent (Glaisyer, 2004). Despite early trade networks operating in a low institutional environment, many networks adhered to social norms which fostered trust between individuals who shared the same business culture (Gómez-Galvarriato, 2008). Of course, there are many different types of trust and when looking into family business networks, historians have often highlighted the concept of 'ascribed' trust, whereby a person is trusted by a network on the basis of attributes other than proven good business practices. Colli (2003) and Haggerty and Haggerty (2009) have each written on this notion of 'ascribed' trust and the family firm; family members were a first source for employees, capital and property and thus were trusted simply because they were related. Other forms of trust were also important to building business networks; *impersonal trust* for instance was trust bestowed upon an individual because of their affiliations (religious groups, i.e., Quaker) or particular social norms which obligated people to act morally (Casson, 2003). These kinds of trust were particularly important in business communities where individuals relied first on family and failing that, had to create new connections.

Aslanian (2006), in a study of early modern Armenian trade networks, argues that the existence of 'trust' amongst business communities was not simply present because of strong ties between business associates but was something that was constructed over time as a result of the accumulation of social capital within a given group. Social capital, a prominent strand of network studies championed by sociologists such as Portes (1998) and Burt (2000) define social capital as the individual or collective benefit gained from one's own relationships and position in a given network. The benefit being that one is trusted within their given network, participates in cooperative relationships that are beneficial rather than detrimental to them and accrues a reputation which will allow them to access new opportunities, information and contacts. Fukuyama (1996) also suggests that 'social capital is the capability that arises from the prevalence of trust in a society or in certain parts of it. It can be embodied in the smallest and most basic social group, the family, as well as the largest of all groups, the nation, and in all groups in between.'

Trust within business networks was also inseparable from reputation. Numerous studies on networks and embeddedness have shown that transactions are most likely to occur between individuals who have knowledge of each other or who have fostered some sort of reputation, usually positive, within a given business community (Granovetter, 1985). As Coleman (1988, p. S107) argues, 'reputation cannot arise in an open structure', it is the network themselves that fosters and transmits reputation and thus it becomes an integral part of exchange within a network. Despite reputation being an essential part of network building and expansion, there are few dedicated business history studies on this topic, although most network histories will touch on it in some form. One of the few but instrumental early studies on medieval trade networks conducted by Avner Grief (1989) explains how a group of traders built trust based on reputation and vice versa. He argues that the mechanisms of reputation reveal a relationship in which trust and reputation must operate together, 'the merchant can thus trust the agent – the agent possesses a reputation as honest agent' (p. 867).

The 'honest agent' is one that is trusted to act in the best interest of the principle (merchant) which then stems the risk of misbehaviour or misconduct. The mechanisms of trust and reputation are in place because businesses are subjected to many different kinds of risk. An interesting strand of the study of historical business networks is examining the ways in which they respond to risks in a variety of forms. This could be market fluctuations, war, financial crises and a host of others. The concept of risk and indeed risk as it relates to business and the economy has its own plentiful literature (Lupton, 1999; Nooteboom, Berger and Noorderhaven, 1997). This has been used to inform our historical conceptions of how businesses of the past have coped with risk. Much of the literature suggests that networks of known and trusted associates were necessary for minimising risk. Especially in times of uncertainty, networks also provided information and knowledge which served to lessen financial and other sorts of risk.

Risk then becomes an important driver for the creation and endurance of networks. Risk as it relates to business networks or simply business relationships can be conceived in numerous ways (risk, hazard, threat, uncertainty, etc.). Haggerty (2013) establishes that a risk is the measure of a hazard occurring and this measure often brings with it a degree of uncertainty. Forrestier (2010) argues that although there were risks that were unavoidable, risks that stem from individual action could be lessened. A strong business culture linked to good business practice and reputation ensured that businessmen and women operated justly without the need for institutions. Therefore, business networks can also be understood as a form of governance because actors become accountable to other actors. While some institutions did help to mitigate risk (government, debtor courts, chambers of commerce, etc.), prior to formal codes governing businesses, actors were forced to deal with risks through their networks. By operating in a network in various forms, individuals ideally could spread risk. This was why, for example, merchants often part-owned vessels, underwrote insurance policy in groups and extended credit to firms they knew and trusted.

Risk also impacts the size and density of an individual's network – individuals may seek out multiple contacts which provide the same good or service in an effort to reduce the risks that come from vertical integration. Some may choose to keep their network small in order to protect their businesses from outside hazards brought about by the unknown (Biggart and Hamilton, 1992). One aspect of business networks which could use more attention in the business history literature is the use of networks to either allow for or restrict malfeasance in a more modern sense (Granovetter, 1992). Networks are the necessary organizational structure through which corruption and collusion occurs and although there have been a number of studies on the history of corruption and fraud, examining the networks that allow for this behaviour would be illuminating.

An important part of mitigating risk is acquiring the appropriate information to deal with potential hazards or uncertainties that may arise. The cotemporary socio-economic literature contains a wealth of research pertaining to the function of networks as the transmitters of information and knowledge (McFadyen and Cannella, 2004; Coleman, 1988). Much of this literature refers to the knowledge accumulated through associations as *human capital* and much like social capital, this remains one of the benefits accrued by being an actor in a network. The business history literature has also adopted theories of human capital accumulation, it being one of the main objectives of network formation (Jacob, 2014; Berghoof and Kohler, 2007; Duguid, 2004). Duguid (2004), in his work on the port commodity chain, emphasizes the information required when business networks engage in the production, procurement and sale of a commodity requiring a wealth of knowledge related to quality, cost and other 'peculiarities' of port. Further to this, actors in this network also had the challenges of cross-cultural business and international regulations with which to contend and thus the ability to access and transmit information was crucial.

Networks and the capital gained (or in some cases, lost) that comes as a result of membership are tied into the factors listed above, as well as many additional subtleties of human behaviour and relationships. The shape and structure of a network depends entirely on the contexts in which they are created and function. How is it then that we can study, in general terms, business networks of the past? Each network will inevitably be different but may display particular patterns related to culture, location, size and industry. The following section will discuss some of the contexts in which business networks arise and the characteristics ascribed to each.

Business networks and clusters in historical context

The contexts in which a business network is created greatly impacts upon the way it functions. It is not enough to say a business network exists and therefore it will contain trustworthy associates who exchange goods and ideas that benefit the group as a whole. Each network will contain a different set of variables, each will be faced with a different set of obstacles, risks, uncertainties, etc. and each will operate on a different scale. This section will examine some of the contexts in which networks in business history have been explored: the family business, local business communities, industrial districts and international trade.

Family business networks have persistently been an important part of business communities. The development of business networks within the context of the family was common as family was, and often still is, the first source of financial capital, property, knowledge and opportunity. Ascribed trust mentioned above was bestowed upon family members and encouraged individuals to participate in business under an informal behavioural code. Family was an expected source of business partners and heirs, as Fukuyama (1996) argues, 'among the numerous forms of social capital that enable people to trust one another and build economic organizations, the most obvious and natural one is the family, with the consequence that the vast majority of businesses, both historically and now, are family businesses'. Of course not all family networks will operate with the same emotional proximity to one another or indeed the same sense of obligation. We must presume that family members may be indifferent to one another and this may influence their actions in business relationships with kin. Even in the same family, members can belong to different 'circles of intimacy,' which can govern the types of relationships that emerge (Firth, 1956). A cousin-cousin business relationship may be the same or different than a brother-brother/sister-sister relationship depending on the level of intimacy between each actor.

The functioning of family-owned businesses and internal networks remains a pressing concern for scholars of contemporary business who have investigated key issues such as agency problems (Morck and Yeung, 2003), gender and small business ownership (Renzulli et al., 2000) and family networks within Asian business (Carney and Gedajlovic, 2002; Yeung, 2000). The multitude of studies featured in *Family Business Review* such as Lambrecht (2005) on transitions between generations in family business and Miemela's (2004) study on family business networking demonstrate the interest in studying family business networks and networks in transition. In business history, literature on the family firm is substantive with Colli (2003, 2011; Colli and Rose, 2003) making some of the greatest contributions to our understanding of the intersection between family and business spheres. The use of network analysis in the study of the family firms provides a fresh perspective on older historiographical questions regarding firm dynamics, agency problems and hereditary business. While many scholars have noted the benefits and persistence of family business (Colli et al., 2013; Mathias, 2000), business historians have started to problematize family networks (Haggerty, 2011; Hancock, 2005). Finding a historical context for problems first recognised by sociologists, business historians such as Haggerty (2011) have examined how individuals chosen as business associates on the basis of familial association may not have always been 'the right man' or woman for the job. In business networks, there was almost an obligatory selection of family member as business partners due to ascribed trust and not always experience or capability. There is scope here then for networks in business history to be problematized further; while networks are often entered into for the benefit of members, the outcomes for networks were certainly not always positive.[2]

Beyond the family, small scale networks formed on the basis of ethnicity and religion also played a substantial role in business. Many studies of local ethnic business networks focus on ethnic diasporas which provides opportunity that examine the formation, function and sometimes dissolution of embedded networks in one environment. Olegario (1999) examines Jewish business groups in New York City in the nineteenth century, combining a discussion of networks and culture for a displaced ethnic group which established a thriving business community. Godley (1996) also turns his attention to the role of Jewish financiers in both New York and London as part of a migrant business community. Hancock's (2005) study of Scots in the Madeira trade paints a different picture of migrant networks, one fraught with problems related to family obligation, hereditary business and cross-cultural communication. A few contemporary studies examine the ways in which minorities bind together to create opportunities for themselves (Model, 1985). This intersection between the history of ethnic minorities and the history of local business networks is one that business historians have yet to fully examine. While these histories may exist under the field of social or cultural history, they have yet to crossover fully to the realms of business history.

Histories of religious networks in business have also been plentiful. Due to the outstanding success of Quaker business in the eighteenth and nineteenth centuries, a number of historians have provided detailed studies of their business and their networks within Quaker communities (Tolles, 1948; Prior and Kirby, 1993; Landes, 2015). Although fewer in number, studies of early French trade in Canada centre on the catholic networks which bound them together against the hordes of protestant/dissenting Anglo-merchants (Bosher, 1998). What at times becomes problematic with histories of ethnic or religious ties is the extent to which networks overlapped. In business communities as intertwined as early modern port cities or industrial towns, one cannot expect that actors 'stuck to their own kind' in all instances. Businessmen and women were often pragmatic, engaging in exchange with whomever regardless of ethnicity or religion, if it appeared profitable to do so.

Much emphasis in the literature is placed on specific ties which created networks; however, spatial proximity also becomes in itself an important factor. Face-to-face interactions, especially in the case of neighbourhoods or industrial districts, was a key feature of business relationship formation and function. As a governance mechanism, it also allowed for reputation building and accountability. One of the ways in which local business networks have been explored in business history is through associations within industrial clusters or industrial district. Studies of clusters have been used to explain particular structures within local business networks or industrially connected networks. According to Wilson and Popp (2003), a cluster can be defined as 'a wider agglomeration of industries that may be connected by common products, technologies, markets (either of supply or demand) or institutional frameworks.' The literature on current and emerging industrial districts is vast, much of it linking back to so-called Marshallian economics (Becattinni, 1990) and for the purposes of this chapter, the description has been kept brief. Industrial districts are 'geographically designed productive systems, characterised by a large number of firms that are involved at various stages, and in various ways, in the production of a homogeneous product' (Pyke et al., 1990); however, recent debates challenge the notion of geographical proximity with regards to districts, stating that resource sharing is accomplished through networks (clusters), regardless of distance, more frequently than in districts (Boschma and ter Wal, 2007).

Influenced greatly by the work of Porter (1990), understanding clusters can help us understand the 'intangible infrastructure of a region' or related industries in many regions (Casson on Regional Business Networks in Wilson and Popp, 2003, p. 23). As Nicols (2014) argues, 'clusters have institutions and culture, industrial structure and corporate organisations that promote innovation and economic development.' The association of similar businesses allows for knowledge-sharing and competition which in turn encourages innovation and development. The formation of a cluster relies on the availability of resources necessary for a particular type of business, available opportunity from the business community and the presence of industry-specific knowledge. Firms forming the cluster also need to be motivated to reduce transport costs and promote the creation of a pooled labour market.

Specific research into innovation clusters has illuminated current geographical spaces in which specific industries have found success, such as Ripcurl and Quicksilver in Torquay, Australia (Stewart, Skinner and Edwards, 2008) and the innovative edge of technology companies in the Silicon Valley (Lee et al., 2000). The study of industrial clusters and districts within business history has also produced many influential works. The edited collection by Wilson and Popp (2003) offers a complete and theoretically rigorous study of the development and characteristics of industrial districts in Great Britain from the eighteenth to twentieth century. Indeed, the theme of industrial districts of Victorian Britain has been a popular one, even if earlier studies apply less of a theoretical framework than Caunce (1997), Popp et al. (2006) and Casson (2003). Since Wilson and Popp's edited collection, the interest in this topic has continued. There has been an increased focus on industrial clusters and districts in East Asian economies (Lee and Jin, 2009) as well as work on the creation of industrial districts in tourism and specific holiday destinations (Cirer-Costa, 2014). Movement away from classical studies of financial and textile clusters in Victorian Britain opens the scope for applying theoretical frameworks of clustering and districts to newer industries and non-western regions, which could potentially inform our understanding of regional development and emergent markets of the past.

Related to the study of intra-sectoral links, work on corporate networks and particularly networks of board interlocks has created a new thread of business history which examines inter-organizational links and corporate governance through the twentieth century. Research into board inter-lock networks gained momentum in the early 1980s with the work of Koenig and Gogel (1981), Scott and Griff (1984), Mintz and Schwartz (1983) and Useem (1980), most focusing in on contemporary American directorate networks. However, some such as Scott (1991) and later Windolf (2002) and Conyon and Muldoon (2006) chose to take a more international as well as longitudinal approach in order to demonstrate how directorate networks compare and how they have changed over the twentieth century in locations such as Great Britain and Germany. In recent years, this research has again become relevant, especially within emergent business history literature. Business historians are now looking to readdress the relationship between industry and finance using the directorate network as an indicator of communication and influence between the two (Schnyder and Wilson, 2014). Da Silva et al. (2016), Del Angel (2016) and Salvaj et al. (2016) have also provided studies of this type of networked relationship in other international contexts, specifically Portugal, Mexico and Chile. This research is a promising bridge between business history and current business research which together could highlight important observations related to governance and policy.

One area of network studies which has received arguably the most attention in business history is international trade networks, likely because, as Divall (2012) argues, a history of globalisation will inevitably lead to a history of business networks. Many historians who examine international business and trade have chosen to adopt social network theories into their work (Haggerty, 2013; Buchnea, 2014). Examining the operation of international business communities through this lens allows historians to more easily negotiate the inner workings of business relationships across vast distances. Especially in the case of what some may term the 'pre-modern' economy, before communication was instantaneous, networks were essential for sustaining connections and ensuring accountability when face-to-face contact was not possible. Unlike other histories of business networks and clusters which have focused largely on the western world, studies of international networks have begun to make a move in earnest towards non-western contexts (Musacchio and Read, 2007; Seland, 2013; Veevers, 2013). That said, much of this literature continues to focus on business networks in the colonial context, especially studies which focus on the Indian Ocean and port economies.

Studies of networks in international business history still have an incredible amount of ground to cover, especially in terms of the development of multi-national enterprise and twentieth century multi-national corporations. That said, the extensive literature on trade networks has pushed historians to adopt approaches beyond simply applying socio-economic theoretical frameworks towards engaging with network analysis technology. The extensive nature of international trade networks makes it difficult to articulate the multitude of bonds formed and the ever-changing nature of business connectivity. To remedy this, scholars have adopted network analysis software to create visualisations of large networks to aid in explaining both the scale and embeddedness of early trade networks (Haggerty, 2010; Buchnea, 2014). This is not to say that visual analytics have not found favour in other areas of historical business network research; for example, interesting work is currently being conducted in corporate network histories (Musacchio and Read, 2007).

The problem with networks in business history

The study of networks in business history, although a natural framework for certain topics, is not without its problems. Histories of business networks have tended to emphasize the advantages obtained by network membership, specifically the access to a variety of resources. This emphasis is not misguided since networks were often created to receive such benefits. However, what has been emphasized less are the ways in which networks have served to disadvantage particular members or the community in which they operate. Too often we view networks as functional business systems, whereby individuals or businesses are connected and these connections offer them multiple forms of capital. Business historians are now looking to problematize networks (Hancock, 2005; Crumplin, 2007). Networks have served many beneficial purposes in historical communities, but what occurs when networks are detrimental to businesses? In sociology, there have been a number of theoretical developments with regards to the disadvantages of networks. In recent years, most influential among these is the concept of *negative social capital* which is the reputational and associational disadvantage obtained from being linked to networks known for bad business practice, dishonesty or failure, to name a few characteristics (Glaeser, Laibson and Sacerdote, 2002). Also linked to this is the negative effects of social capital, 'excessive trust' in a network can lead to pressure on members to be successful and in inherently risky markets can lead to networks as a whole making poor decisions simply because they trust each other too much (Portes, 2014). This side of historical business networks has yet to be engaged with fully but there is incredible scope for further research on the downside of belonging to business networks.

Aside from a need to further problematize networks and perhaps push theoretical boundaries within business history, one must also consider the practicalities of network research within the field of business history. While using network analysis to study the dynamics of business communities and inter-organizational relationships has proved useful, it can present some disadvantages; one of these pertains to sources. Understanding networks is about understanding relationships which allows us to gauge the overall function of a network. In history, we are forced to reconstruct relationships and this can be done using any number of sources. Wills, census data and other genealogical data may tell us whom was related to whom but does this indicate a *relationship*? Corporate network data is often pulled from annual reports or stock exchange year books. This data is robust and gives a clear indication of corporate networks; however, researchers are faced with the challenge of digging out great quantities of qualitative data to actual determine the character of board-director relationships. Further to this, how can we know how the network is utilised and transformed outside of the boardroom without asking the directors themselves? For early studies of international networks, correspondence is the most valued source. Despite the rather formulaic style of business letters, the frequency of firm-to-form correspondence or correspondence between business partners allows researchers to rebuild relationships where such sources are plentiful. However, due to source limitations, there are instances where it may be difficult to reconstruct historical business networks and network data will often be incomplete. That said, even a partial picture of a business network can be useful in understanding business strategy, the behaviour of individual firms and wider business group composition.

While network analysis is a useful tool for studying human interaction, it can sometimes presume that individuals will behave in a determinable way, that they are rational beings. Networks are flexible, they act as informal forms of organizations and allow us to view human behaviour in diverse scenarios. However, if the evidence on business networks is not robust, presumptions regarding the actions of network actors can be dangerous. Business historians now have the task of using networks not only as a way to explain informal business organization but to explain some of problems communities might encounter as a result of network actors. Concepts such as negative social capital or dark networks which have become vogue in current business research can also provide a lens into less favourable network outcomes of the past.

Conclusions: where to next?

To date, business historians have produced monumental studies which demonstrate how social network analysis can be utilised to understand business groups and behaviour in the past.

Established research strands on industrial districts, international trade and Victorian Britain demonstrate how networks can be used successfully to analyse business groups. Emergent research on historical corporate networks and more nuanced historical examinations of social and human capital are strengthening the theoretical fluency of historical network studies by framing business history topics in a manner which current business/management journals will find relevant. That said, there is tremendous scope for further research; subjects which could benefit from social network analysis and network studies which could push the theoretical discussion further.

The use of new techniques such as network visualisation software and network mapping could provide entirely new perspectives of the structure and composition of networks. While visualising static networks is useful, projects which examine network change over time with the use of multiple visualisations would provide important insights into business network development and transformation (Buchnea, 2014). Emerging work on Chinese and South American business networks exposes the dearth of studies of non-western historical business network studies. New studies have revealed that network features which western business and markets have deemed to be problematic, such as cartels, opaqueness and nepotism are at the core of Asian business networks (Biggart and Hamilton, 1988). The importance of *Zaibatsu,* family controlled conglomerates in the Japanese economy through the twentieth century and South Korean *Chaebol* networks of companies or firms owned by a single person or family (Samsung, Hyundai, Goldstar, Daewoo), demonstrates the necessity of networked relationships to East Asian business. If networks are controlled by the intangible values/cultural norms of a given society, then networks in societies with different cultural values should operate differently. Business historians thus need to first grapple with non-western business culture before non-western historical business networks can be interpreted accurately. The amount of work already completed on various network topics is promising and the continued interest in network studies outside of business history indicates that a sustained inter-disciplinary dialogue related to business networks is possible and worthwhile. While business historians must be cautious in interpreting the characteristics of individual business relationships of the past, analysing historical business network behaviour will elucidate many aspects of business group dynamics and business community development over the centuries.

Notes

1 While this is true, historians have also discovered that a range of qualitative sources are also useful in network construction and one need not only work with so-called 'big data.'
2 This can be seen not only in family networks but also in local and regional networks. Family, especially in an early modern sense, was a very fluid organizational construct and often non-family members would develop bonds with a high level of intimacy, occasionally referred to as 'fictive kin' (Socolow, 1978).

References

Aslanian, S. (2006). Social capital, 'trust' and the role of networks in Julfan trade: informal and semi-formal institutions at work. *Journal of Global History, 1*(3), 383–402.

Becattini, G. (1990). 4 The Marshallian industrial. *Industrial districts*, 37.

Berghoff, H. & Köhler, I. (2007). Redesigning a class of its own: social and human capital formation in the German banking elite, 1870–1990. *Financial History Review, 14*(1), 63–87.

Biggart, N. W. & Hamilton, G. G. (1992). On the limits of a firm-based theory to explain business networks. *Networks and Organizations*. Boston: Harvard Business School Press, 471–490.

Boschma, R. A. & Ter Wal, A. L. (2007). Knowledge networks and innovative performance in an industrial district: the case of a footwear district in the South of Italy. *Industry and Innovation, 14*(2), 177–199.

Buchnea, E. (2014). Transatlantic Transformations: Visualizing Change Over Time in the Liverpool–New York Trade Network, 1763–1833. *Enterprise & Society, 15*(4), 687–721.

Burt, R. S. (2000). The network structure of social capital. *Research in Organizational Behavior, 22*, 345–423.

Burt, R. S. (2004). Structural holes and good ideas. *American Journal of Sociology, 110*(2), 349–399.

Carney, M. & Gedajlovic, E. (2002). The co-evolution of institutional environments and organizational strategies: The rise of family business groups in the ASEAN region. *Organization Studies, 23*(1), 1–29.

Casson, M. & Cox, H. (1993). International business networks: theory and history. *Business and Economic History*, 42–53.

Caunce, S. A. (1997). Complexity, community structure and competitive advantage within the Yorkshire woollen industry, c. 1700–1850. *Business History, 39*(4), 26–43.

Cirer-Costa, J. C. (2014). Majorca's tourism cluster: The creation of an industrial district, 1919–36. *Business History, 56*(8), 1243–1261.

Coleman, J. S. (1988). Social capital in the creation of human capital. *American Journal of Sociology*, S95–S120.

Colli, A. (2003). *The History of Family Business, 1850–2000*. Cambridge University Press.

Colli, A. (2011). Contextualizing performances of family firms: The perspective of business history. *Family Business Review, 25*(3), 243–257.

Colli, A., Howorth, C. & Rose, M. (2013). Long-term perspectives on family business. *Business History, 55*(6), 841–854.

Colli, A. & Rose, M. B. (2003). Family Firms in Comparative Perspective. In: *Business History Around the World*. Cambridge: Cambridge University Press, 339–352.

Conyon, M. J. & Muldoon, M. R. (2006). The small world of corporate boards. *Journal of Business Finance & Accounting, 33*(9–10), 1321–1343.

Cookson, G. (1997). Family firms and business networks: textile engineering in Yorkshire, 1780–1830. *Business History, 39*(1), 1–20.

Crumplin, T. E. (2007). Opaque networks: business and community in the Isle of Man, 1840–1900. *Business History, 49*(6), 780–801.

Da Silva, Á. F. & Neves, P. (2016). Business groups in Portugal in the Estado Novo period (1930–1974): family, power and structural change. *Business History, 58*(1), 49–58.

De Nooy, W., Mrvar, A. & Batagelj, V. (2011). *Exploratory Social Network Analysis with Pajek* (Vol. 27). Cambridge University Press.

Del Angel, G. A. (2016). The nexus between business groups and banks: Mexico, 1932–1982. *Business History, 58*(1), 111–128.

Divall, C. (2012). Business history, global networks and the future of mobility. *Business History, 54*(4), 542–555.

Duguid, P. (2005). Networks and knowledge: the beginning and end of the Port Commodity Chain, 1703–1860. *Business History Review, 79*, 493–526.

Firth, R. (ed.) (1956). *Two Studies of Kinship in London*. London: Athlone Press.

Forestier, A. (2010). Risk, kinship and personal relationships in late eighteenth-century West Indian trade: the commercial network of Tobin & Pinney. *Business History, 52*(6), 912–931.

Fukuyama, F. (1996). *Trust: The Social Virtues and the Creation of Prosperity* (Vol. 457). New York: Free Press.

Games, A. (2006). Beyond the Atlantic: English globetrotters and transoceanic connections. *William and Mary Quarterly*, 675–692.

Gestrich, A. & Beerbühl, M. S. (eds.,) (2011). *Cosmopolitan Networks in Commerce and Society: 1660–1914*. London: German Historical Institute.

Glaeser, E. L., Laibson, D. & Sacerdote, B. (2002). An economic approach to social capital*. *The Economic Journal, 112*(483), F437–F458.

Glaisyer, N. (2004). Networking: trade and exchange in the eighteenth-century British empire. *The Historical Journal, 47*(2), 451–476.

Godley, A. (1996). Jewish soft loan societies in New York and London and immigrant entrepreneurship, 1880–1914. *Business History, 38*(3), 101–116.

Gómez-Galvarriato, A. (2008). Networks and entrepreneurship: the modernization of the textile business in Porfirian Mexico. *Business History Review, 82*(3), 475–502.

Granovetter, M. (1985). Economic action and social structure: the problem of embeddedness. *American Journal of Sociology, 91*(3), 481–510.

Granovetter, M. (1992). Economic institutions as social constructions: a framework for analysis. *Acta Sociologica, 35*(1), 3–11.

Granovetter, M. S. (1973). The strength of weak ties. *American Journal of Sociology, 78*(6), 1360–1380.

Granovetter, M. S. & Swedberg, R. (eds.,) (2001). *The Sociology of Economic Life* (Vol. 3). Boulder: Westview press.

Greif, A. (1989). Reputation and coalitions in medieval trade: evidence on the Maghribi traders. *The Journal of Economic History, 49*(4), 857–882.

Haggerty, J. & Haggerty, S. (2011). The life cycle of a metropolitan business network: Liverpool 1750–1810. *Explorations in Economic History, 48*(2), 189–206.

Haggerty, S. (2009). Risk and risk management in the Liverpool slave trade. *Business History, 51*(6), 817–834.

Haggerty, S. (2012). '*Merely for Money'?: Business Culture in the British Atlantic, 1750–1815* (Vol. 2). Liverpool: Liverpool University Press.

Hancock, D. (2005). The trouble with networks: Managing the Scots' early-modern Madeira trade. *Business History Review, 79*(3), 467–491.

Hoppit, J. (2002). *Risk and Failure in English Business 1700–1800*. Cambridge University Press.

Jacob, M. C. (2014). *The First Knowledge Economy: Human Capital and the European Economy, 1750–1850*. Cambridge: Cambridge University Press.

Janzen, O. U. (ed.) (1998). *Merchant Organization and Maritime Trade in the North Atlantic: 1660–1815* (No. 15). St. John's, Newfoundland: International Maritime Economic History Association.

Koenig, T. & Gogel, R. (1981). Interlocking corporate directorships as a social network. *American Journal of Economics and Sociology*, 37–50.

Lambrecht, J. (2005). Multigenerational transition in family businesses: a new explanatory model. *Family Business Review, 18*(4), 267–282.

Lamikiz, X. (2013). *Trade and Trust in the Eighteenth-Century Atlantic World: Spanish Merchants and their Overseas Networks* (Vol. 72). London: Boydell Press.

Landes, J. (2015). Quaker Institutional Structures. In *London Quakers in the Trans-Atlantic World* (pp. 22–36). London: Palgrave Macmillan UK.

Lee, C.M. (2000). *The Silicon Valley Edge: A Habitat for Innovation and Entrepreneurship*. Palo Alto, CA: Stanford University Press.

Lee, K. & Jin, X. (2009). The origins of business groups in China: an empirical testing of the three paths and the three theories. *Business History, 51*(1), 77–99.

Lodhi, A. Q. & Tilly, C. (1973). Urbanization, crime, and collective violence in 19th-century France. *American Journal of Sociology, 79*(2), 296–318.

Lupton, D., (1999). *Risk*. Routledge.

Maclean, M., Harvey, C. & Clegg, S. (2016). Conceptualizing historical organization studies. *Academy of Management Review, 41*(4), 609–632.

Marzagalli, S. (2005). Establishing transatlantic trade networks in time of war: Bordeaux and the United States, 1793–1815. *Business History Review,79*(4), 811–844.

Mathias, P. (2000). 'Risk, credit and kinship in early modern enterprise', in John J. McCusker and K. Morgan (eds), *The Early Modern Atlantic Economy*, 15–35.

McFadyen, M. A. & Cannella, A. A. (2004). Social capital and knowledge creation: Diminishing returns of the number and strength of exchange relationships. *Academy of Management Journal, 47*(5), 735–746.

McWatters, C. S. & Lemarchand, Y. (2013). Merchant networks and accounting discourse: the role of accounting transactions in network relations. *Accounting History Review, 23*(1), 49–83.

Mintz, B. & Schwartz, M. (1983). Financial interest groups and interlocking directorates. *Social Science History, 7*(2), 183–204.

Mitchell, J. C. (1973). 'Networks, norms and institutions', in J. Boissevain and J.C. Mitchell (eds), *Network Analysis Studies in Human Interaction*, Netherlands: Mouton and Co., 15–36.

Model, S. (1985). A comparative perspective on the ethnic enclave: Blacks, Italians, and Jews in New York City. *International Migration Review, 19*(1), 64–81.

Morck, R. & Yeung, B. (2003). Agency problems in large family business groups. *Entrepreneurship Theory and Practice, 27*(4), 367–382.

Muldrew, C. (1998). *The Economy of Obligation: The Culture of Credit and Social Relations in Early Modern England*. London: Palgrave.

Musacchio, A. Read, I. (2007). Bankers, industrialists, and their cliques: elite networks in Mexico and Brazil during early industrialization. *Enterprise and Society, 8*(4), 842–880.

Nicholas, T. (2014). "Technology, Innovation and Economic Growth in Britain since 1870." Chap. 7, Vol. 2 of *The Cambridge Economic History of Modern Britain*. New ed. Edited by Roderick Floud, Jane Humphries, and Paul Johnson, 181–204. Cambridge: Cambridge University Press.

Niemelä, T. (2004). Interfirm cooperation capability in the context of networking family firms: The role of power. *Family Business Review, 17*(4), 319–330.

Nooteboom, B., Berger, H. & Noorderhaven, N. G. (1997). Effects of trust and governance on relational risk. *Academy of Management Journal, 40*(2), 308–338.

Olegario, R., (1999). "That Mysterious People": Jewish merchants, transparency, and community in mid-nineteenth century america. *Business History Review, 73*(2), 161–189.

Parsons, M. & Rose, M. B. (2005). The neglected legacy of Lancashire cotton: industrial clusters and the UK outdoor trade, 1960–1990. *Enterprise and Society, 6*(4), 682–709.

Podolny, J. M. & Page, K. L. (1998). Network forms of organization. *Annual Review of Sociology, 24*(1), 57–76.

Popp, A., Toms, S. & Wilson, J. (2006). Industrial districts as organizational environments: Resources, networks and structures. *Management & Organizational History, 1*(4), 349–370.

Porter, M. E. (1990). *The Competitive Advantage of Nations*. New York: Free Press.

Portes, A. Social Capital: Its Origins and Applications in Modern Sociology, *Annual Review of Sociology, 24*, 1–24.

Prior, A. & Kirby, M. (1993). The Society of Friends and the Family Firm, 1700–1830. *Business History, 35*(4), 66–85.

Pyke, F., Becattini, G. & Sengenberger, W. (eds.) (1990). *Industrial Districts and Inter-Firm Co-Operation in Italy* (pp. 125–154). Geneva: International Institute for Labour Studies.

Rauch, J. E. (2001). Business and social networks in international trade. *Journal of economic literature, 39*(4), 1177–1203.

Renzulli, L. A., Aldrich, H. & Moody, J. (2000). Family matters: gender, networks, and entrepreneurial outcomes. *Social Forces, 79*(2), 523–546.

Rose, M. B. (2000). *Firms, Networks and Business Values: The British and American Cotton Industries since 1750* (No. 8). Cambridge: Cambridge University Press.

Salvaj, E. & Couyoumdjian, J. P. (2016). 'Interlocked'business groups and the state in Chile (1970–2010). *Business History, 58*(1), 129–148.

Scott, J. (1991). Networks of corporate power: a comparative assessment. *Annual Review of Sociology, 17*(1), 181–203.

Scott, J. & Griff, C. (1984). *The Directors of Industry. The British Corporate Network, 1904–76*. Cambridge and New York: Polity Press.

Schnyder, G. & Wilson, J. (2014). 'The Structure of Networks: The transformation of UK business, 1904–2010', in T. David, G. Westerhuis (eds.). *The Power of Corporate Networks: A Comparative and Historical Perspective*. Abingdon: Taylor & Francis.

Seland, E. H. (2013). Networks and social cohesion in ancient Indian Ocean trade: geography, ethnicity, religion. *Journal of Global History, 8*(3), 373–390.

Smith-Doerr, L. & Powell, W. W. (2005). Networks and economic life. *The Handbook of Economic Sociology, 2*, 379–402.

Socolow, S. M. (1978). *Merchants of Buenos Aires 1778–1810: Family and Commerce* (No. 30). Cambridge and New York: Cambridge University Press.

Stewart, B. Skinner, J. & Edwards, A. (2008). Cluster theory and competitive advantage: The Torquay surfing experience. *International Journal of Sport Management and Marketing, 3*(3), 201–220.

Tolles, F. B. (1963). *Meeting House and Counting House: The Quaker Merchants of Colonial Philadelphia, 1682–1783*. New York: The Norton Library.

Toms, S. & Filatotchev, I. (2004). Corporate governance, business strategy, and the dynamics of networks: A theoretical model and application to the British cotton industry, 1830–1980. *Organization Studies, 25*(4), 629–651.

Useem, M. (1980). Corporations and the corporate elite. *Annual Review of Sociology, 6*(1), 41–77.

Watts, D. J. (1999). *Small Worlds: The Dynamics of Networks Between Order and Randomness*. Princeton, NJ: Princeton University Press.

Wetherell, C. (1998). Historical social network analysis. *International Review of Social History, 43*(S6), 125–144.

Wilson, J. F. & Popp, A. (2003). *Industrial Clusters and Regional Business Networks in England, 1750–1970*. Farnham: Ashgate Publishing, Ltd.

Windolf, P. (2002). *Corporate Networks in Europe and the United States*. Oxford: Oxford University Press.

Veevers, D. (2013). 'The Company as Their Lords and the Deputy as a Great Rajah': Imperial Expansion and the English East India Company on the West Coast of Sumatra, 1685–1730. *The Journal of Imperial and Commonwealth History, 41*(5), 687–709.

Yeung, H. W. C. (2000). Limits to the growth of family-owned business? The case of Chinese transnational corporations from Hong Kong. *Family Business Review, 13*(1), 55–70.

Zahedieh, N. (2010). *The Capital and the Colonies: London and the Atlantic Economy 1660–1700*. Cambridge: Cambridge University Press.

18

Business institutions and the state

Robert Millward

Introduction

The business sectors examined here are those which flourished in the nineteenth and twentieth centuries in the economies of Europe, Japan and the USA. The basic setting was one where market transactions and private capital markets came to dominate economic activities. In such a context, the state (i.e government) was an expression of collective action whether at local or central level. Two basic questions thereby arise and form the *leitmotif* of this chapter. Firstly, what did businesses want from governments? Secondly, how far did governments meet those wants and what other pressures prompted government to intervene in the activities of business firms?

The institutional settings in which these issues were resolved varied, but generally fell into one of the following. First was arms' length regulation of businesses on the basis of powers conferred by Parliaments, Senates, etc. An example would be the Sherman Anti-Trust Act in the USA but as well as dealing with competition and monopoly, regulation covered product quality, trade unions and working conditions. Then there was direct government operation of businesses in the form of municipal and state enterprises, such as the Glasgow Electricity Corporation and the French railways, Société Nationale des Chemins de Fer Français. Thirdly, the business sector came to be an important source of taxation and an instrument of economic policy in the form of grants, taxes and subsidies including investment in education and research and development.

The chapter recognises that scholars who have written on these topics come from varying backgrounds. The research method of the classic business historian involves use of company records, archives and accounts with often a focus on the individual firm. Of the topics in 'business institutions and the state' they tend to write about state and municipal enterprise. A good example is Chadeau's work (2000) on French aircraft businesses. Economic historians with a strong background in economics tend to focus on regulation and economic policy using industrial and market data, sometimes econometrically, and on pricing and investment decisions. Such are Hausman and Neufeld's studies (1990, 2002) of US electricity companies. Students of the history of government policy, with a background in history and/or social science (like Tomlinson's work, 1994, on British government industrial policy) use government archives, politicians' diaries, etc. and often write on all three topics though that is true of many of the writers referred to in this chapter.

Early industrialisation and the role of government c. 1815–70

Our starting point is the early nineteenth century as industrialisation takes off. Labour is moving from agriculture and cottage industry to central workshops and the major driving forces for change are the innovative business firms and individual entrepreneurs developing steam engines, blast furnaces, shipping, gas lighting, railways, electricity for telegraphs, new machinery and machine tools in textiles and mining: Boulton and Watt, Schneider Bros., Fielden Brothers in textiles, Lloyds insurance, the Creusot ironworks, the Electric and International Telegraph Company, St Gobern Glassworks. However, such dynamic elements were, in 1820, only a small part of the economy. Many businesses relied still on water power and the spread of factories was very much a British textiles phenomenon. Small unincorporated firms often dominated industries in American woodwork and metal manufacturing, and there were many merchant manufacturers at the heart of putting-out systems in textiles in Russia and Germany. Large scale concentrations of labour were usually found only where labour was cheap, as with unmarried females in New England textiles, and/or coerced, as in American slave cotton plantations, and Russian serf labour cereal growing estates. Agriculture was indeed still the setting for the most numerous business unit: the small tenant farm in Britain, rice paddy in Japan, the peasant farm and sharecropper in Continental Europe and the yeoman farmer in mid North America. Agriculture still accounted for 60% or more of the labour force (except in Britain and Belgium) in 1820 and 50% or more even in 1850. Many industrial activities were still located in rural areas or very small towns. Except for Britain and the Low Countries, more than 80% of the population lived in settlements of less than 5,000 inhabitants in 1820. All was to change with rapid urbanisation which brought congestion and squalor. This was to come first to Britain since it was the first industrialiser, followed closely by Belgium. At the start of the nineteenth century there was a big gap between their industries and those elsewhere, as shown in Table 18.1. Relative to its population, Britain's manufacturing sector was double that of France, Germany, Russia and the USA in 1800, and over the next 60 years it expanded much more quickly than the rest. This was to be important for the governments of these countries who wanted their own industrial sectors to develop, at the least for building up their defence industries.

What then did these business units want from government? Its traditional and indeed central role had been law and order. Protection of trade routes, a good patent system, an effective legal system for business contracts, clear property rights and governance rules were vital. Indeed, Magnusson (2009) has argued convincingly that even in the early modern period (1500–1800) this was precisely what the more advanced countries did to aid the growth of business and markets. Part of Britain's success was that by the end of the eighteenth century it had an effective central administration (embracing all Ireland since 1800), the biggest tonnage of warships of all the major powers and a merchant fleet larger than the rest of the fleets put together.

The advent of rapid industrialisation prompted new demands from business leaders. New forms of communications and energy were emerging, often nation-wide and the railway and telegraph companies, gas and water supply undertakings wanted rights of way for their lines and pipes. Since the land markets always seemed to generate obstacles, the companies appealed to government to force land sales to allow the new networks to emerge. Also as capital requirements grew, entrepreneurs sought to develop joint stock companies with a corporate identity and limited liability for which the sanction of Parliaments or Senates or royalty was needed. What other pressures were put on governments? To grant rights of way by compulsory purchase schemes, effectively gave the newcomer a monopoly position. It was not absolute since other routes could emerge, but in many of the new infrastructure industries duplicate tracks and pipes were not economic and it was not long before complaints from

Table 18.1 Manufacturing output and national income, 1800–1992 (Per head of population: USA 1913 = 100)

	Manufacturing Output[a]					Gross Domestic Product[b]					
	1800	1860	1913	1928	1953	1820	1870	1913	1928	1953	1992
USA	7	17	100	144	281	23	46	100	124	204	407
UK	13	51	91	97	167	33	61	95	96	136	296
Belgium	8	22	70	92	93	30	50	78	78	107	322
France	7	16	47	62	71	23	35	65	83	108	339
Germany	7	12	67	80	106[c]	21	36	72	81	102	363
Sweden	7	12	53	67	129	22	31	58	69	134	317
Italy	6	8	21	31	48	21	28	47	56	78	304
Spain	6	9	17	22	25	20	26	42	53	53	235
Russia	4	6	16	16[d]	58[d]	14	19	28	26	57	89
Japan	5	5	16	24	32	14	14	25	36	45	362
India	4	2	2	2	4[e]	10	11	13	12	12	25

Notes: [a] 1913 boundaries.
[b] 1989 boundaries. The index is derived from Maddison's estimates in 1990 Geary-Khamis dollars.
[c] East plus West.
[d] USSR
[e] India plus Pakistan
Source: Bairoch 1982; Maddison 1995.

customers and other business firms lead to pressure for governments to regulate the prices and profits of the emerging railway, canal, telegraph, gas and water companies. The rise in factory employment in manufacturing itself generated two problems. Working and living conditions were terrible in the new factories and growing urban areas and pressures arose for regulating hours of work and use of child labour, increasingly divorced from the family environment in agriculture. The labour force was also trying to form trade unions and gain the right to strike and picket; business leaders were opposed and governments were pressed to legislate. Finally, industrialisation meant new technology for warfare; metal ships, armoured vehicles, better fire power, quicker transport by rail. Coal, iron and metal manufactures were essential, all available cheaply from Britain but each of the rising nation states wanted their own defence industries so tariff protection, especially against the British, followed, allowing their domestic manufacturing sectors to develop and provide the industrial strength for military power.

Corporate governance and labour conditions

Considering first the issues of corporate governance and the capital market, the legal system was slow to change but this did not seem to have inhibited the rise in capital formation. An increasing number of small businesses wanted transferability of shares and limited liability. Incorporation meant government (or royal charter) recognition of the company as a legal entity separate from the identity of individual shareholders. This seemed for some to be dangerous, bearing in mind past financial scandals, so each firm had to go through a long vetting process and Parliamentary scrutiny before the granting of an Act which itself was filled with due safeguards and initially this privilege was limited to companies deemed to be providing a public service like canals, roads and bridges. What we find then, in France for example, is that resort was made to the legal form of société en commandité (as for the St Gobern Glassworks) which were partnerships where some of the partners had limited liability and where the approval process was very quick. This was allowed in the 1807 Napoleonic Commercial Code which had become the basis of company law in many parts of Western Europe. Over 1848–67 in France we find some 14,400 sociétés en commandité were registered along with some 307 joint stock companies (with limited liability, i.e. the sociétés anonyms) and 52,800 simple partnerships (Fohlen, 1978, pp. 275–6). In Britain, as early as the eighteenth century, joint stock companies (many unincorporated) with transferable shares appeared in a wide variety of industries (Freeman, Pearson and Taylor, 2012, p. 23). By the middle of the nineteenth century pressures arose to make the whole question of incorporation much simpler, so we find in the 1830s in the USA many state governments stopped requiring special acts for each firm and general incorporation laws were passed that enabled incorporation by simple application and payment of fee (Lamoureaux, 2000, p. 473). In Britain the 1844 Companies Act made provision for more routine approvals of corporate status whilst Acts of 1855 and 1862 did the same for limited liability and in France 'full liberation' came in 1863 (Freedman, 1965; for more discussion of corporate governance see Part II of this book).

In the case of labour conditions, the state played a less effective role. For much of human history up to the twentieth century, the years 9–14 were a transition from childhood to remunerative labour (Kirby, 2003, p. 131). In the UK, inspectors were appointed to monitor the effect of the Factory Acts of 1833 and 1844 which specified working hours, schooling and age limits, and the 1842 and 1850 Acts for mining excluded women and children from working underground. Similar laws were passed in Western Europe and the USA. However, this government action probably had limited effects since (quite apart from American slavery and Russian serfdom) the legislation related to a narrow range of sectors-textiles and mining – whilst the bulk of child and female labour worked elsewhere in the traditional sectors of agriculture and small scale workshops in manufacturing and services. By the late nineteenth century, technology had advanced such that simple sweeping and courier duties were becoming redundant, a better educated workforce demanded and family size was starting to fall as the schooling costs of children rose.

Bad working conditions were one of the consistent complaints of trade unions, but for much of the period up to 1870, union activities were severely circumscribed which most business leaders welcomed. In Britain the Combination Laws of 1795 and 1800, passed in wartime, facilitated summary prosecutions against striking workers. Trade union organisation was ruled illegal, but under the 1824–5 Company Laws that was reversed and union activities were recognised albeit limited to questions of hours and wages, and picketing was forbidden as was any use of coercion on workers to join unions. Whilst Britain here was in the vanguard, this legislation left the way open for restrictive interpretations by the courts. It was not until the 1850s that unions started more sustained growth amongst skilled trades and, as a result of a Royal Commission report, an Act of 1871 finally removed all danger of prosecution of unions on the basis of restraint of trade and confirmed their identity by being allowed to register as friendly societies (Rule, 1988; Checkland, 1983). In the ante Civil War period, the majority of American trade unions had short lives and several courts ruled their behaviour criminal. It was from the 1860s that a more sustained growth occurred but again limited to the craft trades. In France the Revolution had swept away, in 1791, all associations of masters and men along with the medieval guilds. Associations of more than 20 persons were forbidden as was picketing and strikes. Article 1781 of the Civic Code had stated that the master's word was final in any dispute whilst the Penal Code classed strikes and picketing as illegal. It was not until 1864 that the Penal Code provision was abolished, and 1868 that the hated 1781 article was revoked. In the German state of Prussia, an Order of 1810 rendered strikes a criminal offence and as Clapham put it, 'obedience was due to the point of absolute servility' (1961, p. 705). Restrictions on union activities in Germany were not relaxed until the 1860s, the first state being heavily industrialised Saxony, and significant growth did not materialise until the early 1900s (Stolper et al., 1967).

International business and tariff protection

As well as suppression of unions and legislation for incorporation, most businesses sought protection from foreign competition. It was, however, a double-edged sword in that if tariffs were levied on raw materials like iron ore as well as final manufactured products like rail track and steam engines, the effective level of protection for manufacturing firms would be so much less. This was the case in Britain in the early years of the nineteenth century in that several protective duties were carried over from the mercantilist eighteenth century practices (glass, silk cloth, Indian cotton cloth) but since there was also duties on raw cotton, timber and iron ore, British manufacturers were not heavily protected even at this early date. But then from the 1820s, and especially in the 1840s which included the Corn Law repeals, import duties fell significantly and quota restrictions revoked. By the 1860s tariffs were largely absent for manufactured imports. Britain had in fact little to fear from foreign competition: it came to dominate world manufactured exports, accounting for 40% by 1870 of which cotton cloth was an important ingredient to the tune of 80% of British output being exported. This consequence of early British industrialisation had potentially devastating effects on manufacturing industries in Continental Europe which prompted pressure groups for tariff protection and with governments especially sympathetic to protection for heavy industrial products like metals and minerals important for the development of domestic defence industries and military power. Britain therefore came to be the exception in not protecting industrial products, which rose consistently elsewhere. Some economic historians have wondered whether some of the tariff protection was motivated by the need to raise government revenues but the evidence does not support that. Customs revenues averaged only 10–15% of total central government revenues in this period. Britain was again the exception where the average was about 35% and reflected the duties on 'luxuries' like wine, tobacco, tea, coffee and sugar (Mitchell, 2003a; Schremmer, 1989; Bairoch, 1982). It is relevant to also record here that the business sector was not a significant source of tax revenues in this period. Direct taxes fell on land, buildings and individuals rather than as company taxes, and direct taxes (save the Russian poll tax) tended to decline in relative importance. Rising revenues came from internal excise taxes on the luxuries plus salt, kerosene, beer, stamp duty, gunpowder.

In Continental Europe, opposition to tariff protection was limited to port merchants (e.g., in Hamburg) who feared a decline in business, and manufacturers at the end of product chains (printed cloth, etc.) who did not want tariffs on raw materials like raw cotton and wool and did not fear competition for their own products which were tailor made for local customers. Another complication was that the still independent German states (like Prussia, Bavaria) were engaged in merging into a new free trade customs area, the Zollverein. Established in 1834, the new common external tariff was kept low (less than 10% on manufactures), despite the protests of Bavarian manufacturers, in part reflecting the vested interests of the powerful eastern Prussian Junker estates whose cereal export markets might have been prejudiced. But from the 1850s the real level of duties was about to rise. Indeed for most businesses in Continental Europe, the more typical position about imports was given, as early as 1816, by the Chamber of Commerce in St Etienne who stated that "...the progress of French industry is mainly due to the prohibition... [of imports]... of large numbers of manufactured articles" (Clapham, 1961, p. 72). French tariffs on iron and steel were 45–50% of import prices as early as 1814 and rose thereafter, buttressed in some products by quota restrictions. By 1841 the average level of duties was 40–60% and by 1858–60, manufactured goods accounted for only 3.8% of French imports. There was a similar pattern in Russia with tariffs on manufactures reaching 50–75% by the mid-1850s (Bairoch, 1989; Crisp, 1976; Gatrell, 1986). For many products, the large transport costs to the USA reduced their competitive edge and there was no doubt some revenue motive to the tariffs levied by the Federal government since the customs was the Fed's only tax source. Tariffs on manufactures averaged 40% in 1832. Textiles, bar iron, refined sugar, pottery, coal, vinegar, candles, paper: all carried duties of the order of 50% for much of this period. At least one industry benefited. The US cotton manufacturing industry, despite claims by several business historians (cf Lazonick, 1983) about its institutional and technological superiority, "would have attained no more than a fraction of its actual size" in the absence of tariffs (Harley, 1992, p. 580). It is true that in mid-century some countries flirted with freer trade, France and Russia in particular, but it did not last long and heavy protection resumed by the end of the 1870s.

Regulation of the new communications networks

So the business sector largely got what it wanted by way of protection from British competition. The other major requirement was for government approval of rights of way for the extensive development of transport, telecoms and energy and this in turn prompted regulation of the quasi monopolies. Whilst the broad pattern of utility regulation was similar in all countries, the way the business/government interface developed reflected three factors: the early British lead; the role of national defence; the amount of free land. The 1838 Prussian Railway Law typified the way governments approached regulation by setting the level of fares and freight rates and, in some countries as here, establishing rights to 24–50% of profits over a stated threshold. There had long been regulation of canal tolls in Britain but whereas competition between the canal barges was feasible, it was not so for railway traffic so conveyance rates also had to be controlled. Parliamentary Acts granted rights of way and set charges for the new British railway companies like the Great Western and North Eastern. In the USA it was state governments, but since networks were spreading beyond state boundaries, there were pressures for Federal intervention which did not arrive until the 1880s. Britain was the leader in railways and also in gas lighting with businesses like London Gas, Light and Coke exploiting the huge potential Britain had for coal gas. The British lead was such that when public lighting came to Berlin in 1826 it was via British engineers and the English company, Imperial Combined Gas Association. The Paris Gas Company started in 1855 as a merger of 8 firms whilst Compagnie des Eaux from 1853 was given the task of developing an integrated water supply for the capital. By 1851 there were 129 statutory gas corporations (i.e. formed by Parliamentary Act) in Britain and there had been a similar large increase in joint stock water companies (Hassan, 1985). Britain also set the lead in the electric telegraph. The domestic market was initially dominated by the Electric International Telegraph Company with competition arriving later with the UK Telegraph Company. In the embryonic international cable market, Britain's technological lead in coal, iron and shipping was so large that most of the new overland and submarine cables were laid by British companies like the Atlantic (later Anglo-American) Company established in 1865–6 such that, whilst cables were strategically sensitive, the government did little, given the pattern of ownership (Headrick and Griset, 2001). It was more concerned about the haphazard development of the domestic market, perhaps also because of worries about Ireland and the industry was nationalised in 1868. The lead in international cables lasted until the 1920s when, as French and German state owned international cable networks grew, the British government became concerned, leading to the establishment of Cable and Wireless Ltd., which later became a wholly state owned enterprise.

Strategic concerns were much to the fore in Continental Europe where new nation states were emerging in Belgium, Italy and eventually Germany. Many states had hostile neighbours on their borders so that links to the borders and armies were vital. Governments were especially nervous about the electric telegraph and all systems (like Postes, Téléphone et Télégraphe) eventually became integrated into government departments. Several of the still independent German states like Wurtemburg and Bavaria, promoted and operated railways, especially the trunk networks. The Prussian government also developed a big trunk network of lines which stretched, by the 1860s, from Berlin to Hamburg, Stettin, Danzig and Breslau. Indeed, so committed was it to strengthening its military power that it became heavily involved in mining and manufacturing, especially in Silesia and the Saar. The Ruhr coal mines were run on a concession and 20% of all German coal was state owned by 1850 (Henderson, 1958; Tilly, 1966). The French government was strongly interventionist from the very beginning. On the basis of an 1842 Act, the 28 rail companies were merged into six networks radiating from Paris. The Codes operated by the elite Corps developed a system of concessions for the whole range of infrastructure services and the concessionaires could be private or publicly owned. Businesses were vetted, their operations scrutinised and even their forecasts challenged as in the case of the Paris-St Germain railway in the 1830s (Radcliffe, 1973).

Both Russia and America had huge land areas to develop, and in this respect differed from Western Europe. In its imperialist drives eastwards and to the south, Russia had to overcome or accommodate some long established communities and the bureaucracy and army were heavily involved. In the midnineteenth century the Tsarist governments were still wary of industrialisation, which they equated with democratisation and revolution. Railways came late. By 1850 only 501 kilometres had been laid as compared to 2,915 in France, 5,656 in Germany and 9,797 in Britain (Mitchell, 2003). Early lines were strategically placed and government backed: Moscow-St Petersburg; Warsaw to the Austrian border. State encouragement gradually increased, if only from fear of external enemies, and it part supported one large multinational, the Grande Société des Chemins de Fer, which was established in 1857 with involvement also by Rothschilds and the Pereire Brothers but which quickly crossed swords with the Russian bureaucracy and was later taken over completely by the state (Cameron, 1961). The USA picture was very different. The Federal government initially owned most of the land and developed a chain of outposts to facilitate rapid settlement. From 1796, land was sold at $2 per acre, lower later. By 1862, Homestead Act settlers with 5 years residence could get a 160 acre patch free. In this respect the Fed was one of world's largest state owned enterprises (Galambos, 2000a). It also approved four trans-continental railroads in the 1860s but credit scandals scotched that and the Fed vowed never again to involve itself in such schemes. Lower levels of government were, however, deeply involved early on with towns competing for stops, and states competing for routes. Dobbin (1994) called it rivalistic state mercantilism. By 1850 some 14,518 kilometres of track had been laid and by 1870 over one half of US railway capital was government owned. The early involvement of the state governments led to corruption and financial scandals. The municipalities then took the lead but their rising debt, in the face of other demands for spending on sanitation, water supply and fire services lead them to pull in their reins. The future lay with private business capital.

Big business and the growth of government, 1870–1930

The period from 1870 witnessed immense advances in industrial technology, productivity and national outputs. Developments in chemicals, electricity, steel and engineering generated more complex products and a shift to more capital intensive processes. Apart from textiles, it was these heavy industries which led. Economies of scale in production and marketing induced businesses to horizontally and vertically integrate to secure raw material sources and spread research and development results, thereby generating large corporations: US Steel, Vickers, Krupps, the Putilov armaments company in Russia. Industrial concentration increased often via mergers and holding companies (like Guest, Keen and Nettlefold in Britain). Nearly 2,000 American manufacturing firms disappeared into consolidations in the years 1895–1904 by which time there were over 300 price fixing agreements (cartels) in Germany. Secondly, communications and energy networks spread to straddle the whole areas of nation states and international links emerged. By 1913 the rail networks had more or less reached their limit. Telephones continued to expand, the telegraph also (internationally by overland and submarine cables), oceanic shipping forged ahead, regional electricity grids were emerging and oil and airlines had entered the picture by the 1920s. In all these sectors again, economies of scale were present with large companies emerging like the Midlands Railway in Britain, Bell telephones in the USA and Thomas Houston in electricity and tramways in both Europe and the USA. Thirdly, populations were rising everywhere, trebling in the USA from 1870–1930 and doubling in Russia and Japan. Since most of this was concentrated in towns, new infrastructures were needed for gas, electricity, water and tramways. Mortality levels and family size were still very high and the congestion and health issues could no longer be ignored. The fourth and final distinctive element, at least in Western Europe, was the rise of trade unions and calls for shorter hours and minimum wages. The size of each union was growing, in part reflecting the labour force's response to the growth of large firms but also from the perceived gains from collective bargaining.

Competition, cartels and anti-trust

The business sector still wanted law and order, especially for commercial transactions, but the new technologies generated pressures on governments to curb monopoly power in both manufacturing and infrastructure industries, to ensure their defence industries kept up with modern technologies, to adjudicate on the rights of trade unions and, for both central and local government, to confront the rising regulatory and financial problems associated with new businesses for urban infrastructure and with the increasing environmental problems which accompanied rapid urbanisation. Let us first consider the advent of large firms in manufacturing, mining and oil and how governments responded. The issue was most obvious in the USA as mass production and continuous throughput methods grew in many sectors, stimulating the growth of huge firms like US Rubber, duPont, American Sugar Refining and Armour & Co.[1] The state governments and the Fed were drawn into monitoring and regulating big business through complaints not only from customers but from small businesses feeling the hard edge of competition. The establishment of the Federal Meat Inspection Service in 1891 followed complaints from butchers in Eastern towns facing severe competition from Chicago butchers on the advent of refrigerated railcars. The 1889 Sherman Anti-Trust Act was triggered by small oil refineries, who used barrels for transport to retail markets, and who resented their loss of markets from Standard Oil's introduction of rail tank cars. The later prosecution of Standard Oil in 1911 was prompted by pressure from competitors like Kansas Oil producers and the Supreme Court ruled that the Standard Oil empire be broken up (so also American Tobacco at the same time). The 1889 Act was actually quite generally worded, which was useful as a guideline, but not for specific practices like tying clauses which were not spelled out until the 1914 Clayton Act. Nor was the onward march of large firms halted particularly, one measure of which was that, by 1927, 97.6% of all US manufacturing firms were incorporated (as opposed to partnerships etc.; Keller, 1990; Gugliemo and Troseken, 2007). Federal regulation and initiatives only applied to inter-state transactions, the Fed did not acquire powers to incorporate until the 1930s and the existence of different regulatory regimes in different US states meant much anti-competitive activity was ignored. The New Jersey state government notoriously ruled that 'business is a private matter'.

The German government also did little to curb concentration and it noticeably sanctioned, if only by default, the growth of cartels. It was only in the 1850s that German industrialisation took off and the new Reich government from 1870 offered no resistance to the Central Association of German manufacturers, a key lobby group for cartels and tariffs. Cartels proliferated in mining, steel, chemicals, glass and cement and the regulation that emerged was limited mainly to a 1923 Ordinance that cartel agreements had to be published and monitored (Maschke, 1963; Marburg, 1964). Mergers did blossom in France in the 1920s (Schneider, Kuhlmann and Westinghouse in electrical machinery) but for most of the 1870–1930 period, it remained the home of small works and family firms with large companies often taking the form of holding companies, as in chemicals where the financial assets of the largest firms were equal to 80% of the value of their real capital assets (Levy-Leboyer, 1978). The apogee of British manufacturing and mining was the 1860s and 1870s when it had little to fear from foreign competition. Although nothing like the scale of the USA, big businesses did grow (Lancashire Cotton Corporation, Distillers, Unilever and Cadburys), some of which were family firms. The common law had traditionally disapproved of restraints of trade so that price fixing and cartels made little headway until the 1920s when Britain's lead came under attack. Then the Lord Chancellor ruled that competition might drive manufacturers out of business and by the end of that decade some 20% of employment was in industries with price fixing agreements (Hannah, 1983; Tolliday, 1986).

Britain in the 1920s therefore was protecting its industry like other countries had done throughout the nineteenth century. At the limit, weak industry meant a weak military. Whereas the size of the army, in continental Europe, had been a traditionally important dimension of military strategy, by the late nineteenth century it was shipyards, warships, rifles and other modernised armaments plus fast rail lines to the borders, secure telegraph and, in the early twentieth century, a new energy infrastructure, the electricity grid. Ensuring there was a minimum of domestic industry to produce shipping, rails and armaments shaped the policy of Continental governments, who also therefore returned to tariff protection after a brief flirtation with freer trade in the mid-nineteenth century. The emphasis was heavy industry but protection there often required accommodating older vested interests in other sectors, especially agriculture. Thus in France, tariffs on manufactures averaged 12–15% of import prices in the 1870s and the Meline tariff of 1892 introduced a wide range of tariffs on manufactured goods which averaged 20% by 1913 (34% for British goods). France still, however, had a big agricultural sector with a huge number of small farms and many opposed, along with small industrial workshops, the rise of big business. Farm businesses with less than 25 acres accounted for 85% of the total in 1892. Agricultural tariffs rose relentlessly from the 1870s, by 1915 the tariff on wheat was 35% and protection continued on all goods into the 1920s. The German Reich had also been raising duties, crowned by the Bülow tariff of 1902 and by 1913 the tariff on manufactures was at about the average level in Europe whilst that on cereals was 'high' (Clapham, 1961; Bairoch, 1989). The most heavily protected country was Russia for whom tariffs were part revenue raising. The more secure inner Russian industries in the Donetz, Ukraine and the Urals were singled out for more protection and subsidy than the industries in politically unreliable Poland (then part of Russia). Tariffs on manufactures were some 15–20% in the 1870s, followed by large increases for iron, coal, pig iron, steel and machinery. By 1913 there were many quota restrictions on imports and the unrestricted duties averaged 29.5% (131% for British goods; Crisp, 1972; Gatrell, 1985; Bairoch, 1989). American industry was developing so well that it would be difficult to characterise the case for tariffs as an infant industry argument. It was straight protection, very important for some sectors like cotton, not needed at all for some others, albeit useful as the Fed's only tax source. Rates were high after the Civil War, and then in 1890 the McKinley tariff raised duties on textiles, tinplate, steel rails, iron and wheat. By 1913 duties averaged 37.6%. The Fordney-McCumber tariff of 1922 raised duties on foods and manufactures by 30% and after the introduction of the 1930 Hawley-Smoot tariff, duties averaged 59.1% (possibly the highest in all American history: Kindleberger, 1989; Bairoch, 1989).

State enterprises in heavy industry, energy and communications

The military issues behind tariff protection were also a prime driving force in the more direct involvement of Continental European governments in their business sectors. Support for heavy industry, energy and communication links were very clearly motivated, not by any modern notions of raising economic growth and living standards, but by defence considerations. This was very clear in Germany where ironworks, shipyards, coal, copper and silver mines, lignite, saltworks and smelters figured prominently in the range of public enterprises in manufacturing and mining set up by Prussia and other state governments with the Reich subsidising shipyards. There was much reflection in Germany on the ill preparedness for World War I with attention shifting in the 1920s to self-sufficiency and Eastern Europe. Import substitutes were developed by state holding companies like VIAG (Vereiningten Industrie Unternehmungen, established 1923) and VEBA (Vereiningten Elektriziitats u. Bergwerk AG, 1929) with extensive interests in tin, lead, oil, coal and electricity (Hentschel, 1989; Henderson, 1958; Overy, 2003; Wengenroth, 2000). The government of Japan, emerging into world trade after the Meiji Restoration of 1868, was also selective in its interventions. The European colonial powers dominated the Far East and prevented Japan from imposing tariffs, which only became possible at the turn of the century. Instead the traditional agricultural sector (silk, etc.) was encouraged to grow and generate export earnings, facilitating the import of heavy machinery. On this basis state shipyards and armaments factories were built up and in 1901 the Yawata state ironworks was established and became a major producer of iron ore by the 1920s (Samuels, 1994). Russia's technical backwardness was exposed several times in the nineteenth century (Crimea 1854–5, Berlin Conference 1878, Japanese war 1904–5) making the Tsarist governments painfully aware of the need to boost industry. State enterprises were started in shipbuilding (the Russian Baltic Ironworks and Machinery Company), naval dockyards (Izhara), armaments factories, mining and iron ore in the Urals. The New Russian Iron Company (actually British owned) benefited from state loans and orders and the government awarded generous contracts to all private firms producing uniforms and armaments or supplying coal, iron, rails and rolling stock to the various state enterprises (Gatrell, 1994). The French government was less directly involved but even here it is clear that the focus was the defence industries. There were already 64 state arsenals in 1870 and shipyards were protected. The weaknesses revealed by WWI lead to the state takeover of Potasses d'Alsace. The Popular Front 1936–7, seemingly committed to wide intervention, limited its action to the aircraft and airline sectors, taking over many of the assets of companies like Hotchkiss, Renault, Schneider-Cresot and Brandt, a two-thirds share in five new aircraft companies and a one quarter of the shares in Air France, establish in 1935 with a 75% subsidy on turnover (Chadeau, 2000; Clarke, 1977). Even the British government had its own naval dockyards (Portsmouth, etc.) and armaments factories (Woolwich). The private sector was however so well developed with companies like Vickers that the government felt able to rely on it in times of war such that in WWI the bulk of the increase in shipping came from the Glasgow and other private yards (Peebles, 1987).

Whereas the governments of Continental Europe and Japan were selective in the parts of manufacturing in which they were involved, this was not true of communications and energy networks. A rising tendency to concentration brought increasing government regulation everywhere, not necessarily public ownership, but rather control on prices and service levels. State ownership did increase for railways, telecoms and electricity but this was motivated by strategic reasons not monopoly. The tendency for concentration in railways is illustrated most vividly in the two countries where strategic factors were largely absent, the UK and the USA. The 1850s and 1860s in the UK saw several amalgamations such as those involving the North Eastern and Great Eastern Railways. Although 'courting' between companies was actually barred by Parliament in 1872, working agreements and conference meetings continued and, by 1907, 13 companies accounted for 86% of track mileage, most of which was owned by the big 4: North Western, Great Western, North Eastern and Midlands (Gourvish, 1980; Irving, 1978). Rail track mileage in the USA reached 250,000 by 1913 with systems organised around connection centres like Chicago and St Louis, involving large companies like Michigan Central. Seven groups accounted for two-thirds of the track mileage and 85% of the revenues, attracting a constant stream of complaints, especially from farmers who had to pay high rates on lines, often short distance, where there was little competition. The 1887 Inter-State Commerce Act had brought in Federal regulation though, given the vague wording of the Act and weak enforcement mechanisms, much was left, as in other industries, for the courts to resolve. In telecoms the dominance of Western Union for telegraph and Bell for telephone also escaped strong state intervention. Bell acquired Western Electric, the major equipment producer, in 1882 and in 1899 vested all its assets in American Telegraph and Telephone which bought out Western Union in 1909. By WWI the Inter-State Commerce Commission had taken powers over telecoms though it was not until the establishment of the Federal Communications Commission in 1934 that a consolidated Federal approach was in place (Fishlow, 2000; Gugliemo and Troesken, 2007; Vietor, 1989).

Regulation was more effective in Continental Europe where the strategic importance of the networks militarily led also to direct state ownership and operation, as had already occurred in telecoms. The planned French rail network was strongly supported by the government which took over the financially threatened Western company (and Paris-Orleans line) and, at the end of WWI, the Alsace and Lorraine network from Germany. The Prussian state government nationalised its railways in 1879, and by 1906 some 93% of German railways were publicly owned, by which time Italy was in a similar position (Doukas, 1945; Stevenson, 1999; Fremdling and Knieps, 1993). Even more remarkable was Japanese progress in communications. Telecoms were operated as a state monopoly from within the Ministry of Communications. Private rail development was slow so that, in 1906, 17 companies were taken over by the state which, by WWI, owned railways also in Korea and Manchuria. The indigenous merchant fleet was tiny in 1870 but, given Japan's ambitions, security of raw materials from the Asian mainland was vital. Two major shipping companies (Nihon Yuzen Kaisha and Osaka Shögen Kaisha) had emerged with state support by the late 1880s and a major subsidy programme was mounted to make Japan self-sufficient in shipping. During 1905–13, 72 out of 78 warships were built in Japan whilst, by 1919, Japan was the world's third largest ship owner (Yamamura, 1977; Andordugoy, 2001). Even the Russian government had shed some of its worries about the political and social upheavals which might follow industrial modernisation and rail track mileage rose from 7,000 in 1870 to 48,000 by 1913. Work on the state owned Trans-Siberian railway was completed in 1901 and by 1913 some two-thirds of the track was owned by the government (Westwood, 1991). In part this shift to state ownership throughout Europe reflected the declining profitability of railways as more remote settlements were targeted and the condition of many systems deteriorated during WWI by over usage and freezing of fares and freight rates. Given their strategic significance, few governments could let their railway systems collapse so the early 1920s saw major government sponsored reorganisations. In America, with less at stake, it was more a matter of streamlining the price structures and other regulatory changes. In 1919 the Deutsche Reichsbann emerged as the imperial railway for all of Germany and managed to survive constant raids for revenue as part of the post-war reparations payments to the allies. In France from 1921, all the net profits of the five private companies and two state owned were pooled into a Fonds Commun with the hope that by cross subsidisation, the whole system would break even. Even Britain, now conscious that it was no longer such a dominant industrial power, passed a Railway Act in 1921 whereby the large number of companies were merged into four regional private regulated monopolies: Southern, Great Western, London North Eastern and London, Midland, Scottish. Few had anticipated the devastating competition on the horizon from road transport. Railway systems were already state owned in some other parts of Europe and the 1930s and 1940s saw this extended to Britain, Spain, Sweden and France.

Similar portents of state ownership were on the horizon in the new infrastructure industries of the early twentieth century: electricity, oil and airlines. The latter two were in only the early stages of development so European governments subsidised aircraft production and airlines (cf Air France) and took shares in multi-national oil companies like the Turkish Petroleum Company (which morphed later into British Petroleum). Electricity was a more urgent case. The development of alternating current facilitated the lengthening of transmission lines for electricity which was fast becoming a key fuel alongside coal. The nineteenth century inheritance was a hotchpotch of small urban private and municipal enterprises which proved difficult to merge into a national system. Britain set the lead in the establishment of the state owned Central Electricity Board in 1926 but strong centralising elements were already present in Swedish and Norwegian hydro-electricity and in Germany the Reich, states and municipalities joined to establish regional networks such that by 1928, public authorities accounted for two-thirds of German electricity output (Hannah, 1979; Mulert, 1929). Surprisingly, electricity was the one area where the French government intervened only tentatively and it was left to the establishment of Électicité de France (EDF) in the late 1940s for full integration to be achieved, as it was similarly in Italy with the formation of Ente Nazionale de l'Energia Elettrica (ENEL) in 1962. Even the American Federal government was able, via the Tennessee Valley Authority in the 1930s, to overcome some of the problems associated with flows across state borders.

Private utilities and municipal enterprise in the new urban infrastructure

In addition to meeting strategic concerns about national defence and fielding complaints about industrial concentration, the third area of concern for government 1870–1930 arose from urbanisation. The issue was congested living and working conditions. New factories were at the heart of air and water pollution but their owners also wanted local government to provide good fire services and reliable water supplies. Some of the new infrastructure was partly supplied by private utilities like the London Gas, Light and Coke Company. But there were also many municipally or state owned enterprises in these sectors like the Cochitate Waterworks in Boston, USA and the Preussische Elektrizitäts in Germany. The responsibility for sanitation, fire and police fell on local governments financed mainly by local property taxes whilst regulation of housing and the environment was shared by local and central government. The focus here will be to explain the pattern of regulation and ownership for gas, water, electricity, tramways and other urban transit and how that related to the finance of local government. Regulation of the environment, including housing, will be touched on but space precludes systematic treatment of this big subject.

It is no accident that the halcyon years of local government, 1870–1930, coincided with a huge increase in urban populations. In 1870 already over one half of the UK population lived in towns with 5,000 or more inhabitants, rising to 70% by 1913. Levels were lower elsewhere but the rate of increase was higher with Germany rising from 25% to 51% and the USA from 25% in 1880 to 47% by 1920 (Bairoch, 1982; US Bureau of the Census, 1875). Mortality was falling as air and water borne diseases came under control but there were still some 17 deaths per 1,000 population and 100 or more infant deaths per 1,000 live births in France, Germany and Ireland just before WWI – and even higher levels in Eastern Europe. Rates had started to fall but many mothers were still having to cope with families of 5 or more children. A significant feature of American towns was the growing number of them with waterworks systems (as opposed to relying on streams and ponds): by 1880 more than one half of all towns with 2,500 inhabitants or more. A concession for the water supply in Paris was given to the Compagnie des Eaux in 1857 but France had nothing like the problems of poor water supplies of Britain where early industrial demand for water added to residential needs so that the first half of the nineteenth century saw a large number of new big joint stock water companies like the New River and Grand Junction in London (Jacobbson, 2000; Hassan, 1985; Melosi, 2000). There were some improvements in the technology of pipes and reservoirs but unit costs and charges for water (relative to other prices) tended to rise as companies had to seek more distant lakes and rivers. Since water quality was increasingly monitored by local and central governments and controls put on prices, there was a financial squeeze on the water companies which seems to have been the most likely trigger for the eventual domination of this industry by publicly owned enterprises. In the USA 47% of waterworks were municipally owned in 1870 and 70% by 1924 (New York, Cincinnati, etc.). The figure for the UK for 1900 was 80%, France 75% in 1913, 100 % in Sweden and Denmark (Millward, 2000, 2005).

It is a rather different picture for the businesses found in gas, electricity and urban transit where there was much less municipal ownership. Real unit costs tended to fall in the nineteenth century as bigger units emerged, serving dense urban populations and with less need to tap natural resources like land and rivers. Privately owned businesses were the prime movers in the development of the gas industry in the early nineteenth century (British Gas Company, Danish Gas Company) and in electricity and tramways at the end of the century (Berlin Tramways Company, Berliner Elektrizitäts, Edison in Milan, Compagnie Générale d'Omnibus in Paris, Thomas Houston, Hydro Electrica Iberia). Municipalisation of gas started in the mid-nineteenth century (and hence, like water supply, well before any possible connection with socialism). In Germany one half of all gas works were municipally owned by 1880 and 30% in the UK by 1885. But the incidence was patchy with little more than 2% in the USA and Italy by the turn of the century. For electricity supply, the UK figure was again fairly high in 1900 at 71.6% as it was in Norway but the rest was generally less than 20% (Millward, 2005). Moreover, within the UK and Germany there were big geographical differences with municipalisation much more common in growing industrial towns. It seems most likely that municipal enterprises in Europe were acting as 'cash cows' and Keller suggests similar factors operated for the smaller number of cases in the USA. Operating profits could be transferred to the cities' coffers to help alleviate the local property taxes which were rising relentlessly in rapidly expanding towns like Darmstadt, Mainz, Mannheim, Bolton, Glasgow and Stoke which faced mounting public health expenditure programmes. Old sleepy rural towns without significant public health problems were happy to remain with private utilities. At the other extreme, some very large town councils were able to obviate municipalisation by making lucrative deals with large private companies as Copenhagen, Paris and Berlin did with the Danish Gas Company, Paris Gas and Deutsche Edison Gesellschaft. Of course the municipalities had themselves to be of significant size and efficiently run and this largely explains why municipalisation was not common in the small communes of France and Belgium and why the London County Council Tramways, the Metropolitan Water Board and the Metropolitan Borough Electricity Corporations did not emerge until the early 1900s after London government had been rescued from its hotchpotch of authorities by the reorganisation of the 1890s.

Business versus trade unions

The final area in 1870–1930 where government was drawn to intervene in the business sector was in relation to trade unions. Britain was in the lead in this respect and many employers, by the end of the nineteenth century, had come to recognise the right of labour to form unions. Whilst the railway and shipping companies notoriously refused, by 1889 official recognition could be found in all craft trades, cotton, iron, steel and some coalfields. It was about this time that 'new unions' emerged covering large numbers of firms and/or sectors and aiming to engage in collective bargaining. In part it gave the unions more strike power but also it reflected the growing industrial concentration; in coal, cotton and iron employers were clearly colluding in setting wage levels (Lovell, 1987, p. 12; Checkland, 1983). Government recognition had come with the 1875 Conspiracy Act and the 1876 Trade Union Act establishing trade unions as voluntary societies with all the rights of unincorporated bodies and allowing combinations and picketing in strike action provided they were specifically related to a trade dispute. The 1896 Conciliation Act facilitated more government scrutiny of strikes by empowering the Board of Trade to investigate the causes of dispute and attempt mediation. These and other changes meant that by 1914 trade unions had significant rights but they could not coerce other workers or strike 'against the community'. This last restraint was reiterated, following the General Strike of 1926, in the Trade Disputes and Trade Union Acts of 1926–7 which explicitly declared illegal all strikes aimed at pressure on government and the community. Notwithstanding these curbs, British trade unions had been allowed to develop much more freely than elsewhere. In America the common law treated workers as free agents who assumed all risks in their workplace, whoever caused them, so strikes and closed shops were declared illegal. Despite the efforts of the American Federation of Labour and some clauses in the Clayton Act of 1914, unions had an uncertain legal status until the 1935 Wagner Act established bargaining rules and the unions' right to organise. High wages in a country with plenty of natural resources and scarce labour probably accounts for the slow growth of unions and the absence of strong political links. In the nineteenth century firms were able to force workers to sign agreements not to join a union and the 1887 Sherman Anti-Trust Act was used on occasion to control strike action, most noticeably in the 1892 strike at the Carnegie Steel Co. in Homestead which ended with the Pennsylvania state governor putting the town under martial law (Margo, 2000). The attitude of both business and government in Japan to trade unions is captured in the 1900 Peace Police Law which barred many group activities, including 'labour organisation' and strikes (Hunter, 1989, p. 241). The legal position of trade unions was at best ambiguous even in the 1920s and by 1931 there was still only 8% of workers in unions. In Germany also, recognition and growth came late. There were only

0.3 million union members in 1895 (1.4 in the UK). Numbers did grow strongly thereafter but the German unions were loose and disjointed and collective bargaining was slow to develop, only taking off in 1906–14. The antagonism of the Reich governments was matched on labour's side by being more strongly linked to political parties than elsewhere. Historians suggest it was the Weimar Republic in the 1920s which first recognised trade unions when the labour contract was acknowledged by government as the normal way to regulate industrial relations (Stolper et al., 1967; Clapham, 1961). The large conservative peasantry was another delaying factor as it was in France where rural trade unions lagged behind the others, with the Vineyard strike of 1904 the first of its kind. Unions had grown strongly in Paris but it was not until 1884 that complete freedom of association had been given to wage earners. By 1911 there were just over 1 million trade union members in France (then over 3m. in the UK). The years 1900–30 were marked by widespread strikes in Western Europe and with the onset of the depression in the 1930s the grievances of labour rose and the business sector came under even more pressure as state intervention really took off.

The state in business: from public ownership to regulation, 1930–2010

The economic depression of the 1930s and the crippling levels of unemployment raised questions about the reliability of the business sector and many countries looked to the state to rescue capitalism. Its role was no longer to be simply promoting law and order, bolstering national defence and unification. It was now also a concern for living standards, employment and economic growth. For the American economic historian Fishback, 1930–45 was a "seemingly endless period of national emergency, to which government, at all levels,...had responded in unprecedented ways...Americans would look to government for more and more sources of security" (2007, p. 507). Such intervention in the USA took the form in part of arms' length regulation and subsidies. It was an addition to the set of interventions for defence, order, property rights, anti-trust and trade union power which continued throughout the twentieth century. There was one area where, even in America, government intervention took the form of direct provision and that was in education and research to promote technological advance and build up human capital. In Europe, the reaction to the depression and WWII took the form of wide scale public ownership of key industrial sectors, plus a competition policy along the lines of American anti-trust. From the 1980s, that concern about the economy was sustained but public ownership was abandoned in many sectors. It was often replaced by tough arms' length regulation so that some observers, by the early 2000s, thought the state had hardly retreated. We shall discuss these issues in three parts, firstly the move to public ownership, secondly the anti-monopoly policies and those restraining the power of trade unions and finally the role of education and R&D (research and development) in the links between business and the state.

Public ownership and planning: rise and fall

A big shift to state ownership of industry and agriculture in Russia had of course started in the 1920s following the Bolshevik Revolution. Initially a form of market socialism emerged in that major parts of the economy had been taken over by the state, but some prices and wages were left to market forces. The so-called 'New Economic Policy' was however introduced under the cloud of civil war conditions 1918–21 (Nove, 1972; Davies, 1989; Davis, 1999). In agriculture little changed and peasants were allowed to leave the land, wage labour was permitted and large estates were broken up. In industry small scale plants were largely left in the private sector and more generally, light industry and the production of consumer goods were given considerable autonomy. Heavy industry, however, was a portent of the future: production quotas and controlled supply of inputs were pervasive in energy, metallurgy and armaments as well as wholesale trade, communications and banking. Even that was too little for the Russian leaders who were increasingly fearful of their strategic weaknesses and moved to build up food supplies and defence industries quickly. Collectivised agriculture and Stalinist planning then followed in the 1930s. The output growth was huge, especially in heavy industry, but of course all semblance of a business sector had disappeared. The skewed nature of the Russian economy thereafter, the mismatch of production and demand and the distorted incentives are now well documented (Gregory, 2004). Some intrinsically dictatorial features of the nineteenth century Russian economy seem to have been carried through to this vampire socialism and indeed to the vampire oligarchic capitalism of modern Russia, 1989 onwards (Rosefielde and Hedlund, 2000).

Space precludes any detail on the eastern European economies under this type of command system (but see Chapter 12). In the 1930s it generated considerable interest in the West whose governments were however opposed to the sort of rules and orders in the Soviet system. Some felt the market needed some support if high long term growth rates were to be achieved and in some countries a form of 'indicative planning' took place geared at providing guidelines for the future, including public investment plans to which private investment might respond. It took off only in France from 1945, Italy and the UK in the 1960s. For France it was mainly a vehicle for showing it was committed to so develop its key resources as to avoid further German invasions (Lynch, 1984). In neither the UK nor Italy did it have any obvious success and did not in any case solve the more short term endemic problems of inflation, balance of payments and unemployment. Public ownership of industry was a different matter, a nuanced story, motivated by some key economic and institutional factors and only partly linked to socialism. For Western Europe, 1930–80 were the halcyon years of the state in business. By the 1950s government owned most of the railways, roads, telecoms, airlines, coal, steel, electricity, gas and water supplies together with significant shares in manufacturing and further state owned enterprises in manufacturing were set up in the 1960s and 1970s. There was not one simple driving force but three quite distinct elements. Even before 1930, some sectors had been taken into public ownership, mainly in Continental Europe, not because of any socialist ideas but because considerations of defence made them strategically significant. Hence 1815–1930, as indicated earlier, saw the public ownership of some trunk railways, practically all telecoms, most national airline flag carriers and some electricity grid networks, coal companies and manufacturing firms. Secondly, to these were added in the immediate post war period, a string of nationalisations, mostly in France and the UK: Électricité de France, Charbonnages de France and Gaz du France were established in 1946, the National Coal Board and the British Transport Commission in 1947, the British Electricity Authority (controlling the Central Electricity Generating Board and the Area Boards) and the British Gas Council (controlling the Area Boards) in 1948. State enterprises were set up in iron and steel, the central banks nationalized in both countries and in France four commercial banks were taken over, along with 36 insurance companies (Millward, 2005). These two countries had lagged behind the rest of Western Europe in public ownership but by the 1950s they were on a par. The post 1945 nationalisations did have a strategic element in them; the focus was on 'basic industries' (not textiles, not even engineering, not land) some of which had been run down during the war and now seen as central to the reconstruction of the war damaged economies. Also the formation of national networks in railways and electricity had been frustrated in the interwar period and the state started to intervene as early as the 1930s in some cases: Société Nationale des Chemins de Fer Français 1937, Statens Järnvägar (1939 Sweden) and

Red Nacional de los Ferrocarriles Españoles in 1941. Thirdly, many infrastructure industries had come to be seen as providing 'public services', albeit commercially, for which the state was expected to take some responsibility (Chick, 1998) whilst coal was the one sector where socialist forces successfully pressed for nationalisation. Note finally that whilst some writers have argued that Germany never experienced the same state intervention in the post-war period, neither did it see any diminution of what was already a big public sector.

The third element underlying state enterprise from 1930–80 relates to manufacturing. We have already recorded how strategic factors prompted a state presence in manufacturing in Germany, Russia and Japan before 1930 and in UK and France in iron and steel post 1945. In a similar vein, in Spain 1941–8 Franco's regime acquired a wide range of holdings in manufacturing and elsewhere via the new state holding company Instituto Nacional de Industria. Even more active was the Italian government from the 1930s, in this case prompted by banking failures and a new explicit commitment to using the state as a source of finance and entrepreneurship. The three key state companies, Istituto per la Ricostruzione Industriale (INI), Ente Finanziamento Industria Manifatturiera (EFIM) and Ente Nazionale Idrocaruri (ENI) held shares in lower level companies (like AGIP) in all sectors of the economy-by 1983, some 367 companies, including 157 in manufacturing (Toninelli and Vasta, 2011). The Italian economy was very successful in the 1950–70 period and, whatever the cause, it attracted the attention of other Western European countries. Whilst there developed a business model of 'national champions', behind some of the interventions was a real fear of competition from the Far East and, if 1970s Britain is any guide, that prestigious parts of the economy, like Rolls Royce, British Shipyards and Jaguar would disappear. State takeovers followed, whilst in France this occurred in the 1980s with firms like Rhone–Poulenc (chemicals), Usinov (steel), St. Gobain (glass) and Matra (missiles) (O'Hara, 2011; Chadeau, 2000).

The way these state enterprises operated has been subject to detailed investigations by many business historians as well as in government reports (Nedo, 1976; Nora, 1976). Whether or not there were sufficient incentives in these big enterprises, whether any different from big private enterprises, whether the managerial structure was too bureaucratic, have been constant themes. Whereas there is some evidence that performance was weaker in those state firms in manufacturing and oil, the evidence on productivity in the grid networks is far from clear. Perhaps of more significance is that all state enterprises were expected to break even financially and yet carried many non-profit burdens. As a result, financial deficits were common and important weapons for those pushing privatisation. Quite apart from ideological positions, several basic economic and technological developments meant that, by the 1980s, changes in structure and ownership were likely. Perhaps most significant was that suspicions hanging over from the 1930s about the private sector had disappeared. So even if some of the infrastructure industries did have potential market failure problems, arms' length regulation might be sufficient. Secondly the strategic parameters had changed. The rise of airline tourism and loss of colonies undermined the role of national airline flag carriers (Air France, British Airways). The old fears about defence security in naval dockyards, telecoms, oil companies and aircraft manufacture were giving way, it seemed, to different methods of screening and spying. This partly reflected technological change with the advent of the micro-chip which also transformed telecoms from the simple, single link line into a complex of data services, telex, email, personal computers. It also prompted the shift out of government departments (PTT, Deutsche Bundespost, British Telecom, etc.). These strategic and technological factors largely explain why the first to be privatised were telecoms, airlines and manufacturing. Grid networks in railways, water, gas and electricity in Continental Europe have tended to remain in the public sector providing a continuing contrast with the USA and the reason why, in Britain, these are the sectors where privatisation has proven most contentious (Köthenbürger, Sinn and Whalley, 2006).

Legislating for monopolies and trade unions

The rise of state enterprises after 1945 coincided with, indeed was partly linked to, the growing power of trade unions. The years from the late 1930s to the end of the 1960s saw unemployment decline and unionism has always risen in response to this kind of cyclical change. Strikes and secondary picketing increased, eventually leading to calls from the business sector for more government controls. At the same time, the initial concern about unemployment generated worries that price agreements, cartels and other monopolistic elements in the product markets, which had proliferated in the inter-war period, would reduce output and employment although in Europe that rationale for robust competition policies soon gave way to the more traditional anti-trust approach which continued unabated in the USA where businesses were facing increasing regulation about product quality and health matters (Vietor, 2000). So whilst 1930–2010 saw a rise and fall in direct government production of goods and services, government regulation saw a sustained increase to control monopolies, product quality, trade unions and general health conditions. For the product markets in West Germany, decartelisation decrees set the agenda though it was not until 1957 that the Law Against Restraint of Competition was passed. In Japan an Anti-Monopoly Law was passed in 1947 whilst in Britain the 1948 Monopolies and Restrictive Practices Act set up a commission to investigate and recommend. It took some time and more legislation for such regulatory activities to have teeth and matters became more complicated in the 1960s when mergers came to be seen in some quarters as beneficial for economies of scale and technological progress. In the event the opening up of markets in the European Union and general globalisation added to the competitive pressures and it was mainly utility companies in energy and communications that felt the continuing pressures from government regulation of prices. In the USA post 1980, regulation declined somewhat but, in the absence of many publicly owned firms to privatise, this was mainly how the push to freer markets manifested itself.

In the case of trade unions, an important benchmark in the promotion of better industrial relations via collective bargaining was Sweden where the 1938 Saltsjöbaden agreement between employers and blue collar workers heralded a long period of regulated wage agreements. This was never achieved in the major powers such as the UK where aggressive confrontations in the 1980s were followed by curbs on unions via Parliamentary Acts. However, the underlying trend was there in other countries where the 'taming' of unions occurred without legislation. There were indeed many common factors in the relations between business, unions and the state. The post 1945 boom saw a huge increase in union membership even in Japan where it reached 20% of the workforce by 1948. In the USA by 1953, it was 26% but, from the 1960s, membership of those working in the private sector declined, in the public sector from the 1980s so that the overall figure by 2000 had fallen to 11.8%. The UK levels were higher with density reaching 63% males and 39% females in 1979 falling to 35% and 30% by 1995. So also in Germany where a level of 36–40% was sustained, 1950–89 falling thereafter (Wrigley, 1997; Hunter, 1989). Several factors were at work strengthening business bargaining power. Perhaps most important was globalisation which meant Third World wages became available to Western businessmen who could also threaten closure of plants, as classically occurred with the Grangemouth oil refinery in Glasgow in October 2013 when the trade union called a strike but had to humiliatingly back off without gains when the firm, INEOS, threatened closure. Large scale manufacturing plants had been a common bastion of unionism. With the shift in the late twentieth century away from Fordist type assembly lines and towards specialist production methods with a more diversified skilled work force, the ability to recruit large numbers into a united union fell. Indeed, the general decline in manufacturing's share of national outputs in the West to little more than 15%, itself brought down union membership as did the employment of women who had tended in the past to be less willing to join a union.

There were significant differences in how these changes mapped out in different countries. The American Federation of Labour acclaimed the years 1930–45 as a revolution in labour relations, including a flurry of work stoppages in 1945/6 but then they came down to earth when in 1948 the Taft-Hartley Act restricted union activities such that firms were increasingly able to enforce the 'right to work' without the pressure of joining a union (Goldin, 2000). Trade unions attempted to have the 'employment relation' excluded from the category of protected property rights of the employer but without success and protection against secondary activities, boycotts and even peaceful picketing, was withdrawn (Tomlins, 2000, p. 627). In Japan, trade unions also finished up in a weak position but in a very different context. Most members were in 'enterprise unions', that is, one for each firm with sector wide unions limited to teaching, railways and civil engineering. Lifetime employment deals, the strike as a demonstration rather than an ultimatum and little unity in union organisation meant they became part of the establishment. The German Trade Union Federation broke its affiliation to political parties and whilst membership rose, full parity between workers and managers was achieved only in coal and steel (Berger, 1995). The German government's initiatives in welfare undermined the influence of the unions whilst in the last quarter of the twentieth century, foreign immigration posed new threats. In France the Confédération Générale du Travail became a representative of mass unionism in 1936 at which stage one half of the workforce in Renault were union members. The labour movement has however always been fairly weak, more interested in strikes as a combative activity than for developing a negotiating position. Women and immigrants were poorly represented and it was left to the state to press employers to engage in collective bargaining (after the fright of the Popular Front in 1936), to recognise unions as institutions (after the 1968 revolts) and accept that workers had a right to 'express themselves' (Milner, 1995, p. 226). Both the state and employers provided subsidies via workers' councils and joint industrial tribunals. By 1982–3 the Auroux law made regular negotiations between unions and employers obligatory. In Britain the pressures tended to be on the other foot with the union a much more recognised part of the institutional fabric and membership so entrenched that 25% of all workers were in closed shops by the end of the 1970s. The unions were as wary as employers about intrusions by the state; they wanted 'voluntarism' but the Labour and Conservative governments of the period from 1964–74 wanted more explicit national arbitration procedures and a series of Parliamentary Acts, some cancelling out others, led eventually to the establishment in 1975 of the Advisory, Conciliation and Arbitration Service. Both employers and workers were drawn, reluctantly, during this period into various forms of formal prices and incomes restraint and to the National Economic Development Council and its associated planning programmes. The Thatcher governments of the 1980s responded to the demands of several business leaders for the activities of trade unions to be restricted and various Acts of 1982–92 removed trade union immunities from civil action for damages, enforced secret ballots before strikes and banned the closed shop (Wrigley, 1997). The irony was that though the strike pattern in Britain in the 1970s was worse than other countries, over the whole post war period working days lost per head of population in the UK was no worse than average and well below Austria, Canada and the USA. Indeed, studies estimating the impact of trade unions on wage levels have found it difficult to record it having more than a small effect. Minimum wage legislation, pushed by trade unions, has tended to favour some sectors or regions more than others and often been correlated with a fall in hours worked. So the trade union/business interface has perhaps been more important symbolically than as a factor in economic performance where international competition has proved much more decisive (Fishback, 2007; Richardson, 1991; Goldin, 2000; Wrigley, 1997; La Croix, 2007).

Education and technical progress

We now turn finally to education, research and development (R&D) where the links between business and the state proved less contentious and more fruitful. By the late nineteenth century industrial technology was becoming more sophisticated and moving away from the single innovating entrepreneur generating factory machinery manned by unskilled workers. Instead innovations were emerging from group research and a more numerate, literate workforce was needed. Some of these needs were met by business firms themselves – on the job training, apprenticeships, in-house R&D – but often the skills could be readily taught as part of a more general education in schools and universities and commercial R&D linked to more basic research. In both cases business firms often looked to the government sector to boost facilities when private provision was limited. This is not a minor economic issue. Economists have argued that 'human capital' is just as important as physical and one estimate, for the USA 1929–82 for example, found that only 5% of the growth in national income per head could be attributed to increases in physical capital and labour but 28% to formal education (Denison, 1985). The scale and effectiveness of R&D has been affected also by two other factors. One is the patent system granting short term monopolies for innovation and the American system has often been seen as bureaucratically better than many others. The other factor is the military. Much R&D since 1945 has been directed to military equipment. It often has important commercial spillovers (the internet came from the US military) but it does mean that in some cases a high R&D effort generates only military benefits. In 1962 for example, R&D spending in Germany, as a % of GDP, was only two thirds that of the USA whereas France was one quarter bigger and the UK 50% bigger. However, Germany, as a WWII aggressor, was forbidden to do military R&D and we find that about one third of all R&D in USA, France and the UK was on aircraft, leaving Germany to allocate the whole of its effort to chemicals, electrical machinery, etc. (Peck, 1968; Freeman, 1979).

The state responses to business needs in education and research did vary considerably across the Western world and reflected a wide range of economic and social factors which we cannot explore here. What stands out however is that some key features reflect well on that part of the American economy which usually attracts few plaudits, the local and state governments, who provided a large part of the funds for universal education, and the Federal government for R&D. For much of the period between 1870–1939, America was way ahead of, for example, Germany and the UK, especially in secondary education (Broadberry, 2004). At primary level Britain was especially slow: only 12% of the population under age 20 in 1870, less than one third that of the USA and Germany and perhaps reflecting the formidable public health spending problems which local government had to face in Victorian Britain. By 1950 the primary gap had disappeared but it took two more decades for the UK and Germany to catch up in secondary education. When we turn to the other needs of business for quality manpower, big differences in technical and higher education are often reflecting different industrial production methods. Large scale assembly lines and big marketing divisions characteristic of US manufacturing from the late nineteenth century could manage with relatively unskilled labour but needed professional management. This largely explains the very high enrolment in higher education in the USA, 5.2% of the population under age 20 in 1950, less than 1% in Britain and Germany. The 1970s and 1980s saw some 'Americanisation' of European industry and the gap narrowed, though in 1998 the USA still had nearly double the European percentage (O'Mahony, 2004).

Business firms in Europe, at least up to the mid-twentieth century, had more need for skilled labour so we find the number of apprenticeships considerably higher than in the USA. Much of this did not involve government, taking the form of on the job training though German governments have been more insistent on provision being made, rather than leaving it voluntary. In Britain in 1889 the Technical Instruction Act facilitated provision of technical training by local authorities but it was the 1944 Education Act and 1964 Industrial Training act which made provision for full time education in Technical Schools. Few resources were allocated and the onus of providing vocational training was left to the choice of either the worker or the firm, leaving many other firms to enjoy a free ride. With the post Fordist shift away from assembly line methods to more specialised computerised production units, the need for basic apprenticeships declined. Finally, we should note that before the take-off of higher education in the 1980s in Europe, the most common form of higher education was in the form of the professional qualification. This was an area where Britain did shine, especially in areas like accounting, giving Britain a distinct human capital advantage in the service sectors.

The other driving force in productivity was R&D. Whether measured as the stocks of qualified manpower or as spending on R&D in total or just in manufacturing, the USA has generally come out on top over the whole 1945–2010 period, especially in sectors like oil, utilities, education and health. Organised group industrial research started on a significant scale in the late nineteenth century in chemicals, glass, rubber and oil. In the USA much was in-house R&D in part because anti-trust laws precluded businesses straddling different product areas in their production activities but for R&D it was fine. Firms linked with local universities who often acted as feeders of the R&D in Europe. Before 1939 the Federal government played a limited role, and this mainly in agriculture (La Croix, 2007; Goldin, 2000). The big spurt started in WWII when the Office of Scientific Research and Development was established, instigating a wave of research contracts with universities and private firms (MIT, Western Electric) in contrast to Europe and Japan where more government sponsored research took place in government laboratories and specialist centres. In the USA, military requirements remained central after 1945 with Federal funds accounting for a very large part of a very large R&D output. Aircraft, missiles and scientific instruments were the focal points for the military but there were spillovers since there were similar performance requirements, especially in micro-electronics. By 1996 universities and federally funded centres are estimated to have been performing 61% of all USA *basic* research (Mowery and Rosenberg, 2000).

Conclusion: some pointers to future research

The last 30 years have seen huge changes across all industrial sectors with the freeing of international capital flows, increasing outsourcing and specialisation in the production of goods and services and a general shift in government activities away from direct production and delivery of services to more financing and arms' length regulation. A fruitful agenda for future research on the history of business/state relations should therefore include studies of past practices with respect to outsourcing, foreign ownership, security and corruption as well as more work on performance. Why, for example, has the construction of buildings (including housing) usually been a specialised sector working on contract for other businesses and government? It contrasts with the huge expansion from the early nineteenth century of sanitary and road infrastructures financed and built in-house by local governments. Was it because sewer and transport technologies were changing rapidly? When comprehensive health schemes were established in Europe after 1945, services were invariably provided by government owned hospitals. Why were they not outsourced like dentistry, optometry and general medical practice? Sectors deemed to have been of strategic importance were traditionally never left to foreign ownership-defence work, railways, telecom, energy—yet the freeing up of capital markets has transformed ownership patterns with governments releasing their golden shares and bodies like the European Union enforcing competition. Research is needed on why, in the past, governments felt, in such sectors, they could not rely on links with private sector businesses (as, exceptionally, the UK did for the international telegraph in the nineteenth century). Even the classic state owned enterprise was regarded as insufficiently secure for postal, telegraph and telephone services in Europe and Japan so they were supplied from government departments for much of the nineteenth and twentieth centuries. Has the technology of monitoring, via the microchip, electronic interceptors and satellites been the prime mover in the increasing lack of concern about who owns airlines, telecoms, railways, prisons and defence establishments?

The distancing of government from the production of goods and services has reflected in part, some perceptions about inefficiencies and corruption in the public sector. A key stimulus has come from America where there has been, in some quarters, an endemic suspicion of government (cf Fishback, 2007b; Higgs, 2007; Hausmann and Neufeld, 2002). Yet history suggests the European and American experiences were different. The conflicting layers of US government and the generally limited powers of the Federal layer rendered government regulation weak for much of the nineteenth and early twentieth centuries. Businesses shopped around the states for the most tolerable regimes and at municipal level generated incentives for graft and corruption. Even the Americans' own local government association acknowledged it was different, more prone to corruption and inefficiency, than its European counterparts (National Civic Federation, 1907). More studies comparing business experience in the two continents are needed. In the same vein the number of high quality studies of performance by private and public enterprises are still limited (Millward, 2005). In particular, we need more comparisons of grid networks under different ownership patterns (EDF versus British Gas), more analysis of whether innovatory activities and marketing, especially in an international context, have indeed been better performed in private businesses and how far there are any differences in productivity performance for sectors like railways and energy in basic delivery of services.

Note

1 The classic big firms like DuPont and US Rubber developed distinctive management structures which Chandler (1990) in particular saw as underling the huge growth in the American economy, illustrated in Table 1 by the USA overtaking the UK in per capita GDP and manufacturing output at the turn of the century. However, Broadberry's research (1993, 1994, etc.) on productivity suggests American resource intensive methods were not necessarily appropriate for Europe and indeed long term productivity growth in *manufacturing* was about the same in the USA for the 100 years from 1870 as in Germany and the UK where smaller scale, sometimes family firm niche production, was more common. America's gains in GDP per head essentially stemmed from the shift from agriculture to industry and significant productivity growth in transport and communications.

References

Anchordoguy, M. (2001). "Nippon Telegraph and Telephone Company (NTT) and the Building of a Telecommunications Industry in Japan", *Business History Review*, 75(3), 507–41.

Bairoch, P. (1982). "International Industrialisation Levels from 1750 to 1980", *Journal of European Economic History*, 11, 269–333.

Bairoch, P. (1989). "European Trade Policy, 1815–1914", in Mathias and Pollard (eds.).

Berger, S. (1995). "Germany" in Berger, S. & Broughton, D. (eds.), *The Force of Labour: The Western European Labour Movement and the Working Class in the Twentieth Century.* Oxford: Berg.

Broadberry, S. N. (1993). "Manufacturing and the Convergence hypothesis: What the Long Run Data Show", *J. Economic History, 53*(4), 772–95.

Broadberry, S. N. (1994a). "Technological Leadership and Productivity Leadership in Manufacturing since the Industrial Revolution: Implications from the Convergence Debate', *Economic Journal, 104,* 291–302.

Broadberry, S. N. (1994b). "Comparative Productivity in Britain and American Manufacturing during the Nineteenth Century", *Explorations in Economic History, 31*(4), 521–8.

Broadberry, S. N. (2004). "Human capital and skills", in Floud, R. & Johnson, P. (eds.), *The Cambridge Economic History of Modern Britain: Volume III, Structural Change and Growth 1939–2000.* Cambridge: Cambridge University Press.

Cameron, R. E. (1961). *France and the Economic Development of Europe 1880–1914: Conquests of Peace and Seeds of War.* Princeton, NJ: Princeton University Press.

Chadeau, E. (2000). "The Rise and Decline of State-Owned Industry in Twentieth Century France" in Toninelli (ed.), *The Rise and Fall of State-Owned Enterprise in the Western World.* Cambridge: Cambridge University Press.

Chandler, A. D. Jr. (1990). *Scale and Scope: The Dynamics of Industrial Capitalism.* Cambridge, MA: Belknap Press of Harvard University.

Checkland, S. (1983). *British Public Policy: An Economic, Social and Political Perspective.* Cambridge: Cambridge University Press.

Chick, M. (1998). *Industrial Policy in Britain 1945–51: Economic Planning, Nationalisation and the Labour Governments.* Cambridge: Cambridge University Press.

Clapham, J. H. (1961). *The Economic Development of France and Germany 1815–1914.* Cambridge: Cambridge University Press.

Clarke, J. J. (1977). "The Nationalisation of War Industries in France, 1935–37: A Case Study", *Journal of Modern History, 49,* 411–30.

Crisp, O. (1976). *Studies in the Russian Economy before 1914.* London: MacMillan.

Daunton, M. (ed.). *The Cambridge Urban History of Britain: Volume III: 1840–1950.* Cambridge University Press.

Davies, R. W. (1989). "Economic and Social Policy in the USSR", in Mathias, P. & Pollard, S. (eds.) *The Cambridge Economic History of Europe: Volume VIII: The Industrial Economies: The Development of Economic and Social Policies.* Cambridge: Cambridge University Press.

Davis, C. M. (1999). "Russia: a Comparative Economic Systems Interpretation", in Foreman-Peck, J. & G. Federico, (eds.), *European Industrial Policy: The Twentieth Century Experience.* Oxford: Oxford University Press.

Denison, E. F. (1985). *Trends in American Economic Growth 1929–82.* Washington: Brookings Institution.

Dobbin, F. (1994). *Forging Industrial Policy: The United States, Britain and France in the Railway Age.* Cambridge: Cambridge University Press.

Doukas, K. (1945). *The French Railroads and the State.* New York: Columbia Press.

Eloranta, J. & Harrison, M. (2010). "War and Disintegration, 1914–1950" in Broadberry, S. & O'Rourke, K. (eds.), *The Cambridge Economic History of Modern Europe, Volume 2: 1870 to the Present.* Cambridge: Cambridge University Press.

Engerman, S. L. & Gallman, R. E. (eds.). (2000). *The Cambridge Economic History of the United States, (Volume II, The Long Nineteenth Century; Volume III: The Twentieth Century).* Cambridge: Cambridge University Press.

Fishback, P. (2007a). "The New Deal" in Fishback, P. and others (eds.) *Government and the American Economy: A New History.* Chicago: University of Chicago Press.

Fishback, P. (2007b). "Seeking Security in the Post War Era" in Fishback, P. and others (eds.) *Government and the American Economy: A New History.* Chicago: University of Chicago Press.

Fishback, P. and others (eds.) (2007). *Government and the American Economy: A New History.* Chicago: University of Chicago Press.

Fishlow, A. (2000). "Internal Transportation in the 19th and 20th Centuries", in Engerman, S. L. & Gallman, R. E. (eds.) *The Cambridge Economic History of the United States, (Volume II, The Long Nineteenth Century).* Cambridge: Cambridge University Press.

Floud, R., Humphries, J. & Johnson P. (eds.) (2014). *The Cambridge Economic History of Modern Britain: Volume II: 1870 to the Present.* Cambridge: Cambridge University Press.

Floud, R. & Johnson, P. (eds.) (2004). *The Cambridge Economic History of Modern Britain: Volume III, Structural Change and Growth 1939–2000*. Cambridge: Cambridge University Press.

Fohlen, C. (1973). "France 1700–1914", in Cipolla (ed.), Part 1.

Freedman, C. E. (1965). "Joint Stock Business Organisation in France 1807–67", *Business History Review, XXXIX*, 184–204.

Freeman, C. (1979). "Technical Innovation and British Trade Performance" in F. T. Blackaby (ed.), *British Economic Policy 1950–64: Demand Management*. Cambridge: Cambridge University Press.

Freeman, M., Pearson, R. & Taylor, J. (2012). *Shareholder Democracies?: Corporate Governance in Britain and Ireland before 1850*. Chicago: The University of Chicago Press.

Fremdling, R. & Knieps, G. (1993). "Competition, Regulation and Nationalisation: The Prussian Railway System in the 19th Century", *Scandinavian Economic History Review, XLI* (1), 129–54.

Galambos, L. (2000a). "State-Owned Enterprise in a Hostile Environment: The US Experience", in Toninelli (ed.) *The Rise and Fall of State-Owned Enterprise in the Western World*. Cambridge: Cambridge University Press.

Galambos, L. (2000b). "The US Corporate Economy in the Twentieth Century", in Engerman, S. L. & Gallman, R. E. (eds.) *The Cambridge Economic History of the United States, (Volume III: The Twentieth Century)*. Cambridge: Cambridge University Press.

Gatrell, P. (1986). *The Tsarist Economy 1850–1917*. London: Batsford.

Gatrell, P. (1994). *Government, Industry and Rearmament in Russia, 1900–1914*. Cambridge: Cambridge University Press.

Goldin, L. (2000). "Labour Markets in the Twentieth Century", in Engerman, S. L. & Gallman, R. E. (eds.) *The Cambridge Economic History of the United States, (Volume III: The Twentieth Century)*. Cambridge: Cambridge University Press.

Gourvish, T. R. (1980). *Railways in the British Economy 1830–1914*. London: Macmillan.

Gregory, P. R. (2004). *The Political Economy of Stalinism*. Cambridge: Cambridge University Press.

Guglielmo, M. & Troesken, W. (2007). "The Gilded Age", in Fishback, P. and others (eds.) *Government and the American Economy: A New History*. Chicago: University of Chicago Press.

Hannah, L. (1979). *Electricity Before Nationalisation*. London: Macmillan.

Hannah, L. (1983). *The Rise of the Corporate Economy*. London: Methuen.

Harley, K. (1992). "International Competitiveness of the Antebellum American Cotton Textile Industry", *Journal of Economic History, 52*, 559–84.

Hassan, J. A. (1985). "The Growth and Impact of the British Water Industry in the Nineteenth Century", *Economic History Review, 38*(4), 531–547.

Hausman, W. J. & Neufeld, J. L. (1990). "The Structure and Profitability of the US Electric Utility Industry at the Turn of the Century", *Business History, 32*(2), 225–43.

Hausman, W. J. & Neufeld, J. L. (2002). "The Market for Capital and the Origins of State Regulation of Electric Utilities in the United States", *Journal of Economic History, 62*(4), 1050–73.

Headrick, D. R. & Griset, P. (2001). "Submarine Telegraph Cables: Business and Politics", *Business History Review, 75*(3), 543–78.

Henderson, W. O. (1958). *The State and the Industrial Revolution in Prussia 1740–1870*. Liverpool: Liverpool University Press.

Hentschel, V. (1989). "German economic and social policy, 1815–1939", in Mathias, P. & Pollard, S. (eds.) *The Cambridge Economic History of Europe: Volume VIII: The Industrial Economies: The Development of Economic and Social Policies*. Cambridge: Cambridge University Press.

Higgs, R. (2007). "The World Wars" in Fishback, P. and others (eds.) *Government and the American Economy: A New History*. Chicago: University of Chicago Press.

Hunter, J. (1989). *The Emergence of Modern Japan: An Introductory History Since 1853*. London: Longman.

Irving, R. J. (1978). "The Profitability and Performance of British Railways 1870–1914", *Economic History Review, 31*, 36–66.

Jacobson, C. D. (2000). *Ties that Bind: Economic and Political Dilemmas of Urban Utility Networks 1800–1990*. Pittsburgh: University of Pittsburgh Press.

Keller, M. (1990). *Regulation and the New Economy: Public Policy and Economic Change in America 1900–1933*. Cambridge, MA: Harvard University Press.

Kindleberger, C. P. (1989). "Commercial Policy between the Wars", in Mathias, P. & Pollard, S. (eds.) *The Cambridge Economic History of Europe: Volume VIII: The Industrial Economies: The Development of Economic and Social Policies*. Cambridge: Cambridge University Press.

Kirby, P. (2003). *Child Labour in Britain 1750–1870*. Basingstoke: Palgrave Macmillan.

Köthenbürger, M., Sinn, H-W. & Whalley, J. (eds.) (2006). *Privatisation Experiences in the European Union*, CESifo Seminar Series. Cambridge: MIT Press.

La Croix, S. J. (2007). "Government and the People: Labor, Education and Health", in Fishback, P. and others (eds.) *Government and the American Economy: A New History*. Chicago: University of Chicago Press.

Lamoureaux, N. R. (2000). "Entrepreneurship, Business Organization and Economic Concentration" in Engerman, S. L. & Gallman, R. E. (eds.) *The Cambridge Economic History of the United States, (Volume II: The Nineteenth Century)*. Cambridge: Cambridge University Press.

Lazonick, W. (1983). "Industrial Organisation and Technological Change: The Decline of the British Cotton Industry". *Business History Review, LVII(2)*, 195–236.

Levy-Leboyer, M. (1980). "The Large Corporation in Modern France", in Chandler and Daems (eds.).

Lovell, J. (1977). *British Trade Unions 1875–1933*. London: Macmillan.

Lynch, F. (1984). "Resolving the Paradox in the Monnet Plan: National and International Planning in French Reconstruction", *Economic History Review, XXXVII(2)*, 229–43.

Maddison, A. (1995). *Monitoring the World Economy 1820–1992*. Paris: Organisation for Economic Cooperation and Development.

Magnusson, L. (2009). *Nation, State and the Industrial Revolution: The Visible Hand*. London: Routledge.

Marburg, T. F. (1964). "Government and Business in Germany: Public Policy towards Cartels", *Business History Review, 38(1)*, 78–101.

Margo, R. A. (2000). "The Labor force in the 19th Century", in Engerman, S. L. & Gallman, R. E. (eds.) *The Cambridge Economic History of the United States, (Volume II: The Nineteenth Century)*. Cambridge: Cambridge University Press.

Maschke, E. (1969). "Outline of the History of German Cartels from 1873 to 1914", in *Essays in European Economic History, 1789–1914*. New York: St. Martin's Press.

Mathias, P. & Pollard, S. (eds.) (1989). *The Cambridge Economic History of Europe: Volume VIII: The Industrial Economies: The Development of Economic and Social Policies*. Cambridge: Cambridge University Press.

Melosi, M. V. (2000). *The Sanitary City: Urban Infrastructure in America from Colonial Times to the Present*. Baltimore: John Hopkins Press.

Millward, R. (2000). "The Political Economy of Urban Utilities in Britain 1840–1950", in Daunton, M., (ed) *The Cambridge Urban History of Britain Volume III, 1840–1950*. Cambridge: Cambridge University Press.

Millward, R. (2005). *Private and Public Enterprise in Europe: Energy, Telecommunications and Transport c.1830–1990*. Cambridge: Cambridge University Press.

Millward, R. (2013). *The State and Business in the Major Powers: An Economic History 1815–1930*. London: Routledge.

Millward, R. (2014). "The Growth of the Public Sector" in Floud, Humphries, and Johnson (eds.) *The Cambridge Economic History of Britain: Volume II*. Cambridge: Cambridge University Press.

Milner, S. (1995). "France", in *The Force of Labour: The Western European Labour Movement and the Working Class in the Twentieth Century*. Oxford: Berg.

Mitchell, B. R. (1988). *British Historical Statistics*. Cambridge: Cambridge University Press.

Mitchell, B. R. (2003). *International Historical Statistics: Europe 1750–2000*. London: Macmillan.

Mowery, D. & Rosenberg, N. (2000). "Twentieth Century Technological Change", in Engerman, S. L. & Gallman, R. E. (eds.) *The Cambridge Economic History of the United States, (Volume III: The Twentieth Century)*. Cambridge: Cambridge University Press.

Mulert, O. (1929). "The Economic Activities of German Municipalities", *Annals of Collective Economy, V*, 209–76.

National Civic Federation (1907). *Municipal and Private Ownership of Public Utilities*. New York: National Civic Federation.

National Economic Development Office (NEDO) (1976). *A Study of UK Nationalised Industries*. London: HMSO.

Nora Report (Groupe de Travail du Comité Interministeriel des Enterprises Publiques) (1967). *Rapport Sur Les Enterprises Publiques*, Paris: La Documentation Française, Editions de Secretariat Général de Gouvernment, Direction de la Documentation.

Nove, A. (1972). An *Economic History of the USSR*. Harmondsworth: Penguin.

O'Hara, G. (2011). "Attempts to Modernise: Nationalisation and the Nationalised Industries in Post War Britain" in F. Amatori, R. Millward and P. Toninelli (eds.), *Reappraising State Enterprise: A Comparison of Italy and the UK*. London: Routledge.

O'Mahony, M. (2004). "Employment, Education and Human Capital", in Floud, R. & Johnson, P. (eds.) *The Cambridge Economic History of Modern Britain: Volume III, Structural Change and Growth 1939–2000*. Cambridge: Cambridge University Press.

Overy, R. J. (2003). "German Business and the Nazi New order", in *Business and Politics in Europe, 1900–1970: Essays in Honour of Alice Teichova*. Cambridge: Cambridge University Press.

Peck, M. J. (1968). "Science and Technology" in R.E.Caves (ed.), *Britain's Economic Prospects*. London: Allen and Unwin.

Peebles, H. B. (1987). *Warshipbuilding on the Clyde: Naval Orders and the Prosperity of the Clyde Shipbuilding Industry, 1889–1939*. Edinburgh: John Donald.

Radcliffe, B. (1973). "The Building of the Paris-Saint Germain Railway", *Journal of Transport History*, 2(1), 20–40.

Richardson, R. (1991). "Trade Unions and Industrial Relations" in N.F.R. Crafts and N.W.C. Woodward (eds.), *The British Economy Since 1945*. Oxford: Clarendon Press.

Rosefielde, S. & Hedlund, S. *Russia Since 1980: Wrestling with Westernisation*. Cambridge: Cambridge University Press.

Rule, J. (1988). *British Trade Unionism 1750–1850: The Formative Years*. London: Longman.

Samuels, R. J. (1994). *'Rich Nation, Strong Army': National Security and the Technological Transformation of Japan*. Ithaca: Cornell University Press.

Schremmer, D. E. (1989). "Taxation and Public finance: Britain, France and Germany", in Mathias, P. & Pollard, S. (eds.) *The Cambridge Economic History of Europe: Volume VIII: The Industrial Economies: The Development of Economic and Social Policies*. Cambridge: Cambridge University Press.

Stevenson, D. (1999). "War by Timetable? The Railway Race before 1914", *Past and Present, 162*, 163–94.

Stolper, G. F., Hauser, K. & Borschadt, K. (1967). *The German Economy: 1870 to the Present*. London: Wiedenfeld and Nicholson.

Tilly, R. H. (1966). "The Political Economy of Public Finance and Prussian Industrialisation 1815–60", *Journal of Economic History, XXVI*, 484–97.

Tolliday, S. (1986). "Steel and Rationalisation Policies 1918–65", in Elbaum and Lazonick, (eds.).

Tomlins, C. (2000). "Labor Law", in Engerman, S. L. & Gallman, R. E. (eds.) *The Cambridge Economic History of the United States, (Volume III: The Twentieth Century)*. Cambridge: Cambridge University Press.

Tomlinson, J. (1994). *Government and the Enterprise since 1900*. Oxford: Clarendon Press.

Toninelli, P.A. (ed) 2000. The Rise and fall of State-Owned Enterprise in the Western World. Cambridge University Press.

Toninelli, P. & Vasta, M. (2011). "Size, Boundaries and Distribution of Italian State. Owned Enterprise", in F. Amatori, R. Millward and P. Toninelli (eds.) *Reappraising State Enterprise: A Comparison of Italy and the UK*. New York: Routledge.

US Bureau of the Census (1976). *The Statistical History of the United States: From Colonial Times to the Present*. New York: Basic Books Inc.

Vietor, R. H. K. (1989). "AT&T and the Public Good: Regulation and Competition in Telecommunications, 1910–1987", in Bradley and Hausman (eds.) *Future Competition in Telecommunications*, Cambridge, MA: Harvard Business School Press.

Vietor, R. H. K. (2000). "Government Regulation of Business", in Engerman, S. L. & Gallman, R. E. (eds.) *The Cambridge Economic History of the United States, (Volume III: The Twentieth Century)*. Cambridge: Cambridge University Press.

Wengenroth, U. (2000). "The Rise and Fall of State Owned Enterprise in Germany", in Toninelli (ed.) *The Rise and Fall of State-Owned Enterprise in the Western World*. Cambridge: Cambridge University Press.

Westwood, J. N. (1991). "The Railways" in Davies, R.W. (ed.), *From Tsarism to the New Economic Policy: Continuity and Change in the Economy of the USSR*. Ithaca, NY: Cornell University Press.

Wrigley, C. (1997). *British Trade Unions 1945–95*. Manchester: Manchester University Press.

Yamamura, K. (ed.) (1997). *The Economic Emergence of Modern Japan*. Cambridge: Cambridge University Press.

19

Evolution of UK corporate ownership and control

Codification, governance, transition and context

Anna Tilba

Overview

Understanding twenty-first century finance is an urgent task for academics, practitioners and policymakers alike. More often than not, the research agendas and debates have been established and taken forward by scholars within the silos of their own academic fields. This chapter highlights the need to re-appraise some of the terminology and methodology we use in relation to charting the evolution of British business and stimulate a more interdisciplinary dialogue between business history and other disciplines. The chapter begins with an account of the evolution of UK ownership and corporate control starting from the middle of nineteenth century to the present day. The emergence of a new class of institutional investor-owners such as pension funds, insurance companies, endowment funds and other asset managers is noted, alongside their increasing significance within academic and policy debates. Turning from the historical to the contemporary, the chapter elaborates on the development of corporate governance codes, which place more emphasis on greater accountability and stewardship both inside and outside the corporate boardroom. Using examples from corporate governance research, the chapter proceeds with a selective overview of the mixed evidence of institutional investor stewardship, but at the same time a lack of voice and influence over the strategic decisions senior managers make. The apparent lack of investor engagement and 'control' undermines the extensive use of labels such as 'Financial Capitalism' or 'The New Financial Capitalism' within the academic literature and popular press. The concluding sections of this chapter cautions against an oversimplified use of such terms and calls for a more contextualised view of ownership where intellectual conversations would attend to both historic contexts, as well as theoretical and practical implications.

Patterns of UK corporate ownership and control

One of the key questions in the history of the modern public company is when exactly did corporate ownership become separate from corporate control? The literature on the evolution of corporate ownership is voluminous,[1] and is highly influenced by the seminal work of Berle and Means (1932) whose view was that US companies were the early movers, with ownership being separated from control at some stage in the early twentieth century followed by the same transition in other Anglo-Saxon economies in the latter part of the twentieth century (Acheson et al., 2015). Subsequently, one of the well-established facts about corporate ownership is that ownership of large listed companies is dispersed in the UK and US and concentrated in most other countries (Franks, Mayer and Rossi, 2005). In the UK, even in the absence of strong investor protection rights dispersed ownership has emerged rapidly in the first half of the twentieth century. In a comprehensive analysis of the evolution of law, finance and ownership of corporations, Franks, Mayer and Rossi associate dispersion of ownership with growth in issued equity, particularly in acquisitions rather than changes to regulations. The authors associate regulation with greater market liquidity in controlling shareholding blocks. The strengthening of regulation in the second half of the twentieth century promoted markets in and for corporate control that undermined relations between owners and managers, which initially were based on trust, but which in turn made it easier for a market for corporate control to emerge. This view is consistent with Cheffins' (2004) study of British evolution of corporate ownership, which considered merger activity to be an important agent of change where regulation of anti-competitive conduct is a potentially key determinant of corporate ownership structures. Hannah and Kay (1977) also link this to levels of concentration in British industry. Indeed, giant firms in the early twentieth century simply could not have existed in the society of 'Personal Capitalism', which had been the norm a century earlier. Crucially, economies of scale and scope, widening markets, technological and managerial innovations and network effects have driven corporate growth and with it the emergence of professional managers and administrators (Foreman-Peck and Hannah, 2012).

It is important to note that in the latest and first broadly representative study for any early twentieth-century economy, Foreman-Peck and Hannah (2012) break conventional wisdom on the separation of ownership from control in the UK by providing evidence of the evolution of managerial control being substantially complete before 1914. The authors report that in the 337 largest independent UK companies in 1911, the directors routinely had control without ownership; management was independent of securities owners and UK investors had large overseas portfolio investments. When combined, these factors indicate that the majority of the corporate securities owned by UK investors were substantially divorced from managerial control, a dispersion which had happened long before Berle and Means (1932) quantified it for the US. Most recently, Acheson et al. (2015) go further and provide an even stronger case for support to the argument that diffuse ownership was present in the UK as early as the second half of the nineteenth century. Moreover, ownership was dispersed not only in large firms but also in medium-sized and small companies. Their argument that ownership diffusion occurred in an era of weak shareholder protection law also undermines the influential law and finance assumptions.[2] All in all, the dispersion of ownership steadily increased over the century and outsiders progressively replaced the insiders as the dominant holders of British equities.

It is also vital to stress that while the UK has for the last 200 years had a robust financial services sector, its expansion was particularly striking in the last two decades of the twentieth century (Daunton, 1989). Deregulation of financial services and the effective privatisation of personal finance prompted a large flow of funds into pension, insurance and property-based financial products (Coggan, 1995). An associated increase in the availability of financial intermediation, in the form of lawyers, underwriters, accountants and other professionals, has facilitated the processes of corporate restructuring. Inefficient capital markets allowed greater tolerance of what Cain and Hopkins (1993) referred to as 'gentlemanly capitalists', which were characterised by reduced accountability to external stakeholders. These groups, indeed, stifled the development of capital markets because they relied on personal contacts and inherited wealth.

Overall, the discourse about the evolution of British business is dominated by the assumptions that it happened in several distinct periods. For over forty years a majority of business historians have relied on Alfred Chandler's model based on differing patterns of ownership and control which were said to develop in stages from *personal* through to *entrepreneurial* and on to *managerial* forms of capitalism (Chandler, 1990). This categorisation was later on complemented by Lazonick's three-stage model which characterised forms of ownership in terms of *proprietal, managerial* and *collective* forms (Lazonick, 1991). Lazonick's thesis, which was more concerned with the nature of decision-making in different business systems, contrasted with the deterministic nature of Chandler's model. The three stages proposed by Lazonick's model represented more the descriptions of different systems at various points in history, where *proprietorial capitalism* related to British business up to the 1940s; *managerial capitalism* mostly described American business for the most part of the twentieth century; and *collective capitalism* described a Japanese business model between the 1940s and 1960s. In other words, Lazonick did not just add another 'stage' to the Chandler's model, by adding a *collective* step, but he was looking at different systems over time.

However, both Chandlerian and Lazoncick's models have been criticized by business historians for a lack of universal appeal. For example, Toms and Wilson (2003) argue that Chandler's model fails to accommodate national cultures and national institutions, as well as a constantly changing flow of power. Furthermore, Wilson (1995) observes that both Chandler's and Lazonick's models fail to link these stages to the overall state of economic development. Interestingly, Wilson (1995) argues that different forms of capitalism could be operating alongside each other. For example, personal (or proprietorial) firms can be operating alongside *managerial* or *collective* corporations, that in-spite of a bias towards large-scale firms, the existing models offer only a very simplistic insight into the dynamics of management structure and decision making, ignoring the differences between strategic, functional and operational management. We will revisit these important arguments later in the chapter.

Notwithstanding a significant amount of criticism[3] that Chandler's and Lazonick's work has had from business historians, there is general agreement among scholars that the separation of ownership from control has resulted in a shift to 'managerial capitalism' (Aguilera et al., 2006), which in turn has encouraged ownership diversification to the point where most shareholders only held small stakes within companies (Mayer, 2000). The changed pattern of share ownership in the UK and US has over the past 30 years led to a greater concentration of ownership in the hands of institutional investors such as insurance companies and pension funds (Mallin et al., 2005). Table 19.1 demonstrates the changes in UK ownership patterns that took place between 1963 and 2010. While analysing the evolution of direct ownership structures in the UK for the decade 1991–2001, Marchica and Mura (2005) document that whilst outside ownership was relatively stable over time, ranging from about 22% in 1991 to 32% in 2001, there was a steady decrease in insider ownership. For example, executive director ownership has been declining from 14.22% in 1991 to 7.57% in 2001. According to Mallin (2008), institutional investors such as insurance companies, pension funds, banks, unit and investment trusts and other financial institutions owned approximately 45% of UK equities, with overseas institutional investors owning 40% and individuals owning only 13% of UK equity. This reflects a broader trend where share ownership by individuals has been decreasing, from 54% in 1963 to 11.5% in 2010 (ONS).

Table 19.1 Percentage of total market value of UK quoted shares by sector of beneficial owner 1963–2010

Sector	1963	1975	1981	1991	1997	2001	2010
Rest of the world	7.0	5.6	3.6	12.8	28.0	35.7	41.2
Insurance companies	10.0	15.9	20.5	20.8	23.6	20.0	8.6
Pension funds	6.4	16.8	26.7	31.3	22.1	16.1	5.1
Individuals	54.0	37.5	28.2	19.9	16.5	14.8	11.5
Unit trusts	1.3	4.1	3.6	5.7	4.2	1.3	6.7
Investment trusts	...	...	...	1.5	1.2	1.6	2.1
Other financial institutions	11.3	10.5	6.8	0.8	1.3	7.2	16.0
Charities	2.1	2.3	2.2	2.4	1.9	1.0	0.9
Private non-financial companies	5.1	3.0	5.1	3.3	1.2	1.0	2.3
Public sector	1.5	3.6	3.0	1.3	0.1	-	3.1
Banks	1.3	0.7	0.3	0.2	0.1	1.3	2.5
Total	100.0	100.0	100.0	100.0	100.0	100.0	100.0

By 2015, out of £6.6 trillion of assets under management in the UK, approximately £2.1 trillion were invested through pension funds, £1.2 trillion were in retail investment products and £0.4 trillion in public sector and charity investments. There is a further £1 trillion investment in insurance products and £1 trillion invested in non-mainstream asset management products, which include pension fund investments (FCA, 2015). In 2010, UK pension funds invested around 43% of their assets in UK equities, a figure that amounted to nearly £400 billion (The Pension Protection Fund, 2010). Considering this significant amount of capital under institutional investor's management, it is unsurprising that both academics and policy makers have assigned a greater role to institutional investors within both the policy agenda and scholarly debates.

Development of corporate governance codes

A variety of factors have put corporate governance research and policy under the spotlight, including the changing nature of the UK ownership landscape, the dynamics of power and influence in and around corporate boardrooms, and an apparent inability of boards to oversee and discipline managers, which was becoming evident in persistent spectacular and surprising British corporate failures in the final quarter of the twentieth century. A chapter by Steven Toms in this book analyses the history of fraud and financial scandals in the United Kingdom, identifying some common features. Corporate collapses of firms such as Bank of Credit and Commerce International (BCCI) have been investigated in detail, demonstrating that this arose because of weak oversight within a complex multinational organisation. Other cases-Barings, Blue Arrow, British and Commonwealth/Atlantic Computers, Coloroll, Guinness, Lloyd's of London, Mirror Group/Maxwell, Polly Peck, Queen's Moat House Hotels and Ferranti represented the examples of wider contemporary failures in auditing and financial reporting. These failures precipitated efforts to improve governance and accountability, which began with the Cadbury Report in 1992 (Billings et al., 2015).

The Committee on Financial Aspects of Corporate Governance, also known as the Cadbury Committee, was set up in May 1991 to address the increasingly voiced concerns about the conduct of the UK companies and how they dealt with financial reporting, accountability and the wider implications of these issues. The Committee was sponsored by the London Stock Exchange (LSE), the Financial Reporting Council (FRC) and the accountancy profession. It produced a draft Report in May 1992 and, after further consultation, published its final Report and recommendations in December 1992. Central to these was the code of best practice in corporate governance (the Cadbury Code) and the requirement for companies to comply with it or explain to their shareholders why they had not done so.

The Cadbury Report played a crucial role in influencing thinking about corporate governance around the world. The Report had identified 'corporate governance' as 'the system by which the companies are directed and controlled. Boards of directors are responsible for the governance of their companies'. Notwithstanding the significance of this report, however, many critics have argued that it did not go far enough to improve corporate governance practices by simply introducing a 'comply or explain' culture. Tilba (2015) suggests that the narrative around Cadbury was framed mostly in terms of resolving the issues arising between shareholders and boards, excluding, for example, the employees. In their review of the history of Cadbury Committee, Spira and Slinn were also reluctant to highlight that the 'comply or explain' agenda might indicate that the membership of the committee did not seem to be interested in changing anything substantial (Tilba, 2015).

Perhaps not surprisingly, more governance reports that followed[4] focused on preventing the potential abuse of corporate power and called for greater accountability, compliance and independence at board level, the separation of the role of chairman of the board from that of chief executive as well as more effective participation by non-executive directors on boards. The Higgs Review, which particularly focused on the roles and effectiveness of non-executive directors (2003) has led to the changes to the UK Combined Code and served as a basis for new governance regulation in other countries. Since the publication of Cadbury in 1992 and the UK Combined Code, corporate governance codes have become an important global phenomenon informing how both businesses set policy and governments assess the need for regulation (Aguilera and Cuervo-Cazurra, 2004). In the US, for example, Institutional Shareholder Services and Investor Responsibility Research Center have emerged, while by 2002 the US Sarbanes-Oxley Act was rushed through following yet more corporate scandals such as Enron, Worldcom, Tyco and Arthur Andersen. The Act significantly raised corporate governance requirements for all companies listed in the US.

However, despite the developments in governance regulation through 'hard' laws in the US or 'soft' law (code-based) in the UK, the financial crisis of 2007–2009 has demonstrated that poor conduct and governance failures still persisted. The impact of recurring collapses, especially the loss of pensions savings of employees, raised questions on the social legitimacy of corporations, prompting further reconsiderations of what constitutes good (even, best) corporate governance practices in the UK and around the world. In 2009 the UK's FRC commissioned a fresh revision of the Combined Code, which was conducted in parallel with a review of corporate governance in UK banks (Walker Review, 2009). The outcome of these reviews was the new UK Corporate Governance Code. Nordberg and McNulty (2013) observe a shifting discourse in the codification within UK corporate governance away from board structures, composition and procedures in Cadbury towards 'behaviour', as the code seeks to improve board effectiveness as a mechanism of governance. The revised version of the Code now explicates that compliance is not enough; what is also important is the substance of compliance, which is context-specific and involves the behaviour of actors both in and around boards.

The emergence of institutional investors such as insurance companies and pension funds, as well as the arrival of non-traditional investors such as hedge funds and investors outside the UK (see Table 19.1), have also altered the character of the codes. Greater attention is now being given to the role that institutional investors in the UK and the US *ought* to perform in corporate governance (Mallin, 2008), highlighting the degree of disengagement currently pursued by these bodies. Following governance scandals relating to Enron in 2001 and leading up to the collapse of Lehman Brothers in 2008, a number of 'voluntary' codes have prescribed greater investor monitoring and engagement vis-à-vis investee companies (the Myners Review, 2001; HM Treasury Review of Myners Principles, 2004). By 2006, the Combined Code on Corporate Governance was requiring institutional investors to make considered use of their votes; enter into a dialogue with investee companies based on the mutual understanding of objectives; and give due consideration to all relevant factors drawn to their attention when evaluating corporate governance arrangements of their investee companies. Similar requirements have been published by the ISC's Responsibilities of Institutional Shareholders and Agents: Statements of Principles (Institutional Shareholders' Committee, 2007). In the UK the financial crisis has served to heighten the expectations of policy-makers that institutional investors should act as stewards and engaged owners of shares (Ownership Commission, 2012; The Stewardship Code, 2010).

A year-long review by John Kay of UK equity markets (2012) was especially critical of investment short-termism and a lack of investor ownership behaviour. The Kay Review emphasized the need for a shift towards long-term and fiduciary standards, necessitating loyalty and prudence within the investment world. This also prompted the UK Law Commissions' inquiry into fiduciary duties of investment intermediaries, resulting in a report (2014) that defines stewardship activities as including the monitoring of and engaging with companies on matters such as strategy, performance, risk, capital structure and corporate governance, including culture and remuneration. In November 2015, the Financial Conduct Authority launched an Asset Management Market Study in order to to understand whether competition within the capital market is working effectively to enable both institutional and retail investors to generate value for money when purchasing asset management services. All in all, the current landscape of UK ownership, and the legal and regulatory environment of shareholder protection, are seen to create receptive conditions for investor involvement in corporate governance, while the 'soft' codes have placed expectations on institutional investors to act not as shareholders but as shareowners. The next section of this chapter explores conflicting evidence of investor engagement practices vis-à-vis investee corporations.

Corporate governance, investor stewardship and disengagement

Long before corporate governance developed as a research discipline, Berle and Means (1932) left an intellectual legacy to the subject of corporate ownership by drawing attention to the growing separation of power between the executive management of publicly-listed corporations and the increasingly diverse and remote shareholders. The separation of corporate ownership from control created information asymmetries and the associated agency problems, which represent core issues in corporate governance research. Information asymmetry in this case means that incumbent managers are in a position to pursue their own objectives, such as increasing corporate size, at the expense of shareholders' interests, for example, the value of the company (Fama and Jensen, 1983). Following this agency perspective, a principal concern of corporate governance is to employ governance mechanisms that resolve or minimize a conflict of interests between managers and shareholders.

A significant body of theoretical and empirical literature about corporate governance exists on the principal-agent relationships, resulting in the formulation of several hypotheses about various governance mechanisms capable of minimizing agency costs. One way of differentiating between governance mechanisms is to refer to them as internal (incentives and monitoring) governance mechanisms and external (monitoring and disciplinary) mechanisms. Internal mechanisms include managerial share ownership (Jensen and Meckling, 1976) and oversight by a board of directors (Fama, 1980; Fama and Jensen, 1983; Baysinger and Butler, 1985), while external mechanisms include managerial labour markets (Fama, 1980), the existence of large external shareholders (Shleifer and Vishny, 1986), mergers, buyouts and takeovers (Hirschey, 1986) and the market for corporate control which acts as a mechanism of last resort (Jensen, 1986; Grossman and Hart, 1987). Fama and Jensen (1983) consider the board of directors to be the most central governance mechanism, arguing that managerial opportunism can be countered by a board of directors that exercises decision control and subsequent oversight of management.

On the other hand, increasingly institutional investors have been seen by scholars as an important governance mechanism associated with monitoring and disciplining management (Mallin, 1994; Gillian and Starks, 2000; David et al., 2001; Hoskisson et al., 2002; Anabtawi, 2006; Johnson et al. 2010). In his seminal work, Hirschman (1970) identified the investor-company relationship within the 'exit' or 'voice' framework, where investors either sell shares ('exit') if they are dissatisfied, or express concerns to management though 'voice' or engagement. However, the evidence of investors behaving as stewards in the spirit of the codes appears more assumed than demonstrated as managerial decision making is still left to professionally trained managers and executives. The empirical evidence investigating this relationship is decidedly mixed (Bainbridge, 2003; Dalton et al., 2007; Tilba, 2011; McNulty, 2015). On the one hand, there is much written about 'active' and engaging investors, yet on the other hand, the case is made that institutional investors tend to be 'passive' in their approach to corporations.[5] Tilba and McNulty (2013) provide further support for this argument when they examine investment practices of UK pension funds, finding them to be distant and more concerned with the performance of the portfolios of their investment managers, rather than the performance of individual companies in which they hold shares. Although one might expect pension funds to act as long-term and engaged share owners because of their supposedly long-term investment horizons (Ryan and Schneider, 2002), Tilba and McNulty (2013) found that pension funds do not seek to influence their investee companies because they operate at a considerable distance from their investee corporations with a high dependency on a chain of financial market intermediaries.

It is also vital to stress, however, that in benchmarking the behaviour of institutional investors over this period, one should highlight how, since the 1970s, it was apparent that in spite of their dominance, investment strategies were determined largely by generating short-term financial rewards, while rarely did they engage much with the management of firms in which they invested (Wilson, 1995). The change in duration of shareholding and the apparent lack of investor involvement with investee companies, despite revisions of investor engagement codes, suggests an 'absentee ownership' (Daily, Dalton and Rajagopalan, 2003). An impression of 'ownerless' companies (The Ownership Commission Report, 2012), and of the distant and disengaged institutional investor, is puzzling and runs counter to the theoretical assumptions and normative prescriptions of the codes of best practice.

In the context of investor-company relationships, a number of scholars have been articulating concerns about the ability and inclination of investors to act as principals and monitor and control investee companies. For example, Webb et al. (2003) argue that it is not the role of the institutional investors to act like banks in developing a long-term relationship with investee companies, because institutional investors have different time horizons and abilities.

Similarly, Hellman (2005) suggests that even large institutional investors cannot assume active ownership because these organisations do not have the organisational capacity or design to acquire adequate knowledge about specific investee companies, so as to make any genuine or worthwhile contribution to discussions on corporate strategy. Furthermore, Hendry et al. (2006; 2007) find that the traditional conceptualisations of investment fund managers as 'owners' bears little resemblance to the day-to-day practices of these actors, who primarily behave and view themselves as traders. This is evident from the shortening of average duration of equity holding periods which have been steadily decreasing from 5 years in 1960s to just over 7 months in 2009 (Haldane, 2010). The latest figures of the Ownership Commission (2012) indicate that average duration of equity holding in 2012 was just 2 months. The most recent academic review of the shareholder activism literature by Goranova and Ryan (2014) suggests that the research on shareholder activism (both financial and social) offers conflicting perspectives. There is evidence of shareholder activism and engagement and at the same time there is also a persistent absence of investor influence vis-à-vis investee corporations. Highly publicized cases of excessive management risk-taking in the financial sector and persistent corporate failures further add uncertainty about institutional investor ability to act as owners.

A transition from 'managerial' to 'New Financial Capitalism'?

In tracking British business dynamics over time, one should draw a distinction between the work of Foreman-Peck and Hannah (2012) on the early twentieth century business, which highlights an early divorce between control and ownership and what Davis (2008) and Jackson (2008) characterise in the later twentieth and early twenty first century as the ear of 'New Financial Capitalism'. The key difference between these periods relates to the nature of the management in each period: the early twentieth century is characterised by a continued presence of former family owners within the firm even though they've sold out to investors (Wilson, 1995); while in the late-twentieth and early-twenty first century, ownership and control is dominated by professional managers (Wilson and Thomson, 2006). Acknowledging these distinctions, we move on to see further changes within UK ownership landscape over the course of the last fifty years, which is characterised by the dominance of institutional investors such as insurance companies and pension funds, which represent enormous pools of money invested in the stock market (Cheffins, 2004; Franks, Mayer and Rossi, 2005; Marchica and Mura, 2005; Mallin et al., 2005). These changes have been tracked in some detail by Wilson (1995) and Wilson and Thomson (2006). For this reason, many scholars have argued that traditional *'managerial capitalism'* has been supplanted by the so-called *'financial capitalism'*, a regime characterised by active markets for corporate control, flexible labour markets, the primacy of shareholder value and dispersed share-ownership (Aguilera et al., 2006; Clark and Hebb, 2004; Dore et al, 1999; Useem, 1996). A number of corporate governance scholars have also argued that in this new era of capitalism it would be rational for institutional investors to act as share 'owners' and use their 'voice', as opposed to 'exiting' by selling large blocks of shares on the market, which would have a negative impact on the performance of the investment portfolio as a whole (Hawley and Williams 2000). Clark and Hebb (2004) have argued that institutional shareholders such as pension funds are evolving into a new stage of Anglo-American capitalism characterised by the increased significance of the shareholders in corporate governance. They assert that pension funds can act with a unified force, demonstrating an ability to reflect a power shift within a firm away from managers and towards shareholders and the pension funds which represent them.

However, it is important to note that paradoxically, while institutional investors seem to be growing in size and in the concentration of their stakes, which gives them potential influence over corporate managers, their use of equity-holdings generally lacks the corresponding or desirable investor engagement with investee corporations. Indeed, it is increasingly apparent that there is extensive evidence of both high levels of share liquidity and the absence of 'voice' in investor behaviour. Davis (2008) and Jackson (2008) have referred to this process as the emergence of 'New Financial Capitalism', highlighting the reluctance of institutional investors to engage with those firms in which they have invested. More recently, Haldane (2010), Knyght et al. (2011), Nicholson et al. (2011) and Tilba and McNulty (2013) have also noted that despite public concerns and government reaction, financial sector behaviour appears largely unchanged and geared towards the short-term. This is reflected in the trend towards increased stock turnover and shorter average stock-holding periods (Tomorrow's Owners, 2008; Ownership Commission, 2012). In the US, for example, Société Générale Cross Asset Research (2008) shows that the average period of holding stock on the New York Stock Exchange (NYSE) was just seven months, while in the UK institutional investors' portfolio turnover reached 56% (Jackson, 2008).

Although a number of scholars have argued that this so-called 'new era' of capitalism ought to be characterised by institutional investors (particularly pension funds) acting as share 'owners', the existing evidence of institutional investor distance and investment short-termism indicates that the reality of business ownership and control is more consistent with the prevalence of control by managers rather than institutional owners. This supports Martin et al.'s (2007) conclusion that managers rather than owners determine the destiny of the firm. This is also something that Foreman-Peck and Hannah (2012) have observed happening in the first half of the twentieth century. Furthermore, the authors also provide evidence of increases in personal ownership in a wide range of societies (US, Sweden, Italy, France and ex-communist countries), suggesting that personal capitalism is alive and well everywhere. This brings into question the frequently evoked, but rarely analysed, generalisation that traditional managerial capitalism has been supplanted by so-called 'Financial Capitalism'.

While labels such as 'Financial Capitalism' or 'The New Financial Capitalism' have been used extensively, it is apparent from existing research that corporate management are rarely exposed to the full impact of the influence institutional shareholders have over either strategic or operational decision-making. Indeed, such is the extent of disengagement in corporate decision-making by institutional shareholders one might conclude that, in effect, very little had changed in British business over the course of the twentieth century. In the first place, it is well known that executives are able to control a company when holding much less than 50% of the equity, while as a result of the growing importance of institutional investment and the appointment of financial representatives onto the board of most publicly-floated companies, one might argue that there had been no substantial divorce between control and ownership. Zeitlin (1974, p. 1107) confirms this by noting that with regard to American corporations, the alleged separation of ownership and control could well be described as a 'pseudofact', because all that had happened was a change in controlling interest. With specific regard to post-1945 trends in British business, while the long history of family boardroom domination might have ended in all but a few of the large businesses which dominated the industrial landscape by that time. In effect, institutional investors rarely engaged much with management, leaving the latter free to dictate strategy and other aspects such as remuneration. This is consistent with Cheffins (2001; 2004), who demonstrates that companies both in the US and the UK are run by professional managers and are configured on the 'outsider/arm's-length' basis, where publicly traded shares are being traded amongst dispersed and passive shareholders. Cheffins (2001) suggests that the arm's-length approach prevails because investors are more concerned with the overall performance of their portfolio of shares, rather than with developments affecting any one particular company.

Based on these important observations one can conclude that when terms like 'Financial Capitalism' or 'The New Financial Capitalism' emerge in the literature, but do not sufficiently reflect reality, we need to challenge such notions. Specifically, one can conclude that managerial capitalism has prevailed in British business since early twentieth century (Foreman-Peck and Hannah, 2012). While there has been a transformation in the ownership of especially large-scale British firms, management continues to exert control over strategic and operational direction, albeit in the context of a financial environment dominated by the need to sustain short-term performance indicators, while financial institutions remain primarily concerned with short-term investment returns and practices. In spite of frequent exhortations to change their orientation, institutional owners choose to disengage from the firms in which they invest, preferring instead to focus on financial trading as their principal modus operandi. There is an argument to be made here that in order to understand the complex nature of relationships between managers and owners in British business in the twenty-first century, a radical re-appraisal of terminology and methodology is therefore required.

Forces of transition in business history: the importance of context

Foreman-Peck and Hannah (2012) caution against generalisations about industrial systems and varieties of capitalism which foundered because international differences have been casually diagnosed. The authors highlight a need to develop alternative models of governance/performance interactions within nations in order to understand the chequered evolution of managerial capitalism. Within the corporate governance literature, several scholars have also emphasized the lack of attention to context (Aguilera and Jackson, 2003; Johnson et al., 2010; Renders and Garemynck, 2012; Jansson, 2013). Ahrens et al. (2011) point out that the financial crisis of 2007–09 was a wake-up call for corporate governance research, introducing factors such as the influence of national and institutional environments on company behaviour and performance. Most recently, in their review of the field of corporate governance research McNulty, Zattoni and Douglas (2013) highlight a need for more rigorous and relevant qualitative studies exploring the array of interactions and processes involved in corporate governance across different levels of analysis and contexts.

Johns defines context as 'situational opportunities and constraints that affect the occurrence and meaning of organisational behaviour as well as functional relationships between variables' (2006, p. 386). Despite the fact that context can have both subtle and powerful effects, the impact of context on organisational behaviour has not been sufficiently recognised or appreciated by researchers, resulting in a general lack of refined, systematic language for expressing context (Johns, 2006). In management research the focus on explaining lower rather than higher levels of analysis comes at the expense of overlooking industrial macro-cultures. Studying context also means exploring manifestations or facets of context as related, rather than independent, and over time (Johns, 2006).

In order to gain a better understanding of both the nature of business development and the total environment in which that activity occurs, one needs to employ models and conceptual frameworks that would encompass the clues about issues such as: the nature of decision-making within a firm: the nature of ownership and control in a company; and the clues about internal values and external pressures. It seems sensible to re-visit earlier arguments made by Toms and Wilson (2003) who emphasized the need for a comparative analysis of financial institutions and their relationships to corporate business policy and revise older and more static models that ignore the dynamics associated with business evolution and accountability relationships within the UK system of corporate governance (Toms and Wilson, 2003). Toms and Wright (2002) suggest that the strategy and structure of British business is closely linked to the relative effectiveness of governance and accountability mechanisms.

Significantly, Toms and Wilson (2003) have developed a conceptual framework (illustrated in Figure 19.1), which might be helpful to this line of inquiry. The framework is based on 'the notion that business is always in transition, strategically and structurally, governed by interaction of scale and scope economy exploitation and accountability of external stakeholders'. This framework holds potential for further analysis and empirical testing because it allows researchers to move beyond the static descriptors like *'managerial capitalism'* or *'personal capitalism'* which have been used to illustrate either the common ownership type or a locus of power within business firms.

Toms and Wilson (2003) provide several compelling arguments against using the typical 'stages' approach to the evolution of British business. Firstly, they argued that many business historians have applied these stages in a rather atheoretical manner, attempting to find suitable adjectives to describe different types of 'capitalisms', and in so doing fail to make any theoretical contribution, neglecting interesting and causal processes of *transition* from one 'stage' to the next. Secondly, they find 'the Darwinian' nature of these stages limited, as it views businesses being capable of merely adapting to changes in their environment. This assumption is problematic because, as history lessons have shown, businesses (especially

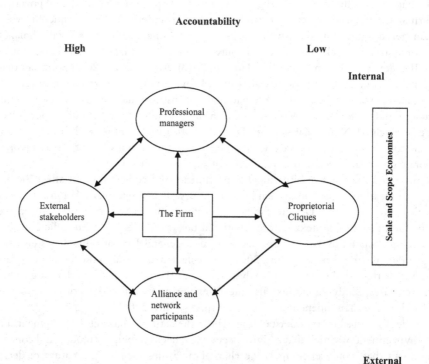

Figure 19.1 Forces of transition in business history
Source: Toms and Wilson (2003).

large-scale) have successfully fashioned their own environments.[6] Thirdly, the static stages omit the significant role played by external arrangements like networks and clusters.

In place of this static analysis, Toms and Wilson propose a more flexible way of understanding the evolution of British ownership and control by mapping out the forces of transition in business history. More specifically, the framework is based on the incorporation of corporate governance and accountability relationships and the analysis of scale and scope economies in the internal and external components. The strength of this conceptual framework comes primarily from being flexible enough to allow for different firms and industries of *different types of capitalism* to co-exist within *the same economy* and *in the same historical period*. Crucially, Toms and Wilson (2003) highlight that there does not have to be an inevitable progression from inefficient to efficient capital markets, or from low accountability to high. In other words, although the framework is capable of accommodating the 'stages' approach, it does not imply a teleological perspective that everything moves towards what we can observe today. In short, this means that different forms of capitalism could be operating alongside each other.

Using this approach offers the possibility of coming to terms with the existing complexity of capital markets, and at the same time with contradictory evidence of a lack of owner-investor control of managerial decision-making. It is then possible to argue that the current elements of *'financial capitalism'* like shareholder primacy, financialisation of business strategy and the power of large financial intermediaries can co-exist alongside dispersed share-ownership, and a lack of investor engagement and control of managerial decision-making-characteristics mainly associated with *'managerial capitalism'*. Using Toms and Wilson's historical example of textile mills of Oldham in the 1860–1890 period, it is also equally possible to see how the democratic ownership of local mills using the one-share-one-vote mechanism, alongside extensive financial disclosure that held relatively powerless directors to account – a trend that today is associated with *'financial capitalism'*.

Conclusions

Over the past 25 years, we have witnessed an endless flow of corporate scandals accompanied by criticisms of financial markets and indeed the nature of 'capitalism' itself. While governance codes of best practice have been evolving since Cadbury 1992, there is still very little to show for all this activity (Keating, 2015). McNulty, Zattoni and Douglas (2013) have also reviewed the field of corporate governance research, observing that after over two decades of research, reform and prescription via codes and other forms of regulation, problems of corporate governance practice still remain. One of the key problems of studying 'varieties of capitalism' (Useem, 1996; Whitley, 2000; Morgan and Whitley, 2012) is its concentration on a small number of variables across different environments and a consequent tendency to ignore variations in context and combinations of institutions that lead to these variables behaving differently when set in different ensembles. Comparative institutional analysis needs to step back and identify the conditions under which different levels of outcomes and relationships occur. There is a need to build more dynamic models of the relationships between actors and across different sorts of contexts. By emphasizing the fluidity of business evolution and crucial links with corporate governance and transaction-cost economics, Toms and Wilson's (2003) theoretical framework sets out a substantial agenda for future empirical research.

What remains empirically unresolved is that on the one hand much of the corporate governance debates have neglected historical evidence, while on the other hand few historians have incorporated corporate governance theories into their analyses. A way forward would be for both disciplines to engage in an intellectual conversation that would attend to both historic context as well as theoretical and practical implications. Important questions to address would be: what is the nature of current ownership and how is control exercised; what are the implications of national and organisational contexts; and ultimately, when we conceive capitalism as a system of economic organisation. In particular, future research questions should explore which of the 'varieties of capitalism' (shareowner or stakeholder) is less flawed as a means of generating wealth and ensuring that it is distributed equitably and effectively.

Notes

1 For an overview see J. F. Wilson (1995) *British Business History, 1720–1994* (Manchester, 1995). For thorough surveys of historical trends influencing the development of Britain's current system of corporate governance see Cheffins, B. (2001). 'Law, Economics and the UK's System of Corporate Governance: Lessons from History', *Journal of Corporate Law Studies, 71* and Cheffins, B. (2004). 'Mergers and the Evolution of Patterns of Corporate Ownership and Control: The British Experience', *Business History, 46*:2, 256–284. For a political and historical account of corporate governance see Mar Roe (2004). 'Institutions of Corporate Governance' in Menard, C. and Shirley, M., eds., *Handbook for New Institutional Economics*' (Norwell, MA: Kluwer Academic Publishers).
2 La Porta, Lopez-de-Silanes and Shleifer,'Corproate ownership around the world' and 'The economic consequences of legal origins'; La Porta, Lopez-de-Silanes and Shleifer and Vishny, 'Law and Finance'.
3 See the work of Steven Toms and John F. Wilson on 'Revisiting Chandler on the Theory of the Firm' and 'Scale, Scope and Accountability: Towards a New Paradigm of British Business History' and John F. Wilson's 'Modelling the Evolution of British Business: New and Old Approaches'.
4 For an overview of the development of UK corporate governance codes see Nordberg and McNulty (2013). 'Creating better boards through codification: Possibilities and limitations in UK corporate governance, 1992–2010', *Business History, 55*:3, 348–374.
5 For a review of evidence of both investor engagement and disengagement see Tilba (2011), 'Pension Funds' Investment Practice and Corporate Engagement' PhD Thesis, University of Liverpool Management School, 126.
6 For example, N. Fligstein, *The Transformation of Corporate Control*, (Cambridge, MA, 1990); D. Korten, *When Corporations Rule the World*, (London, 1995); G. Monbiot, Captive State: *The Corporate Take over of Britain*, (London, 2000).

References

Acheson, G., Campbell, G., Turner, J. & Vanteeva, N. (2015). 'Corporate Ownership and Control in Victorian Britain', *The Economic History Review, 68*(3), 911–936.

Aguilera, R. V. & Cuervo-Cazurra, A. (2004). 'Codes of Good Governance Worldwide; What is the Trigger?' *Organization Studies, 25*(3), 417–446.

Aguilera, R. V. & Jackson, G. (2003). 'The Cross-National Diversity of Corporate Governance: Dimensions and Determinants', *Academy of Management Review, 28*, 451–465.

Aguilera, R. V., FIlatotchev, I., Gospel, H. & Jackson, G. (2008). 'An Organizational Approach to Comparative Corporate Governance: Costs, Contingencies, and Complementarities', *Organization Science, 19*, 475–492.

Aguilera, R. V., Williams, C. A., Conley, J. M. & Rupp, D. E. (2006). 'Corporate Governance and Social Responsibility: A Comparative Analysis of the UK and the US', *Corporate Governance: An International Review, 14*(3), 147–158.

Ahrens, T., Filatotchev, I. & Thomsen, S. (2011). 'The Research Frontier in Corporate Governance', *Journal of Management and Governance, 15*, 311–325.

Anabtawi, I. (2006). 'Some Scepticism About Increasing Shareholder Power', *Ucla Law Review, 53*(3), 561–599.

Bainbridge, S. M. (2003). 'Director Primacy: The Means and Ends of Corporate Governance', *Northwestern University Law Review, 97*, 547–601.

Bamberger, P. (2008). 'Beyond Contextualization: Using Context Theories to Narrow the Micro-Macro Gap in Management Research', *Academy of Management Journal, 51*, 839–846.

Baysinger, B. & Butler, H. (1985). 'Corporate Governance and Board of Directors: Performance Effects of Changes in Board Composition', *Journal of Law, Economics and Organization, 1*, 101–124.

Berle, A. A. & Means, G. C. (1932). *The Modern Corporation and Private Property.* New York: Macmillan.

Billings, M., Tilba, A. & Wilson, J. (2015). 'To invite disappointment or worse': governance, audit and due diligence in the Ferranti-ISC merger. *Business History* 2015, (ePub ahead of print).

Cain, P. J. & Hopkins, A. G. (1993). 'British Imperialism: Innovation and Expansion, 1688–1914', Longman.

Chandler, A. D. Jr. (1990). *Scale and Scope. The Dynamics of Industrial Capitalism.* Cambridge: Belknap Press.

Cheffins, B. R. (2004). 'Mergers and the Evolution of Patterns of Corporate Ownership and Control: The British Experience', *Business History, 46*(2), 256–284.

Clark, G. & Hebb, T. (2004). 'Pension Fund Corporate Engagement: The Fifth Stage of Capitalism', *Industrial Relations, 59*(1), 142–171.

Coggan, P. (1995). *The Money Machine: How the City Works'.* Harmondsworth: Penguin.

Daily, C., Dalton, D. R. & Rajagopalan, N. (2003). 'Governance through Ownership: Centuries of Practice, Decades of Research', *Academy of Management Journal, 46*, 151–158.

Dalton, D. R., Hitt, M. A., Certo, T. S. & Dalton, C. M. (2007). 'The Fundamental Agency Problem and Its Mitigation: Independence, Equity, and the Market for Corporate Control', *The Academy of Management Annals, 1*, 1–64.

Daunton, M. J. (1989). 'Gentlemanly Capitalism and British Industry, 1820–1914', *Past and Present, 122*, 119–58.

David, P., Hitt, M. A. & Gimeno, J. (2001). 'The Role of Institutional Investors in Influencing R&D', *Academy of Management Journal, 44*, 144–57.

Davis, G. (2008). 'A New Finance Capitalism? Mutual Funds and Ownership Re-Concentration in the United States', *European Management Review, 5*(1), 11–21.

Dore, R., Lazonick, W. & O'Sullivan, M. (1999). 'Varieties of Capitalism in the Twentieth Century', *Oxford Review of Economic Policy, 15*(4), 102–120.

Fama, E. F. (1980). 'Agency Problems and the Theory of the Firm', *The Journal of Political Economy, 88*(2): 288–307.

Fama, E. F. & Jensen, M. (1983). 'Separation of Ownership and Control', *Journal of Law and Economics, 26*, 301–325.

FCA (2015). 'The Asset Management Market Study'. https://www.fca.org.uk/news/asset-management-market-study.

Foreman-Peck, J. & Hannah, L. (2012). 'Extreme Divorce: The Managerial Revolution in UK Companies before 1914', *The Economic History Review, 65*(4), 1217–1238.

Franks, J., Mayer, C. & Rossi, S. (2005). 'Ownership: Evolution and Regulation', *Social Science Research Network*.

Gillian, S. L. & Starks, L. T. (2000). 'Corporate Governance Proposals and Shareholder Activism: The Role of Institutional Investors', *Journal of Financial Economics, 57*, 275–305.

Goranova, M. & Ryan, L. V. (2014). 'Shareholder Activism: A Multidisciplinary Review', *Journal of Management, 40*(5), 1230–1268.

Grossman, S. J. & Hart, O. D. (1987). 'One-Share Vote and the Market for Corporate Control', *Journal of Financial Economics, 20*, 175–202.

Haldane, A. (2010). *Patience and Finance.* Beijing: Oxford China Business Forum.

Hannah, L. & Kay, J. A. (1977). *'Concentration in Modern Industry: Theory, Measurement and the UK Experience'.* London: Macmillan.

Hawley, J. & Williams, A. (2000). 'The Emergence of Universal Owners: Some Implications of Institutional Equity Ownership', *Challenge (05775132), 43*(4), 43–61.

Hellman, N. (2005). 'Can We Expect Institutional Investors to Improve Corporate Governance?', *Scandinavian Journal of Management, 21*(3), 293–327.

Hendry, J., Sanderson, P., Barker, R. & Roberts, J. (2006). 'Owners or Traders? Conceptualizations of Institutional Investors and Their Relationship With Corporate Managers', *Human Relations, 59*, 1101–1132.

Hendry, J., Sanderson, P., Barker, R. & Roberts, J. (2007). 'Responsible Ownership, Shareholder Value and the New Shareholder Activism', *Competition & Change, 11*(3), 223–240.

Higgs, D. (2003). 'Review of the Role and Effectiveness of Non-Executive Directors', *Department of Trade and Industry/* HMSO, London, http://dti.gov.uk/cld/non_exec_review.

Hirschey, M. (1986). 'Mergers, Buyouts and Takeouts', *American Economic Review, 76*(2), 317.

Hirschman, A. O. (1970). *Exit, Voice and Loyalty: Responses to Decline in Firms, Organizations, and States.* Cambridge: Harvard University Press.

HM Treasury (2001). *Myners Review of the Governance of Life Mutuals.*

HM Treasury (2004). *Myners Review of the Governance of Life Mutuals – Final Report.*

Hoskisson, R. E., Hitt, M. A., Johnson, R. A. & Grossman, W. (2002). 'Conflicting Voices: The Effects of Institutional Ownership Heterogeneity and Internal Governance on Corporate Innovation Strategies', *Academy of Management Journal, 45*, 697–716.

Institutional Shareholders Committee (2007). *The Responsibilities of Institutional Shareholders and Agents – Statement of Principles.*

Jackson, G. (2008). 'A New Financial Capitalism? Explaining the Persistence of Exit over Voice in Contemporary Corporate Governance', *European Management Review,5*, 23–26.

Jansson, A. (2013). 'Real Owners' and 'Common Investors': Institutional Logics and the Media as a Governance Mechanism. *Corporate Governance: An International Review, 21*, 7–25.

Jensen, M. C. (1986). 'Agency Cost Of Free Cash Flow, Corporate Finance, and Takeovers'. *American Economic Review, 76*(2).

Jensen, M. C. & Meckling. W. H. (1976). 'Theory of the Firm: Managerial Behaviour, Agency Costs and Ownership Structure', *Journal of Financial Economics, 3*(4), 305–360.

Johns, G. (2006). 'The Essential Impact of Context on Organizational Behaviour', *Academy of Management Review, 31*, 386–408.

Johnson, R., Schnatterly, K., Johnson, S. & Chiu, S.C. (2010). 'Institutional Investors and Institutional Environment: A Comparative Analysis and Review'. *Journal of Management Studies, 47*, 1590–1613.

The Kay Review (2012). '*The Kay Review of UK Equity Markets and Long-Term Decision Making*'. http://www.bis.gov.uk/assets/biscore/business-law/docs/k/12-631-kay-review-of-equity-markets-interim-report.pdf.

Knyght, R., Kakabadze, N., Kakabadze, A. & Kouzmin, A. (2011). 'When Rules and Principles and Not Enough: Insider's Views and Narratives on the Global Financial Crisis', *Journal of Change Management, 11*, 45–67.

The Law Commission (2014). '*Fiduciary Duties of Investment Intermediaries*' https://www.gov.uk/government/uploads/system/uploads/attachment_data/file/325509/41342_HC_368_LC350_Print_Ready.pdf.

Lazonick, W. (1999). *Business Organisation and the Myth of the Market Economy.* Cambridge: Cambridge University Press.

Mallin, C. (1994). *The Role of Institutional Investors in Corporate Governance*, London: ICAEW Research Board Monograph, Institute of Chartered Accountants in England & Wales.

Mallin, C. (2008). 'Institutional Shareholders: Their Role in the Shaping of Corporate Governance', *International Journal of Corporate Governance, 1*(1), 97–105.

Mallin, C., Mullineux, A. & Wihlborg, C. (2005). 'The Financial Sector and Corporate Governance: the UK Case', *Corporate Governance: An International Review, 13*(4), 532–541.

Marchica, M.-T. & Mura, R. (2005). 'Direct and Ultimate Ownership Structures in the UK: An Intertemporal Perspective Over the Last Decade', *Corporate Governance: An International Review, 13*(1), 26–45.

Martin, R., Casson, P. D. & Nisar, T. M. (2007). '*Investor Engagement: Investors and Management Practice Under Shareholder Value.* Oxford University Press.

Mayer, C. (2000). 'Corporate Governance in the UK', *Hume Papers on Public Policy, 8*(1), 54–69.

McNulty, T. (2015). 'Ownership, activism and engagement: Institutional investors as active owners'. *Corporate Governance: An International Review, forthcoming.*

McNulty, T., Zattoni, A. & Douglas, T. (2013). 'Developing Corporate Governance Research Through Qualitative Research: A Review of Previous Studies', *Corporate Governance: An International Review, 21*(2), 183–196.

Nicholson, G., Kiel, G., & Kiel-Chisholm, S. (2011). 'The Contribution of Social Norms to the Global Financial Crisis: A Systemic Actor Focused Model and Proposal for Regulatory Change', *Corporate Governance: An International Review, 19*, 471–488.

Nordberg, D. & McNulty, T. (2013). 'Creating better boards through codification: Possibilities and limitations in UK corporate governance 1992–2010', *Business History*, *55*(3), 348–374.

The Ownership Commission Report (2012), *Plurality, Stewardship and Engagement. The Ownership Commission*. http://www.ownershipcomm.org/files/ownership_commission_2012.pdf.

The Pension Protection Fund (2010). *'The Purple Book'*. http://www.pensionprotectionfund.org.uk/Pages/ThePurpleBook.aspx.

Renders, A. & Gaeremynck, A. (2012). 'Corporate Governance, Principal-Principal Agency Conflicts, and Firm Value in European Listed Companies', *Corporate Governance: An International Review*, 20, 125–143.

Ryan, L. V. & Schneider, M. (2002). 'The Antecedents of Institutional Investor Activism', *Academy of Management*, *27*(4), 554–573.

Ryan, L. V. & Schneider, M. (2003). 'Institutional Investor Power and Heterogeneity: Implications for Agency and Stakeholder Theories', *Business & Society, 42*, 398–429.

Shleifer, A. & Vishny, R. W. (1986). 'Large Shareholders and Corporate Control', *Journal of Political Economy, 94*(3), 461–488.

Stewardship Code (2010). Financial Reporting Council. London.

Tilba, A. (2011). *Pension Fund's Investment Practice and Corporate Engagement. PhD Thesis*. University of Liverpool Management School, 126.

Tilba, A. (2015). 'The Cadbury Committee: A History', by Laura F. Spira and Judy Slinn, Oxford University Press, 2013, xii, 257. Book Review, *Business History*, December 2015.

Tilba, A. & McNulty, T. (2013). 'Engaged versus Disengaged Ownership: The Case of Pension Funds in the UK', *Corporate Governance: An International Review, 21,* 165–182.

Tomorrow's Owners (2008). 'Stewardship of Tomorrow's Company', *Tomorrow's Company Report.*

Toms, S. & Wilson, J. F. (2003). 'Scale, Scope and Accountability: Towards A New Paradigm of British Business History', *Business History, (45)*4, 1–23.

Tonello, M. (2006). *Revisiting Stock Market Short-Termism*. The Conference Board Report No. R-1386-06-RR.

Useem, M. (1996). *Investor Capitalism: How Money Managers are Changing the Face of Corporate America*. New York: BasicBooks/Harper Collins.

The Walker's Review (2009). Financial Reporting Council. London: Financial Reporting Council.

Webb, R., Beck, M. & McKinnon, R. (2003). 'Problems and Limitations of Institutional Investor Participation in Corporate Governance'. *Corporate Governance-an International Review, 11*(1): 65–73.

Wilson, J. F. (1995). *British Business History, 1720–1994*. Manchester: Manchester University Press.

Wilson, J. F. & Thomson, A. (2006). *The Making of Modern Management*. Oxford University Press.

Zeitlin, M. (1974). 'Economic Concentration, Industrial Structure, National and Foreign Capital in Chile, 1966', *International Industrial Organisation Review*, 195–205.

20

Globalisation

Pierre Gervais and Cheryl S. McWatters

Introduction: the many faces of globalisation

Business history has a built-in tendency to favour the recent and the localised—even when it comes to multinational corporations. The business case study is the form of choice, and strategic lessons for the present a recurring goal, whereas the relevance of past connections and past contexts to contemporary business seem tenuous at best, at least at first sight. As a result, while worldwide interconnections and their rapid intensification can serve as a backdrop against which internationalising business strategies should be assessed, they rarely constitute a topic of research *per se*, a point recently and forcefully made by Ekberg and Lange (2014). In the ambitious overview of the field by Scranton and Fridenson (2013), the notion did not even make it as a chapter heading. Presented in their introduction as the defining element of an era of contemporary capitalism dating back to the 1970s, as an environmental sea change in the way that business is done, and as a decisive shift towards financialisation and instability, globalisation is quickly subsumed under a variety of discrete flows or connections which the authors themselves present as 'lacking a script'—basically a phenomenon as important as it is unexplained (3–4, 7).

Hence, globalisation in business history, even among the proponents of its usefulness as a concept, often appears as a very recent phenomenon, mostly concerning large multinational enterprises, or MNEs (Friedman and Jones 2011; Fitzgerald 2015; see also Wilkins, 2009 for a comprehensive review of the history of the MNE from this perspective). In the Chandlerian tradition, these large businesses would be not only a symptom of it, but its cause (Chandler, Amatori and Ikino, 1997; also Jones, 2005). In this narrative, MNEs in the past few decades have managed to increase their impact through ever greater amounts of foreign direct investment to the point where flows of goods, capital, people and ideas (both technical and cultural) can no longer be controlled by nation-states. A spill-over effect of this evolution is also considered to be that national firm cultures are being slowly transformed, and possibly replaced, by a new transnational or post-national entrepreneurial environment (Ōmae, 1990; see also the classic statements by Levitt, 1983). Thus, globalisation would express the ultimate form of modernity, a unified world in which homogenised firms would join forces to achieve maximum efficiency, and bring all kinds of technological and social benefits to humankind, while breaking down local isolation and barriers to free circulation of capital, men, ideas and goods. While far from complete, international free-trade treaties notwithstanding, it would still be on the march, more or less irresistibly.

If viewed historically, however, globalisation is a somewhat murkier phenomenon. Economic historians, as well as many business historians, have long assumed that a first globalisation actually took place from the end of the nineteenth century (O'Rourke and Williamson, 1998). This 'first globalisation', which spanned the years from 1870 to 1914, was followed by a 'second globalisation', which has been under way since the 1940s and 1950s, and was both similar and different from the first (Baldwin and Martin, 1999). Yet more recently, historians of earlier periods have called attention to the considerable enlargement of the sphere of merchant activity from the Lower Middle Ages on. For many specialists in 'Atlantic' history, and its successor 'global' history, globalisation actually started in the thirteenth or fourteenth century, with the development of European trade networks and their subsequent taking over of vast swaths of other continents (Braudel, 1982–84; Wallerstein, 1974; Wallerstein, 1978–89; Bailyn, 2005; Hopkins, 2002). Economic historians have contributed to this shift towards the long run, erasing the distinction between industrial and pre-industrial periods and finding key shifts towards market liberalisation in the Early Modern era (Berg, 1994; Mokyr, 2002; Landes, 2003; Greif, 2005, 2006; Casson and Lee, 2011; Ogilvie, 2011). Dependency theorists have largely shared the same timeline, and for some of them, have ended up pushing even further into the past, turning the entirety of recent humankind history into one extended globalisation process (Gunder Frank, 1998).

What is globalisation – a definitional conundrum

The globalisation debate is not only chronological, but also definitional; it is hard to come up with a description of globalisation that adequately accommodates phenomena as different as the European expansion of the 1500s and the recent rise of the BRICS in world trade. Narrowly economic as well as broader sociological definitions tend to focus on a two-dimensional process of intensification, of movement (of goods, people, ideas) and convergence (of economies, societies, cultures). In Anthony Giddens' words, globalisation can be defined as 'the intensification of worldwide social relations which link distant localities in such a way that local happenings are shaped by events occurring many miles away and vice versa' (Giddens, 1990, p. 64). Related notions such as 'deterritorialisation' or the 'connected world' can be seen as variants of these two dimensions pushed to the extreme in terms of space and time compressions. Spatial homogenisation reaches such an extent that a new type of social or economic space is created in which physical localisation becomes irrelevant or even unidentifiable; movement becomes so fast that it disappears altogether and is replaced by quasi instantaneous interaction, with interconnectedness and interdependence turning into essential unity (Appadurai, 1996; see examples in Chanda and Froetschel, 2012).

A problem with this broad definitional context is that any increase in connections or similarities between any two spaces at any point in time qualifies as a step in globalisation. Logically, this leads to the observation of globalisation-generating phenomena at any point in human history, from capitalist developments in Greece and Rome to the birth of MNEs in Ancient Assyria (Neal and Williamson, 2014; Moore and Lewis, 2009). Globalisation begins to look much like the rise of the bourgeoisie in social history, a historical phenomenon having taken place repeatedly since the dawn of times, and yet somehow never completed.

Long-run descriptions of globalisation also tend to have an almost positivist quality of 'necessarily better' or 'necessarily occurring' progress. This perspective leads to largely

Whiggish narratives, usually Euro-centric or quasi-providentialist, with false or at least overly stressed dichotomies between closed and open (often conflated with some version of the archaic/modern society, going back all the way to *gemeinschaft/gesellschaft*). The drift toward the very long run also generates an agency-less history, in which capitalist development takes an unavoidable quality, even when the idea of a recent 'take-off' is maintained (Straw and Glennie, 2012; Maddison, 2001). In globalisation history outside business history, these two pitfalls have generated counter-narratives, mostly around post-colonial and dependency theories (Kapoor, 2002); a few attempts have been made recently at introducing these counter-narratives into business history (Wilkin, 2008; Crawford, 2015). Yet both dependency theory and post-colonial theory share the same timeless quality evinced by the more positive versions of globalisation, and ultimately end up focusing on the present. The production process whereby this present came into being remains little problematised, and remarkably continuous.

In this presentation, we attempt to order what discussion there has been around globalisation in business history around a different paradigm, stressing discontinuous periodisation and exploring the various implications of business history research for the conceptualisation of globalisation within each period. We will consider that one can speak of globalisation only insofar as long-distance economic relationships ended up significantly restructuring regional political economies—an externally driven process, observable locally on a large enough scale to make a difference, either in the behaviour of economic agents and their way of doing business, or in the political/institutional sphere within which they operated. This definition rules out early phenomena of long-distance trade connections up to the Middle Ages, since local societies were only marginally modified by the introduction of small quantities of luxury goods from afar, while even larger-volume trade between neighbouring regions did not generate any major change in the way in which institutions operated. It leads us to identify two main waves of transformative connectivity in business history.

The first wave

The first wave was more limited, and took place in the Early Modern era. European long-distance trade, backed by European military power, created from the fourteenth century onwards an entirely new world of powerful, gate-keeper merchant firms, the activities of which reoriented production spheres in some, but not all, local societies both within Europe and in a significant number of colonised areas, while giving rise to the imperial-military States which dominated the eighteenth century.

The second wave

The second wave dates back roughly to the middle of the eighteenth to end of the nineteenth century. It also brought its share of innovations in terms of business history, and was much more deeply transformative. Local social relationships were more or less slowly but universally marginalised by industrial capitalism, the modern business firm and wage labour, with all their associated phenomena (productivity gains, commodification, large-scale production and the business processes associated with all of this, primarily cost control); while the political-institutional environment was entirely transformed by the rise of the large business as a major, and possibly dominant actor. While economists often distinguish within this second period, for macro-economic reasons, a 'first' and a 'second' era of globalisation in the end of the nineteenth century and after World War II, and sometimes even a post-1980s 'third wave' associated with information technologies, the heuristic value of such sub-periodisation in business history is not altogether clear.

The first globalisation: trade, European expansion, and the rise of the merchant firm

Bearing in mind the various approaches outlined above, whatever globalisation there was before the nineteenth century mostly took place through merchant activity, from the end of the Middle Ages onward. The story usually starts with Northern Italian cities, late Middle Ages fairs in Northern France, Flanders and Western Germany, and the merchants and bankers who organised and financed this long-distance trade. These men, for they were almost all men, developed an entire set of business instruments at the heart of the later growth of commercial capitalism. Most notably, they invented new instruments of payment, allowing for long-distance compensation and transfers of funds outside of the usual, cumbersome and risky method of carrying precious metals from one place to the next (de Roover, 1948, 1953; Rogers, 1995; Denzel, 2008). The establishment of credit instruments and networks of finance were requisite to the further development of global trade, since a key element of this globalisation was access to capital and financing. As Lemarchand and McWatters have argued with respect to the Atlantic world,

> [T]rade and its development in the Atlantic world required capital and financing, directly or indirectly, as credit was allocated, extended, used and abused to further growth in various commercial sectors. While the circulation of capital was a requisite feature of trade activity, with implications on both sides of and across the Atlantic, it was also a very human activity involving networks of partners and players across time and space. By its very human nature, issues of credit and debt cannot be isolated from the broader institutional context: technical, social, and cultural. … Equally, credit networks were social relations within extensive and extended networks of actors subject to social and cultural norms. These norms can be apprehended more readily through the examination of the attitudes, perceptions, and values of those involved in granting and securing credit. Credit evokes questions of confidence, insolvency, risk, reputation, and trust. How these concepts were interpreted, perceived and operationalised are important in understanding the evolving nature of the broader institutional context. (Lemarchand and McWatters, 2013)

New firm structures also emerged, with the Italian *commenda* at the root of all subsequent modern forms of business, from joint-stock corporations to private partnerships (de Roover, 1958, 1966; Goldthwaite, 1968, 1987).

Last but not least, an Italian monk named Luca Pacioli popularised a cleverly designed way of accounting for transfers of value, indeed so cleverly designed that the 'double-entry accounting' system was quickly adopted, and adapted, by the major economic agents of the Early Modern period. It provides much of the basis for contemporary economic activity, having thus held up in slightly modified form for over half a millennium. While not our focus, the role of double-entry bookkeeping in the emergence of global capitalism has been a dominant theme in business history writ large, and more recently a source of significant controversy, as the complexity of its social uses in the first globalisation came into sharper focus (See Bryer, 2000a, 2000b; Edwards, Dean and Clarke, 2009; *a contrario* Funnell and Robertson, 2011; Toms, 2010; Gervais, 2014; Goldthwaite, 2015; Yamey, 1949, 1964, 2000, 2005).

From a globalisation point of view, the period of 1350–1850 seems to have been a seamless forward march, with European merchants taking over trade routes the world over, first around Africa and across the Atlantic islands as early as the fourteenth and fifteenth centuries, then throughout the American continent from the sixteenth to the nineteenth century and finally in continental Asia, in the Pacific Ocean and within Africa from the eighteenth century on. In terms of firm organisation, however, after the first bout of innovation described earlier, one has to wait until the 1600s to again find European economic actors being pushed into innovative practices by the development of their commercial empire. Most notably, the rise of the publicly-sanctioned joint-stock corporation led to the appearance of the first multinational, multidivisional firms.

Corporations were created at first specifically for long-distance trade, as with the various East and West Indian, African or North American companies, so that the form can be said to be a direct product of the first European expansion; the few forerunners in production, such as the Bazacle Milling Co., were much smaller ventures of only local interest, and ephemeral as a rule (Sicard, 2015). They offered the various nation-States an entirely new tool of economic intervention, with stockholders attracted to risky ventures by the guarantee of the sovereign. As noted by Jones and Ville:

> Perhaps the most celebrated of these are the English and Dutch East India companies, established in 1600 and 1602, respectively, with a national monopoly of trade with Asia. Other English companies to be granted trading monopoly charters included the Muscovy Company (1553), the Hudson's Bay Company (1670), and the Royal African Company (1672), and similar rights were granted to foreign companies by the governments of France, Spain, Sweden, and Denmark. (1996a, 898)

Their role, however, went far beyond State promotion of foreign ventures. Indeed, it is hard to overstate the importance of the corporation in business history. While always semi-public in nature, and significantly different in some respects from the post-nineteenth-century private business corporations (limited liability was not a feature of most early public corporations, for instance), these firms were very large, compared to the usual partnerships numerically dominant at the time. They were also the first to experiment with new ways to control far-flung agents (Carlos and Nicholas, 1988, 1990; Brenner, 1993; Bowen, 2006; Gaastra, 2003; Robins, 2006; Jones and Ville, 1996b; Chaudhury, 1965, 1978; Prakash, 1985, 1994; Davies, 1957).

The corporation form was also linked to the birth of two crucial elements of modern capitalism: the bank and the stock exchange. While banking activity had been a natural outgrowth of earlier long-distance trade activities, what created the banking system was the granting of a sovereign warranty, either directly through regulation or indirectly through incorporation, of key banking activities such as metallic currency exchange, minting or discounting commercial paper as a banker of last resort (Quinn and Roberds, 2009; Desan, 2014; Rousseau and Sylla, 2005). With this warranty, banks were to create a new kind of currency, the banknote, far less cumbersome than precious metals, yet far more secure, and hence far more liquid, than any private commercial paper. Stock exchanges, alternatively, had been developed in Northern Italy earlier; but as a place providing a public record of trades in private stock, as opposed to State or local securities, the stock exchange was at first a direct outgrowth of the development of large, transoceanic private corporations, starting in Amsterdam, then London in the seventeenth century (Neal, 1990; Poitras, 2000; Murphy, 2009).

As for commodities exchanges, their origins are less clear-cut, but every indication points to the large merchant communities of the lower Middle Ages, from Northern Italy again to the Hanseatic town along the Baltic Sea (Poitras, 2009, pp. 17–20; also Gelderblom and Jonker, 2005), then to the ports of the Atlantic dealing in colonial crops such as sugar, tobacco or indigo. At any rate, by 1800, commodities, banknotes and commercial paper were circulating throughout the world among European, American and Asian merchants and bankers, so that a first, limited version of a global universe had indeed been created in several regions of the world (Tracy, 1990; Chaudhury and Morineau, 1999; Hancock, 1995; also Gervais, 2008).

The first globalisation also had a significant effect on the relationship of producers and merchants to their customers, and to society in general. It has been argued that the Industrial Revolution was no revolution at all, but merely the tail end of a process whereby multiple forms of labour organisations were experimented with throughout the seventeenth and eighteenth centuries (Berg, 1994). Putting-out, flexible specialisation, central workshops, *kaufsystem* and manufactures were developed in part as an answer to the growth of a vibrant international market spanning four continents. Savvy entrepreneurs developed product innovation and substitution, enlarging the choices of newly interested consumers; in this so-called 'consumer revolution', city and country dwellers took advantage of their improved means of subsistence to buy through cash, barter, or (mostly) credit, exotic goods such as tea, coffee or sugar, or imitations of foreign manufactures such as calico, and a new middle class started to assert itself, throwing out medieval strictures against the acquisitive impulse and 'bourgeois virtue' and breaking new ground in technical, intellectual and political innovation, particularly in the era of Revolution (Brewer and Porter, 1993; Berg, 2002, 2010; Hancock, 2009; DuPlessis, 2016; McCloskey, 2010; Landes, 2003; Mokyr, 2002).

However, all these studies tend to overlook or marginalise many actors in the process, especially Amerindian and Indigenous groups who do not fit well into Euro-centric models of rational market behaviour (Cohen, 2008; Ray and Freeman, 1978; Ray, 1998; Carlos and Lewis, 2010). As argued by Cohen,

> The very sinews of Atlantic history – transatlantic commerce, seaborne migration, the circulation of commodities, capital flows, colonial settlement, European geopolitics, the African slave trade, and the plantation complex – have left little space for Amerindians. The Atlantic narrative has privileged maritime mobility and particular kinds of actors who in some way had a direct stake in the ocean itself—explorers, conquistadors, merchants, colonial settlers, seamen, African slaves, and Atlantic diasporas. (Cohen, 2008, p. 394)

Other actors tend also to be written off, and Cohen points out that the global world was more than an Atlantic one.

> '[I]n certain periods Dutch and Portuguese commerce with Asia exceeded that of Atlantic trade, that in the mid-eighteenth century England and the Netherlands imported more goods from Asia and the Indian Ocean than from the Americas, and that the Dutch sent over 20 times as many colonists east as they did to the Americas. The Atlantic, then, may not have been quite as decisive or influential as its champions claim … primarily an Anglo-American paradigm, well-suited to the specificities of British patterns of commercial exchange, overseas settlement, and colonial policy in North America, but little representative of the varied patterns of the basin as a whole'. (Cohen, 2008, p. 394)

In several regions, especially the Caribbean, some parts of the American continent and several islands in South-East Asia and the Indian Ocean, international flows of trade gave rise to savagely oppressive plantation economies based on newly developed forms of chattel slavery, fed by one of the most massive forced displacement of populations ever witnessed in pre-industrial times. One of the results of the first globalisation was a plantation economy which represented a unique blend of modern capitalist acquisitiveness and barbarous violence, the shadow of which loomed large on labour management techniques well after its demise (Johnson, 2001, 2013; Rosenthal, 2013).

The advent of industrial capitalism: from Chandlerian national firms to the converging MNEs and beyond

For all intents and purposes, business history was born with the Industrial Revolution, and indeed to this day most of its focus postdates the beginning of the nineteenth century. From the original shift that Marx observed toward wage labour, down to the organisational revolution and the Chandlerian synthesis of Big Business and the multidivisional firm, throughout the rise of modern cost and financial accounting methods or the emergence of Schumpeterian innovation as a key business objective, the period between roughly 1830 and 1920 has seen enough changes to keep business historians busy for centuries to come.

None of these phenomena are particularly dependent on the degree of openness and transnational connectivity developed within business communities, however, and indeed most of them are studied in a national or regional context (Chandler, 1977, 1990, 1993 are good examples). We do not have room here to present more than a synoptic review of the Chandlerian framework (see for example, Lamoreaux, Raff and Temin, 2003; Supple, 1991; Scranton, 2008; Whittington, 2008; Wilkins, 2008; Walton, 2010 for various debates and interpretations) and its adoption and diffusion by many scholars of globalisation and markets. Chandler's core argument is that technological improvements enabled firms to benefit from economies of scale. Yet to reap the benefits of these economies of scale, it was necessary for firms to integrate effectively and efficiently activities both upstream and downstream in the supply chain, and to develop parallel management hierarchies to co-ordinate them. This framework has been adopted, debated, reframed and re-energised by a generation of scholars of business history including those examining firms that entered international markets, or failed in their attempts to do so. Chandler's synthesis remains appealing, a descriptive alternative to the theory of the firm, transaction costs and institutions à la Coase and Williamson. Nonetheless, new and more nuanced research has motivated research that looks at firm and market structures in alternate ways, for instance in terms of the entrepreneurial function and process as theorised by Coase, Knight and Schumpeter (see for example, Casson and Godley, 2007). Such re-examinations offer the potential to overcome what Aldous describes as the teleological nature of the Chandlerian view, in which 'other than large integrated firms organised as corporations were poor substitutes either waiting to be replaced or retardants of economic growth' (Aldous, 2015, p. 651).

'Going global'

Still, with this new stress on the large firm, business history seemingly has 'gone global' in terms of its examination of business strategy, retailing, marketing and branding. The rise of mass merchandising and marketing have led to interest about globalisation and how firms adapted to global markets, changing consumer preferences and the effects of market-driven imperialism (De Grazia, 2005; Trentmann, 2006, and the much earlier work of Porter and Livesay, 1971). Business historians celebrate the diffusion of sewing machines and other consumer products (Godley, 2006, but also the earlier work of Davies, 1969; Church and Clark, 2003; Fitzgerald, 2005; Koese, 2008), the development of commodity chains, and of the eminently present-day issues of quality control, supply chains and government relations (Bair, 2006; Duguid, 2003, 2005; Jones, 2007 with respect to Unilever in Turkey and India). These topics link also to earlier concerns with the interconnectedness of business and markets as argued by Beckert (2004, 2014).

While most of these works take globalisation as a given, as we pointed out in the introduction, and focus rather on firm reactions to it, some business historians have indeed questioned the process itself. One of the first, and most widespread, discussions in classic business history was why globalisation took place at all, that is, why would firms invest abroad rather than operate through market exchanges (Dunning, 1958; Wilkins, 1970, 1974). This line of analysis was already present in the examination of the 'Industrial Revolution', often focusing on investment flows from specific nations, in particular on the trading companies of Britain and how they developed trading links and then manufacturing entities abroad, before retreating in the eighteenth century; Jones (2000), for instance, has viewed the later demise of the global firm in the UK as the result of the preference for commission income versus equity investment. These firms did not 'go global' but rather failed to diversify and to develop managerial talent. This interpretation aligns with the prevalent Chandlerian view that British firms did not develop into the multidivisional form claimed to be prevalent in the USA. Amongst others, Casson and Lee (2011) and Scott and Walker (2010, 2012) offer an alternate assessment.

More generally, the cost of doing business abroad, including the so-called 'liability of foreignness', its possible quantification, and the various hypotheses on which factors would best compensate it, spawned a massive comparative literature with primarily empirical goals, but which includes often a historical dimension (e.g., Ōmae, 1995; Zaheer and Mosakowski, 1997; Lubinski, 2014). Researchers have probed everything, from the possible transaction costs of being forced to get groups of managers from different cultural backgrounds to work together, to the multi-layered variety of consumer reactions to foreign firms, through the process whereby technical breakthroughs and management practices developed and were subsequently modified by their circulation in a global world (Barkema and Vermeulen, 1997; Cantwell, 1995; Christiansen, 2012; on a more empirical note, see Hetrick, 2002; Zhou and Guillén, 2015).

Another locus of heated debate is the extent to which globalisation unfolded, and still unfolds, not only in terms of markets, suppliers and production cycles, but also in terms of regulation and management. The fierce battles surrounding the accounting standards to be used throughout Europe and in the United States, and whether they should converge toward a global model, are particularly egregious (Hansmann and Kraakman, 2001; Camfferman and Zeff, 2015). Yet there is a similar, although often more muted, discussion at every level of formalisation relating to the internal organisation of the firm, as well as its interaction with society and the institutional-political sphere. In management studies, in particular, the 'convergence' argument assumes that firms in an interlinked economy will eventually adopt, and push for the adoption of, rules and methods at least formally similar, even when functional differences linger in local practices (Gilson, 2004; Morck and Steier, 2005; Khanna, Kogan and Palepu, 2006; Yoshikawa and Rasheed, 2009). Others will predictably see a half-empty bottle, and contend that even in large MNEs, national political-institutional arrangements from the country in which any given MNE was born, such as business regulations and the shape of the financing system, have far more influence on the corresponding corporate culture than commonly recognised, even after decades spent operating on so-called 'global' markets (Doremus, Keller, Pauly and Reich, 1998).

As far as globalised business is concerned, then, there is no consensus on whether one size should fit all, or indeed whether it could ever do so, and the real impact of globalisation, even on the MNEs which are supposed to carry it on, is still hotly debated. Recent work by Lichenstein (2012) makes a strong case for the 'return of merchant capitalism'. Mass retailers such as Carrefour and Walmart dominate supply chains across the globe with products transformed into mere commodities. These firms bear striking resemblance in terms of market power and practices to their antecedents, the antebellum merchants of New York and Liverpool (see also Lichtenstein, 2006).

Summary

In our view, the various stages identified by macroeconomists, the 'first globalisation' of 1870–1990, an interconnected world economy developing in the second half of the twentieth century during the 'second globalisation', and maybe even a third chapter with the new 'information age' ushered in by computers and the internet do not appear to have been very relevant for business historians, who see more a rather continuous development of modern firms. Even the apparent backtracking of the interwar period and its rejection of open, free trade is downplayed in recent research, which points out that it did not necessarily slow down internationalising trends in the business branches in which such trends existed (Miller, 2012).

As the previous section underscores, much of the recent business history on globalisation stems from management studies rather than business history proper. In the latter, most studies focus on one firm or at most a group of firms or an industrial branch, whereas researchers in management have conducted a plethora of national or comparative analyses of one or the other of the firm functions affected by globalisation. Certainly a useful endeavour would be to integrate the results of such empirical research into the broader narrative of business history. However, this approach would require a higher level of problematisation of globalisation itself, which, whatever the field or sub-field, tends to remain a given. As such it generates as its natural sub-product a self-evident drive to capture opportunities everywhere, or, for the slower denizens of the business world, a (usually welcome) set of new pressures on economic actors to adapt. There is no agency in contemporary globalisation: nobody especially pushes it as a political or social program, nobody even especially wants it, although it has its apologists, yet it is nonetheless there, as a mental horizon against which every move should be gauged. The result of this disembodiment is that in many ways, business historians studying the past century have less to say on globalisation itself, its sources and the paths it took, than historians of the Early Modern era.

The limited analytic relevance of globalisation for recent business history points to a larger shortcoming of the concept itself. While it has provided the theoretical horizon of many case studies, and quite a few grandiose syntheses, either on twentieth and twenty-first century developments or on the longer history of capitalism, it is difficult to find in any of these works a convincing model which could be borrowed by business historians and applied to the history of particular firms or set of firms.

In this regard, chiding business historians for their lack of engagement with the notion on the grounds that they 'are uniquely placed to understand the inner workings of the globalisation process', providing they would merely use 'existing knowledge developed at the macro-level', seems rather unfair (Ekberg and Lange, 2014, p. 102). For using globalisation does not require only knowledge of the development path that it has supposedly been following, it also requires some idea as to how the phenomenon can be explained, what its roots are, and which processes have been pushing it forward (or hampering it). The least of which can be said is that no consensus exists among either historians or economists on this score (see for instance Baddeley, 2006 and *a contrario* Williamson, 1998). In a way, the reluctance of business historians to engage the notion may be a collective, though implicit, recognition by specialists, whose subject matter forces them to pay particularly close attention to the strategies, goals and motives of the economic agents that they study, that these same agents never really thought in those terms. Ian Steele, researching Early Modern globalisation, once remarked that 'no one ever lived, prayed, or died for the Atlantic world' (Steele, 1998, p. 83). One could paraphrase him by pointing out that nobody ever invests globally, either; foreign direct investment has always been localised, both at its point of departure and at its target location, and business historians may be forced more than other researchers to keep this rather un-global fact in mind.

References

Aldous, M. (2015). "Avoiding Negligence and Profusion: The Failure of the Joint-Stock Form in the Anglo-Indian Tea Trade, 1840–1870". *Enterprise and Society, 16*(3), 648–685.

Appadurai, A. (1996). *Modernity at Large: Cultural Dimensions of Globalization*. Minneapolis: University of Minnesota Press.

Baddeley, M. (2006). "Convergence or Divergence? The Impacts of Globalisation on Growth and Inequality in Less Developed Countries." *International Review of Applied Economics, 20*(3), 391–410.

Bailyn, B. (2005). *Atlantic History. Concepts and Contours*. Cambridge: Harvard University Press.

Bair, J. (2006). "Global Capitalism and Commodity Chains: Looking Back, Going Forward". *Competition and Change, 9*(2), 129–156.

Baldwin, R. E. & Philippe. (1999). "Two Waves of Globalisation: Superficial Similarities, Fundamental Differences". In *Globalization and Labor*, edited by Horst Siebert, 3–58. Tübingen: Mohr Siebeck.

Barkema, H. G. & Vermeulen, F. (1997). "What Differences in the Cultural Backgrounds of Partners are Detrimental for International Joint Ventures?" *Journal of International Business Studies, 28*(4), 845–864.

Beckert, S. (2004). "Emancipation and Empire: Reconstructing the Worldwide Web of Cotton Production in the Age of the American Civil War". *American Historical Review, 109*(5), 1405–1438.

Beckert, S. (2014). *Empire of Cotton: A Global History*. New York: Alfred A. Knopf.

Berg, M. (1994). *The Age of Manufactures, 1700–1820*. London: Routledge.

Berg, M. (2002). "From Imitation to Invention: Creating Commodities in Eighteenth-Century Britain". *Economic History Review, 55*(1), 1–30.

Berg, M. (2010). "The British Product Revolution of the Eighteenth Century". In *Reconceptualizing the Industrial Revolution*, edited by Jeff Horn, Leonard N. Rosenband and Merritt Roe Smith, 47–64. Cambridge (Mass.): MIT Press.

Bowen, H.V. (2006). *The Business of Empire: The East India Company and Imperial Britain, 1756–1833*. Cambridge (G.-B.): Cambridge University Press.

Braudel, F. (1992). *Civilization and Capitalism, 15th–18th Century*. 3 vols. Berkeley: University of California Press.

Brenner, R. (1993). *Merchants and Revolution: Commercial Change, Political Conflict, and London's Overseas Traders, 1550–1653*. Princeton: Princeton University Press.

Brewer, J. & Porter, R. (1993). *Consumption and the World of Goods*. London: Routledge.

Bryer, R. A. (2000a). "The History of Accounting and the Transition to Capitalism in England. Part One: Theory". *Accounting, Organizations and Society, 25*(2), 131–162.

Bryer, R. A. (2000b). "The History of Accounting and the Transition to Capitalism in England. Part Two: Evidence". *Accounting, Organizations and Society, 25*(4), 327–381.

Camfferman, K. & Zeff, S. A. (2015). *Aiming for Global Accounting Standards: The International Accounting Standards Board 2001–2011*. Oxford: Oxford University Press.

Cantwell, J. (1995). "The Globalisation of Technology: What Remains of the Product Cycle Model?" *Cambridge Journal of Economics, 19*(1), 155–174.

Carlos, A. M., & Lewis, F. D. (2010). *Commerce by a Frozen Sea: Native Americans and the European Fur Trade*. Philadelphia: University of Pennsylvania Press.

Carlos, A. M. & Nicholas, S. (1988). "Giants of an Earlier Capitalism: The Chartered Trading Companies as Modern Multinationals". *Business History Review, 62*(3), 398–419.

Carlos, A. M. & Nicholas, S. (1990). "Agency Problems in Early Chartered Companies: The Case of the Hudson's Bay Company". *Journal of Economic History, 50*(4), 853–875.

Casson, M. & Godley, A. (2007). "Revisiting the Emergence of the Modern Business Enterprise: Entrepreneurship and the Singer Global Distribution System". *Journal of Management Studies, 44*(7), 1064–1077.

Casson, M. & Lee, J. S. (2011). "The Origin and Development of Markets: A Business History Perspective". *Business History Review, 85*(1), 9–37.

Chanda, N. & Froetschel, S. (eds.) (2012). *A World Connected: Globalization in the 21st Century*. New Haven: Yale Global Online Books.

Chandler, A. D., Amatori, F. & Hikino, T. (eds.) (1997). *Big Business and the Wealth of Nations*. Cambridge: Cambridge University Press.

Chandler, A. D., Jr. (1977). *The Visible Hand: The Managerial Revolution in American Business*. Cambridge (Mass.): Harvard Belknap.

Chandler, A. D., Jr. (1990). *Scale and Scope: The Dynamics of Industrial Capitalism*. Cambridge: Harvard Belknap.

Chandler, A. D., Jr. (1993). "Organizational Capabilities and Industrial Restructuring: A Historical Analysis". *Journal of Comparative Economics, 17*(2), 309–337.

Chaudhuri, K. N. (1965). *The English East India Company: The Study of an Early Joint Stock Company, 1600–1640*. London: Frank Cass.

Chaudhuri, K. N. (1978). *The Trading World of Asia and the English East India Company, 1660–1760*. Cambridge (G.-B.): Cambridge University Press.

Chaudhury, S. & Morineau, M. (eds.) (1999). *Merchants, Companies, and Trade: Europe and Asia in the Early Modern Era*. Cambridge (G.-B.): Cambridge University Press.

Christiansen, B. (ed.) (2012). *Cultural Variations and Business Performance: Contemporary Globalism*. Hershey: Business Science Reference.

Church, R. & Clark, C. (2003). "Purposive Strategy or Serendipity? Development and Diversification in Three Consumer Product Companies, 1918–39: J.&J. Colman, Reckitt & Sons and Lever Bros./ Unilever". *Business History, 45*(1), 23–59.

Cohen, P. (2008). "Was there an Amerindian Atlantic? Reflections on the Limits of a Historiographical Concept". *History of European Ideas, 34*(4), 388–410.

Crawford, R. (2015). "Relocating Centers and Peripheries: Transnational Advertising Agencies and Singapore in the 1950s and 1960s". *Enterprise and Society, 16*(1), 51–73.

Davies, K. G. (1957). *The Royal African Company*. London: Longmans Green.

Davies, R. B. (1969). "'Peacefully Working to Conquer the World:' The Singer Manufacturing Company in Foreign Markets, 1854–1889". *Business History Review, 43*(3), 299–325.

De Grazia, V. (2005). *Irresistible Empire: America's Advance through Twentieth-Century Europe*. Cambridge (Mass.): Belknap Press.

Denzel, M. A. (2008). "The European Bill of Exchange: Its Development from the Middle Ages to 1914". In *Cashless Payments and Transactions from the Middle Ages to 1914*, edited by Sushil Chaudhuri and Markus A. Denzel, 153–191. Stuttgart: Franz Steiner Verlag.

Desan, C. (2014). *Making Money. Coin, Currency, and the Coming of Capitalism*. Oxford: Oxford University Press.

Doremus, P. N., Keller, W. W., Pauly, L. W. & Reich, S. (1998). *The Myth of the Global Corporation*. Princeton: Princeton University Press.

Duguid, P. (2003). "Developing the Brand: The Case of Alcohol, 1800–1880". *Enterprise and Society, 4*(3), 405–441.

Duguid, P. (2005). "Networks and Knowledge: The Beginning and End of the Port Commodity Chain, 1703–1860". *Business History Review, 79*(3), 493–526.

Dunning, J. H. (1958). *American Investment in British Manufacturing Industry*. London: George Allen & Unwin.

DuPlessis, R. S. (2016). *The Material Atlantic: Clothing, Commerce, and Colonization in the Atlantic World, 1650–1800*. Cambridge (G.-B.): Cambridge University Press.

Edwards, J. R., Dean, G. & Clarke, F. (2009). "Merchants' Accounts, Performance Assessment and Decision Making in Mercantilist Britain". *Accounting, Organizations and Society, 34*(5), 551–570.

Ekberg, E. & Lange, E. (2014). "Business History and Economic Globalisation". *Business History, 56*(1),101–115.

Fitzgerald, R. (2005). "Products, Firms and Consumption: Cadbury and the Development of Marketing, 1900–1939". *Business History, 47*(4), 511–531.

Fitzgerald, R. (2015). *Rise of the Global Company: Multinational Enterprise and the Making of the Modern World*. Cambridge (G.B.): Cambridge University Press.

Frank, A. G. (1998). *ReOrient: Global Economy in the Asian Age*. Berkeley: University of California Press.

Friedman, W. & Jones, G. (2011). "Business History: Time for Debate". *Business History Review, 85*(1), 1–8.

Funnell, W. & Robertson, J. (2011). "Capitalist Accounting in Sixteenth Century Holland". *Accounting, Auditing and Accountability Journal, 24*(5), 560–586.

Gaastra, F. S. (2003). *The Dutch East India Company: Expansion and Decline*. Zutphen: Walburg Pers.

Gelderblom, O. & Jonker, J. (2005). "Amsterdam as the Cradle of Futures Trading". In *The Origins of Value: the Financial Innovations that Created Modern Capital Markets*, edited by William M. Goetzmann and K. Geert Rouwenhorst. Oxford: Oxford University Press, 189–205.

Gervais, P. (2008). "Neither Imperial, nor Atlantic: A Merchant Perspective on International Trade in the Eighteenth Century". *History of European Ideas, 34*(4), 465–473.

Gervais, P. (2014). "Why Profit and Loss Didn't Matter: The Historicized Rationality of Early Modern Commerce". In *Merchants and Profit in the Age of Commerce, 1680–1830*, edited by Pierre Gervais, Yannick Lemarchand and Dominique Margairaz, 33–52. London: Pickering & Chatto.

Giddens, A. (1990). *The Consequences of Modernity*. Cambridge (G.-B.): Polity.

Gilson, R. J. (2004). "Globalizing Corporate Governance: Convergence in Form or Function". In *Convergence and Persistence in Corporate Governance*, edited by Jeffrey N. Gordon and Mark J. Roe, 128–158. Cambridge: Cambridge University Press.

Godley, A. (2006). "Selling the Sewing Machine Around the World: Singer's International Marketing Strategies, 1850–1920". *Enterprise & Society, 7*(2), 266–314.

Goldthwaite, R. A. (1968). *Private Wealth in Renaissance Florence: A Study of Four Families*. Princeton: Princeton University Press.

Goldthwaite, R. A. (1987). "The Medici bank and the world of Florentine Capitalism". *Past and Present 114*, 3–31.

Goldthwaite, R. A. (2015). "The Practice and Culture of Accounting in Renaissance Florence". *Enterprise and Society, 16*(3), 611–647.

Greif, A. (2005). "Commitment, Coercion, and Markets: The Nature and Dynamics of Institutions Supporting Exchange". In *Handbook of New Institutional Economics*, edited by Claude Ménard, and Mary M. Shirley, 727–786. Norwell: Kluwer Academic Publishers.

Greif, A. (2006). *Institutions and the Path to the Modern Economy: Lessons from Medieval Trade*. Cambridge: Cambridge University Press.

Hancock, D. (1995). *Citizens of the World: London Merchants and the Integration of the British Atlantic Community, 1735–1785*. Cambridge (G.-B.): Cambridge University Press.

Hancock, D. (2009). *Oceans of Wine: Madeira and the Emergence of American Trade and Taste*. New Haven: Yale University Press.

Hansmann, H. & Kraakman, R. (2001). "The End of History for Corporate Law". *Georgetown Law Journal, 89*(2), 439–68.

Hetrick, S. (2002). "Transferring HR Ideas and Practices: Globalization and Convergence in Poland". *Human Resource Development International, 5*(3), 2002.

Hopkins, A. G. (2002). *Globalization in World History*. New York: Norton.

Johnson, W. (2001). *Soul by Soul: Life inside the Antebellum Slave Market*. Cambridge (Mass.): Harvard University Press.

Johnson, W. (2013). *River of Dark Dreams. Slavery and Empire in the Cotton Kingdom*. Cambridge (Mass.): Harvard University Press.

Jones, G. (2000). *Merchants to Multinationals: British Trading Companies in the Nineteenth and Twentieth Centuries*. Oxford: Oxford University Press.

Jones, G. (2005). *Multinationals and Global Capitalism: From the Nineteenth to the Twenty-First Century*. New York. Oxford: Oxford University Press.

Jones, G. (2007). "Learning to Live with Governments: Unilever in India and Turkey, 1950–1980". *Entreprises et Histoire, 49*(4), 78–101.

Jones, S. R. H. & Ville, S. P. (1996a). "Efficient Transactors or Rent-Seeking Monopolists? The Rationale for Early Chartered Companies". *Journal of Economic History 56*(4), 898–915.

Jones, S. R. H. & Ville, S. P. (1996b). "Theory and Evidence: Understanding Chartered Trading Companies". *Journal of Economic History, 56*(4), 925–927.

Kapoor, I. (2002). "Capitalism, Culture, Agency: Dependency Versus Postcolonial Theory". *Third World Quarterly, 23*(4), 647–664.

Khanna, T., Kogan J. & Palepu, K. (2006). "Globalization and Similarities in Corporate Governance: A Cross-Country Analysis". *Review of Economics and Statistics, 88*(1), 69–90.

Koese, Y. (2008). "Nestlé in the Ottoman Empire: Global Marketing with Local Flavor 1870–1927". *Enterprise and Society, 9*(4), 724–761.

Lamoreaux, N. R., Raff, D. M. G. & Temin, P. (2003). "Beyond Markets and Hierarchies: Towards a New Synthesis of American Business History". *American Historical Review, 108*(2), 404–433.

Landes, D. (2003). *The Unbound Prometheus: Technological Change and Industrial Development in Western Europe from 1750 to Present.* 2nd ed. Cambridge (G.B.): Cambridge University Press.

Lemarchand, Y. & McWatters, C. (2013). "Credit and Debt". In *Oxford Bibliographies in Atlantic History*, edited by Trevor Burnard. New York: Oxford University Press. http://www.oxfordbibliographies. com.

Levitt, T. (1983). "The Globalization of Markets". *Harvard Business Review 61*(3), 92–102.

Lichenstein, N. (ed.) (2006). *Wal-Mart: The Face of Twenty-First-Century Capitalism.* New York: The New Press.

Lichtenstein, N. (2012). "The Return of Merchant Capitalism". *International Labor and Working Class History, 81*, 8–27.

Lubinski, C. (2014). "Liability of Foreignness in Historical Context: German Business in Preindependence India (1880–1940)". *Enterprise and Society, 15*(4), 722–58.

Maddison, A. (2001). *The World Economy: A Millennial Perspective.* Paris: OECD.

McCloskey, D. N. (2010). *Bourgeois Dignity: Why Economics Can't Explain the Modern World.* Chicago: The University of Chicago Press.

Miller, M. B. (2012). *Europe and the Maritime World. A Twentieth Century History.* Cambridge (G.-B.): Cambridge University Press.

Mokyr, J. (2002). *The Gifts of Athena: Historical Origins of the Knowledge Economy.* Princeton: Princeton University Press.

Moore, K. & Lewis, D. (2009). *The Origins of Globalization.* London: Routledge.

Morck, R. K. & Steier, L. (2005). "The Global History of Corporate Governance: An Introduction". *NBER Working Paper 11062.* Cambridge (Mass.): National Bureau of Economic Research.

Murphy, A. L. (2009). *The Origins of English Financial Markets. Investment and Speculation before the South Sea Bubble.* Cambridge (G.-B.): Cambridge University Press.

Neal, L. (1990). *The Rise of Financial Capitalism. International Capital Markets in the Age of Reason.* Cambridge (G.-B.): Cambridge University Press.

Neal, L. & Williamson, J. G. (eds.) (2014). *The Rise of Capitalism: From Ancient Origins to 1848.* Vol. 1 of *The Cambridge History of Capitalism.* Cambridge (G.-B.): Cambridge University Press.

O'Rourke, K. H. & Williamson, J. G. (1998). *Globalisation and History: The Evolution of the Nineteenth-Century Atlantic Economy.* Cambridge (Mass.): M.I.T. Press.

Ogilvie, S. (2011). *Institutions and European Trade: Merchant Guilds, 1000–1800.* Cambridge (G.-B.): Cambridge University Press.

Ōmae, K. (1990). *The Borderless World.* London: Collins.

Ōmae, K. (1995). *The End of the Nation State: The Rise of Regional Economies.* New York: Free Press.

Poitras, G. (2000). *The Early History of Financial Economics, 1478–1776.* Cheltenham: Edward Elgar.

Poitras, G. (2009). "From Antwerp to Chicago: the History of Exchange Traded Derivative Security Contracts". *Revue d'Histoire des Sciences Humaines, 20*(1), 11–50.

Porter, G. & Livesay, H. C. (1971). *Studies in the Changing Structure of Nineteenth-Century Marketing.* Chicago: Ivan R. Dee.

Prakash, O. (1985). *The Dutch East India Company and the Economy of Bengal, 1630–1720.* Princeton: Princeton University Press.

Prakash, O. (1994). *Precious Metals and Commerce. The Dutch East India Company in the Indian Ocean Trade.* Aldershot: Variorum.

Quinn, S. & Roberds, W. (2009). "An Economic Explanation of the Early Bank of Amsterdam, Debasement, Bills of Exchange and the Emergence of the First Central Bank". In *The Origins and Development of Financial Markets and Institutions From the Seventeenth Century to the Present*, edited by Jeremy Atack and Larry Neals, 32–70. Cambridge (G.B.): Cambridge University Press.

Ray, A. J. (1998). *Indians in the Fur Trade: Their Role as Trappers, Hunters, and Middlemen in the Lands Southwest of Hudson Bay, 1660–1870*. Toronto: University of Toronto Press. Ray, A. J. & Freeman, D. B. (1978). *"Give us Good Measure": An Economic Analysis of Relations Between the Indians and the Hudson's Bay Company before 1763*. Toronto: University of Toronto Press.

Robins, N. (2006). *The Corporation that Changed the World: How the East India Company Shaped the Modern Multinational*. London: Pluto Press.

Rogers, J. S. (1995). *The Early History of the Law of Bills and Notes: A Study of the Origins of Anglo-American Commercial Law*. Cambridge: Cambridge University Press.

de Roover, R. (1948). *Money, Banking and Credit in Mediaeval Bruges; Italian Merchant Bankers, Lombards and Money-Changers, a Study in the Origins of Banking*. Cambridge (Mass.): Mediaeval Academy of America.

de Roover, R. (1953). *L'évolution de la lettre de change: XIVe-XVIIIe siècle*. Paris: Armand Colin.

de Roover, R. (1958). "The Story of the Alberti Company of Florence, 1302–1348, as Revealed in its Account Books". *Business History Review, 32*(1), 14–59.

de Roover, R. (1966). *The Rise and Decline of the Medici Bank*. New York: Norton.

Rosenthal, C. C. (2013). "From Memory to Mastery: Accounting for Control in America, 1750–1880". *Enterprise and Society, 14*(4), 732–748.

Rousseau, P. L. & Sylla, R. (2005). "Emerging Financial Markets and Early US Growth". *Explorations in Economic History, 42*(1), 1–26.

Scott, P. & Walker, J. (2010). "Advertising, Promotion, and the Competitive Advantage of Interwar British Department Stores". *Economic History Review 63*(4), 1105–128.

Scott, P. & Walker, J. (2012). "The British 'Failure' That Never Was? The Anglo-American 'Productivity Gap' in Large-scale Interwar Retailing—Evidence from the Department Store Sector". *Economic History Review 65*(1), 277–303.

Scranton, P. (2008). "Beyond Chandler?" *Enterprise and Society, 9*(3), 426–429.

Scranton, P. & Fridenson, P. (2014). *Reimagining Business History*. Baltimore: Johns Hopkins University Press.

Sicard, G. (1953). 2015. *The Origins of Corporations. The Mills of Toulouse in the Middle Ages*. Translated by Matthew Landry. New Haven: Yale University Press.

Steele, I. K. (1998). "Exploding Colonial American History: Amerindian, Atlantic, and Global Perspectives". *Reviews in American History, 26*(1), 70–95.

Straw, W. & Glennie, A. (2012). *The Third Wave of Globalisation*. London: Institute for Public Policy Research.

Supple, B. (1991). "Essays in Bibliography and Criticism. Scale and Scope: Alfred Chandler and the Dynamics of Industrial Capitalism". *Economic History Review, 44*(3), 500–514.

Toms, S. J. (2010). "Calculating Profit: A Historical Perspective on the Development of Capitalism". *Accounting, Organizations and Society, 35*(2), 205–221.

Tracy, J. D. (ed.) (1990). *The Rise of Merchant Empires: Long-Distance Trade in the Early Modern World, 1350–1750*. Cambridge (G.-B.): Cambridge University Press.

Trentmann, F. (2006). *The Making of the Consumer: Knowledge, Power and Identity in the Modern World*. Cultures of Consumption Series. Oxford; New York: Berg.

Wallerstein, I. (1974). "The Rise and Future Demise of the Word-Capitalist System: Concepts for Comparative Analysis". *Comparative Studies in Society and History, 16*(4), 387–415.

Wallerstein, I. (1974–1989). *The Modern World System*. 3 vols. New York: Academic Press.

Walton, J. K. (2010). "New Directions in Business History: Themes, Approaches and Opportunities". *Business History, 52*(1), 1–16.

Whittington, R. (2008). "Alfred Chandler, Founder of Strategy: Lost Tradition and Renewed Inspiration". *Business History Review, 82*(2), 267–277.

Wilkin, P. (2008). "Global Communication and Political Culture in the Semi-periphery: The Rise of the Globo Corporation". *Review of International Studies, 34* (Supplement S1), 93–113.

Wilkins, M.. (1970). *The Emergence of Multinational Enterprise: American Business Abroad from the Colonial Era to 1914*. Cambridge (Mass.): Harvard University Press.

Wilkins, M. (1974). *The Maturing of Multinational Enterprise. American Business Abroad from 1914 to 1970*. Cambridge (Mass.): Harvard University Press.

Wilkins, M. (2008). "Chandler and Global Business History". *Business History Review, 82*(2): 251–266.
Wilkins, M. (2009). "The History of the Multinational Enterprise". In *The Oxford Handbook of International Business*, edited by Alan M. Rugman, 3–38. Oxford: Oxford University Press.
Williamson, J. G. (1998). "Growth, Distribution, and Demography: Some Lessons from History". *Explorations in Economic History, 35*(3), 241–271.
Yamey, B. S. (1949). "Scientific Bookkeeping and the Rise of Capitalism". *Economic History Review, 1*(2–3), 99–113.
Yamey, B. S. (1964). "Accounting and the Rise of Capitalism: Further Notes on a Theme by Sombart". *Journal of Accounting Research, 2*(2), 117–136.
Yamey, B. S. (2000). "The 'Particular Gain or Loss Upon Each Article we deal in': An Aspect of Mercantile Accounting, 1300–1800". *Accounting, Business and Financial History, 10*(1), 1–12.
Yamey, B. S. (2005). "The Historical Significance of Double-entry Bookkeeping: Some Non-Sombartian Claims". *The Accounting Historians Journal 32*(1), 77–85.
Yoshikawa, T. & Rasheed, A. A. (2009). "Convergence of Corporate Governance: Critical Review and Future Directions". *Corporate Governance: An International Review 17*(3), 388–404.
Zaheer, S. & Mosakowski, E. (1997). "The Dynamics of the Liability of Foreignness: A Global Study of Survival in Financial Services". *Strategic Management Journal, 18*(6), 439–463.
Zhou, N. & Guillén, M. (2015). "From Home Country to Home Base: A Dynamic Approach to the Liability of Foreignness". *Strategic Management Journal, 36*(6), 907–917.

Part V
Management and ethics

21

The challenge of management professionalization

Mitchell J. Larson

This chapter traces the historical background behind the long effort to professionalize British management in the twentieth century. As the title suggests, this process has been contested throughout this period when even the concept of 'management' itself as a defined body of knowledge was challenged; these questions over the existence and contents of a distinct 'management' field of study made claims for professionalization that much harder, especially when compared to long-standing professions such as the law or medicine. This chapter therefore attempts to reinvigorate these debates by looking back at changing ideas of professionalization as well as specific instances where groups or individuals have advocated for the professionalization of management workers.

Drawing upon published books and articles, research theses, newspapers and trade publications, the chapter continues as follows. The first section discusses the professionalization effort by British management and highlights a number of prominent concepts in this long debate. The second section concentrates on the sociology of professionalization and how this has interacted with the efforts of managers in the United Kingdom (UK) to secure greater professional recognition during the twentieth century. The third section pursues a particular line of thinking expounded by one of the leading British management consultants and professionalization advocates of the second half of the century, Edward Brech. The chapter concludes with some final thoughts on how some elements of business history might fit into management teaching taking place in business schools to assist the professionalization effort.

The professionalization debate and British management

A variety of authors, predictably, have weighed in on the management professionalization debate over the years. Some management writers dismiss it out of hand: Henry Mintzberg joyfully steps past the issue in the first chapter of his book *Managers Not MBAs*, claiming that because in his view management cannot be 'taught in advance of practice, out of context' (Mintzberg, 2004, p. 11) in the same way that medicine or engineering might be, it cannot, by definition, be a profession. Indeed, business history offers many examples of 'managers' without a day of formal training who experience considerable success, while many of the most highly trained people suffer business or career reverses because of their inability to match their training with the complexities of actual practice. While hardly alone in his critiques of various programmes, Mintzberg has been particularly vocal about the failings of management training programmes for a long time, and his refusal to consider management as a profession akin to others such as medicine, law or education comes as no surprise to long-term readers in the field.[1]

If we move beyond those who refuse to engage in the debate in the first place – and overlooking this argument does not deny Mintzberg's substantial contributions to thinking about management, management education and 'the work managers do' – there remains significant literature about the professionalization process and management's efforts to raise its public status to the level of other established professional groups. At the turn of the twentieth century, Sidney and Beatrice Webb discussed the relationship between trade unionism and democratic society in their book *Industrial Democracy*. They argued that trade unions would increasingly be nationalised in the public interest, and those who worked on behalf of the 'citizen-consumer' would begin to 'assume the character of professional associations' (Webb and Webb, 1920, pp. 825–6). Coincidentally, Keeble (Keeble, 1992) reports that the first attempts at what we now consider management education began during this period in London, Birmingham and elsewhere suggesting the Webbs may have been even more prescient than previously believed.

Edward T. Elbourne leapt onto the management scene with the 1914 publication of his book *Factory Administration and Accounts*. The book outlined his ideas to codify 'management' and make its principles comprehensible to businessmen, accountants and engineers alike. A career factory-level manager without upper management experience, he still felt strongly that management could be studied and learned like many other disciplines. Elbourne, in short, wished to professionalize industrial managers. The outbreak of the war in late summer of that year led him to become an assistant general manager at the Ponders End National Shell Factory in 1915 and Elbourne held that post until 1919. During the war Elbourne's book sold over ten thousand copies across Britain and its success encouraged him further in his quest. In 1919 he formed an engineering consulting business with his former boss Harry Brindley, but more importantly they decided to pursue the formation of a central management institute. Activities of others made the timing seem right: in 1919 the Manchester School of Technology began its first courses in management subjects, and businessman Seebohm Rowntree used his influence to begin a series of annual conferences on management topics, later held at Oxford. But Elbourne and Brindley alone called for a central institute catering specifically to the needs and interests of managers. They moved quickly in order to make use of the mood surrounding management: by August of that year they had sent out 5,000 copies of a provisional prospectus for a management body that would become the Institute of Industrial Administration (IIA) in 1920.[2]

The study of industrial management did not abate during the interwar years. Oliver Sheldon's 1923 volume *The Philosophy of Management* began to talk about general management as a profession emerging out of earlier work done by people such as Frederick W. Taylor and others (Sheldon, 1923). The establishment of the Institute for Industrial Administration and similar activities began a new phase of the parallel development of management as a discipline and its attempts to professionalize. Management consultancies began to appear in the UK run by Charles Bedaux, Lyndall Urwick and others (Kreis, 1992; Fitzgerald, 1995; Larson, 2003. For Bedaux, see Chapter 3 of Weatherburn, 2014. For more on Urwick, see Brech et al., 2010). In parallel, research on the sociology of professions progressed also: an article by Talcott Parsons (Parsons, 1939) examined their function(s) within modern society and questioned whether individual motivational differences account for the perceived differences between 'professionals' (traditionally seen as prioritizing altruism) and normal 'business men' (seen as prioritizing self-interest). His interwar juxtaposition of 'professionals' with 'business men' reflected the difficulty managers and directors had faced, and therefore might continue to face, in any serious professionalizing mission. Alongside his other works, Parsons's functionalist construct became part of the sociological lexicon at least until the 1970s.[3] In spite of the efforts of the IIA and subsequent writers, during the interwar period in Britain it remained impossible to speak of a professional class of manager in the way Elbourne envisioned.

The post-war re-examination of Britain's industrial management capabilities began a chain of events which seemed to promise great things for managers in business enterprises. The Second World War had shown the usefulness of skilled technical people in improving industrial productivity, and the rise of 'technocrats' within governments and other organizations began. Once the war ended British industrialists immediately made efforts to retain and expand such expertise with the creation of the Administrative Staff College at Henley-on-Thames in 1946 (Larson, 2003), the establishment of which had been under discussion since 1943; the Staff College – a direct parallel for businessmen and Civil Service personnel to the military colleges at Sandhurst and elsewhere – aimed to enhance managers' job skills and offered the chance for students to communicate with their peers about common problems. Another college opened a few years later with the establishment in 1959 of the Ashridge College in Berkhamstead. Located away from major conurbations and the distractions of students' everyday business concerns, these colleges created small groups or 'syndicates' of men from the world of business with similar levels of experience and training, and enabled them to confer with each other to share solutions, reflect on problems and gain exposure to concerns outside of their own organizations or industries. As 'proto-professionals' these men (students at these colleges were all men in those days) shared a great deal in common and could have, had they chosen or been guided by tutors to do so, adopted a perspective which encouraged them to advocate and pursue a more thoroughgoing agenda of professionalization.

Such small operations, however, did not possess sufficient scale to make sweeping changes by themselves in the landscape of British management. They were both highly selective in terms of their students while also intellectually narrow – there was no attempt to conduct research or do much more than facilitate discussion and reflection among the syndicate members. The cost of the programme erected a barrier to more widespread participation; furthermore, nearly all students were nominated by their companies and interviewing by Henley staff played a large role in admissions. But the creation of these small cohorts of like-minded men of similar age, work experience and career trajectory may have been a tiny example of an effort to create a sense of professional co-responsibility for the success of at least large-scale firms of the day (see Chapter 4 of Larson, 2003). Various companies made their own internal efforts at management preparation through things like job rotation and other development techniques, but these remained embryonic, localised and therefore small in scale. These early attempts, however, arguably paved the way for the advent of the first university business schools in the middle of the 1960s and their subsequent spread across the university sector in the United Kingdom. Over time the increased size and number of management courses meant that the exclusivity of student admission and the opportunity to form strong and durable bonds with others on one's course, so prominent in the Henley and Ashridge colleges, decreased. One possible element of the justification for the establishment of formal degree-granting management education programmes within universities in the UK arose from the search for professional status to combat the widely-held view in British society that management, especially manufacturing management, did not represent a socially-desirable career as was the case for the military, (higher) civil service or the financial industry. This may have resulted from the fact that two of the roles, the military and finance, are concerned with *directing* resources in the same way as social elites had done for centuries rather than actually *employing* these resources themselves, which may have served to make these activities more desirable or acceptable.

Yet Britain wanted (and some believed, needed) more business experts, managers whose companies would produce goods for domestic but especially foreign consumption and managers who could keep the peace between themselves and organized labour. The emphasis here fell upon productivity, wage restraint and various financial measures, usually of a short-term nature; there was no time or motivation for managers across the wide range of industrial sectors (some of which found themselves nationalized by the Attlee Labour Government shortly after the war ended) to compose and instil a professional sense of responsibility for growing the national wealth. Two things occurred in 1960 that would dramatically alter the path of the management professionalization debate in the UK: the first was the wide dissemination of the Ford Foundation (Gordon and Howell, 1959) and Carnegie Foundation (Pierson, 1959) reports on management education, which began to change the way management education was conceived and taught in the US and elsewhere. The second was the beginning of attempts to formalize management education in the UK which resulted in the London and Manchester business schools in the middle of the 1960s (Wilson and Manchester Business School, 1992; Larson, 2003). The professionalization debate continued into the 1960s and researchers grew more sophisticated in their approach to the subject.

Quickening the pace

Harold Wilensky's provocatively titled "The Professionalization of Everyone?" (Wilensky, 1964) posited a number of substantial points and reflected the changing nature of post-war society when it appeared in 1964. Wilensky's paper heralded a beginning of the end to earlier definitional debates about professionalization and signalled a shift into a more complex sociological examination of the activities of interest groups in society. He talks of a 'technical service ideal' (Wilensky, 1964, p. 141) and how this is based upon two key pillars: specialist technical knowledge and agreed professional norms. He studied eighteen professional groups to determine if there was a common process of professionalization and derived a five-step process which he claimed applied to most, if not all, professions. From Wilensky's list of five stages, some of them, such as the fourth – that of seeking legal protection for certified practitioners in the field – do not easily apply in business management. He even pointed out that 'many occupations will be tempted to try everything at once [all the stages concurrently] or anything opportunity or expediency dictate. The "professionalization" of labor, management and commerce is largely of this kind' (Wilensky, 1964, p. 146). Although he was writing about the situation in the United States, this last observation is particularly telling. Wilensky's research did not specifically address the professionalization process for management as such but after analysing the trajectories of a number of professional groups, he argued that management along with several other activist groups had not yet navigated the professionalization process successfully.

During the 1960s and 1970s, Britain's national economic situation began to shift in numerous ways which continued to undermine any effort to create a conventionally 'professional' managerial class on a national scale. While in previous generations the highest management ranks of business tended to be significantly if not exclusively populated by those from the higher social classes in the country (Quail, 1998), the post-war 'baby boom' generation would help to democratize management enormously with respect to social class background in the 1970s as those children reached maturity and began to enter organizations of all sizes. In the 1940s and 1950s, the hand-picked students at the Henley or Ashridge colleges might have expected to have broadly similar educational backgrounds to their classmates due to family or class advantages, but by the 1970s and 1980s for most cohorts of business students this was no longer the case. Britain had embarked upon a long and slow path toward a more meritocratic system, but privileged social elites continued to rise highest in British companies. Company directorships especially attracted those with titles and considerable social capital, and these directors unsurprisingly appointed senior managers who reflected similar perspectives and opinions to those they held themselves (see for example Whitley et al., 1981).

As the demographics and economic conditions evolved so did the nation's understanding of the relationships between management, labour and government. The steady erosion of the so-called 'post-war consensus' about the desirability of full employment and rising standards of living as a reward for the sacrifices during wartime meant that labour strife rose and the difficulties of management grew, especially within mature industries like textiles, coal and automobiles. The rise of the welfare state encouraged a growth in bureaucracy with its concomitant hierarchical organization, antithetical to the forms of work valued – if not always enjoyed – by professionals (Perkin, 1989). Very slowly, companies demonstrated more interest in managers with educational credentials purporting to show that they prepared for the challenges they would face in their careers; if nothing else, qualifications suggested an agreement with the basic ethos of management. In the tense industrial relations atmosphere, perhaps people felt that educational qualifications helped to justify managers' places at the bargaining table or enabled them to assemble sophisticated financial information to bolster arguments with either the government or labour unions. However public perception of the poor performance of many British industries did little to boost the social esteem managers and directors held in British society. The search for social status consonant with similar professional groups continued.

A growing interest in hiring business graduates arose alongside an expansion in management education opportunities in British universities. The increase in the number of universities in the 1960s gradually allowed more students to attend courses, thus feeding nascent business and management education programmes which themselves took some inspiration from the London and Manchester business schools started during the middle of this decade. Early business school degree recipients in the UK knew about the higher pay and status enjoyed by graduates of American Master of Business Administration (MBA) programmes and sought that sort of recognition from the firms that hired them; for their part, firms had yet to be convinced that these allegedly well-trained and 'slick' graduates deserved premium pay and other benefits. Press criticism of MBAs reflected business community sentiments, ranging from wariness to outright disapproval, regarding the MBA graduate. The more disturbing ones for MBAs had headlines such as "MBA: Mediocre But Arrogant" or "Means Bugger All" (i.e., worthless) (Robertson, 1970; Roeber, 1971; Wills, 1971; Mosson, 1972; Lester, 1991; Shipman, 2002; Stern, 2002). The disconnection between the elevated expectations of recent graduates and the more critical attitudes of employers generated a lasting tension which, ironically, further undermined professional status recognition efforts by managers by constructing barriers for mutual professional cooperation even within the same companies. While those tensions have faded away over the past three decades, new critics have surfaced who question the value of management education to business in terms of its intellectual content and its usefulness to business: the works of Henry Mintzberg in particular criticize the content of management training and education (Mintzberg, 1973, 1989, 2004). There is a long literature that holds business schools responsible for failing to inculcate successfully not just the technical skills needed for business but also the code of conduct or ethical element that has recently risen to the forefront of public consciousness. Books such as Robert Locke's *Confronting Managerialism: How the Business Elite and Their Schools Threw Our Lives Out of Balance* (Locke and Spender, 2011) and other recent publications by Starkey and Tiratsoo (Starkey and Tiratsoo, 2007), Khurana (Khurana, 2007) and Morsing and Rovira (Morsing et al., 2011) highlight these critiques, coming from both within and outside of business schools. Such criticisms have not helped the professionalization cause.

Simultaneously the sociology of professionalization rapidly produced some further, and more seminal, contributions to the field. Eliot Freidson's *Profession of Medicine: A Study of the Sociology of Applied Knowledge* (Freidson, 1970) was soon followed by Magali Sarfatti Larson's *The Rise of Professionalism: A Sociological Analysis* (Sarfatti Larson, 1977).[4] Together these books helped to update and reshape views of existing accepted professions (medicine, teaching, law, etc.) by studying the professionalization process itself combined with the ideology(s) that defined it, a theme discussed previously decades earlier by such authors as Sheldon and Parsons mentioned above. As a reconceptualization of the professions advanced alongside macro-level social changes in the wake of the Second World War, these later books by Freidson and Larson took a more sophisticated sociological view of the world of professions and what it might mean to be a 'professional' or to undertake a 'professional project', that is, the effort to acquire high status for individual professionals regardless of their organizational affiliation. Sarfatti Larson's Marxist-inspired interpretation in particular received praise for being well grounded historically (Wood, 1977; Mills, 1978; Barber, 1979; Riggs, 1982). In contrast, Schudson voiced more criticism (1980).

Around the same time Terence Johnson published *Professions and Power* in Britain in 1972 (Johnson, 1972). In it, Johnson explicitly asked whether the professions played specific roles (economic, political or social) in modern society. Johnson points out historically- and culturally-bound elements of earlier models like those affecting Parsons's distinction between professionals and businessmen. Others had previously questioned the level of 'altruistic' behaviour allegedly shown by people in established professions, specifically medicine (Wilensky, 1964, p. 148). His main contribution however suggested flaws in the conventional sociology of the professions and these flaws arose from one of two sources, depending on the approach used. Either the flaws came from the limitations of the functionalist focus (e.g. Talcott Parsons) on professions acting within a society, or arose from the 'traits' of individual professions, including those arising from the 'professionalization' process itself (e.g., Wilensky, Freidson and others). In their place Johnson offered another explanation which attempted to overcome these concerns by accounting for variations within the institutional framework of professional practice(s), in part by addressing the relationship with clients coming from a wide range of social backgrounds. For Johnson, the differences can be explained, at least in part, by looking closely at the forms of institutional control and how these are exercised within, and in part outside of, the professional group itself.

Another decade passed before Andrew Abbott's *The System of the Professions* produced considerable reaction when it was published in 1988 (Abbott, 1988). Another major publication on the topic of professionalization, it took an ecological view of the many (more than 50) professions he identified. Instead of outlining the alleged 'professional' characteristics that appeared to stretch across numerous occupational categories as others had done using the 'trait' approach, he took a view that professions competed against each other for specific spaces in the public arena; that is, they often fought for 'territory' both tangible and intangible that the individual profession could call its own. This territory, once won, could be defended against intruders by the construction of barriers to entry, such as legal rights to practice negotiated with the state, possession and demonstration of a closely guarded body of knowledge (usually but not exclusively acquired in a university setting) and demands to adhere to a set of behavioural norms set within the profession. This hard-won territory could also be lost, however, to a more powerful competing professional group or it could be given up willingly as the profession itself found 'greener pastures' ripe for colonization. Abbott's view reads in many ways as a more advanced 'functionalist' approach to the professions, but only in the sense that the 'function' the professions are performing is not limited merely to the services performed on behalf of clients for the greater good of society, but also on behalf of the profession overall in competition with other professions for the most valuable or prestigious 'territory' available in the relevant sphere of activity.

Abbott's book generated a good deal of further discussion and examination of the issues he raised. The 'ecosystem' view outlining the evolution of *interlocking communities of professions* represented an original approach to understanding the phenomenon that he set out to examine. Closer inspection by later authors revealed some of the problems of this view for mainstream business managers and directors. For example, Christopher Grey pointed out that under the Abbott model a 'profession' needed to possess a specific technical body of knowledge which was sufficiently abstracted from individual circumstances to empower its practitioners to apply this knowledge across a broad range of cases or situations (Grey, 1997). Abbott, with the (unrelated) support of authors like Richard Whitley (see Grey, 1997; Whitley, 1984), denied that managers could prove that management studies constituted an academic discipline in the same manner as other fields like law, engineering or education. The paradox for Grey is that despite this apparently fatal flaw, the occupational 'territory' in which management beliefs and practices are dominant or in the ascendancy continued to expand. According to Abbott, that should be something only a profession is able to accomplish, and yet management – which Mintzberg, Abbott and Whitley all independently posit is most definitely *not* a profession – keeps expanding the territory in which its values and dominant perspectives prevail.

Grey explains the process by claiming that in the case of management the professionalization mission has primarily been one of seeking status rather than defining a technical body of knowledge. He admits that efforts have been made in this latter area in the past by the early management gurus of their day, including Henri Fayol, Frederick W. Taylor, Lyndall Urwick and Edward Brech (Grey, 1997, p. 708). But instead of focusing on the success or failure of these efforts, he concentrates on the intentional (re-)positioning of management studies in the scientific realm and notes repeated emphasis on the *science* aspects of the term *social science*. Management studies, he says, have been labelled and conceived in very positivistic ways specifically to transfer the legitimacy of more established scientific disciplines onto management. This process of transferring status shows signs of success, though the effort is mitigated by three main factors. First, management as a group is internally fragmented because of the nature of the work itself and the tensions that exist between various levels of managers, even within the same company. Likewise, state support for a professionalising mission, which Timmons (Timmons, 2010, p. 339) highlighted as an important element in the process, has been absent. Second, managers are organizationally dependent for their work in a way that individual practitioners of other professions, such as law, are not (the teaching profession might run aground on this same issue). This means their autonomy as professionals is constrained by factors outside of their control; the vast majority of managers are, after all, employees. Finally, most managers – especially those embedded in the middle levels of larger organisations – are subject to increased monitoring activity as their work becomes ever more bureaucratic and less open to contextual application of systematic knowledge, which was previously identified as a conventional hallmark of professional activity. Grey then shows that the first two of these arguments against professionalization of managers can be solidly questioned, and then addresses the third – the routinization of management work – in greater depth.

This third element deals with what Grey calls the 'responsibilization' of managers, that is, the process of socialising them into a collection of values and behaviours sufficiently in agreement with the employer's preferences to render them 'trustworthy and predictable by virtue of their beliefs and behaviours' to become stewards of the company's resources (Grey, 1997, p. 719). If this is true, Grey has brought us full circle and seems to endorse the views of people like Mintzberg and Whitley mentioned earlier: it is not the *content* of management education which gives it a 'professional' aura but instead the *values transmitted through it* to students of the subject. Grey, like others before and since, recognised that the socialization process that management students undergo represented a large if usually misunderstood portion of students' educational experiences. Instead of business-friendly values being infused into the student as a sort of by-product of studying the 'science' of management, infusing those values is instead posited as the main purpose of business education where the teaching of particular theories and techniques relevant to business operations serves merely as an excuse for the opportunity to imbue values in the next generation of 'responsibilized' managers. As shown above, the titles of recent books studying the situation in both America and Europe have picked up on the two main aspects of this issue, both the lack of effective management content within management schools as well as their function as transmitters of social values useful to, or at least not incompatible with, the core values of corporations and their leaders.

'Responsibilization' and the views of Edward Brech

In June 2005, a Management History Research Group workshop was held at Queen Mary, University of London, to discuss participants' research ideas and projects related to management history. I was asked by the organiser to serve as chairperson for the first session of the day, and thus had the honour of introducing the management consultant turned business historian Edward Brech as a panellist in this session. As is common at such events, I introduced him briefly, explained that each presenter would have about twenty minutes to present and said that we would take questions immediately after each person had spoken. Brech stood up, graciously thanked 'our chairman' for the introduction, and proceeded to explain why he felt that Britain needed not only professional management qualifications but also that he wanted to see a thorough-going professionalization of management, encompassing all managers and directors in the United Kingdom. Brech was well aware of much of the professionalization literature discussed above, of course, having contributed to it himself over many years. Brech spoke for only about 10 or 12 minutes, finished his presentation and sat down. After a moment of confusion at this unexpectedly swift conclusion, I announced that we were ready to take questions. Though my memory of the event has faded somewhat, I remember everyone in the room quickly raising a hand to dispute Brech's stated position on the wisdom, necessity or viability of the professionalization agenda he had just briefly outlined for businesspeople in the British economy.

It is possible that the nonagenarian Edward Brech, a seasoned veteran of British industrial management who had worked alongside some of the biggest names in British management consultancy and who had played a notable role in the evolution of post-war management training, was simply testing the younger generation by deliberately provoking them with his professionalization arguments. Most of the participants in the room knew the basic story of British management education, and this does not bear reviewing here; other sources provide rich and insightful histories of these events (Wilson and Manchester Business School, 1992; Keeble, 1992; Larson, 2003; Workman, 2004; Wilson and Thomson, 2006; Williams, 2010). But in general Brech's comments were only partly historical and it appears that he may have been looking to the future for the realisation of a goal which had heretofore proved elusive throughout the twentieth century: the creation and implementation of a true professionalization *process* for British managers.

Brech himself had more than weighed in on the topic of the history of management in the UK with the completion of his enormous five-volume work entitled *The Evolution of Modern Management in Britain 1832–1979* which naturally included discussion of educational programmes for current or aspiring managers (Brech, 2002). Arising from his PhD (Brech, then 85 years old, was among the first Britons to complete a doctorate explicitly in the field of 'business history'), the work represents an enormous investment of time and energy in trying to bring a definitive voice to the history of management in the UK. His passion for the topic was obvious – but as the hands shot up from people in the audience, it became obvious that the rationale for professionalizing British management in the twenty-first century did not appear as clear to everyone else as it might have been for Brech. His presentation outlined a particular type of professionalization for British managers which could, arguably, have brought them centre-stage in British national life. How did he believe this could be accomplished?

Brech's short paper says volumes in its two typed pages.[5] While he acknowledges that politicians and policy makers eagerly took credit for what in 2005 appeared to be several years of reasonably strong economic performance from the middle 1990s onwards, his paper focused primarily upon those he believed genuinely created wealth in the British economy: industrial and commercial managers and directors. Brech noted that these same self-congratulating politicians were content to leave blame for the general (long-term) decline of Britain's economic power "where it belonged professionally", that is, with those same directors and managers of businesses. His paper painted a sobering picture of the economy in the early years of the new millennium, highlighting the loss of Britain's former industrial and commercial power, pointing out that then-current [2005] unemployment figures continued to show nearly 1.5 million people out of work which Brech noted as "a figure higher than in the depression years of 1971–72", and lamenting the near-constant refrain in public discourse of the inability to "afford the initiation of a desirable new service, or the construction of even much-needed new premises … and not infrequently important improvements in existing public services". The Great Britain to which Brech referred was not so 'great' after all, and given the actual economic reality described above he suggested that it was time, in effect, for Britain's managerial class to 'grow up'.

He argued that the three main hallmarks of professionalization could easily be applied to business. The first, that there was "a pertinent body of specialist knowledge and know-how that can be taught and learned", has itself been a topic of strenuous discussion both in Britain and abroad (see above discussion as well as others such as Grey, 1997; Reed and Anthony, 1992; Wilson and Thomson, 2006). Brech himself had participated in these debates along-side such vocal supporters as management consultant Lyndall Urwick (Brech et al., 2010); both, not surprisingly, came down on the affirmative side of the discussion. The advent of formal management education within universities at graduate degree level in the 1960s had generated considerable doubt among both academics and the business community regarding whether 'management' was an academic subject worthy of inclusion within the pre-expansion university system that existed in the UK in that period (Larson, 2003, p. 115). In the end, however, through a combination of building upon earlier expertise in London and Manchester and some small help from American management educators, the beginnings of British postgraduate business schools took shape and with it the construction within the university sector of an identifiable body of knowledge relevant to management specialists. Thus the first hallmark of professionalization could claim to have been addressed, even if it did not fully convince everyone.

Brech's second and third hallmarks of professionalization are two sides of the same coin. The second hallmark claims that a profession "has an objective in service to other persons and/or to the community". It was this point that served as the crux of Brech's argument that day in 2005: he was arguing that a true 'profession' serves the community first and itself and its members second. The third hallmark, he wrote, demanded that the members of a profession "value and pursue that objective [service to others] in manifest preference to their own personal gain, benefit, or advantage". That is to say, professionals demonstrate, through their own actions, that the needs of the community and (or) their clients are prioritized ahead of their own desires. For some established professions these patterns have been demonstrated and accepted by the society surrounding them for a long time. The usual examples are law, where there is steady professional pressure for lawyers to abide by an agreed code of professional conduct regarding such things as client confidences, and medicine, where the efforts of medical professionals attending the patient are wholly intended for the patient's benefit (this has been questioned occasionally; see Wilensky, 1964). Given the differences in environment, expectations and *raison d'etre*, what can the business community do in order to satisfy these two hallmarks of professionalization?

Brech's answer, and perhaps the point that was not expressed verbally during his presentation as effectively as he might have wished, called for Britain's managerial class to 'grow up' and assume main responsibility for the wealth-creation process on behalf of the country. In his own words, he wanted both managers and directors together to "recognise, accept and acknowledge their inherent fundamental responsibility for the attainment and maintenance of wealth-creation in provision for the livelihood and well-being of the nation's community". This view does not dismiss the important groundwork carried out by politicians who create an environment designed to provide opportunities for businesses to succeed. Brech imagined businesspeople becoming the advisors to these policy makers in this respect and thus playing a central role in securing the future economic well-being of the nation.

He saw clearly that his vision of an enhanced role for a business 'profession' advising policy makers on the best way forward economically within British society remained a long way from realization. He frankly admitted that there was a desperate need for Britain's managerial class to address their own "totally inadequate recognition of [their] professional responsibility for the wealth and well-being of the community". To address this successfully would require a number of institutional changes across the whole field of management, including bringing the previously separate managerial and directorial organizations either fully together (or at least much more directly in harmony with each other), and by bringing the academic business schools – by 2005 these were ubiquitous within British universities – and management practitioners into a much closer relationship. Brech called for nothing less than a total revolution in the way managers received their training, behaved on the job and understood their role in society.

Here, then, we have arrived at the fundamental element of the challenge referred to in the title of this chapter: how can all of these groups of people, all with different agendas and perspectives, come together to agree on what the role(s) of managers will be in modern life and thereby get managers and directors, as a sort of 'officer class' within UK business, to internalise responsibility for carrying out the nation's long-term wealth-creation function? How, in short, can they be brought together to form a single, if diverse, 'profession' of management?

Final thoughts

The changes that Brech sought in 2005 are not qualitatively unlike those sought by Elbourne during the 1920s, Lyndall Urwick during the 1950s or the advocates of university management education in the 1960s. All of them sought to elevate the status of managers in the esteem of British society by doing two main things: associating the activity of management with a codified body of knowledge general enough for use by all managers thereby creating a 'science' of management, and establishing a code of conduct which could inspire confidence in outsiders that qualified managers behaved ethically and correctly with respect to the law but perhaps more importantly the needs of the nation as a whole. After the 1980s the prevalence of collective action in economic activity declined as union membership decreased and workers of all levels, including managers, grew more individualized. Thus for the past thirty years it has been hard to conceive of a united management profession of the sort envisaged by Brech. As the forgoing tried to illustrate, Brech took a long-term view along the lines of those writing in the first three-quarters of the twentieth century.

Like Brech, Wilson and Thomson (Wilson and Thomson, 2006) revived the long-standing discussion of the theme of the professionalization of managers in *Making of Modern Management*. As one of four main themes in the book, they trace the difficult history of British management professionalization in a valuable way by outlining how inadequate training, weak professional institutes, poor social status of managers and ineffective dissemination of important writings by management theorists combined to undermine professionalization efforts through the end of the twentieth century. Although the Chartered Management Institute received its royal charter in 2002, the CMI remains a long way from realizing the goals set for its predecessor body, the British Institute of Management; the BIM was established shortly after the Second World War by the Attlee Labour Government in a largely failed attempt to repair the perceived deficiencies of Britain's industrial and commercial leaders. Poor choices of leaders early in the Institute's life and the stigma of being a Labour Party creation hampered its progress and severely limited its effectiveness for more than two decades (Larson, 2003).

There are, of course, substantial obstacles in the way of this transformation today and they operate on a variety of levels. Conversely, we have seen recently that a large and complex economic crisis led people to reconsider the goals of management education; this is a necessary process for Brech's professionalization dream to be realised. The codification and transmission of a body of specialist technical knowledge about management happens primarily, though not exclusively by any means, in business schools. In wake of the 2008 banking crisis there arose a significant call for a thorough restructuring of the economic system and, therefore necessarily, of the educational systems which cater to it. Advocates of that restructuring must be disappointed today in the small amount of change that has taken place in formal management education institutions. Syllabi for management courses remain largely as they were before the crisis, though with perhaps slightly more emphasis on corporate governance or ethical business practices. The 'quantification' of management education decried by authors like Locke and Spender (2011) continues to dominate the leading business schools; whether this results from what students want to learn, what staff want to teach, or for some other reason is hard to say. This chapter highlights the importance of *contextualizing* the learning that students do in business schools in order to overcome both a strong presentist bias in management education as well as the quantification bias identified above. Pursuing this contextualizing mission is a contribution to the education of future managers for which historians are eminently well qualified, yet for many years business historians remained marginalized in both business and management schools and, to a slightly lesser degree, in history departments. Therefore, few universities have programmes directly in the area of business history, and these tend to be based in history departments rather than business schools. Business historians, therefore, would be wise to follow advice offered from a number of voices both within and outside of business history to make their research and publications more relevant for a wider management studies audience.

Publications like those of Maclean, Harvey and Clegg (Maclean et al., forthcoming), Bucheli and Wadhwani (Bucheli and Wadhwani, 2014) and others offer guidance about how scholars might do that. They call for a better integration of historical techniques with organizational theorizing so that business and management theory is better grounded in historical reality while making the field of business history more meaningful to future generations of scholars and students. Ideally the contextualization process will help practitioners gradually become more sensitive to the needs of the business as well as the community in which the business operates. It would be unrealistic to think that someday every management decision would be made in favour of the 'big picture' issues facing practicing managers, but it could represent a reasonable and rational advancement of a process which made slow progress throughout the previous century. Today, student numbers in university business and management courses in the United Kingdom remain healthy at over 220,000 students across full-time and part-time programmes, representing just under 10% of the total number of undergraduates registered at UK universities.[6] Not all of those students will rise to positions of prominence within the world of business, but if the ones who will could be educated with the sort of historically-informed community-mindedness that Brech advocated, it might begin to turn the tide in favour of the sort of developments he hoped to see.

Notes

1 He illustrates this with an amusing comparison: schoolchildren must often contend with 'substitute' teachers, but would businesspeople ever consider employing a 'substitute manager' for a day a week in a business while they were ill or travelling for business? Mintzberg's point is the importance of *context* to managerial capabilities and performance. See page 12 of Mintzberg, H. 2004. *Managers Not MBAs: A Hard Look at the Soft Practice of Managing and Management Development,* Harlow, England, Pearson Education Ltd.

2 For a thorough history of the development of the Institute, see Rose, T. G. and Institute of Industrial Administration, 1954. *A History of the Institute of Industrial Administration, 1919–1951,* London, Institute of Industrial Administration. Edward Brech also explored the IIA's growth and its later merger with the British Institute of Management; see Chapters 2–5 of Brech, E. F. L. and Dempster, A. 1999. *A History of Management,* Corby, Northants, Institute of Management.

3 This is not surprising given Parsons's long career and productivity. In her review of Freidson's book (see below), Geraldine Tate Clausen wrote that 'There is a work-orientation stemming from the practitioner's role...which makes him far less likely than the scholar or researcher to manifest the Parsonian professional values...'. This suggests that she assumed most readers of the *American Sociological Review* would know what these 'Parsonian' (functionalist) values were. Clausen, G. T. 1971. Review of Eliot Freidson's 'Profession of Medicine: A Study of the Sociology of Applied Knowledge'. *American Sociological Review, 36,* 1166–7.

4 There is no relation between Sarfatti Larson and the author of this chapter.

5 E.F.L. Brech, 'Historical Lessons for the Advancement of Management in Britain's Twenty-First Century'. Paper circulated to delegates to the 2005 Management History Research Group meeting held at Queen Mary, University of London, on 13–14 June. All quotations presented here within double quotation marks come from this short paper unless otherwise stated.

6 See Table 4 at https://www.hesa.ac.uk/free-statistics. The figure is over 11% for full-time students and half of that (5.6%) for part-time students. Accessed on 8 Feb 2016.

References

Abbott, A. D. (1988). *The system of professions: an essay on the division of expert labor.* Chicago, University of Chicago Press.

Barber, B. (1979). Review of Magali Sarfatti Larson's 'The Rise of Professionalism: A Sociological Analysis'. *Political Science Quarterly, 94,* 155–156.

Brech, E. F. L. (2002). *The evolution of modern management in Britain, 1852–1979,* five volumes. Bristol, UK, Thoemmes Press.

Brech, E. F. L. & Dempster, A. (1999). *A history of management,* Corby, Northants, Institute of Management.

Brech, E. F. L., Thomson, A. & Wilson, J. F. (2010). *Lyndall Urwick, management pioneer: a biography.* Oxford, Oxford University Press.

Bucheli, M. & Wadhwani, R. D. (eds.) (2014). *Organizations in time: history, theory, methods.* Oxford: Oxford University Press.

Clausen, G. T. (1971). Review of Eliot Freidson's 'Profession of Medicine: A Study of the Sociology of Applied Knowledge'. *American Sociological Review, 36,* 1166–1167.

Fitzgerald, R. (1995). *Rowntree and the marketing revolution, 1862–1969.* Cambridge, Cambridge University Press.

Freidson, E. (1970). *Profession of medicine: a study of the sociology of applied knowledge.* New York, Dodd, Mead & Co.

Gordon, R. A. & Howell, J. E. (1959). *Higher education for business.* New York, Columbia University Press.

Grey, C. (1997). Management as a Technical Practice: Professionalization or Responsibilization? *Systems Practice, 10,* 703–725.

Johnson, T. J. (1972). *Professions and power.* London, Macmillan Press for the British Sociological Association.

Keeble, S. P. (1992). *The ability to manage: a study of British management, 1890–1990.* Manchester, Manchester University Press.

Khurana, R. (2007). *From higher aims to hired hands: the social transformation of american business schools and the unfulfilled promise of management as a profession.* Princeton, NJ, Princeton University Press.

Kreis, S. (1992). The Diffusion of Scientific Management: The Bedaux Company in America and Britain, 1926–1945. *In:* Nelson, D. (ed.) *A Mental revolution: scientific management since Taylor.* Columbus, Ohio State University Press.

Larson, M. J. (2003). *Practically Academic: the formation of the british business school.* Unpublished doctoral thesis, University of Wisconsin-Madison.

Lester, T. 1991. The Great Divide. *Management Today,* 77–79.

Locke, R. R. & Spender, J.-C. (2011). *Confronting managerialism: how the business elite and their schools threw our lives out of balance.* London, Zed.

Maclean, M., Harvey, C. & Clegg, S. (2015). Conceptualizing Historical Organization Studies. *Academy of Management Review, 41*(4), (Oct 2016), 609–632.

Mills, D. L. (1978). Review of Magali Sarfatti Larson's 'The Rise of Professionalism: A Sociological Analysis'. *Contemporary Sociology, 7,* 654–655.

Mintzberg, H. (1973). *The nature of managerial work,* New York, Harper & Row.

Mintzberg, H. (1989). *Mintzberg on management: inside our strange world of organizations.* New York, Free Press.

Mintzberg, H. (2004). *Managers not MBAs: a hard look at the soft practice of managing and management development.* Harlow, England, Pearson Education Ltd.

Morsing, M., Sauquet Rovira, A. & Community of European Management Schools. (2011). *Business schools and their contribution to society.* Los Angeles; London, SAGE.

Mosson, T. M. (1972). And Now a Word from Our Sponsors... *Management Education and Development*, *3*, 74–78.

Parsons, T. (1939). The Professions and Social Structure. *Social Forces, 17*, 457–467.

Perkin, H. J. (1989). *The rise of professional society in England since 1880*, London, New York, Routledge.

Pierson, F. C. (1959). *The education of American businessmen; a study of university-college programs in business administration*. New York, McGraw-Hill.

Quail, J. (1998). From Personal Patronage to Public School Privilege – Social Closure in the Recruitment of Managers in the United Kingdom from the Late Nineteenth Century to 1930. *In:* Kidd, A. & Nicholls, D. (eds.) *The rise of the british middle class?: studies of regional and cultural diversity since the eighteenth century.* Stroud: Sutton.

Reed, M. I. & Anthony, P. (1992). Professionalizing Management and Managing Professionalization: British Management in the 1980s. *Journal of Management Studies, 29*, 591–613.

Riggs, R. R. (1982). Review of Magali Sarfatti Larson's 'The Rise of Professionalism: A Sociological Analysis'. *Southern Review of Public Administration, 82*, 255–256.

Robertson, A. B. (1970). Business Schools: Is the Backlash Justified? *Management Decision, 4*, 13.

Roeber, J. (1971). Crisis in Business schools. *The Times Educational Supplement*, November 19.

Rose, T. G. & Institute of Industrial Administration (1954). *A history of the Institute of Industrial Administration, 1919–1951.* London, Institute of Industrial Administration.

Sarfatti Larson, M. (1977). *The rise of professionalism: a sociological analysis.* Berkeley, University of California Press.

Schudson, M. (1980). Review Essay of Magali Sarfatti Larson's 'The Rise of Professionalism: A Sociological Analysis'. *Theory and Society, 9*, 215–29.

Sheldon, O. (1923). *The philosophy of management.* London, Pitman & Sons.

Shipman, A. (2002). Is the Masterplan Coming Unstuck? *The Times Higher Education Supplement*, November 8.

Starkey, K. & Tiratsoo, N. (2007). *The business school and the bottom line.* Cambridge, Cambridge University Press.

Stern, S. (2002). What did Business School do for them? *Management Today*, 40–45.

Timmons, S. (2010). Professionalization and its Discontents. *Health, 15*, 337–352.

Weatherburn, M. R. (2014). *Scientific management at work: the bedaux system, management consulting, and worker efficiency in british industry, 1914–48.* Unpublished doctoral thesis, Imperial College London.

Webb, S. & Webb, B. (1920). *Industrial Democracy.* New York, Augustus M. Kelley.

Whitley, R. 1984. The Fragmented State of Management Studies: Reasons and Consequences. *Journal of Management Studies, 21*, 331–348.

Whitley, R., Thomas, A. & Marceau, J. (1981). *Masters of business?: business schools and business graduates in Britain and France.* London, Tavistock Publications.

Wilensky, H. (1964). The Professionalization of Everyone? *The American Journal of Sociology, 70*, 137–158.

Williams, A. P. O. (2010). *The history of UK business and management education*, London, Emerald for the Association of Business Schools.

Wills, G. (1971). 'Arrogance' of 'National' Business Schools Attacked. *The Times Higher Education Supplement*, December 3.

Wilson, J. F. & Manchester Business School (University of Manchester) (1992). *The Manchester experiment: a history of Manchester Business School, 1965–1990.* London, Paul Chapman Publishing for Manchester Business School.

Wilson, J. F. & Thomson, A. (2006). *The making of modern management: British management in historical perspective.* Oxford, Oxford University Press.

Wood, S. W. (1977). Review of Magali Sarfatti Larson's 'The Rise of Professionalism: A Sociological Analysis'. *Library Journal, 102*, 2174–2175.

Workman, J. (2004). *Paying for pedigree? British business schools and the master of business administration degree.* Unpublished doctoral thesis, University of Sussex.

22

Gender and business

Women in business or businesswomen? An assessment of the history of entrepreneurial women

Helen Doe

Historians of businesswomen face more than a few challenges in uncovering women in business. In order to find them, they must first find the man. For example, William Wright had a ropemaking business in Birmingham in the early years of the nineteenth century. Unfortunately, he was a chronic alcoholic and this meant that in practise it was his wife, Ann, who ran the business while bringing up the children. This fact would not have been apparent except for Ann's application in 1838 to the local magistrates for an order banning William and leaving her to run the business out of which she would pay him an income (Jenns, 1997, pp. 187–92). So even if a man was feckless, drunk or incapable and his wife in reality ran the business, it was still his name above the door. In 1813 a list of the shipbuilders based on the Thames was provided to parliament for an enquiry into shipping. These were the largest industrial organisations of their time. The clerk who drew up the list included Francis Barnard and son who employed in excess of 400 men, but he made a mistake; the owner and driver of the business was Mrs Frances Barnard (Doe, 2009, p. 179).

Second, the vast majority of women ran small businesses which left few records. Business history, in general, has tended to feature large business and particularly so in America. Wendy Gamber challenged US business historians:

> Unless one concentrates on the exceptional – the woman bank president, the rare female millionaire – studying the history of women in business (especially in the nineteenth century) means studying the history of small business, indeed the history of very small business. Such a perspective has been anathema to U.S. business history, which until quite recently took the large corporation as its subject.
>
> *(Gamber, 1998, p. 192)*

Big businesses are seen as symbols of success and also tend to be the ones for which there is most evidence. The large numbers of small family run businesses left little trace, often leaving just a name in a directory. Combine that with laws and social conventions that subsumed a woman's name and property into that of her husband's and it demonstrates why finding businesswomen is such a challenge, yet since the 1990s this world of the female-run business is gradually being uncovered.

Does it matter whether a business is primarily run by a man or a woman? The aim of all business is surely gender neutral since all enterprises need to achieve a profit. But it is attitudes, aims and ambitions that shape a business and these can be affected by the circumstances of the owner and the environment, political or social, in which he or she lives. This chapter looks at the questions raised by historians when examining female-led business and women in the world of financial risk. It looks at the historiography and the main debates and poses further questions.

'Women as a group appear to share more similarities than differences but the business experiences of men and women are allegedly more different than similar. These hypotheses remain to be tested' (Yeager, 1999). These are words from Yeager's review of Angel Kwoleck-Folland's book, *Incorporating Women,* and 16 years later they still remain to be tested. Kwoleck-Folland's book was a torch bearer for the study of women in business and her scope was wide. She felt constrained by a definition of business as economic activity in a market to seek profit and 'assuming the financial responsibility for that activity' (Kwoleck-Folland, 1998, p. 5). This definition, which included shareholders, owners of business and market traders, excluded the waged. In her wide-ranging examination of women in business, Kwoleck-Folland included wage earners, the self-employed and those engaging in forms of barter. She saw a complex arena for women in which business experience came from women as entrepreneurs, as members of family businesses and women's roles as slaves, labourers, wage earners and managers (Kwoleck-Folland, 1998, p. 11). In American business history the corporation dominated and obscured small firms, family firms, barter and trade. In all of these forms women were active. Additionally, Kwoleck-Folland accused business historians of ignoring the history of workers and leaving that arena to labour historians who were anti-business (Kwoleck-Folland, 1998, p. 10).

The businesswoman in European history remained hidden. The focus was on women's work rather than the risk takers, entrepreneurs and investors. The Marxist-feminist view of waged women struggling against male patriarchy had plenty of supporters, but was described as 'too sweeping' by Pamela Sharpe in a useful article on change and continuity (Sharpe, 1995, p. 354). While Bridget Hill's contribution challenged the theory that there had been a 'golden age' for women in work in the early modern era and in a second, very useful, article laid out the challenges in using the census as a source on women and work in the nineteenth century (Hill, 1993a, 1993b).

The influential publication for English gender historians was Davidoff and Hall's *Family Fortunes* (Davidoff and Hall, 1987). This pioneering study promoted the notion that women were the hidden investment in many family businesses (Davidoff and Hall, 1987, pp. 272–315). It also promulgated the theory of separate spheres, where women were increasingly marginalised into domestic life. Although Davidoff and Hall also pointed out that it was 'a matter for negotiation, rather than a fixed code', the striking image provided by separate spheres has proved lasting (Davidoff and Hall, 1987, p. 117; Gleadle, 2007). It has continued to be a useful target for later historians. There remained what Gamber referred to as 'the inattention of women's historians to the history of women in business' (Gamber, 1998, p. 199). Despite Amanda Vickery's lively attack, the theories of a lost golden age and separate spheres held sway (Vickery, 1993). Pamela Sharpe highlighted several case studies of women entrepreneurs from 1600 to 1850. Her findings generally supported the notion of separate spheres in the nineteenth century. Women, she found, were edged out of merchant roles into more feminine retail trades (Sharpe, 2001).

It seemed as if in Europe, certainly in Britain, the female entrepreneur was to remain in the margins. This changed with Hannah Barker and Nicola Phillips who provided the first full length treatment of women in business and challenged several images. They covered much the same period, the late eighteenth century to the early nineteenth century, but with different locations. Barker focussed on Northern England and Phillips mainly on London. Barker challenged models of 'women's shifting economic and social status' and saw a broad continuity in women's commercial activity (Barker, 2006, p. 168.) Her conclusion was that her findings complicated, rather than negated, the separate spheres theory (Barker, 2006, p. 171). Phillips took a different tack and criticised the arguments on capitalism and patriarchy as too narrow and encouraging the widespread assumption that there are only two ways to discuss women's economic opportunities; 'that is that they were always limited, or that they became more so after the industrial revolution' (Phillips, 2006, p. 173).

As Vickery put it: 'assumption prevails that it is helpful to examine culture and society in terms of intrinsically male and female spheres' (Vickery, 1993, p. 267). The continued attack on separate spheres moved the story further into the nineteenth century. Kay, like Phillips, used the Sun Life insurance records and found significant numbers of women running small businesses. While many were in feminine related trades they built up strong business reputations and used their family and local networks for capital (Kay, 2009). In the nineteenth century maritime sector, women and their male counterparts had a more flexible approach to what was required of the typical masculine or feminine role. Research on maritime communities across England and Wales showed a continuity of female – led business activity from 1780 to 1880 (Doe, 2006). As Vickery reminds us 'Victorian women emerge as no less spirited, capable and most importantly, diverse a crew as women in any century' and demonstrated that independence of 'spirit, brains and capability were not and are not limited to just one half of mankind' (Vickery, 1993, p. 300). Melanie Buddle continued the theme in Canada taking the story up to the Second World War (Buddle, 2010).

In general, the businesswoman in the twentieth century has had less attention. In the USA, Kwoleck-Folland found a narrowing of prospects as 'industries matured, requiring more capital, adopting professional management and addressing larger markets' (Kwoleck-Folland, 1998, p. 126). It did see women heading large cosmetics companies. Estee Lauder was one of several women who moved from the kitchen table to Wall Street (Kwoleck-Folland, 1998, pp. 128–130). If there was a narrowing of opportunity, Kwoleck-Folland shows a change in the type of industry in which women ran businesses. In a survey in 1954, the largest sector for women-owned businesses was retail 32.5%, personal service 11.2%, real estate, insurance and finance 10.7%, educational 10.1% and manufacturing and construction 3%. By 1991 those percentages were over turned, with a 19% increase in women in construction and a 3.5% decline in retail (Kwoleck-Folland, pp. 157, 192).

Many of these women succeeded despite the obstacles in their path. All business historians need to understand the economic, political, social and technological frameworks within which business institutions operate, which constrain business or provide opportunities. For historians of women in business there are the additional frameworks provided by marriage, property rights, probate, political franchise and exclusion from position (Finn, 1986; Holcombe, 1983; Morris, 1994; Shanley, 1989). For women to earn an income from whatever means these restrictions (and they were more often restrictions than opportunities) must be examined. The ability to earn money brings independence and the control of money earning opportunities brings power. For much of history that control has been in male hands. But that does not mean that men have not co-operated, supported and encouraged independent women. Indeed, there are plenty of ways in which men and women have used the law selectively and opportunistically to further their own needs, for themselves or for the family, or to avoid the consequences of financial loss (Erickson, 1990; Doe, 2009, pp. 13–16, 94; Phillips, 2006, pp. 37, 67–68). Detailed examination of post-mortem distribution of wealth in the early industrial period in England uncovered family strategies that took advantage of the legal system governing inheritance and demonstrated that they were adept in 'exploiting (and sometimes ignoring) the law to realise family ambitions that was based on a popular awareness of property law' (Barker and Ishizu, 2012, p. 239).

There is no disagreement that coverture, when a woman's property, earnings and very existence was merged on marriage with that of her husband, was a restriction. As seen in the earlier example of Ann Wright, it poses additional hurdles for the historian. Even if the wife was the main driving force, manager and accountant her existence remains hidden by her husband's name on business activities. Some historians have fallen with delight on the English system in some urban areas of *feme sole* status mainly during the late medieval and early modern periods. The practise lingered on in London until the 1850s (Phillips, 2006, p. 53). For married women, *feme sole* status gave a unique opportunity to have a separate economic life and acquire legal agency in running a business (McIntosh, 2005; Phillips 2006). Mrs Janet Taylor was a high profile businesswoman. She ran navigation schools, published navigation charts and books and set the compasses on the SS *Great Eastern*. She corresponded with admirals and parliamentary committees in her own name as a married woman (Alger, 1987; Doe, 2009, pp. 246–7). Assertions or denials of *feme sole* status joined the diverse array of other legal or illegal strategies practiced by both women and men across the centuries (Macintosh, 2005). Local practise could and did ignore legal restrictions as Erickson found in her study of early modern England and in the examples of married women who registered shares in shipping in their own right before the passing of the Married Women's Property Acts in 1870 and 1882 (Erickson, 1990; Doe, 2009, p. 96).

Studies in other countries reveal differences. In nineteenth century Russia, married women took advantage of a more open legal system for women that enabled greater business independence, which led to increasing numbers of female factory owners (Ulianova, 2009). Germany has been epitomised as a highly conservative culture when it comes to married women. *Küche, Kirche, und Kinder* (kitchen, church and children) were the traditional roles for women. German guilds restricted women's commercial activities and the civil code of 1900 broadly established the husband as the patriarchal head of house (Beachy, 2001, p. 322). Yet there were many contradictions. Despite apparent guild restrictions, local studies found that 'women were represented in larger eighteenth-century business communities at rates of up to 10 per cent' (Beachy, 2001, p. 315). As a nation of small merchant firms, wives and daughters gained their commercial training within the family based business, acting as helpmate and support. In nineteenth century Cologne the reality of most family businesses was in contrast to legal and guild diktats (Beachy, 2001, pp. 313, 323).

Women proved adept at exploiting small niche markets. Examples from post 1850 America and Germany demonstrate how increasing consumerism and market segmentation provided opportunities for kitchen businesses which expanded on demand into substantial enterprises. Such as Melitta Bentz, a grocer from Düsseldorf, who 'invented and marketed the eponymous coffee filter, or the Cologne seamstress Käthe Kruse, who initially stitched felt dolls as simple gifts and later mass-produced them for a national market' (Beachy, 2001, p. 325).

Women it seemed were mainly in sectors linked to domesticity such as hostelries, pubs, lodging houses, millinery and dressmaking. But this apparent relegation to the feminine trades in previous centuries has also undergone a re-appraisal. Women appear as business owners in manufacturing, notably in Birmingham, then a major cluster of small workshops and businesses. Berg found women were apparent in significant numbers in the metal trades (Berg, 1993). Katherine Jenns' detailed examination of women in the metal trades in Birmingham supported and extended Berg's brief findings (Jenns, 1997). A recent study found that 33% of female-led business in nineteenth century Leeds and Birmingham, which on the surface appeared to be retail concerns, actually involved the manufacturing of various items (Aston, 2012, p. 226). Mrs Frances Barnard was not alone in running a shipyard. Women can be found in charge of shipyards from the early modern to the nineteenth century. They were able to hold their own in the masculine world of maritime business, running sailmaking lofts, chandleries, ropemaking and blockmaking businesses and shipyards. They managed fleets of ships and made the key business decisions (Doe, 2009).

In early twentieth century Canada, there were many women running tearooms, schools and similar 'womanly trades' (Buddle, 2010, pp. 62–63). But there were also other examples such as Wendy Macdonald who on widowhood took over B. C. Bearings, a major industrial company, from 1950 to 1998. Wanda Ziegler took over her husband's chocolate shops in 1923 and expanded them from three to eleven stores (Buddle, 2010, p. 63). Then there was Sophie Henschel who ran a major locomotive business in Germany from 1894 to 1912 (Beachy, 2006). This expansion of our understanding of the range of business in which women were in charge has led to new thoughts on family, property and power.

Pre-World War Two wage earning women in Canada were 'very likely to be single, less likely to be married, and even less likely to be widowed or divorced' on the other hand self-employed women were 'more likely to be married or once-married (widowed or divorced) than single and more likely to have children to support'. Economic necessity rather than individual choice was the key factor in Canadian womens' self-employment (Buddle, 2010, pp. 22, 49). Which brings us to the family tie. Women managed households, brought up children and also ran businesses. Yeager posed an excellent question that still needs to be fully explored:

> Women are described as having been more continuously and often circumscribed in their choices and activities by the "family claim" then men have been. Yet, histories of businessmen in the pre-industrial period have suggested that the family claim also structured the economic activity of men. We need to know whether women and men interpreted the claim differently and how their interpretations influenced economic outcomes (Yeager, 1999).

There are consistent findings on women and their involvement in family firms. In some quite large and often technical industries widows appeared to be able to take on a going concern without apparent difficulty. Such a smooth transition following the death of the husband suggests their deep involvement prior to their husband's deaths (Barker, 2006, p. 133; Doe, 2009, pp. 172–215). It was indeed vital to have such a smooth transition in order to retain important and highly influential customers. It is also clear that power once gained was not easily given up. Even when sons came of age, women remained in charge in family firms, partnerships and independent traders (Barker, 2006, pp. 109–115; Doe, 2009, p. 222).

The definition of a successful business has largely been to champion size and market share (Mandel, 2014, p. 503). This is where gender studies have opened up new debates and have combined with studies of small business and family firms (Rose, 1994; Jones and Rose, 1993; Kirby and Rose, 1994). Buddle argues that running a business to support the family even if it did not become a major enterprise was a success in itself. 'Their accomplishments were small by conventional standards of financial success or individual ambition, but they succeeded at the two jobs of "home" and business if they managed to keep the former afloat with the latter, no matter how small the enterprise' (Buddle, 2010, pp. 49–50). Maintaining the family firm was often seen as a priority by widows, but so were notions of honour, duty and respectability rather than pure financial profit (Kay, 2009, p. 99.).

Business continuity is a measurement of success and there was use of both formal and informal methods of handing over the family business, showing greater continuity in the family business. Handing over control to the widow was not just due to underage sons. Age was less relevant it seems than business experience to ensure business continuity. There is plenty of evidence of widows with close and active involvement with a firm before their husbands' death. As the son or sons came of age they might join the business as a junior partner alongside the experienced widow. There were, however, situations where business continuity might not be possible after the death of the husband and forethought was needed in order for family security. In his will in 1820 James Dixon gave his wife a choice. Dixon was a joiner and cabinet maker, a highly skilled craftsman. He requested that all orders be completed on his death (presumably by an apprentice), then the business was to be sold and Mary was to use the money to 'carry on whatever business she might think most conducive for the Maintainance Education and bringing up of my Dear Children' (Barker and Ishizu, 2012, p. 239). What the authors do not mention was the sound business sense in this will. A small owner-run business such as this required the skills of the owner. Mary's sex precluded her from training as a joiner even if she had the skill or inclination. She would have been forced to employ someone which added an extra salary to the overheads of a small family business as in the case of Mary Ellery. Mary inherited the family ship which was all very well but she could not take her husband's place as the master so, again, she would need to employ someone. Such businesses were subsistence businesses providing income for the family and occasionally some spare cash. The biggest asset was the ship itself and this was sold enabling Mary to invest the money elsewhere for the sake of her family (Doe, 2009, p. 117). James Dixon gave his widow the freedom to pursue a business career that was more likely to give her a better income.

Other ways of measuring success are highlighted by the case of Gladys Adams who ran a highly effective factory restaurant as a private concession. She was praised for her contribution to reducing factory staff turnover and improving productivity. She had zero turnover among her own staff but her business model was not based on ever-increasing profits. "I'm not making a fortune", she reported, "if I should, it would be by taking advantage of the men". In 1919 an American national business magazine hailed Mrs Adams' enterprise as a business success, alongside much larger more conventional businesses (Mandel, 2014, pp. 499–501).

Rebecca Pennock Lukens led an American ironworks for 22 years in the first half of the nineteenth century. Her husband left it in deep debt in 1825. Rebecca survived recession and raised the enterprise to regional prominence and financial stability. She fought 'legal battles over water rights, fended off her mother's attempts to hand business control to her brother and raised two children' (Kwoleck-Folland, 1998, pp. 46–47). In the case of Frances Barnard, she ran the yard as a successful enterprise from the time of her husband's death in 1795 until her own death in 1825. She extended the business and maintained a good relationship with the, wholly male, Admiralty. She built warships and large armed ships for the East India Company. Less than 10 years after her death her son was bankrupt having borrowed heavily on the business to fund a lavish country lifestyle and a place in parliament (Doe, 2009, pp. 184–187). Many female-led businesses had similar longevity, a business achievement in itself in an era of business bankruptcies (Doe, 2009; Aston, 2012, p. 227).

Not all female-led large businesses were successful. Few women had the education or the right industry grounding to manage the enormous changes wrought by technological and industry changes. There is no shame in that, many men with better education failed at the same time. But historians do women's history no favours by ignoring business failure. Lady Charlotte Guest has been hailed as a successful businesswoman. She managed the Dowlais ironworks in South Wales from 1851 on the illness and later death of her husband. It was a big concern supplying iron bars across the world (Sharpe, 2001, pp. 304–5). Her diary shows the great enthusiasm with which she engaged with the business, but she was forced to give it up on her remarriage (Guest and John, 1989). Her diary, inevitably, gives a one-sided viewpoint. A closer examination of the business accounts shows a very different picture. Charlotte simply took over where her husband had left off and the business was severely undercapitalised. After Charlotte's departure, dramatic intervention and heavy borrowing put this major industrial concern back on track and enabled it to continue into the twentieth century (Boyns and Edwards, 1997). Not all widows were happy to be left in charge. The Oxford Dictionary of National Biography hails Isabella Elder as a shipbuilder. When her husband died in 1869 she was left in charge of a major Clyde shipbuilding yard with over 4,000 men. The reality was that she coped for barely nine months until she was able to handover all business matters to her brother. Childless, Isabella then devoted herself to lifelong philanthropic work, spending her share of the money generated by the business (MacAlpine, 1997; MacAlpine, 2004).

In traditional terms of financial business success, Christine Wiskin's study of three businesswomen in the eighteenth century shows two women who were certainly not mere business figureheads. Eleanor Coad had a monumental stone business dealing with the rich and well-connected while Charlotte Matthews was a financier in the City of London. Charlotte dealt with major City of London banking and merchant houses and survived the financial crisis of war with France. Both women demonstrated sound business judgment and financial management, particularly of credit. This is contrasted by the third example, Jane Tait, who was forced into bankruptcy despite a large millinery and dressmaking business with international connections. The conclusion was that her attention to bookkeeping was not effective (Wiskin, 2006).

Walsh argues that a business endeavour is more than a 'rational search for profit, growth and stability. It is part of a social environment in which people live together and where communal values count'. She champions Helen Schultz who made her way from humble origins as a stenographer to set up a bus company in 1920s America. When banks refused to lend to her she persuaded a private investor. Her company was successful for eight years in an extremely competitive industry when many other similar companies went to the wall. She was in the end forced to sell out, but Walsh argues that she should not be judged by the male historians' benchmarks of 'internal administration, financial credibility and market command' (Walsh, 2005, p. 184). This is a statement that deserves a greater debate between business historians.

Women and investment has proved a good seam of historical writing and women have been investors certainly from the eighteenth century. They invested in the South Sea Company, the East India Company and in wartime, in privateers (Maltby and Rutterford, 2006a). The number of women shareholders increased in the nineteenth century with changes in the types of shares on offer and those brought about by the Women's Property Acts. They held shares in banks, utility firms, canals, railways and many other companies (Green and Owens, 2003, pp. 510–536; Acheson and Turner, 2006, p. 334; Freeman, Pearson and Taylor, 2006). The debate has centred on attitudes to investment risk. Green and Owens saw women as preferring, or being advised, to stay risk averse (Green and Owens, 2003). In shipping communities between 1780 and 1880 women shareholders controlled thirteen percent of the available shares in ships. They actively managed their share portfolios, buying and selling shares. Under maritime law ship owners had a direct connection to their investment and acted as the board of directors. These women were not merely passive contributors, but active players in an industry sector known for its risks (Doe, 2010). Women were also managing owners, a role unique to shipping where the shareholders elected one of their own to manage all the business affairs of the ship. It was a role that required considerable specialised industry knowledge and an ability to manage men (Doe, 2013).

We need to know more about male attitudes to these female entrepreneurs. Solidly male establishments could be gender blind when it was pragmatically necessary. Philippa Walton ran a gunpowder factory, a highly dangerous undertaking. As one of the major suppliers to government at a time of constant war during the eighteenth century, hers was a vital role. She took over from her late husband in 1711 at the age of 36 and at that time she had ten young children. It was not until 1723 that she took one of her sons into partnership with her (Fairclough, 2004). During the Napoleonic Wars, the Admiralty, a male bastion of power and control, continued to give shipbuilding contracts to the forthright and determined Mrs Ross because hers were the best bids in a competitive tendering system. She, on the other hand, was not averse to mentioning her widowed status as a potential extra inducement to winning contracts (Doe, 2006). The government owned Post Office knew who was actually in charge of some businesses. William Forster married Ms Norman, the postmistress of Fenny Stratford in Buckinghamshire in 1815. This meant that in legal terms he was now officially the Postmaster and therefore the name on the contract. Twenty years later it was obvious that the Post Office was fully aware that Mrs Forster had performed the 'whole duty' of his office since their marriage (Mawdsley, 2013, p. 82.). The Post Office could and did place women in positions of authority over men and with considerable financial responsibility. These were prominent, influential and important positions within a community (Mawdsley, 2013, pp. 38–41). Between 1771 and 1841 the percentage of women postmasters ranged from 15 to 23% in the post offices in England and Wales. The peak was in 1830 when is reached its highest point at 28% (Mawdsley, 2013, p. 43).

Admiral Beaufort, head of the Royal Navy's hydrographic service, commissioned work from Mrs Taylor, the publisher of navigation charts and books, and he was understanding when she was severely delayed in completing the work by family illness, including a very sick baby. He continued to use her services (Doe, 2009, p. 162). James Downs was recruited in 1859 as the manager and technical expert of the Hull foundry owned by mother and daughter, Mrs Christiana Rose and Mrs Susan Thompson. After some initial tense negotiations over business decisions between employer and employee matters settled down. Downs' role took as surprising turn in 1867 when, despite the prevailing laws that favoured the husband's rights, he became the main intermediary, negotiator and advisor to Susan Thompson when her marriage broke down (Doe, 2009, p. 160).

Mrs Rose and Ms Thompson had to learn how to work with, and delegate to, a highly qualified senior business manager and it is clear they needed to adapt. Women could be tough employers. In dressmaking and millinery trades examples of brutal exploitation of the workforce proved to one US historian that 'unadulterated maternalism rarely guided work-room management'. Like their male counterparts, female employers could be by turn both tyrannical and considerate (Gamber, p. 202).

Small firms and self-employment opportunities have been essential to women entre-preneurs but greater quantification of the role played by small firms in national economies would help to provide a better context to the contribution of businesswomen. Small firms are critically important to economies, providing essential specialist services and flexibility to the bigger businesses. The American perception of a US economy based on big business is now seen to be a more complex jigsaw of firms of a variety of sizes working together (Mandell, 2014, p. 501). We need to reassess the definition of a small business in relative terms in different periods in history. In Britain, the home of small business, micro businesses (those employing less than nine people) have always formed a majority of the whole business industry. Even in 2013 the UK small medium enterprise sector (those employing less than 250 employees) comprised over 99% of the total number of enterprises. They employed 60% of all employees and had 47% of total turnover. Microbusiness made up 96% of the total. The European Commission's SME Performance Review estimates the Gross Value Added of SMEs as €473 billion or 49.8% of the UK economy (Ward and Rhodes, 2014). If this is the situation now what was the significance of the SME sector in previous centuries? In 2014 women business owners in the UK accounted for 17% of all businesses and a third of all were self-employed. In the US 29% of businesses are female owned (Prowess, 2014; Atlantic, 2014).

Historians of women in business have challenged mainstream business history and still have a distance to travel. A criticism of the first full length history of US businesswomen was that it did not interrogate activities or roles. This made it difficult to 'distinguish one businesswoman or type of business activity from another, except insofar as production differs from trade and sales and service' (Yeager, 1999). The study of gender and business has moved on since then. Historians no longer merely report the existence of women in business but consider whether they assumed financial responsibility and were accountable as business leaders and entrepreneurs. Questions still abound on definitions of business success, the quantification of female-led businesses and their economic contribution. How did business institutions deal with notions of 'masculine' and 'feminine', and how did women deal with and view the business world and the world of risk? Women cannot be considered in isolation. Men were not just enforcers of the rules in a male dominated society. Women inherited their business from men, had male advisors, male mentors, male customers, male suppliers and male employees. These interactions deserve more attention. The field is wide open for future researchers to build on the existing evidence, to challenge it and to explore new avenues, new sources and new methods. It is an exciting stage in the debate on whether women were nominally in business or were true businesswomen.

References

Theses and dissertations

Aston, J. (2012). 'Female Business Owners in England, 1849–1901', (unpublished PhD thesis, University of Birmingham).

Jenns, K. R. P. (1997). 'Female Business Enterprise in and Around Birmingham', (unpublished PhD thesis, University of Birmingham).

Mawdsley, H. (2012). 'The Invisible Postmaster: Women and the Post Office, 1771–1851', (unpublished MA dissertation, University of Exeter).

Books and articles

Acheson, G. G. & Turner, J. D. (2006). The Impact of Limited Liability on Ownership and Control: Irish Banking, 1877–1914. *Economic History Review*, LIX.

Alger, K. R. (1982). *Mrs Janet Taylor "Authoress and Instructress in Navigation and Nautical Astronomy", 1804–1870, Fawcett Library Papers No 6.* London.

Barker, H. (2006). *The Business of Women: Female Enterprise and Urban Development in Northern England, 1760–1830*. Oxford: Oxford University Press.

Barker, H. & Ishizu, M. (2012). Inheritance and Continuity in Small Family Businesses during the Early Industrial Revolution, *Business History, 54*(2), 227–244.

Beachy, R. (2001). Business was a Family Affair: Women of Commerce in Central Europe, 1650–1880, *Histoire Sociale/Social History, 34*(68), 307–330.

Beachy, R. (2006). Profit and Propriety: Sophie Henschel and Gender Management in the German Locomotive Industry. In Beachy, R, Craig, B. and Owens, A. (eds), *Women, Business and Finance in Nineteenth-Century Europe: Rethinking Separate Spheres*, Oxford, 67–80.

Berg, M. (1987). Women's Work; Mechanisation and the Early Phases of Industrialisation in England. In Joyce, P. (ed). *The Historical Meanings of Work*. Cambridge: Cambridge University Press, 64–98.

Berg, M. (1993). Women's Property and the Industrial Revolution, *Journal of Interdisciplinary History, XXIV*, 233–50.

Bowen, H. V. (1989). Investment and Empire in the Later Eighteenth Century: East India Stockholding, 1756–1791, *Economic History Review, XLII*(2), 186–206.

Boyns, T. & Edwards, J. R. (1997). Cost and Management Accounting in Early Victorian Britain: A Chandleresque Analysis? *Management Accounting Research, 8*, 19–46.

Buddle, M. (2010). *The Business of Women: Marriage, Family and Entrepreneurship in British Columbia, 1901–51*. Vancouver: UBC Press.

Davidoff, L. & Hall, C. (1987). *Family Fortunes: Men and Women of the English Middle Class, 1780–1850*. London: Hutchinson.

Doe, H. (2006). Challenging Images: Mrs Mary Ross of Rochester, Nineteenth Century Businesswoman and Warship Builder. *Journal for Maritime Research, 8*, 49–60.

Doe, H. (2009). *Enterprising Women and Shipping in the Nineteenth Century*. Woodbridge: Boydell and Brewer.

Doe, H. (2010). Waiting for Her Ship to Come In: The Female Investor in Nineteenth Century Shipping, *Economic History Review, 63*(1), 85–106.

Doe, H. (2013). Power, Authority and Communications: The Role of the Master and the Managing Owner in Nineteenth Century Merchant Shipping, *International Journal of Maritime History, XXV*(1).

Erickson, A. L. (1990). Common Law Versus Common Practice: The Use Of Marriage Settlements. In Early Modern England. *Economic History Review, 53*(1), 21–39.

Finn, M. (1996). 'Women, Consumption and Coverture in England, C. 1760–1860', *The Historical Journal, 39*, 703–22.

Freeman, M., Pearson, R. & Taylor, J. (2006). A Doe in the City: Women Shareholders in Eighteenth- and Early Nineteenth-Century Britain, *Accounting, Business and Financial History, 16*(2), 265–291.

Gamber, W. (1998). A Gendered Enterprise: Placing Nineteenth-Century Businesswomen in History. *The Business History Review, 72*, 188–217.

Gleadle, K. (2007). Revisiting *Family Fortunes*: Reflections on the Twentieth Anniversary of the Publication of L. Davidoff & C. Hall (1987). *Family Fortunes: Men and Women of the English Middle Class, 1780–1850* (London: Hutchinson), *Women's History Review, 16*(5), 773–782.

Green, D. R. & Owens, A. (2003). Gentlewomanly Capitalism? Spinsters, Widows, and Wealth Holding in England and Wales, C. 1800–1860, *Economic History Review, 56*, 510–36.

Green, D. R., Owens, A., Rutterford, J. & Maltby, J. (2011). 'Who comprised the nation of shareholders? Gender and investment in Great Britain, c. 1870–1935' *Economic History Review, 64*(1), 157–187.

Guest, R. & John, A. (1989). *Lady Charlotte: A Biography of the Nineteenth Century*. London: Weidenfield & Nicolson.

Heemskerk, E.M. & Fennema, M. (2014). Women on Board: Female Board Membership as a Form of Elite Democratization. *Enterprise & Society, 15*(2).

Hill, B. (1993a). Women, Work and the Census: A Problem for Historians of Women, *History Workshop Journal, 35*, 78–94.

Hill, B. (1993b). Women's History: A Study in Change, Continuity or Standing Still?, *Women's History Review, 2*, 5–22.

Holcombe, L. (1983). *Wives and Property: Reform of the Married Women's Property Law in Nineteenth Century England*. Toronto: University of Toronto Press.

Horrell, S. & Humphries, J. (1995). Women's Labour Force Participation and the Transition to the Male-Breadwinner Family, 1765–1865, *Economic History Review, 48*, 89–117.

Jones, G. & Rose, M. B. (1993). Family Capitalism, *Business History, 35*, 1–16.

Kay, A.C. (2009). *The Foundations of Female Entrepreneurship: Enterprise, Home and Household in London, c. 1800–1870.* London and New York: Routledge.

Kirby, M. W. & Rose, M. B. (eds.) (1994). *Business Enterprise in Modern Britain from 18th to 20th Century.* London: Routledge.

Kwolek-Folland, A, (1998). *Incorporating Women: A History of Women and Business in the United States.* New York: Palgrave.

Maltby, J. & Rutterford, J. (2006). Editorial: 'Women, Accounting and Investment', *Accounting, Business and Financial History, 16*, 133–42.

Maltby, J. & Rutterford, J. (2006). She Possessed Her Own Fortune: Women Investors from the Late Nineteenth Century to the Early Twentieth Century, *Business History, 48*, 220–53.

Mandell, N. (2014). Will the Real Businessman/Businesswoman Stand Up?: The Historical Implications of Regendering Business Success in the Early Twentieth Century, *Enterprise & Society, 15*(3).

McAlpine, J. (1997). *The Lady of Claremont House: Isabella Elder, Pioneer and Philanthropist.* Argyll: Argyll Publishing.

McAlpine, J. (2004). Isabella Elder, (1828–1905), *Oxford Dictionary of National Biography.* Oxford University Press.

McIntosh, M. K. (2005). The Benefits and Drawbacks of Femme Sole Status in England, 1300–1630, *Journal of British Studies, 44*, 410–38.

Morris, R. J. (1994). 'Men, Women and Property: The Reform of the Married Women's Property Act 1870'. In Thompson, F. M. L. (ed.) *Landowners, Capitalists, and Entrepreneurs: Essays for Sir John Habakkuk.* Oxford: Clarendon Press, 171–91.

Phillips, N. (2006). *Women in Business, 1700–1850.* Woodbridge: Boydell & Brewer.

Rose, M. B. (1994). The Family Firm in British Business, 1780–1914. In Kirby, M. W. and Rose, M. B. (eds.) *Business Enterprise in Modern Britain.* London: Routledge, 61–87.

Rutterford, J., Green, D., Maltby, J. & Owens, A. (2011). Who Comprised the Nation of Shareholders? Gender and Investment in Great Britain, 1870–1935, *Economic History Review, 61*(1), 157–187.

Shanley, M. L. (1989). *Feminism, Marriage and the Law in Victorian England, 1850–1895.* London: Princeton University Press.

Sharpe, P. (1995). Continuity and Change: Women's History and Economic History in Britain, *Economic History Review, XLVIII*, 353–69.

Sharpe, P. (ed.) (1998). *Women's Work: The English Experience 1650–1914.* London: Arnold.

Sharpe, P. (2001). 'Gender in the Economy; Female Merchants and Family Businesses in the British Isles, 1600–1850', *Histoire Sociale/Social History, 34*(68), 283–306.

Ulianova, G. (2009). *Female Entrepreneurs in Nineteenth-Century Russia.* London: Pickering and Chatto.

Vickery, A. (1993). Golden Age to Separate Spheres? A Review of the Categories and Chronology of English Women's History, *The Historical Journal, 36*, 383–414.

Walsh, M. (2005). Gendered Endeavours: Women and the Reshaping of Business Culture, *Women's History Review, 14*(2), 181–202.

Ward, M. & Rhodes, C. (2014). 'Small businesses and the UK Economy', House of Commons Briefing Paper, December 2014. http://researchbriefings.parliament.uk/ResearchBriefing/Summary/SN06078 [accessed 18 August 2015].

Wiskin, C. (2006). Businesswomen and Financial Management: Three Eighteenth-Century Case Studies, *Accounting, Business & Financial History, 16*(2), 143–161.

Yeager, M. A. (1999). Review of Angel Kwolek-Folland, *Incorporating Business* https://networks.h-net.org/node/24846/reviews/25631/yeager-kwolek-folland-incorporating-women-history-women-and-business [accessed 28 July 2015].

Websites

Prowess https://www.prowess.org.uk/facts [accessed 15 July 2015].

The Atlantic http://www.theatlantic.com/business/archive/2015/04/women-are-owning-more-and-more-small-businesses/390642/ [accessed 15 July 2015].

23

Fraud and financial scandals

Steven Toms

Overview

The chapter illustrates the benefits of using business history to gain perspective on a significant problem for present day business and regulators: the continuing occurrence of financial fraud and financial scandals. To do so, it presents a conceptual framework of financial fraud based on the historical interaction of opportunity and impediment. In the long run, the character of opportunity is determined by the technical characteristics of assets and their unique, unknowable or unverifiable features. Impediment is promoted by consensus about the real value of assets, such that through *active* governance processes, fraudulent deviations from real, or consensus value, can be easily monitored. Active governance requires individuals in positions of responsibility to exercise a duty of care beyond merely being honest themselves. Taking a long run historical perspective and reviewing a selection of British financial frauds and scandals, from the South Sea Bubble to the global financial crisis, the chapter notes the periodic occurrence of waves of opportunity and the evolutionary response of passive governance mechanisms. In doing so, it provides an overview of the business history and related literatures that have addressed this recurrent 'dark side' of business behaviour.

Introduction

To paraphrase Santayana's famous aphorism, those who do not learn from history are doomed to repeat their mistakes. Yet historical mistakes are repeated perhaps most commonly in the case of fraud and financial scandal. To devise effective mechanisms to combat fraud, whether based on improved regulation or more efficient market mechanisms, requires us to learn from past mistakes. Yet fraud seems to be the most perennial feature of business activity and its most intractable problem.

The chapter analyses the history of fraud and financial scandal and identifies some common features. To do so, it develops a conceptual framework based on the long run interaction of technology and market development. These features lead respectively to problems of context specific asset valuation and value verification, which taken together define the environment of mispricing opportunities. Such opportunities do not in themselves lead to specific fraudulent transactions, but do influence the probability of their occurrence and their character. Thus, whereas particular frauds vary in terms of the specific opportunity, motivation and ex post rationalisations of the individuals involved (Cressey, 1953), historians might focus on the factors that make frauds more or less likely.

A historical approach may accordingly explain why frauds and scandals tend to cluster in certain time periods. The chapter begins by developing a conceptual framework based on the dynamic interaction of opportunity and impediment. It then presents a brief history of fraud and financial scandal in the United Kingdom, in three broad periods. The first, on manias and frauds before and during industrialisation, examines the features of frauds that became common in subsequent events. The second period begins by considering Victorian frauds and the notions of reasonable business behaviour and honesty as substitutes for direct intervention in corporation's affairs, which have survived largely unmodified through a series of twentieth century frauds. The third details the period since 1980 during which time the process of financialisation compounded earlier circumstances leading to fraud opportunity, culminating in the financial crash of 2007–2008. The final section draws conclusions referring to limitations of the conceptual framework whilst noting the value of a historical approach for the purposes of identifying the long run determinants of fraud and financial scandal.

Conceptual framework

Taking a long view of financial fraud allows systemic causes to be more easily identified, leaving aside the psychological and individual circumstances surrounding specific cases. Most notably, frauds and scandals appear to occur in clusters, which are also cyclical in nature. The first of these, the South Sea Bubble of 1720, featured a large number of similar fraudulent projects. The same could be said of mispriced railway floatations of the nineteenth century, the accounting frauds in the UK in the late 1980s and in the US in the late 1990s, or the scandals that came in the wake of the global financial crisis of 2007–2008.

Such intermittent clusters are suggestive of common features, based on the balance of opportunity and impediment. To structure our analysis, it is useful to consider what these might be from a conceptual point of view. If we begin by considering any financial misdemeanour, a common attribute is the opportunity to mislead a third party about the value of an asset or collection of assets. Such opportunities are mitigated where there is agreement about asset value and such agreement is transparent. Note there are two conditions. The first, agreement about asset value, is, for example, more difficult in the market for second hand cars and easier in for new ones. Newly produced cars possess a common cost base and uniform quality assured features. The second dimension complements these asset features, which is the transparency of the basis of agreement. New cars are more easily subjected to standard and independent testing, industry association kite-marking and warranty provisions. Second hand car values are less easy to verify, leading to individual but costly quality signalling, as in the famous 'market for lemons' argument (Akerlof, 1970). Price lists for second-hand cars can be constructed on the basis of common and verifiable features, such as age, but in general verification of true asset value is problematic or costly and such assets present opportunities for the unscrupulous seller, or demand additional vigilance, or activism, on the part of the buyer.

The complexity of the asset, and the ability to verify its value, therefore present important challenges to those who would enforce financial fair play. Technological change alters the nature of net assets, and the character of future cash flows, either as a function of new assets with unknown properties or their effect on the obsolescence of existing assets. Technological change therefore poses a fundamental problem for *accounting valuation*. At the same time, the presence of information asymmetry creates the problem of *dominant insiders*, either as market operators, or senior managers. Note that the dominant insider is a function of market inefficiency and may exist even where technology is stable. Where technology is also dynamic, market inefficiencies are compounded.

From the perspective of history, technology and value verification have important properties. Technology can advance steadily within a given paradigm, or change suddenly through new breakthrough discoveries. In the case of steady advance, the market and market participants have the opportunity to value and refine notions of accurate value. In the case of disruptive periods of rapid technological change, the old rules of valuation no longer apply, and indeed established technology loses value suddenly through obsolescence. New technology is at the earliest phase understood by only a minority of innovators who may themselves be uncertain of market potential and therefore value. Mispricing opportunities, which might occur with or without fraudulent intent, are consequently more prevalent in periods of technological discontinuity.

Value verification is similarly historically contingent. Early phases of market development impose limits on accurate pricing, for example where there are small numbers of buyers and sellers, thin trading and so on. Even so, market development through historical time and greater market depth do not in themselves promote market transparency. Over the long run, there is what might be described as a process of 'financialisation' of society, in which financial market participants, financial institutions and financial elites gain greater influence over economic policy and economic outcomes (Palley, 2011). Such processes can be reversed, but also tend to reappear and therefore recur at different times in history, for example in the decades before 1914 and more recently with financial deregulation since 1980. Features of financialisation that compound the problem of value verification include multiple principal agent relationships, differential access to information by elites and insiders and perverse incentives. Sub-prime lending prior to the global financial crisis of 2007–2008 contained all three of these features. Financial obligations were packaged and resold, at a time when interest rates and market prices were subject to insider manipulation and accountants and ratings agencies subjected to incentives to produce optimistic valuations of complex assets.

Drawing these concepts together leads to a general conceptual framework based on opportunity and impediment. As the discussion has so far suggested, technology and market development can be linked to the prevalence of fraud opportunity, but are themselves governed by broader exogenous factors. Nonetheless, each leads to the more specific issues of asset complexity and value verification. The interaction of these two features then gives rise to specific opportunities for mispricing, which include the technical characteristics of assets, the nature of principal agent relationships, the role of elites and insiders and the effects of incentives. Conversely, from a regulatory point of view, each of these opportunities for fraud could be envisioned as an area for setting fraud impediments, using a variety of legal and institutional mechanisms. The relationship between opportunity and impediment is viewed as dynamic, with the former creating a reaction for the latter, which in turn is undermined by new sets of opportunity. To examine the interaction of these relationships through time, a specific country focus is required. The next section reviews the history of the relationship, based on an analysis of selected leading cases from British business and economic history.

A short history of financial fraud

Manias and frauds before and during industrialisation

The South Sea Bubble provided an early illustration of the power of insiders in possession of difficult to value assets in the absence of effective market scrutiny. At the centre of the scandal was the transfer of government debt to the South Sea Company, whose shares were then subjected to a speculative mania. The scheme was contrived such that all stakeholders, including shareholders, but also the government and annuity holders, had a collective interest in the share price increasing (Chancellor, 2000). The proceeds of share issues were used to fund dividend payments, with the intention of attracting further investment, so that the bubble had some of the features of a Ponzi scheme (Garber, 2001). Consequently, the lack of underlying value being created by the company and therefore the degree of mispricing became quickly obvious and the unsustainable share price collapsed. The victims of the bubble were those shareholders left with worthless shares and capital losses in the absence of any scrutiny, objective judgement or advice from market operators and institutions. For the first time in history, an auditor was employed to investigate fraudulent practices (Giroux, 2014), and found that the directors of the company and also government officials, including the Chancellor of the Exchequer, John Aislabie, were implicated in bribery and corrupt share dealing (Dale, 2004).

The bubble extended well beyond the South Sea Company itself, and included a large range of "bubble" companies. In some cases, these represented genuine investment opportunities where the value of the proposed investment could be easily verified. In most cases however, either one of both of these features were absent. Some, for example Puckle's machine gun, were based on apparently elaborate technical specifications, but which, by corollary were difficult for non-expert investors to verify. Others were difficult to verify for reasons other than technical specification, such as geographical distance, for example related to the exploitation of mineral rights or monopoly trading rights in overseas locations. Some were simply implausible, such as the proposed machine for perpetual motion. Many were bizarre, such as the scheme for importing jackasses from Spain in the name of a deceased clergyman (for these and other examples, see: South Sea Company, 1825, pp. 70–84).

The practical effect of these schemes was that the probability of future cash flows and profits could not be easily verified. Notwithstanding the development of discount-based methods, such as risk adjusted years' purchase (Harrison, 2001), valuation was problematic because either the technical specification was complex or there was no practical way of verifying the existence and value of the assets being sold. A further complication was the pricing of calls on subscription shares (Dale et al. 2005, but c.f. Shea, 2007). In such an environment, opportunities for fraud arose from the uncertainly of valuation of the underlying asset and the absence of agreed and transparent valuation methods. The reaction, which was to outlaw incorporation other than through charter under the *Bubble Act* of 1720,[1] was not extreme in this respect, although it had wider ramifications for economic development. The regulatory reaction was reasonable in an environment where information asymmetries suggested in promotion schemes appeared beyond practical regulation. At the same time, information asymmetry and the lack of access to information for the typical investor significantly inhibited market efficiency and transparency.

By the first half of the nineteenth century the situation had changed somewhat. Industrialisation brought common replications of technical solutions with standardised components and units of output, which were increasingly common by 1850. Centralisation of production in factories reduced the opportunities for embezzlement that had prevailed in the putting out system, enabling the complementary functioning of surveillance and accounting controls (Toms, 2005). Increased scale and accumulated wealth also meant that joint stock based finance could once again be accorded legal legitimacy.

The environment in which new companies were now allowed to operate, was, nonetheless, inauspicious. Railway promoters like George Hudson were at the centre of new scandals, once again exploiting a new wave of technology that was not well understood by investors. A contemporary journalist, David Morier Evans described the railway mania as a new alliance between dishonesty and financial sophistication (Wilson and Wilson, 2013, p. 15). Cash flows expected from investments were not well understood, and uncertainties were compounded by the use of creative accounting methods. For example, uncertainty over the division of expenditure between capital and revenue was exploited by unregulated directors and company promoters (McCartney and Arnold, 2000). Railway companies would reduce their depreciation charges to justify dividend payments. In turn, dividend distributions were instrumental in attracting new investors. In the absence of shareholder protection regulation, investors rationally demanded high dividend payments (Campbell and Turner, 2011). Many of the investors had accumulated profits from unincorporated businesses in other industries, and notably included the cotton merchants and manufacturers of Liverpool and Manchester (Chapman, 2003, pp. 103–104).

As the state receded from interference, as in the first half of the nineteenth century, the risk of expropriation for minority shareholders increased. Sunk investments, like railways and manufacturing, require permanent capital and therefore restrictions on capital withdrawals (Lamoreaux, 2009) to protect minority investors and third party creditors. Such pressures placed limitations on dividends, whilst legal protection for minority shareholders who might otherwise suffer from the domination of powerful insiders was minimal, as the judgement in *Foss v Harbottle* case demonstrated.[2] By the mid nineteenth century, the dominant insider was well established, with decisive influence on value and its distribution.

Victorian frauds and the origins of modern regulation

Following the railway mania there were the beginnings of legal mechanisms designed to counter this dominance. Some re-regulation in the form of the Companies Act of 1862[3] inaugurated improvements in shareholder protection. An important feature was the specimen articles of association that allowed limitations on directors' power, such as democratic (one shareholder one vote) or graduated voting rights, voluntary shareholder audits, low thresholds (10%) to exercise rights to call extraordinary company meetings and so on. These were relatively weak protections and investors therefore restricted directors' power by structuring their incentives and requiring most profits to be distributed as dividends (Campbell and Turner, 2011). Although the features of the 1862 Act were permissive, their effect was to encourage shareholders to play an active role in the governance of their companies, for example using shareholder committees to conduct audits. The Act also promoted the use of private companies, which did not depend on raising capital through issues to the public (Watson, 2012, p. 58), and therefore had less opportunity to mislead third party investors. The post 1860 environment consequently ushered in features of corporate governance that provided some protection to investors.

Simultaneously the economy modernised further, but primarily though incremental improvements to the established coal and iron technological paradigm. Where technology is stable or incremental, the main opportunities from fraud come from market manipulations, such as market rigging or abuse of insider knowledge arising from market inefficiencies and lack of transparency. In the 1860s for example there were cases affecting banks, including Overend Gurney, 1866, which issued a prospectus whilst technically insolvent and collapsed soon afterwards (Ackrill and Hannah, 2001) and also the railways and money markets. Again, these were subject to market manipulation style activities by insiders (Johnston, 1934). New legislation for railway accounting in 1868 failed to address fundamental issues of capital and revenue distinctions and associated valuation issues (Georgiou and Jack, 2011). Even so, there were no significant waves of corporate scandal in the period immediately after the reintroduction of limited liability.

There were nonetheless individual and damaging cases. In the months before its collapse in 1878, the City of Glasgow Bank had been using company funds to purchase its shares, thereby deceiving investors about its true value (Acheson and Turner, 2008). The practice was declared illegal in the subsequent case of *Trevor v Whitworth* (1887).[4] Following legislation in the form of the Acts of 1879 (Prosecution of Public Offences) and 1890 (Winding-up),[5] standards expected of directors became higher, such that criminal prosecutions of promoters or directors could be instigated by the Director of Public Prosecutions or the Board of Trade (Taylor, 2013). A distinction was made between the criminalisation of dishonesty and intent to defraud, and what might be considered normal trading transactions (Wilson and Wilson, 2013). These mechanisms reduced the burdens on shareholders, who, with increasingly liquid markets and diverse portfolios, had less time to actively participate in company affairs, leading to a decline in shareholder activism. Even so, as a consequence, dishonesty might go undetected in the absence of responsibilities for vigilance in audit and other oversight functions.

In the 1890s a new wave of technical progress based on electricity, tramways, the internal combustion engine, pneumatic tyres, cycles and oil presented opportunities for the fraudulent promoter and challenges for the evolved legal framework. The career of broker and promoter Ernest Terah Hooley provides useful illustration. In 1896 he purchased the Pneumatic Tyre Company for £3m using borrowed money. He created a new board of honorary directors, with impressive aristocratic pedigree using financial inducements. The Earl de al Warr was listed as the chairman (in return, it was alleged for £25,000), and fellow directors were his Grace the Duke of Somerset and the Earl of Albemarle.[6] None of these directors had any knowledge of the business of cycle or tyre manufacturing, a pattern repeated across a series of flotations in the sector in the mid-1890s. Hooley floated the Dunlop Pneumatic Tyre Company for £5m one month later. The directors retained significant ownership through the use of deferred shares.[7] Hooley had not created any value from this operation, but relied instead on inducements to journalists to publish favourable accounts of the firm's prospects, benefiting from a wider boom in the promotion of cycle industry shares. These techniques were designed to manage investors' risk perceptions (Harrison, 1980). Hooley used inside information about Dunlop licenses held by the Beeston and Grappler cycle companies, as part of a share rigging scheme, from which Hooley profited personally (Stratmann, 2012). Such details were unknowable to the investing public, particularly those relying on press reports. In such fashion, Hooley moved from one scheme to another, including the development of Trafford Park in Manchester and a plan to purchase Cuba. He was successfully prosecuted and served several terms in jail, each time returning, undeterred, to concoct new financial schemes.

Notwithstanding these shenanigans, the balance between fraud opportunity, shareholder protection and criminal prosecution operated without significant modification until well into the twentieth century. Criminal prosecution mitigated the requirement for direct shareholder vigilance, as did the emergence of the accounting profession in the late nineteenth century. The 1900 Companies Act made incorporation more expensive and demanded greater financial disclosure, resulting in a reduction in the number of publicly traded corporations (Lamoreaux, 2009, p. 27). Prudent accounting promoted the rise of professional auditors to replace amateur shareholder committees. These safeguards did not however directly protect investors, and by offering advice, professional audit firms became complicit with management and inside investors, to the exclusion of small investors (Maltby, 1999). At the height of Hooley's first round of share pushing in 1896, Lord Justice Lopes famously declared, the auditor is 'a watchdog, not a bloodhound',[8] signalling the law's limited interpretation of shareholder protection. Indeed, the law took a favourable view of the insider trader, seeing their profits as a legitimate reward for risk taking, for example on the promotion of new companies, a situation that was tolerated until 1980.[9]

Insiders exploited the situation, which gave rise to a whole series of scandals in the 1920s. There were few major technological breakthroughs in this period. Indeed, the 1920s represented a crisis in the valuation of established technologies. As a consequence, the main opportunity for fraudsters was the exploitation of inside market knowledge based on the permissive regime for insiders, who indulged in market manipulations and mis-selling share issues. They included the recapitalisation of established cotton firms and newly established combines, none of which lived up to their prospectuses and often left innocent investors holding worthless assets (Higgins et al., 2015). Hooley was prosecuted again, this time for mis-selling shares in a relatively worthless cotton mill.[10] Horatio Bottomley and Clarence Hatry promoted other notorious schemes (Johnston, 1934). The activities of another fraudster, Gerard Lee Bevan at City Equitable Fire Insurance, illustrated two important sources of power of insiders. The first was the use of associated companies to move funds to cover losses. Hence Bevan transferred money to City Equitable from his stockbroking firm, Ellis and Company, and vice versa (Vander Weyer, 2011). The second was the lack of vigilance from his fellow directors, who were nominees and oblivious to the fraud. Moreover, the law upheld the view that their office imposed no such requirements of additional vigilance, only a duty of care to act honestly with a reasonable level of knowledge and skill.[11] In *City Equitable*, as in *Kingston Cotton*, a standard of 'reasonableness' was wheeled out, in an environment where managers and auditors had strong incentives to limit the extent of their responsibilities.

The Bevan case demonstrated that outside investors were extremely vulnerable to accounting manipulations by powerful corporate directors. In the absence of clear accounting rules and regulations, these risks persisted, and were well illustrated by the activities of Lord Kylsant in the Royal Mail Steam Packet (RSMP) case. Like the South Sea scheme promoters and George Hudson in the railway mania respectively, Kylsant paid dividends out of capital. He also used connections between companies to massage profits. By manipulating the accounts in this fashion, he went one step further than previous fraudsters. His main method was to use secret reserves to boost corporate income such that what should have been losses in 1926 and 1927 were reported as profits (Davies and Bourne, 1972). Kyslant then used these false accounts to underpin the prospectus for a new share issue in 1928.

The RMSP case differed in some further important respects from earlier scandals. Kylsant had to rely on the auditors to accept the accounting manipulation, a problem that had not troubled Hudson or Hooley. His secret reserves scheme was also designed to exploit a specific loophole. In the absence of enforceable accounting regulations on disclosure, including any requirement to publish a profit and loss account, the concealment of financial balances in secret reserves was acceptable under the law (Jones, 2011). Kylsant was convicted, but only on matters relating to the prospectus.[12] Accounting remained largely unregulated even after the Companies Act 1929, although disclosure requirements grew in successive Companies Acts from 1948 to 1967.[13]

Opportunities to move and disguise assets, liabilities, income and expenditure that had been features of frauds like City Equitable were compounded in the 1960s by the development of the market for corporate control. Contested takeover bids and complex group structures provided important context for the fraudster. A crucial issue in takeover bids is the underlying value of the target company's assets and associated opportunities for manipulation. When the General Electric Company (GEC) launched a bid for Associated Electrical Industries (AEI) in 1967, the directors of AEI overvalued their stocks and contract work in progress, with the result that a £10m profit was turned into a £4.5m loss, post takeover. The flexibility of accounting practice led to the establishment of accounting rules for the first time in the UK, with consequential establishment of the Accounting Standards Committee (ASC) in 1970 (Jones, 2011, pp. 129, 486–487).

The development of accounting standards became a work in progress for the ASC in the 1970s and 1980s. Meanwhile, the Slater Walker (SW) scandal, which broke in 1974, was facilitated, like GEC/AEI, by the lack of accounting regulation. SW also demonstrated further problematic consequences of the emergence of the market for corporate control. SW's main function was the buying and selling of businesses, with the prime objective of raising its share price. Such transactions were often conducted in haste, with little knowledge demonstrated of the underlying business or their inherent value (Toms et al., 2015). SW's chief executive, Jim Slater, used creative accounting to present a rosy picture and increase his own reputation in the City. After the scandal, investigative journalist Charles Raw (1977, pp. 235–238) demonstrated the effect of creative accounting on profits and apparent value in the SW subsidiary, Crittall Hope Ltd. In addition to manipulations in individual company accounts, Slater used the complex group structure to hide liabilities and losses. His use of Ralli bank as his own banking division to underwrite the dubious assets of other subsidiaries created further opportunities to disguise the true position of the business in the short term, but ultimately left the group insolvent and at the centre of the secondary banking crisis of 1974.

James Goldsmith succeeded Slater and commissioned accountancy firms Price Waterhouse and Peat Marwick to investigate SW's finances and report to the Department of Trade and Industry (DTI). His motive was to prevent a DTI investigation (Raw, 1977, p. 346). Only later did it become apparent that Goldsmith was Slater's nominee.[14] Slater's manoeuvrings were indicative of new problems for regulation and oversight arising from the personal connections of the financial elite. SW also demonstrated the problems of valuing individual company assets, how those problems are compounded by complex group structures and how they are difficult to verify in the absence of accounting standards, corporate governance and effective regulatory scrutiny.

Although the consequences of SW were serious, they had relatively little effect on the governance of City institutions. SW certainly contributed to the establishment of the Roskill Committee and the creation of the Serious Fraud Office (SFO) in 1987.[15] Moreover, the first legislation on banking supervision followed the SW case in an Act of 1979.[16] However, the objectives of that supervision were not specified until 1997 (Foot, 2003, p. 251). Indeed, the Slater Walker aftermath was a precursor for the wave of deregulation and the associated financialisation of the economy after 1980.

Financialisation and the financial crash

From 1980, greater financialisation implied changes in the structure of financial markets, lack of policy control over markets and the concentration of power amongst a financial elite (Palley, 2011). The end of corporatism and dirigisme in Europe, withdrawal of the state from the management of firms, and the advent of laissez faire and deregulation led to waves of corporate governance scandals in Europe and the US (Lamoreaux, 2009, p. 30). Resulting concentrations of elite power proved problematic for regulators, and also for the efficient functioning of transparent markets.

These problems were well illustrated by the Guinness scandal of 1986. Insider trading had been a feature of the SW scandal and loomed large once again in the Guinness case.[17] The directors of Guinness and their associates, who included Wall Street financier Ivan Boesky, operated a share support scheme during the takeover battle for Distillers (Augur, 2006). Guinness directors used the company's funds to write cheques for associates to buy Guinness shares, thereby increasing the share price and the value of the share for share offer. Such practices were already illegal, based on precedent, and also new regulation against insider trading introduced in 1980.[18] To be enforced these rules required the identification of connectedness between insiders and nominees, which established a high burden of proof for prosecutions. In the Guinness case there were successful prosecutions by the SFO following a long trial, but the connectedness insider trading rules were subsequently abandoned in 1993 in favour of information access (Loke, 2006).[19]

Guinness was the precursor of a further wave of accounting scandals and frauds that broke in the late 1980s. These included Robert Maxwell and Mirror Group Newspapers, Bank of Credit Commerce International, Coloroll and Polly Peck. Once again these scandals revealed the problems of subjective asset valuation. Like RMSP and SW, in all these cases profits were reported immediately before the business went bust (Smith, 1992), and were compounded by the deregulated institutional environment and complex group structures that made verification more difficult. The Polly Peck case was illustrative (Jones, 2011). The firm expanded rapidly through a series of takeover transactions between 1982 and 1989. Accounting standards were in force, but nonetheless allowed the Polly Peck Chief Executive and main shareholder, Asil Nadir, significant opportunities to manipulate his firm's accounts, particularly using the options created by foreign currency fluctuations in his group of companies. Nadir channelled funds via overseas subsidiaries to his private bank accounts, which he covered by overvaluing the subsidiary assets in the consolidated accounts.

Polly Peck and other frauds posed serious challenges for regulators in the late 1980s. Roskill (1986, p. 15) commented that serious fraud was one 'in which the dishonesty is buried in a series on inter-related transactions, most frequently in a market offering highly-specialised services, or in areas of high-finance involving (for example) manipulation of the ownership of companies'. Such frauds, Roskill argued, were beyond the understanding of members of the public and by implication, beyond the purview of jury trials. Instead regulation and oversight became voluntary, based on insiders sharing similar expertise.

In the wake of Polly Peck, a new Accounting Standards Board was established, with the aim of tightening accounting rules. At the same time, with the 1992 Cadbury Report, there began a process of codification of practice in corporate governance (Jones, 2011). The process was only completed in 2003, with the creation of the Combined Code as a collection of self-regulatory principles.

Much of the Combined Code came too late for the Dot.com crash of 2001. Again, as with the South Sea Bubble and the railway mania, new technology presented the markets with difficult to value assets. The decline of traditional manufacturing and its replacement with new economy firms switched value decisively from the physical and tangible to the ephemeral and intangible in firms' balance sheets. For these reasons, particularly in the US but also elsewhere, there was a retreat from historical cost based valuation in favour of market based fair value (Georgiou and Jack, 2011). New firms were, for example, priced according to website traffic forecasts rather than traditional financial metrics. These difficult to value assets left a deficit of trust between inside promoters and naïve investors (Dale, 2004). The effect was to increase reliance on regulatory mechanisms.

However, the response to this demand was partial and based on voluntarism. New regulatory authorities, supplemented what later became the Combined Code. Most important was the Financial Services Authority (FSA). Established in 1997, under the Bank of England Act, the agency progressively embodied European laws aimed at restricting market abuse based on equality of access to information (Wilson, 2014). Post-1980 legislation on insider trading proved difficult to enforce because it relied upon detecting connections between parties, and was ineffective, as the Guinness scandal demonstrated. The information parity approach, which followed, further reflected European legislation, and relied on windows during which directors were barred from trading.[20] Under the FSA, regulatory oversight was enforced through administrative sanction and fines, with less emphasis on prosecution relative to the US and more on cost effectiveness and the preservation of the competitive position of the city of London (Jackson, 2005). Leading investment bankers provided the necessary expertise to staff the agency, but to provide such expertise they were necessarily drawn from banking institutions that were 'too big to fail'.

Such compromises meant that regulatory bodies were subject to capture by the political and financial elites. A leading example was Versailles Trade Finance, a partnership of businessman Carl Cushnie, a close associate of Prime Minister Tony Blair and career criminal Fred Clough. Like Polly Peck, they exploited the latitude within accounting standards, in this case to inflate turnover and assets, thereby defrauding investors. Political favour had promoted the reputation of the company, whilst the Combined Code failed to prevent the operation of the fraud. As in the City Equitable case, Cushnie and Clough obstructed fellow directors, in this case the non-executives. The auditors, Nunn Hayward, were also implicated by the Joint Disciplinary Scheme (JDS) for turning a blind eye to the gross inflation of turnover through the use of fictitious insider transactions.[21] These auditors lacked independence due to over-reliance of this relatively small second tier firm on what had apparently become a large client.[22]

The Versailles case was relatively small beer compared to what had meanwhile unfolded across the Atlantic and the subsequent global financial crisis. The Enron scandal, and a wave of others including Global Crossing, Tyco and Worldcom, to some extent reflected the absence of the corporate governance reforms that had evolved in the UK during the period 1992–2003. Indeed, in the early 1990s, US business successfully resisted most of the recommendations from the Treadway Report on corporate governance, preferring a model where the firm's internal hierarchy selected board members and monitored performance (Toms and Wright, 2005, p. 248). The power of dominant insiders was therefore reinforced at a vital moment in US corporate history.

However, as the Versailles case in the UK demonstrated, as did the Parmalat case in Italy, neither corporate governance rules nor EU directives on market regulation were sufficient to prevent significant frauds. The effects of the Dot.com crash added to the impetus for stronger regulations, which were tightened dramatically in the US in 2003 with Sarbanes Oxley Act (Sarbox), and more marginally in the UK with further additions to corporate governance codes with the Higgs (Non-Executive Directors) and Smith (Audit Committees) Reports (2003), and marginal changes to rules on auditor rotation after the Parmalat scandal in Italy in 2005. Notwithstanding these changes, the 'watchdog not bloodhound' principle established in the *Kingston Cotton* case remained, and indeed might be characterised as 'see no evil, speak no evil'. In legal cases and auditing standards,[23] auditors were absolved from specific duty to detect fraud. Instead the responsibility was placed directly onto the senior management through their administration of internal controls (Lee et al., 2009). History demonstrates clearly however, from the earliest scandals, that dominant insiders, themselves responsible for detection of fraud, were its most frequent instigators, a point demonstrated once again in the wave of corporate scandals of the early 2000s and the global financial crisis of 2008.

Frauds were also facilitated however, by the nineteenth century principles that remained embedded in accounting and auditing standards. In the Enron led wave of scandals, the finger of blame was pointed at dominant senior managers. With attention focused on the individual scapegoats, lax accounting rules, it was argued, were not at fault. Features present in previous frauds and scandals were now writ large and indeed appeared to have become systemic. Asset misvaluation was widespread, but occurred within the accounting rules that had developed through the various scandals since 1980, and indeed the significant tightening post Sarbox and Combined Code. As in the South Sea Bubble, the railway scandals and the Dot.com bust, new difficult to value assets posed a new set of problems for valuation specialists and a new set of opportunities for market manipulators. Financial derivatives, including options, futures and swaps, but also complex combinations of these were valued by mathematical algorithms. Their complexity posed problems even for their developers, as the $4.6bn bail out of the Long Term Capital Management hedge fund in 1998 revealed. The firm's directors included Myron Scholes and Robert Merton who had been instrumental in creating derivative valuation models (Lowenstein, 2000). To be accurate these models needed deep markets and frequent trading data as their inputs. Many of the more complex derivatives, such as collaterised debt obligations were, however, traded over the counter on a bilateral basis. In the absence of market values, accountants resorted to valuation models based on often heroically optimistic assumptions (Toms, 2016).

As in previous decades, regulators were slow to catch up. New regulations tended to follow in the wake of scandals rather than anticipate their effects. In 2007–2008 and the aftermath, the effect was catastrophic. Expanded and deeper capital markets did not guarantee market efficiency or transparency. Instead, deregulation and financialisation empowered corporate insiders, who were only weakly counteracted by restrictions on their activities. The scale of the moral hazard problem was compounded by bank executive incentives, which were associated with bonus scheme complexity and bank profits, but not the level of risk exposure (Bruce and Skovoroda, 2013). Under such circumstances, 'reasonable behaviour' might be conflated with opportunities to engage in risky lending to achieve growth and shareholder returns.

Ahead of the failure of Halifax Bank of Scotland (HBOS) in 2008, as in the South Sea Bubble, all major stakeholders stood to gain from growth through further risky lending, whether executives receiving bonuses, shareholders increasing their wealth and non-executives and regulators drawn from senior positions in the Banking industry, credulous about the responsible behaviour of everyone else (Bank of England, 2015, for example, pp. 217–222).[24] For some of the period immediately before the crisis, James Crosby was both HBOS Chief Executive and a member of the FSA board. Although the accounts stated that the 'performance and effectiveness of the Board and each of its Committees is evaluated annually', there was no evidence of such reviews having been carried out by the Chairman and Non Executive Directors in line with the *Combined Code* on corporate governance. In their reports, the auditors, KPMG, referred frequently to the 'reasonable' nature of the firm's risk policies and disclosures. Individual executives themselves did what was reasonable, but were not incentivised to challenge the reasonableness of others (Bank of England, 2015, pp. 33, 175, 189–192, 217–218). In short, oversight amounted to a collection of 'watchdogs' with strict tunnel vision, such that resulting blind spots undermined collective responsibility.

During this time, the FSA's regulatory policy was to rely on out of court processes and administrative fines, thereby attracting criticism for failure to prosecute frauds involving pension and endowment mis-selling, or to effectively police individual financial institutions like Northern Rock. An important reason was that the burden of proof in complex cases required even greater levels of expertise than noted by Roskill two decades earlier. Prosecution was therefore expensive and risky (Croal, 2004, p. 48; Wilson and Wilson, 2013). At the same time, voluntary codes of corporate social responsibility, third party regulatory agencies and multi-national firms whose activities span individual state jurisdictions have led to the rise of 'private regulation' (Bakan, 2015). Even where investigations were pursued, for example HSBC was investigated for permitting money laundering involving Mexican drug cartels and terrorist organizations, criminal prosecutions were deferred in favour of fines, in this case at the instigation of senior politicians.[25] Private sector interests were conflated with the policy process through regulatory capture, applying apolitical transnational standards through informal governance processes (Tsingou, 2010, p. 5). Difficult to value assets, then, coupled with misplaced incentives for insiders and their capture of the regulatory process created significant opportunities for fraud during and after the financial crisis.

Complexity, as before, benefitted insiders, particularly market operators. Market rigging scandals occurred on a regular basis. In the UK, the LIBOR rate and FOREX markets were subject to serious and fraudulent manipulations market insiders. The FOREX scandal was operated by a cartel of senior traders ("the bandits' club"), with significant influences in the Bank of England, using inside information about client positions against the setting of market exchange rates for daily publication carried out at 4pm (Fields, 2014). There was no statutory monitoring of their activities. For example, WM, the private organisation administering the '4pm fix' was outside any regulatory authority, and the changes introduced in the wake of LIBOR had not been applied to FOREX (O'Brien, 2014). In short, the traders were operating a complex transaction that was poorly understood by outsiders and subjected only to voluntary codes of regulation.

Conclusions

The above discussion has been wide ranging and has necessarily been selective in its choices of illustrative cases. Also missing has been any analysis of counter arguments against regulation, which has been implied throughout to be desirable. Certainly in the model presented here, the cat and mouse evolution of opportunity and impediment is suggestive of the reduction of the former and the enhancement of the latter. However, without technological advances from which opportunity arises, economic growth is compromised and likewise too much regulation potentially damages market efficiency. In this view, fraud is a by-product of an otherwise successful market economy, and is to be tolerated as such. To be sustainable, this perspective must show that the costs of fraud are sufficiently small and that the economy is successful notwithstanding its presence. However, where fraud damages the reputational capital of individual firms, the write offs are potentially larger than the conventionally accumulated capital arising from normal trading. Where systemic, the loss of reputation spreads to institutions. The combined effects of fraud can thus significantly raise the cost of capital for all firms and damage economic growth.

As a consequence, the effect of the financial crisis has increased the demand for historical studies such that lessons can be learned and recent mistakes prevented. In the cases illustrated, the regulatory institutions have tended to lag the opportunities presented to fraudsters. The *Bubble Act* was ex-post the speculation, railway mania attracted railway regulation and Slater Walker led to the SFO. In the long run, and in more recent decades, regulatory impediments have been watered down, mainly as a result of reduced expectations placed on senior managers, auditors and market insiders.

The lessons of history are clear. The criminal law has throughout most of history, punished dishonesty, yes, but without imposing responsibility for its detection on senior staff within business organisations. Like everyone else, senior managers are expected to behave reasonably and exercise a duty of care, but if someone acts dishonestly, that need be of no direct concern to them, if they can show themselves to have acted honestly. No one is therefore expected to explicitly check for the dishonesty of others. However, this collective action problem compounds moral hazard problems resulting in a multiplication of opportunity with absence of impediment. Such problems have been most pronounced in periods of rapid technological changes, which have also coincided with deregulation. Their coincidence is most pronounced today, even post financial crisis. Many of history's apparently obvious lessons remain to be learned.

A balance is thus required, not just between the costs of fraud against the costs of regulation, but between the dominant narrative of deregulation and a counter narrative suggesting duties for regulators and high paid executives that might go beyond what is expected of the ordinary businessman or woman. Board members, in return for high salaries, should expect rigorous and frequent challenge, taking full responsibility for those in their charge as well as for their own behaviour. In other words, *active* governance; 'bloodhounds' are needed as well as 'watchdogs'.

Notes

1 *Bubble Act* [1720] 6 Geo I, c 18.
2 *Foss v Harbottle* [1843] 67 ER 189. The court will not interfere with the wishes of the majority of members in a general meeting.
3 *Companies Act* [1862] 25 & 26 Vict. c.89.
4 *Trevor v Whitworth* [1887] 12 App Cas 409.
5 *Prosecution of Offences Act*, [1879] 42 & 43 Vict. c.22. *Companies (Winding Up) Act* [1890] 53 & 54 Vict c 63.
6 Dunlop Prospectus, 11 May 1896, *Times Book of Prospectuses*.
7 Founders or deferred shares were shares held by directors (who were usually the founders of the company) which received no dividend until a pre-established dividend had been paid to ordinary shareholders, and sometimes they gave the holders a right to a high share of profits once the pre-established dividend had been met (Campbell & Turner, 2011).
8 *Re Kingston Cotton Mills*, [1896] 2 Ch. 279.
9 *Percival v Wright* [1902] 2 Ch. 401.
10 *Jubilee Cotton Mills, Ltd. v. Lewis*, [1924] A. C. 958.
11 *Re City Equitable Fire Insurance Co* [1925] Ch. 407.
12 *R v Kylsant* [1931] 1KB 442.
13 *Companies Act* [1929] 19 & 20 Geo.5 c.23. *Companies Act*, [1948] II & 12 Geo. 6. *Companies Act* [1967] c. 81.
14 HM Treasury Papers, Unwin to Bridgeman, 27th October, 1975. http://www.hm-treasury.gov.uk/d/slaterwalker_part1.pdf.
15 *Criminal Justice Act* [1987]. The SFO was accountable to the Attorney General for prosecuting criminal cases of fraud and corruption.
16 *Banking Act*, [1979] c.37.
17 Slater had been convicted under s.54 *Companies Act 1948* which prohibited the provision of financial assistance for the purchase of the firm's own shares.

18 *Companies Act* [1980].
19 *Criminal Justice Act* [1993], s.52.
20 *Financial Services and Markets Act* [2000]; *Market Abuse Directive* [2005].
21 'Nunn Hayward faces questions', *The Times*, 8 April, 2003. The JDS was a created in 1979 by the accountancy profession for the purposes of professional self-regulation (Matthews, 2000, p. 70).
22 *The Times*, 10 June, 2004.
23 *Hedley Byrne & Co Ltd v Heller* & Partners Ltd [1964] AC 465; *Caparo Industries plc* v *Dickman* [*1990*] UKHL 2; *International Standard on Auditing* 240, 'Auditors' Responsibilities Relating to Fraud in an Audit of Financial Statements' (APB, 2010).
24 Bank of England, for example pp. 217–222.
25 *Breitbart*, 20 April 2015.

References

Acheson, G. & Turner, J. (2008). 'The Death Blow to Unlimited Liability in Victorian Britain: The City of Glasgow Failure', *Explorations in Economic History*, *45*, 235–53.
Ackrill, M. & Hannah, L. (2001). *Barclays: The Business of Banking, 1690–1996*. Cambridge: Cambridge University Press.
Akerlof, G. A. (1970). 'The Market for "lemons": Quality Uncertainty and the Market Mechanism'. *The Quarterly Journal of Economics*, 488–500.
Augur, P. (2006). *The Greed Merchants: How the Investment Banks played the Free Market Game*. London: Penguin.
Bakan, J. (2015) 'The Invisible Hand of Law: Private Regulation and the Rule of Law', *Cornell International Law Journal*, *48*, 279–451.
Bank of England (2015). *The Failure of HBOS plc (HBOS)*, http://www.bankofengland.co.uk/pra/Documents/publications/reports/hbos.pdf.
Bruce, A. & Skovoroda, R. (2013). 'Bankers' Bonuses and the Financial Crisis: Context, Evidence and the Rhetoric – Policy Gap'. *Business History*, *55*(2), 139–160.
Campbell, G. & Turner, J. D. (2011). 'Substitutes for Legal Protection: Corporate Governance and Dividends in Victorian Britain', *Economic History Review*, *64*(2), 571–597.
Chancellor, E. (2000). *Devil Take the Hindmost: A History of Financial Speculation*. New York: Plume.
Chapman, S. (2003). *Merchant Enterprise in Britain: From the Industrial Revolution to World War I*. Cambridge: Cambridge University Press.
Cressey, D. R. (1953). *Other People's Money: A Study of the Social Psychology of Embezzlement*. New Jersey: Patterson Smith.
Croall, H. (2004). 'Combating Financial Crime: Regulatory Versus Crime Control Approaches', *Journal of Financial Crime*, *11*(1), 45–55.
Dale, R. S. (2004). *The First Crash: Lessons from the South Sea Bubble*. Princeton: Princeton University Press.
Dale, R. S., Johnson, J. E. & Tang, L. (2005). 'Financial Markets Can Go Mad: Evidence of Irrational Behaviour during the South Sea Bubble', *Economic History Review*, *58*(2), 233–271.
Davies, P. N. & Bourne, A. M. (1972). 'Lord Kylsant and the Royal Mail', *Business History*, *14*(2), 103–123.
Fields, G. (2014). 'Common Cause: Institutional Corruption's Role in the Libor and the 4pm Fix Scandals'. *Law and Financial Markets Review*, *8*(1), 8–12.
Foot, M. (2003). 'Working with Market Forces', in Mizen, P. (ed.) *Monetary History, Exchange Rates and Financial Markets*. Cheltenham: Edward Elgar.
Garber, P. (2001). *Famous First Bubbles: The Fundamentals of Early Manias*. Cambridge: MIT.
Georgiou, O. & Jack, L. (2011). 'In Pursuit of Legitimacy: A History behind Fair Value Accounting', *The British Accounting Review*, *43*(4), 311–323.
Giroux, G. (2014). *Business Scandals, Corruption, and Reform: An Encyclopedia*. California: Greenwood.
Harrison, A. E. (1981). 'Joint-Stock Company Flotation in the Cycle, Motor-Vehicle and Related Industries, 1882–1914', *Business History*, *23*(2), 165–190.
Harrison, P. (2001). 'Rational Equity Valuation at the Time of the South Sea Bubble', *History of Political Economy*, *33*(2), 269–281.
Higgins, D., Toms, S. & Filatotchev, I. (2015). 'Ownership, Financial Strategy and Performance: The Lancashire Cotton Textile industry, 1918–1938', *Business History*, *57*(1), 96–120.

Jackson, H. E. (2005). An American Perspective on the UK Financial Services Authority: Politics, Goals & Regulatory Intensity. *Harvard Law and Economics Discussion Paper*, (522).

Johnston, T. (1934). *The Financiers and the Nation*. London: Methuen.

Jones, M. (2011). *Creative Accounting, Fraud and International Accounting Scandals*. Chichester: Wiley.

Lamoreaux, N. R. (2009). 'Scylla or Charybdis? Historical Reflections on Two Basic Problems of Corporate Governance', *Business History Review*, *83*(1), 9–34.

Lee, T., Clarke, F. & Dean, G. (2009). 'Scandals' in Edwards, J. R. and Walker, S. (eds.) *The Routledge Companion to Accounting History*. Abingdon: Routledge.

Loke, A. F. (2006). 'From the Fiduciary Theory to Information Abuse: The Changing Fabric of Insider Trading Law in the U.K., Australia and Singapore', *American Journal of Comparative Law*, *54*(1),123–172.

Lowenstein, R. (2000). *When Genius Failed: The Rise and Fall of Long-Term Capital Management*. Random House Trade Paperbacks.

Maltby, J. (1999). 'A Sort of Guide, Philosopher and Friend': The Rise of the Professional Auditor in Britain. *Accounting, Business & Financial History*, *9*(1), 29–50.

Matthews, D. (2000). 'Oral history, accounting history and an interview with Sir John Grenside', *Accounting, Business & Financial History*, *10*(1), 57–83.

McCartney, S. & Arnold, A. J. (2000). 'George Hudson's financial reporting practices: putting the Eastern Counties Railway in context', *Accounting, Business & Financial History*, *10*(3), 293–316.

O'Brien, J. (2014). 'Fixing the Fix: Governance, Culture, Ethics and the Extending Perimeter of Financial Regulation', *Law and Financial Markets Review*, *8*(4), 373–388.

Palley, T. (2011). 'America's Flawed Paradigm: Macroeconomic Causes of the Financial Crisis and Great Recession' *Empirica*, *38*(1), 3–17.

Raw, C. (1977). *Slater Walker: An Investigation of a Financial Phenomenon*. London: Andre Deutsch.

Roskill (1986). *Fraud Trials Committee Report*. Great Britain. Fraud Trials Committee London: HMSO.

Shea, G. S. (2007). 'Financial Market Analysis can go Mad (In the Search for Irrational Behaviour During the South Sea Bubble)', *Economic History Review*, *60*(4), 742–765.

Smith, T. (1992). *Accounting for Growth: Stripping the Camouflage from Company Accounts*. Century Business.

South Sea Company (1825). *The South Sea Bubble, and the Numerous Fraudulent Projects to Which it Gave Rise in 1720, Historically Detailed as a Beacon to the Unwary Against Modern Schemes*. London: T Boys.

Stratmann, L. (2012). *Fraudsters and Charlatans*. Stroud: History Press.

Taylor, J. (2013). *Boardroom Scandal: The Criminalization of Company Fraud in Nineteenth-Century Britain*. Oxford University Press.

Toms, S. (2005). 'Financial Control, Managerial Control and Accountability: Evidence from the British Cotton Industry, 1700–2000', *Accounting, Organizations and Society*, *30*(7), 627–653.

Toms, S., Wilson, N. & Wright, M. (2015). 'The Evolution of Private Equity: Corporate Restructuring in the UK, c.1945–2010', *Business History,* *57*(7): 736–768.

Toms, S. & Wright, M. (2005). 'Divergence and Convergence within Anglo-American Corporate Governance Systems: Evidence from the US and UK, 1950–2000', *Business History*, *47*(2), 267–295.

Tsingou, E. (2010). Regulatory Reactions to the Global Credit Crisis: Analyzing a Policy Community Under Stress. *Global Finance in Crisis. The Politics of International Regulatory Change*. London and New York: Routledge, 21–36.

Vander Weyer, M. (2011). *Fortune's Spear: The Story of the Blue-Blooded Rogue Behind the Most Notorious City Scandal of the 1920s*. Elliott & Thompson.

Watson, S. (2012). 'Derivation of powers of boards of directors in UK companies', in Vasudev, P and Watson S. (eds), *Corporate Governance After the Financial Crisis*. Cheltenham: Edward Elgar, 47–67.

Wilson, G. & Wilson, S. (2013). 'Criminal Responses and Financial Misconduct in Twenty-First Century Britain: Tradition and Points Of Departure, and the Significance of the Conscious Past', *Law, Crime & History*, *3*(3).

Wilson, S. (2014). *The Origins of Modern Financial Crime: Historical Foundations and Current Problems in Britain*. Abingdon: Routledge.

24

Changing approaches
to business ethics

Bernard Mees

An arch over one of the exits from Greenwich Market in the east of London bears a sign which reads "A false balance is an abomination to the Lord but a just weight is his delight". Erected in the nineteenth century, this quote from the Biblical Book of Proverbs (11:1) underlines the traditionally religious nature of most thinking regarding the proper conduct of business internationally. Greenwich is also the home of the Old Royal Naval College and the Greenwich Meridian – it was the military centre of the British Empire, the Pentagon of the nineteenth century. Greenwich is also the site of the parish where Joseph F. Mees served as a lay reader until his death during the outbreak of the Spanish flu at the end of the First World War. I would like to imagine that my great uncle had a hand in erecting the Old Testament quote over that exit to Greenwich Market, but it seems more likely that it is older than that. In 1849, an Act of Parliament gave the Commissioners of Greenwich Hospital the right to set up and manage Greenwich Market and I suspect that the biblical warning against falsifying balances was erected then as merely one of the many acts of Victorian epigraphic piety that still dot the British built environment today.

The quote still on display at Greenwich Market is one of several biblical sources around which the Christian concept of business ethics was built and may be taken to epitomise the two manners in which business ethics is typically encountered in business history today: in the history of business institutions and business biography. Most religions retain comparable traditions of admonition regarding greed and unfairness in commercial dealings. From a survey of recent handbooks of business ethics, however, one would think that religion had very little to do with business ethics. Modern business ethics is construed in recent textbook accounts as a form of cosmopolitan "practical ethics" of the kind that the Australian Jewish ethicist (and outspoken atheist) Peter Singer first advocated in 1979.

According to Singer, the problem with ethics as it had been taught in university philosophy departments before the 1970s was its lack of practical application. Singer first made his name as a radical proponent of animal rights (Singer, 1975) and has more recently been associated with the "new atheism" rather than any business or religious tradition. Neither ancient Greek nor Chinese philosophy, however, has as strong traditions of business ethics as do the major world religions. Hence much of the history of business ethics is best seen as an extension of religious history, even if criticism of the moral shortcomings of business is more often imagined to be a particular feature of the nineteenth-century worker movement and its contemporary reflection in the political left. The history of business ethics, taken in Nietzsche's (1887) sense of a genealogy of morals, is punctuated by religious concerns wherever it is found, many of the key contributions to the topic having clear foundations in institutional religion and religious thinking, whether clerical, personal or secularised.

Perhaps the most obvious example of the link between religion and contemporary business ethics is the Institute of Business Ethics in London. As is recorded in the "brief history" on its website, the Institute was founded in 1986 under the umbrella of the Christian Association of Business Executives, which itself dates back to 1938. But the Christian Association of Business Executives was established originally as the British Catholic Industrialists' Conference, an expression of a broader movement that developed in light of the 1891 Papal encyclical *De rerum novarum* (Gremillion, 1961). Scratch the surface of many apparently secular business ethics bodies and the influence of organised religion readily becomes apparent. Business ethics is largely a secularised form of religion which developed outside the tradition of Western philosophical ethics or the movements which gave rise to contemporary socialism.

This connection can be seen more explicitly in the United States. The founder of modern business philanthropy is generally acknowledged to have been John D. Rockefeller, Sr. whose pioneering Standard Oil was the forerunner of ExxonMobil, still one of the largest corporations in the world by market capitalization today. Rockefeller was a Baptist and as he recounted in 1900 had got into the habit of giving money each week to his local church as a young man (Chernow, 1998). The Rockefeller Foundation that he set up in 1913 was established to administer his (and his son's) charitable activities. As the preeminent philanthropic organisation of its type, the Rockefeller Foundation developed the first public giving principles and remains one of the most influential business charities internationally, having disbursed over $15 billion in funds over the last century. But business philanthropy is only one aspect of business ethics, and is not as celebrated in Europe and other parts of the world that have more developed traditions of state support for the provision of public welfare.

Nonetheless similar initiatives by British industrialists were often associated with religious tradition. Lord Leverhulme who established the Leverhulme trust in 1925 was noted for his running of Lever Brothers (now Unilever) along Congregationalist grounds, and a long tradition of Quaker capitalism is shared by both the United Kingdom and the United States (Lewis, 2008; King, 2014). The notion that the concept of business ethics was an oxymoron was first declared by a columnist in the *Wall Street Journal* in 1983 (Tannenbaum, 1983). But it had always made considerable sense to industrialists who took their religion seriously.

The Islamic world has similarly long witnessed obvious influences of religion on business ethics (Rice, 1999; Mohammed, 2013). The most notable to external eyes is clearly that of Islamic finance, a movement that has developed based on a prohibition on usury that was once also shared in the Christian West. Where the sixteenth-century Papacy was convinced by business interests to weaken the prohibition on the charging of interest (the 'pound of flesh' of Shakespeare's *Merchant of Venice*), Islamic clerical opinion has not proved so bending to the needs of finance capitalism. The Islamic tradition of Zakat (alms-giving) is also institutionalized in most of the Islamic world, but has yet to receive a proper academic study. Much of the history of business ethics outside the US and Britain remains unwritten, the failure of business historians to deal with issues of such scope reflecting the traditional focus of business history on the history of individual companies or biographies of industrialists, as if thematic issues such as business ethics are of lesser importance than writing narrative histories informed principally by personal archives or those of large business concerns.

Similar traditions of business philanthropy are also found in China – the notion that individuals made rich by business success should give back to society is not a Western or Islamic preserve. Chinese industrialisation, however, has often been conceived in very Western terms, with received Confucian and Taoist traditions rejected as holding China back. In the 1920s, the Confucian tradition was actively opposed by Chinese nationalists and suppressed in the 1950s and 60s at the height of Maoism (Lin, 1979; Sun, 2005; Hu, 2007). Philanthropy in mainland China today is often arraigned instead around expressions of the Communist Party such as the cult of the soldier-hero Lei Feng (Funari and Mees, 2013). Lei Feng charities, although ad hoc, are the only large-scale public institution in the People's Republic that could be taken to mirror the scale of the Islamic Zakat charities or the similar mixture of private endowments and Christian charities which receive much business philanthropy in Western countries today.

Similar institutions are not as evident in countries such as India. The Sir Dorabji Tata Trust was established in 1932 and operates along Western lines, but rates of business giving in India remain notoriously low. That one of India's most disgraced companies called itself "truthfulness" (Sanskrit *satyam*) underlines much of the concern regarding how Hindu traditions of benevolence and fairness should inform the Indian tradition of business giving in the future. Hindu religious tracts (like the Bhagavad Gita) tend to the general rather than the specific and hence accusations of ethical relativism (Chakraborty, 1997). Recent public support by the chairman of Wipro and the founder of the Sobha group to the Giving Pledge campaign started by Bill Gates and Warren Buffett (inspired ultimately by figures such as Rockefeller) highlight the lack of a culturally distinct tradition of business philanthropy in India. Why this has remained so remains an unrealised desideratum of Indian business history.

Yet business philanthropy has long been criticised as merely a sop to the lack of ethics more generally in business. Rockefeller's approach to philanthropy first fell afoul of US public opinion in the 1890s when it was revealed that he was giving money to religious institutions – as if they were being asked somehow to condone the behaviour of his monopoly kerosene producer. Rockefeller's main early critics were often Protestant pastors who thought he was using his religious bequests in order to inflate his reputation and hence his profits. Rockefeller's solution was to stop giving money to religious foundations and instead form the country's first formal corporate giving programme (Soskis, 2010).

That other titan of American business philanthropy of the day, Andrew Carnegie, was a less publicly devout man. A Scotsman by birth, Carnegie sat somewhat outside the overtly religious environment that has always characterised American public life. Carnegie argued instead for a business philanthropy based on more evidently Social Darwinist principles. Where Rockefeller had at first given out money in a somewhat ad hoc manner to institutions which approached him, Carnegie (1901) argued for a more functional and measured style of business giving – one that would improve American society in a more clearly Benthamite and stewardly way. Carnegie's manner of corporate giving would aim to avoid the pitfalls of Rockefeller's less instrumental approach to philanthropy, with Carnegie arguing that commercial men like himself were better stewards of the public good than publically elected officials.

The period of Rockefeller and Carnegie, however, is better known today as a time of robber barons, of unscrupulous business conduct and competition run mad (Josephson, 1934). By the 1920s it had come quite clear to US society at large that the business practices of the late Victorian era were no longer acceptable – or at least that is what we read in the works of the first generations of writers on American business ethics. Edgar Heermance's *The Ethics of*

Business (1926) represents the first attempt at a general survey of the issue of business morals and as Heermance notes in his introductory chapter, a substantial change had occurred in public attitudes to the ethics of business practice since the early 1900s. What Heermance was describing, later writers would call the emergence of the "progressive era" – a time of US social reform led by civically minded figures (mostly) of a politically liberal persuasion who rejected the extreme *laissez faire* capitalist allowance characteristic of a previous age.

The main feature that Heermance focuses on in his 1926 work is the emergence of an American movement of business ethics codes. There is no hint of R.H. Tawney's *The Acquisitive Society* (1921) or other prominent contemporary works of social democracy in Heermance's book. The early 1920s had seen a plethora of business ethics statements and codes emerging in the US and Heermance saw the development of this movement as a sign of an increased commitment to moral standards in US business (cf. Heald, 1970, pp. 92–95). Heermance's book also contains chapters on ethical philosophy and above all religious ethics. Heermance was a former Protestant preacher and it is quite clear where the root of his interest in business ethics lay.

Nonetheless by the early 1930s, the many scandals which had emerged with the onset of the Great Depression seemed to have put the lie to the promise of business reform suggested during the progressive era. The new focus in business ethics in the US was instead most clearly that proposed by Chester Barnard in his *Functions of the Executive* (1938) – the duty of moral leadership. Barnard was the first properly systematic American thinker in the emerging field of management studies and refined the earlier notion of business stewardship into a more suitably sociologised and corporate form. As a supporter of what would later be recognised as a form of paternalistic managerialism, Barnard was the most noted proponent from his era of what is now studied in business schools as "ethical leadership".

The first survey of American business education (prepared for the Wharton School in 1929/30) noted that moral questions were only rarely addressed specifically in business school curricula at the time (Bosshard and Dewhurst, 1931; Abend, 2013). But as the turbulent 1930s and 40s gave way to a more confident and prosperous period, a new focus emerged in what at the time was styled US "business and society" thinking. The 1940s and 50s produced many and varied studies and polemics in the US regarding the proper conduct of businessmen; yet the most famous contribution to this new discursive strand remains Howard R. Bowen's *Social Responsibilities of the Businessman* (1953). Where earlier authors had suggested that the social responsibility of business was to help rebuild Europe after the war (Merill, 1948) or simply, even, to focus on lowering consumer prices (Filene, 1922), Bowen's book laid the foundation for the broader field of what today is known as corporate social responsibility or CSR (Carroll, 1999).

It is not often recognised, however, that Bowen, an economist, had been asked to write the book by a committee of the Federal Council of Churches (Acquier et al., 2011). The monograph also includes a response to Bowen's survey (which was begun with the support of a 1949 Rockefeller Foundation grant) by F. Ernest Johnson, a leading American religious studies educator (Bowen, 1959, pp. 233–59; Limbert, 1969). The movement which encouraged American businesses to accept some social responsibility was a distinctly religious expression, mirrored by comparable developments in Western Europe where a Catholic tradition had emerged of promoting socially responsible commercial behaviour through organisations such as the Catholic industrial associations (Gremillion, 1961). The Protestant reaction of the day obviously represented a form of keeping up with the Catholic Joneses.

With its roots stretching back into late antiquity, the Catholic Church has been the longest-standing institutional promoter of business ethics. A fortune honestly made was considered a virtue in ancient Greece, but there is no sense of a particularly nuanced or developed tradition of business ethics in classical philosophy. The ancient Greeks were a mercantile race, yet the ethics of business practice does not seem to have been of much concern in the writings of ancient philosophers which have come down to us today. There is no sense, for example, from St Thomas Aquinas, the medieval philosopher who might well be considered the founder of Western business ethics, that he had any classical predecessors when he considered the notion of what was a just price in his *Summa theologica* (ed. O'Sullivan, 1952). Aquinas would seem to be the inaugurator of a continuous tradition of discussing fairness in Western business activity from a considered philosophical position.

Aquinas's just price theory was followed by a series of further writings on how a good Christian might undertake business honourably. Indeed, medievalists such as Davis (2012) have been able to point to the writings of a Christine de Pizan (trans. Forhan, 1994) or one of the many medieval trade manuals for signs of an ethical facet to business discourse already in Aquinas's day (Davis, 2012). But unlike his late medieval continuator Johannes Nider (trans. Reeves, 1966; Wren, 2000), Aquinas was the king of Christian philosophers, aiming to reconcile as he did the Greek tradition (as articulated in Aristotle) with the teachings of Scripture. Although Christian philosophers are often written out of ethics texts today (and not only in an effort to keep things cosmopolitan), Aquinas remains a towering figure in the history of Western philosophy (Stump, 2003).

Pope Leo XIII's *De rerum novarum* or "On Capital and Labour" (1891) was a development the neo-Thomist tradition of late nineteenth-century Catholicism which promoted the Church as a public guarantor of moral behaviour. The papal encyclical which forms the basis of Catholic social justice teaching recognises the role of trade unions in mitigating the worse effects of industrial capitalism and seeks to stake out a middle ground between revolutionary socialism ("working on the poor man's envy of the rich"; *Rer. nov.* 4) and a society ruled by "men of greed, who use human beings as mere instruments for money-making" (*Rer. nov.* 42). Singer's form of practical ethics ignores the very active tradition of applied philosophy that has been typical of the Catholic approach since the nineteenth century.

The influence of the Catholic tradition is particularly obvious in the US American business ethics remained a very public concern throughout much of the 1950s and 60s, but perhaps most famously in terms of an article penned by a Jesuit doctoral student Raymond Baumhart for the *Harvard Business Review* in 1961 (McMahon, 2002). The first American business ethics conference was hosted by the University of Kansas in 1976 (De George and Pischler, eds., 1978). Yet by the 1970s the movement to reform business practice on overtly religious grounds was already giving way to a broader stream of protest associated with mainline Protestant student groups and the re-emergence of a popular anti-corporate movement whose most famous member was the consumer activist Ralph Nader (Graham, 2000; Marcello, 2004). A searching critique of the US automobile industry, Nader's celebrated *Unsafe at Any Speed* (1965) would inspire many campaigns and protests against the unscrupulous behaviour of large US corporations at the time. And two new fields of business ethics duly grew out of the anti-corporate movement of the 1960s and 70s: corporate governance and stakeholder theory.

The term "corporate governance" had first been coined by Richard Eells, a former manager of social policy at General Electric whose first book *Corporation Giving in a Free Society* (1956) had launched his career as a business ethicist. In 1960, Eells bemoaned the "excessive materialism", the "cynical disregard for moral and religious standards" and the "undemocratic values" of US business of the time, and called instead for the development of "a theory of corporate governance consistent with the ideals of a democratic society" (Eells, 1960, p. 52).

Nader and his colleagues further developed this call for reform in the 1970s, complaining of the "failure of modern corporate governance" in their bid to "constitutionalise" large US corporations as part of a struggle for "corporate democracy" (Nader et al., 1976, p. 86). Corporate governance first emerged as a concern of business ethics before it was reduced to the preserve of commercial lawyers and financial economists.

Stakeholder theory was first proposed (similarly) as a method for companies to deal with critics such as Nader. While Nader and his colleagues were unmasking the many moral shortcomings of American corporate life, business school theorists such as William R. Dill (1975) proposed strategies to accommodate "Naderites" in corporate strategy (Freeman et al., 2010). The first articulation of "stakeholder theory" employed the "corporate democracy" language of Nader and his colleagues as part of a proposed strategy to manage corporate critics. Although now typically seen as a form of ethical business practice, stakeholder theory has a rather perverse origin as an expression of American management scholarship.

Despite Heermance's much earlier call, the entry of philosophical ethics into the business curriculum is a rather late development. W. Michael Hoffmann, director of the Center for Business Ethics at Bentley College, Massachusetts, convened the first national business ethics conference in 1977 (ed. Hoffman, 1978) as chairman of the Philosophy Department at Bentley College (now Bentley University). Speakers at the conference included such luminaries as the Jewish sociologist (and futurologist) Daniel Bell who had linked the criticism of business which characterised the 1960s and 70s to the emergence of his post-industrial or information society – like most sociologists of the day, he ignored the fundamental religious underpinnings of business ethics (Bell, 1973). Yet the entry of philosophers into US business schools seems to have been concomitant with a retreat of clergy as the theologians of Hoffmann's early conferences were replaced by neo-Kantians such as Norman Bowie who sought to develop a more cosmopolitan form of applied business ethics (Bowie, 1997).

The surveys of American business ethics of authors such as Carroll et al. (2012) seem to forget how decidedly non-secular US discourses of business ethics have long remained. Abend (2014) has more insightfully focussed on the very Christian nature of American business ethics, but religion is not the only influence on the discourse and practice of ethical behaviour in the Anglo-Saxon business tradition. The early Welsh socialist Robert Owen was an anti-clerical deist and consorted with freethinkers such as Jeremy Bentham (Harrison, 1969; Donnachie, 2000) and Adam Smith's negative assessment of religion is well known (Ward, 2004). More radically still, Marx and Engels (1848) were proponents of atheism claiming that nineteenth-century businessmen had "left remaining no other nexus between man and man than naked self-interest" and "veiled by religious and political illusions ... substituted naked, shameless, direct, brutal exploitation" (Marx and Engels, 1848, p. 15). Immanuel Kant is the figure who has most clearly usurped the throne of Aquinas in the Western tradition (Kuehn, 2001; Hunter, 2001). But unlike Aquinas, Kant was quite unconcerned with the world of business, and the Marxisant left has made few inroads into discourses of commercial ethics, set as it has largely been against the capitalist business establishment. When overtly ethical developments have arisen in mainstream business practice, they have usually done so as a reflection of religion, one of the key social institutions from which business communities have proved overtly receptive to in a prominent and continuous way.

More recently, however, the business ethics canon has been especially influenced by the environmental notion of sustainability, an idea usually linked with the Brundtland Commission (1987), which like much United Nations thinking in this area has obvious Kantian overtones. Sustainability is a discourse with which anti-clerical and liberal activists can engage which is not as clearly Western in its articulation as are earlier expressions of business ethics, and the various international ethics initiatives from the Principles of Business issued by the Caux Round Table (in 1994) to the Ten Principles of the UN Global Compact (first issued in 2000) have done much to globalise originally American and European ethical concerns. The promotion of companies as ethical to consumers, however, such as by the Body Shop, found in 1976 by the British entrepreneur Anita Roddick, has tended to reflect broader expressions of social criticism which more properly reflect notions first raised by figures from the anti-capitalist and often anti-religious left such as Singer.

Yet rather than a reflection of the Western political left, a historical perspective on business ethics suggests that it has (most clearly in the American tradition) largely been an expression of religion, an attempt (as Heermance proposed in the 1920s) to marry the realities of business practice with the moral teachings of Christianity. In terms of the writing of business history (and business biography), however, the approach to ethics has usually only veered between exculpation and omission. Although Roddick's (2005) autobiography is perhaps an exception here, usually such works (and commissioned company histories) have tended to pass over the ethical dimension of business practice. Spectacular failures such as the Penn Central collapse of 1970 have tended to attract more critical accounts (Sobel, 1977) and works like Edwin Black's investigation of the role of IBM in the Holocaust provide searching criticisms of significant moral failure (Black, 2001). But it would not be true to say that any typology or formal analysis of the historiography of business ethics has yet been developed by academic investigators.

Nonetheless changing approaches to and understandings of ethics underline how varied the concept of business morals can be. The institution of slavery was once held as normal and acceptable until religious objections to it became dominant in the nineteenth century. For many American and British businessmen, the Puritan notion of stewardship, glorified in Weber's (1904/5) notion of a Protestant work ethic, had already become justification enough by the 1950s to reconcile the exigencies of their daily business life with the broader moral behaviour expected of them in majority church-going societies (Sutton et al., 1956; Worden, 2010). Similarly, the Aristotlean notion of prudence (Greek *phronêsis*, Latin *providentia*) has long been associated with business practice, but usually in an etiolated manner – either in purely financial (or fiduciary) terms or as an aspect of business strategy (Fayol's *prévoyance*, usually mistranslated into English as 'planning'; see Fayol, 1916, 1949). Yet even in the less publicly devout European West, much of the recent discourse of business ethics has remained decidedly Christian in its formulation. For example, the British peer Lord Griffiths of Fforestfach (a former consultant to Margaret Thatcher) expresses many of the key issues of business and morality in his 1982 work *Morality and the Market Place* in terms of a business practice which eschews both the "semi-atheism" of neo-liberal mainstays such as Friedrich Hayek (1944) and Milton Friedman (1962) as well the unacceptably deadly and radical path of Marxism (as "the utopian dream of a Christian heresy"; Griffiths, 1982, p. 58). That institutions such as London's Institute of Business Ethics have firm Christian roots and that many discourses of business ethics remain rooted in older clerical contributions is not always clear in the broader field today. But despite the secularisation of the discursive formation, it is its roots in a progressive Christianity which seems most fundamentally to characterise business ethics as an aspect of Western intellectual history, not the neo-Kantian or utilitarian pretensions of many of its more recent advocates.

The main problem with the cosmopolitan approach to business ethics prevalent in American academic discourse since the 1980s has been its tendency to crowd out other approaches. And a similar forgetting of the history of business ethics seems also to be reflected in recent approaches to other regional traditions such those which apply in Asia. Confucius and his many followers (including later Confucian scholars such as Mencius) shared a disdain of business. The notion of a Confucian business ethics reflected in leading Western academic organs such as the *Journal of Business Ethics* (founded in 1982) often reflects a reconfiguration of the Confucian heritage by members of the Chinese diaspora, and historically seems to have its origin in the need for immigrants to develop discourses of hard work and thrift in order to succeed in alien societies (Yao, 2002; Wang, 2004). In the nineteenth century, the Chinese were largely seen as less hard working than was the norm in the West, and much of contemporary Confucianism reflects a form of nationalism dating particularly to the 1980s (Dirlik, 1995; Makeham, 2003). A form of business ethics has been manufactured in recent Confucianist accounts which reflects what Hill (2002) has characterised as a "reverse Orientalism". As Giddens (1999) stresses, local cultural and religious revivals (often in the form of "invented" traditions; see Hobsbawm and Ranger, eds., 1983) are an expected response to globalization, with attempts to form regional business ethics traditions informed more by Westernisation than any truly native genealogy of morals.

Arguably then, institutions such as the Catholic Church have had more historical influence over business ethics than have comparable non-Western ones. The abolition of the Muslim Caliphate in 1924 and the lateness of the coming of industrialisation to much of Asia has seen traditional religious teachings on business morality muted with the globalization of business concerns. Historically, the main discourses of business ethics developed as a form of self-regulation in American business. Yet by the 1950s, the field had become caught up in a broader reform movement with a clear religious sensibility that was particularly expressed in the form of calls for businessmen to act in socially responsible manners. Notions of social responsibility produced academic articulations of this ideal such as CSR which were later adopted in corporate programmes and globalized by the adoption of corporate responsibility initiatives by international institutions. Never articulated, however, in anything other than liberal and conservative political terms, most crucially business ethics also remains a justification for undertaking business activity – as part of the social license of business. A response to critics of business scandal and greed, business ethics remains mostly an attempt to sail the politically centrist waters between the Scylla of neo-liberal excess and the Charybdis of socialist overreaction.

References

Abend, G. (2013). 'The origins of business ethics in American universities, 1902–1936', *Business Ethics Quarterly, 23*(2), 171–205.

Abend, G. (2014). *The Moral Background: An Inquiry into the History of Business Ethics*. Princeton: Princeton University Press.

Acquier, A., Gond, J-P. & Pasquero, J. (2011). 'Rediscovering Howard R. Bowen's legacy: the unachieved agenda and continuing relevance of *Social Responsibilities of the Businessman*', *Business and Society, 50*, 607–46.

Barnard, C. I. (1934). *The Functions of the Executive*. Cambridge: Harvard University Press.

Baumhart, R. C. (1961). 'How ethical are businessmen?', *Harvard Business Review 39*(4), 6–19 and 156–76.

Bell, D. (1973). *The Coming of Post-Industrial Society: A Venture in Social Forecasting*. New York: Basic Books.

Black, E. (2001). *IBM and the Holocaust: The Strategic Alliance Between Nazi Germany and America's Most Powerful Corporation*. New York: Crown.

Bossard, J. H. & Frederick Dewhurst, J. (1931). *University Education for Business*. Philadelphia: University of Pennsylvania Press.

Bowen, H. T. (1953). *Social Responsibilities of the Businessman*. New York: Harper & Bros.

Bowie, N. E. (1997). *Business Ethics: A Kantian Perspective*. Maiden: Blackwell.

Brundtland, G. H. (1987). *Our Common Future*. Oxford: Oxford University Press.

Carnegie, A. (1901). *The Gospel of Wealth and Other Timely Essays*. London: Warne.

Carroll, A. B. (1999). 'Corporate social responsibility: evolution of a definitional construct', *Business and Society, 38*, 268–95.

Carroll, A. B., Lipartio, K. J., Post, J. E. & Werhane, P. H. (2012). *Corporate Social Responsibility: The American Experience*. Cambridge: Cambridge University Press.

Chakraborty, S. K. (1997) 'Business ethics in India', *Journal of Business Ethics, 16*(14), 1529–38.

Chernow, R. (1998). *Titan: The Life of John D. Rockefeller, Sr.* New York: Random House.

Davis, J. (2012). *Medieval Market Morality: Life, Law and Ethics in the English Marketplace, 1200–1500*. Cambridge: Cambridge University Press.

De George, R. T. & Pichler, J. A. (eds.) (1978). *Ethics, Free Enterprise, and Public Policy: Original Essays on Moral Issues in Business*. New York: Oxford University Press.

Dill, W. R. (1975). 'Public participation in corporate planning—strategic management in a Kibitzer's world', *Long Range Planning, 8*, 57–63.

Dirlik, A. (1995). 'Confucius in the borderlands: global capitalism and the reinvention of Confucianism', *Boundary 2, 22*(3), 229–73.

Donnachie, I. L. (2000). *Robert Owen: Owen of New Lanark and New Harmony*. East Linton: Tuckwell.

Eells, R. (1956). *Corporation Giving in a Free Society*. New York: Harper.

Eells, R. (1960). *The Meaning of Modern Business: An Introduction to the Philosophy of Large Corporate Enterprise*. New York: Columbia University Press.

Fayol, H. (1916). *Administration Industrielle et Générale: Prévoyance, Organisation, Commandement, Coordination, Controle*. Paris: Dunod & Pinat.

Fayol, H. (1949). *General and Industrial Management*, trans. C. Storrs. London: Pitmann.

Filene, E. A. (1922). 'A simple code of business ethics', *Annals of the American Academy of Political and Social Science, 101*(196), 223–28.

Forhan, K. L. (trans.) (1987). Christine de Pizan, *The Book of the Body Politic*. Cambridge: Cambridge University Press.

Freeman, R. E. et al. (2010). 'The development of stakeholder theory: A brief history', in *Stakeholder Theory: The State of the Art*. Cambridge: Cambridge University Press, 30–62.

Friedman, M. (1962). *Capitalism and Freedom*. Chicago: University of Chicago Press.

Funari, R. & Mees, B. (2013). 'Socialist emulation in China: worker heroes yesterday and today', *Labor History, 54*(3), 240–255.

Giddens, A. (1999). *Runaway World: How Globalization is Reshaping Our Lives*. London: Profile.

Graham, K. (2000). *Ralph Nader: Batling for Democracy*. Denver: Windham.

Gremillion, J. B. (1961). *The Catholic Movement of Employers and Managers* (Studia socialia 5), Rome: Gregorian University Press.

Griffiths, B. (1982). *Morality and the Market Place* (London Lectures in Contemporary Christianity, 1980). London: Hodder & Stoughton.

Harrison, J. F. C. (1969). *Quest for the New Moral World: Robert Owen and the Owenites in Britain and America*. New York: Scribner.

Hayek, F. A. (1944). *The Road to Serfdom*. London: Routledge.

Heald, M. (1970). *The Social Responsibilities of Business: Company and Community, 1900–1960*. Cleveland: Press of Case Western University.

Heermance, E. L. (1926). *The Ethics of Business: A survey of Current Standards*. New York: Harper & Bros.

Hill, M. (2002). '"Asian values" as reverse orientalism: Singapore', *Asia Pacific Viewpoint, 41*(2), 177–190.

Hobsbawm, E. &Ranger, T. (ed.) (1983). *The Invention of Tradition*. Cambridge: Cambridge University Press.

Hoffmann, M. W. (ed.) (1977). *Business Values and Social Justice: Compatibility or Contradiction? Proceedings of the First National Conference on Business Ethics, March 11 and 12, 1977*. Waltham, Mass.: The Center for Business Ethics, Bentley College.

Hu, S. (2007). 'Confucianism and contemporary Chinese politics', *Politics & Policy, 35*(1), 136–153.

Hunter, I. (2001). *Rival Enlightenments: Civil and Metaphysical Philosophy in Early Modern Germany*. Cambridge: Cambridge University Press.

Josephson, M. (1934). *The Robber Barons: The Great American Capitalists, 1861–1901*. New York: Harcourt, Brace.

King, M. (2014). *Quakernomics: An Ethical Capitalism*. London: Anthem.

Kuehn, M. (2001). *Kant: A Biography*. Cambridge: Cambridge University Press.

Lewis, B. (2008). *So Clean: Lord Leverhulme, Soap and Civilization*. Manchester: Manchester University Press.

Limbert, P. M. (1969). 'F. Ernest Johnson: prophetic interpreter of Christian ethics (1885–1969)', *Religious Education, 64,* 499–500.

Lin, Y. (1979). *The Crisis of Chinese Consciousness: Radical Antitraditionalism in the May Fourth Era.* Madison: University of Wisconsin Press.

Makeham, J. (2003). 'The retrospective creation of New Confucianism', in idem (ed.), *New Confucianism: A Critical Examination.* New York: Palgrave Macmillan, 25–53.

Marcello, P. C. (2004). *Ralph Nader: A Biography*. Westport: Greenwood Press.

Marx, K. & Engels, F. (1888 [1848]). *Manifesto of the Communist Party*, trans. S. Moore. London: Reeves.

McMahon, T. F. (2002). 'A brief history of American business ethics', in R. Frederick (ed.), *A Companion to Business Ethics*. Oxford: Blackwell, 342–52.

Merill, H. F. (ed.) (1948). *The Responsibilities of Business Leadership*. Cambridge: Harvard University Press.

Mohammed, J. A. (2013). 'The ethical system in Islam – implications for business practices', in C. Luetge (ed.), *Handbook of the Philosophical Foundations of Business Ethics*, 3 vols, Dordrecht: Springer, 873–82.

Nader, R. (1965). *Unsafe At Any Speed: The Designed-In Dangers of the American Automobile*. New York: Grossmann.

Nader, R., Green, M. J. & Seligman, J. (1976). *Taming the Giant Corporation*. New York: Norton.

Nietzsche, F. (1887). *Zur Genealogie der Moral: Eine Streitschrift*. Leipzig: Naumann.

O'Sullivan, D. J. (ed.) (1952). Thomas Aquinas, *The Summa Theologica* (Great Books of the Western World, 19–20). Chicago: Encyclopedia Britannica.

Reeves, C. H. (trans.) (1966). Johannes Nider, *On the Contracts of Merchants*. Norman: University of Oklahoma Press.

Rice, G. (1999). 'Islamic ethics and the implication for business', *Journal of Business Ethics, 18*(4), 345–358.

Singer, P. (1975). *Animal Liberation: A New Ethics for our Treatment of Animals*. New York: Random House.

Singer, P. (1979). *Practical Ethics*. Cambridge: Cambridge University Press.

Sobel, R. (1977). *The Fallen Colossus: The Great Crash of the Penn Central*. New York: Weybright & Talley.

Soskis, B. J. (2010). *The Problem of Charity in Industrial America, 1873–1915*. Unpublished PhD dissertation, Columbia University.

Stump, E. (2003). *Aquinas*. London: Routledge.

Sun, A. X. D. (2005). 'The fate of Confucianism as a religion in socialist China: controversies and paradoxes', in Fenggang Yang and Joseph B. Tamney (eds.), *State, Market and Religions in Chinese Societies*. Leiden: Brill, 229–253.

Sutton, F. X. et al. (1956). *The American Business Creed*. Harvard: Harvard University Press.

Tannenbaum, J. A. (1983). 'Business bulletin', *Wall Street Journal*, May 5.

Tawney, R. H. (1921). *The Acquisitive Society*. London: Bell & Sons.

Wang, G. W. (2004). 'The uses of dynastic ideology: Confucianism in contemporary business', in Frank-Jürgen Richter and Pamela C.M. Marr (eds.), *Asia's New Crisis: Renewal Through Total Ethical Management*. Singapore: Wiley, 51–62.

Ward, T. J. (2004). 'Adam Smith's views on religion and social justice', *International Journal on World Peace, 21*(2), 43–62.

Weber, M. (1904/5). 'Die protestantische Ethik und der "Geist" des Kapitalismus', *Archiv für Sozialwissenschaft und Sozialpolitik*, v. 20, 1–54 and v. 21, 1–110.

Worden, S. (2010). *Godliness and Greed: Shifting Christian Thought on Profit and Wealth*. Lanham: Lexington Books.

Wren, D. A. (2000). 'Medieval or modern? A scholiast's view of business ethics, circa 1430', *Journal of Business Ethics, 28*(2), 109–119.

Yao, S. (2002). *Confucian Capitalism: Discourse, Practice, and the Myth of Chinese Enterprise*. London: RoutledgeCurzon.

Index

Printed in the United States
by Baker & Taylor Publisher Services